Transactions of the RHS (2023), **1**, 1–3
doi:10.1017/S0080440123000208

EDITORIAL

Welcome from the Editors

Harshan Kumarasingham[1] and Kate Smith[2]

[1]School of Social and Political Science, University of Edinburgh, Edinburgh, UK and
[2]Department of History, University of Birmingham, Edgbaston, Birmingham, UK
Email: trhs@royalhistsoc.org

Welcome to volume one of the seventh series of the *Transactions of the Royal Historical Society*. We hope this series, and more particularly, this volume, marks a new departure for the *Transactions*. We have been working as the editors of the journal since January 2022, the year that marked its 150th anniversary. From the beginning of our tenure, we have been keen to shape the journal in new ways to ensure it represents the relevance, dynamism and diversity of the historical discipline today. We have worked together with our UK Editorial Board and International Advisory Board to foster such change.

At its core, the purpose of the *Transactions* remains to publish excellent historical scholarship. Academic journals are fundamental to the ecology of the discipline, providing a space where original research is shared, reviewed, communicated and discussed. They create spaces in which scholars come together and talk with each other. The ways in which journals foster such engagements are not always obvious. Peer review is the lifeblood of academic journals. It continues quietly in the background of academic life, but often shapes our research anew, generating fresh lines of enquiry and prompting different questions or approaches. We are deeply grateful to our peer reviewers who make ready their expertise and set to reading, analysing and commenting on submissions. The engagements with research begun at the peer review stage continue as the piece is reworked, published and read. In publishing new research, the *Transactions* seeks out work that is methodologically exciting and geographically, conceptually and chronologically diverse. It does so and will continue to do so by identifying and promoting new voices, approaches and ways of working across the discipline.

In editing the journal, we are particularly committed to ensuring it reflects the full diversity of geographical and chronological areas at stake in the field. We seek to further the journal's current work in this area by particularly welcoming submissions from historians whose research sits outside British and European history. Alongside geographical diversity, we want the *Transactions* to demonstrate the dynamic nature of the field. We are particularly energised by methodologically innovative and cutting-edge work and have sought to encourage such publications through our workshop scheme. Begun in 2022 and funded by the Royal Historical Society, we have set up an annual call for proposals for workshops. The purpose of this scheme is to support scholars at different career stages by providing the funds needed to bring colleagues together to discuss a particular historical, historiographical or methodological problem. The organisers of funded workshops work closely with us as editors to also develop a publication which has the potential to be included in the journal. The scheme funded four workshops last year on topics such as environmental history and parliamentary culture in colonial contexts. In 2023 the scheme has allocated funds to five workshops on topics such as barter in the Global Middle Ages, the role of historical scholarship in video games, and mothers and motherhood on the left in the twentieth century. Rather than simply benefiting UK-based scholars, the workshops support the work of historians in different countries. For instance, a workshop considering 'Collective Reflection on Oral Histories of Pakistan's Women Constitution-Makers' will take place at the Institute of Development & Economic Alternatives in Lahore, Pakistan, in November this year.

As well as the workshop scheme providing support to enable new discussions to take place, we have also worked to create new spaces for different forms of publication. The Common Room is a new section within the *Transactions* and has been introduced this issue. The name of the section plays upon the long history of the journal and the changing nature of the institutions in which we work. With perhaps fewer common rooms in which to sit and discuss (and less time to do it), the *Transactions'* Common Room creates an alternative site in which issues pertinent to our discipline can be shared, discussed and collectively worked through. It is a space open to all interested in History, which welcomes shorter pieces that might focus on methodological problems, historiographical issues, intellectual debates or engage with recent publications.

While we have made these changes and seen their fruition in this issue, we have further plans afoot for the next volume. With one volume a year, it is not feasible for *Transactions* to host special issues, but we are introducing the possibility of a 'Special Section'. There will be one Special Section per issue made up of around four articles and a brief introductory text explaining the theme at stake. The Special Section will allow scholars to contribute a range of research articles on a particular theme or problem, giving more space for different perspectives to be represented. As such they provide the possibility of unpacking the different facets of an issue from various angles and to work together to show their complexities.

Together we seek to ensure that the *Transactions* publishes research which is original and vital. It is a space where we come together as a field to see what is new and where we might be going next. In an age when humanities scholarship seems to be under threat, the *Transactions* seeks to underscore the ways in which our discipline is thriving, a place in which historical scholarship is seen to be ever more relevant. With over 150 years of publishing the highest-quality pieces across the discipline we hope that *Transactions* will not only build on those traditions, but with its changes in scope and approach will reach a wider readership and represent the full diversity and dynamism found in History.

Cite this article: Kumarasingham H, Smith K (2023). Welcome from the Editors. *Transactions of the Royal Historical Society* **1**, 1–3. https://doi.org/10.1017/S0080440123000208

Transactions of the RHS (2023), **1**, 5–22
doi:10.1017/S0080440122000159

ARTICLE

Monks and the Muslim Enemy: Conversion, Polemic and Resistance in Monastic Hagiography in the Age of the Crusades, c. 1000–1250

Andrew Jotischky

Department of History, Royal Holloway University of London, Egham, Surrey, UK
Email: Andrew.Jotischky@rhul.ac.uk

(Received 7 October 2022; accepted 17 October 2022; first published online 16 November 2022)

Abstract

Although most accounts of Christian encounters with Muslims in the period between the eleventh and thirteenth centuries pay particular attention to conflict and violence, a body of hagiographical texts emanating from monastic circles points to a different kind of approach. In this article I foreground three examples of Italo-Greek saints' lives from the tenth and early eleventh centuries in which the saints in question treat Muslims whom they encounter as potential converts, and explain to them the tenets of Christian theology. These texts are examined as precursors of the Cluniac 'dossier' compiled about Abbot Maiolus's encounter with Muslims in the 990s. Two of the three saints' lives were translated from Greek into Latin, one in the late eleventh, the other in the late twelfth century. The motives for and circumstances of these translations are discussed in light of growing hostility towards the Islamic world during the period of the crusades.

Keywords: monasticism; Italo-Greek; Islam; conversion; polemic

Conventionally, historians writing about the relations between Christians and the Islamic world in the period between the eleventh and thirteenth centuries have thought more about war, particularly holy war, than about dialogue and conversion. We tend to think of the Christian world – at least, outside the Iberian peninsula – as having little knowledge or understanding of, and little interest in, the Islamic world before the first crusade (1095–9) and the settlement of western Europeans in the eastern Mediterranean in its wake.[1] This lack

---

[1] The classic statement of this is R. W. Southern, *Western Views of Islam in the Middle Ages* (Cambridge, MA, 1962), 1–33, esp. 14; see also Norman Daniel, *Islam and the West: The Making of*

of knowledge has often been seen by historians as a characteristic feature of the western approach to the target enemy. As has often been said, most crusading narratives referred to the crusaders' adversaries either as Turks or by deploying labels drawn from the Old Testament, focusing on their ethnic rather than religious identity. Where religious identity is invoked, crusade narratives are just as likely to draw attention to the Turks as pagans, barbarians or indeed as heretics. This apparent lack of interest can sometimes seem odd on the part of participants in what is usually characterised – in current historiography, at least - as a religious war, fought for spiritual reasons. The spirituality of contemporary narratives of crusading appears to be invested less in a clash between different religious systems – still less a 'clash of civilisations'[2] – than in the holiness of the sites to be reconquered from an enemy in possession, and the purity of intent on the part of those dedicated to their recovery.

This consideration made the question of dialogic exchange, polemic and conversion bulk less large than we might expect in a 'holy war', especially given that so many of the contemporary narratives originated in monasteries. Until the middle of the thirteenth century, remarkably little attention was paid to the potential of crusading for the conversion of Muslims, or indeed to the prospect of using conquest of territory as a means of enforcing conversion.[3] Indeed, in the mid-thirteenth century a papal legate to the East complained that Frankish landowners in the kingdom of Jerusalem were passing up opportunities to bring Muslim peasants on their estates to Christianity. The reason for this lack of interest in conversion – paralleled in other regions, notably Sicily – has been well explained by historians in terms of economic advantage, in light of the *consuetudo terre* in operation in the kingdom of Jerusalem that Muslim slaves who sought baptism could thereby evade servile status.[4] But

---

an Image (Edinburgh, 1960), 11–23; John Tolan, *Saracens: Islam in the Medieval European Imagination* (New York, 2002), 12–20, 69–104. For the first crusade specifically, see Svetlana Luchitskaja, 'Barbarae nationes: Les peuples musulmans dans les chroniques de la première croisade', in *Autour de la Première Croisade: Actes du Colloque de la Society for the Study of the Crusades and the Latin East, Clermont-Ferrand, 22–25 juin, 1995*, ed. Michel Balard (Paris, 1996), 99–107; Tom Asbridge, 'Knowing the Enemy: Latin Relations with Islam at the Time of the First Crusade', in *Knighthoods of Christ*, ed. Norman Housley (Aldershot, 2007), 18–19. On the development of these themes in the twelfth century, see Sini Kangas, 'Inimicus Dei et sanctae Christianitatis? Saracens and their Prophet in Twelfth-Century Crusade Propaganda and Western Travesties of Muhammad's Life', in *The Crusades and the Near East: Cultural Histories*, ed. Conor Kostick (2011), 131–60; Margaret Jubb, 'The Crusaders' Perception of Their Opponents', in *Palgrave Advances in the Crusades*, ed. Helen Nicholson (Basingstoke, 2005), 225–44.

[2] Kurt Villads Jensen, 'Cultural Encounters and Clash of Civilisations: Huntingdon and Modern Crusading Studies', in *Cultural Encounters during the Crusades*, ed. Kurt Villads Jensen, Kirsi Salonen and Helle Vogt (Odense, 2013), 15–26.

[3] Benjamin Z. Kedar, *Crusade and Mission: European Approaches towards the Muslims* (Princeton, 1984), 57–74, argues that while conversion was barely discernible as an avowed aim of crusading before the middle of the twelfth century, thereafter it was increasingly cited as a desirable potential outcome of crusades by some writers. The consensus among canon lawyers was that Muslims should not be forced into conversion as an outcome of war, though conversions thus obtained were to be regarded as valid.

[4] *Ibid.*, 151, citing the threat by Odo of Chateauroux in 1253 to excommunicate those who obstructed the baptism of Muslims. In 1216/17 Jacques de Vitry, newly installed as bishop of

acceptance of this reason has perhaps made historians reluctant to consider more fully questions of polemic and conversion in encounters between Christians and Muslims. There are, of course, exceptions, most notably Benjamin Kedar's seminal *Crusade and Mission*. William Chester Jordan has shown in a recent book, *The Apple of His Eye*, that Louis IX not only took conversion of Muslims seriously as a potential outcome of his crusade, but brought Muslim converts – in some cases, whole families – back to France with him in 1254.[5] But Louis, after all, was a saint, and perhaps his saintliness consisted partly in his understanding of holy war precisely as an opportunity for evangelism.

Louis IX's sanctity is invoked here with only a tinge of irony, because this paper will explore some earlier instances of polemic and conversion in encounters with Muslims in hagiographical texts emanating from monasteries, and suggest that, in some parts of the Christian world at least, confrontation with Muslims was already an important feature of the construction of Christian sanctity for at least 100 years before the crusades. At the heart of this discussion are examples from three early medieval Italo-Greek hagiographies: in other words, saints' lives written in Greek and about Greek-speaking monks whose careers played out in southern Italy in the ninth and tenth centuries. The significance of these texts lies not only in the encounters with Muslims narrated in them, but also in the rediscovery and reuse of these texts in the period of the crusades, from the late eleventh century onwards.

These episodes of Italo-Greek monastic encounters with Muslims are not unusual in Greek hagiographical texts from the ninth to the eleventh centuries, but they have not yet been absorbed into the putative landscape of Christian–Islamic interactions before the first crusade. So far as I am aware, they have not been mentioned by any historian discussing Christian attitudes to Muslims in the pre-crusade period. Inevitably, much – though not all – of that landscape has been sketched by historians of the crusades, and perhaps for that reason the discussion can have a rather deterministic character, appearing as a search for the roots of a phenomenon that came to characterise western views of the Islamic world in the twelfth and thirteenth centuries. In recent years, for example, we have seen renewed appeals to see the Norman conquest of Sicily in the late eleventh century as 'a crusade' before the fact, as though the conflicts in the eastern Mediterranean initiated by the papacy

---

Acre, complained that Christians refused baptism to their Muslim servants even when it was asked for, on the grounds that they would then be unable to exploit them as they wished (*Lettres de Jacques de Vitry*, ed. R. B. C. Huygens (Leiden, 1960), 79–97, no. 2). Such obstruction evidently persisted despite the ruling by Pope Gregory IX in 1237 that baptised slaves could continue to be held in servile status. See now Benjamin Z. Kedar, 'Muslim Conversion in Canon Law', in *Proceedings of the Sixth International Congress of Medieval Canon Law: Berkeley, California, 28 July–2 August 1980*, Monumenta Iuris Canonici, Series C, Subsidia, vii, ed. Stephan Kuttner and Kenneth Pennington (Vatican City, 1985), 321–32.

[5] William Chester Jordan, *The Apple of His Eye: Converts from Islam in the Reign of Louis IX* (Princeton, 2019), 61–96.

in 1095 formed a normative framework within which a global set of relationships was formulated and can be tested.[6]

In one sense this approach to Christian views of Muslims is not surprising. Reading the words of Thomas Madden – 'The Crusades were in every way a defensive war. They were the West's belated response to the Muslim conquest of fully two-thirds of the Christian world' – we might be reminded of the opening chapter of Guibert de Nogent's *Dei gesta per Francos*. Here, in a theological retelling of the first crusade written in *c.* 1108/9, Guibert talks about 'Europe' as an isolated corner of Christian civilisation, assailed on three sides by 'enemies'.[7] This view from a northern French monastery places the 'defence of civilisation' as a feature of the cultural *habitus* of reform monasticism. Historians of monasticism have also picked up on this theme; and there has been considerable interest in exploring the role of the monastery of Cluny in the construction of a matrix of 'Christendom on the defensive'. The classic exposition of this theme was proposed by Dominique Iogna-Prat, who saw the twelfth-century abbot of Cluny Peter the Venerable, the commissioner of the first Latin translation of the Qur'an and compiler of a dossier of anti-Islamic polemic, as the guiding figure behind the construction of a 'Cluniac identity' in which the monastery formed the intellectual and spiritual engine-room of the defence of Christendom against the challenges posed by heresy and unbelief.[8] Peter invokes the same siege mentality as Guibert. In his long letter to Bernard of Clairvaux in 1144 about the Latin translations of the Qur'an and other Arabic works, he pointed out that the Arab conquests of 'the greater part of Asia, the whole of Africa and part of Spain' mimicked the 'infection' of those same regions by heresy.[9]

More recently, Scott Bruce has explored the origins of this theme in earlier generations of Cluniac writers. Starting with the notable episode of the capture of Abbot Maiolus of Cluny in 972 by Muslim raiders based in Fraxinetum, in southern France, Bruce traces the retelling of this story by subsequent Cluniac writers from the late tenth century to the twelfth. Bruce's model sees Peter the Venerable as the culminating point of a project that had begun in the 990s, with a series of hagiographical studies of Abbot Maiolus that explored the significance of his kidnapping, his confrontation with the Muslim raiders and his eventual release on payment of a ransom, and the final outcome, the destruction of the raiders' base of Fraxinetum by William I of Provence.[10] Cluniacs were not alone in reflecting these interests.

---

[6] Paul Chevedden, 'A Crusade from the First: The Norman Conquest of Islamic Sicily, 1060–1091', *Al Masaq*, 22 (2010), 190–210.

[7] Guibert de Nogent, *Dei gesta per Francos*, II, Corpus Christianorum Continuatio Medievalis (CCCM) 127A, ed. R. B. C. Huygens (Turnhout, 1996), 89–90.

[8] Dominique Iogna-Prat, *Ordonner et exclure: Cluny et la société chrétienne face à l'hérésie, au judaisme et à l'islam, 1000–1150* (Paris, 1998).

[9] *The Letters of Peter the Venerable*, ed. Giles Constable (2 vols., Cambridge, MA, 1967), CXI, at I, 298, and II, 275–84 for discussion; James Kritzeck, *Peter the Venerable and Islam*, Princeton Oriental Studies 23 (Princeton, 1964), 220.

[10] Scott G. Bruce, *Cluny and the Muslims of La Garde-Fraxinet* (Ithaca, 2015), esp. 10–62; see also M. Meickle, 'Wolves and Saracens in Odilo's *Life of Mayeul*', in *Latin Culture in the Eleventh Century*, ed. M. W. Herven, C. McDonagh and R. Arthur (Turnhout, 2002), II, 116–28.

Other hagiographical texts from the eleventh century appear to corroborate a growing concern with the need for defence against Muslims. The Provençal knight Bobo devoted much of his life to fighting the Muslims of Fraxinetum, and was venerated as a saint at Voghera, in the Po Valley near Pavia; a *Life* of Bobo from the early eleventh century makes clear that his sanctity lay in the use to which he put his arms in defending Christendom.[11]

Bruce's study challenges an accepted model of western Europe in the period before the crusades largely – outside the Hispanic peninsula – ignorant of and oblivious to the Muslim world and Islamic beliefs. He finds the second *Life* of Abbot Maiolus (BHL5177/9),[12] written by 1010 by the Cluniac monk Syrus, particularly significant in this respect. In this version of the story, the captive Maiolus is subjected to attacks by his kidnappers not only on his person but on Christian doctrines. He defends himself by seizing the initiative and preaching to them. 'He seized the shield of faith and, making the case for the Christian religion, pierced the enemies of Christ with the blade of God's word.' More specifically, Maiolus argued that his captors' conception of God was false, that they were worshipping a human construct and that their God did not have the power to free himself from punishment, let alone to help his worshippers.[13] By the time the story was retold by the Cluniac monk Ralph Glaber in *c.* 1040, further details had been added. In this version, there is an exchange among the raiders over how to treat Maiolus: was he a genuine man of God, and should he be shown reverence as such? In Glaber's version, some of the Muslims examined the Bible Maiolus had with him, and recognised the prophets of the Old Testament as the same venerated by them. The interchange then becomes charged with a sharper glimmer of mutual recognition between the Muslims and the Christian.[14] It has been suggested – first, to my knowledge, by a past president of the Royal Historical Society, Sir Richard Southern – that this exchange contains the first mention of the Prophet Muhammad by any writer north of the Alps. And, according to Scott Bruce, 'the debate between the abbot of Cluny and his Muslim captors about the principles of the Christian faith in Syrus's *Life* was unprecedented in Latin literature composed north of the Pyrenees in the early Middle Ages'.[15] Southern and Bruce were both conscious of the necessary exemption from their claims for texts produced in regions where Christians were more likely to come into actual contact with Muslims – notably the Iberian peninsula after the Arab

---

[11] *De S. Bobone seu Bovo*, Acta Sanctorum Augusti ... Collecta [hereafter AASS] (68 vols., Antwerp, 1643–1940) May II, 184–91; C. Carozzi, 'La *Vita boboni*, un jalon vers une mentalité de croisade', *Publications du Centre Européen d'Etudes Bourguignonees*, 11 (1969), 30–5; M. A. Casagrande Mazzoli, 'La tradizione testuale della Vita Sancti Bobonis', *Annali di storia pavese*, 16–17 (1988), 21–6; see now Adrian Cornell du Houx, 'Journeys to Holiness: Lay Sanctity in the Central Middle Ages, *c.*970–*c.*1120' (Ph.D. thesis, Lancaster University, 2015), 73–106.

[12] Syrus, *Vita sancti Maioli*, in *Agni Immaculati: Recherches sur les sources hagiographiques relatives à saint Maieul de Cluny (954–994)*, ed. Dominique Iogna-Prat (Paris, 1988), 163–285.

[13] Syrus, *Vita sancti Maioli*, III, 2, *ibid.*, 249–50.

[14] Rodolfus Glaber, *Historiarum Libri Quinque*, ed. and trans. John France (Oxford, 1989), I.19, pp. 20–2.

[15] Southern, *Western Views of Islam*, 28 n. 25; Bruce, *Cluny and the Muslims*, 54.

conquest and settlement of the eighth century, and southern Italy after the Arab conquest of Sicily in the ninth century. Iberian sources will not be addressed directly in this discussion, but I offer, by way of further contribution to the studies of Iogna-Prat and Bruce, the Italo-Greek hagiographical tradition as a means of shedding further light on Christian–Islamic interchange in the West.

Although the primary purpose of these texts was to establish the sanctity of the protagonists of the *Lives* within the set parameters of the genre, and thereby to provide liturgical material for the celebration of the saints' feast days and exemplary material for monastic reading, the human landscape in which that sanctity was earned was one in which the saints had to show their mettle in different ways in dealing with challenges from Muslims. The saints' lives under discussion therefore feature set-piece encounters between Muslims and Christians in which polemical dialogue – and, in one case at least, conversion – play important roles. Such an encounter can be understood as a feature of the construction of sanctity in this tradition.

These three Italo-Greek *vitae* from the tenth and eleventh centuries are the *Life* of Elias the Younger (Elias of Enna), the *Life* of Elias Speleota (Elias the Troglodyte) and the *Life* of Vitalis of Castronuovo.[16] All three derive from the orbit of Calabrian monasticism and reflect a period of disruption and political turmoil during the aftermath of the conquest of Sicily from Ifriqiya in the ninth century.[17] All three are set within a context of conquest, raids and continual insecurity in Sicily and Calabria. The ever-present threat of raids and violence against Christian communities is a theme, indeed the narrative backcloth, in all three *Lives*. Italo-Greek hagiographical traditions were strongly coloured by the ninth-century Aghlabid conquest of Sicily and the subsequent Byzantine attempts at reconquest, which seem, at least in so far as the hagiographical texts present the situation, to have caused widespread migration of Greek-speaking Christians from urban centres in Sicily to rural Calabria and Apulia.[18] This is a feature of other Italo-Greek saints, such as St John Theristes, or St Sabas the Younger. More broadly, Byzantine hagiography of the period often deploys suffering at the hands of Arab raiders as a stage in the journey to sanctity. Three ninth-century female saints, Theodora of Thessaloniki, Athanasia of Aegina and Theoktiste of Lesbos, all suffered at the hands of Arab raiders. Theodora and Athanasia were forced to flee their

---

[16] *Vita sancti Eliae junioris*, AASS Aug. III, cols. 489–509; *Vita di sant'Elia il giovane*, ed. M. Taibi (Palermo, 1962); M. V. Strattezeri, 'Una traduzione dal Greco ad uso dei normanni: la *vita latina* di sant'Elia lo Speleota', *Archivio storico per la Calabria e la Lucania*, 59 (1992), 1–108, with edition at 42–86; *Vita sancti Vitalis Siculi*, AASS Mar II, cols. 26–34.

[17] For a brief overview of these events, see Alex Metcalfe, *Muslims and Christians in Norman Sicily: Arabic Speakers and the End of Islam* (Edinburgh, 2003), 8–29.

[18] Léon-Robert Ménager, 'La "Byzantinisation religieuse de l'Italie méridionale (IXe – XIIe siècles) et la politique monastique des Normands de l'Italie', *Revue d'Histoire Ecclésiastique*, 53 (1958), 747–74; but see now the scepticism expressed by André Guillou (ed.), *Les actes grecs de S. Maria di Messina*, Istituto Siciliano di Studi Bizantini e Neoellenici 8 (Palermo, 1963), 19–33, over the usefulness of these texts. Metcalfe, *Muslims and Christians*, 14, suggests that onomastic evidence for Sicilian refugees is limited, and that the period of flight may have been quite short.

native island of Aegina as a consequence of the Arab conquest of the 820s, and both subsequently became nuns. Theoktiste was captured by Arab pirates and escaped to lead a life of solitary asceticism.[19] St Euthymius the Younger, a ninth-century monk of Mount Athos, was captured by Arab raiders but returned to his hermitage unharmed when the kidnappers realised his holiness.[20]

The Italo-Greek *vitae* are linked in other ways that indicate shared traditions and probably shared textual knowledge; for example, the *Life* of Elias Speleota contains an account of the death of Elias of Enna, and Elias Speleota is directed in the eremitic life by Daniel, a monastic disciple of Elias of Enna. Vitalis of Castronuovo is said to have been related to Elias of Enna, perhaps his nephew. Spiritual kinship is a characteristic feature of Greek Orthodox monasticism, and the network drawn by the *vitae* encompasses many of the notable Italo-Greek monastic figures of the period: Luke of Armentum, Phantino the Younger, Nilus of Rossano and Nikephorus the Nude.[21] But there are also links to the major monastic figures and trends in the orbit of Constantinople; thus Nikephorus the Nude, who through discipleship from Phantino is linked to Elias Speleota, was also the disciple of Athanasius the Athonite, the founder of cenobitic monasticism on Mount Athos. This distinctive networking character reminds us of the gravitational pull of Constantinople in Italo-Greek monasticism. Annick Peters-Custot has argued that the ideals of eremitism and personal austerity so characteristic of Italo-Greek hagiography should be seen not only as a response to remote rural settlement in the mainland, but also as a sign of connections with contemporary monastic reform in Constantinople.[22] And as Agostino Pertusi observed, in Apulia in particular, the influence of the Studite reform of the ninth century in Constantinople can be seen in the manuscripts of Studite ascetic texts copied in Greek monasteries in the region.[23]

In this light it is striking to note textual influences on the *Life* of Elias of Enna not only from what we might call 'universal' early texts known widely across the monastic world, such as Athanasius' *Life* of Anthony, but also from texts specific to Syria and the Holy Land: the fifth-century accounts of Syrian monks in Theodoret of Cyrrhus's *Historia Religiosa*, and Cyril of Scythopolis's sixth-century *Lives* of Euthymius and Sabas.[24] Cyril in particular

---

[19] *Holy Women of Byzantium: Ten Saints' Lives in Translation*, Byzantine Saints Lives in Translation 1, ed. and trans Alice-Mary Talbot (Washington, DC, 1996), 110–16, 143, 168.

[20] *Life of Euthymios the Younger*, xxiv–xxv, ed. Alexander Alexakis, trans. Alice-Mary Talbot, in *Holy Men of Mount Athos*, ed. Richard P. Greenfield and Alice-Mary Talbot, Dumbarton Oaks Medieval Library (Cambridge, MA, 2016), 68–77. Not all relocations from Sicily to the mainland were attributed to Muslim incursions. SS Sabas and Macarios were induced to leave Sicily because of famine (Metcalfe, *Muslims of Sicily*, 14).

[21] Annick Peters-Custot, *Les Grecs de l'Italie méridionale post-Byzantine* (Paris, 2009), 177.

[22] Ibid., 176.

[23] Agostino Pertusi, 'La spiritualite gréco-byzantine en Italie meridionale', in Pertusi, *Scritti sulla Calabria greca medieval*, 99–116, at 103.

[24] Theoderet of Cyrrhus, *Historia Religiosa*, ed. P. Canivet and A. Leroy-Molinghen, Sources Chrétiennes (Paris, 1977–9); English translation: *A History of the Monks of Syria*, trans. Richard M. Price (Kalamazoo, 1985); *Kyrillos von Skythopolis*, ed. E. Schwarz (Leipzig, 1939); English translation: Cyril of Scythopolis, *Lives of the Monks of Palestine*, trans. Richard M. Price (Kalamazoo, 1991).

provided models for the kinds of fluidity between settled and wandering monasticism so typical of Italo-Greek hagiography – and, of course, so inimical to Benedictine monasticism. Typical spiritual traits in Italo-Greek hagiography are the master–disciple relationship; hesychasm; fasting; the gift of tears; nudity or sparse clothing; and the practice of 'grazing' – in imitation of the *boschoi* of Palestine and Syria – that is, living off vegetation that grew in the wild.[25] In the *Lives* of these three saints, we also find a streak of prophecy, particularly in relation to the threat of Arab raids, sometimes tinged with eschatological concerns. Pertusi has characterised Italo-Greek monasticism of the period before the eleventh century as 'a perpetual oscillation between a type of anchoritism or hesychastic eremitism and a lavra or cenobitic community'.[26]

In all three of these *Lives*, encounters with Muslims of the kind under discussion – exchanges of views about their faith – although they are fleeting and brief, nonetheless form significant points within the narrative. The whole course of Elias of Enna's life was shaped by the experience of the Aghlabid conquest of his homeland, Sicily. Captured as a boy of twelve during the conquest, he was enslaved but sold to a Christian family in North Africa; he was eventually able to buy his freedom and set out on a pilgrimage to Jerusalem, where he adopted the habit of a monk at the Holy Sepulchre, before continuing his pilgrimage to the Jordan, Galilee and Mount Sinai. He subsequently returned to Sicily, but his career was characterised by mobility: from Palermo to Taormina; then to Greece; a pilgrimage to Rome (885/91); then Calabria, where he founded a monastery at Reggio; finally dying at Thessaloniki en route to a meeting with the emperor. The encounter with Muslims occurs during his pilgrimage in the Holy Land. He comes across twelve Agarenes who, in a threatening manner, ask him to explain the principles of the Christian religion, and especially the Trinity. Elias delivers a lengthy sermon that includes a statement of faith drawn from the Nicene creed. He then goes on to explain that the false belief of the Ishmaelites has no coherence, drawn as it is from different sects. Their view of Christ as only a pure human and not God makes them Arians; their practices, such as circumcision, make them followers of the Jewish law. There follows an attack on the Prophet, who has simply cobbled together the worst of different sects, and for whose revelation there is no verifiable authority. The outcome of this encounter is the conversion and baptism of the twelve Muslims, before Elias completes his pilgrimage and returns to Sicily.[27]

The encounters with Muslims in the two other texts are briefer; more ephemeral perhaps, but nonetheless significant in the context of polemical exchanges. Elias the Troglodyte was a Calabrian by birth, who lived as a hermit after the woman his parents had tried to make him marry was killed in an Aghlabid raid, before taking the habit under the senior monk Arsenius at Reggio; both Elias and Arsenius fled to Greece to escape Muslim raids and

---

[25] John Wortley, '"Grazers" (βοσχοι) in the Judaean Desert', in *The Sabaite Heritage in the Orthodox Church from the Fifth Century to the Present*, Orientalia Lovaniensia Analecta 98, ed. Joseph Patrich (Louvain, 2001), 37–48.

[26] Pertusi, 'La spiritualité', 102.

[27] *Vita sancti Eliae*, xxi–xxii, col. 494.

lived for eight years in an abandoned tower at Patras where they disposed of a demon who had been tormenting the populace. They returned to Calabria after attracting too much of the attention of the powerful. First the wife of the archon tried to seduce Elias, then a bishop made advances towards Arsenius. When they tried to leave Patras, the bishop detained them with a false accusation of the theft of liturgical books.[28] Eventually they were able to return to Calabria, but Arsenius died soon thereafter, and Elias re-entered the monastery of S. Eustratius. On a further raid by Muslims from Sicily, Arsenius's tomb at S. Eustratius was attacked. The raiders broke it open, thinking they might find lucrative precious metals inside, but what they found instead was the incorrupt body of the monk; his body and clothing in exactly the state in which they had been when he was buried. The point of interest for us comes in the words put in the mouths of the Muslims when they come upon the body of Arsenius. 'Look, here is one of those who stupid Christians say will, at the day of judgement, judge the living and the dead.'[29]

The earliest manuscript of the text compresses the episode into a concise couple of sentences. Nevertheless, there is enough to hear mockery on the part of the Muslims both of Christian ideas of sanctity and of the doctrine of the resurrection of the body. Having initially opened the tomb to rob it of any treasure, they decide to burn the body because Christians believe in the resurrection of the body, and if it is burned it will presumably not be raised. For them, the body of the dead monk represents the body of Christ – 'the deceiver' – and the attempt to destroy it by fire is a deliberate act of repudiation of Christian beliefs.[30] The attempt at burning the body of Arsenius is a trope of early Christian monastic martyrology; a parallel is found, though without the mockery of the resurrection, in the sixth-century *Life* of Chariton, where Arab raiders attempt to burn the bodies of Chariton and his monastic followers.[31] Elias himself had further adventures – including one with a levitating Ethiopian demoniac – but that is the extent of the involvement with Muslims. He eventually founded the cave monastery from which he took his name.[32]

---

[28] *Vita sancti Helye*, viii, ed. Strattezeri, 52–4.

[29] *Ibid.*, xv, 59: 'Ecce hic de illis est de quibus stulti aiunt Christiani iudicaturos ad iudicium vivos et mortuos.'

[30] *Ibid.*, xv, 59: 'Igitur illis servientibus et plurimum ignis super sanctam glebam accendentibus nec etiam vestimenti eius ustus fuit pilus. Videntes itaque suam perfidiam ad id quod temptabant nichil valere admirantes et stupentes nimium a loco recessere.'

[31] 'La vie prémétaphrastique de St Chariton', ed. G. Garitte, *Bulletin de l'Institut historique belge de Rome*, 21 (1940–1), ii–xxiii, 17–33, at 30–1. For western medieval knowledge of this tradition, *Descriptio locorum* (1131–43), xxxiv, *Itinera Hierosolymitana Crucesignatorum* (*IHC*), ed. Sabino de Sandoli (4 vols., Jerusalem, 1987–94), ii, 100; *Rorgo Fretellus de Nazareth et sa description de la Terre Sainte*, ed. P. C. Boeren (Amsterdam, 1980), 30; John of Würzburg, *Descriptio locorum*, cccm 139, 137, Anon VI, *IHC*, iii, 68; Eugesippus, *Tractatus de distantiis locorum Terrae Sanctae*, Patrologia Cursus Completus, Series Graeca (161 vols., Paris, 1857–66), cxxxiii, 996. The legend of the founder's incorruptible body was also known by Peter de Pennis in the 1330s (Charles Kohler, 'Libellus de Pierre de Pennis de locis ultramarinis', *Revue de l'Orient latin*, 9 (1902), 367).

[32] *Vita sancti Helye*, xix, ed. Strattezeri, 69; Agostino Pertusi, 'Soprarvivenze pagane e pietà religiosa nella società bizantina dell' Italia meridionale', in *Calabria bizantina: Tradizione di pietà e tradizione scrittoria nella Calabria greca medievale*, Mezzogiorno e democrazia 11 (Reggio Calabria, 1983), 17–46.

The third *Life*, that of Vitalis of Castronuovo, follows a broadly similar pattern. Vitalis, a Sicilian, became a monk in youth, made a pilgrimage to Rome, then became an eremitical monk in Calabria before settling in Apulia. He built a monastery, but withdrew into the wilderness again; he tamed wild animals, mortified his flesh and diverted a flood that threatened to destroy crops. He was visited by the great abbot Luke of Armentum, whom he cured of stomach complaints after he had fed him wild mushrooms. He attracted eremitical followers; restored a ruined church which he then refounded as a *coenobium*; performed miracles and healings; and spared Bari from a violent storm.[33] Back in Calabria, he was captured in a raid from Sicily. The Muslims – who are interchangeably referred to as *barbarians*, *Agarenes* and *Saracens* – were initially interested in the material wealth of the monastery before realising that Vitalis had no livestock, no barn full of crops, vineyards or moveable treasures. They tried instead to kill Vitalis, but the 'barbarian' who laid hands on him was struck by a lightning bolt and fell on his face. The other raiders saw a column of fire in front of Vitalis stretching into the heavens, and while they were in this terrified state Vitalis took the opportunity to deliver a short homily:

'Cease from shedding the blood of Christians, and stop wanting to capture their homes; almighty God will not permit you to do this ... he wants you, like wise and well-taught men, to leave behind these bad ways, to convert and live according to his holy precepts; he does not will the death of the sinner, but that he should convert and live in knowledge of him and in penance. For it was for this that the Son of God came down from heaven to earth; and although he was truly God, through his immense goodness he became truly man. You, however, are ignorant of all contrition, and you do not want to know that holy and life-giving destiny. For he will come again from heaven, to where he ascended, and destroy all pride, and all those who blaspheme his name.'[34]

Vitalis continued by drawing parallels between the Saracens and the Egyptians of the Old Testament who were drowned in the Red Sea, warning that they will

---

[33] Ibid., i–iv, AASS Mar II, cols. 26–32.

[34] *Vita S. Vitalis*, iii, 14, AASS Mar II, col. 30: 'Cessate vlterius ab effusione sanguinis Christianorum, & nolite eorum habitacula captiuare: nam Deus omnipotens non vobis permittet hoc facere, vt illos videlicet destruatis, sed vult, vt, sicut bene eruditi & docti, derelinquant vias suas malas, & conuertantur & viuant in sanctis præceptis eius; non enim vult mortem peccatoris, sed vt conuertatur & viuat in ipso secundum cognitionem & pœnitentiam. Nam propter hoc Dei Filius inclinauit cælos & descendit in terram, atque; cum esset verus Deus, per immensam bonitatem suæ magnitudinis verus homo factus est: quæ quidem vos omnia penitus ignoratis, nolentes scire sacram & salutiferam illius præordinationem. Venturus est enim e cælo, quo ascendit, ad destruendam omnem superbiam, & elatos & blasphemantes sanctum nomen eius. Hic profecto deponet in breui, & ad nihilum valde rediget vestræ gentis elationem & audaciam: demerget vos ipsos infelices & miseros in abyssum, cum brachio quoque virtutis suæ, vtpote sanctus & fortis Dominus & excelsus & insuperabilis, vos dispergere non cessabit. Sicut olim vestrum Principem cum suo equitatu in mari rubro demersit, Tyrannum scilicet illum & duri cordis Pharaonem: similiter ira Dei subito veniet super vos, nisi recesseritis a populo Christiano.'

similarly suffer the anger of God, unless they desist from persecuting the Christian people.

In all three texts, then, there is an encounter with Muslims that features some explanation of or reference to the central tenets of Christian teaching. In all three, Muslims are a people associated with violence, robbery and murder of Christians; although in the *Life* of Elias of Enna, the encounter in which Christianity is explained turns out despite Elias's foreboding to be entirely peaceful; indeed the exchange with them is at the invitation of the Muslims. In two of the texts, a violent attempt is made by the Muslims against a saint, in one case living, in another dead; in both, the violence is overcome by miraculous power. In two of the texts, Elias of Enna and Vitalis of Castronuovo, the encounter becomes an occasion of conversion or attempted conversion. In all three, the encounter is a constituent element, even if a relatively minor one, in the construction of sanctity (in the *Life* of Elias the Troglodyte, not so much his own but that of the dead Arsenius).

Attention has already been drawn to some elements in the *Lives* that indicate the influence of Palestinian, to some extent Syrian, monastic traditions. The polemical nature of the encounters with Muslims also suggests this milieu. It may be significant, for example, that Elias of Enna's conversion of the Muslims occurs not in his homeland but in the Holy Land, a location that may consciously recall the corpus of about sixty Christian Arabic hagiographical and polemic texts from the mid-ninth to the end of the tenth centuries studied by Sidney Griffith. The exchange between Elias and the Muslims has something in common with an episode retold in the *Life* of Theodore of Edessa, featuring a set-piece debate about the merits of Christianity over Islam. The text survives in both a Greek and Arabic version, and probably dates from the early tenth century.[35] We might also be reminded of the ninth-century *Passio* of the monk of St Sabas, George, and the martyrs of Cordoba, in which George tells the qadi before whom he is arraigned:

'Do you think I could believe anything good of your master, the disciple of Satan? I believe that he who had appeared to him in the guise of an angel had in reality been a demon. He is in fact a perfidious and worthless believer in the Devil, a minister of Antichrist and a labyrinth of all the vices.'[36]

The striking difference between these examples and the *Life* of Elias lies in the irenic quality of the Italo-Greek *Life* in contrast with the *Life* of Theodore, in

---

[35] Sidney H. Griffith, 'The *Life of Theodore of Edessa*: History, Hagiography and Religious Apologetics in Mar Saba Monastery in Early Abbasid Times', in *The Sabaite Heritage*, ed. Patrich, 147–70

[36] Cited from the *Memoriale sanctorum* by Milka Levy-Rubin and Benjamin Z. Kedar, 'A Spanish Source on the Mid-Ninth Century Mar Saba and a Neglected Sabaite Martyr', in *The Sabaite Heritage*, ed. Patrich, 63–72, at 69; see also R. J. Pedrajas, 'San Eulogio de Córdoba, autor de la Pasión Francesca de los mártires mozárabes cordobeses Jotge, Aurelio y Natalia', *Anthologica Annua*, 17 (1970), 465–583; Edward P. Colbert, *The Martyrs of Cordoba (850–859): A Study of the Sources* (Washington, DC, 1962); Jessica A. Coope, *The Martyrs of Cordoba* (Lincoln, NE, 1995).

which the saint is martyred when he seems to be prevailing in debate against his Muslim captors – and indeed with the *Passio* of George and the Martyrs of Cordoba. The argument deployed by Elias, particularly the accusation that Islamic teaching is basically Arianism, and that its practices are judaising, seems to be taken by the author of the *Life* from the eighth-century author John of Damascus – again, an indication of an intellectual and textual milieu with connections to Constantinople and to the Holy Land, since John had been a monk in the desert monastery of St Sabas.[37]

The harmonious exchange in the encounter with Muslims in the *Life* of Elias of Enna should not mislead us, however. In two of the three Italo-Greek hagiographies – the *Life* of Elias of Enna and the *Life* of Vitalis – the terms used for Muslims are 'barbarians', Agarenes, Ishmaelites or Saracens. This is fairly standard terminology, shared by Greek monastic texts from the eastern Mediterranean and from Constantinople dealing with Arab incursions that seek to draw attention to violence and conquest. We find similar language in, for example, the ninth-century *Passion of the Twenty Martyrs of St Sabas*, the *Chronographia* of Theophanes (*c.* 814) and the *Lives* of Theodora of Thesssaloniki, Athanasia of Aegina and Theoktiste of Lesbos, all of which describe Christians suffering at the hands of Arab raiders.[38] Just to pick two eleventh-century Greek monastic texts, the *Life* of Lazaros of Mount Galesion and the *Testament* of the monastic founder Christodoulos, again we find Muslim conquerors described in the same terms, even though the contexts are different – the passage in the *Life* of Lazaros is set in the first decade of the eleventh century, when Lazaros fled the Holy Land from the Fatimid caliph al-Hakim's persecution of Christians, whereas Christodoulos was recounting his flight from the Holy Land in the face of the Seljuq invasion.[39] Just as two of the Italo-Greek hagiographies, the *Life* of Elias the Troglodyte and the *Life* of Vitalis, emphasise the preoccupation of the Aghlabid raiders from Sicily with sacrilegious robbery, so the *Life* of Lazaros characterises the Fatimids carrying out the destruction of the Holy Sepulchre in Jerusalem in 1009 as 'sacrilegious and thieving'.[40]

The *Testament* of Christodoulos, an account of how the founder came to establish his monastery on Patmos, tells briefly but in vivid tones of his flight from Jerusalem. For him, the Seljuqs were 'the Saracen swarm ... a barbarian phalanx ... spreading like a monstrous hailstorm, with a baneful rattling and gibbering, destroying and annihilating the whole Christian society'.[41]

---

[37] Levy-Rubin and Kedar, 'A Spanish Source', 69 and n. 36; John of Damascus, *Liber de haeresibus*, Patrologia Graeca 94, col. 764, trans. D. J. Sahas, *John of Damascus on Islam* (Leiden, 1972), 133.

[38] *Passio SS XX martyrum S.Sabae*, ed. A. Papadopoulos-Kerameos, *Pravoslavnii Palestinski Sbornik*, 57 (1907), 1–41 [Greek text], AASS Mar III, cols. 165–79 [Latin translation]; *Theophanis Chronographia*, ed. C. de Boor, (2 vols., Hildesheim, 1963), ι, 484, 499; *The Chronicle of Theophanes*, ed. and trans. C. Mango and R. Scott (Oxford, 1997), 665, 693, and see above, note 18.

[39] *The Life of Lazarus of Mt Galesion, an Eleventh-Century Pillar Saint*, Byzantine Saints' Lives in Translation 3, ed. and trans. Richard P. Greenfield (Washington, DC, 2000), 101–3; *Rule, Testament and Codicil of Christodoulos*, trans. Patricia Karlin-Hayter, in *Byzantine Monastic Foundation Documents*, ed. John P. Thomas and Angela Hero (5 vols., Washington, DC, 2000), ιν, 564–606.

[40] *Life of Lazarus*, 102.

[41] *Testament of Christodoulos*, 579.

The Italo-Greek texts all merit a more systematic comparison of their polemical content with earlier or contemporary Byzantine polemics against Islam, but the passage in which Vitalis compares the Muslims with the Egyptians of the Old Testament is particularly striking. As Katherine Allen Smith has recently shown, Latin crusade narratives and papal letters from the twelfth century exploit such parallels, and, in Latin monastic discourse more generally, 'Egypt' is found as a term of opprobrium for sinfulness.[42] But the sentiment expressed in the *Life* of Vitalis that God will not allow the Muslim raiders to prevail against Christians is also found in a very similar context in an eleventh-century Latin text from Italy. In the *Dialogi* of Desiderius of Monte Cassino, a Muslim raiding fleet that had burned Monte Cassino in 846 was destroyed by the miraculous appearance of SS Benedict and Peter, with an accompanying speech by St Peter to the effect that the Agarenes, who are described as *heretici atque Iudei* (heretics and Jews), are God's instrument to inflict punishment on Christians but not to defeat them utterly.[43] The labelling of the Muslim raiders as heretics and Jews is, to my mind, particularly striking, since it echoes the identification of Muslims with Jews made by Elias of Enna, and of course shows the longevity of John of Damascus's profiling of Islam as a Christian heresy.

It will not have escaped attention that the citations from the *Life* of Elias the Troglodyte and the *Life* of Vitalis are in Latin, not Greek. The question of the reception and readership of these Italo-Greek hagiographies brings the discussion back to wider questions about western monastic attitudes to Islam. Both the *Life* of Elias the Troglodyte and the *Life* of Vitalis of Castronuovo were translated into Latin, the *Life* of Elias in *c.* 1080, the *Life* of Vitalis in 1194. Indeed, the Greek original of the *Life* of Elias the Troglodyte no longer survives, so the Latin translation is the earliest text we have, although a subsequent Greek version was made from a retranslation of the Latin in the early fourteenth century.

What were the circumstances of these translations into Latin? The Latin version of the *Life* of Elias the Troglodyte was made at the monastery of Sta Eufemia in Calabria. The manuscript containing the *vita* dates from the twelfth century, and contains hagiographical lives according to the calendar mid-April to mid-September. The presence of saints such as Audoenus (d.684), archbishop of Rouen, indicates a Norman influence on the calendar. But other *vitae* in the manuscript, including the *Life* of Elias, also show a southern Italian influence: *Translatio s. Bartholomaei de India in insulam Lypparim, Passio ss.mm. Senatoris, Viatoris, Cassiodori et Dominatae matris eorum* and of course *Vita e i Miracula di Sant'Elia lo Speleota*. The monastery of Sta Eufemia was founded in 1062 with an endowment from Robert Guiscard, on the site of the cave monastery founded by Elias, and its first abbot was Robert of Grandmesnil, formerly abbot of St Evroul, who had been exiled from Normandy after incurring

---

[42] Katherine Allen Smith, *The Bible and Crusade Narrative in the Twelfth Century* (Woodbridge, 2020), 174–80.

[43] Desiderius of Monte Cassino, *Dialogi*, ɪ, Monumenta Germaniae Historica (MGH) (SS), xxx, 1118–19.

the suspicion of William the Conqueror.[44] The endowment for the monastery seems to have been considerable. Like other Hauteville foundations, it was directly subject to the papacy. It was probably during Robert of Grandmesnil's abbacy that the translation of the *Life* of Elias was undertaken.

Not only was Sta Eufemia founded on the site of an older Greek house, but among its endowments was the still functioning cave monastery of Elias the Troglodyte. The translation may have been in part an attempt to appropriate the cult of Elias, perhaps to ensure the transfer of property, and this indeed sounds perfectly plausible as a reason.[45] The appropriation of the cave monastery might be seen as the sort of example that historians arguing a case for the enforced latinisation of the indigenous monastic landscape would usefully deploy, but this is not really a sustainable inference, given that what we seem to be witnessing is the transfer of a functioning Greek community to Latin possession. Moreover, Norman interest in the veneration of local saints was already well established by the 1080s. As Paul Oldfield has argued, promoting a local cult helped to reconcile the largely Greek urban community with the new Norman lords.[46]

The *Life* of Vitalis of Castronuovo was translated at the request of Robert, bishop of Tricarico (1187–94), and the translation is addressed to him. Tricarico, in the Basilicata, was a diocese with a strongly Greek cultural orbit. The cathedral chapter included Greek- as well as Latin-speakers – in fact the Epistle and Gospel was chanted in Greek by some canons as late as 1758. Liturgical rites were sometimes celebrated in Greek instead of Latin – there is evidence of payments being made for this to be done at funerals; and, as also happened in crusader states, auxiliary Greek-rite bishops were appointed to administer sacraments to Greek-speakers. In 1203, just a few years after the *Life* of Vitalis was translated, the cathedral cantor of Tricarica, the son of a Greek priest and someone who had received minor orders according to the Greek rite, was elected bishop of Anglona. The archbishop of the province wrote to Innocent III to ask if this was acceptable, and the pope ruled that it was, as long as it did not cause outrage to the chapter.[47]

These translations of Greek texts in the Norman period obviously raise wider questions about the religious politics of the Norman settlement in the *mezzogiorno*; questions over which there has of course been considerable scholarly debate and disagreement. To summarise the historiography very crudely, the traditional view was that the Normans effectively liquidated Greek monasteries, or denuded them of property which they gave to their own Latin foundations, and put an end to Greeks holding episcopal

---

[44] Orderic Vitalis, *Historia Ecclesiastica*, v, 16, ed. and trans. Marjorie Chibnall (6 vols., Oxford, 1969–80), III, 158–61; Graham Loud, *The Latin Church in Norman Italy* (Cambridge, 2007), 85–7; Peters-Custot, *Les grecs d'Italie*, 271.

[45] Loud, *Latin Church in Norman Sicily*, 506.

[46] Paul Oldfield, *Sanctity and Pilgrimage in Medieval Southern Italy 1100-1200* (Cambridge, 2014), 51–106.

[47] *Die Register Innocenz' III*, Osterreichische Akademie der Wissenschaften VI, 1203/4, ed. O. Hageneder, John Moore and A. Sommerlechner (Vienna, 1995), 228–9, no. 139.

office.[48] With regard to bishoprics, this view has been rejected, particularly by Graham Loud and Vera von Falkenhausen, and more recently by Annick Peters-Custot.[49] It is now accepted that there were remarkably few forced latinisations of sees, and that in most cases Latins were appointed only after a see had become vacant; it was only when a Greek bishop refused to accept Roman authority, as was the case with Basil, the metropolitan of Reggio, that he was deprived. There are examples of pragmatism in appointments; for example, John de Niceforo, the first Latin bishop of Squillace (1096), was of mixed Greek and Latin origins, perhaps bilingual. The cathedral of Anglona – whose chapter elected the Greek cantor – was enlarged at the end of the twelfth or beginning of the thirteenth century, perhaps because of the addition of the Greek chapter from Tursi. The sees of Crotone and Sta Severina had a Greek bishop until the end of the thirteenth century, Oppido Mamertina as late as 1400, and Gallipoli and Bova into the sixteenth century.[50] Annick Peters-Custot has recently cautioned against too positivist a view that sees no rupture at all in the 'politique religieuse' of the eleventh and twelfth centuries; nevertheless, there is ample reason to understand the translations of Italo-Greek hagiographies within a hybridising culture.

In emphasising the Norman pragmatic modus vivendi as the context of these acts of translation, however, we must be careful not to miss the significance of the context in which I have framed this discussion, the landscape of Muslim/Christian encounters. The significance of the texts in the form in which we have them is not only that Greek hagiographical texts were being translated into Latin, but about the content of the texts. Presumably they were read and used by their Latin communities in similar ways to Latin hagiographical texts; in other words, liturgically, and for didactic and instructive purposes. No Latin audience could miss the fact that part of the construction of sanctity in these texts is the polemical confrontation with Muslims in which the tenets of the faith are either presented, or demonstrated miraculously, or in the case of the *Life* of Vitalis, both. So what might the instances of Christian–Muslim interaction in these texts have told Latin audiences? As suggested at the start, the underlying message in respect of Christian–Muslim dynamics in the hagiographies is concerned with expounding the principles of Christian doctrine, particularly on the Trinity and the Resurrection. One might say, in fact, the message of those episodes at least is concerned with conversion. What it is *not* concerned with is holy war.

In the 1080s, when the *Life* of Elias the Troglodyte was translated, a preoccupation with the tenets of the faith, even conversion, does not seem out of line

---

[48] Louis-Robert Ménager, 'La "byzantinisation" religieuse de l'Italie méridionale et la politique monastique des Normands d'Italie (IXe – XIIe s.) *Revue d'histoire ecclésiastique*, 53 (1958), 747–74; 54 (1959), 5–40, repr. in *Hommes et institutions de l'Italie normande* (1981).

[49] Graham Loud, 'Byzantine Italy and the Normans', *Byzantinische Forschungen*, 13 (1988), 215–33, esp. 227–32; Vera von Falkenhausen, 'I monasteri greci dell'Italia meridionale e della Sicilia dopo l'avvenuto dei normanni: continuità e mutamenti', in *Il Passagio dal domino bizantino allo stato normanno nell'Italia meridionale* (Taranto, 1997), 197–229; Peters-Custot, *Les grecs*, 234, 271.

[50] Peters-Custot, *Les grecs*, 257–9.

with concerns in other Norman sources. An example from roughly the same period helps to make the point. In a well-known passage in Eadmer's *Life* of Anselm, the archbishop, in exile from England, was present at the siege of Capua in 1098. He encountered the Sicilian Muslims in the service of Count Roger, whom he so impressed by his conduct and his words that, according to Eadmer, they would have converted to Christianity if Roger himself had not forbidden this.[51] We are not obliged to believe that this was at all likely in order to appreciate the point that in a hagiographical text, more or less contemporary with the Italo-Greek texts under discussion, and written in a Norman orbit, Muslims are encountered as non-Christians ripe for conversion rather than as a legitimate enemy.

Some historians, of course, tend to view the Norman conquest of Sicily as part of a wider phenomenon of the aggressive 'defence of Christendom', or indeed as a precursor of the crusading phenomenon.[52] Doubtless there are plentiful examples of violence rather than evangelism offered to Muslims in Sicily. But this example seems closer to the dynamic of witness and conversion that we have seen in the Italo-Greek texts, or indeed in the Cluniac *Lives* of Abbot Maiolus, than to holy war. As I remarked at the beginning of this paper, when we look closely at holy war narratives – especially the first-crusade chronicles – we see very little interest in the conversion of Muslims. An exception is the episode of the betrayal of the walls of Antioch to the crusader Bohemond by the Turkish emir Pirus/Firuz. In the earliest crusade narrative, the anonymous *Gesta Francorum*, Pirus is prepared to do this in return for material riches and baptism.[53] In the version of the story by Raymond d'Aguilers, Firuz is a *Turcatus*, or Christian renegade – in other words, an Armenian Christian in Turkish service, or even a convert to Islam.[54] It is surely significant that the author of the *Gesta* was a south Italian follower of Bohemond; and therefore someone to whom the notion of alliances and agreements between Christians and Muslims was a defining feature of their interaction. As Joshua Birk has pointed out, by 1095 southern Italians were used to fighting alongside Muslims as well as against them because they had frequently made use of Muslim soldiers in their campaigns of conquest. Moreover, a parallel can be found between the Firuz episode in the siege of Antioch and the Norman siege of Castrogiovanni in Sicily in 1087.[55] The conversion story is also followed, and extended, in the slightly

---

[51] *Eadmeri vita sancti Anselmi*, xxxiii, ed. and trans. R. W. Southern (1962), 111–12.

[52] Chevedden, 'A Crusade from the First', 190–210.

[53] *Gesta Francorum et Aliorum Hierosolimitanorum*, viii, ed. Rosalind Hill (1962), 44–7; see also Joshua Birk, 'The Betrayal of Antioch: Narratives of Conversion and Conquest during the First Crusade', *Journal of Medieval and Early Modern Studies*, 41 (2011), 463–85.

[54] Raymond d'Aguilers, *Historia Hierosolymitana*, Patrologia Latina, ed. J.-P. Migne, 215 vols., clv, 608.

[55] Joshua Birk, 'Imagining the Enemy: Southern Italian Perceptions of Islam at the Time of the First Crusade', in *Just Wars, Holy Wars and Jihads: Christian, Jewish and Muslims Encounters and Exchanges*, ed. Sobhail H. Hashmi (Oxford, 2012), 91–106, at 101, citing Geoffrey Malaterra, *De rebus gestis Rogerii Calabriae et Siciliae comitis et Roberti Guiscardi ducis fratris eius*, Rerum Italicarum Scriptores, 2nd edn, v, pt 1, ed. Ernesto Pontieri (Bologna, 1927–8), 87–8.

later account of the first crusade by Robert the Monk, written in *c.* 1108. In this northern French version, Pirus asks Bohemond how it can be that, as he has heard the Christians say, the crusaders will be helped by an army of saints. How, specifically, can saints in heaven carry the material equipment of a warrior? Bohemond consults his chaplain and obtains the answer that saints carry weapons as a sign of divine sanction for the coming battle. Pirus is sufficiently satisfied by this to convert, out of conviction that God's hand will be seen at work in a crusader victory; he subsequently becomes a model of faithfulness.[56] There are other examples of early crusaders bearing witness against Islamic belief, specifically in a context of martyrdom: for example the *Passio* of Thiemo, archbishop of Salzburg, who when captured by Turks on the crusade of 1101 smashed a golden statue that he saw them worshipping and that he claimed held a demon.[57]

These episodes are exceptional and anomalous in early crusade narratives. When we look forward in time to the context in which the *Life* of Vitalis was translated from Greek into Latin, in the episcopate of Robert of Tricarico, witness and conversion seems even more exceptional. Robert became bishop in the year that Saladin conquered Jerusalem and the third crusade was launched, 1187. None of the crusading rhetoric of that period – chronicles, papal bulls, even treatises such as Peter of Blois's *De peregrinatione Ierusalem* – talks seriously about conversion as part of the framework of Christian responses to Islam.[58]

Yet the story may not be as simple as this. By way of conclusion, I suggest that if we fail to see an interest in witness and conversion in texts written around the time of the first and third crusades, it may be because we are not looking in the right places. What is most striking in the Christian–Muslim dynamic discussed in the Italo-Greek and Cluniac texts is the expression of fundamentals of doctrine: the Muslim scepticism about Christianity as expressed in the *Life* of Elias the Troglodyte and the *Life* of Maiolus, and Christian profession of faith in the *Life* of Elias of Enna and *Life* of Vitalis, and in Maiolus's resistance to his captors. These 'polemical debate' passages form a distinct aspect of some hagiographies of the late tenth and eleventh centuries, examples of which can be found in both Greek and Latin texts. But there is also an example to be found in a hagiographical text that circulated far more widely than either the Cluniac dossier on Maiolus or the Italo-Greek saints' lives, and that can be found in both Greek and Latin versions in the eleventh century, and subsequently in the vernacular as well – but which we might not immediately associate with Christian–Muslim polemic –

---

[56] *The Historia Ihersolimitana of Robert the Monk*, v, ed. Damien Kempf and Marcus Bull (Woodbridge, 2013), 51–5.

[57] *Passio Thiemonis archiepiscopi*, xi, MGH (SS) 11, 51–62; John V. Tolan, 'Muslims as Pagan Idolaters in Chronicles of the First Crusade', in *Western Views of Islam and Medieval and Early Modern Europe*, ed. David R. Blanks and Michael Frassetto (New York, 1999), 97–117, at 97–8; Suzanne Akbari, *Idols in the East: European Representations of Islam and the Orient, 1100-1450* (Ithaca, 2009), 245–7.

[58] See e.g. John D. Cotts, 'The Exegesis of Violence in the Crusade Rhetoric of Ralph Niger and Peter of Blois', in *Uses of the Bible in Crusader Sources*, ed. Elizabeth Lapina and Nicholas Morton (Leiden, 2017), 273–95.

namely the *Life* of St Katherine of Alexandria. The earliest known versions are Greek, but Latin versions, originating from the mid-eleventh century from Monte Cassino, became phenomenally popular in Normandy and England in the twelfth century, and later in German-speaking territories. There are numerous spin-off versions, and also prayers, hymns and a (now lost) liturgical drama from the early twelfth century.[59] Of course, the *Life* of St Katherine has, ostensibly, nothing to do with Christian–Muslim encounters, but the centre-piece of the text is the debate Katherine holds with pagan philosophers sent by the emperor to argue her out of her foolish adherence to Christian teaching. Katherine ends up, through flouting the philosophers' arguments, converting them to Christianity. The theology in her argument is similar to that in Elias of Enna's homily to the Muslims, namely that the gods worshipped by the pagans are not real, but human constructs. In essentials, the same dynamic is at work here as in the Italo-Greek hagiographies: the saint suffers violence or the threat of violence at the hands of a non-Christian power, and responds by verbal demonstration of the tenets of Christian doctrine, and an attempt to convert the wielders of violence.[60]

In thinking about Christian–Muslim interactions in the period before and during the crusades, we have at our disposal a wider set of writings than has usually been deployed. Like the *Lives* of Elias the Troglodyte and Vitalis of Castronuovo, the *Life* of St Katherine and other texts significant for the spread of her cult were circulating in monastic circles in the West at the same time as texts that presented Christian/non-Christian contacts in purely bellicose ways. Furthermore, these writings are distinctively monastic. They were produced in monasteries, and largely for monastic communities and their clients. While portraying Muslims as hostile to Christians, sacrilegious, even barbaric, they emphasise polemical dialogue and conversion as legitimate forms of resistance, rather than violence. The protagonists of these texts are unarmed, and prepared for martyrdom. If we consider what is happening in such texts from the point of view of the communities that produced and used them, we can see that confrontation with Muslims, with the demands such encounters make on the saint's fortitude, faith and resources of persuasion, is an inherent part of the construction of monastic sanctity.

Acknowledgements. A version of this article was first presented as a Royal Historical Society lecture, read on 4 February 2022.

---

[59] The best guide is Christine Walsh, *The Cult of St Katherine of Alexandria in Early Medieval Europe* (Aldershot, 2007).

[60] For fuller discussion, see Andrew Jotischky, 'Saint's Cults and Devotions on the Norman Edge: The Case of St Katherine of Alexandria', in *The Normans and the 'Norman Edge': People, Polities and Identities on the Frontiers of Medieval Europe*, ed. Keith J. Stringer and Andrew Jotischky (2019), 191–218, esp. 212–18.

Cite this article: Jotischky A (2023). Monks and the Muslim Enemy: Conversion, Polemic and Resistance in Monastic Hagiography in the Age of the Crusades, c. 1000–1250. *Transactions of the Royal Historical Society* 1, 5–22. https://doi.org/10.1017/S0080440122000159

Transactions of the RHS (2023), **1**, 23–43
doi:10.1017/S0080440122000160

ARTICLE

The 'Dying' Bourbon Dynasty: The Diplomatic Role of the Spanish Monarchy in the Long Nineteenth Century

David San Narciso

Departamento de Historia Moderna y Contemporánea, Universidad de Valencia, Valencia, Spain
Email: dasanar@uv.es

(Received 30 March 2022; revised 27 September 2022; accepted 7 November 2022; first published online 9 December 2022)

Abstract

This article explores one of the main arenas in which change came over the role of the monarchy as part of Europe's transition to a modern political system: diplomacy. Traditionally, there had been a dual aspect to monarchy that merged dynastic and state interests. The creation of modern constitutional political systems in the nineteenth century forced European crowns to modify their prerogatives and effective power, sharing this with elected politicians. This included foreign policy, which thenceforward pursued national interests that did not always agree with dynastic ones. Focusing on the Spanish branch of the house of Bourbon, I examine this involved and controversial process. Firstly, I trace the breaking of the Bourbon alliance which had been dominant in the eighteenth century and its unsettled reconfiguration into the worldwide system created by the Congress of Vienna. I then discuss the complex imposition of the nation-state interest over the dynastic one in a time of deep ideological division – between constitutional and absolutist systems – and traumatic revolutions that overthrew Bourbon monarchs. From the mid-nineteenth century onwards, the liberal and nationalist wave forced transnational family ties to succumb to national interest.

Keywords: monarchy; nineteenth century; diplomacy; nationalism; Spain

On 4 May 1898, Lord Salisbury gave a controversial speech dividing 'the nations of the world as the living and the dying'.[1] The former were those great countries 'growing in power every year, growing in wealth, dominion, and

---

[1] *The Times*, 5 May 1898.

the perfection of their organization', whereas the latter were states characterised by disorganisation, decay, misgovernment and corruption. 'Decade after decade,' he said, 'they are weaker, poorer, and less provided with leading men or institutions in which they can trust.' In his opinion, 'the inevitable result' was quite obvious. Amidst his colleagues' laughter and cheers, he stated, 'the living nations will gradually encroach on the territory of the dying'. Thus, they would cure or cut up 'these unfortunate patients', removing 'desolation and sterility by means of this aggrandisement'. Nobody was unaware that the prime minister was alluding to Spain.[2] Just a fortnight earlier, US ships had attacked Spanish possessions in America and Asia to consummate its 'manifest destiny'.

That conflict exposed the definitive retreat of Spain to second-class power status,[3] but it also confirmed the end of an era when sovereigns claimed the right to play a leading diplomatic role. As monarchs throughout the century had done, Maria Cristina of Habsburg–Lorraine promptly corresponded with her royal cousins to request their support. The Spanish queen regent thus invoked a sort of monarchic, supranational fraternity to oppose the republican United States. Months before the war broke out, in 1898, she wrote to Queen Victoria 'to expose my complicated situation' to her but also to seek 'her powerful support and great advice'.[4] Maria Cristina went into all the outrages committed by the United States in financing the Cuban independence fighters to provoke a war and exclaimed, 'I can no longer allow my country to be humiliated.' Appealing for peacekeeping, she begged Victoria 'not to deny me her powerful protection'. Victoria's response foreshadowed the kind of tensions her grandson, George V, would be exposed to sixteen years later. After consulting her government, Victoria responded in terms of the strictest neutrality. However, in her journal, she wrote: 'it is monstrous of America'.[5] Informal contacts between monarchs might continue, but their personal preferences were already outweighed by state interest.

In 1898, Spain was reduced to a 'dying nation', a lesser and decayed country that had lost its former powerful international presence. However, the same certainly did not apply to its monarchy and dynasty.[6] The Bourbons restoration in 1874 succeeded in stabilising the Spanish monarchy with the explicit support of other European sovereigns.[7] Fears, after the Paris Commune, of revolutionary excesses and the republic undoubtedly helped. The Spanish

---

[2] Rosario de la Torre, 'La prensa madrileña y el discurso de Lord Salisbury sobre las naciones moribundas', *Cuadernos de Historia Moderna y Contemporánea*, 6 (1985), 163–80.

[3] James W. Cortada (ed.), *Spain in the Nineteenth-Century World: Essays on Spanish Diplomacy, 1789-1898* (Westport, 1994); Alfred W. McCoy, Josep M. Fradera and Stephen Jacobson (eds.), *Endless Empires: Spain's Retreat, Europe's Eclipse, America's Decline* (Madison, 2012).

[4] Queen Maria Cristina to Queen Victoria, 17 March, 1898, in *The Letters of Queen Victoria. Third Series*, ed. George Early Buckle (1932), iii, 236–7.

[5] Queen Maria Cristina to Queen Victoria, 21 April 1898, *ibid.*, 244.

[6] David San Narciso, Margarita Barral and Carolina Armenteros (eds.), *Monarchy and Liberalism in Spain: The Building of the Nation State, 1780-1931* (2021).

[7] Julio Salom, *España en la Europa de Bismarck. La política exterior de Cánovas, 1871-1881* (Madrid, 1967).

monarchy now participated as one of the cosmopolitan European royal families in a way that had never been seen before. In 1906, Alfonso XIII actually married Victoria Eugenie of Battenberg, one of Queen Victoria's most cherished granddaughters. This was far from the previous image of the Bourbon monarchy. In 1857, Victoria and Albert urged the young newly crowned Pedro V of Portugal to marry, avoiding especially the Bourbons. In their opinion, the dynasty 'had not only a simple education', but 'it was also corrupted by the Court's incest'.[8] Four years later, Albert again advised him not to marry a Spanish princess. Her blood, he claimed, 'promised little spiritual, moral, and physical health'.[9] The Neapolitan branch of the family was not spared censure either. In 1857, Pedro wrote to the Portuguese ambassador in London discussing possible marriage alliances for his sister. In his opinion, they had to reject the proposal of the duke of Calabria because 'it would make us, through the bond of kinship, partners in the intrigues that fly from Naples to Madrid and from Madrid to Naples'.[10] Political reasons strongly discouraged the match. As he wrote, 'we are one of the few princes who have accepted the representative regime wisely and sincerely', while the Bourbons 'represent diametrically opposed principles'. Their counterpoint was 'the house of Savoy which, since 1848, has given highly regarded proof of its adherence to the constitutional regime'.[11]

The image of the Bourbons as a degenerate dynasty circulated throughout Europe and created a body of opinion that associated moral excesses with the purest political absolutism. Hence, following Lord Salisbury's analogy, there were living and dying dynasties. Among them, there was a clear winner: the Coburgs. From the 1830s onwards, that family extended its tentacles steadily around Europe until its infiltration into the innermost realms.[12] On the other side, the identity of the corresponding dying dynasty, over the top of which they built their power, was evident: the Bourbons. Decade after decade, revolution after revolution, this family saw its power and international influence progressively decline. Historians have focused primarily on the winners. However, there are almost no studies dealing with the losers. This article proposes a global analysis of the house of Bourbon, centred on its Spanish branch. Based on a wide range of sources, I study the role that the monarchy played in the modern diplomatic system. Firstly, I trace the breaking of the Bourbon alliance which had been dominant in the eighteenth century. But I also locate it in the worldwide system reconfiguration that followed the Congress of Vienna. I

---

[8] Prince Albert to Pedro V, 13 Feb. 1857, in *Correspondência entre D. Pedro V e seu tio, o príncipe Alberto*, ed. Maria Filomena Mónica (Lisbon, 2000), 188.

[9] Prince Albert to Pedro V, 16 May 1861, *ibid.*, 367.

[10] Pedro V to Francisco de Almeida, 7 Dec. 1857, in *Cartas de D. Pedro V ao conde de Lavradio*, ed. Ruben Andresen Leitâo (Porto, 1949), 167–8.

[11] Bernardo de Sá da Bandeira to Luís I, 22 Dec. 1861, in Julio de Vilhena, *D. Pedro V e o seu reinado: novos documentos* (Coimbra, 1922), 174–5.

[12] Olivier Defrance, *Léopold Ier et le clan Cobourg* (Brussels, 2004); Karina Urbach (ed.), *Royal Kinship: Anglo-German Family Networks, 1815-1918* (Munich, 2008); Patrick Weber, *La saga des Saxe-Cobourg* (Paris, 2016).

then discuss the complex imposition of the nation-state interest over the dynastic one in foreign affairs.

The monarchy in the modern diplomatic world

Its role in international affairs was one of the most relevant and lasting powers of the monarchy. Historiography has traditionally defended an idealised model of royal adaptation to the modern world, according to which liberalism restricted monarchy to its symbolic place throughout the nineteenth century. Thus, it is said, the institution relinquished its active and effective political role, avoiding political struggles and becoming apolitical. The reality, however, was somewhat different. The transition was much more complicated and less peaceful. Liberal politicians all around Europe fought to impose themselves over monarchies and repurpose the institution.[13] The battles between parliaments, monarchs and governments were sometimes extraordinarily intense.[14] However, it was the executive branch that was central to these fights. Notwithstanding the separation of powers, no constitution enshrined what the nature of the monarch's coexistence with ministers should be. It was primarily a process achieved through political practice. Sovereigns were reluctant to yield even a whit of their sovereignty, prerogatives or effective exercise of power. To that end, they would use their constitutional prerogative of appointing and dismissing ministers and take advantage of the cabinet's need for royal support to survive. Thus, ministers had to get the upper hand over the monarchy. And this was only possible with strong political parties and parliamentary forms of government.[15] The result was frequent tensions between monarchs and politicians throughout the whole of the century.

Diplomacy was one of the main battlefields. Traditionally, this was the monarchy's dominion par excellence, in which state politics merged with dynastic considerations. The established account would have it that the government progressively appropriated and absorbed the sovereign's role in foreign affairs. While this process might be apparent in theory, it was much tougher in practice. The monarch's removal from active power in foreign affairs was a convoluted and lengthy process all over Europe and almost up to 1914.[16] Sovereigns' day-to-day involvement in policy could be progressively reduced, but their governments always required their consent for their most consequential policies. In the end, the cabinet had to have royal support to survive. In that

---

[13] Dieter Langewiesche, *Die Monarchie im Jahrhundert Europas. Selbstbehauptung durch Wandel im 19 Jahrhundert* (Heidelberg, 2013); Volker Sellin, *Violence and Legitimacy: European Monarchy in the Age of Revolutions* (Berlin, 2018).

[14] Martin Kirsch, *Monarch und Parlament im 19. Jahrhundert. Der monarchische Konstitutionalismus als europäischer Verfassungstyp* (Göttingen, 1999).

[15] Petra Schleiter and Edward Morgan-Jones, 'Constitutional Power and Competing Risks: Monarchs, Presidents, Prime Ministers, and the Termination of East and West European Cabinets', *American Political Science Review*, 103 (2009), 496–91; Carsten Anckar, 'Constitutional Monarchies and Semi-constitutional Monarchies: A Global Historical Study, 1800–2017', *Contemporary Politics*, 27 (2021), 23–40.

[16] Roderick McLean, *Royalty and Diplomacy in Europe, 1890-1914* (Cambridge, 2001).

sense, as the new diplomatic history has emphasised, it is necessary to reconsider the importance of agency,[17] especially in a field that was controlled by few people and demanded the utmost secrecy. Besides monarchs being intent on defending their prerogatives, governments of all political stripes also understood that informal royal networks could be useful to them, so they favoured correspondence and international meetings between sovereigns to mediate in the governmental interest.

Beyond the direct involvement of monarchs in diplomacy, the nineteenth century saw an intensified struggle for the direction and conditioning of foreign policy. The first decades were presided over by a 'royal international', as Johannes Paulmann has called it.[18] European monarchs still formed a 'fraternity' to promote political equilibrium, thwart revolution and stabilise the monarchical principle. After the revolutions of 1848, this situation changed radically. For this to happen, as Eric Hobsbawm pointed out, European crowns had 'to provide a new, or at least, a supplementary national foundation', as opposed to the traditional one.[19] Both in new and former states, dynastic and personal bonds between sovereigns slowly ceased to structure foreign affairs and state relations. Modern diplomacy would be distinguished by bureaucratisation, professionalisation, the growth of government control and greater openness to parliamentary and even public scrutiny.[20] But above all, it was characterised by the imposition of a prevailing national interest. As Emperor Franz Joseph I wrote to his mother during the Crimean War (1853–6), 'leaving aside Emperor Nicholas as a person, I am pleased with the weakness Russia is now showing'.[21] 'Even if it is hard to have to stand up against former friends,' he continued, 'there is no other way in politics.' Ultimately, 'it is urgent to be Austrian above all'. In that sense, Johannes Paulmann concluded that the *fin de siècle* monarchs 'still acted on an international stage, but their role was now that of figures from national dynasties'.[22] Also, there was no longer a direct connection 'between dynastic and inter-State relations'. Thus it happened that three cousins fought on two sides in the Great War despite their close relationships.[23]

The very constitutional British monarchy illustrates this struggle for influence over domestic and, notably, international policy. Many historians have placed in Queen Victoria's reign the diminution of the monarchy's political role and its

---

[17] David Reynolds, 'International History, the Cultural Turn, and the Diplomatic Twitch', *Cultural and Social History*, 3 (2006), 75–91.

[18] Johannes Paulmann, 'Searching for a "Royal International": The Mechanics of Monarchical Relations in Nineteenth-Century Europe', in *The Mechanics of Internationalism: Culture, Society, and Politics from the 1840s to the First World War*, ed. Martin Geyer and Johannes Paulmann (Oxford, 2001), 156–8.

[19] Eric Hobsbawm, *Nations and Nationalism since 1780* (Cambridge, 1990), 84; Charlotte Backerra, Milinda Banerjee and Cathleen Sarti (eds.), *Transnational Histories of the 'Royal Nation'* (2017).

[20] Matthew Anderson, *The Rise of Modern Diplomacy, 1450–1919* (New York, 2013), 142–8.

[21] Franz Schnürer (ed.), *Briefe Kaiser Franz Josephs I. an seine Mutter, 1838–1872* (Munich, 1930), 232.

[22] Paulmann, 'Searching for a "Royal International"', 176.

[23] Catrine Clay, *King, Kaiser, Tsar: Three Royal Cousins Who Led the World to War* (New York, 2008); Matthew Glencross and Judith Rowbotham (eds.), *Monarchies and the Great War* (2018).

seclusion into a symbolic sphere. The reality was far more intricate. Encouraged by her husband, Prince Albert, and his 'Coburg model' of a powerful monarchy, she firmly believed that sovereigns had an active role in the cabinet.[24] They understood the Crown as the only institution qualified to protect the general interest of the nation. For that reason, there was no place for insignificant political squabbles. They sought to build a strong monarchy that might govern above politics and supervise them. Both Victoria and Albert shared this vision in the diplomatic field. To quote David Cannadine, they 'regarded foreign affairs as the crown's special preserve'.[25] Their contemporaries could see this too. Lord Clarendon wrote in 1856 that the royal couple 'labour under the curious mistake that the Foreign Office is their particular department and that they have a right to control, if not to direct, foreign policy'.[26]

This fact evidenced a deep problem with the constitutional procedures and the political competencies of the monarchy. Albert wrote to the prime minister in 1850 stating that the queen 'has a right to demand from him [the foreign secretary] that she be made thoroughly acquainted with the whole object and tendency of the policy to which her consent is required'.[27] She also should have assurances 'that the policy is not arbitrarily altered from the original line, that important steps be not concealed from her, nor her name used without her sanction'. Queen Victoria stuck to these views throughout her reign. For example, during the Polish uprising against Russia and during the Schleswig–Holstein crisis (1863),[28] she wrote to the foreign secretary expressing 'her desire that no step is taken in foreign affairs without her previous sanction being obtained'.[29] Even so, over the course of her reign the monarch's prerogatives and effective power progressively gave way to a new form of influence. In the latter part of her reign, responsible ministers took charge of foreign policy and imposed the state interest. For this to happen, however, it was necessary to have strong, vigorous political structures. Thus, as Vernon Bogdanor has pointed out, from 1868 onwards, 'the growth of organized parties pushed the sovereign, somewhat against her will, above party'.[30]

British monarchs were not exceptional in their practices. Their European cousins reproduced these dynamics in articulating international policy. In

---

[24] Richard Williams, *The Contentious Crown: Public Discussion of the British Monarchy in the Reign of Queen Victoria* (Aldershot, 1997), 92–107.

[25] David Cannadine, 'The Last Hanoverian Sovereign? The Victorian Monarchy in Historical Perspective, 1688–1988', in *The First Modern Society: Essays in English History in Honor of Lawrence Stone*, ed. Augustus Lee Beier, David Cannadine and James Rosenheim (Cambridge, 1989), 143.

[26] Lord Clarendon to George Cornewall Lewis, 26 Dec. 1856, in Herbert Maxwell, *The Life and Letters of George Willian Frederick* (1913), I, 340–1.

[27] Prince Albert to John Russell, 1 Apr. 1850, in Frank Eyck, *The Prince Consort: A Political Biography* (Bath, 1975), 132–3.

[28] W. E. Mosse, 'Queen Victoria and Her Ministers in the Schleswig–Holstein Crisis 1863–1864', *English Historical Review*, 307 (1963), 263–83.

[29] Queen Victoria to Lord Palmerston, 11 Aug. 1863, in *The Letters of Queen Victoria. Second Series*, ed. George Early Buckle (1926), I, 102.

[30] Vernon Bogdanor, *The Monarchy and the Constitution* (Oxford, 1995), 27.

France, for example, Louis Philippe was reluctant to lose any vestige of his power.[31] When there was a powerful prime minister, the king would mount a defensive resistance, and if the government was weak, he went on the offensive. Thus, when André Dupin insisted on the need for a real prime minister and the king's political seclusion, Louis Philippe 'sternly responded that he did not intend to put himself under tutelage by appointing a viceroy'.[32] This fact was especially noticeable in foreign policy. As Adolphe Thiers attested in 1835, 'the king wants to do everything, talks and never listens, pretends to manage foreign affairs personally'.[33] He even corresponded secretly with some of his ambassadors, such as Talleyrand. Napoleon III continued this practice and took it to its fullest extent. In his mind, he had both to reign and to govern. As he wrote to his minister of war in 1856, 'I want and have to know everything because I alone am responsible for the facts of government.'[34] Respecting international politics, Napoleon III not only maintained secret correspondence, his parallel diplomacy went as far as his having direct contact with sovereigns or their ambassadors in Paris.[35] He did not require the mediation of his minister for foreign affairs, or even his presence or knowledge. He told the Prussian ambassador, 'a statement written by my foreign minister would be of no importance. I alone know what France's foreign policy will be.'[36]

Examples were widespread across Europe. In Belgium, King Leopold was directly involved in shaping Europe through his family ties for much of the nineteenth century.[37] Personal diplomacy went on until 1909, based on parallel networks and developed without their government's knowledge, particularly in colonial aspects.[38] Something similar applies to the house of Savoy after the unification of Italy in 1861,[39] and even to the Austro-Hungarian Empire. As Emperor Franz Joseph told the militarist count Franz Graf Conrad von Hötzendorf in 1911, 'I do foreign policy' and 'my policy is a policy of peace. So, my minister of foreign affairs conducts my politics in this sense.'[40] The Spanish monarchs were integrated into these very same general dynamics.

---

[31] Charles H. Pouthas, 'Les ministères de Louis-Philippe', *Revue d'histoire moderne et contemporaine*, 1 (1954), 102–30.

[32] André Dupin, *Mémoires* (Paris, 1856), II, 441.

[33] *Journal et correspondance intimes de Cuvillier-Fleury*, ed. Ernest Betin (Paris, 1903), II, 18 Feb. 1835, 129.

[34] Napoleon III to Jean-Baptiste Philibert Vaillant, 8 Sep. 1856, quoted in Émile Ollivier, 'Napoléon III. Création et procédés du gouvernement impérial', *Revue des Deux Mondes*, 145 (1898), 801.

[35] Yves Bruley, *La diplomatie du sphinx. Napoléon III et sa politique internationale* (Paris, 2015).

[36] Count Von der Goltz to Otto von Bismarck, 27 Feb. 1858, quoted in Émile Ollivier, 'Napoléon III. Son dessein international', *Revue des Deux Mondes*, 146 (1898), 69.

[37] Frédéric Marchesani, *Léopold Ier, roi diplomate, 1850-1865* (Brussels, 2007); Gita Deneckere, *Leopold I: De Eerste Koning Van Europa 1790-1865* (Antwerp, 2012).

[38] Jean Stengers, *L'action du roi en Belgique depuis 1831: pouvoir et influence* (Brussels, 2008).

[39] Paolo Colombo, *Il re d'Italia. Prerogative costituzionali e potere politico della Corona, 1848-1922* (Milan, 1999), 320–34.

[40] Friedrich Engel-Janosi, 'Der Monarch und seine Ratgeber', in *Probleme der franziskojosephinischen Zeit 1848-1916*, ed. Friedrich Engel-Janosi and Helmut Rumpler (Munich, 1967), 17.

Like the rest of their royal counterparts, the Bourbons had to find a new role in the liberal system. On international affairs, they competed fiercely with their ministers to define their competencies in diplomacy. But also, as I will demonstrate, they struggled to impose the national or family interest as a structuring principle for foreign affairs.

The Bourbons' dynastic dynamics in the age of revolutions

The French Revolution and the Napoleonic Wars dynamited the alliances maintained by the Bourbons during the eighteenth century. The so-called *Pacte de Famille* rhetorically appealed to a supra-state dynastic identity but created a political system of balance against England.[41] In 1761, during the Seven Years' War, Carlos III of Spain and Louis XV of France reaffirmed their mutual commitment and updated their offensive–defensive alliance. The imbalance created by England's conquest of Canada required this. In this way, based on 'the close ties of blood that unite the two monarchs', they made 'permanent and indissoluble' the duties 'that naturally bring kinship and friendship'.[42] The agreement perpetuated 'the distinguished mentality of Louis XIV', which prioritised the union against England. The Italian branch of the Bourbons – the king of the Two Sicilies and the duke of Parma – joined the new covenant. As the seventh article stated, the Spanish monarch exercised a direct influence on them as father and elder brother, respectively.

The alliance was still in force in 1789 when the system collapsed. Carlos IV initially upheld an ambiguous policy towards the revolutionary governments. The death of Louis XVI made him radically change his position and join the First Coalition. However, once the Directory stabilised, Spain renewed the traditional alliance. The eighteenth-century logic of union against England prevailed over any dynastic dynamic to preserve Spain's power.[43] Thus, in 1801, Carlos IV signed with Napoleon Bonaparte, then First Consul, an important agreement. In addition to Spain's ceding Louisiana and several warships to France, they also divided up the northern Italian states.[44] Spain guaranteed that Ferdinando of Bourbon would cede to France the duchy of Parma. In exchange, his son – married to Carlos IV's daughter, Maria Luisa of Bourbon – received the duchy of Tuscany with the new status of the kingdom of Etruria. The alliance changed drastically after the defeat at Trafalgar (1805) when English ships destroyed the Spanish navy. In 1808 Napoleon decided to intervene directly and appoint his brother, Joseph Bonaparte, as king of

---

[41] Didier Ozanam, 'Dinastía, diplomacia y política exterior', in *Los Borbones: Dinastía y memoria de la nación en la España del siglo XVIII*, ed. Pablo Fernández-Albadalejo (Madrid, 2002), 17–46; María Victoria López-Cordón, 'Pacte de famille ou intérêts d'État? La monarchie française et la diplomatie espagnole du XVIIᵉ siècle', in *La présence des Bourbons en Europe XVIᵉ–XXIᵉ siècle*, ed. Lucien Bély (Paris, 2003), 185–220.

[42] Alejandro del Cantillo, *Tratados, convenios y declaraciones de paz y de comercio que han hecho los monarcas españoles de la Casa de Borbón desde el año de 1700* (Madrid, 1843), 468–81.

[43] Emilio La Parra, *La alianza de Godoy con los revolucionarios: España y Francia a fines del siglo XVIII* (Madrid, 1992).

[44] Cantillo, *Tratados, convenios*, 697–8.

Spain. An agitated political situation compounded the loss of military power. Fernando VII supported a riot against his father, forcing Carlos IV to abdicate. Meanwhile, French troops invaded Italy. Napoleon proclaimed Joachim Murat as king of Naples while the Bourbons secluded themselves in Sicily, under British protection.[45]

From that moment, the dynastic alliance survived more as a rhetorical appeal than an effective action, despite fighting together against Napoleon. As Paul Schroeder has shown, between 1813 and 1815 Europe abandoned the competitive balance-of-power politics of the previous century.[46] A new equilibrium was established based on a system of rights and obligations underpinned by a security alliance among the five major powers. While the new international system arose, the Bourbons' dynastic community collapsed, generating intense civil wars and clashing legitimacies.[47] The Spanish branch had to find a new place in a world where many of the territorial, social and political changes introduced by Napoleon endured.[48] The process was especially involved, mainly due to a lack of perspective and political reality on the part of Fernando VII and his ministers. They went into the treaty negotiations following the Napoleonic Wars with a false sense of returning to 1808. The instructions received by the ambassadors were highly eloquent. They demanded Louisiana, economic compensation and the restitution of plundered artworks, but the emphasis was on reclaiming the dynastic Bourbons' rights in Italy.[49] Against this fiction, the great powers merely invited Spain to accede to the treaties already signed. Fernando was obliged to contribute men during the Hundred Days in order to be a signatory party. In other words, he should have participated as a true regulatory power; instead, the reality after decades of struggle was a decomposed empire, economically bankrupt, in demographic decline and with its military power in decay.

Nevertheless, the phantom of the *Pacte de Famille* and its renewal remained ever present. Chateaubriand mentioned it in a pamphlet supporting the Bourbons' restoration in France. In his opinion, Napoleon's great mistake was his 'impious, sacrilegious, hateful, and above all anti-French actions' in Spain.[50] Not content with 'ruling it as a province from which to extract blood and gold', he wanted to 'rule the throne personally'.[51] To do so, 'he sowed discord in the royal family, kidnapped it in defiance of all human and

---

[45] John Davis, *Naples and Napoleon: Southern Italy and the European Revolutions, 1780-1860* (Oxford, 2006); Pierre-Marie Delpu, Igor Moullier and Mélanie Traversier (eds.), *Le royaume de Naples à l'heure française, 1806-1815* (Villeneuve-d'Ascq, 2018).

[46] Paul Schroeder, *The Transformation of European Politics, 1763-1848* (Oxford, 1994).

[47] Carmine Pinto, 'Sovranità, guerre e nazioni. La crisi del mondo borbonico e la formazione degli Stati moderni (1806-1920)', *Meridiana*, 81 (2014), 9-25.

[48] David Laven and Lucy Riall (eds.), *Napoleon's Legacy: Problems of Government in Restoration Europe* (Oxford, 2000).

[49] Pedro Gómez Labrador, *Mélanges sur la vie privée et publique du Marquis de Labrador écrits par lui-même* (Paris, 1849).

[50] François-René de Chateaubriand, *De Buonaparte, des Bourbons, et de la nécessité de se rallier à nos princes légitimes* (Paris, 1814), 13.

[51] *Ibid.*, 33.

divine laws, and invaded the territory of a faithful people who had fought for him'.[52] Thus, France must re-establish the *Pacte de Famille* to regain its power. For its part, England feared a revival of the alliance. In a treaty in 1814, it included a secret article whereby Spain undertook 'not to enter any obligation of the so-called *Pacte de Famille* that would encroach upon its Independence or prejudice the English interests'.[53] However, a few days later, the Franco-Spanish peace and friendship treaty included Talleyrand's classified commitment in this regard. He promised to mediate 'on behalf of the Spanish Bourbon princes who had possessions in Italy and make an order for Spain to obtain compensation'.[54] They thus attended the Congress of Vienna together. Consequently, the loss of power of one had a negative influence on the other. Despite the favourable international image Spain enjoyed for defeating Napoleon in 1812, it did not achieve its objectives.

Following the king's instructions, Spanish diplomats refused to agree to the Treaties of Paris and the Final Act of Vienna. It was the reaction of a power that neither understood its international degradation nor its consequences. Two factors conditioned the Spanish integration into the Restoration system: the Bourbons' request in Italy and the territorial integrity of its empire in America. In other words, Spain followed the eighteenth-century logic of competition with Austria for hegemony in Italy and with England in America. In both cases, it started from a precarious situation. Firstly, the Bourbons had been restored in Naples by Austrian arms and not by Spanish diplomacy.[55] And secondly, England had taken advantage of the Latin American independence revolutions to extend its informal empire and economic influence in the region.[56] Fernando sought to continue the spirit of the *Pacte de Famille* with France, at least officially and rhetorically, to achieve his aims. However, their international position had changed radically. Besides, thorough ideological differences weakened the Bourbons' solidarity: Louis XVIII in France promoted a policy of forgetting, and Ferdinando I accepted in Naples many of the Napoleonic reforms, whereas the Spanish monarch maintained an intransigent counter-revolutionary absolutism.[57]

Given these complications with the traditional alliance, Fernando VII did not hesitate to approach Tsar Alexander I. A confluence of interests facilitated the agreement.[58] Spain offered Russia the prospect of establishing a foothold in the Mediterranean and curbing Austrian supremacy in Italy. At the same time, it allowed the Russian–American Company along the California coast to

---

[52] *Ibid.*, 34.

[53] Cantillo, *Tratados, convenios*, 732–4.

[54] *Ibid.*, 734–41.

[55] Marco Mugnaini, *Italia e Spagna nell'età contemporanea. Cultura, politica e diplomazia, 1814-1870* (Turin, 1994), 68–9.

[56] Gabriel Paquette, 'The Dissolution of the Spanish Atlantic Monarchy', *The Historical Journal*, 52 (2009), 175–212.

[57] Juan Luis Simal, '"Strange Means of Governing": The Spanish Restoration in European Perspective (1813–1820)', *Journal of Modern European History*, 15 (2017), 197–220.

[58] Ana María Schop, *Un siglo de relaciones diplomáticas y comerciales entre España y Rusia, 1733-1833* (Madrid, 1984).

strengthen its commercial power. For his part, the tsar could facilitate Bourbon pretensions in Italy and help Spain's pacification efforts in Latin America. Fernando established a direct, secret correspondence with Alexander. In summer 1814, the Spanish ambassador to Russia received instructions to arrange the king's marriage to the grand duchess Anna Pavlova. Alexander rejected the proposal, however, due to its diplomatic complications and 'the very terrible system adopted in Spain under the excessive influence of clergy and friars'.[59]

Rapprochement strengthened after the signing of the Holy Alliance. On 31 March 1816, the tsar sent the Spanish king a letter, both inviting him to agree to the pact and advising him to take 'moderation measures to forget the past and consolidate the future'.[60] Fernando replied instantly, and secretly agreed to join the alliance. Barely three months later, he directly requested the tsar's mediation on behalf of the queen of Etruria.[61] The issue was too tangled by then. In the Treaty of Fontainebleau (1814) and the Final Act of Vienna, Russia granted the duchy of Parma to Maria Theresa of Habsburg – Napoleon's wife and the Austrian emperor's sister – to the detriment of María Luisa of Bourbon.[62] On the tsar's advice, Spain now began to accede to the treaties, except for the articles on the Parma question.[63] European chancelleries resumed negotiations, reaching an agreement that was only relatively satisfactory for Bourbon dynastic interests.[64] The duchy of Parma would be passed to María Luisa when the Austrian princess died, something that did not happen until 1847. However, the modification finally settled the Italian question.

Personal relationships between the monarchs changed drastically and dramatically in 1820 when a liberal revolution triumphed in Spain. Fernando VII had to swear the Constitution of 1812 and restore the institutions and persons harshly repressed in 1814. The liberal shock wave drove a constitutional shift across Europe, notably in the Mediterranean.[65] Ferdinando I of Naples was forced to swear the same constitution as his Spanish nephew. This new situation prompted the European powers to react swiftly. Later that year, the Holy Alliance agreed on the right to intervene in a country whose revolution could cause instability to the others. England and France provided legitimacy for this by abstaining. In 1821, after the Congress of Laibach, the Austrian military intervened in Naples and restored monarchical 'normality'. However, this also demonstrated Austrian hegemony in the Italian peninsula vis-à-vis the Bourbons.[66]

---

[59] *Ibid.*, 151–2.

[60] Jerónimo Becker, *Historia de las relaciones exteriores de España durante el siglo XIX* (Madrid, 1924), I, 418.

[61] Wenceslao Ramírez de Villaurrutia, *La reina de Etruria* (Madrid, 1923), 134–5.

[62] Marco Meriggi, *Ducato di Parma, Piacenza & Guastalla, 1731-1859* (Milan, 1995).

[63] Cantillo, *Tratados, convenios*, 745–84.

[64] *Ibid.*, 794–5.

[65] Maurizio Isabella and Konstantina Zanou (eds.), *Mediterranean Diasporas: Politics and Ideas in the Long Nineteenth Century* (2016).

[66] Paul Schroeder, *Metternich's Diplomacy at Its Zenith, 1820-1823* (Austin, 1973).

The intervention in Spain was slightly more intricate. Russia could not act directly, as it wished, or it would arouse the misgivings of the other powers and encourage France to take the initiative. At the Congress of Verona, the Holy Alliance pledged to help Louis XVIII to intervene in Spain if revolutionaries attacked it, put Fernando VII's life in danger or modified the line of succession.[67] Besides, they agreed to send the Spanish government formal notes threatening to intervene. As Metternich wrote, the revolution there had posed a danger to Europe, serving as 'a model everywhere'.[68] Its constitution, moreover, provided that it was necessary 'to move towards moderation'. It 'required, above all, the king to be free' in both physical and political terms by restoring his sovereignty. Behind these words lurked Fernando VII's own shadow. He personally led the counter-revolution from the outset, even engaging in two thwarted putsches.[69] To this end, he sought the support of his cousins. Through his diplomats, he conveyed to the European courts a victimising discourse of a king held captive by the liberals.

Following the above dynamic, Fernando first sought Tsar Alexander's support. However, the Russian ambassador advised him to seek help from France. Dynastic ties as head of the house of Bourbon, as well as their being neighbours, suggested this. In December 1821, the Spanish king requested one of his mediators to make 'the foreign sovereigns know his very critical and painful situation'[70] so that, he continued, 'they may come to free me from the slavery and danger I am currently suffering'. His already liberated uncle, Ferdinando I of Naples, promptly wrote to the other kings communicating the request for help. France finally intervened in 1823 after ascertaining England's neutrality.[71] Rather than the threat to European order, the French government favoured a discourse that appealed to monarchical solidarity and dynastic ties. At the state opening of parliament, Louis XVIII announced that 'a hundred thousand Frenchmen, commanded by a prince of my family, are ready to march invoking the name of Saint Louis to safeguard the Spanish throne for a grandson of Henry IV'.[72] Wellington noted with surprise to Metternich that the French government did not base 'its action on the revolutionary question, as agreed at Verona, but on the house of Bourbon, wishing to re-establish influence and relations with the Spanish branch as they had been before'.[73] An eventual revival of the *Pacte de Famille* would be an attack on England's honour, inasmuch as 'it sought to oppose its maritime power', but also that of Austria. Ultimately, he added, 'you are European and not a Bourbon', and France should not use international legitimacy to 'promote family views outside Europe's general interest'. In barely six months, the French army – supported by internal counter-revolutionary forces – managed to

---

[67] Irby Nichols, *The European Pentarchy and the Congress of Verona, 1822* (The Hague, 1971).

[68] 9 Jan. 1823, Madrid, Diario de Sesiones de Cortes (DSC), no. 98, 1298.

[69] Emilio La Parra, *Fernando VII. Un rey deseado y detestado* (Barcelona, 2018), 420–32.

[70] Wenceslao Ramírez de Villaurrutia, *Fernando VII, rey constitucional* (Madrid, 1922), 301.

[71] Emmanuel Larroche, *L'Expédition d'Espagne. 1823: de la guerra selon la Charte* (Rennes, 2013).

[72] François-René de Chateaubriand, *Congrès de Vérone. Guerre d'Espagne* (Paris, 1838), I, 281–2.

[73] Duke of Wellington to Prince Metternich, 1 Apr. 1823, in Arthur Wellesley Wellington (ed.), *Dispatches, Correspondence, and Memoranda* (1867), II, 83–6.

defeat liberalism and 'freed' Fernando VII. To avoid uprisings, as in 1808, they were careful to present themselves as the monarch's collaborators. Thus, as Chateaubriand wrote retrospectively, 'legitimism burns gunpowder under the [Bourbon] white flag for the first time since the Napoleonic Empire', succeeding 'where his army failed'.[74]

French diplomacy not only sought to restore Fernando VII in Spain; it also wanted to face down the challenge of Spanish American independence, for its own and the Bourbons' benefit. Chateaubriand proposed creating new constitutional monarchies in America, headed up by Spanish princes, to halt both the republican and British expansion.[75] The idea was not entirely original. In 1821, American deputies in the Cortes proposed a solution to the conflict. They argued for the creation of a federal empire, wherein the Spanish Cortes would have three sections in America: Mexico, Santa Fé and Lima. Each of them would be governed 'in the king's name' by a person, 'among them members of the royal family', responsible to Fernando VII and the Cortes.[76] However, the monarch perceived the problem in quite the opposite way. Fernando even considered of moving to Mexico in 1820, to escape the liberal revolution.[77] The obstinacy with which he closed off the transatlantic monarchical solidarity solution exasperated the diplomats, mainly because, as the French minister for foreign affairs pointed out, 'to place Spanish princes at the head of the government in this vast colony is not relevant to Spain alone'.[78] The question was 'of great interest to all European countries, which did not want the republican system to be established throughout the American continent'. Besides, he concluded, this federal monarchical solution was the only way for Spain 'to preserve its relationships with its overseas possessions'.

The second restoration of Fernando VII proceeded under this rhetoric of dynastic cooperation. The reality was quite different. Between 1823 and 1828, France maintained a standing army in Spain to 'ensure prosperity and tranquillity', allow the reorganisation of the armed forces and 'strengthen the government'.[79] The request came from the Spanish king himself, aware of his vulnerability to liberal insurrections. The relationship between the two Bourbon branches, and between their countries, was no longer on the equal terms posited in the *Pacte de Famille*.[80] France used the campaign to rebuild its international prestige and expand into areas previously controlled by Spain, such as North Africa. It also exerted a direct influence on Spanish politics, trying to moderate the reactionary, counter-revolutionary regime – assimilating it to the tempered 'constitutionalism' present in the French *Charte* of 1814 – and establish its economic interests. This tutelage created manifold tensions between Fernando VII and Charles X and

---

[74] François-René de Chateaubriand, *Mémoires d'outre-tombre* (Brussels, 1849), IV, 215.

[75] Chateaubriand, *Congrès de Vérone*, II, 260–4.

[76] 25 June 1821, DSC, no. 118, 2476–7.

[77] Josep Escrig, *Contrarrevolución y antiliberalismo en la independencia de México, 1810-1823* (Zaragoza, 2021), 267–71.

[78] Baron of Pasquier to Count of La Garde, 30 Nov. 1821, quoted in Carlos Villanueva, *La monarquía en América. Fernando VII y los nuevos Estados* (París, 1912), 107.

[79] Cantillo, *Tratados, convenios*, 833–8.

[80] Gonzalo Butrón, *La ocupación francesa de España, 1823-1828* (Cádiz, 1996).

broke the dynastic understanding after the Portuguese crisis (1826). Matters went far better between the Spanish and the Neapolitan branch.[81] As soon as he was freed, the Spanish king wrote to his uncle, Ferdinando I, assuring him that he would do 'everything possible to preserve and increase the relations that unite us'.[82] Ultimately, he continued, 'the similarity of our misfortunes' had made him feel 'very close to you'. This harmony paid off in 1829 when Fernando married his niece, Maria Cristina of Two Sicilies. Nevertheless, this unsteady Bourbon 'royal international' was about to collapse definitively.

The national turn and dynastic contradictions

The 1830s were a turning point in the decline of the Bourbon dynasty. The loss of power in foreign affairs was compounded by a profound crisis of legitimacy within the family. In March 1830, Fernando VII abolished the Salic Law of Succession a few months before his consort gave birth for the first time. Introduced in Spain by the Bourbons in 1713, this law forbade women from reigning, against Castilian tradition. Therefore, the birth of Princess Isabel in October opened a grave legal and dynastic dispute. The hitherto heir to the throne, Prince Carlos, did not accept his niece as Fernando's legitimate successor. For his part, Francesco I of Naples also protested. He mobilised his diplomacy to try to make a joint Bourbon complaint with Charles X. The change could endanger the dynasty's hold on the Spanish throne, compromise the European equilibrium and undermine their rights in the succession.[83]

The July Revolution in 1830 changed the main actors and altered this dynastic united front. In contrast to the liberal coherence shown by the Coburgs, the Bourbons' ideological consensus broke down. In France, the revolution dethroned Charles X and replaced him with his relative the liberal Louis Philippe of Orléans. Fear of revolutionary contagion, knowledge of his political moderation, and the consummated facts persuaded both Spanish and Neapolitan Bourbons to recognise him. Fernando VII hesitated at first and mobilised his army on the border. However, Louis Philippe used the Spanish liberal exiles, whom he supported morally and financially, to pressure the government and compel recognition.[84] For his part, Francesco I promptly accepted the king of the French. He knew Louis Philippe very well. Barely a month before, the hitherto duke of Orléans had given a party in his honour on his return from Madrid.[85] In addition to his well-known moderate disposition, the revolutionary echoes in northern Italy, stifled by Austria, persuaded the duke to recognise him quickly.[86] Thus, fear of the revolution spreading to

---

[81] Mugnaini, *Italia e Spagna*, 101–14.

[82] Fernando VII to Ferdinando I, 9 Oct. 1823, Naples, Archivio di Stato, Archivio Borbone, 178, quoted in Pedro Rújula, 'El rey', in *El Trienio Liberal (1820-1823). Una mirada política*, ed. Pedro Rújula and Ivana Fraasquet (Granada, 2020), 35.

[83] Becker, *Historia de las relaciones*, I, 597–8.

[84] Rafael Sánchez, 'L'Espagne et la Révolution de 1830', *Mélanges de la Casa de Velázquez*, 9 (1973), 567–79.

[85] Francesco Michitelli, *Storia delle rivoluzioni ne' Reami delle Due Sicilie* (Rome, 1860), I, 505–7.

[86] Acton Harold, *The Last Bourbons of Naples, 1825-1861* (New York, 1961).

their countries was more influential than dynastic ties. Fernando VII told the deposed Charles X, through a confidential agent, that he wanted to help him, but circumstances obliged him not to get involved. The Bourbons' solidarity broke, and a rift was created between a liberal branch of the family and another reactionary, legitimist one.[87]

In 1833, this fracture became even more acute. When Fernando VII died without male offspring, his daughter was proclaimed queen by the moderate absolutists and the liberals under the regency of his mother, Queen Maria Cristina of Bourbon–Two Sicilies. A dynastic and political civil war ensued in Spain. Supported by reactionary forces, Prince Carlos rose against Isabel II. The domestic dispute promptly fed into the international fight between liberal and reactionary powers, showing the tensions within the dynasty. Ferdinando II of Naples took diplomatic action before the European courts and called for the recognition of Prince Carlos.[88] On one side, he directed his efforts at enlisting Holy Alliance support, especially that of Austria. The leading conservative power preferred to wait for events to unfold before recognising Carlos, while supporting him financially. Metternich requested military victories and popular shows of support for the Carlist cause to even intervene diplomatically.

On the other side, Ferdinando set himself up as the mediator for the Bourbon family, arranging a three-way correspondence with his sister, Maria Cristina, and Louis Philippe to seek a negotiated end to the war. The formula always involved a marriage between Isabel II and Prince Carlos's heir, Carlos Luis of Bourbon. However, the other conditions varied according to the fortunes of war and the consolidation and deepening of liberalism. At times of great tension, such as in 1836, when progressive liberalism seized power through revolution, Maria Cristina asked her French and Neapolitan relatives to mediate. On several occasions, she even wrote requesting their intervention and help to get out of Spain.[89] When victory came within reach, she threw out the agreements and denied that a marriage alone would solve the problem. Obstacles were not only dynastic but also ideological. The determining factor was Louis Philippe's ambiguous attitude and the course of the war. In his early days, he had to approach England and even joined forces with the liberal Coburg dynasty. Despite being favourable to the Bourbon marriage pact solution, France's international policy was heavily dependent on British support, limiting its scope for action.[90] As a result, England, France, Portugal, and Spain signed a crucial alliance in 1834.[91] The first two gave economic, diplomatic, and military aid to the liberal sides in both civil conflicts. The

---

[87] Jean-Paul Bled, *Les lys en exil ou la seconde mort de l'Ancien Régime* (Paris, 1992); Bruno Dumons and Hilaire Multon (eds.), *«Blancs» et contre-révolutionnaires en Europe. Espaces, réseaux, cultures et mémoires, XVIIᵉ-XXᵉ siècles* (Rome, 2011).

[88] José Ramón Urquijo, *Relaciones entre España y Nápoles durante la primera guerra carlista* (Madrid, 1998).

[89] Isabel Burdiel, *Isabel II. Una biografía, 1830-1904* (Madrid, 2011), 40–51.

[90] Roger Bullen, 'France and the Problem of Intervention in Spain, 1834–1836', *The Historical Journal*, 20 (1977), 363–93.

[91] María Teresa Menchén, 'La Cuádruple Alianza (1834). La Península en un sistema occidental', *Cuadernos de la Escuela Diplomática*, 2 (1989), 31–51.

development of the war led to the victory of the liberals in 1839 and shaped a European Western constitutional, liberal system facing an absolutist Eastern one. The Carlists thus joined the list of the transnational legitimist dynasties oriented towards clearly reactionary positions, and the Bourbon family further aggravated its differences and loss of power.

Louis Philippe's political consolidation would progressively legitimise his dynasty within the traditional royal families. He then tried a rapprochement between the branches of the Bourbon family to rupture the watertight blocks of powers established in Vienna. His primary tool for this was the marriages of his offspring according to one international recognition policy.[92] In the beginning, he could only join the liberal dynasties, particularly the Coburgs. Thus, several marriages took place, merging the two families. In 1832, the king of the Belgians and head of the dynasty, Leopold, actually married the eldest daughter of Louis Philippe. However, Louis Philippe began to explore the possibility of joining an ancient dynasty. In 1837, he succeeded in marrying his heir to the niece of the king of Prussia. As Alphonse Lamartine stated, Louis Philippe's aim might be rightful according to 'the legitimate solicitousness that his royal paternity entails'.[93] He thus sought to 'royalize his blood more and more, to place his young sons in the high aristocracy of thrones'. But his goal was essentially political. He wanted 'to reconstitute a kind of universal monarchical family in a house of Bourbon resurrected from its ruins'.

In this context, the ghost of the *Pacte de Famille* appeared for the last time as a plausible strategic alliance dangerous to both English and Coburg interests. The idea was to shape a coherent, homogeneous and mighty south of Europe united by family ties.[94] As before, Louis Philippe used the marriages of his extensive progeny as a political instrument. He planned a triple alliance that involved union with the Neapolitan and Spanish Bourbons. As Guizot wrote, 'this triple combination would bind the three crowns, the three countries, very closely together and make the house of Bourbon more strongly constituted than ever'.[95] Despite Austria's reluctance, Louis Philippe succeeded in marrying Henry of Orléans to Maria Carolina of Bourbon–Two Sicilies in 1844. However, the third vertex of the triangle, the Spanish one, generated enormous difficulties. The balance between French international ambition and its agreement with Britain was by far the most complex. In 1843, Queen Victoria visited Louis Philippe in the Château d'Eu. Besides staging the Entente Cordiale, the visit aimed to discuss the marriage of the Spanish queen. In order to maintain the balance of diplomatic influence, they agreed that she could marry neither a Coburg nor a son of Louis Philippe. They also decided that Princess Luisa Fernanda, sister of Isabel II and heir to the throne, could marry Antoine of Orléans only when the queen's succession

---

[92] Grégoire Franconie, *Les lys et la cocarde. Royauté et Nation à l'âge romantique, 1830–1848* (Paris, 2021), 179–234.

[93] *Le Courrier Français*, 8 Oct. 1846.

[94] Salvo Mastellone, *La politica estera del Guizot (1840–1847). L'unione doganale, la lega borbónica* (Florence, 1957).

[95] Ernest Jones Parry, *The Spanish Marriages 1841–1846: A Study of the Influence of Dynastic Ambition upon Foreign Policy* (1936), 179.

was assured. Thus, neither the young queen's tastes nor the opinion of Spanish politicians was taken into account.

The candidate proposed by Louis Philippe was Francesco of Bourbon–Two Sicilies, the younger brother of both Ferdinando II and Maria Cristina. The triangle closed with the marriages of Isabel II and her sister to Neapolitan and French princes, respectively. This political movement led to the official recognition by Naples of the Spanish liberal monarchy, to the great indignation of Austria.[96] However, the count of Trapani displeased Spanish public opinion so much that it made his candidacy impossible. Many diplomatic manoeuvres to marry the queen of Spain began. Maria Cristina even wrote to the king of the Belgians and the duke of Saxony–Coburg to propose the marriage of Isabel II to Prince Leopold.[97] However, the vetoes between the two powers and the change in England's international policy with the advent of Palmerston left marriage to a Spanish Bourbon as the only possibility. In 1846, Queen Isabel finally married her cousin, Francisco de Asis of Bourbon. Simultaneously, and contravening what was agreed in Eu, Luisa Fernanda married Antoine of Orléans. Thus, France's alliance with England did not survive, nor was the Bourbon union planned by Louis Philippe consummated.[98]

The family entered less powerful and only partially united a turbulent political time during which their thrones began to fall one after the other, engulfed by the liberal, nationalist wave. As Lamartine concluded, 'it is no longer time for family pacts but between people'.[99] The coexistence of the monarchy and the nation was only possible insofar as 'the spirit of family and dynasty disappeared for the sake of the national essence and interest crowned by the revolution'. The Bourbon solidarity and dynastic interest should be subordinated to nationalism, while the monarchy was being nationalised.[100] The political earthquake of 1848 was felt throughout Europe, including in the Bourbon territories. It started in Naples, where Ferdinando II had to promulgate a liberal constitution and put a stop to the Sicilian insurrection, which lasted sixteenth long months. The newly appointed duke of Parma, Carlo II of Bourbon-Parma, had to abdicate in favour of his son Carlo and go into exile. Finally, the revolution dethroned Louis Philippe accused, among many things, of putting his personal and family interests before national ones.[101] The first Bourbon piece on the international chessboard had fallen.

The Italian unification process was the last and most complex challenge the dynasty would have to face. Neapolitan participation in the First Italian War of Independence (1848–9) against Austria, and its subsequent withdrawal, showed the contradictions and tensions that the dynasty experienced in trying to

---

[96] Federico Curato, *Il Regno delle Due Sicilie nella politica estera europea, 1830–1861* (Palermo, 1989).

[97] Burdiel, *Isabel II*, 164–6.

[98] Roger Bullen, *Palmerston, Guizot, and the Collapse of the Entente Cordiale* (1974).

[99] *Le Courrier Français*, 8 Oct. 1846.

[100] David San Narciso, 'Being a Nation through the Crown: Banal Monarchism and Nation-Building in Spain, 1833–68', *European Review of History*, 27 (2020), 474–93.

[101] Jo Burr Margadant, 'Gender, Vice, and the Political Imaginary in Postrevolutionary France: Reinterpreting the Failure of the July Monarchy, 1830–1848', *American Historical Review*, 104 (1999), 1461–96.

maintain its independence in face of the Italian nationalist, liberal wave. In the second war (1859), these contradictions became a significant challenge for its continuity. Isabel II tried to assume leadership of the family interests at this difficult juncture. However, Bourbon solidarity was increasingly conditioned by the prevalence of national interest[102] and the limitations of their reduced foreign power, particularly after their fall in France. In northern Italy, popular revolutions supported by the Sardinian army dethroned the monarchs of the small states, including the duchy of Parma, and created a confederation which finally joined Piedmont in 1860. Spain mobilised to defend the rights of the Bourbons and formally protested.[103] Its position, however, was too precarious for it to be able to impose on the other powers. In the south, likewise, Garibaldi landed in Sicily and began the conquest of the Two Sicilies. Both France and England supported, or at least consented to, the action, due to Ferdinando II's reactionary turn and his harsh political repression in the post-1848 context. His son, Francesco II, quickly turned to his Spanish cousin for help. The government repeated its strategy of providing diplomatic aid but no material or military assistance. Thus, it protested in the European chancelleries more at the way the royal family was expelled from Naples in 1861 – without a negotiated solution, when Spain had proposed itself as a mediator – than for its substance.[104]

Bourbon family connections went from structuring and underpinning their foreign power to becoming a serious political problem. With her French and Italian cousins in exile and her political positions increasingly anti-liberal, Queen Isabel II found herself in a critical dilemma. She refused to recognise the new kingdom of Italy and offered to host Francesco II despite the government's firm opposition. After a deep political crisis, the cabinet finally asserted the national interest over the queen's dynastic one. However, she continued to lend symbolic support to her reactionary relatives. The astonishment of the Coburgs and the opposition of Spanish liberalism were colossal. In 1864, she tried to name the deposed king and queen of Naples as godfather and godmother of her new offspring. Four years later, she arranged the marriage of her first-born daughter to the count of Girgenti, Francesco II's brother. As the French ambassador in Madrid wrote then, Isabel seemed not to understand that 'she is the queen of Spain rather than the cousin of the fallen sovereigns of Naples'.[105] Thus, he continued, 'she could not sacrifice to family considerations the duties imposed on her by her dignity as queen'. As Benito Pérez Galdós summarised after her death, Isabel II had an exclusive private world where 'the invisible political spirit of the nation never entered' but only royalty based on dynastic spirit.[106] Like a house of cards, the Spanish Bourbons finally fell in 1868, also overwhelmed by the national, liberal wave.

---

[102] Mark Mazower, *Governing the World. The History of an Idea, 1815 to the Present* (New York, 2012)

[103] Becker, *Historia de las relaciones*, II, 630–1.

[104] *Ibid.*, 634–5.

[105] 29 Jan. 1864, Paris, Archive du Ministère des Affaires Étrangères, Correspondance Politique de l'Espagne, vol. 865.

[106] Benito Pérez Galdós, *Memoranda* (Madrid, 1906), 22.

After a difficult six-year period of exile, the dynasty succeeded in returning to the Spanish throne in the person of Alfonso XII. The young king was free of those contradictions experienced by his mother, Isabel II, on account of her relatives. At this point in the century, the Bourbons were an outdated residue among the reigning European families, some of them royals without a kingdom, associated, most of the time, with reactionary political solutions. This fact made the Spanish monarchs definitively detach themselves from dynastic interests. Nevertheless, by no means did it inhibit their participation in foreign policy. They continued to use their constitutional prerogative and played a direct role in diplomacy. Alfonso XII tried to break free from the traditional international dynamics of Spain to join the rising monarchical power, the German Empire. After a meeting with Kaiser Wilhelm II in Berlin and the journey of the crown prince to Spain in 1883, they reached a verbal, secret and personal agreement on mutual aid against possible attacks from France.[107] The government, however, thwarted their plans and stopped the alliance, upholding the primary principle that had guided Spanish international policy since 1834: act only in conjunction with France and Britain.[108] For his part, Alfonso's heir continued participating in foreign affairs, intervening in the decision-making process and even negotiating bilateral treaties. But Alfonso XIII's actions coincided with those of his ministers, prioritising the paradigm of the nation state over dynastic interests.[109] As he wrote to his prime minister in 1913, 'this monarchical solidarity was already history'.[110] The clearest evidence of this, he continued, was precisely 'our conflict in Cuba (1898) in which no one came to Spain's defence' despite the desperate appeals of his mother, Maria Cristina of Habsburg–Lorraine. At the gates of the contemporary world, the Spanish Bourbons found themselves alone, freed from all ties, and subject to the national interest.

Conclusion

In 1885, amid rising tensions in the Anglo-Russian rivalry, the German parliament discussed the role of its royal family in this quandary. Ultimately, the close royal kinship with both contenders was able to force an intervention. Prince Bismarck angrily objected to 'the association of dynastic relationship and its influence on questions of foreign policy on which two nations might differ'.[111] He acknowledged, of course, the legitimate authority of the German dynasty in politics. However, it should 'always be exerted on the side of the national interest and never of princely relationships'. As an English journalist commented at the time, the same thing would happen in

---

[107] Ingrid Schulze, 'La diplomacia personal de Alfonso XII: una proyectada alianza con el Imperio alemán', *Boletín de la Real Academia de la Historia*, 183 (1985), 473–50.

[108] José María Jover, *España en la política internacional, siglos XVIII–XX* (Madrid, 1999), 136.

[109] Antonio Niño, 'El rey embajador. Alfonso XIII en la política internacional', in *Alfonso XIII. Un político en el trono*, ed. Javier Moreno (Madrid, 2003), 239–76.

[110] Alfonso XIII to Eduardo Dato, 2 Dec. 1913, quoted in Carlos Seco, *Estudios sobre el reinado de Alfonso XIII* (Madrid, 1998), 158–9.

[111] *Leicester Chronicle*, 21 March 1885.

Britain: Queen Victoria's 'long reign has been to such a large extent a recognition of the spirit and fact of nationality'. Thus, modern royalties 'may still win a new lease of power in yielding to the influence of a royalty that has already put itself in harmony with nationality'. At this point in the nineteenth century, monarchs still maintained a legitimate and essential influence on their country's foreign politics. But the increasing prevalence of nationalism and imperialism changed the relations between the monarchs even despite their close family ties. As Johannes Paulmann highlighted, supra-monarchical solidarity could no longer exist in this modern world.[112] Liberalism managed to nationalise the crowns, but it also imposed the predominance of the national interest in foreign relationships over the dynastic one.

In this struggle for European domination at the *fin de siècle*, the Coburgs had to face contradictions and challenges quite similar to those that the Bourbons experienced a few decades earlier. The difference, now, was that the competition did not confront two different dynasties and two antagonist political models but some imperialist nations reigned over by the same family. The Bourbons, meanwhile, extended their bonds of solidarity to support each other in their respective exiles. Their thrones had gradually fallen as the years passed, and revolutions succeeded from 1830. The family that had dominated the world during the eighteenth century was expelled from most of its territories. Strongly associated with the counter-revolution, from the 1860s the dynasty was primarily in exile throughout Europe. By 1885, only modest Spain, after many difficulties, remained under the Bourbons. But their position was much reduced from that of global dominance to a secondary, dependent one that aimed solely at maintaining the status quo. Besides, the Spanish Bourbons had to distance themselves from their openly reactionary, legitimist relatives. Freed from family commitments, they tried to maintain a clearly liberal facet and get closer to the triumphant royal families. It was the only possible way to survive the challenges posed by liberalism.

The political evolution of Europe from the French Revolution to the unification of Italy was evident in that sense. Structured on the so-called *Pacte de Famille*, the Bourbon dynasty reached the apogee of its foreign power in the eighteenth century based on the offensive–defensive alliance among Spain, France, and the Italian states. The spectre of this alliance was kept alive until the 1840s, not only in the minds of the Bourbons themselves but of all their royal counterparts. Chateaubriand even fantasised about the idea of establishing 'two or three Bourbon monarchies in America, working for our benefit as a counterpoint to the influence and commerce of the United States and Britain'.[113] Certainly, Spain did not cease trying to place a Bourbon prince in the newly independent states, particularly in Mexico, until as late as 1864.[114] However, like one of those phantasmagorias so popular

---

[112] Paulmann, 'Searching for a "Royal International"', 175–6.

[113] Chateaubriand, *Congrès de Vérone*, II, 425.

[114] Víctor Alberto Villavicencio, *El camino del monarquismo mexicano decimonónico* (Ph.D. thesis, Universidad Nacional Autónoma de México, 2015); Marcela Ternavasio, *Candidata a la Corona: La infanta Carlota Joaquina en el laberinto de las revoluciones hispanoamericanas* (Buenos Aires, 2015).

at that time, this possibility was pure fiction. Spain lost the international role that it had played in Mediterranean and American politics, after the Congress of Vienna (1815) and the independence of Latin America in the 1820s. For its part, France on its own could not maintain the family hegemony. In this context, revolutions directly attacked the theoretical and ideological foundations of the dynasty. In contrast to the coherence of principles shown by the expanding Coburgs, the Bourbons were divided between those who had to assume liberalism and those who advocated reaction. Although they still played an active role in their countries' diplomacy, the Bourbon monarchs saw their scope of action to help their relatives wholly constrained. Their loss of power and mere survival meant that Bourbon solidarity lasted more as rhetoric than an effective policy. Transnational family ties have thus succumbed to the prevalence of the national interest.

Acknowledgements. I thank Josep Escrig for his comments and suggestions, especially concerning American issues, and Rosario de la Torre, who masterfully taught me and inspired my engagement with many of the issues raised in this article.

Financial support. My research was funded by the European Research Council under the European Union's Horizon 2020 research and innovation programme (ERC Grant Agreement No. 787015) and the Ministry of Science, Innovation and Universities of Spain under the Knowledge Generation Project (PGC2018-093698-B-I00) and the Juan de la Cierva–Formación programme (FJC2020-042753-I).

Cite this article: San Narciso D (2023). The 'Dying' Bourbon Dynasty: The Diplomatic Role of the Spanish Monarchy in the Long Nineteenth Century. *Transactions of the Royal Historical Society* **1**, 23–43. https://doi.org/10.1017/S0080440122000160

Transactions of the RHS (2023), 1, 45–67
doi:10.1017/S0080440122000172

ARTICLE

The Historical Lecture: Past, Present and Future

Toby Green

Departments of History and Languages, Literatures and Cultures, King's College,
London, UK
Email: toby.green@kcl.ac.uk

(Received 6 November 2022; accepted 7 November 2022; first published online 9 December 2022)

Abstract

The oral performance of history has been common to many societies from Herodotus and
the histories of Beowulf, to the griots of West Africa. The lecture in Western history
emerged from these histories of orality, with its name showing the close connection in
its origins to reading, and to the lecturer's expertise in that domain. From this starting
point, lectures grew to be associated with frameworks of academic authority, as well as
markers of community and shared academic, religious and civic identity. From the late
eighteenth century onwards, the role of the historical lecture widened to involve public
education, and was also later incorporated into political contestations by anticolonial orators such as Maya Angelou, Amílcar Cabral and Fidel Castro. In the twenty-first century,
the rise of transnational technology has seen the increasing atomisation of the lecture
into a space of performative and disembodied information. As technologies change, in
the future the knowledge and thematic being explored in historical lectures may change.
What is embraced may prove to be demonstration of mastery of the commercial technology involved in a lecture's delivery, as much as the exposition related to the lecture or
reading from which knowledge and academic communities historically have built.

Keywords: lecture; history; orality; feminism; technology

The opening lines of the old Anglo-Saxon epic poem *Beowulf*, as rendered in
Michael Alexander's translation, offer a good starting point for the discussion
which I hope to develop here:

> *Attend!*
> *We have heard of the thriving throne of Denmark,*
> *how the folk-kings flourished in former days,*
> *how those royal athelings crowned that glory.*

Was it not Scyld Shefing *that shook the halls,*
took mead-benches, taught encroaching
foes to fear him – who, found in childhood,
lacked clothing. Yet he lived and prospered,
grew in strength and stature under the heavens
until the clans settled in the sea-coasts neighbouring
over the whale-road all must obey him
and give tribute. He was a good king![1]

The context of the relationship between the historian and audience for *Beowulf* is made clear in Alexander's introduction. As he notes, 'much of the characteristic power and beauty comes from what I take to be the traditional poetic and narrative forms of public oral performance. Like the "winged words" of Homer, *Beowulf* was composed to be projected in public performance – to be sung or spoken aloud.'[2] Thus in the context of the late seventh and early eighth century in which the version which we now have was formalised in script, the relationship between the historian and their public was an oral, performative one. Should the audience choose to attend, or listen, then they would be recounted a history which sharpened and made sense of their collective identity, whilst offering an Anglo-Saxon version of the twentieth-century 'American dream', in which the impoverished child becomes a great king – all the while dwelling in the nether regions between fact and myth in which history has so often resided.

This relationship between history and myth is well attended to in linguistic terms by the words in many European languages for 'history' – the French *histoire*, Spanish *historia*, Italian *istoria*, all refer both to the field of history and to the story which is at its heart, the oral storytelling from which history as a field has been born. By contrast, our familiar English 'history' suggests at once a field and practice which is more objective and measured than any mere story. And yet oral stories, and storytelling, lie at the origins of what communities understand as history – not only in the old Anglo-Saxon, but also as we will shortly see in many world cultures.

Indeed, to consider the lecture in a historical analysis, it straightaway becomes apparent that this is a global history – something which unites peoples from the Pacific Ocean and Asia to West Africa and Europe. Historical frameworks and understandings emerged in Sri Lanka, the Pacific Islands, the civilisations of West Africa and the symposia of ancient Greece, as oral. Speech gave power to history, gave it shape and told the stories through which it became real – and this is something that unites civilisations in all parts of the world. Over time, that speech became inscribed in texts, and texts came to be privileged in the historical canon – and yet the authority of those written texts very often derived from the proficiency of their authors

---

[1] *Beowulf*, trans. Michael Alexander (Harmondsworth, 1973), 51.
[2] *Ibid.*, 9.

in delivering speech in a public setting, in the theatre of performance and the interaction with the audience which that required.[3]

The twentieth-century Western privileging of written sources – the 'documents' – in the construction of history is therefore something of a historical outlier. While it may speak to the tyranny of the written word, it cannot supplant the underlying structure of the relationship between the written and the oral. And while that tyranny may indeed also be very old – here I recall R. I. Moore's classic book *The Formations of a Persecuting Society*,[4] where persecution is linked by Moore to the spread of the scribal class – the oral underpinnings are even older.

All of this is to give some context to the present lecture. Orality and the oral performance of history have always been at the heart of the relationship between the historian and their audience. That relationship is fundamentally a dynamic, interactive one. Through the means of the lecture, that relationship has been institutionalised for many centuries. The oral relationship remains in place, because it is through the means of speech that lectures are delivered in 2022, as they have been for thousands of years. However the mode of delivery of that speech has changed radically in the past two decades – and especially during the past two years of the pandemic.

The historian-speaker in many instances refers now to their presentation, rather than their lecture. Hence, the digital lecture has now taken its place within the production of economic value, through the role of algorithms in harvesting data from Zoom attendees. And indeed, there is nothing new in the place of historical production in capitalist accumulation, as historians of nineteenth-century 'print capitalism' can attest. Nevertheless, the online lecture fundamentally reframes the relationship between orator and audience. It's my argument this evening that by attending to the nature of this transformation, we can think more carefully about the historian's craft as a whole – and also the nature of our present time in particular.

However, this will not be a presentation – a word which smacks of the technological interface linking speaker to audience in a boardroom, committee or corporate conference hall, rather than of the interaction of speaker and public which used to be connoted by the concept of the 'illustrated lecture'. It will be a lecture – because I have nothing to sell, except for the idea of speech as a performance of historical knowledge, rather than one more mode of the conveying of information.

We can begin by extending further our understanding of the importance of orality in the relationship between the historian and their audience. This is something that has tended to characterise the historian in all cultures. Indeed it is something that can help us to draw strong connections between cultures and world regions which have traditionally been seen as quite distinct.

---

[3] On the relationship of orality to the history of the lecture, see W. Ong, *Orality and Literacy: The Technologizing of the Word* (1982).

[4] R. I. Moore, *The Formation of a Persecuting Society: Authority and Deviance in Western Europe, 950–1250* (Oxford, 1987).

In previous research, I have dwelt on the significance of the oral histories told by West African griots for modern historical reconstruction of the West African past.[5] The reality of history as an oral genre in West Africa has long been recognised by historians.[6] In a series of extraordinary works, the historian and specialist on Bamana society David Conrad has highlighted the significance of the oral epics in which the histories of the Mali empire and the kingdom of Segu can best be located.[7] Further work building on the pathfinding research of Bakary Sidibeh has highlighted the significance of repositories of oral histories in The Gambia both for documenting and detailing the historical past, and for recontextualising and providing new perspectives upon that past.[8]

In a recent book the historian Michael A. Gomez suggested that the oral histories recounted by griots had emerged interdependently with the textual historical culture of the empire of Mali – now known to have been widespread.[9] This is an intriguing observation, since if true it would suggest that the interdependence between a historian's oral performance and written practice is very long-standing in many cultures. There is a phenomenon well known to scholars of oral history, known as 'feedback', where materials from written histories find their way into oral histories, and it could be that such a phenomenon is in fact very old. What becomes important is the word, and its fixity, in developing a historical outlook or discourse that can then be widely shared.

This interrelationship is of course as much modern as older. Once set in text, a standardised version of the oral performance or lecture can begin to circulate to a wider audience, as also happened in early Anglo-Saxon England once the stories of *Beowulf* that began to circulate probably in the sixth century were codified in text by the later seventh or early eighth century. In the twentieth and twenty-first century, moreover, it has been standard practice for historians to develop their own writing on the basis of lectures.[10] This essay itself began life as a lecture that was given remotely, and the process of transforming that lecture into a written text has proved valuable in considering how the relationship between orality and text takes shape. What is gained

---

[5] See Toby Green, *A Fistful of Shells: West Africa from the Rise of the Slave Trade to the Age of Revolution* (London and Chicago, 2019).

[6] Jan Vansina, *Oral Tradition as History* (Madison, 1985); P. F. de Moraes Farias, 'The Gesere of Borgu: A Neglected Type of Manding Diaspora', in *In Search of Sunjata: The Mande Oral Epic as History, Literature and Performance*, ed. Ralph A. Austen (Bloomington, 1998), 141–69; Donald Wright, 'The Epic of *Kelefa Sane* as a Guide to the Nature of Precolonial Senegambian Society – and Vice Versa', *History in Africa*, 14 (1989), 287–309.

[7] David C. Conrad (ed.), *A State of Intrigue: The Epic of Bamana Segu According to Tayiru Banbera* (Oxford, 1990); David C. Conrad (ed.), *Great Sogolon's House* (Oxford, forthcoming).

[8] Toby Green, 'From Essentialisms to Pluralisms: New Directions in West African History from the Oral History Archive at Fajara, The Gambia', in *Landscapes, Sources and Intellectual Projects from the West African Past: Essays in Honour of Paulo Fernando de Moraes Farias*, ed. Toby Green and Benedetta Rossi (Leiden, 2018), 332–52.

[9] Michael A. Gomez, *African Dominion: A New History of Empire in Early and Medieval West Africa* (Princeton, 2018).

[10] See e.g. Ngũgĩ wa Thiong'o, *Decolonizing the Mind* (1986); Keith Thomas, *In Pursuit of Civility: Manners and Civilization in Early Modern England* (New Haven, 2018).

in the transformation from speech to text is perhaps consistency of argument and style, and the logical framework of an argument; whereas what is lost is the way in which emphasis in an argument can also be produced by inconsistency, pause and digression. On the other hand, the act of writing forces the speaker into a concentrated focus on harnessing a range of knowledge and sources which is not required by a lecture in the same way.

In terms of the relationship of oral and written historical texts, we can indeed move to more distant reaches of time and place than the West African historical past and Anglo-Saxon England. According to Paul Cartledge, the so-called 'father of history',[11] Herodotus, also developed his famous *Histories* through oral performance. Cartledge suggests that Herodotus – who was born near what is now Bodrum, in Turkey – may have recited portions of his *Histories* in front of large audiences at the quadrennial Olympic Games in Athens. Cartledge writes: 'The work [*Histories*] at any rate gives the strong impression in a number of ways – its strung-together rather than periodic structure, its devotion to storytelling narration, and above all its aggressively personal presentation – that it was composed for oral, public recitation rather than for a private reading audience.'[12] However, gradually Herodotus' *Histories* became available in part in written papyrus, and other works were also sold in this manner in Athens by the fifth century BCE.[13]

This relationship between orality and writing allows for further reflection as to the role of the historian and of the oral performance of history. Textual codification enables a standardised wide circulation of a historical discourse or idea, but the fact that in many cultures this codification has been based on an initial oral formulation is significant. It shows that oral performance of historical ideas has often conferred a certain legitimacy on the historian and their approach. Once a historian has been invited to offer an oral discourse on the past, that discourse may then be codified in written text, but authority is derived in part from the oral delivery in the first place.

That's to say: performance matters. We may not recall the content of a lecture delivered years ago, just as we probably won't remember the information we learnt thirty years ago, but we certainly may remember the performance style. The pauses, coughs, or whether the lecturer looked to the heavens or directly at us. The authority of the performance lends significance to a later written text, because the lecture – like the historical narrative – is also a form of theatre that has to be imagined.

This can help us now to begin to identify the significance of the lecture in the historical canon. The lecture derives from this tradition of oral storytelling in many cultures, in which the role of the storyteller is to splice myth and hearsay into a narrative story which provides a new sense or understanding of the identity and past of a political community. Just as Herodotus' authority to codify his work in text appears to have derived from oral presentations of it,

---

[11] Attributed to Cicero – see Paul Cartledge, 'Introduction', in *Herodotus: The Histories*, trans. Tom Holland, xix.

[12] *Ibid.*, xvii.

[13] *Ibid.*, xviii.

so it is the lecturer's oral speech which then confers the acceptance of a written text, or book. Thus in fact the lecture is an essential aspect of the practice of written history – and this reproduces a very ancient relationship between orality and written text.

At the same time, we can see important elements of transformation in modern practices when we reflect on the examples we have considered so far. There is a strong element of the mythic, as many have observed of Herodotus' work for example. Tall tales make good stories, but over the past century as the discipline of History has professionalised, these tales have been seen not to make for 'good history'. The advance of what Isaiah Berlin called 'scientific history',[14] alongside the professional historian's arsenal of what we call objective evidence, means that the conscious presentation of myth in twenty-first-century history should certainly be enough for any self-respecting historian to be dismissed from the collective. So I want to be clear that there is no myth involved in this presentation – unless that claim is also part of my mythos.

Certainly, the mythic endures in historical discourse, albeit in a different form. It survives today in ideas of progress, nation and honour which derive in part from the significance of the emerging arena of History during what is traditionally called the European Enlightenment, when historical-national myths supplanted religious ones.

We move now from the global frameworks of orality and their relationship to text, to something more specific. The concept of the 'lecture' with which most people attending this evening are familiar emerged in Western Europe in the fifteenth century.[15] When it comes to the origins of this new concept in Europe, several elements of genesis are important. We must acknowledge the role of the Church, clerical orders and monastic libraries, the new printing technologies which expanded the production and availability of written texts, and also the origins of traditions of speech in the earlier frameworks of orality and learning which we have just considered. In sum, at a time of technological revolution, a new concept and practice emerged to convey the changing relationship of speech, knowledge and audience – something that may sound familiar.

The relationship between institutions of learning and what became known as the lecture in the West was certainly very old. Following the lead of nineteenth-century rewritings of history, many modern historians have traced this lineage to pre-modern Athens. In his study *The First Universities*, Olaf Pedersen discussed the development of learning in Athens, and distinguished the methods of education developed by Plato and his pupil Aristotle. The works of Plato and Xenophon were testament to the dialogic method of instruction, with, as we may note, orality the first principle – as the preservation of his works has shown. The writings of Aristotle, by contrast, are evidence of a

---

[14] Isaiah Berlin, 'History and Theory: The Concept of Scientific History', *History and Theory*, 1 (1960), 1–31.

[15] https://logeion.uchicago.edu/lectura.

different method, and indeed, suggests Pedersen, emerged from 'dry lectures written down by Aristotle himself or his pupils'.[16]

Here we see the ancient nature of oral educational instruction, as we would understand it, and at the same time run up against some of the assumptions that have limited the appreciation of the lecture in recent times. Certainly dialogue of the Platonic style is more engaging than monologue. Yet are lectures necessarily dry? I expect that many people have attended lectures in which they or someone near them has fallen asleep. But is this response any different to the disconnection that can also take place during online lectures? Does the online lecture retain the space to awaken people from their – albeit metaphorical – dozing, in the way that this digression has tried to do?

In fact, that process of awakening in a lecture is very important. It is one of the things that a lecture and a lecturer tries to do – to awaken in an audience an awareness of the significance of the topic at hand. Along those lines, the process of actual sleep and then waking is an embodiment of the lecture's potential. Whatever listeners may make of this, I think that everyone would agree that Pedersen's view, published in 1997, certainly predates the era of the online presentation. Had he spent two years living on Zoom, he might have had a very different perspective on the dryness of the lecture.

Circling back to the origins of this digression, we find ourselves in what Plato would have called a process of recollection, recovering something we knew already (albeit not necessarily from a previous lifetime, as he conjectured in *Meno*). Orality, discussion and the lecture all characterised education in Athens. In the case of both Plato and Aristotle, these methods emerged from the educational institutions that they developed. Here we can trace several key elements of the nascent lecture. For Plato, the *Republic* not only laid out the ground rules of what was for him an ideal-type educational institution; it also integrated physical experience into this schema, for as Pedersen notes gymnastics were central to the practice of education in Plato's worldview.[17] Meanwhile, discussion and orality were key to the school developed by Aristotle, in which monthly symposia were arranged around defined topics. In other words, on the one hand, the lecture and education as a whole were linked to the physicality of experience and the integration of mind and body; and on the other they were linked to orality and discussion alongside scholarship.

How, then, did this relationship of oral speech and history transform itself in Western Europe into a concept so closely connected to reading – the 'lecture'? The development of bibliographic cultures – and paradoxically their decline during the Middle Ages – was central to this change. At the high point of Athenian learning, the library at Alexandria, on the Egyptian Mediterranean, is estimated to have held anywhere between 100,000 and 700,000 manuscripts.[18] Teams of scholars worked here, and it was in

---

[16] Olaf Pedersen, *The First Universities: Studium Generale and the Origins of University Education in Europe*, trans. Richard North (Cambridge, 1997).

[17] *Ibid.*, 12.

[18] *Ibid.*, 17.

Alexandria that some of the epics that circulated in Athens and beyond were codified to what became their standardised form, with the final redaction of Homer's *Iliad* and *Odyssey* made there, alongside the version of Herodotus' *Histories* that was passed down to posterity.[19]

This begins to show the relationship between textual scholarship on the one hand and the codification of oral histories on the other, which we have already been exploring. As we have seen, it is in the codification and circulation of oral texts that wider publics were reached – and created – and this was an attempt to fix and circulate oral texts which until then had been indeterminate. Of course, textual manuscripts circulated prior to the emergence of the scholarly culture in Alexandria. Yet it was there that they were finally codified, and preserved – and this relationship between orality and scribal scholarship based in the library was one which would become very important in the era immediately preceding the emergence of the concept of the 'lecture'.

Nevertheless, in the Mediterranean world, this flourishing textual and manuscript culture did not survive the decline of Roman power. From a scholarly and educational library of hundreds of thousands of volumes in Alexandria, the quantity of available books fell into decline over the next several hundred years – and also became confined in European societies to religious settings, including monastic orders and cathedral chapters, as the commercial book trade disappeared. The reduction was such that Pedersen estimates that, by the seventh century, in Western Europe 'all things considered, we have to conclude that a library could have been a source of national pride without exceeding 200 works'.[20]

This process of the reducing of learning to ecclesiastical circles was not however confined to Europe. Indeed, the place of religious institutions in this practice of codification of texts was often also central outside of European cultural pasts, and, as in Europe, this monopoly was often retained until the dawn of the modern era. In Asia, Buddhist and Sanskrit texts were also initially preserved orally before being committed to writing; and in this role Buddhist monasteries were essential in adopting technologies of book-making.[21] In West Africa, scholarship and the collection of books remained the preserve of the clerical class in Timbuktu until the fall of the Songhay empire in 1591.[22] Thus over this period of time, in many world cultural contexts, access to manuscripts became circumscribed, within monastic and scholastic centres, while at the same time the number of available works declined dramatically – making reading into both a rare and refined knowledge.

As Elias Canetti, the Nobel Prize-winning writer, put it in his masterpiece *Crowds and Power*, 'secrecy lies at the very core of power'.[23] The relationship which this insight has to books and the culture of reading in medieval

---

[19] *Ibid.*, 18.

[20] *Ibid.*, 59.

[21] See e.g. Xinjiang Rong, 'The Nature of the Dunhuang Library Cave and the Reasons for Its Sealing', *Cahiers d'Extrême Asie*, 11 (1999), 247–75.

[22] See e.g. Sékéné Mody Cissoko, *Tombouctou et l'Empire Songhay: Épanouissement du Soudan Nigérien aux XVe - XVIe siècles* (Paris, 1974).

[23] Elias Canetti, *Crowds and Power*, trans. Carol Stuart (New York, 1981), 290.

Europe was explored by Umberto Eco in his famous novel *The Name of the Rose*. In Eco's rendering, knowledge of forbidden texts, and their location in the byways of the labyrinthine monastic library which is hidden from all but a select number of monks, become the key to understanding a series of violent murders which take place in an abbey in northern Italy in 1327. And how was access granted to these books, but through authority – and the authority then to sermonise drawing upon the contents of the hidden books, which the blind murderer Jorge proceeds to do shortly before he is caught.

Thus, when we consider the emergence of the lecture in Europe in the sixteenth century, several factors must be borne in mind. In the first place there is the culture of the ecclesiastical institutions which had in previous centuries acted as the major centres for both learning and bibliophilia on the European continent, much as Buddhist monasteries served the same function in many parts of Eastern and Southern Asia. This culture then shaped the relation of biblical-centred learning to the oral exposition of that knowledge through preaching in the European monastic tradition. In the second place there is the long-established relationship of libraries to the preservation of and curating of oral knowledge. And thirdly, there is the reduced availability of texts, and the centrality of knowledge of these to the authority of anyone who might expound orally to others.

In other words, by the dawn of the fifteenth century, reading and the knowledge of literature had become central to the authority of the Christian preacher. That authority was jealously guarded. However, with the development of new printing technologies in the late fifteenth century, and as the number and availability of books grew exponentially, a new concept emerged to capture this relationship between a privileged or unusual knowledge of published written material on the one hand, and the authority to deliver this knowledge orally on the other. This was the lecture.

What little attention has been given to the historical evolution of the lecture attests to this relationship between the lecture and the huge expansion of the availability of books in the sixteenth century. It was this expansion which gave rise to a culture of secular rhetoric, which distinguished the art of lecturing from that of preaching. It was during this century that the concept of the lecture became widespread – and this was connected to the lecturer's practice of expounding their expertise from a lectern, the stand from which they would read. The skill and expertise of the lecturer in the art of reading derived from the 'specialist' – or we might say, secret – knowledge through which their authority to speak had been conferred. Access to reading, guidance through teaching in its highways and byways, and the development of a range of skills and expertise on which the lecturer could draw, were all related to the validation of their oral performance.

Here at once the relationship between the Western lecturer's practice and Christian tradition must be acknowledged – one that is significant, but not unique. This religious connection is indeed a thread which connects many aspects of lecturing and education through the centuries. In this case, the lectern – the object from which the lecturer reads, or read, in the sixteenth century – is a sibling to the pulpit from which the preacher would speak.

We can compare this structural relationship of lecturing and preaching to the late nineteenth century where, as the Finnish scholar Matti Klinge has noted, the relationship of university professors to their students was often modelled on the relationship of bourgeois Lutheran pastors to their congregations:

> the academic teacher ... worked at home and gave his lectures in an auditorium, normally in the main building of the university. He received his students and colleagues mostly at home, where he had his own studio or library. This familiar atmosphere was a heritage from the classical vicar's house of the bourgeois tradition.[24]

In the early modern period, this framework inherited from religious practice was central to the structuring of the lecture, and the relationship which this had to university life. Universities in Europe – Paris, Pisa, Salamanca and beyond – were deeply intertwined with the religious world. It was not that natural sciences were not taught, but that their exposition was always subordinate to religious life. This emerged most clearly in the career of Galileo Galilei in the first half of the seventeenth century, and the controversies which emerged surrounding his work on astronomy – and the obligation that the work which he produced must be approved by the cardinals of Rome.[25]

Thus in this period the relationship between religious and academic power was essential, something that embraced not only the lecturer's oral presentation of their topics, but also their integration into the expanding and professionalising fields of education in the early modern period. However it is important here to acknowledge the stubborn persistence of more ancient forms of orality even as this pattern of professionalisation and subordination within a patriarchal religious hierarchy emerged. While the scholar Walter Ong has taken a Whiggish approach to orality's history in education – recognising the lecture's origins in oral cultures but seeing them as superseded by advances in technology, something which I will come back to[26] – my argument here this evening is that orality has not been superseded but rather has endured and underpinned the evolution of historical learning and exposition. And we can see that very clearly as professionalised lectures expanded in the sixteenth, seventeenth and eighteenth centuries.

This emerges in the centrality of rhetoric and oratory to the lecturer's craft in this period. By the late eighteenth century, the religious framework still endured not only in the relationship of the lecture to scholarship and its expounding from a lectern/pulpit, but also in the role of orality and rhetoric in aspects of the lecturer's appointment within university systems. As Klinge notes: 'The early process, even if not always practised, derived from the clerical world: applicants had to give special lectures and take part in disputations.'[27]

---

[24] Matti Klinge, 'On Teachers', in A History of the University in Europe, III: Universities in the Nineteenth and Early Twentieth Centuries, ed. Walter Rüegg (Cambridge, 2004), 123–62, at 145.

[25] Dava Sobel, Galileo's Daughter: A Historical Memoir of Science, Faith and Love (New York, 1999).

[26] Ong, Orality and Literacy.

[27] Klinge, 'On Teachers', 134.

Thus the capacity to lecture was not only one which relied on specialist knowledge of texts, but also on the ability to deploy rhetoric in oral disputation – much as had been the standard norm in theological disputes, also of course grounded in book knowledge – in preceding times.

We can indeed see legacies of this framework of the *disputatio* in academic practice to this day. The standard framework of the lecture or seminar followed by questions, whether in the job talk, seminar room or Zoom lecture, emerges from the practice of oral disputation. This clearly shows the limits of seeing the expounding of knowledge through the lens of Whiggish history as 'improving' or transforming with advanced technologies. While technologies of delivery may change, the oral and its historical traditions remain central. Moreover, the idea that technologies may radically transform and improve education is revealed as a profoundly imperial one, lurking in discourse from our own era of the pandemic, back through the ethnographic studies of the twentieth century and beyond: the privileging of textual source and exposition in the historical canon was of course a means of distinguishing 'scientific' and 'rational' European societies from those which could be dismissed as 'pre-literate', where in fact the craft, technique and authority of the lecturer still relied upon oral frameworks.

This power of oratory and rhetoric thus remained central, a testimony to the power of the orator and of oral culture within Western society that endured after the rise of the Enlightenment. A further symptom of the framework within which this came to be viewed is the connection drawn by Western scholars from this oral framework to classical Rome. Marcus Tullius Cicero is seen by many as the doyen of oratory, from which much of European rhetorical culture followed.

Cicero indeed expounded beautifully on the importance of oratory:

> The art of speaking beautifully is greater and composed of more sciences and study than people can imagine ... [N]o person can become a speaker accomplished with any laudable capacity unless he has acquired knowledge of all significant objects and all liberal arts ... for unless there is something beautiful beneath the surface that the speaker feels and understands, rhetoric will remain an empty and childish stream of words.[28]

Yet as we have already seen, this beautiful relationship between orality and knowledge is not something that inhered only to Rome; it has rather been a universal trait in human societies, and remains so to this day.

Drawing these threads together, we can see many important aspects of the emergence of the lecture in the early modern period. The relationship with books, and the historical connection of books to religious institutions, was a fairly universal one, linking Christian traditions in Europe, Islamic traditions in West Africa, and Buddhist traditions in Asia. In colonial Latin America, the profusion of universities – certainly in comparison to British colonial North America, as the late J. H. Elliott pointed out – was closely connected

---

[28] Pedersen, *The First Universities*, 20–1.

to the requirement to train and equip the proselytising clergy of the New World.[29] Thus many aspects of the lecturer's art derived from both the authority and practice of religious institutions. At the same time orality and rhetoric were central both to the development of knowledge and to the means through which the practices of the lecture gained social approval.

What, however, of the *historical* lecture itself? The rise of bourgeois society in the eighteenth century, and the technological and materialist frameworks associated with it, went with the institutionalisation of the field of history. These changes also began to revolutionise the purpose both of the lecture and of education in Europe, as the technical requirements of colonial societies changed. Already at the start of the eighteenth century, these changes were both predicted and lampooned by Jonathan Swift in *Gulliver's Travels*, which was published in 1726. In the Third Book, Swift's protagonist is introduced to a number of extraordinary professors in the Academy of Balnibarbi, who have attempted to develop new technologies to reduce human excrement to its original food, replace silkworms with spiders, produce sunbeams from cucumbers, and transform labour and architecture so that it is immeasurably more productive. However, as Swift put it:

> The only inconvenience is, that none of these projects are yet brought to perfection, and in the meantime the whole country lies miserably to waste, the houses in ruins, and the people without food or clothes. By all which, instead of being discouraged, they are fifty times more violently bent upon prosecuting their schemes.[30]

Yet in spite of the hiccoughs, the materialist advance proceeded, and with it the development of a place for the field of history. Before eviscerating Swift's reactionary Luddite approach, however, we should recall that, as I argued in my book *A Fistful of Shells*, the scientific and material advances of liberal societies were the other side of the coin of economic warfare in West Africa, among other locations.[31] The technical progress of the eighteenth century did also lead to economic ruination as described by Swift, for economic violence beyond Europe was ever the hidden face of liberal progress.

By the end of the eighteenth century, in Friedrich Schiller's inaugural lecture at the University of Jena in 1789, the purpose and nature of both modern Western history and the lecture began to become clear. In Schiller's introduction to his lecture, entitled, 'The Nature and Value of Universal History', he said: 'The sight of so many excellent young men, gathered here eager for knowledge and already revealing the talents which the approaching era will need, makes my duty a pleasure, but also makes me sensible of the burden

---

[29] J. H. Elliott, *Empires of the Atlantic World: Britain and Spain in America, 1492-1830* (New Haven, 2006).

[30] Jonathan Swift, *Gulliver's Travels* (Harmondsworth, 1985), 220.

[31] Green, *A Fistful of Shells*.

and importance of that duty.'[32] Schiller more or less avers that the lecture, and its education, had become designed to produce the skills that bourgeois society needed in its material advancement – and as the nineteenth century unfolded, the discipline of History would become a handmaiden in that task, as it produced mythographies of nation that encouraged European colonial societies to hierarchise the world, and thereby materially to exploit the resources of those civilisations which were located in what today has become the Global South.

It's now possible to come directly to something that has been a permanent feature of this lecture so far, but that I have not yet confronted directly. This is the question of the patriarchal nature of much of the discourse regarding lecturing – that is, the patriarchal nature of oral power in many world historical societies, and who has held the authority to declaim.

One of the features of the cultures splicing orality and scribal reproductions of knowledge that we have considered is central: whether in the Buddhist or Christian monastery, or the Islamic madrasa of Timbuktu, the patriarchal monopoly on access to restricted knowledge, and the authority to speak that comes with this, is to say the very least striking. While in Christian convents women did have access to books, and could write, they had no power to speak. In general, book-learning, and the orality which was connected to it, and the speech of the lecture, was in very many world cultures the preserve of men. And in this sense we must conclude that not only did the lecture emerge from cultures of patriarchal oral authority, but that the lecture up to the time of the nineteenth century also helped to reinforce this patriarchal framework. As we have seen, orality is a marker of power, but also lends authority to written texts which then circulate – thereby reinscribing the power and authority of those (men) who speak.

Of course, the lecture's origins in religious institutions may help us to understand at least some of this process. The figure of the male priest, whether in Rome or in China, and the power of that priest to intercede between this realm and others, is reflected in the patriarchal hold on the lecture which, as we have seen, grew out of religious institutions. However, what may be significant is that in the nineteenth century, in the high age of European imperialism and the rise of the modern nation state and the public sphere, this tradition of patriarchal speech expanded alongside the expansion of what we may call publics. Women had long had to listen to male preachers in religious settings; however, now, as the role of the public lecture emerged, and the role of the lecturer grew, this patriarchal framing of society grew too.

This role of the lecture in the public sphere may indeed be one as-yet unexplored factor behind the acceleration of gendered inequalities in the nineteenth century. The place of the lecture in creating a public sphere has been widely discussed: from the public tours of famous nineteenth-century authors such as Charles Dickens and Mark Twain to the vigorous exhortations of travelling preachers such as William Booth, founder of the Salvation Army, the

---

[32] Friedrich von Schiller, 'The Nature and Value of Universal History: An Inaugural Lecture', delivered at Jena in 1789, *History and Theory*, 11 (1972), 321–34, at 322.

greater mobility provided by rail and steam was fundamental in the construction of new identities – alongside the print cultures in which all these lecturers of course also participated. Nevertheless, the role of the lecture in also accentuating patriarchal structures has been less widely discussed.

How this affected individuals is suggested in Juliet Barker's collective biography of Anne, Charlotte and Emily Brontë.[33] Barker describes the excitement with which at times the young Brontës would head from their home in Haworth to nearby towns such as Halifax to hear visiting preachers and lecturers. The rise of female education was of course one important aspect of social change in the nineteenth century, and yet on the other hand that went with the expansion of the reality of public speech as almost entirely a masculine pursuit. This was indeed what one historian has called 'the great period of civic participation',[34] and yet with that civic society shaped through patriarchal relationships, it was hard for this civic culture not to reproduce them at least in part.

This nineteenth-century expansion of the lecture's role in Europe is of course a key feature of its history. Yet it was also an era of contradictions. On the one hand, the role of public lectures and discussions expanded greatly. And yet on the other, the rhetorical and oratorical skill of the lecturer began to decline in significance, to be replaced by what was seen as 'pure scholarship'. Matti Klinge suggests that 'this evolution can be seen in linguistics: chairs in rhetoric and poetry increasingly became chairs of Latin and Greek philology ... and thus prowess as a poet, translator [or] orator became less important than scholarly merits'.[35] Perhaps the best person to exemplify this change was Friedrich Nietzsche, appointed to a chair of philology in Basel at the age of twenty-four, and yet found by many in person to be a poor and insubstantial speaker in public.

Nevertheless, as far as historians were concerned the lecture was very important. Asa Briggs discusses the significance of the lecture in striking terms, noting that: 'In the nineteenth century the lecture was a main instrument of inspiration as well as of instruction, and there are many accounts of the impacts of professorial lectures and lecturers on the seen audience.'[36] Briggs recounts a number of instances of this, and it is clear that while the disciplines of rhetoric and oratory may have been in decline, the appreciation of them was not. By the later nineteenth century, the academic discipline of history was fully formed, and the relationship between the historical lecture, political and gendered power and the pursuit of knowledge was fully established in colonising European societies.

Moreover, just as the lecture played a central role in embedding patriarchy in modern nation states, so its role in constructing imperial ideologies should not be underestimated. We can consider for instance the History tripos at

---

[33] Juliet Barker, *The Brontës* (1996).

[34] Klinge, 'On Teachers', 127.

[35] *Ibid.*, 134.

[36] Asa Briggs, 'History and the Social Sciences', in *A History of the University in Europe*, ed. Rüegg, 459–91, at 467.

Cambridge, inaugurated in 1873. Only in 1897 was the first essential course even in European history introduced to the degree, which speaks volumes about the extent to which the construction of national identities of exceptionalism was an essential part of the professionalisation of the discipline.[37] In time, reforms of the History syllabus would incorporate the wider world through the lens of the expansion of Europe, but there was no sense that it could be included as a field of study on its own merits. Meanwhile, historians were becoming public figures, as the role of the public lecture grew and historians developed a growing presence in the burgeoning print media, and in a role as public speakers to a general audience.[38] Where Chairs were established in non-European history, they fell largely within the frame of imperial history: thus what mattered to European societies in the late nineteenth and early twentieth centuries was not to attend lectures which might expand their grasp of world history and culture, but to listen to expositions of myths of national and imperial exceptionalism.

In this sense, we can see that the great era of the creation of civic publics, from the start of the nineteenth century through the first third of the twentieth century, saw the lecture playing several key roles. It helped to build publics, and a sense of a shared public sphere which went far beyond the pre-existing hierarchies of aristocracy, church, and state. This was through the way in which the lecture hall was a space in which all could meet, and discuss – and through the physical experience of that proximity, and observation of the embodied performance of the lecturer. As we have seen this evening, this was not however a new phenomenon, but rather a continuity of a long global history of the social status and awakening power ascribed to the oratorical performance.

On the other hand, the nineteenth-century lecture was deeply connected to the establishment of a canon which was constructing gendered hierarchies and ethnocentrism. And there was a sense in which this too represented the continuity of a long tradition. The mythic had not departed the lecture with the rise of so-called scientific history: it was in fact very much alive. In the twentieth century, the lecture would prove to be a malleable form, that would be deployed by those marginalised in these hierarchies, as female and colonised subjects talked back.

As is widely known, the early twentieth century saw the dawn of the movement of women's suffrage, and naturally the lecture was a key element of this movement. In 1908, Edith Morley became the first female professor in a British university, as professor of English at Reading.[39] Similar changes were taking place across Europe. In Spain, for instance, a change to the law in 1910 allowed women to be appointed as university professors. Shortly afterwards the writer Emilia Pardo Bazán was appointed a lecturer on the Ph.D. programme at the University of Madrid, and such movements spread also around the continent.[40]

---

[37] *Ibid.*, 469–70.

[38] Klinge, 'On Teachers', 143.

[39] https://www.kcl.ac.uk/celebrating-legacy-of-englands-first-female-professor.

[40] Consuelo Flecha-García, 'The First Female Lecturers at Spanish Universities', *International Journal of the History of Education*, 56 (2020), 769–86.

For the first time, the power of women's voices was institutionalised and given the authority that they had long been demanding. As many will know, this gave expression to a dynamic which was as old as human society itself. In *The Exaltation of Inanna*, one of the earliest of all surviving poems, from 2300 BCE, the priestess Enheduanna from Mesopotamia spoke thus:

> *Truly I entered the cloister at your command.*
> *I the priestess*   *I Enheduanna*
> *carried the basket*   *intoned the paean*
> *but now I'm consigned*   *to the leper's ward.*[41]

The power of women's writings to challenge patriarchal voices recurred throughout the ages in text, as with Sor Juana de la Cruz's evisceration of her confessor Father António Núñez de Miranda in early eighteenth-century Mexico:

> Of what envy am I not the target? Of what malice am I not the object? What actions do I take without fear? What word do I speak without misgiving? Women feel that men surpass them, and that I seem to place myself on a level with men; some wish that I did not know so much; others say that I ought to know more to merit such applause ... What else can I say or instance? – for even having a reasonably good handwriting has caused me worrisome and lengthy persecution, for no reason other than they said it looked like a man's writing, and that it was not proper, whereupon they forced me to deform it purposely, and of this the entire community is witness; all of which should not be the subject for a letter but for many copious volumes.[42]

Politically, women had held power at various times and places, but as I have argued for the West African context in *A Fistful of Shells*, in the early nineteenth century this power was eroded by the twin vectors of patriarchal Christian missionary movements and the renewed power of the Salafiya revival movement that had emerged in Arabia in the eighteenth century.[43] In Britain, as we have seen, the public space and the continuation of the religious patriarchal framework saw an accentuation of a similar pattern of the erosion of women's power. Finally, in the early twentieth century, a line was marked in the sand.

At Reading, Professor Morley became closely involved in the women's suffrage movement, in the years following the award of her Chair. It was in these years that lectures and speeches became a key element of the movement – at once broadening and subverting the patriarchal public space which had been the province of the lecture in the nineteenth century. In 1913, Emmeline

---

[41] https://babylonian-collection.yale.edu/sites/default/files/files/Hallo_Van%20Dijk%20(1968)%20-%20Exaltation%20of%20Inanna_YNER%203.pdf.

[42] Octavio Paz, *Sor Juana, or the Traps of Faith*, trans. Margaret Sayer Peden (Cambridge, MA, 1990), 496.

[43] Green, *A Fistful of Shells*, ch. 11.

Pankhurst gave a famous lecture at Hartford, Connecticut, entitled 'Freedom or Death', which showed the cause for women's suffrage in the starkest terms. But this was just a part of the extraordinary role of lectures and speeches in the suffrage movement, and Pankhurst's work was prefigured by American pioneer lecturers such as Susan B. Anthony, Elizabeth Cady Stanton and Ida B. Wells who spoke widely in the later nineteenth century.[44]

As opportunities for women expanded in societies, and the place of women's speech became further embedded, History as a field grew to encompass the study of gender – though this would take many decades to be fully realised. The same was true of anticolonial speech. With the rise of anticolonial movements and their growing power in the years after the end of the Second World War, anticolonial oratory became a powerful element of the historical lecture.

The independence of Ghana in 1957 provides a good illustration of this. Leading African American intellectuals and activists including W. E. B Du Bois and the young Maya Angelou moved to Accra, which became a centre for the development of Afrocentric philosophies and pan-Africanism.[45] Angelou would later draw on her experiences as she became one of the best-known orators in American public life in the late twentieth and early twenty-first centuries.

In his lecture inaugurating the new Centre for African Studies at the University of Ghana, Kwame Nkrumah made clear how much this heritage and discussion played a part in the formulation of the ideas that drove the new Centre, and the community that was growing up around it:

> First and foremost, I would emphasise the need for a reinterpretation of our past ... We have to recognize frankly that African Studies, in the form in which they have been developed in the universities and centres of learning in the West ... still to some extent remain under the shadow of colonial ideologies and mentality ... [T]he history, culture and institutions, languages and arts of Ghana and of Africa [should be studied] in new African centred ways.[46]

As we can see, historical elements were often embedded into the context and content of these lectures. Two years after Ghana's independence, Fidel Castro led the revolution in Cuba in 1959. His success led to the institutionalisation of the Castro lecture, which went with the trademark oratorical stamina of a leader whose 26 September 1960 speech at the United Nations of 4 hours and 29 minutes remains the longest ever recorded in the institution's history.[47] Castro's ringing tones and declamatory style entranced audiences with a

---

[44] See https://dianavroeginday.files.wordpress.com/2016/04/diana-vroeginday-text-image-final1.pdf.

[45] Kevin K. Gaines, *American Africans in Ghana: Black Expatriates and the Civil Rights Era* (Chapel Hill, 2006).

[46] Kwame Nkrumah, *The African Genius: Speech Delivered by Osagyefo Dr Kwame Nkrumah at the Opening of the Institute of African Studies, 25th October 1963* (Accra, 1963), 2–3.

[47] https://ask.un.org/faq/37127.

hallucinatory power; but the contents often related to history, the history of slavery, the contribution of Africa and Africans to Cuban society, and the systemic racism which had excluded that reality. It was indeed because of that history that Cuba played such a key role in decolonisation movements in Angola and Guinea-Bissau, following the famous Tricontinental Conference in Havana in 1966.[48]

One of the attendees at the Tricontinental Conference was Amílcar Cabral, leader of the PAICV, the anticolonial movement in the Portuguese colonies of Cabo Verde and Guinea-Bissau. As Portugal refused to decolonise in the manner of Belgium, France and the UK, Cabral became a figurehead of the global anticolonial movement in the late 1960s and 1970s. He lectured widely across the world, and in these lectures the cultural and historical framework of the Portuguese colonial reality was placed side by side with his movement's anticolonial struggle.[49]

Another leading anticolonial orator in this era was Walter Rodney, the Guyanese historian who completed his Ph.D. at the School of Oriental and African Studies in London in the late 1960s. After this, Rodney moved to teach at the University of Dar-es-Salaam, and it was in Tanzania that he wrote the now classic book *How Europe Underdeveloped Africa*, published in 1972.[50] Throughout the rest of the decade, Rodney became a speaker in high demand, whether at the University of the West Indies in Jamaica or as an invited speaker on American campuses at the height of the discussions surrounding the Vietnam War in the 1970s. Rodney was a historian par excellence, whose powerful evocations of history as part of the continuity of global struggles against imperialism and racism were hugely popular.

Thus the twentieth century saw the lecture as an oral form change in its social role. Instead of embedding hierarchies of gender and ethnocentrism, it was deployed by many to challenge those hierarchies. Given the place of the oral form in validating text, as we have seen, this was also fundamental in breaking down the discipline of History so that it no longer focused on the myths of nation and empire. Moreover, these challenges did not simply emerge because of the content of those lectures, but because of the presence of the lecturers and their audiences on campuses. The physical space of the lecture hall became one which itself could challenge the authorities and hierarchies which prefigured them.

However, not everyone responded positively to these challenges, and as we shall now see in the concluding part of this lecture, the rise of remote technologies has made it easier to place such challenges 'out of sight, out of mind'.

Two of the figures we have just discussed passed away during the era which saw the dawn of neoliberalism. Amílcar Cabral was assassinated in Conakry in 1973, and Walter Rodney in Georgetown in 1981. The 1980s saw the

---

[48] See e.g. Aditya Nigam, 'Fidel and the Tricontinental Imagination', *Cultural Critique*, 98 (2018), 320–3.

[49] António Tomás, *Amílcar Cabral: The Life of a Reluctant Nationalist* (2021).

[50] Walter Rodney, *How Europe Underdeveloped Africa* (London and Dar-es-Salaam, 1972).

inexorable rise of computing technology, and the rise of computing platforms, which brings us to the present day.

Some will of course have noticed that this lecture was billed as dealing with the past, present and future of the lecture – and perhaps I have not got all that long left, therefore, to address two-thirds of the contents. I am a historian after all. But when we come to the question of the lecture, the present and the future are inevitably conjoined through the experience of the pandemic, and the accelerated use of the digital technologies.

As we have seen, the lecture has a very long and in some ways a universal history, one which connects many different cultures and their traditions of textual learning, oral performance and social renewal. During the 1980s and 1990s, some scholars of education such as Diana Laurillard took a Whiggish approach to the form, and saw it as an outdated and antiquated form of transmission of information, one which was being superseded through the new technologies then emerging.[51] By the turn of the millennium, some scholars, for instance the art historian Robert Nelson, recognised already that these technologies might change the form of the lecture permanently.[52] Advocates of new online models saw the lecture as an antiquated form now effectively being replaced by new media and the audiovisual experience which that could provide; and yet, as Norm Friesen has noted, in spite of all the discussion around this, the reality on the ground remained different until the pandemic, with the old lecture hall circuit stubbornly enduring.[53]

This would place the modern history of the lecture as part of a continuity. To be sure, there are continuities. But there are also ruptures.

We can start with the work of Laurillard. Laurillard argued that the lecture was indeed a residue of ancient cultures of orality – as we have seen this evening. However this was for her a kind of atavistic throwback to residual orality in a world where text was the most efficient mode of communication.[54] And yet as we have seen this evening, this kind of privileging of text over orality derives from nineteenth-century cultures of patriarchy and ethnocentrism. It assumes that the purpose of the lecture is to provide information, rather than understanding it as part of a performance – the performance of knowledge and what it may mean, and the tics which may make that memorable. Laurillard's approach also follows a decidedly Whiggish ideology of human 'improvement' over time. As a historian, one of the things that strikes me more and more is just how similar human behaviour is over time – so the liberal ideal of human progress is not one which to me seems grounded wholly in reality. So rather than progress, I do indeed see some kind of rupture, and one which is worth exploring.

---

[51] Diana Laurillard, *Rethinking University Teaching: A Conversational Approach for the Effective Use of Learning Technologies* (1993).

[52] Robert S. Nelson, 'The Slide Lecture, or the Work of Art *History* in the Age of Mechanical Reproduction', *Critical Inquiry*, 26 (2000), 414–34.

[53] Norm Friesen, 'A Brief History of the Lecture: A Multi-media Analysis', *Medien Pädagogik*, 24 (2014), 136–153, at 136.

[54] Laurillard, *Rethinking University Teaching*, 93.

Some might argue that the rupture lies in the relationship of the lecture to capital. The new online format for many lectures is after all deeply connected to technologies which both accumulate capital and increase social inequalities. In a new book, *Pandemic Response and the Cost of Lockdowns*, the scholar of inclusive artificial intelligence Mark Wong makes clear how far the turn to online has exacerbated inequalities during the pandemic, and the means through which this has been achieved. As Wong notes, algorithmic harm has been shown by many scholars to affect the 'people who are most marginalised in society'.[55] During the pandemic, the turn to online has radically increased inequalities through the algorithmic harms produced by the very use of these digital platforms. Wong explains:

> The vast amount of new data being collected by online platforms, data processes, and AI that we encounter as part of our everyday interactions in the pandemic is unfair and unjust. By using these platforms and services more intensively during the pandemic, people are trading in their data, or more accurately, the *datafication* of their habits and behaviours, to these platforms – free of charge or at an inversed cost to themselves. More users, across the world, are essentially turning into free labour to generate the data that data-driven innovation mines, sells, trains AI, and generates huge profits from. This is a form of exploitative global operation termed *data extractivism*.

Thus the use of online platforms for the delivery of lectures such as this is part of the process of massively increased inequality that has been associated with the response to the pandemic. By giving online lectures and attending them, we are directly increasing inequalities, and stoking the massive increase in wealth which digital entrepreneurs such as Jeff Bezos, Bill Gates and Mark Zuckerberg have accumulated during the pandemic. Clearly, if we are serious about addressing the massive inequalities in society, we should not participate in online lectures, and indeed should reduce our online activity in many ways.

And yet, some might argue that the role of lectures in accumulating capital may not be the complete rupture that it appears. The expansion of the lecture in the late nineteenth- and early twentieth-century public sphere was part of the explosion of what historians call print capitalism. As Matti Klinge puts it of late nineteenth-century Germany, 'Not for the first or last time, academic teaching and research, universities and professors, were seen as tools in the general economic and production process.'[56] Given the role of the lecture in publications, as we have seen, and the place of emerging technologies in creating modern capitalism in the early twentieth century, one cannot say that the lecture sat apart from this process in that era.

---

[55] Mark Wong, 'Digital Society, Algorithmic Harm, and the Pandemic Response', in *Pandemic Response and the Cost of Lockdowns: Global Debates from Humanities and Social Sciences*, ed. Peter Sutoris, Sinéad Murphy, Aleida Mendes Borges and Yossi Nehushstan (2018).

[56] Klinge, 'On Teachers', 135.

Nevertheless, I would argue that there is indeed a distinctive new element in the relation of the Zoom lecture to capital. The production of data about people's online habits is now a direct tool for digital marketing and the production of online profits. It is therefore directly a part of the productive process for modern capital, in a way in which the oral performance in an auditorium never was. Its online presence connects it also to the major forms of capital accumulation in the twenty-first century, whereas in the era of print capitalism accumulation was connected more directly to natural resources. Thus there is a clear difference in the role of the online lecture in the production of capital and inequality today – one where it has been drawn directly into the process of capital production and thereby the enhancement of inequalities.

Another element of rupture might be seen in the form of technology. And yet as we have seen this evening, the history of the lecture is deeply connected to the ability to be conversant with and manipulate the latest technologies. In the monasteries of medieval Europe and Asia this was connected to the technologies of writing, and later of printing. In our era, it is related to the digital technologies of production. And hence what is being reinscribed through the Zoom lecture is not a new relationship between human beings and the world but a different manifestation of it.

These new technologies produce what is deemed to be knowledge, just as book-learning did in the past. However, whereas it is knowledge of books and literature which attests to the lecturer's prowess, this element is now accompanied by their skill in technical wizardry. The nature of expertise changes, and with it the nature of the academic, public and scholarly communities which historically have been formed.

Beyond technology, what changes is the relationship of the production of knowledge to the lecture. This is reinscribed in the relationship of human subjects to the objects which they perceive – and what changes, as Marshall McLuhan might have put it, is the medium and thus the message. The knowledge created remains mediated by human technologies, just as it did in the past with text; and yet it is still unable to bridge the gulf between human subjects and the world around them which is the origin of the quest for knowledge, and which yet seems to grow with each new medium devised to bridge it. Far from making knowledge transmission accessible, it becomes more alienating, remote – and irrelevant. However much we may record and capture images of the world and of our engagement with it, and try to find new meaning in these fragments, the gulf remains, and is even expanded.

Beyond capital or technology, wherein lies the transformation of the modern lecture as it has moved online? I will close this lecture this evening with the proposition that this transformation is in the nature of the human experience. As we have seen, physicality and the physical space has an important part to play in the history of the lecture – and was seen by Plato to have an important role in the process of education itself. This physicality was true of the collective spaces in which epics of the past were performed by griots in West Africa, bards in Denmark, or at the Olympic Games at which Herodotus may have spoken. But it was also true in the packed lecture halls which came to hear Emmeline Pankhurst, Walter Rodney and Amílcar Cabral. The shared physical experience brought people together, whatever their social class. It was one which was more likely to produce commitment, energy, life-long friendships, relationships – and change.

Certainly, the online space also provokes huge change, as we have seen in the past twenty years. But it is a form of change which is privatised, as the public sphere retreats from its role as a provider of shared spaces and this responsibility is placed on the shoulders of the private citizen, whatever their means – in this sense closely related to the logical praxis of the neoliberal capitalist retreat from the state as a provider of public goods. The quality of experience is privatised as it does not take place in a shared physical space, but in a privatised personal space which is inevitably qualitatively present, even if apparently absent. I am speaking this evening from my living room, which is reasonably comfortable, and provides the space that someone who has been far too lucky in their career, as I have, might be expected to have: the common space which is shared is however a virtual one, and class and historical inequalities now structure the way in which people are listening – or sleeping – alongside whatever I have to say.

Another change in the quality of the experience is that it becomes more homogeneous. Whereas the physical act of attending a lecture, in an auditorium, is qualitatively different to many other forms of human experience, the same cannot be said of the online lecture. As we spend more time online, interacting with computers, the lecture becomes just another mode of interacting with the machine's audiovisual potential. This offers an experience which is ultimately controlled by the computer's mechanical structure and not by whatever the speaker may have to say, and the ways in which the audience may respond – as we all discover when 'the technology goes wrong'.

Others will respond that the online lecture is a more democratic mode of participation, since it is open to many more people who could not otherwise attend. This is of course true. Yet as we have seen this evening, the physical space of the lecture hall in the twentieth century was a principal conduit which opened the way to social change. This was a mode of delivery which worked. Thus far, the online replacement has achieved the mass enrichment of a few people, which cannot be to the long-term benefit of social and human progress – it's not a good start, or a framework which at the moment suggests that it can have the same beneficial ends.

Nor am I alone in holding this view, it would appear, since shares in Zoom have fallen 80 per cent since its 2020 peak,[57] as people – as we so often hear these days – 'have had enough of Zoom'. Thus it could be that the future of the lecture is not as online as its evangelists have been promising for the past three decades or more. And this may be because, I have suggested here this evening, they have not understood the role of the lecture: this is not just to provide information, but to provide a shared social space and a performance wherein knowledge and its performance becomes memorable.

---

[57] https://www.barrons.com/articles/zoom-stock-growth-downgrade-51646244535.

I would conclude by suggesting that, if we want to understand ourselves as human beings and our relationship with societies, we have to attend not only to how to interact with changes, but also how to safeguard the core of what has produced healthy societies in human history until now. In sum my aim this evening has been to furnish just a small part of what Herodotus averred to be his aim at the opening of the *Histories* that were at length set down from the oral to the print form:

Herodotus, from Halicarnassus, here displays his enquiries, that human achievement may be spared the ravages of time, and that everything great and astounding, and all the glory of those exploits ... be kept alive.[58]

Acknowledgements. An oral version of this article was first presented as a Royal Historical Society lecture, read on 6 May 2022.

---

[58] Herodotus, *Histories*, 3.

Cite this article: Green T (2023). The Historical Lecture: Past, Present and Future. *Transactions of the Royal Historical Society* **1**, 45–67. https://doi.org/10.1017/S0080440122000172

Transactions of the RHS (2023), **1**, 69–93
doi:10.1017/S0080440122000184

ARTICLE

The Gaiety Girl and the Matinee Idol: Constructing Celebrity, Glamour and Sexuality in the West End of London, 1890–1914

Rohan McWilliam

Department of Humanities and Social Sciences, Anglia Ruskin University, Cambridge, UK
Email: rohan.mcwilliam@anglia.ac.uk

(Received 30 November 2022; accepted 5 December 2022; first published online 11 January 2023)

Abstract

This study examines the role that musical comedy on stage played in shaping popular culture in the long Edwardian period (1890–1914). It is based around two iconic theatrical types of the period: the Gaiety Girl and the matinee idol. Historians have underestimated their importance and what they represented. These two are decoded as a way of understanding the development of a culture based upon glamour, celebrity, fashion, display and public forms of sexuality which started to break with Victorianism. It looks in particular at the musical comedies produced by the West End impresario George Edwardes and explores their links to the developing fashion and beauty industries of the period.

Keywords: musical comedy; glamour; celebrity; fashion; West End of London

In 1908, a young boy at the age of just four fell in love. The object of his adoration was not a person but a picture postcard, which he discovered one morning as he crawled onto his mother's bed as she was opening her letters. It depicted the actress Lily Elsie (Figure 1) who had shot to fame the previous year by taking the lead role in the first London production of Lehár's operetta *The Merry Widow*, at Daly's Theatre, a major venue for musical theatre just off Leicester Square. The show, amongst other things, had sparked the Edwardian craze for the Viennese waltz. In the picture on the card, Elsie's jewels were dotted 'with sparkling tinsel' which a young child might have enjoyed for its tactile quality. Her cheeks were tinted with a translucent pink that was beyond anything that his box of crayons could achieve. As he later recalled, 'the beauty of it caused my heart to leap'. He saw her as the embodiment of romance, requiring women to imitate her and men to chivalrously protect her.

PHILCO SERIES 3197 D   MISS LILY ELSIE.

Figure 1. Lily Elsie (author collection).

The boy became obsessed with the actress, spending his pocket money on more postcards, treasuring images taken of her at her home near Henley, or of her walking behind a plough in a chiffon dress (evidence that she was 'leading a country life'). He devoured issue after issue of the *Play Pictorial* as well as other popular periodicals, which featured, for example, pictures of Elsie on holiday in Stanmore posing in front of Dorothy Perkins rambler roses

The young boy was the future designer and photographer Cecil Beaton. It seems this encounter with Elsie stirred his interest in both images of beauty and in photography as a medium. He later admitted that his tastes in fashion and style were rooted in the Edwardian era into which he was born, and it is not too fanciful to view his adoration of Elsie as presaging the designs he produced for the stage production and film of *My Fair Lady*.[1]

Lily Elsie herself was one of a wave of stars who emerged from the management of George Edwardes, who ran the Gaiety Theatre, Daly's Theatre and other West End venues and who shaped British popular culture in profound ways between 1890 and 1914. But the Edwardes productions were part of a larger wave of spectacle and performance that helped define West End entertainment. This new West End was shaped by entrepreneurs such as Richard D'Oyly Carte of the Savoy, Augustus Harris of Drury Lane, and Harry Gordon Selfridge whose department store opened in 1909.[2] As John Pick argues, 'Between 1890 and 1914 the term "West End" became a synonym for high sophistication and expense, a term which could be used by advertisers to sell fashionable clothes, luxury, make-up, perfumes, and entertainment equally.'[3]

If we look at the 1890s we see the West End helping produce a new category within popular culture: glamour. Was this new? There are undoubted continuities but the new West End had a different sensory and emotional weight to what had gone before, partly because the technology that shaped fame was changing. The word 'glamour' did not acquire its modern meaning of physical allure till at least the 1930s but it will become clear that 'glamour' is a term we can retrospectively apply.[4]

This article looks more closely at one particular aspect of this process: the role that musical theatre played in constructing a new culture of sexual attraction. By focusing on the iconography of performance emerging from Daly's Theatre and the Gaiety, it adds to current discussions of the mass image and of celebrity culture with its qualities of enchantment and sensual appeal. I could make a similar argument about other West End locations and forms of theatre but there was something distinctive about these theatres. Neither survives today but they had a huge impact on their time. Whilst this article focuses on the West End, it is worth remembering that this new culture of glamour was part of a cultural conversation between London and popular theatre elsewhere: notably the Folies-Bergère in Paris and the Ziegfeld Follies in New York.[5] It was a transnational phenomenon.

The figure of the Gaiety Girl entered the popular imagination in a dramatic way in the 1890s. This study explores a moment populated by female

---

[1] Cecil Beaton, *Photobiography* (1951), 13–14; Beaton, *The Glass of Fashion* (1954), 26–7; Beaton, 'Lovely Lily Elsie', in *The Rise and Fall of the Matinee Idol: Past Deities of Stage and Screen, Their Roles, Their Magic, and Their Worshippers*, ed. Anthony Curtis (1976), 13–14; Hugo Vickers, *Cecil Beaton: The Authorised Biography* (1985), 9. As a boy Beaton managed, through a family connection, to actually meet Elsie and this became the prelude to a friendship that would last for the rest of her life.

[2] Rohan McWilliam, *London's West End: Creating the Pleasure District, 1800-1914* (Oxford, 2020); McWilliam, 'The Electric Pleasure District: The West End of London in the Age of Empire, 1880–1914', *London Journal*, 46 (2021), 229–48.

[3] John Pick, *The West End: Mismanagement and Snobbery* (1983), 99.

[4] Stephen Gundle and Clino T. Castelli, *The Glamour System* (Basingstoke, 2006); Stephen Gundle, *Glamour: A History* (Oxford, 2008); Carol Dyhouse, *Glamour: Women, History, Feminism* (2011).

[5] Linda Mizejewski, *Ziegfield Girl: Image and Icon in Culture and Cinema* (Durham, NC, 1999).

performers such as Gabrielle Ray and matinee idols like Hayden Coffin. Both produced influential constructions of gender that proliferated through mass media in the long Edwardian period (1890–1914) yet have not been sufficiently explored by historians. Decoding their iconic images allows us to trace the development of glamour, with its connections to consumerism and notions of sensual sophistication, developed through clothing, appearance, scent and, perhaps above all, what we would now call 'attitude'. In the period, as we will see, these images fed their way into material culture through the souvenir, the postcard, the illustrated magazine and the advertisement.[6] They reflect the shift to an age of mass consumption which possessed new forms of enchantment.[7] Glamour was one of the things that drew visitors to the West End and helped construct the idea of the night out. For that reason, the figures of the carefree Gaiety Girl and the debonair matinee idol constitute a small building block of modern culture.

The Gaiety Girl as icon

Let us start with the figure of the 'Gaiety Girl' who emerged through George Edwardes's pioneering role in musical comedy.[8] She succeeded earlier icons of independent femininity such as the figure of the 'Girl of the Period'.

Edwardes originally worked as a manager for Richard D'Oyly Carte at the Savoy Theatre, overseeing the spectacular success of the Gilbert and Sullivan operas.[9] He wanted to go into management for himself and decided to become joint owner with John Hollingshead of the Gaiety Theatre across the road from the Savoy in 1885. He became sole owner the following year. As Eilidh Innes has shown, Hollingshead had turned the Gaiety Theatre (since its opening in 1868) into a major West End venue, which attracted an upscale audience and was associated with burlesque.[10] The Gaiety aimed to compete with music halls in its brightness and feeling of comfort (but suited middle-class people who would not have lowered themselves to attend the halls). It was known for its shows in which performers like Nellie Farren and Kate Vaughan performed in stockings and figure-hugging clothing which went down well with a largely male audience.

The Edwardes management shifted the emphasis in a different direction in the early 1890s, abandoning the use of women in skimpy clothing. Thus, if we discuss here the sexuality of the Gaiety Girl, it is worth saying that Edwardes's productions were arguably less raunchy than what had gone before. The term

---

[6] I explore the issue of postcards more deeply in a companion article, 'Theatrical Celebrity and the Coming of the Picture Postcard' (forthcoming).

[7] Anat Roseneberg, *The Rise of Mass Advertising: Law, Enchantment and the Cultural Boundaries of British Modernity* (Oxford, 2022).

[8] Peter Bailey, 'Musical Comedy and the Rhetoric of the Girl, 1892–1914', in *Popular Culture and Performance in the Victorian City*, ed. Peter Bailey (Cambridge, 1998), 175–93.

[9] We lack a major modern study of George Edwardes, but see Alan Hyman, *The Gaiety Years* (1975).

[10] Eilidh Innes, 'The Many Lives of John Hollingshead' (D.Phil. thesis, Anglia Ruskin University, 2021).

'Gaiety Girl' does not seem to have been much used before the 1890s (which is why I am only going to look at Gaiety females in the post-Hollingshead era), but the imagery in Edwardes's new shows clearly traded on the memory of what the high-kicking women at the Gaiety had been. *The Sketch* in 1896 noted that the days when the Gaiety was renowned for its 'absence of dress' were gone and maintained that 'a Sunday School meeting, or a prize-distribution at a girls' school, could not have been more free from offence'.[11]

Edwardes developed the genre of musical comedy in what was a mini-revolution between 1892 and 1894 when new forms of musical theatre emerged to sweep away the world of burlesque.[12] Edwardes was, of course, not a playwright, composer or lyricist; nor was he a director (though the modern concept of the director barely existed at that point). Nevertheless, he can be considered a creator of the form because he developed each show with an eye on public taste and every element of a production needed to be achieved to his satisfaction. He certainly managed a business which knocked out hit after hit working with a set of composers such as Ivan Caryll and Lionel Monckton whose melodies appealed to the middle-class suburbanites who flocked to the West End. Edwardes also maintained Hollingshead's practice of drawing on music hall performers, blending drama and what were considered more vulgar entertainments.[13] Although musical comedy was a major point of origin for the modern musical, it is unfamiliar today because, as a specific genre, it barely survived the Great War and has rarely been subject to revival.

Edwardes understood that a night out required entertainment that was breezy: mildly irreverent but still classy. He spent large sums on his productions so that the audience would be ravished by both music and spectacle. Shows like *The Shop Girl* (1894) at the Gaiety were defined by their strong sense of up-to-dateness, cosmopolitanism, striking fashion aimed at a female audience, and, increasingly, an American influence. When the Broadway musical *The Belle of New York* opened at the Shaftesbury in 1898, he was so impressed by its fast pace and the 'pep' of the chorus girls that he sent his female performers to learn from it and speeded up the tempo of the dance routines in his productions.[14]

---

[11] *The Sketch*, 22 Apr. 1896, 571.

[12] On musical comedy in this period, see Bailey, 'Musical Comedy and the Rhetoric of the Girl'; Erika Diane Rappaport, *Shopping for Pleasure: Women in the Making of London's West End* (Princeton, NJ, 2000), 178–214; Jeffrey Richards, *Imperialism and Music: Britain, 1876–1953* (Manchester, 2001), 261–77; Len Platt, *Musical Comedy on the West End Stage, 1890–1939* (Basingstoke, 2004); J. Brian Singleton, *Oscar Asche, Orientalism and British Musical Comedy* (Westport, CT, 2004); Thomas Postlewait, 'George Edwardes and Musical Comedy: The Transformation of London Theatre and Society, 1878–1914', in *The Performing Century: Nineteenth-Century Theatre's History*, ed. Tracy C. Davis and Peter Holland (Basingstoke, 2007), 80–102; Len Platt, Tobias Becker and David Linton (eds.), *Popular Musical Theatre in London and Berlin, 1890–1939* (Cambridge, 2014); Stephen Banfield, 'English Musical Comedy, 1890–1924', in *The Oxford Handbook of the British Musical*, ed. Robert Gordon and Olaf Jubin (Oxford, 2016), 117–42; Ben Macpherson, *Cultural Identity in British Musical Theatre, 1890–1939: Knowing One's Place* (Basingstoke, 2018).

[13] *Entr'Acte*, 19 Aug. 1898, 4; 21 Oct. 1893, 4.

[14] Hyman, *The Gaiety Years*, 124.

Following *A Gaiety Girl* (1893) and *The Shop Girl*, Edwardes produced a succession of shows with the word 'girl' in the title, demonstrating the construction of a discernible brand. These included *The Circus Girl* (1896), *A Runaway Girl* (1898) and *The Sunshine Girl* (1912). The shows were essentially farces in which a good-hearted girl achieves riches and the love of a good man (a matinee idol often played by Seymour Hicks or Hayden Coffin). As Peter Bailey argues, the presentation of women was based around the idea that they were 'naughty but nice'.[15] Stories could be exotic or turn the everyday into an urban fairy-tale.

What was distinctive about these shows is that they particularly suited the imaginative world of the pleasure district: they existed as part of a continuum that included upscale restaurants, department stores and grand hotels. They were geared up to offer a good package for a night out. The Gaiety Theatre even had its own restaurant attached to it. Some of these musicals were actually set in the West End, endowing the location with romance and flattering the audience which came in. Act three of *The Girl from Kay's* (1902) took place in the restaurant of the Savoy Hotel. The show was originally meant to be called 'The Girl from Jay's', the Bond Street milliner (hence another West End location), but the firm objected, which required a subtle change of title.[16] These references enhanced the reputation of the pleasure district, giving it an allure even for those who could not afford to go to the Savoy or shop on Bond Street.

Edwardes quickly established an entertainment empire. He came to manage Daly's in Leicester Square, where he developed operettas like *The Merry Widow* and shows that were less irreverent than those at the Gaiety. An evening at Daly's was more geared up to romance and the exotic. It offered orientalist extravaganzas like *The Geisha* (1896), *San Toy* (1899), set in China, or *The Cingalee* (1904) set in 'Sunny Ceylon'. He also managed the Adelphi Theatre and the Empire music hall, where the raunchiness of the ballet as well as the notorious presence of prostitution led to confrontations with social purity reformers.[17] In other words, his productions managed to appeal to high society whilst sometimes pushing at the boundaries of respectability, giving them a mildly transgressive appeal. They toured the country, went to Broadway and circled the globe. In 1894–5 a touring version of *A Gaiety Girl* featuring Decima Moore went all over the United States and on to Australia.[18] *The Toreador* (1901) and *The Geisha* both played at the Moulin Rouge in Paris. This was important because, even with a long run, Edwardes's productions cost so much to mount (roughly £10,000 in 1911) that they could not make their money back from the West End alone but required national and international tours to generate true profit (although it was important for these

---

[15] Bailey, 'Musical Comedy and the Rhetoric of the Girl'.

[16] *Referee*, 2 Feb. 1902, 3; Ken Reeves, *Gertie Millar and the Edwardesian Legacy* (Dagenham, 2004), 121.

[17] Joseph Donohue, *Fantasies of Empire: The Empire Theatre of Varieties and the Licensing Controversy of 1894* (Iowa City, 2005); Judith R. Walkowitz, *Nights Out: Life in Cosmopolitan London* (2012), 44–63.

[18] Granville Bantock and F. G. Aflalo, *Round the World with 'A Gaiety Girl'* (1896).

plays to have been a hit in London in order to succeed elsewhere).[19] The impact of Edwardes was that very quickly other producers were offering musical comedies that could have been mounted by him. This is why he was one of the key cultural figures of his day.

But who was the Gaiety Girl? As a theatrical character, she was an unchaperoned young woman who was open to the delights of the city, someone who could find her way around pleasure districts like the West End. In addition, she was a challenging female figure who did not seem to revere the domestic. She benefited from the increased respectability of the stage, which had particular importance for actresses (who had effectively been equated with prostitutes earlier in the century).[20] The Gaiety Girl became a brand which was recognised on an international stage. As early as 1897 the Gaiety Theatre in Brisbane, Australia, offered a musical comedietta titled *The Giddy Curate and the Gaiety Girl*.[21] Similarly, the American composer Percy Gaunt penned a song titled 'Rosey Is a Gaiety Girl' which features a poor girl who takes to the stage as she loves the tights and the spangles that performers wear.[22]

The presentation of carefree femininity in musical comedy contrasted with that exhibited by some of the formidable actresses who were also bold actor-managers at that time such as Ellen Terry, Madge Kendall or, indeed, Sarah Bernhardt. Gaiety actresses like Ellaline Terriss or Gertie Millar were more akin to the confident female voices developed by music hall performers like Marie Lloyd; they had immense vivacity on stage. Millar insisted that the key to success in musical comedy was making the performance look easy when it was really based on extensive rehearsal and hard work.[23] The fact that some of these figures such as Constance Collier and Gladys Cooper went on to have enduring theatrical careers confirms that they were able to develop their acting skills at the Gaiety very effectively.

As a term, the 'Gaiety Girl' has a certain amount of slippage. It did not necessarily mean the leading performers such as Ada Reeve or Ellaline Terriss (although I will treat them as part of the Gaiety Girl phenomenon); not did it mean the chorus girls (although that is how Gaiety Girls are sometimes seen). Rather, the shows were often known for their supporting female players, whose purpose was not to act but to dance and look decorative. They embodied a commodified form of femininity that was invented by Edwardes and by male writers and composers but successfully sold to an audience of both sexes. We can see them in the picture from *Our Miss Gibbs* (1909) (Figure 2) where the chorus are on the upper floor whilst the Gaiety Girls decorate the main stage.

---

[19] George Edwardes, 'My Reminiscences', *Strand Magazine*, 39 (1910), 526; Jerrard Grant Allen, 'What It Costs to Run a Theatre', *Strand Magazine*, 42 (1911), 341.

[20] Tracy C. Davis, *Actresses as Working Women: Their Social Identity in Victorian Culture* (1991); Kerry Powell, *Women and Victorian Theatre* (Cambridge, 1997).

[21] Australian Variety Theatre Archive: https://ozvta.com/wp-content/uploads/2019/01/1897-1812019.pdf (accessed 29 June 2022).

[22] Percy Gaunt, *Rosey Is a Gaiety Girl* (Boston, MA, 1895).

[23] Gertie Millar, 'Musical-Comedy Recollections and Reflections', *Strand Magazine*, 44 (1912), 50.

Figure 2. Our Miss Gibbs: *Play Pictorial* Vol XIV no. 85 (1909) (©British Library Board P.P.5224.db).

Discussing this show, Max Beerbohm was struck by 'the splendid nonchalance of these queens, all so proud, so fatigued, all seeming to wonder why they were born, and born so beautiful'.[24] Ada Reeve, who became a star after appearing in *The Shop Girl*, recalled that 'The Gaiety Girls of those days really were more important than the principals in the show, and were quite as well known to the public'.[25]

Their impact can be gauged from the wages that they enjoyed. The chorus got £2 a week but the Gaiety Girls got £15, evidence of their ability to pull in an audience.[26] Ellalline Terriss recalled that when she was a leading player at the Gaiety in the 1890s, she got £35 (while Seymour Hicks, her leading man and also her husband, got no more than £25).[27] For comparison, the greatest female star of the period, Ellen Terry, made £200 a week in the 1890s.[28] In 1911 it was estimated that the leading lady in a musical comedy made £85 a week, evidence of their ability to draw in an audience.[29]

To give a flavour of what these productions were like, let us look at the show *A Gaiety Girl*, which premiered at the Prince of Wales Theatre in 1893 and ran for 413 performances. The musical comedy cemented the Gaiety Girl brand as one based on clothing, style and a fun-loving disposition. Written by the solicitor Jimmy Davis (under the name 'Owen Hall'), it is a frothy tale of amatory

[24] *Saturday Review*, 30 Oct. 1909, 529.
[25] Ada Reeve, *Take It for a Fact: A Record of My Seventy-Five Years on the Stage* (1954), 80.
[26] Hyman, *The Gaiety Years*, 96.
[27] Ellaline Terriss, *Just a Little Bit of String* (1955), 150.
[28] Davis, *Actresses as Working Women*, 4.
[29] Allen, 'What It Costs to Run a Theatre', 341.

mix-ups strong on cheesecake. The show's premise was that the Gaiety Girl had an ambivalent relationship with respectability. *Entr'Acte* quipped that the show had a good title 'but is hardly one that would be suggested by an author of any great delicacy'.[30] One reviewer noted it had a 'smoking room feel' to it.[31]

Opening at the barracks at what is meant to be Windsor (called Winbridge here), the show features an officer, Captain Goldfield, who is in love with a Gaiety Girl called Alma Somerset. We immediately understand that Alma is good-hearted, because, just before her entrance, we are told she is outside feeding sweets to a horse. She feels, however, that she cannot marry Goldfield because she is just a Gaiety Girl and does not want to damage his prospects.[32] During the action a group of Gaiety Girls arrive with a major who has picked them up at the Savoy Hotel. They sing a song about themselves:

> For we're the Gaiety Girls who are giddy and gay,
> And we've come for a lark to the Barracks to-day,
>   We're as pretty a lot
>   As the Gaiety's got,
> And we don't care a jot what we do and we say.[33]

The carefree nature of the Gaiety Girls contrasts with the more buttoned-up young ladies of high society who are also at Winbridge with a chaperone. The use of the term 'Gaiety Girl' was a reference back to the presentations of femininity at the Gaiety in the Hollingshead era, signalling a hedonistic love of pleasure. Indeed, the iconic value of images of this kind is to suggest these are young women who are totally taken up with having a good time. They have relatively little dialogue and are there to look pretty and dance gracefully.

Alma is framed for the theft of a diamond comb by a scheming French maid. The action then moves to the Riviera, which allows for scenes where the Gaiety Girls sport bathing costumes. This is followed by a carnival where the cast dress as pierrots, the maid's scheming is exposed and lovers are united. As *The Era* noted, the moral of the show was that 'the average "Gaiety girl" is as good as the ordinary society damsel, and a good deal better too'.[34]

The opening song features a girl admiring the glittering appeal of a soldier's uniform:

> When a masculine stranger goes by
>   Arrayed in a uniform smart,
> The appeal to the feminine eye
>   takes effect on the feminine heart.

---

[30] *Entr'Acte*, 21 Oct. 1893, 4.

[31] *The Gentlewoman*, 21 Oct. 1893, 39.

[32] Owen Hall, 'A Gaiety Girl', Lord Chamberlain's Plays 53535 I (British Library).

[33] Owen Hall (book) and Harry Greenback (lyrics), *A Gaiety Girl, New Musical Comedy* (1893?), 5.

[34] *The Era*, 21 October 1893, 8.

In the song 'The Gaiety Girl and the Soldier' (introduced later in the run of the show), Letty Lind sings of how a soldier fell in love with a Gaiety Girl but she spurns him as such relationships only end in divorce, the girl being a pretty but fickle sprite bent on hedonism.[35] The plot of the show and these songs remind us that military men were an important part of the West End audience, especially army officers. The reviewer for *The Stage* saw Hayden Coffin as Captain Goldfield receive an encore for his performance of the song 'Tommy Atkins'. The production elevated him into a leading matinee idol and included this verse about the average British soldier:

> And whether he's on India's coral strand,
>   or pouring out his blood in the Soudan,
> To keep our flag a-flying, he's a doing and a-dying,
>   Every inch of him a soldier and a man![36]

At one level, therefore, the show manifested a strong sense of patriotism and imperial supremacy. At another, it gently mocked institutions like the clergy and the army; thus it featured a worldly clergyman who is clearly familiar with the latest variety shows. Audiences responded well to the optimistic feel of the show, including Owen Hall's bright dialogue which teemed with up-to-date references to socialism and the recently opened play *Charley's Aunt*. The light and breezy score itself expressed a feeling about the world: it was cheerful and coquettish, a musical reimagining of courtship. The visual and sonic dimensions of these shows made them perfect for a night out.

The Gaiety Girl figure was not confined to the stage. She was embodied on the posters and souvenirs for the shows, many of which were created by the artist Dudley Hardy. This was the moment when poster art rather than text-based playbills began to adorn the walls of cities and of public transport.[37] Posters lured people in through images that captured the essence of the show. Hardy had been influenced by French graphic design and, in particular, the work of Jules Chéret, the great poster painter of the belle époque whose work featured frivolous women eager to dance the cancan and quaff champagne.[38]

The image on the posters and souvenir covers for *A Gaiety Girl* suggests the abandonment of middle-class forms of female propriety and puritanism (which had never been a marked feature of the West End). (See Figure 3.) They call time on Victorianism and break the connection between leisure and self-improvement; instead, they reassure viewers that it is okay to just have fun.[39]

---

[35] Harry Greenback (lyrics) and Sydney Jones (music), *The Gaiety Girl and the Soldier* (1895).

[36] Hall and Greenback, *A Gaiety Girl*, 5, 17.

[37] George Lander, 'The Humours of Theatrical Posters', *Strand Magazine*, 33 (1907), 209–14; Rachel Teukolsky, *Picture World: Image, Aesthetics and Victorian New Media* (New York, 2020), 355–60.

[38] Marcus Verhagen, 'The Poster in *fin-de-siècle* Paris: "That Mobile and Degenerative Art"', in *Cinema and the Invention of Modern Life*, ed. Leo Charney and Vanessa R. Schwartz (Berkeley, 1995), 103–29.

[39] Peter Bailey, 'The Victorian Middle Class and the Problem of Leisure', in *Popular Culture and Performance*, ed. Bailey, 13–29.

Figure 3. *A Gaiety Girl* souvenir cover (©British Library Board: BL callmark:1874 b7 p.1).

Thus the image of femininity in the poster is carefree and free-spirited, linked to a notion of excess. The girl displays her ankles in the dance with her feet apparently off the ground. Her eyes are shut, suggesting enjoyment of the intensity of her revel. She owes nothing to anybody but invites male attention. Hardy's lettering seems to actually dance around her. The picture suggests that Montmartre has come to London.

At the same time there is clearly an overlap with representations of prostitution. A walk through the West End was impossible without encountering sex workers. Like prostitutes, the fashion of Gaiety Girls could be seen as a parody of what aristocratic women wore.[40] The outspokenness of the Gaiety Girl, not caring what she says, may have reproduced the badinage of sex workers soliciting clients. Thus the moral that a Gaiety Girl is as good as a high society lady may have been a more transgressive message than it might appear today.

The Dudley Hardy posters are also important not just in their depiction of Gaiety Girls but in how they constructed the viewer: principally male and endowed with a worldly quality integral to such entertainments. These qualities can be associated with the man about town who populated the West End.[41] By 'worldly' I mean a sense of sophistication and possession of cultural capital, an ability to require only hints about sexuality. At one level, images of the Gaiety Girl are perfectly innocent but, at another, they can be constructed as a form of sexual enticement.

This linkage with prostitution can be pursued further as it aligns with Peter Bailey's analysis of barmaids in pictorial representations. Bailey argues that these images present women as an apparently paradoxical combination of the good woman and the prostitute: a zone which he terms 'para-sexual'.[42] The Gaiety Girl was clearly presented in para-sexual terms; indeed this liminal blurring of boundaries may have been what turned her into an object of fascination.

Women were deployed as a form of decorative adornment in musical comedy. This can be illustrated by *The Beauty of Bath* at the Aldwych in 1906 (not a George Edwardes production but very much influenced by him). This featured a scene in which beautiful girls appeared on stage bringing paintings by artists such as Reynolds and Gainsborough to life.[43] This parade would have been familiar to an audience used to *poses plastiques* in music hall where models recreated great works of art. Another context for these representations is that this was the period when the fashion model was just coming into existence as the dress designer 'Lucile' (Lady Lucy Duff Gordon) abandoned mannequins and created fashion parades at her shop in Hanover Square.[44] In the 1890s mannequins or paintings thus came to life. There was continuity between popular theatre and the developing fashion sector.

Sexuality and courtship

By the 1890s Britain was well into the age of mass production and there was an element of factory production in the Edwardes shows as he turned his female

[40] Mariana Valverde, 'The Love of Finery: Fashion and the Fallen Woman in Nineteenth Century Social Discourse', *Victorian Studies*, 32 (1989), 168–88.

[41] Rohan McWilliam, 'Man about Town: Victorian Night Life and the Haymarket Saturnalia, 1840–1880', *History*, 103 (2018), 758–76.

[42] Peter Bailey, 'The Victorian Barmaid as Cultural Prototype', in *Popular Culture and Performance*, ed. Bailey, 151–74.

[43] *The Era*, 18 Aug. 1906, 15; Terriss, *Just a Little Bit of String*, 196.

[44] Meredith Etherington-Smith and Jeremy Pilcher, *The 'It' Girls: Lucy, Lady Duff Gordon, the Coutourière 'Lucile', and Elinor Glyn, Romantic Novelist* (1986), 75.

performers into a mechanised unit.[45] They were taught acting, dancing, deportment and fencing, though some of the girls found the work hard and discipline difficult to sustain.[46] He paid for their teeth to be looked after by a London dentist called Forsyth (an acknowledgement that bad British teeth were the opposite of beauty), not least because the smile was an important part of their appeal. Edwardes even allegedly asked his talent scouts if an actress they had found was someone they would want to sleep with.[47] Constance Collier admitted that she got on at the Gaiety because of her looks rather than her voice.[48]

There was clearly a mildly risqué form of sexuality in some shows. In *The Orchid* (1903), Gabrielle Ray sang a song clad in pink pyjamas:

I'm a pink pyjama girl, all pink and rosy,
I'm a lovely little lady to adore!
If you're a pink pyjama Girlie, You're allrighty,
And you'll never wear a Nightie anymore![49]

In *The Lady Dandies* (1906) she wore a gown fastened at her thigh which gave way when she did a high kick showing off the silk stockings on her legs. Five years later in the Gaiety show *Peggy*, Ray would arrive on stage wearing a cape which would then be abandoned to show off her swimsuit.[50]

Ada Reeve insisted on the essential respectability of the form, maintaining that female performers barely showed their ankles (although the example of Gabrielle Ray in Figure 4 suggests this was not always the case). However, when Reeve produced the musical *Butterflies* (Apollo Theatre, 1908), a well-known performer refused to appear in the butterfly dance as the costume was too revealing: a skirt of transparent black gauze with bare flesh showing at the sides. The young actress Phyllis Monkman then volunteered to take over the role in the dress and made a success of it.[51] There was clearly a sexual allure that ran through musical comedy.

We can gauge the cultural impact of the Gaiety Girl by the fact that in 1905–6 there seems to have been a concerted effort by other West End producers to come up with their own equivalents. Seymour Hicks's musical comedy *The Talk of the Town* at the Lyric in 1905 offered the Vaudeville Girls. *The Dairymaids* at the Apollo featured the Sandow Girls, named after the bodybuilder Eugene Sandow, who engaged in gymnastic exercises on stage. *The Beauty of Bath* at the Aldwych featured the Bun Girls, with different ladies named after various

---

[45] Bailey, 'Musical Comedy and the Rhetoric of the Girl', 178–9.

[46] Constance Collier, *Harlequinade: The Story of My Life* (1929), 46–7.

[47] Walter MacQueen-Pope, *Shirtfronts and Sables: A Story of the Days when Money Could Be Spent* (1953), 140.

[48] Collier, *Harlequinade*, 50–1.

[49] Information from Robert Waters in the file BTC 2011/0031, University of Bristol Theatre Collection.

[50] Newspaper cutting, *ibid.* (second folder).

[51] Reeve, *Take It for a Fact*, 121.

Figure 4. Gabrielle Ray (author collection).

buns: hence there was Spice Bun, Plum Bun, Iced Bun and the inevitable Currant Bun.

This was also the moment when the West End took account of the American Gibson Girl, a comparable figure in some respects, who had been popularised in the United States through the illustrations of artist Charles Dana Gibson (reproduced in Britain in the magazine *Pictorial Comedy*).[52] Drawn with an S-shape physique, she was athletic, free-spirited, independent but also a less threatening figure than the New Woman. The American actress Camille

---

[52] Martha H. Patterson, *Beyond the Gibson Girl: Reimagining the American New Woman, 1895–1915* (Urbana, 2005).

Figure 5. Camille Clifford (author collection).

Clifford (Figure 5) won a contest in New York to find the perfect embodiment of the Gibson Girl in real life (partly because of her bosomy physique). She then came to London with the show *The Prince of Pilsen* in 1904 and stayed on as she found she could exploit her fame. That year she appeared in Seymour Hicks's *The Catch of the Season* at the Vaudeville, which ran until 1906 and deployed a variety of actresses (including Clifford) playing Gibson Girls, wearing costumes designed by Lady Lucy Duff Gordon and bringing Dana's pictures to life. Following this, Clifford went into another successful show, *The Belle of Mayfair*, where she sang the song 'Why Do They Call Me a Gibson Girl?'. She had so much impact that the star of the show Edna May left as she felt she was being overshadowed by Clifford; she was also notorious enough to be burlesqued in *The Beauty of Bath*.[53] The Edwardian stage was therefore alive with images of independent but commodified femininity.

Musical comedies had a strong impact on the audience. The actor-manager Robert Courtneidge recalled a young man who saw *The Arcadians* (1909) over 300 times.[54] Male aristocrats were truly mesmerised by Gaiety Girls, a reminder that the word 'glamour' in the nineteenth century was linked to magic or sorcery. Some men would book seats at the Gaiety for an entire season.[55] The term 'stage door johnny' was imported from the United States to describe the numerous titled figures who would swarm around the stage door after the show, asking to meet one of the female performers and to take them out to dinner usually at the Savoy.[56] There is some evidence that the big stars kept the youngest girls (such as Constance Collier who started at the Gaiety aged fifteen) away from the attentions of the johnnies. Collier claimed 'they guarded me as if I were in a convent' and 'were the best of chaperones'.[57]

This was therefore an atmosphere based both on male entitlement but also class entitlement. Between 1892 and 1914, some twenty-four actresses (many of them Gaiety Girls) married peers of the realm.[58] Thus Rosie Boote became Marchioness of Headfort, Constance Gilchrist married the Earl of Orkney, Olive May became Countess Drogheda and Denise Orme became Baroness Churston. Ada Reeve counted among her admirers Lord Stavordale and Prince Jitendra, second son of the Maharajah of Cooch Bahar.[59] In 1895, Birdie Sutherland sued the Honourable Dudley Marjoribanks for breach of promise (Marjoribanks's father, Lord Tweedmouth, seems to have prevented his son from marrying a showgirl).[60] One article about the case was titled 'Jilting a Gaiety Girl'.[61]

Relationships between actresses and aristocrats and even monarchs were of course nothing new and these associations need to be seen as part of a longer historical trajectory. The fact that these women became wives rather than mistresses was, however, a departure. George Edwardes apparently believed that the future of the peerage lay in the Gaiety chorus: in eugenic terms, it raised the prospect of fit, attractive children.[62] As early as 1893, the *Sheffield Weekly Telegraph* ran an article titled 'In Love with a Gaiety Girl', commenting 'In smart society's matrimonial market, Gaiety Girls are snapping up the eligible

---

[53] Reeves, *Gertie Millar and the Edwardesian Legacy*, 107–9; Terriss, *Just a Little Bit of String*, 195.

[54] Robert Courtneidge, *I Was an Actor Once* (1930), 204.

[55] Collier, *Harlequinade*, 50

[56] See, for example, *The Sketch*, 22 April 1896, 571; James Jupp, *The Gaiety Stage Door: Thirty Years' Reminiscences of the Theatre* (1923), 13.

[57] Collier, *Harlequinade*, 49.

[58] See http://www.stagebeauty.net/th-frames.html?http&&&www.stagebeauty.net/th-peerge.html (accessed 19 June 2022).

[59] Reeve, *Take It for a Fact*, 88, 121–2.

[60] *Aberdeen Press and Journal*, 20 May 1895, 5.

[61] *Liverpool Weekly Courier*, 25 May 1895, 2.

[62] J. B. Booth, *London Town* (1929), 80.

Table 1. The background of some key Gaiety Girls

Name	Dates	Parental background (father's occupation)	Gaiety or musical appearances include:
Constance Collier	1878–1955	Dancer	*The Shop Girl*
Gladys Cooper	1888–1971	Journalist	*Girls of Gottenburg, Havana, Our Miss Gibbs*
Phyllis Dare	1890–1975	Barrister's clerk	*Peggy, The Sunshine Girl*
Gertie Millar	1879–1952	Wool merchant (illegitimate)	*The Orchid, The Girls of Gottenberg*
Decima Moore	1871–1964	Chemist	*A Gaiety Girl*
Denise Orme	1885–1960	Lawyer's servant	*Our Miss Gibbs, The Quaker Girl, The Orchid*
Gabrielle Ray	1883–1973	Iron merchant	*The Orchid, Peggy, The Dollar Princess*
Ada Reeve	1874–1966	Actor	*The Shop Girl*
Marie Studholme	1872–1930	Auctioneer	*A Gaiety Girl* (revival), *An Artist's Model, The Geisha, The Messenger Boy, The School Girl, The Toreador*
Ellaline Terriss	1871–1971	Actor	*The Shop Girl, A Runaway Girl, My Girl, The Circus Girl*

bargains.'[63] The use of the word 'bargain' was presumably meant ironically but it epitomised the commercial atmosphere which shaped these connections. A similar phenomenon was notable in the United States where a number of Ziegfeld Girls married millionaires.[64] Stage door johnnies even started to feature in shows. In *The Beauty of Bath*, the Duke says that he has winked his eye at the girls in the 'dear old Gaiety'.[65]

The journalist Claud Jenkins recalled going to the Gaiety as a boy and rushing round to the stage door afterwards to see if the girls were as beautiful off-stage: 'I used to gaze with awe at the "Stagedoor Johnnies" so well dressed, tall hat, white gloves, opera cloak and monocle, with the inevitable bouquet in

[63] *Sheffield Weekly Telegraph*, 12 May 1893, 3.

[64] Derek and Julia Parker, *The Natural History of the Chorus Girl* (Newton Abbot, 1975), 91.

[65] Ken Reeves, *Gertie Millar and the Edwardesian Legacy*, 199.

their hands, hanging around in profusion, waiting hopefully to take one of the beauties to supper.'[66] Ada Reeve allowed herself to be taken out for dinner at the Savoy Grill Room after a show but insisted there were no demands for sexual congress although she received diamond bracelets, necklaces and tiaras as gifts: 'In those days the young bloods were so glad – so proud, in fact – of being seen with beautiful and talented ladies of our profession that they were willing to pay well for the privilege.' On the other hand, she recalled an incident in 1903 at Romano's restaurant on the Strand where a chorus girl turned up wearing luxurious clothing which she could not have afforded herself. She wore a black-sequined gown, carried a cane with a diamond top and sported a hat with a Paradise feather. She then lewdly shouted, 'People call me fast, but ... I can count the men I've had on my two hands.'[67] Sometimes these connections could be positively dark. The young bachelor Baron Gunther Rau von Holzhausen became infatuated with Gertie Millar whom he got to know. In 1905, having lost all his money on the horses, he broke into her boudoir (she was out) and shot himself.[68]

There is another way of looking at these aristocratic marriages. Most Gaiety Girls came from relatively modest backgrounds. (See Table 1.) Part of their mystique was that they appeared in rags-to-riches stories on stage and then seemed to live that experience in real life. When she got older, Constance Collier found herself in the incongruous situation of being wined and dined at the Savoy and then returning to her family's working-class flat in Kennington.[69]

The matinee idol as icon

But what about the male stars? The comparable equivalent to the Gaiety Girl was the 'matinee idol'. This is in many ways an unsatisfactory term, not least because I am talking about performances that did not just take place at matinees. However, it does capture an important feature of the West End. Matinees were increasingly offered in West End theatres from the 1880s onwards and they were particularly suitable for a middle-class female audience from the suburbs who could come into town, shop in a major department store and then take in a play. Or they might appeal to younger un-chaperoned women who would not be allowed out in the evening but would feel safe if they came into town in the afternoons. A lot of West End theatre increasingly serviced this public.[70]

The matinee idol was a male leading player whose handsomeness was thought to be especially attractive to women. This in turn produced images

---

[66] The Stage, 1 Feb. 1962, 15.

[67] Reeve, Take It for a Fact, 74, 75–6, 88

[68] The Stage, 2 Nov. 1905, 3.

[69] Collier, Harlequinade, 57.

[70] McWilliam, London's West End; Susan Torrey Barstow, 'Hedda Is All of Us: Late Victorian Women at the Matinee', Victorian Studies, 43 (2002), 387–411.

Figure 6. Hayden Coffin (author collection).

that were comparable to those of women in pictorial representations.[71] One could argue that the term 'matinee idol' was used to infantilise women by portraying them as subject to love-sickness and hysteria. Similar language was used about women and shopping at that time.

The leading men in George Edwardes's musical comedies were essentially matinee idols and marketed as such: actors like Hayden Coffin (Figure 6), Seymour Hicks and George Grossmith junior. Hicks turned the song 'Her Golden Hair Was Hanging down Her Back' (sung in *The Shop Girl*) into a popular standard. Grossmith was described as 'the schoolgirl's dream'. He gained a

---

[71] Paul R. Deslandes, *The Culture of Male Beauty in Britain: From the First Photographs to David Beckham* (Chicago, 2021), 27.

reputation from always playing the dude or 'masher' figure in musical comedy. His dapper taste in clothing was thought to have rubbed off on many suburban lower-middle-class males who were visible in the pit at West End shows.[72] The term 'masher' seems to have come over from the United States around 1882 and referred to the kind of foppish young men who would be seen on the promenades of music halls. They were interested both in looking sharp and in the fair sex. In *The Shop Girl*, Grossmith's Bertie Boyd (clearly an ancestor of both Burlington Bertie and Bertie Wooster) sang:

> I've joined the 'Junior Pothouse' and drop in when I am by,
> I don't possess much brain, but I have got the latest tie.
> When I've done my morning Bond Street crawl, I do the thing in style,
> And give the cabbie half-a-crown to drive me half-a-mile.

In another verse he opines:

> I must confess in 'Hamlet' no interest I've found,
> I much prefer 'The Gaiety Girl', or else 'Morocco Bound'.[73]

The swell or masher type was a demotic approximation of the aristocratic man about town. The masher was mocked in these shows but also was seen as embodying a form of stylish behaviour that could be emulated through wearing the right kind of clothing and possessing his *savoir faire*.

The mass image

What became distinctive about the cultural work of the West End after about 1890 was the way it became supported by a range of mass media that generated an emotional feeling amongst spectators.[74] We have already seen the importance of the souvenir, but the mass image manifested itself in a growing number of magazines (as well as press content) devoted to theatre, which helped generate an emotional response. Stars felt increasingly accessible. Gertie Millar claimed she had to spend several hours a day dealing with correspondence, including requests for signed photographs and, inevitably, letters asking for help getting on the stage.[75]

---

[72] Seymour Hicks, *Twenty Four Years of an Actor's Life* (1910), 188; William Archer, *The Theatrical World of 1896* (1897), 298–301; Peter Bailey, 'Theatres of Entertainment/Spaces of Modernity', *Nineteenth-Century Theatre*, 26 (1998), 14.

[73] H. J. W. Dam (words) and Ivan Carryll (music), *The Shop-Girl* (1894), 166–7. *Morocco Bound* played at the Shaftesbury and the Trafalgar Square theatres in 1893–4.

[74] On the mass image in this period see, amongst a vast literature, Thomas Richards, *The Commodity Culture of Victorian England: Advertising and Spectacle* (1991); Vanessa R. Schwartz, *Spectacular Realities: Early Mass Culture in* fin-de-siècle *Paris* (Berkeley, 1998); Gerry Beegan, *The Mass Image: A Social History of Photomechanical Reproduction in Victorian London* (Basingstoke, 2008); Teukolsky, *Picture World*; Rosenberg, *The Rise of Mass Advertising*.

[75] Millar, 'Musical-Comedy Recollections and Reflections', 50.

Founded in 1902, the *Play Pictorial* was one of a number of periodicals that fed this culture of glamour. Each monthly issue was devoted to a specific production. It did not cover touring productions but promoted the West End as the essential site of theatregoing. The periodical was clearly aimed at a female audience as is evident from the advertisements. These were often for shops in West End locations aimed at female consumers. Thus a 1903 issue features advertisements for the Bond Street Corset Company and the shop Ernest of Regent Street which sold ball gowns. One issue featured a promotion for the shops on the Burlington Arcade in Piccadilly.[76] This made it an aspirational read for women who could not afford to shop there. It also reaffirmed a connection between playgoing and other forms of consumption. The word 'pictorial' in the title was crucial. Advances in lighting and photography enabled it to present pictures of a production in a theatre (rather than in a studio). Most pages were devoted to large pictures of the stars, which could be cut out and used in scrapbooks. The impact of the magazine can be deduced from the information that it had to reprint its issue devoted to *The Merry Widow* three times and it regularly advertised back issues so that fans could find the photographs of the stars or productions that most interested them.[77]

The *Play Pictorial* had a regular feature called 'Dress at the Play' (or some variant of the same title) which looked at the dresses on stage which were frequently explored in exuberant detail.[78] Thus, in the second act of *The Dollar Princess* (1909), we are told 'Miss Gabrielle Ray wins all hearts in a pink satin and lace confection that is a triumph of grace and skill. With it she wears a very captivating little Juliet cap which sets off her fair hair to great advantage.'[79] Ellaline Terriss's coat in *The Beauty of Bath* was judged a '*pièce de résistance*':

> a truly lovely garment of hyacinth blue voile, arranged in tucks over the shoulders, and fitted with long wing sleeves; a band of pink silk, embroidered in silver, borders the inside of cloak and sleeves, while upon the outside appears a narrowband of blue silk embroidered in pink, and edged by a tiny blue ribbon pleating.[80]

In the case of Phyllis Dare in *The Girl in the Train* (1910) we are informed that her dress is from Robe de Madame Margaine-Lacroix, 19 Boulevard Haussmann, Paris.[81]

Theatre took on a new role as the instigator of fashion and style. The fashion press worked carefully with West End impresarios and turned the act of watching a play into an opportunity to see the coming fashions on stage and perhaps to check out what other members of the audience were wearing.

---

[76] *Play Pictorial*, 4 no. 19 (1903), v–vi; 14 no. 82 (1909), x.

[77] *Ibid.*, 14 no. 85 (1909), i.

[78] For example, *Play Pictorial*, 5 no. 32 (1905), 274–9. See Joel Kaplan and Sheila Stowell, *Theatre and Fashion: Oscar Wilde to the Suffragettes* (Cambridge, 1994).

[79] *Play Pictorial*, 15 no. 88 (1909), 23.

[80] *Ibid.*, 7 no. 45 (1906), 164.

[81] *Ibid.*, 16 no. 96 (1910), 71.

Significantly, it was female rather than male dress that was explored in detail. West End theatre was intended partly as a showcase for changes in female fashion, which is why leading designers such as Lady Lucy Duff Gordon were increasingly called upon for the dresses. Their impact can be gauged, to give just one example, from the way the author Dodie Smith recalled how, at St Paul's Girls' School in this period, she sported a hairstyle worn with side combs copied from Zena and Phyllis Dare and would wear a white V-necked blouse ('worn open as low as I dared') of the sort popularised by Lily Elsie.[82]

Theatre turned fashion into a form of fantasy. Reviewing the clothes at *The Merry Widow*, the fashion writer for the *Play Pictorial* had this to say:

> They appealed to me especially because they are so unlike the frocks you meet in everyday life ... This colour scheme throughout is really beautiful, and it is worthy of notice to mention that all the gowns in the first and third acts are, without exception, made in the Empire style. The high-waisted bodices, the long trailing skirts, the tinted aigrette floating from perfectly dressed heads, how well they suit the tall, graceful Daly girls and the Daly stage! but alas! how very little practicable for the average woman with the average dress allowance. But still, let us admit it, their effect is undoubtedly artistic.[83]

This focus on clothing produced a complaint from Marie Corelli about the reckless extravagance of clothes and the way they detracted from the play:

> The 'faked' woman has everything on her side. Drama supports her. The Press encourages her. Whole columns in seemingly sane journals are devoted to the description of her attire. Very little space is given to the actual criticism of a new play *as* a play, but any amount of room is awarded to glorified 'gushers' concerning the actresses' gowns.[84]

This emphasis on fashion was part of a process where West End theatre was seen as the preserve of the middle classes (and above), rather than working-class people who had earlier in the nineteenth century been part of the audience, if only in the gallery.

Fashion and theatre became increasingly interconnected, reflecting the way in which dress was becoming a way of negotiating the strangeness of metropolitan life. Actresses in this period enjoyed an enduring relationship with the West End fashion industry. In *Our Miss Gibbs*, the millinery firm Maison Lewis of Regent's Street provided hats that were so expensive that they were only given to the actresses immediately before they were about to go on stage and were afterwards stored back at the firm's shop in hatboxes.[85] Even touring productions of these shows produced the same interest in female

---

[82] Dodie Smith, *Look Back with Mixed Feelings* (1978), 4, 28.
[83] *Play Pictorial*, 10 no. 61 (1907), 106.
[84] *The Bystander*, 27 July 1904, 436.
[85] MacQueen-Pope, *Shirtfronts and Sables*, 140.

fashions.[86] The clothing of actresses was believed to be of interest to a female audience because they provided evidence of 'the coming modes'.

To put this in perspective, up to the 1880s it was common for actors to provide their own costumes. Yet by 1911 the management for a musical comedy paid an estimated £1,200 for the principal actresses' dress bill alone during a run. The cost of female costumes on *The Dollar Princess* ran to £6,000, with one dress for one of the principals costing £80.[87] Lavish costumes were in turn one reason why West End theatres felt they could charge more.

At the same time, the shows reflected new forms of body politics. An increasingly metropolitan culture produced new visual codes about how to move through the city. It also reflected the fact that women were becoming more prominent in the public sphere. As Jessica Clark argues, the expanding socio-economic opportunities for women in the later nineteenth century made greater demands upon them in terms of appearance. Clothing, hair, make-up and deportment all became subject to visual codes as people negotiated the challenges of city life.[88] This fed into the commodification of beauty that both the fashion and cosmetics industry served. This is also the context in which we should see the rise of musical comedy and the Gaiety Girl. It also reinforced the notion of the West End as a space for display.

Appearance clearly mattered. Gertie Millar claimed she received a letter from an admirer that said: 'Dear Miss Millar, "Why on earth don't you always part your hair in the same way? I really do dislike not knowing how to expect to see your hair done next."'[89] Lily Elsie, with whom we commenced, was not originally meant to star in *The Merry Widow*. George Edwardes had signed Mizzie Gunther, who had created the lead role at its première in Vienna in 1905, without looking at a photograph. When she turned up in London, he was shocked by her outsize appearance and had to pay her compensation.[90] He gave the role to the relatively unknown but attractive Elsie even though she had difficulty singing some of the music.

The focus on appearance accounts for the success of Gabrielle Ray whose appearances for George Edwardes included *The Orchid* and *The Dollar Princess*. Cecil Beaton recalled that her appearance was heavily contrived to give a semblance of innocence combined with 'an intriguing perversity about such excessive prettiness'. Lily Elsie informed him about how artfully she went about creating her image on stage:

A past mistress of pointillisme, Gabrielle Ray would, for her stage appearance, put mauve and green dots at the edges of her eyes, with little red and mauve dots at the corner of her nostrils. As meticulously as Seurat working over one of his canvases, she shaded her eyelids and temples in different colours of the mushroom, while her cheeks were tinted with varying

---

[86] *South Wales Daily News*, 11 Sept. 1895, 6.

[87] Allen, 'What It Costs to Run a Theatre', 341.

[88] Jessica P. Clark, *The Business of Beauty: Gender and the Body in Modern London* (2020), 172.

[89] Millar, 'Musical-Comedy Recollections and Reflections', 48.

[90] Hyman, *The Gaiety Years*, 146

pinks from coral to *bois de rose*. The chin was touched with a hare-foot brush dipped in terracotta powder, and the lobes of the ears and the tip of the nose would be flicked with salmon colour. Thus painted, Gabrielle Ray appeared before the audience enamelled like a china doll ... With little talent but much imagination Gabrielle Ray, during her brief career, turned herself into a small work of art.[91]

There was therefore an important relationship between actresses and the beauty industry.

Helena Rubinstein deployed photographs of actresses in the advertisements for her cosmetics. Thus one advertisement featured a letter from Gaiety Girl Marie Studholme which read 'Your Valaze preparations are really wonderful & delightfully effective to use.'[92] Lily Elsie also advertised Rubinstein's Valaze Toilet preparations.[93] Constance Collier found herself advertising face creams and soaps as well as providing advice in the press on how to stay beautiful and young-looking.[94] Gabrielle Ray advertised Atkinson's Poinsetta perfume in *The Tatler* in 1912, a reminder that glamour is connected not just with appearance but with smell.[95] Rimmell, the perfumier on the Strand, actually helped provide the Gaiety with scented programmes. The hugely successful show *Floradora* (1899) significantly centred on a perfume, again showing the conjunction of beauty, glamour and scent. This culture of fame had both sensory and sensual qualities.

These advertisements were mutually beneficial for the star, the producer of beauty goods and (arguably) the consumer. Celebrity endorsements made customers feel they shared something with stars. They also humanised stars in a way that reassured consumers, acknowledging that, no matter how beautiful they appeared, they still needed a bit of help.

Conclusion

If we focus on these bold images derived from the stage, it is worth adding that this was the moment when images started to move. Through the Gaiety Girl and the matinee idol we see the emergence of forms of attractiveness that would be taken over by the cinema. Film found ways of extending the power of these mass images which were appropriate because they linked sensuality to consumerism.

The George Edwardes-inspired brand of musical comedy in turn came to seem old-fashioned. Around 1910 we see the coming of musical forms derived from the United States, especially ragtime and a new form of popular theatre, the musical revue. The Gaiety and Daly's Theatre both continued after the war but they felt dated and were later demolished. Yet Gaiety Girls lingered in the memory. Richard Greene played George Edwardes in a fictionalised film biopic, called

---

[91] Beaton, *Glass of Fashion*, 34–5.
[92] *Black and White*, 26 June 1909, 951.
[93] *Play Pictorial*, 15 no. 88 (1909), xv.
[94] Collier, *Harlequinade*, 61.
[95] *The Tatler*, 6 Mar. 1912, 110.

Gaiety George, in 1946. Another film, *Trottie True*, in 1949 portrayed the adventures of a Gaiety Girl. In 1957, the proprietor of a pub near Hyde Park turned his bar into a replica of the Gaiety in its glory days. Significantly, despite a varied career, Ada Reeve was still referred to at the end of her life as a Gaiety Girl. As late as 1973, *Punch* offered an image of Gaiety Girls in an advertisement for sparkling wine.[96]

What I have traced is a form of sensual consumerism allied to new forms of visual culture. This was the cultural work provided by London's West End. Both the Gaiety Girl and the matinee idol proclaimed their modernity, underscoring a way of life based upon the consumption of images. They were both constructions of glamour, which has become one of the most important forms of cultural capital since then. Their beauty and handsomeness was a statement of their character: fun-loving, style-driven but also good-hearted, optimistic and open to romance. They were expressions of a new consumer culture in which the focus on appearance was viewed as integral to obtaining success in life.[97]

This study has focused mainly on the Gaiety Girl exploring her iconographic meanings. At one level she was a figure constructed by men for male pleasure. At the same time, many of these female stars were admired by women: a feature that remains true even if one allows that women are socialised to view the world through the male gaze.[98] There is, however, a tension that has emerged in looking at these figures. On stage, some of the Gaiety Girls were lively and full of banter even if they were unlikely to join the Suffragettes (if they had offered a more challenging image of femininity they would probably not have drawn the attention of stage door johnnies). Yet when they were refigured as images within mass media (though magazines and advertising) they were often objectified and reduced to a form of adornment, avatars of para-sexuality.

The idiom of musical comedy in the long Edwardian era provided a discourse through which the joys of courtship could be understood, with its coquettish battles of the sexes. It was made possible by the new mass media and by the developing beauty industry. Icons like the Gaiety Girl and the matinee idol were a resource to help young men and women negotiate urban life. They hailed viewers with the promise that if they were able to participate in a night out, they would not only see glamorous images but would become glamorous themselves.

Acknowledgements. A version of this article was first presented as the Royal Historical Society's 2022 Prothero Lecture, read on 6 July 2022.

---

[96] Gaiety Theatre aka Gaiety Bar Beware: Pathé newsreel 1957: https://www.youtube.com/watch?v=8P57n_CVleU&t=1s (accessed 29 June 2022); 'The Gaiety Girl Who Always Said No', clipping in Ada Reeve papers, MM/REF/PE/AC/AMR/3 (press cuttings) box 1180, University of Bristol Theatre Collection; *Punch*, 18 July 1973, v. See also Martina Lipton, 'Memorialization, Memorabilia and the Mediated Afterlife of Ada Reeve', *New Theatre Quarterly*, 29 no. 2 (2013), 132–45.

[97] Deslandes, *The Culture of Male Beauty in Britain*, 23.

[98] Laura Mulvey, 'Visual Pleasure and Narrative Cinema', *Screen*, 16 (1975), 6–18.

Cite this article: McWilliam R (2023). The Gaiety Girl and the Matinee Idol: Constructing Celebrity, Glamour and Sexuality in the West End of London, 1890–1914. *Transactions of the Royal Historical Society* 1, 69–93. https://doi.org/10.1017/S0080440122000184

Transactions of the RHS (2023), 1, 95–120
doi:10.1017/S0080440123000014

ARTICLE

Enclosure as Internal Colonisation: The Subaltern Commoner, *Terra Nullius* and the Settling of England's 'Wastes'

Carl J. Griffin (iD)

Department of Geography, University of Sussex, Brighton, UK
Email: Carl.Griffin@sussex.ac.uk

(Received 16 July 2022; revised 14 January 2023; accepted 20 January 2023; first published online 14 February 2023)

Abstract

In the past decade, scholars of the here-and-now have (re)discovered the concept of enclosure, applying it with considerable zeal and in a bewildering variety of situations: from the securitisation of the Internet, and patenting genes, to attempts to privatise urban 'public' spaces, the English 'enclosure story' is presented as a given, a narrative that is set in stone. One critical aspect of this account is that enclosure was exported to Britain's overseas colonies in a one-way process. This paper shows, however, that from the early sixteenth century – and insistently so from the late eighteenth century – arguments for the enclosure of English commons and wastes were framed using techniques and discourses deployed overseas: the languages and practices of colonialism. Commons and wastes, so the paper argues, were not just increasingly seen as empty spaces, but the peoples that inhabited them were written as if they were uncivilised and unable to manage the land. Further, arguments for the enclosure of wastes were made as an alternative to Britain's overseas imperialism. The paper traces a variety of debates and proposals that collectively constitute a coherent body of 'internal colonial' thought.

Keywords: enclosure; internal colonialism; commons; wastes; England

In a pioneering paper published in 2008, Stephen Thompson argued that historians of enclosure have tended to fixate either on the processes of enclosure or on the impacts of enclosure on the poorest members of rural society, whilst the broader political contexts and languages of enclosure have been all but ignored.[1] The point still holds. This paper heeds Thompson's call in addressing the political settings of enclosure, not in a Wrightsonian sense at the level of the parish,[2] but in terms of wider political discourses that drew directly on the practices of colonialism and on the political languages of colonialism. This paper argues that from the latter decades of the eighteenth century, commons and wastes were explained as empty spaces, *terra nullius*, the claim made in the language – and often in relation to examples – of British overseas colonialism. This is not to say that the idea of wastes being empty spaces was altogether new, this being a discourse used to explain and justify the enclosure of large swathes of fen and forest from at least the turn of the seventeenth century,[3] but rather the influences and modes of making claims had shifted. As part of this process the peoples that inhabited commons and wastes were inscribed as uncivilised and unable to manage the land, natives of the place but with no title. Enclosure was thus increasingly conceived of as a form of internal colonisation, something that paralleled settler colonialism abroad, and according to influential thinkers like Arthur Young a counter-movement that did away with the need to establish colonies beyond the bounds of the Metropole.

That the connection between the 'enclosure movement' in England and Wales and the experience of (re)settling colonial territories has not been made by historians is in many ways extraordinary.[4] Doubly so given that no less a figure than E. P. Thompson suggestively made the link, albeit in a rarely referenced passage in 1991's *Customs in Common* in which he noted that 'the concept of exclusive property in land' which was central to enclosure was 'carried across the Atlantic, to the Indian sub-continent, and into the South Pacific, by British colonists, administrators, and lawyers'.[5] E. P. Thompson's point, that local customs in territories under British colonial rule were made to yield – or were entirely reinvented – to embrace British conceptions of private property in land and the primacy of exclusive title as necessary conditions for 'improvement', rests on the idea that the legal technologies of enclosure were exported from the Metropole, this following the Lockean model whereby

---

[1] S. Thompson, 'Parliamentary Enclosure, Property, Population, and the Decline of Classical Republicanism in Eighteenth-Century Britain', *Historical Journal*, 51 (2008), 621–42.

[2] K. Wrightson, 'The Politics of the Parish in Early Modern England', in *The Experience of Authority in Early Modern England*, ed. P. Griffiths, A. Fox and S. Hindle (1996), 10–46.

[3] For instance see K. Lindley, *Fenland Riots and the English Revolution* (1982), esp. ch. 1; E. Robson, 'Improvement and Epistemologies of Landscape in Seventeenth-Century English Forest Enclosure', *Historical Journal*, 60 (2017), 597–632.

[4] The one exception can be found in one sentence (with a supporting footnote) in Jeanette Neeson's masterful study of common right: Jeanette Neeson, *Commoners: Common Right, Enclosure and Social Change in England, 1700-1820* (Cambridge, 1993), 30 n. 46.

[5] E. P. Thompson, *Customs in Common* (New York, 1991), 163. The relevant passage can be found on pp. 164–75. The same argument is repeated in Peter Linebaugh and Marcus Rediker, *The Many-Headed Hydra: Sailors, Slaves, Commoners, and the Hidden History of the Revolutionary Atlantic* (Boston, MA, 2000), esp. 99.

the productivity of enclosed English land provided justification for the colonisation and dispossession of territories overseas.[6]

This is not to say that scholars have been entirely remiss in analysing the way lessons from colonial conquest informed English and Welsh enclosure. In a recent paper in *Legal Studies*, Henry Jones makes the point that the 'development of both English colonialism and land as property are best understood together' given that, as he sees it, '[early English] colonialism drove the development of practices of private property that are essential for enclosure and capitalism'.[7] Jones's point is perhaps overplayed, not least in relation to the supposed novelty of new surveying techniques devised in English colonies and exported back to the Metropole. But in his emphasis on the emergence of new legal devices that allowed the clash of jurisdictions between the settler colonial state and the indigenous people to be settled in favour of the state, we see a critical parallel with the clash of jurisdictions between those who wished to project enclosure and those who might suffer the loss of their common rights and its 'resolution' in the passing of dedicated Acts of Parliament. Likewise, Allan Greer has noted in his study of 'commons and enclosure' in the colonisation of North America that English 'pro-enclosure propagandists' believed that 'improvement' was 'equally at odds with common fields in England and uncleared forests in America'.[8]

This paper speaks to a particular historical moment, or rather set of moments, that followed the challenge of funding and running Britain's North American colonies and their subsequent loss after the American War of Independence. This moment, so it is argued, gave rise to new models of how Britain's lands might be more profitably managed, something that, conversely, Britain's subsequent colonial endeavours provided the inspiration, example and justification for. Colonialism was thus both the target and the inspiration. If the specific focus is the late eighteenth and early nineteenth centuries, it is important to understand the deeper histories and genealogies of the ideas and dynamics that informed these discourses and practices of internal colonialism, not least given the paucity of studies on the central concepts that underpin the paper. As such, before analysing how these ideas were framed and articulated, and how detailed schemes to settle the wastes of the Metropole – paying attention to a variety of proposals supported by the Board of Agriculture from the late eighteenth century – were implemented, the paper explores these foundational contexts. It starts by detailing our

---

[6] John Locke, *Two Treatises of Government*, ed. Peter Laslett (Cambridge, 1960), see 133–46. This relationship has recently been problematised by Allan Greer who has argued that the practices of settler colonialists were often rooted in forms of custom and common property, the idea, then, that settler colonialism as a form of 'enclosure' is problematic: A. Greer, 'Commons and Enclosure in the Colonization of North America', *American Historical Review*, 117 (2012), 365–86. For a similar point in relation to the making of new commons in Australia see B. Maddison, 'Radical Commons Discourse and the Challenges of Colonialism', *Radical History Review*, 108 (2010), 29–48.

[7] H. Jones, 'Property, Territory, and Colonialism: An International Legal History of Enclosure', *Legal Studies*, 39 (2019), 187–203.

[8] Greer, 'Commons and Enclosure', 67.

state of knowledge of the 'enclosure story', goes on to evaluate the concept of internal colonisation, before examining the process of the inferiorisation of the commoner. These contexts established, the paper in the second half examines three settings of internal colonisation: first, Young's schemes to colonise English wastes as an alternative to the (failed) example of the North American colonies; second, the persistence of the claims and schemes in relation to debates around 'general enclosure' at the turn of the nineteenth century; and third, the legacy of the logics of internal colonisation in the 'back to the land' projects of the mid- to late nineteenth century.

As a history of an idea – and of the on-the-ground experiments in settling the commons – the paper necessarily draws upon a wide range of sources. It makes particular use of pamphlet literature and the extensive archive of the Board of Agriculture and Arthur Young's *Annals of Agriculture* in teasing out how the idea was framed and asserted, as well as biography, newspaper reports, parish records and parliamentary papers in analysing the experiments. In what follows, the word 'waste' is used to describe all commons and waste lands, this being both legally correct and a reflection of the way in which waste, as a word, was used in relation to debates about enclosure.

On enclosure

As a concept, enclosure was once confined to the heavily economistic branch of the 'ploughs and cows' approach to the study of rural England. Now it has shed its contextual shackles and can be found deployed in a bewildering array of contexts. Enclosure, so this approach goes, is no longer just about land, let alone the act of consolidating landholdings and making that which was once commonable exclusive, but is a process that has become a kind of shorthand for privatisation, or at least the acts of making private. From the regulation and securitisation of the Internet; assertions of intellectual property and patent claims in the mammalian genome; the imposition of new forms of control and restriction by property developers on hitherto 'public space'; to ongoing neo-imperial land-grabs in Africa and Latin America, spaces and things told as commons, so the story goes, are becoming private, use rights limited, barriers – literal and figurative – erected, the collective treasury sold off, enclosed. Such work draws – albeit often in a rather skewed and narrow way – on the English 'enclosure story' both as conceptual inspiration and as a salutary warning. In this the English historical context is just that, context; the nuts and the bolts, the nuances and complexities of the case are often lost. Indeed, that before enclosure the open fields, commons and other wastes of England were already in private ownership is a point that is often either not understood or just ignored.[9] By reducing a complex series of processes, incomplete and in some ways ongoing as they are, to the one

---

[9] A. Jeffrey, C. McFarlane and A. Vasudevan, 'Rethinking Enclosure: Space, Subjectivity and the Common', *Antipode*, 44 (2012), 1247–67; C. Corson and K. Iain MacDonald, 'Enclosing the Global Commons: The Convention on Biological Diversity and Green Grabbing', *Journal of Peasant Studies*, 39 (2012), 263–83. For an example of such decontextualisation see R. Sánchez and B. Pita,

narrative – 'the enclosure story' – it renders histories of enclosure intellectually inert; the story, as it were, 'enclosed', the fences erected, the limits placed. *Enclosure happened.*

The very existence of this paper is testament to the fact that there is much which remains unknown and untold. But what is the state of the enclosure story? We know that the first dedicated Act of Parliament for the enclosure of land was passed in 1604 (although this was not strictly agricultural, the Act allowing for the enclosure of a small parcel of the waste for the creation of a new burial ground in the Dorset parish of Radipole).[10] This legislative moment, however obscure, matters because it prefaced a major shift in state policy from opposition to enclosure as a depopulating social wickedness to actively supporting it as an economic good. Of course, this is to paint with a broad brush, medievalists and early modernists rightly noting the ebbs and flows in the Crown's role as projector of enclosure on its own estate.[11] Further, Elly Robson's recent study of the enclosure of Gillingham Forest in 1624 relates that such policy could turn on the head of a pin: the 1620s at once marking the end of the long-established policy of holding commissions into depopulation and enclosure and, from Charles I's accession to the throne in 1625, the extension of disafforestation to royal forests across England in one of the 'first major projects of state-sanctioned enclosure and "improvement" of "waste" commons'.[12]

By the time of the first attempt to systematise and make more straightforward enclosure by parliamentary Act in the form of the 1773 Inclosure Act,[13] a decisive shift had occurred: the state was not just projector of enclosure on its own estate but also facilitator across the realm. As Wordie has calculated, between 1604 and 1760 some 228 enclosure Acts were passed (these enclosing 1.1 per cent of the area of England and Monmouthshire). Thereafter, so it was understood, the demand for parliamentary support accelerated. Of the residual 25 per cent of land that remained unenclosed in 1760, the vast majority was subsequently enclosed by parliamentary Acts, the last such enclosure being passed in 1914 at which point only 4.6 per cent of England and Monmouthshire remained unenclosed.[14] Such figures, as Wordie has suggested, overestimate the area actually enclosed by parliamentary means, allowing for areas enclosed by agreement – which for

'Rethinking Settler Colonialism', *American Quarterly*, 66 (2014), 1043 ('Of course enclosures can be established internally, as in the case of displaced serfs in early modern England').

[10] The earliest statute is 4 Hen. 8 c.19 (1487), the last is 39 Eliz. 1 c.2 (1597). The story of the Acts may be found in, for example, P. Ramsey, *Tudor Economic Problems* (1963) chs. 1 and 5; M. W. Beresford, *The Lost Villages of England* (Lutterworth, 1954), ch. 4. For evidence of enclosure (by agreement), apparently despite the Acts, see A. Baker and R. Butler, *Studies in Field Systems in the British Isles* (Cambridge, 1973), esp. 647–8.

[11] R. Hoyle, 'Disafforestation and Drainage: The Crown as Entrepreneur?', in *The Estates of the English Crown, 1558–1640*, ed. R. Hoyle (Cambridge, 1992), 353–88.

[12] Robson, 'Improvement and Epistemologies of Landscape'.

[13] 13 Geo. 3. c. 81.

[14] J. R. Wordie, 'The Chronology of English Enclosure, 1500–1914', *Economic History Review*, 36 (1983), 501.

Hampshire, as John Chapman and Sylvia Seeliger have shown, covered some 2.23 per cent of the whole county – through informal means without agreement, and wherein parliamentary awards either wholly or partly confirmed lands already enclosed by whatever other means.[15] From the start of the Napoleonic Wars, the proportion of land enclosed shifted decisively in favour of the enclosure of commons and wastes against an earlier balance in favour of open fields. This in part reflected a diminution of the area left in open field systems but also reflected that the higher farm-gate prices of the war years made cultivation of once marginal lands now viable.[16]

The charting of these complex chronologies and geographies of enclosure dominated the historiography of enclosure until the publication of Jeanette Neeson's *Commoners*, her 1993 study of the role that common rights played in English rural society.[17] Offering a critical rebuke to the long-standing assertion of Chambers and Mingay that the loss of common rights on enclosure represented no great material loss to the rural poor,[18] Neeson's book has done more than any other study to invigorate the study of enclosure, variably provoking critiques and supportive studies around her central thesis.[19] More recently, a sustained body of work has also returned to issues of process, either in terms of complicating our understandings of how it was enacted – Ronan O'Donnell's application of Actor Network Theory to the study of enclosure in the post-medieval north-east and Nick Blomley's highly influential study of the work of enclosure hedges notable examples[20] – or how it was opposed, the latter category, though, largely confined to the pre-parliamentary enclosure era.[21] A series of articles by Briony McDonagh has also usefully, in her words, engaged in 'thickening the concept of enclosure' by placing examples of enclosure into complex *longue durée* narratives and drawing in humans and non-human things often excluded from established enclosure

---

[15] *Ibid.*, 487–8; J. Chapman and S. Seeliger, 'Formal Agreements and the Enclosure Process: The Evidence from Hampshire', *Agricultural History Review*, 43 (1995), 39.

[16] For an analysis of Hampshire see E. L. Jones, 'Eighteenth-Century Changes in Hampshire Chalkland Farming', *Agricultural History Review*, 8 (1960), esp. 11.

[17] Neeson, *Commoners*.

[18] J. D. Chambers and G. Mingay, *The Agricultural Revolution, 1750–1880* (1966).

[19] L. Shaw-Taylor, 'Parliamentary Enclosure and the Emergence of an English Agricultural Proletariat', *Journal of Economic History*, 61 (2001), 640–62; G. Clark and A. Clark, 'Common Rights to Land in England, 1475–1839', *Journal of Economic History*, 61 (2001), 1009–36; A. Howkins, 'The Use and Abuse of the English Commons, 1845–1914', *History Workshop Journal*, 78 (2014), 107–32; J. Handy, '"The Enchantment of Property": Arthur Young, Enclosure, and the Cottage Economy in England, 1770–1840', *Journal of Agrarian Change*, 19 (2019), 711–28.

[20] R. O'Donnell, *Assembling Enclosure: Transformations in the Rural Landscape of Post-medieval North-east England* (Hatfield, 2015); N. Blomley, 'Making Private Property: Enclosure, Common Right and the Work of Hedges', *Rural History*, 18 (2007), 1–21.

[21] S. Hindle, 'Imagining Insurrection in Seventeenth-Century England: Representations of the Midland Rising of 1607', *History Workshop Journal*, 66 (2008), 21–61; B. McDonagh, 'Making and Breaking Property: Negotiating Enclosure and Common Rights in Sixteenth-Century England', *History Workshop Journal*, 76 (2013), 32–56; J. Bowen, '"Before the Breaking of the Day, in a Riotous Manner and With Great Shouts and Outcries": Disputes over Common Land in Shropshire in the Sixteenth and Seventeenth Centuries', *Rural History*, 26 (2015), 133–59.

stories.[22] Yet, beyond the aforementioned paper by Stephen Thompson,[23] the politics of enclosure in the very era of parliamentary enclosure (and in the age of enclosure by dispossession overseas that became known as settler colonialism) remains remarkably little studied, the study of enclosure itself in many ways 'enclosed'.

Conceiving the colony

The Latin *colōnia* meant 'farm', 'landed estate' or 'settlement'. Strictly, it related to a settlement of Romans in a 'hostile or newly conquered country' which also acted as a garrison. It was in this sense that the concept of a colony – and the Roman word *colōniae* – was first transmuted into modern languages as the planting of settlements in newly discovered lands, this meaning solidified in the sixteenth century by Latin and Italian writers and rendered into English by the geographical thinker Richard Eden in his 1555 translation of Peter Matyr's *The Decades of the Newe Worlde*. The more strictly agrarian *colonie* ('tiller, farmer, cultivator ...') was older still, having its English roots in Middle English, and was in use into the seventeenth century, but the impact of the Irish Plantations and the Virginia Plantation meant that the broader-based meaning in use today instead assumed commonplace usage. It was at the same time that the conception of (and the actual word) colonising came into circulation, colonisation (as the action of colonising) a far later addition to the lexicon in the middle decades of the eighteenth century. Thus, the abstract concept and the actual practice of creating colonies was rooted in the idea of settling and making productive, this invariably (at first at least) meaning improving the land through cultivation and the creation of pasture, the integration of lands into the economy. Further, the idea of making productive colonies, of growing the economy (and population) through expanding the settled area, came into political thinking at the same time that enclosure was no longer viewed by the English state as an evil, that is to say the early decades of the seventeenth century.[24]

It is not a huge leap, then, to draw conceptual similarities between 'planting' colonies overseas and planting farmers on wastes and commons at home. Indeed, the idea of 'internal colonialism' has a long history. This has been figured as an articulation of dissent at being subject to the imposition of seemingly distant and arbitrary state power; for example, Gramsci noted of communists in 1920s Italy that the 'bourgeoisie of the North' had 'subjected

---

[22] B. McDonagh and S. Daniels, 'Enclosure Stories: Narratives from Northamptonshire', *Cultural Geographies*, 19 (2012), 107–21; B. McDonagh and C. Griffin, 'Occupy! Historical Geographies of Property, Protest and the Commons, 1500–1850', *Journal of Historical Geography*, 53 (2016), 1–10; B. McDonagh, 'Disobedient Objects: Material Readings of Enclosure Protest in Sixteenth-Century England', *Journal of Medieval History*, 45 (2019), 254–75.

[23] Thompson, 'Parliamentary Enclosure'.

[24] Colony, n. OED Online, June 2022, Oxford University Press, https://www.oed.com/view/Entry/36547?rskey=FJeWXy&result=1 (accessed 15 July 2022); M. Ferro, *Colonization: A Global History* (2005), 1–3; Peter Matyr, *The Decades of the Newe Worlde*, trans. Richard Eden (1555).

southern Italy and the Islands... to the status of exploited colonies'.[25] It has also been articulated as state policy, and as an academic concept, something first articulated by Leo Marquard in relation to South Africa in 1957 and gaining a degree of prominence in the late 1970s amongst post- and de-colonial theorists.[26] The same languages were picked up by scholars of popular protest in that remarkably fecund era for the subject, the late 1970s and early 1980s. Keith Lindley asserted of the drainage and enclosure of the Cambridgeshire fens in the late seventeenth century that they represented a form of internal colonialism, although the idea is not explored in any detail nor the source of his inspiration for the phrase related.[27] Tellingly though, Lindley draws upon an important example. As the drainer's poet, to use Keith Lindley's description, put it in 1685 of the chance to make money in the enclosure of the Cambridgeshire fens:

And ye, whom hopes of sudden Wealth allure,
Or wants into Virginia, force to fly,
Ev'n spare your pains; here's Florida hard by.
All ye that Treasures either want, or love,
(And who is he, who Profit will not move?)
Would you repair your fortunes, would you make,
To this most fruitful Land yourselves betake.[28]

Evidently, the example – the challenge even – of Britain's North American colonies made a stark contrast with the hitherto unexploited opportunities to make money through draining and enclosure at home.

In relation to the 'union' of England and Wales, then the Kingdoms of England and Scotland in 1706/7, and from 1801 the United Kingdom of Britain and Ireland (and from 1922 the United Kingdom of Great Britain and Northern Ireland), the idea of internal colonialism has been used only in relation to the acts of subordination carried out by English elites and the Westminster Parliament.[29] Most recently Iain MacKinnon has argued that the Gàidhealtachd (the Gaelic-speaking Highlands and Islands of Scotland) was a site of repeated internal colonialisms of which multiple territorial dispossession and later clearances and 'improvements' were continuums. The practice of colonisation, so MacKinnon claims, was at once paralleled by and made possible by the inferiorisation and racialisation of the Gaels, this systematic demeaning part of the process of colonialism being, as Barbara Arneil has

---

[25] Antonio Gramsci, The Modern Prince and Other Writings, trans. L. Marks (1957), 28.

[26] Leo Marquard, South Africa's Colonial Policy (Johannesburg, 1957). On this genealogy see R. Hind, 'The Internal Colonial Concept', Comparative Studies in Society and History, 26 (1984), 543–68.

[27] Lindley, Fenland Riots, 3–4.

[28] Anonymous, The History or Narrative of the Great Level of the Fens, called the Bedford Level (1685), 80–1, cited in ibid., 4.

[29] The point is also made in relation to Cornwall, a part of the 'Celtic fringe': Michael Hechter, Internal Colonialism: The Celtic Fringe in British National Development, 1536-1966 (Berkeley, CA, 1977).

put it, 'the theoretical and ideological framework by which ... colonisation is justified'.[30]

This is one of the fundamental practices of colonisation: discredit and debase indigenous peoples; deny their agency and ability to manage the space and its resources; and make assertions that this inability to make the land productive in ways analogous to the system of English enclosed exclusive title agriculture is evidence of being 'backward', unable to comprehend anything beyond their own situation and intellectually incapable of conceiving of how they might change their lot.[31] The idea that the colonial other was savage, the brute creation, the human animal, has a deep history, a history as long as the practice of colonisation itself. Paul Slack has recently taken the idea further. We might usefully think, so he claims, of the making of colonies both as an act of 'improvement' and as integral to the development of the idea of improvement in seventeenth-century England. Empowered by biblical decrees 'to go forth and multiply and replenish the earth', the colonial project was underwritten by what Slack has labelled a 'natural right ... to exercise dominion over empty spaces'. Such colonised spaces were empty in the sense that indigenous peoples were portrayed as 'barbarous' and must be brought to a state of Christian civility.[32] As Brenna Bhandar has it, these parallel processes rely on twin abstractions: the abstraction of turning land into fungible property, into a commodity; and racialising of the landholding of the indigenous people who are abstracted into savages. This, Bhandar asserts, is a constant of settler colonialism in all settings and all temporal contexts, starting with the plantations of Ireland and North America.[33] And, as the next section shows, we see precisely this dynamic in rural England too.

The commoner as savage

Outside of times of national crisis, the agricultural labourer – the largest occupational group in England through the eighteenth century and until the time of the 1871 Census – was written as a bucolic fool, comfortable and content yet comic, object and subject of humour, this savant trope established by the time of – and further promulgated by – Shakespeare.[34] If this is a generalisation, the deeper point holds: the labourer always became what the nation needed, but was only viewed positively if positioned out of actual

---

[30] I. MacKinnon, 'Colonialism and the Highland Clearances', *Northern Scotland*, 8 (2017), 22–48; Barbara Arneil, 'Liberal Colonialism, Domestic Colonies and Citizenship', *History of Political Thought*, 33 (2012), 491–2.

[31] For important assertions of these dynamics in a variety of colonial contexts see Merete Borch, *Conciliation, Compulsion, Conversion: British Attitudes towards Indigenous Peoples, 1763-1814* (Rodopi, 2004); Karl Jacoby, *Crimes against Nature: Squatters, Poachers, Thieves, and the Hidden History of American Conservation* (Berkeley, CA, 2014), esp. ch. 7.

[32] P. Slack, *The Invention of Improvement: Information and Material Progress in Seventeenth-Century England* (Oxford, 2014), 31–2, 68.

[33] B. Bhandar 'Property, Law, and Race: Modes of Abstraction', *UC Irvine Law Review*, 4 (2014), 203–18.

[34] A. Howkins, 'From Hodge to Lob: Reconstructing the English Farm Labourer 1870–1914', in *Living and Learning: Essays in Honour of JFC Harrison*, ed. M. Chase and I. Dyck (1996), 218–35.

sight. Even during the Revolutionary Wars and subsequent Napoleonic Wars when politically those that laboured in the fields were represented as the loyal, well-fed John Bull – the representational polar and political opposite of the oppressed, shackled French – no less a figure than the field marshal the Duke of Wellington viewed these men as 'the scum of the earth'.[35] By the late eighteenth century, as I have explored elsewhere, the labourer was being thought of not just as an over-procreating, poor-rate-dependent problem but also as apart from other rural and urban citizens, a process that used racial explanation and language to define the labourer as a racial other.[36] The commoner, as we will see, was understood as a different sort of problem, although the processes and language have striking parallels, their relative independence from the structures of agrarian capitalism by dint of finding other ways of getting by outside of the offering of their labour at the heart of why they were viewed with such disdain.

Through the de facto anti-enclosure policy of the Tudor years, the shift to the support of enclosure in the early years of Stuart rule, and then during the Civil War and the Commonwealth where the figure of the commoner took on a particular political charge (amplified by the Leveller and Digger movements), the commoner had an important political stake at the heart of the nation. Of course, this is at once a simplification and a conflation: commoner at once the generic label for the 'common people', those undistinguished by rank, and those who held and/or practised common rights. But, outside of the fact that some high-profile regicides such as Major General Edward Whalley were active promoters of enclosure and introduced legislation to Parliament supporting universal enclosure, the distinction, politically, was broadly an irrelevance.[37] Indeed, there is an important case to be made that given that so large a proportion of the population was enrolled in Manor Courts and were otherwise in some way reliant on the use of commons, there was no dual meaning, just one: a shared loathing of the copyhold services, obligations and fines, that 'ancient and almost antiquated badge of slavery' as a Leveller tract had it.[38]

While the commoner was both political subject and powerful lobby, the seeds of the making of the commoner as a barrier to enclosure and improvement were evident from the moment of the Ulster Plantations and the Colony of Virginia. To surveyor and cartographer John Norden, commoners

---

[35] J. Barrell, 'Sportive Labour: The Farmworker in Eighteenth Century Poetry and Painting', in *The English Rural Community: Image and Analysis*, ed. B. Short (Cambridge, 1992), 105–32; D. Lowenthal, 'British National Identity and the English Landscape', *Rural History*, 2 (1991), 205–30, at 211.

[36] C. Griffin, *The Politics of Hunger: Protest, Poverty and Policy in England, c. 1750–c. 1850* (Manchester, 2020), ch. 5.

[37] W. E. Tate, *The English Village Community and the Enclosure Movements* (1967), ch. 11; J. Healey, 'The Political Culture of the English Commons, c. 1550–1650', *Agricultural History Review*, 60 (2012), 266–87. On Whalley see *The Agrarian History of England and Wales*, v.ii: *1640–1750* (Cambridge, 1985), ed. Joan Thirsk, 319–21.

[38] Anon., *A New Engagement, or, Manifesto Wherein is Declared the Sence and Resolution of Many Thousands of Well-affected People in and About London, and Some Adjacent Counties (viz. Kent, Hartford, Buckingham, and Berks, &c.)* (1648).

were 'as ignorant of God … as the very savages amongst the infidels', although Norden was not advocating enclosure, the first edition (1607) of his famed *The Surveyor's Dialogue* making only one reference to it, while the 1618 edition added a further critical reference to the 'devastation' that enclosure could cause.[39] From the middle of the seventeenth century, anti-commoner discourse became shackled to pro-enclosure rhetoric during the great debates about enclosure of the Commonwealth. For instance, Adam Moore's 1653 pro-enclosure tract *Bread for the Poor* asserted that those who lived on the commons were rapt in 'idleness': 'our poorer people bordering on these Lands, account it to be a sufficient Trade of living to be only a Borderer: and so many Strategems (forsooth) have they to get thrift here, that to seeke other mysteries of gaining, were to incur the danger of sweat, and a laborious life'.[40] Of course, there is no little irony here in that Moore also claimed that commons were 'fruitless, naked, and desolate', Arabia to enclosure's 'pleasant fruitful fields of Canaan', and that the poor already subject to enclosure might be usefully employed in diking, hedging and fencing new enclosures to save them from '*Begging, Filching, Robbing, Roguing,* [and] *Murthering* and whatsoever other Villainies their unexercised brains and hands undertake'.[41] Similarly, John Evelyn in his famed *Sylva* concluded that the enclosure of the remnant Crown forests 'would be the most likely expedient to *civilize* those wild and poor *Bordurers*; and to secure the vast and spreading heart of the *Forest*'. To Evelyn such forest commoners were 'clamorous and rude' and 'are generally not so civil and reasonable, as might be wished'.[42] This mirrored pro-enclosure John Locke's belief that those who lived in forests and woods were 'irrational, untaught',[43] this itself an established discourse well rooted in popular culture.[44] There is also an irony here in that commons were, at least in part, peopled by those displaced by earlier waves of enclosure, their eking out an existence on the common now justified as the reason for a new wave of enclosure.

The discourse was already ingrained by the turn of the eighteenth century.[45] Timothy Nourse in his *Campania Foelix* (1699), subtitled 'a discourse of the benefits and improvements of husbandry', denounced commoners as:

---

[39] J. Norden, *The Surveyors Dialogue* (1618), 103; *John Norden's The Surveyor's Dialogue (1618): A Critical Edition*, ed. M. Netzloff (2016).

[40] A. Moore, *Bread for the Poor and Advancement of the English Nation Promised by Enclosure of the Wastes and Common Grounds of England* (1653), 6.

[41] *Ibid.*, 30.

[42] J. Evelyn, *Sylva* (1670), 208, 213.

[43] J. Locke, *Two Treatises of Government*, ed. Peter Laslett (Cambridge, 1988), 183. As Neal Wood has argued, Locke was wary of enclosure by parliamentary Act but was a keen advocate of enclosure when agreement could be reached, although waste was fair game and enclosure by any means the only way to make such land yield to improvement through the exercise of labour: N. Wood, *John Locke and Agrarian Capitalism* (Berkeley, CA, 1984), esp. 57–66.

[44] For instance in *As You Like It*, Silvius is referred to by Orlando as 'forest-born, and hath been tutored in the rudiments of desperate studies': W. Shakespeare, *As You Like It* (2003, first published 1623), 160.

[45] It is important to note, though, that the argument that enclosures were depopulating continued into the eighteenth century, but this fear related to open fields, not wastes:

[V]ery rough and savage in their Dispositions, being of levelling Principles, and refractory to Government, insolent and tumultuous: What Gentleman soever then shall have the Misfortune to fall into the Neighbourhood of such Boors, let him never think to win them by Civilities; it will be much more easie for him to teach a Hog to play upon the Bagpipes, than to soften such *Brutes* by *Courtesie*; for they will presently interpret a Man's Gentleness to be the Effect of a timorous and easie Nature, which will presently make them bold and saucy ... The Saying of an *English* Gentleman was much to the purpose, That Three things ought always to be kept under, our Mastiff-Dog, a Stone-Horse, and a Clown.

'Such Men', Nourse went on, 'are to be look'd upon as trashy Weeds or Nettles, growing usually upon Dunghills, which if touch'd gently will sting, but being squeez'd hard will never hurt us.'[46] Fifteen years later, John Bellers took this process of inferiorisation one step further by making an explicit comparison with other subaltern figures of British oppression, substituting Nourse's generic 'brutes' – although note the elision between hogs and the Scots ('to teach a Hog to play upon the Bagpipes') – with 'Indians'. 'Our Forrests and great Commons (make the Poor that are upon them too much like the *Indians*) being a hindrance to Industry, and are Nurseries of Idleness and Insolence'.[47] W. Pennington returned to precisely the same theme in 1769 – the costs and fallout of the Seven Years War in North America fresh in the mind – in his treatise on the importance of enclosure: 'Let the poor native Indians (though something more savage than many in the fens) enjoy all their ancient privileges, and cultivate their own country in their own way.' This was not an anti-colonial plea but laced with irony, the 'savage' commoners and Indians alike not to be trusted to manage the land.[48] We shall return to Pennington later.

The discourse of the commoner as savage persisted. Edward Hasted in his survey of Kentish parishes noted in 1799 of the commoners of the 'minnises' between Elham, Lyminge and Stelling parishes that they were 'as wild, and in as rough a state as the country they dwell in'.[49] Likewise, William Gilpin, the famed theorist of the picturesque, on coming across a squatter's hovel at Exbury in his ethnographic enquiries into the 'savage of the woods' of the New Forest related that:[50]

J. Howlett, *Enquiry into the Influence which Enclosures have had Upon the Population of this Kingdom*, 2nd edn (1786); Thompson, 'Parliamentary Enclosure', esp. 627–8.

[46] Timothy Nourse, *Campania Foelix, or a Discourse of the Benefits and Improvements of Husbandry* (1700; 2nd edn 1706), 15–16.

[47] John Bellers, *About the Improvement of Physick ... with an Essay for Imploying the Able Poor* (1714), 40.

[48] W. Pennington, *Reflections on the Various Advantages Resulting from the Draining, Inclosing and Allotting of Large Commons and Common Fields* (1769), 35.

[49] Edward Hasted, *History and Topographical Survey of the County of Kent*, vol. VIII (Canterbury, 1799), 79. Minnis is a name peculiar to south-east Kent for a common, and potentially derives from the Middle English *gemænnes*, 'land held in common'.

[50] William Gilpin, *Remarks on Forest Scenery, and Other Woodland Views* (1791), I, 272.

At the door stood two or three squalid children, with eager famished countenances staring through matted hair. On entering the hovel, it was so dark, that we could at first see nothing. By degrees a scene of misery opened. We saw other ragged children within, and were soon struck with a female figure, grovelling, at full length, by the side of a few embers upon the hearth. Her arms were naked to her shoulders, and her rags scarce covered her body. On our speaking to her, she uttered, in return, a mixture of obscenity and imprecations. We had never seen so deplorable a maniac.

On making later enquiries, the women was understood not to be 'a maniac' but the victim of a blow from her husband, he being 'one of the most hardened, abandoned, mischievous fellows in the country' and she no less 'infamous'.[51] Or as agricultural writer Charles Vancouver put it of the forest commoners, they were an 'idle, useless and disorderly set of people' who subsisted only by their systematic abuse of the vert and venison of the forest.[52] The idleness of the indigenes was one thing, that of immigrants and newcomers attracted to squat on the wastes of the parish yet another. The Thatcham (Berkshire) vestry complained to the lord of the manor in 1826 that 'non-parishioners' were 'enclosing parts of the wastelands' and in the process gaining settlement, thus becoming chargeable to the parish.[53]

The temptations of unenclosed land, so reckoned John Middleton in his survey of the agricultural state of Middlesex, actively encouraged and thus bred the wrong sort of people, which became a danger to all agriculturalists. Land without fencing, so he claimed, encouraged 'hunters, who are another species of destroyers: those imitators of the life of savages, are as destructive in a well cultivated country, as foxes and wolves would be in a hen-roost or a sheep-fold'.[54] The discourse of wastes as not only a breeding and training ground for savagery also extended to their *attracting* criminals. For example, Cranborne Chase, on the border between Dorset and Wiltshire, had a reputation as 'a nursery for and a temptation to all kinds of vice, profligacy and immorality' and was 'a great harbour for smugglers, the woods being very commodious for secreting their goods'.[55] The abuses of such persons, so the discourse went, devalued commons, and preventing their 'illegal' use was, in turn, a frequent justification for enclosure. For instance, at Chillington in Somerset enclosure was proposed as the solution to the 'down being overstocked and trespassed by strange cattle', whilst the problem of overstocking on Cambridge's commons led a meeting of the town council to conclude the only solution was 'to sell or lease certain parts thereof', i.e. enclosure.[56]

---

[51] *Ibid.*, II, 181.

[52] Charles Vancouver, *General View of the Agriculture of Hampshire* (1813), 496.

[53] Berkshire Record Office, D/P130/8/1, Thatcham Vestry Minute, 25 Mar. 1826.

[54] John Middleton, *General View of the Agriculture of Middlesex* (1807), 152.

[55] Anthony Chapman, *A Letter to the Noblemen, and Gentlemen, Proprietors of Lands in Cranborne Chace ... for the Disenfranchisement of the Said Chace ...* (Tarrant Gunville, 1791), 22–3.

[56] Howkins, 'The Use and Abuse', 119; *Cambridge Independent Press*, 19 May 1849.

In 'improving' the common through enclosure, the commoner too would be reformed, made to yield, made useful. As William Mavor put it of Berkshire commoners in 1813, 'Wherever there are large wastes, and particularly near forests, the lazy industry and beggarly independence of the lower orders of people, who enjoy commons, is a source of misery to themselves, and of loss to the community.' Enclosure would allow them to 'employ their time in productive labour, which is now so frequently wasted on objects … incompatible with their duty'.[57] John Knight, who purchased Exmoor from the Crown in 1818 and proceeded to enclose it, was more pessimistic though. He perceived the residents of the one-time Royal Forest to suffer from, as Leonard Baker has recently put it, 'moral turpitude' and as only able to 'exploit' the moor. Being unable to yoke them to his scheme to 'reclaim' Exmoor for 'improved' agriculture, Knight instead settled the enclosed Exmoor with tenant farmers from Lincolnshire and labour from his family's Irish estate.[58] Improvement when shackled to enclosure was never just about managing the land, it was also about managing the people: the human resource must be improved too.

Internal colonisation: ideas and applications

Making wastes work

In sum, the enclosure of wastes was a moral act: it made the wasteful productive; it settled the right sort of people on the land; it purified and removed the beggarly and criminal; it colonised the empty – and its proponents relied upon these discourses to justify it. Given that overseas colonial experiments, as we have seen, were also written in precisely this language – extending and deepening the dominion and making it productive – it is not hugely surprising that the two settings became conflated. As Pennington, having placed the English commoner and the 'native Indians' of North America on the same scale of savagery, reflected:

> It seems very strange to encourage the peopling and cultivation of that extensive region [North America] as a national concern, and at the same time permit large forests, commons and open fields in the mother country to remain in pretty much the same condition as when agriculture and commerce were not half so well understood, or half the consequence they are at present.[59]

While it is beyond the immediate scope of this paper to tease out precisely when this wider discourse of 'improve our lands first' was first manifest, it is telling that Evelyn in *Sylva* makes the point that a reliance on foreign timber might prove 'a greater mischief to the Publick, than the last diminution of the

---

[57] William Mavor, *General View of the Agriculture of Berkshire* (1813), 328–9.

[58] Leonard Baker, 'The Reclamation of Exmoor Forest', *Rural History Today*, 41 (2021), 5.

[59] Pennington, *Reflections*, 35.

Coin', ergo that the Crown forests need to be enclosed and planted alongside a greater campaign of planting the barren wastes.[60] Indeed, we know that colonial thinking started to permeate through writings encouraging enclosure and other agricultural treatises, Evelyn detailing colonial planting successes: cider-making in the Connecticut Colony and silk-making from successful mulberry trees in Virginia, the mulberry being recommended to be planted in England and 'even in the Moist places of Ireland'.[61]

By 1783, Arthur Young, then the chair of the agriculture committee of the Royal Society and with an already established reputation as a prolific commentator on agriculture and wider political matters, could note that: 'For a century past the colonial scheme has been that which guided the administration of the British government.' To Young, writing in the immediate aftermath of the American War of Independence, this concept had been proved to be an expensive fallacy. Foreign colonies – and in this Young excluded Ireland – were not creating wealth for Britain but instead creating commercial rivals. '[L]et not the possession of these countries deceive us into an idea that they can be worth colonizing. If they continue poor they will be no markets. If rich they will revolt; and that perhaps is the best thing they can do for our interest.'[62] Two wars – 'one undertaken to defend our colonies, and the other to reduce them' – had cost 'no less than ONE HUNDRED AND SIXTY MILLION', a scandal, as Young saw it, in itself, but doubly so given that this sum at the rate of £5 per acre 'would have improved no less than thirty-two millions of waste acres, that is a KINGdom as large as the uncultivated parts of England and Wales ... The money went for America – The wastes remain.'[63]

This argument formed the central basis for Young's extended opening essay in the first volume of his *Annals of Agriculture*. His plea was for a form of internal colonialism, the 'failure' of the adventure in North America being linked to the 'old system of colonizing' and, by inference, the enclosure of the wastes at home to the new. The premise was simple:

> If noxious islands in another hemisphere are to be manured with African blood that Englishmen may raise a monument not of profit, but of bankruptcy and ruin. If with less flattering appearances we are to colonise the deserts, marshes and snows of Canada and Nova Scotia, that the congress of a future period may reap the harvest. If we look to the Ganges tinged with the blood which rapine sheds to gain the wealth that humanity might gather on the Severn.[64]

This might be difficult to achieve but there could be 'no doubt of its propriety' and as such it should be the 'very greatest object of British policy.'[65] The

---

[60] Evelyn, *Sylva*, 278.

[61] *Ibid.*, 310, 26.

[62] Arthur Young, 'An Inquiry into the Situation of the Kingdom on the Conclusion to the Late Treaty', *Annals of Agriculture*, 1 (1783), 15.

[63] *Ibid.*, 44.

[64] *Ibid.*, 47.

[65] *Ibid.*, 53.

solution was to settle the wastes, to found internal colonies. The particular scheme envisaged by Young drew on the example of Sir William Osbourne's settlement of the wastes and mountains on his estate in Clonmel, County Tipperary – visited by Young in October 1776 during his tour of Ireland[66] – which had involved granting plots of unimproved wasteland to the poor, from which 'ragged beggars became farmers'.[67] Note, Young's plan was intended for former soldiers and those then resident in poorhouses. At no point are the commoners who would be dispossessed by such a state-sponsored scheme mentioned. They, it is inferred, in the same way as indigenous peoples in North America and in the emergent colonies of India, had no claim to the land which was their home.

Young proposed that the British state would assign a dwelling and ten acres to every family and further support them with a £10 allowance and further cash for fencing, tools, seed as well as a cow and a calf and two ewes (or in some places pigs). The total cash outlay was £27 2s. per family, which Young rounded up to £30. To encourage industry, those who were so settled would forgo any right to poor relief but neither would they pay poor rates or tithes. On this basis, at a cost of £500,000 per year, 16,666 'men' would establish the same number of farms and bring 166,660 acres of waste into cultivation. Over the ten years that Young envisaged the scheme would run for, 166,000 farms would be settled, which at five people per house would increase the population by 833,000 – this at a time of concerns that the population was decreasing, a situation turned on its head by the time of Malthus's famous *Essay* published just fifteen years later.[68]

> This establishment would be a new colony, where the principles of American population would be brought into these desert parts of Britain. Fifteen millions of produce would in ten years be created, and an income of 3,333,200l. a year. And all this for a less sum than it now costs us to keep Gibraltar, a barren rock of impregnable defence ... Comparing it with the expence we have been at for colonies, it is but a drop of water to the ocean.[69]

Indeed, Young concluded, the scheme could be further extended and would take 'but a short period to improve the eight millions and upwards of waste acres in England'. This would be a 'much greater addition to our wealth, income, population, and strength, than we now receive from our brilliant oriental dominions of Bengal, Bahar, and Orixa, though an empire as large as France'.[70]

---

[66] Arthur Young, *A Tour in Ireland, 1776-1779*, ed. Henry Morley (1897), 124–6.

[67] Young, 'An Inquiry into the Situation', 54–5; T. Malthus, *An Essay on the Principle of Population* (1798).

[68] Young, 'An Inquiry into the Situation', 54–7.

[69] *Ibid.*, 58.

[70] *Ibid.*, 60.

Young's attitude to the commoner was a complex and in some ways contradictory one. He believed that 'commoners *without property* are notorious rogues', but once property owners commoners became 'honest men'.[71] In this qualification Young asserted that owning a cottage was not sufficient property, 'for the common is a very bad support':

A man with a cottage and a goose is a rogue, who would be honest with a cow and land to feed it. This is not theory, it is fact.: I inquired for the families of the worst character at Farnham, and others against whom nothing was suspected; the one had hovels and chickens, the others houses and cows.

Upon enclosure, commoners with property needed to be 'respected' otherwise the consequences were 'fatal'.[72] In short, there were small farmers and petty producers and then there was the property-less poor. Herein the tension in Young's proposals becomes apparent. Wastes were at once empty and yet certain types of people were admitted to be usefully present, but in future the basis of their presence would need to yield to the logics of enclosure and the vicissitudes of agrarian capitalism. Indeed, it is telling that, in his calculations for settlement upon wastes, no allowance is made for existing peopling, whilst it is assumed in terms of cost that those who were to be settled had no property: the 'honest men' ignored and the 'notorious rogues' given title to make them 'honest'.[73] Indeed, as Jim Handy has artfully shown, Young's obsession with the decline of the 'cottage economy', this a byword for sturdy self-sufficiency and a dutiful deference and rooted in the disciplining effects of being a property owner, did not make him an advocate for the preservation of commons and the protection of the commoner. If his early pro-enclosure stance softened, even in his later writings Young's advocacy was for the reinvigoration of the peasant who got by through farming their plot, not for the commoner who got by through their use of common land. Property was all.[74]

Young's scheme, as flawed and dystopic as it was – the idea that anybody could be a successful farmer ironically exposed as nonsense by Young's own failings to make his several farms a financial success – drew on a deeper history of the idea of settling the forests. In 1709, Daniel Defoe – that great hater of wastes and lover of improvement – proposed that the Palatine refugees

may be planted in small townships, like little colonies, in the several forests and wastes of England, where the lands being rich and good,

---

[71] Arthur Young, *An Inquiry Into the Propriety of Applying Wastes to the Better Maintenance and Support of the Poor* (1801), 49.

[72] *Ibid.*, 49, 50–1.

[73] Young, 'An Inquiry into the Situation', *passim*.

[74] Handy, '"The Enchantment of Property"'; J. Handy, *Apostles of Inequality: Rural Poverty, Political Economy, and the Economist, 1760-1860* (Toronto, 2022), esp. chs. 2–4.

will upon their application to husbandry and cultivation of the ground, soon not only subsist them but encourage them.[75]

On further reflection, Defoe settled on the New Forest where a new town might be created, not so much a little colony but a large one. To Defoe, as Richard Hoyle puts it, 'commons were empty spaces calling out for colonisation', the poor gaining nothing from them and as such having no meaningful title.[76]

General enclosure

If the scope of such schemes fell out of favour, the principles that fed them did not and nor did less ambitious schemes. Mavor in his 1813 *General View of the Agriculture of Berkshire* claimed that the 40,000 acres of waste – used dismissively as shorthand for all common land and wastes – 'yields hardly anything to the community ... in no direct way returns one penny to the state'.[77] Rather than 'throwing them to farms already too large', 'throwing them' being a euphemism for enclosure, Mavor suggested that the land be divided into 'new farms, of a moderate extent' and let on long leases. From this, 'smiling villages would rise where desolate heaths now tire the eye'.[78] There is a sense that the county reports, commissioned by the Board of Agriculture under Young's secretaryship, and the *Annals of Agriculture*, edited by Young, simply replicated Young's line on enclosure. The boosterish essay by Young published as part of volume 31 in 1798 – the same volume that notoriously included the paper 'On the Uselessness of Commons to the Poor'[79] – collating anti-commons commentary from the county reports certainly attests to a doggedness to promote enclosure.[80]

To read this exclusively as the belief and work of Young, however prolific, energetic and influential he was, is to deny the critical point that the promotion of 'colonising' English wastes assumed a broader platform. Sir John Sinclair, the founding president of the Board of Agriculture and commissioner of the county reports, wrote in 1795 that the only impediment to improvement in British agriculture was a want of capital, it being 'diverted from its natural means of employment, *domestic improvement*, to remote and foreign speculations'.[81] In this context it is particularly telling that Sinclair initially wanted to call what became the Board of Agriculture 'The Board of Agriculture and Internal Improvement'.[82] His thinking, his motivations, were

---

[75] *A Review of the State of the British Nation*, 2 July 1709, 154, cited in R. Hoyle, 'Daniel Defoe, the Palatine Refugees and a Projected New Town in the New Forest, 1709', *Southern History*, 38 (2016), 135.

[76] *Ibid.*, 136.

[77] Mavor, *General View of Berkshire*, 329–30.

[78] *Ibid.*, 327.

[79] J. Billingsley, 'On the Uselessness of Commons to the Poor', *Annals of Agriculture*, 31 (1798), 27–32.

[80] A. Young, 'Of Enclosures', *Annals of Agriculture*, 31 (1798), 529–54.

[81] J. Sinclair, 'Plan for Reprinting the Agricultural Surveys', *Annals of Agriculture*, 24 (1795), 554. Emphasis in original.

[82] John Sinclair, *Plan for Establishing a Board of Agriculture and Internal Improvement* (1793); R. Mitchison, 'The Old Board of Agriculture (1793–1822)', *English Historical Review*, 74 (1959), 42.

further spelt out in 1803 in commenting on Britain ending the Treaty of Amiens and declaring war on France that May:

> We have begun another campaign against the foreign enemies of this country ... Why should we not attempt a campaign also against our great domestic foe, I mean the hitherto unconquered sterility of so large a proportion of the surface of the Kingdom? ... let us not be satisfied with the liberation of Egypt, or the subjugation of Malta, but less us subdue Finchley Common; let us conquer Hounslow Heath; let us compel Epping Forest to submit to the yoke of improvement.[83]

Another aspect of many of the county reports was the claim that an extension of the cultivable area would not only act to reduce the poor rates dramatically but also increase the supply of grain and other foods – this a Lockean refrain that punctuated much pro-enclosure writing in the period – and help to prevent future famines.[84] So much is understandable in the context of the period. A particularly severe subsistence crisis in 1766, followed soon after by another crisis in 1772, meant that issues around the food supply assumed a particular political potency. When conditions again deteriorated to a point of near famine in 1795,[85] the Board of Agriculture and others were quick to suggest enclosure of wastes as a way of not only increasing agricultural production but also through settlement schemes reducing labouring dependency on the parish state. In the context of declining real wages for rural workers during the Napoleonic Wars as well as the horrific famine-like conditions of 1795 and 1800, and the problem of provisioning the huge military force both fighting on the continent and keeping order at home, the need to increase the production of food assumed critical levels of political importance. The timing of Sinclair's campaign in 1795 to persuade Parliament to pass a general enclosure Act was motivated precisely by the opportunity the specific crisis of 1795 presented as well as these other wartime contexts. The initial bill stipulated that on enclosure a certain proportion of the waste should be set aside in the form of rent-free allotments, these then being made available to all adult labourers on a fifty-year lease, thus increasing production and turning the labourer into a de facto peasant.[86]

If the bill ultimately failed on Parliament being dissolved in May 1797, the debate generated significant publicity for the idea of internal colonisation, the committee report detailing that there were some 6,259,670 acres of 'waste' (this figure including all commons) in England and another 1,639,307 acres of waste in Wales, thereby highlighting the scope for settlement.[87]

---

[83] John Sinclair, *Memoirs of Sir John Sinclair*, vol. II (1837), 111, cited in Neeson, *Commoners*, 31.

[84] Mavor, *General View of Berkshire*, 327.

[85] R. Wells, *Wretched Faces: Famine in Wartime England, 1793–1803* (Stroud, 1988), esp. ch. 8.

[86] Rosalind Mitchison, *Agricultural Sir John: The Life of Sir John Sinclair of Ulbster, 1754–1835* (1962), 154–8 and 163–4; Jeremy Burchardt, *The Allotment Movement in England, 1793–1873* (Woodbridge, 2002), 29.

[87] Arthur Young, *General Report on Enclosures Drawn up by Order of the Board of Agriculture* (1808), 2–3, 139–40.

Provincial agricultural societies were quick to support the line of the Board of Agriculture, and such endorsements often adopted a broadly 'internal colonisation' line. A petition in support of Sinclair's bill from the Bath and West of England Society, drafted in December 1795, asserted: 'the natural source of internal strength and happiness, is to be derived from such a plan of cultivating the soil of this country as may most fully and effectually employ, in its fruitful fields, the laborious industry of an active and persevering people'.[88] The Kent Agricultural Society went further, holding a meeting in February 1796 to 'propose the enclosure of all wastes' as a measure 'of the highest public utility'.[89]

The failure of Sinclair's bill was followed by other proposals that sought to both 'improve' wastes and, as Jeremy Burchardt has put it, restore the fabled 'hardy peasantry'.[90] One high-profile scheme initially proposed by Young and then taken up by the Earl of Winchilsea – and duly given publicity by Sinclair's Board of Agriculture – was to enclose waste to provide the poor with cow pastures. Yet notwithstanding Winchilsea's assertion that 'except the haymaking, the rest of the business is done by his [the labourer's] wife and his labour is not interrupted', the scheme failed to secure any parliamentary backing.[91] Likewise a proposal to establish a 'Society for the Cultivation of Waste Land', their preferred method involving extensive house-building, came to nought.[92] Even a proposal by Prime Minister Pitt which would have allowed the poor to rent three acres on which to keep a cow was met with a wall of criticism – including from Jeremy Bentham who saw the 'cow money' as an assault on capital.[93] Whatever the energy devoted to such schemes, 'more acres of print were devoted to the issue', as Roger Wells has put it, 'than acres of land to farmworkers'.[94] Indeed, it is telling that when a General Enclosure Act was eventually passed in 1801[95] – following another desperate subsistence crisis in 1800, with food rioting inflaming the capital in midsummer, and further campaigning and lobbying by Young and

---

[88] *Bath Chronicle*, 7 Jan. 1796.

[89] Mitchison, *Agricultural Sir John*, 154–8 and 163–4; *Kentish Gazette*, 19 Feb. 1796; see also *Maidstone Journal*, 12 Jan. 1796 for an example of local reportage.

[90] Burchardt, *Allotment Movement*, 12–13.

[91] Lord Winchilsea, 'Letter from the Earl of Winchilsea, to the President of the Board of Agriculture, on the Advantages of Cottagers Renting Land', *Communications to the Board of Agriculture*, 1 (1797), 80. On schemes to promote cow-keeping by the poor see Jane Humphries, 'Enclosures, Common Rights, and Women: The Proletarianization of Families in the Late Eighteenth and Early Nineteenth Centuries', *Journal of Economic History*, 50 (1990), 17–42.

[92] Anon., 'Proposals for Establishing a Society for the Cultivation of Waste Land in Great Britain', *Annals of Agriculture*, 25 (1796), 131–5. A similar, if more fully fleshed-out, scheme was projected by Dorset MP William Morton Pitt with the backing of the Society for the Betterment of the Condition of the Poor: William Morton Pitt, 'Observations on the Situations of Cottages, with a Plan for Enabling Cottagers to Build Them. Extracted from "An Address to the Landed Interest"', *Reports of the Society for the Bettering the Condition and Increasing the Comforts of the Poor*, vol. I (1798), 239–43.

[93] G. Stedman-Jones, *An End to Poverty? A Historical Debate* (New York, 2005), 77–8.

[94] R. Wells, 'Historical Trajectories: English Welfare Systems, Rural Riots, Popular Politics, Agrarian Trade Unions, and Allotment Provision, 1793–1896', *Southern History*, 25 (2003), 90.

[95] 41 Geo. III c.109.

Sinclair – it contained no dedicated provisions to settle poor labourers on enclosed wastes.[96]

Mingay has called the 1801 Act a 'dismal half-measure', a reflection of the fact that private Acts were still necessary for each enclosure and the overall enclosure process was little simplified.[97] Certainly, it is hard to discern what impact the Act had, given that high wartime farm-gate prices already provided a huge incentive to enclose uncultivated lands. Even Young's *Annals* gave no explicit publicity to the provisions of the Act; instead the 1801 and 1802 volumes contained letters and reports – including one by Sinclair – on the worth of enclosing and settling wastes.[98] Indeed, this remained a constant refrain until the final volume of the *Annals* was published in 1808, a paucity of copy beyond that provided by Young ultimately proving to be the *Annals'* undoing.[99] If the direct influence of Young waned – the same being true of Sinclair after he was displaced as chair of the Board of Agriculture in 1798 when the Board rebelled against his treating the organisation as his own personal fiefdom[100] – the legacy of their language of enclosure persisted. For instance, the recently established Royal Agricultural Society of England – founded with the intention of promoting the application of science to agriculture – gave a prize to an essay by farmer John Watson entitled 'On Reclaiming Heath Land', the award-winning article being published in the journal of the society in 1845. Watson's essay drew on decidedly Youngian tropes. '[W]ealthy landowners' were 'squandering their time and capital on the Continent' whilst a 'great number of farmers and agricultural labourers' were 'driven through dire compulsion' to emigrate to 'foreign climes and far distant colonies'. What was needed, so Watson argued, was the 'drainage and reclamation of extensive heaths' which would enhance the value and produce of the country, at the same time 'diffusing peace and plenty around the cottage hearth', ergo capital should be used not overseas but in settling and making productive the wastes of Britain.[101]

Later schemes

The recurrent theme of settling British workers on British soil as opposed to supporting them to emigrate was also played out in wider debates about migration in the early nineteenth century. The 1827 House of Commons Select Committee on Emigration was charged with finding, in the words of Callington MP Alexander Baring, a 'permanent' solution 'for the benefit of the country' to the problem of 'not only the manufacturing, but the agricultural, districts, particularly Sussex, which was overloaded with a

---

[96] Young, *An Inquiry Into the Propriety*; Mitchison, 'The Old Board of Agriculture', 57.

[97] G. E. Mingay, *Parliamentary Enclosure in England* (1997), 29.

[98] *Annals of Agriculture*, 37 (1801), esp. 32–46 and 231–49; *Annals of Agriculture*, 38 (1802), esp. 26–7.

[99] *Annals of Agriculture*, 45 (1808); John Gerow Gazley, *The Life of Arthur Young, 1741-1820* (Philadelphia, 1973), 464.

[100] Mitchison, 'The Old Board of Agriculture', 55–6.

[101] John Watson, 'On Reclaiming Heath Land', *Journal of the Royal Agricultural Society of England*, 6 (1845), 101–2.

wretched population, living on charity and the poor-rates ... constituting, by their wretchedness, an enormous charge on the cultivators of the land'.[102] Starting from this Malthusian position, one of the possible solutions the select committee explored was the enclosure, settlement and cultivation of waste lands as an alternative to emigration. This was given strong support in evidence provided by two founders of the recently formed General Association for the Purpose of Bettering the Condition of the Manufacturing and Agricultural Labourers who advocated the systematic enclosing of all waste lands that would yield to the application of labour through spade husbandry. The 3,454,000 acres in England that the association reckoned suitable would be divided up into four-acre plots on which a cottage would be built and a poor family 'located', with financial support given in the first year for equipment, seeds, animals and their food. In total, so the association estimated, the cost of settling one family, comprising two adults and three children, totalled £75, a sum that would either be paid out of the poor rates in lieu of monies that would otherwise have been spent on relieving the 'located' family or would be advanced by individual capital. The scheme betrayed a strong similarity to that advanced by Young four decades previously, although the context was rather different as it was proffered as a solution to the issues of 'surplus population' – to use the constant refrain of the committee – rather than the encouragement to population growth that Young had proposed in the 1780s.[103] As with Young's earlier scheme, the association's proposal came to nothing, the committee believing that emigration offered a cheaper alternative to enclosing wastes at home, the evidence – or rather opinion – of Revd Malthus being that settling waste land would 'greatly aggravate the evil intended to be remedied, and after a short time there would be a much greater redundancy of population than before'. Further, the committee was convinced that any capital outlay would be more profitably spent for the economy of the Empire on settling British émigrés on colonial wastes rather than on settling British wastes.[104]

We also find the language of internal colonisation in later proposals – and in actual enacted schemes – to improve the lot of the poor by settling them on the land. Indeed, in Robert Owen's Home Colonization Society, the prospectus for which was launched by Owen and his friends in September 1840, we see the first explicit labelling of a settlement scheme as an act of internal colonialism.

---

[102] Hansard, HC Debate, 21 May 1827, vol. 17, col. 930.

[103] General Association for the Purpose of Bettering the Condition of Manufacturing and Agricultural Labourers, *A Narrative and Exposition of the Origin, Progress, Principles, Objects, &c. &c. of the General Association Established in London, for the Purpose of Bettering the Condition of Manufacturing & Agricultural Labourers* (1827); Evidence of R. J. Wilmot Horton, 12 May 1827, and Benjamin Willis, 12 May 1827, and appendix 5 (copy of 'An appeal to the nation from the Directors and Central Committee of the General Association'), Third Report from House of Commons Select Committee on Emigration from U.K., c.13 (234) [herein Third Report], 358–68, 368–74 and 576–9. For an analysis of the operation of the General Association see Burchardt, *Allotment Movement*, 75–6.

[104] Select Committee report and evidence of Revd Malthus, 5 May 1827, Third Report, 10–11, 40 and 81.

It is important to note, though, that Owen's society – and his vision – was not concerned with the enclosure of wastes per se but rather an attempt to convert poor labouring men into independent small farmers on already enclosed land. The material manifestation of Owen's vision was the Harmony Hall estate settlement at East Tytherley, west Hampshire, the initial lease being taken out in April 1839, thus predating the Home Colonization Society. Leases were initially taken on three pre-existing farms totalling some 776 acres, before adding two extensions in the summer of 1842 totalling a further 360 acres. At the centre of the community was a huge mansion, the Harmony Hall – the building of which started in the summer of 1841 but was not completed until two years later – which acted as the centre of the community and a de facto hub for Owen's organisations. By September 1845 Harmony Hall had closed, the community having run up large debts and having 'settled' fewer than 100 people, the original intention having been to create a community of 500 souls.[105] If the Chartist Land Plan bore a family resemblance to the Owenite community in Hampshire, the language of the plan's proponents was not figured in terms of home colonisation – although occasionally the settlements were referred to as 'colonies', evidence of the wider influence of the languages of internal colonisation.[106]

It was not until the late nineteenth century that radical interest in poverty alleviation schemes again turned explicitly to languages of internal colonisation, Unitarian minister and Poor Law reform campaigner Herbert Mills in 1887 founding a new Home Colonization Society. Mills's Poor Law critique and manifesto *Poverty and the State* (1886) detailed a scheme wherein 4,000 farm 'colonies' of 2,000 acres would each support 4,000 people who would otherwise be living in workhouses or urban slums and trapped in a cycle of under- and unemployment. Unlike Owen's earlier society, Mills *did* advocate the turning of wastes into productive land, drawing on the example of the 'beggar colonies' created on one-time waste land in the Netherlands, but as with Owen's Harmony Hall Community the solitary attempt to create a colony – the so-called Westmorland Commune, established at Starnthwaite in 1892 – also ultimately folded, Mills abandoning the colony in 1901.[107] The Westmorland Commune was, as Jan Marsh has detailed, one of several turn-of-the-century attempts to settle the urban, industrial worker 'back' on

---

[105] Edward Royle, *Robert Owen and the Commencement of the Millennium: The Harmony Community at Queenwood Farm, Hampshire, 1839-1845* (Manchester, 1998). Also see Malcolm Chase, *The People's Farm: English Radical Agrarianism 1775-1840* (Oxford, 1988), ch. 6. An Owen-inspired, but not -backed, agrarian community was also set up at the same time at Manea Fen in Cambridgeshire. This was even shorter-lived, collapsing in 1841: J. Langdon, '"A Monument of Union": Social Change and Personal Experience at the Manea Fen Community, 1839-1841', *Utopian Studies*, 23 (2012), 504-31.

[106] For example, *Northern Star*, 13 Nov. 1847 and 3 Feb. 1849.

[107] Herbert V. Mills, *Poverty and the State, Or, Work for the Unemployed: An Enquiry Into the Causes and Extent of Enforced Idleness, Together with the Statement of a Remedy Practicable Here and Now* (1886), esp. ch. 10 ('The colonies in the Netherlands'); H. G. Willink, 'The Dutch Labour Colonies', *Charity Organisation Review*, 4 (1888), 241-59; L. Smith, 'A Failed Utopia: H.V. Mills and the Westmorland Commune', *Transactions of the Unitarian Historical Society*, 20 (1991), 297-303.

the land, such schemes united by the use of the term 'colony' in describing their intentions, but these were, including Mills's schemes whatever his advocacy of using unenclosed waste land, neither concerned with enclosure nor based on a critique of the imperial system.[108] Still, their existence points to the persistence of Young's ideal that the solution to social problems lay on the land, and with a deeper sense that the land, and access to working the land, should not be the exclusive preserve of the rich; that the land might be more effectively made to yield for the good of the country and meet issues of poverty.

Conclusions

The account given here has a critical legacy that goes beyond the internal colonial languages and logics of later 'back to the land' schemes. Debates surrounding the projection of internal colonialism had major effects in shifting both the tenor of the debate on enclosure and in altering practices of enclosure, including being instrumental in the passing of the 1801 General Enclosure Act. Indeed, notwithstanding Mingay's critique of the effectiveness of the Sinclair-sponsored Act of 1801, it did help the projectors of enclosure ride roughshod over the opposition and to ignore the wishes of countless commoners in that it required a lower level of consent from landowners. Whilst it is beyond the scope of this paper to delineate the influence such thinking had on the projectors of actual enclosures, we can see that it had an influence on debates surrounding actual enclosures. The following two examples from 1817–18 are instructive. In the aforementioned case of the enclosure of Exmoor, John Knight, the purchaser of the forest from the Crown, created the new village of Simonsbath as the central settlement of the scheme, a literal ordering and (re)peopling of the one-time waste.[109] Elsewhere, plans to enclose Epping Forest provoked considerable public debate, both sides drawing on ideas of internal colonialism. One supporter argued that it

> ought not to be continued in a state of waste, whilst millions of their fellow-subjects are placed upon a short allowance of its produce ... [It is] in the interest of the country and the capital, that nothing but gardens, grass, and corn fields should be within a hundred miles of its gates.

An opponent, conversely, drew upon the squatters' 'colonies' at Stratford, then in Essex on the east London fringe, where 'you will witness scenes at which humanity shudders', to suggest that settling Epping with '36,000 ... idle paupers' was unlikely to 'improve the morals of the lower orders, residing within its boundaries'.[110] Together, such enclosures meant that from 1800 to

---

[108] Jan Marsh, *Back to the Land: The Pastoral Impulse in England, from 1880 to 1914* (1982), esp. ch. 8.

[109] M. Williams, 'The Enclosure of Waste Land in Somerset, 1700–1900', *Transactions of the Institute of British Geographers*, 57 (1972), 106–7.

[110] *Morning Post*, 25 Dec. 1817; *Weekly Dispatch*, 18 Jan. 1818; Anon., *Enclosure of Waltham Forest* (1818), 23.

1873 the area of England and Wales covered in 'wastes' fell from 21.3 per cent to 6.4 per cent.[111]

We do well to remember that the history of state-sponsored or state-encouraged acts of internal colonialism in other parts of Britain – notably in late thirteenth-century Wales, and in Scotland after the Act of Union – was bitter and brutal and leaves a toxic legacy that shapes the politics of today. Further, it is important to note that Young and Sinclair and their wider circle were not altogether anticolonial. Indeed, they make pretty poor heroes for post- and de-colonial politics. For instance, Charles Vancouver, author of the Board of Agriculture county reports for Cambridge (1794), Essex (1795), Devon (1808) and Hampshire (1813), having learnt agriculture in his native Norfolk was found a position working for Lord Shelburne at Rahan in King's County (now County Offaly) in 1776 by no less a person than Arthur Young. From here Vancouver moved to Kentucky where as well as taking on a 57,000-acre farm he applied his expertise in land draining and improvement learnt in Ireland. Thereafter he flitted between Kentucky, Sussex, the Netherlands, Kentucky, back to England, and then finally Virginia where he died in 1815. Vancouver was a classic settler colonialist, and whilst Young may have preferred that he use his capital in acts of internal colonisation he was at least not using British public funds.[112]

Arguably what is more striking still is the way in which debates about the nature of enclosure and improvement were quick to draw upon the colonial experience overseas, both in terms of the languages used but also in terms of making direct comparisons. Enclosure was not simply something forged in the fields and wastes of England (and Wales and Scotland) and imposed on Britain's colonies. Rather, enclosure became a two-way process, the languages of British settler colonialism used not only to describe the enclosure of wastes in the Metropole but also to inspire and justify it. The very practice – and cost – of dispossession and enclosure in Britain's overseas colonies was also used by Young and others to argue that such speculations (and violences) were both unnecessary given the millions of acres of waste at home and a betrayal of the needs of the British people and economy. Moving beyond the confines of a solitary paper, the challenge, now, is to dig deeply into the archive and to explore every internal colonisation scheme in micro-historical detail.

Beyond this, the process of the inferiorisation of the commoner was not only vital in the project of internal colonialism but also part of the making of the rural poor – the poor commoner and pauperised wage labourer alike – as the internal subaltern. As I have shown elsewhere, by the 1830s this was used to justify the imposition of a variety of biopolitical acts of statecraft that rendered the dispossessed commoner not just subaltern – excluded,

---

[111] M. Williams, 'The Enclosure and Reclamation of Waste Land in England and Wales in the Eighteenth and Nineteenth Centuries', *Transactions of the Institute of British Geographers*, 51 (1970), 61.

[112] H. Fox, 'Vancouver, Charles (bap. 1756, d. 1815?), agricultural improver and writer', *Oxford Dictionary of National Biography*, retrieved 15 Jul. 2022, from https://www.oxforddnb.com/view/10.1093/ref:odnb/9780198614128.001.0001/odnb-9780198614128-e-28061.

denied – but reduced to a state of just bodily existing; to, after Giorgio Agamben, bare life.[113] Internal colonisation schemes thereby created a hierarchy of not just land but of life itself: a hierarchy in which waste must be converted to improved farmed land and in which the property-less commoner must be eliminated and the pauperised labourer turned into a sturdy peasant. This account, then, matters well beyond the contexts of rural Britain and to an audience well beyond scholars of enclosure and the making of private property in land. Indeed, ultimately the narrative offered here speaks to a broader point about colonisation never being a one-way process, something just enacted in overseas colonies. Rather, it was to engage in a two-way flow of ideas and practices that challenged understandings of how the Metropole was governed (and who it was governed for). The Empire was not just 'at home' but it reimagined and refigured home: it made it the setting for experiments that drew on colonial learnings and turned it into a laboratory for new forms of colonial ideas, practices and spaces. Colonialism was, as this paper shows, to place all subjects and things, at home and abroad, on the same hierarchy of worth and value.

Acknowledgements. An earlier version of this paper was presented at the Graduate Seminar in History, 1680–1850, University of Oxford, in March 2021. I would like to thank Perry Gauci and those who attended the seminar for their comments. My thanks are also due to Kate Smith and the anonymous reviewers for their perceptive feedback and helpful suggestions.

Author biography. Carl Griffin is Professor of Historical Geography at the University of Sussex and Visiting Professor in the Centre for History at the University of the Highlands and Islands. A historian of rural England, the main foci of his work are protest and popular politics, agrarian change and human–environment relations in the eighteenth and early nineteenth centuries. His latest books are *Moral Ecologies* (2019) and *The Politics of Hunger* (2020).

---

[113] Griffin, *The Politics of Hunger*, ch. 5. On bare life see G. Agamben, *Homo Sacer: Sovereign Power and Bare Life* (Stanford, 1998).

Cite this article: Griffin CJ (2023). Enclosure as Internal Colonisation: The Subaltern Commoner, Terra Nullius and the Settling of England's 'Wastes'. *Transactions of the Royal Historical Society* 1, 95–120. https://doi.org/10.1017/S0080440123000014

Transactions of the RHS (2023), **1**, 121–144
doi:10.1017/S0080440123000026

ARTICLE

The Idea of Asia in British Geographical Thought, 1652–1832

Paul Stock

International History Department, The London School of Economics and Political
Science, London, UK
Email: p.stock@lse.ac.uk

(Received 29 July 2022; revised 24 January 2023; accepted 21 February 2023; first published
online 20 March 2023)

Abstract

This article explores popular British ideas about Asia from the mid-seventeenth century to
the early nineteenth century, using largely neglected sources: geography books. Thanks to
their popularity and focus on conventional knowledge, this genre of texts – geographical
reference works, gazetteers, encyclopaedias and schoolbooks – allows us to glimpse the
commonplace mentalities of the period, and consequently to understand how Asia was
perceived by ordinary literate Britons and not just by prominent intellectuals.
Geography books typically regard Asia as a 'place of origin' for the cultural and societal
achievements of Europe. They also assume that Asia possesses plentiful natural resources
and is thus ripe for economic exploitation. At the same time, however, Asia is understood
to be degenerate and corrupt, usually due to a combination of climactic decay, religious
failings and government mismanagement. Asia is thus alien and entirely distinct from
Europe, and, simultaneously, it is intimately connected to Europe's rise and future imperial
progress. British geography books can tell us a great deal about how ordinary literate people understood Asian peoples and places in the formative age of British empire-building.

Keywords: Britain; history of geography; Asia.

What did the literate British public think about Asia in the seventeenth, eighteenth and early nineteenth centuries? This article offers some answers to that
question using largely neglected sources: British geography books. Scholars
have long discussed how early modern European understandings of Asia are
organised around particular tropes. In broad terms, Asia is often presented
as a sclerotic continent resistant to historical progress; its torpid climate is
said to promote languor and licentiousness among the populace; and its

arbitrary social structures purportedly give rise to brutal despotisms and fanatical, superstitious religions, if not to outright lawlessness.[1] Many of these ideas – notably those concerned with climatic influence and so-called oriental despotism – have very long legacies, some even dating from classical antiquity.[2] But much scholarship on the textual adaptation, expression and dissemination of such ideas tends to use, as its source material, literature or works on political thought.[3] Such texts were not necessarily rarefied or elite: novels and travel literature in particular increased in popularity throughout the eighteenth century. But there is nonetheless a propensity to understand European ideas about Asia through the perspectives of prominent intellectual and literary figures, especially key Enlightenment thinkers. The works of Montesquieu or Volney, Smith or Hume – with all their undoubted sophistication – are sometimes presented if not exactly as direct representatives of their period's thought, then as foundations for the comprehension of contemporary ideas.[4]

It cannot always be assumed, however, that celebrated intellectuals epitomise the commonplace opinions of their age; at the very least this assumption must be tested by examining a wider range of source material. This article's purpose is therefore to explore the characterisation of Asia in a different genre of texts designed for the broadest possible readership in early modern Britain. To what extent are certain ideas about the continent reproduced in books for a general audience? Are there notable patterns and complications in public discourse about Asia? Geography books – a genre of texts which includes geographical reference works, gazetteers, encyclopaedias and schoolbooks – are a useful medium through which to consider these questions. Such works have largely been neglected by historians, or treated condescendingly, dismissed as 'second- and third-rate books' which are 'useless for any practical purpose'.[5]

---

[1] Foundational works on European attitudes to Asia include V. G. Kiernan, *The Lords of Human Kind: European Attitudes towards the Outside World in the Imperial Age* (1969); Edward Said, *Orientalism* (1978), revd edn (2003); Alain Grosrichard, *The Sultan's Court: European Fantasies of the East* (1979), trans. Liz Heron, intro. Mladen Dolar (1998); P. J. Marshall and Glyndwr Williams, *The Great Map of Mankind: British Perceptions of the World in the Age of Enlightenment* (1982).

[2] See David N. Livingstone, 'Environmental Determinism', in *The Sage Handbook of Geographical Knowledge*, ed. John A. Agnew and David N. Livingstone (2011), 368–80; Melvin Richter, 'Aristotle and the Classical Greek Concept of Despotism', *History of European Ideas*, 12 (1990), 175–87.

[3] Frederick G. Whelan, *Enlightenment Political Thought and Non-Western Societies: Sultans and Savages* (New York, 2009); Srinivas Aravanmudan, *Enlightenment Orientalism: Resisting the Rise of the Novel* (Chicago, 2012); Sankar Muthu (ed.), *Empire and Modern Political Thought* (Cambridge, 2012); Geoffrey P. Nash (ed.), *Orientalism and Literature* (Cambridge, 2019).

[4] See, for example, Bruce Buchan, 'Asia and the Modern Geography of European Enlightenment Political Thought c. 1600–1800', in *Western Political Thought in Dialogue with Asia*, ed. Takashi Shogimen and Cary J. Nederman (Plymouth, 2009), 65–86; Michael Curtis, *Orientalism and Islam: European Thinkers on Oriental Despotism in the Middle East and India* (Cambridge, 2009); Urs App, *The Birth of Orientalism* (Philadelphia, 2010); Phil Dodds, 'One Vast Empire': China, Progress and the Scottish Enlightenment', *Global Intellectual History*, 3 (2018), 47–70.

[5] Lester Jesse Cappon, 'Geographers and Map-Makers, British and American, from about 1750 to 1798', *Proceedings of the American Antiquarian Society*, 81 (1972), 243–71, at 245; J. K. Wright 'Some British "Grandfathers" of American Geography', in *Geographical Essays in Memory of A. G. Ogilvie*, ed. R. Miller and J. Wreford Watson (Edinburgh, 1959), 144–65, at 147.

But thanks to their popularity and focus on conventional knowledge, they allow us to glimpse the commonplace mentalities circulating in the period. My purpose is not to imply that geography books offer startlingly original understandings of Asia. Indeed, many geographical texts relay perspectives which were deeply familiar or even clichéd in their period. But herein lies the books' principal usefulness: their wide readership and tendency to present commonplace knowledge help us to identify more precisely the ideas about Asia which circulated in popular British literate culture from the mid-seventeenth to the early nineteenth centuries.

The first books in English which seek to describe the entire world appeared in the late fifteenth century; about fifty were published prior to 1650, many being translations of works originally published in Greek, Latin, French and Spanish.[6] The 'first large-scale ... geography by an English author', however, was Peter Heylyn's *Cosmographie* published in 1652.[7] From then the numbers of new works increased steadily: another forty-four before 1700, just under 140 between 1700 and 1800 (including forty in the 1790s alone), and around another 140 in the first three decades of the nineteenth century.[8] These figures leave out reprints and new editions, numbers of which could be substantial – some books were revised or reissued upwards of thirty times.[9]

The growth in geographical material can be attributed partly to general expansions in literacy and book production, but also to flourishing cultural interests in travel, tourism, exploration and, consequently, foreign lands.[10] Most importantly, geography books were read by many different groups of people. Many were produced specifically for educational use, most often for children – either at school or studying privately – but some served as university textbooks or emerged from public lecture courses for adults.[11] People with recreational or professional interests in travel and overseas places were another important audience. This included armchair tourists interested in exotic locales, but also actual travellers – merchants, sailors, naturalists, tourists – some of whom used geographical works as practical guidebooks.[12] Amid

---

[6] The following paragraphs on the characteristics of geographical texts draw on arguments and examples from Paul Stock, *Europe and the British Geographical Imagination, 1760-1830* (Oxford, 2019), 17–37.

[7] O. F. G. Sitwell, *Four Centuries of Special Geography* (Vancouver, 1993), 301.

[8] Figures are approximations based on the bibliographical lists in Sitwell, *Special Geography*, 619–30. Titles published in the United States are excluded.

[9] Richard Brookes's *The General Gazetteer* reached six principal editions between 1762 and 1815, with thirty-five 'other versions' between 1771 and 1842, some with further editions of their own. William Guthrie's *A New Geographical, Historical and Commercial Grammar* (1770) had reached its forty-sixth edition by 1843. Sitwell, *Special Geography*, 120–4, 273–84.

[10] Among many works on these topics see Lawrence Stone, 'Literacy and Education in England 1640-1900', *Past & Present*, 42 (1969), 60–139; James Raven, *The Business of Books: Booksellers and the English Book Trade 1450-1850* (New Haven, 2007), esp. 221–56; David N. Livingstone, *The Geographical Tradition: Episodes in the History of a Contested Enterprise* (Oxford, 1992), esp. 127–33; John Towner, *An Historical Geography of Recreation and Tourism in the Western World 1540-1940* (Chichester, 1996), 96–138.

[11] Sitwell, *Special Geography*, 17–18; Robert J. Mayhew, 'Geography in Eighteenth-Century British Education', *Paedagogica Historica*, 34 (1998), 731–69, at 753–66.

[12] For the popularity of travel and geography books as reading material see Paul Kaufman, *Libraries and Their Users* (1969), 80, 138, 173; John Feather, 'British Publishing in the Eighteenth

this wide market, geography books were read by individuals of all ages and at every social level from monarchs to labourers. The future Queen Victoria is known to have read a geographical primer as part of her early education;[13] and similar works were also consumed by working- and middle-class readers: the labourer Francis Place and the shopkeeper Thomas Turner both read geography books for self-improvement and general interest.[14] The range of editions – from lavish folios to mass-produced cheap versions costing a few pence – is also evidence of a broad readership. Some books were high-end luxury products: Millar's *New and Universal System of Geography* (1782) was sold in eighty serialised parts for 6*d.* each, making the total cost 40s., or two-and-a-half to four times the weekly wage of a shop manager or office worker. Indeed, its published list of subscribers included aristocrats alongside senior military officers, clergy and doctors.[15] But other books were significantly cheaper: Lenglet du Fresnoy's much-reprinted *Geography for Children* (1737) could be purchased for as little as 9*d.*[16] Christopher Kelly's *New and Complete System of Universal Geography* (1814–17) was not exaggerating when it claimed that geography books were aimed at 'people of *every* rank and description, from the prince to the peasant'; they were equally suitable for 'the lady's library, the tradesman's parlour, and the peaceful retirement of the sequestered cottage'.[17]

Like many books from this period, geographical works typically have unclear authorships. In some cases, the books are simply anonymous, but in others the authorship details are obscure or misleading. It is questionable, for example, whether William Guthrie actually wrote the *Geographical Grammar* which was published six months after his death, and it is entirely unknown who revised it through forty-six subsequent editions.[18] Daniel Fenning and J. Collyer's *New System of Geography* (1765–6) lists nameless 'others' as co-authors on its title page.[19] And the anonymous translator of Büsching's *New System of Geography* (1762) admits to editing and reorganising the material,

Century: A Preliminary Subject Analysis', *The Library*, n.s. 8 (1986), 32–46. For a traveller reading a geography book while travelling see Janet Schaw, *Journal of a Lady of Quality [...] in the Years 1774 to 1776*, ed. Evangeline Walker Andrews with Charles MacLean Andrews (New Haven, 1934), 60–1, http://www.open.ac.uk/Arts/reading/UK/record_details.php?id=19056 (accessed 12 January 2023).

[13] Megan A. Norcia, *X Marks the Spot: Writers Map the Empire for British Children* (Athens, OH, 2010), 130–1. The text in question is *Geography in Easy Dialogues for Young Children, by a Lady* (1816).

[14] Francis Place, *The Autobiography of Francis Place (1771–1854)*, ed. Mary Thrale (Cambridge, 1972), 109, http://www.open.ac.uk/Arts/reading/UK/record_details.php?id=2093 (accessed 12 January 2023); Thomas Turner, *The Diary of Thomas Turner*, ed. David Vasey (Oxford, 1984), 37, http://www.open.ac.uk/Arts/reading/UK/record_details.php?id=6240 (accessed 12 January 2023).

[15] George Henry Millar, *New and Universal System of Geography* [1st edn] (1782), iv, subscriber list bound after 812. The wage information is from J. E. Elliot, 'The Cost of Reading in Eighteenth-Century Britain', *English Literary History*, 77 (2010), 353–84, at 372–3.

[16] [William Baynes], *W. Baynes's Catalogue for 1799* (1799), 42. Lenglet du Fresnoy's volume continued to be printed until 1852: see Sitwell, *Special Geography*, 347–50.

[17] Christopher Kelly, *New and Complete System of Universal Geography* [1st edn] (2 vols., 1814–17), I, preface.

[18] Richard B. Sher, *Enlightenment and the Book: Scottish Authors and Their Publishers in Eighteenth-Century Britain, Ireland and America* (Chicago, 2006), 155–6.

[19] D[aniel] Fenning, J. Collyer and others, *A New System of Geography* [1st edn] (2 vols., 1764–5).

but does not explain the criteria for doing so.[20] Indeed, various geographical works present themselves as 'compilations', and a great many plagiarise text from each other, sometimes with brief acknowledgement but usually without it.[21] Kelly's *New and Complete System of Universal Geography* (1814–17), for instance, includes material from Pinkerton's *Modern Geography* (1802) both within and outside quotation marks.[22] And a discussion of 'Political Geography' in the anonymous *New and Commercial System of Geography* (1800) paraphrases and copies an essay in Guthrie's *Geographical Grammar* (1770) on 'The Origins of Nations, Laws, Government and Commerce'.[23]

These qualities are disconcerting to those methodologies in intellectual and cultural history which place a high premium on originality and authorial intent. Clearly, it is unsound to premise interpretations of the books' contents on authorial intent; and seeking to establish the novelty or the genealogy of their contents is often speculative and, at times, impossible. Indeed, to attempt such tasks may be to misunderstand the roles of generic conventions, market expectations and the publishing procedures of early modern hack writing. But rather than seeing the books' unoriginality and repetitiousness as regrettable hindrances, we can instead view their tendency to recycle text and ideas as advantages. Their borrowings and repetitions allow us to identify and analyse the cultural conventions circulating in Britain in that period. These are books which deliberately set out to accumulate and disseminate conventional knowledge, something which makes them extremely useful for tracing wider cultural mentalities. Naturally, we cannot assume that these works replicate the view of any individual reader; but by understanding geographical works as repositories of commonplace notions, we can use them to investigate broad cultural assumptions about Asia.

The discussion which follows is distilled from my reading of nearly 350 geography books published between 1652 and 1832, ranging from educational primers a few score pages long, through to multi-volume geographical encyclopaedias.[24] The opening date is set by Heylyn's *Cosmographie* (1652), though I have also consulted a few English translations of atlases published earlier in the seventeenth century. The date range ends with the publication of James Bell's *System of Geography* in 1832, 'the last British example of a massive description of all the countries in the world' purporting to be written by a

---

[20] A[nton] F[riedrich] Büsching, *A New System of Geography* (6 vols., 1762), I, iii. The translator is probably Patrick Murdoch: see Gordon Goodwin, 'Murdoch, Patrick (d.1774)', rev. Alexander Du Toit, *Oxford Dictionary of National Biography* (Oxford, 2004), https://doi.org/10.1093/ref:odnb/19559 (accessed 12 January 2023).

[21] *New and Complete System of Universal Geography* [1st edn] (2 vols., Edinburgh, 1796), I, v; Alexander Adam, *A Summary of Geography and History* [1st edn] (Edinburgh, 1794), iii.

[22] Kelly, *New and Complete System of Universal Geography* (1814–17), II, 1–4; John Pinkerton, *Modern Geography* [1st edn] (2 vols., 1802), II, 7–16.

[23] *A New Historical and Commercial System of Geography* (Manchester, 1800), xiv–xxiv; Guthrie, *A New Geographical, Historical and Commercial Grammar* (1770), xxxiv–xxxv, xxxix–xl.

[24] For bibliographical information on geographical texts, including notes on authorship and edition numbers, see Stock, *Europe and the British Geographical Imagination*, 261–83.

single author.[25] My purpose is not to catalogue understandings of every region or polity in Asia from the Ottoman Empire to Japan. Instead, I have sought to show how geography books discern and characterise the continent of 'Asia' overall: to delineate the features which, they claim, homogenise the continent and make its natural environment, cultures, states and peoples distinctive. I have therefore focused my analysis on the books' main entries on 'Asia': the articles which head the section on that continent, or the entries on 'Asia' in alphabetical gazetteers. By identifying the trends in these introductory articles, we can establish the core information which readers would encounter when reading about Asia.

One crucial such trend is that even when ostensibly talking about the whole continent, the books tend to focus on those parts of the Ottoman Empire which would later be called the Near and Middle East. In some respects, this emphasis is unsurprising. The rise of Ottoman military and economic power in the sixteenth century, and the creation of the Levant Company in 1581, prompted sustained (and often anxious) British interest in the societies, politics and commerce of the region.[26] In part, that interest pivots on the ambiguous position of the Ottoman Empire in wider British thought and culture. It is often denigrated as 'an unfamiliar space at the margins of Europe', principally due to its distinctive (and supposedly inferior) governmental system and religious culture. But the presence of Greece and the Holy Land within its territory complicates matters as these regions are frequently seen as central to 'European history, culture and self-definition'.[27] The Ottoman Empire is thus at the heart and the periphery of ideas about Europe, and this dual role also influences how geographical texts conceptualise Asia. At times, Asia is presented as the parent of Europe's later cultural achievements; at others it is seen as the antithesis of Europe's supposedly superior civilisations. The Ottoman territories around the Mediterranean – especially the Holy Land – play an especially important role in facilitating both these narratives, and they thus receive considerable attention in general articles on Asia.

As we shall see, Asia is also woven into broader narratives about both European and universal history. These include: the role of environmental conditions in shaping social progress; the privileging of certain governmental systems, particularly non-despotic monarchy; and the relative access of certain cultures to religious truths.[28] It might be tempting, therefore, to see the 'Asia' of British geography books largely as an ideological construction framed by Eurocentric assumptions. We might even see Europe and Asia as mutually

---

[25] Sitwell, *Special Geography*, 95.

[26] See Gerald MacLean, *Looking East: English Writing and the Ottoman Empire before 1800* (Basingstoke, 2007); Christine Laidlaw, *The British in the Levant: Trade and Perceptions of the Ottoman Empire in the Eighteenth Century* (2010); Anders Ingram, *Writing the Ottomans: Turkish History in Early Modern England* (New York, 2015).

[27] Paul Stock, 'The Real-and-Imagined Spaces of Philhellenic Travel', *European Review of History – Revue Européenne d'histoire*, 20 (2009), 523–37, at 523.

[28] For elisions of European and universal history see Michael A. Peters, 'Eurocentrism and the Critique of "Universal World History": The Eastern Origins of Western Civilisation', *Geopolitics, History and International Relations*, 6 (2014), 63–77.

Geographical and Historical View of the World (1810) reinforces Europe's relative unimportance with a quotation from Voltaire: 'our European battles are only petty skirmishes in comparison of the numbers that have fought and fallen in the plains of Asia'.[42]

However, for all that these texts stress the apparent pre-eminence of Asia, they also present a version of history in which Asian achievements facilitate the European present. The 1807 *System of Geography*'s article on Asia quickly becomes an account of how the continent has influenced and attracted Europeans. Alexander the Great 'laid open to Europeans the more remote parts of that continent', and the article continues by showing how successive Mediterranean societies – the Romans, the Italian city states – benefited from commerce with Asia.[43] In this example, Asia is not simply seen through a European lens; it is also an instrument for European development. This sentiment is common to geographical texts, even if the details can vary. According to one work, perhaps adapting a comparable argument made by William Robertson in *The History of the Reign of the Emperor Charles V* (1769), it was the encounter with Asian cultures during the Crusades which first galvanised Europeans' 'spirit of enterprise'. The Crusades 'opened a state of existence which astonished the barbarians of Europe', and their desire to obtain 'luxuries' and a 'state of life, which ... appeared to be so much superior' then led to greater interest in commercial exchange and global adventurism.[44] Although ostensibly a reflection on European inadequacies, the narrative treats Asia largely as a vehicle for European betterment. Asia remains defined by its past, and by its role in facilitating Europe's more recent accomplishments.

European priorities are also at work in the characterisation of Asia's natural environment: the continent apparently enjoys particular advantages, but these are presented in terms of European opportunity. One recurring phrase describes Asia as 'rich and fruitful', and the general idea that it possesses a superior climate and plentiful natural resources is widespread.[45] Echoing Hippocrates, Asia is said to be the 'most temperate' continent; and it is also blessed with the 'bounties of Providence, which are here dispensed in vast variety, as well as superabundance'.[46] As one text says, 'the most precious things that the world doth yield are found in this noble parte thereof, as besides great varietie & divers kyndes of beastes, & birds, excelent sortes of spices, frutes,

---

[42] John Bigland, *A Geographical and Historical View of the World* [2nd edn] (5 vols., 1810), IV, 118. The quotation is a loose translation from [Voltaire], *Essai sur l'histoire générale et sur les moeurs et l'esprit des nations* (10 vols., [Geneva?], 1757), II, 200.

[43] *System of Geography* (1807), II, 256–61.

[44] *The Glasgow Geography* [1st edn?] (5 vols., Glasgow, 1819), II, 3–4. This work reproduces text from *System of Geography* (1807). Compare William Robertson, *The History of the Reign of the Emperor Charles V* (3 vols., 1769), I, 77–9.

[45] George Henry Millar, *The New, Complete, Authentic, and Universal System of Geography* [3rd edn.?] (n.d. [1785?]), 6. See also George Augustus Baldwyn, *A New, Royal, Authentic, Complete and Universal System of Geography* (n.d. [1794?]), 2; *A New General Atlas* (1721), 141.

[46] Richard Blome, *Geographical Description of the Four Parts of the World*, pt 1, p. 1; *New Historical and Commercial System of Geography* (1800), 329. Hippocrates claims that Asia possesses the ideal median temperature: see *Ancient Medicine*, trans W. H. S. Jones (Cambridge, MA, 1923), 107.

medicinall herbes, rootes, & other things, As also the moste precious metals, precious stones, and pearles'.[47] Asia exceeds other parts of the world in

> the Richness and Fertility of its Soil, the Serenity of Air, the Delicousness of its Fruits, the Salubriousness of its Drugs, Fragrancy and Balsamick Quality of its Plants, Spices, Gums, &c. the Quantity, Variety, Beauty and Value of its Gems, Fineness of its Silks, Cottons, &c. the Richness of its Metals, and many more of the like Nature.[48]

The continent, in short, produces 'a great abundance of all things necessary for Humane Life'.[49]

For many geography books, therefore, Asia is defined by the superiority of its natural environment. This is complicated by that fact that these books also often use very similar terms of reference to describe Europe's natural environment.[50] 'Europe', says one,

> surpasseth all other parts of the world, not only in abundance of all things through the admirable and sweete temperature of the aire, pleasant prospect, and multitudes of people, but also for the fertility of fruits, trees, plants, all sorts of beasts, metals and other things necessary for man's life.[51]

Many texts make observations about 'the fertility of the soil' in Europe and the 'abundance of its productions'.[52] On one level, these correspondences seem contradictory: Asia and Europe surely cannot both possess the best climate and natural resources. But these overlapping qualities are perhaps better understood in terms of the chronological priority which casts Asia as the progenitor of modern Europe. Just as Asia was the location for religious and social events which contextualise and facilitate Europe's subsequent development, so too does Europe succeed Asia in natural and climatological advantages. Those environmental qualities – temperate climate, rich soil – which formerly defined Asia are now more applicable to Europe, in the same way that the guardianship of religious truths and the growth of advanced commercial states have also migrated from one continent to the other. This developmental logic is evident when one book says that, at the time of writing, 'Asia enjoys a temperature similar to that of Europe', and that 'this may be one reason ... why

---

[47] [Abraham Ortelius], An Epitome of Ortelius His Theatre of the World [1st edn] ([1601/2?]), 3.

[48] Complete System of Geography (1747), II, 67.

[49] Thesaurus Geographicus [1st edn] (1695), 412.

[50] There are classical precedents for prioritising the European natural environment: Strabo, The Geography of Strabo, trans. Horace Leonard Jones (8 vols., Cambridge, MA, 1917–32), I, 489; Pliny, Natural History, trans. H. Rackham, W. H. S. Jones and D. E. Eichholz (10 vols., Cambridge, MA, 1938–62), II, 5.

[51] Gerhard Mercator [and Jocodus Hondius], Atlas [1st edn] (Amsterdam, 1636), 42.

[52] J. W. Clarke, A New Geographical Dictionary [1st edn] (2 vols., 1814), I, 779. See also [Richard] Turner [Sr], A View of the Earth [1st edn] (1762), 9; Clement Cruttwell, The New Universal Gazetteer [2nd edn] (Dublin, 1800), 260.

Europeans generally find this continent to agree with their constitution'.[53] By the modern period, Europe defines the ideal environment, and Asia is understood in European terms rather than the reverse.

Asia's subordination to Europe is most clearly on display when geography books discuss the exploitation of Asian resources. In its introductory article on the continent, the anonymous *System of Geography* (1807) devotes considerable space to ancient and modern commerce with Asia, tracing the rise and fall of Mediterranean powers – ancient Rome, the Italian states, Portugal – to the 'acquisition of trade' in the continent.[54] According to this narrative, Asia is a repository of riches and a means to achieve and consolidate wealth. For some texts, the connections between commerce and imperial ambition are outlined even more explicitly. Several tabulate commercial activities in Asia, listing the regions which 'trade with or belong to' certain European states. Hence, Japan is said to 'trade with or belong to' the Dutch, the Philippines to Spain, and Bombay to the English.[55] By blurring the distinction between commercial exchange and imperial possession, the books present Asian resources as the instruments of European empires.[56]

For many texts, Asia is defined largely as a venue for imperial adventure and acquisition. Peter Heylyn's *Cosmographie* (1652) begins its account of Asia with a description of its physical geography and some remarks on its role in Christian history and practice. The next paragraph details the Roman Empire's incursions into the continent; the Roman provinces are thus itemised even before the entry mentions the 'great monarchs' of Tartary, China and Burma. Indeed, ancient Rome still defines modern states: the Ottoman Empire commands 'all these parts and Provinces which antiently belonged to the Roman Empire'.[57] A similar logic is on display when it is claimed that Asia's northward limits 'were not discovered till the reign of the Czar Peter the Great'; or when another book outlines the 'progressive geography' of Asia by listing incremental incursions into the continent by Europeans, starting in antiquity and ending with contemporary explorers.[58] For some books, Asia is merely an addendum to European empires. James Playfair's *System of Geography* (1808–14) is one of several which absorb non-European colonies into their sections on European states. The article on Britain thus concludes with its 'possessions and settlements' in Asia and elsewhere, presenting

[53] *System of Geography* (1807), II, 267.

[54] *Ibid.*, 256–61.

[55] John Payne, *Universal Geography* [1st edn] (2 vols., 1791), I, 6; John Smith, *A System of Modern Geography* (2 vols., 1810–11), II, 757.

[56] Stock, *Europe and the British Geographical Imagination*, 224–5. For an overview of European imperial and commercial engagements with Asia see Om Prakash (ed.), *European Commercial Expansion in Early Modern Asia* (Aldershot, 1997).

[57] Heylyn, *Cosmographie*, bk 3, p. 4.

[58] Thomas Bankes, Edward Warren Blake and Alexander Cook, *By the King's Royal Licence and Authority. A New Royal, Authentic and Complete System of Geography* [1st edn?] (n.d. [1787/88/90?]), 107; Bell, *System of Geography* (1832), IV, 28–33.

those regions as outposts of the European metropole.[59] On occasion, a geography book is self-conscious about the exploitative consequences of imperialism. Guthrie's *Geographical Grammar* (1770), for example, castigates 'the avarice and profligacy of the Europeans, who resort thither [to Asia] in search of wealth and dominion'.[60] But even that text still casts Asia as an imperial resource.

Overall, then, geographical works often present Asia in an apparently positive light, possessed of notable – sometimes unique – environmental qualities or cultural and religious achievements. But these advantages are habitually understood in European terms. This frequently involves empirical and teleological assertions: Asia possesses an environment which Europe can exploit; Asian societies instituted practices which Europeans have perfected. John Pinkerton's *Modern Geography* (1802) praises Asia for 'its intimate connexion with the destinies of Europe, which it has frequently overawed, while the savage tribes of Africa and America can never become formidable to European arts or happiness'.[61] Ostensibly, this is a compliment: unlike other continents, Asia can both impress and intimidate Europeans. But its significance still ultimately lies in its connections with Europe. Just as with assertions about Asia's chronological primacy, Asia is superficially pre-eminent but is subsumed within a Eurocentric epistemological framework.

All of this carries substantive conceptual complications because Asia not only acts as a source and inspiration for Europe, but at the same time serves as its subject, waiting to be discovered, labelled and exploited. On one level, we might argue that Asia defines Europe, as much as Europe defines Asia. In some respects, this appears persuasive: after all, geography books delineate Europe's history, achievements and prospects via comparison with Asia. But while there is credence in this view, to assert reciprocity too strongly would be to mistake Europe's and Asia's relationship as an equal one. Ultimately, for most geographical texts, Asia's past facilitates contemporary Europe, and Asia's present and future enables further European growth. No geography book that I have examined reverses these positions.

Geography books, then, often present Asia as the predecessor and foundation of Europe. But Asia is also seen more negatively, in particular as an alien space, significantly different from Europe. One key theme is Asia's recent degeneration: whatever the glories of the past, the modern continent is now degraded and corrupt. For some books, the natural environment prompted this decline. Repeating an oft-made argument, the anonymous *New Historical and Commercial System of Geography* (1800) says that 'a considerable part of Asia ... has lost much of its ancient splendour'. Some parts are 'still in a flourishing condition, which is rather to be attributed to the richness of the soil,

---

[59] James Playfair, *A System of Geography* (6 vols., Edinburgh, 1808–14), III, 96. See also F. Francis, *An Introduction to Geography* [2nd edn] (1818), 23–4; Richmal Magnall, *A Compendium of Geography* [3rd edn] (1829), 12–17.

[60] Guthrie, *Geographical Grammar* (1770), 441. See Smith, *System of Modern Geography* (1810–11), II, 755. For critiques of empire see Sankar Muthu, *Enlightenment against Empire* (Princeton, 2003).

[61] Pinkerton, *Modern Geography* (1802), II, 8.

than to the industry of the inhabitants, who are remarkable for their indolence, luxury and effeminacy. This effeminacy is chiefly owing to the warmth of the climate, though in some measure heightened by custom and education.'[62] Malte-Brun's *Universal Geography* (1822–33) similarly asserts that the 'climates no industry can sensibly ameliorate ... must have an influence on the moral character of the Asiatics, as well as uniformly modifying their nervous and muscular system'. The book goes on to quote and update Hippocrates, the ancient Greek exponent of climatic influence on the human body, concluding that 'the people of Asia owe to geographical circumstances some political and moral features very different from those which exist in Europe', not least because in Asia 'the uniform fertility of the soil, and the constant mildness of the climate, in recompensing too rapidly the most trifling labour, have stifled almost in its birth the energy of the human mind'. This torpor has various consequences, from 'mental and bodily inactivity' and the prevalence of 'religious superstition' to the construction of poor-quality houses – all of which can be attributed to 'the uniform influence of a climate'.[63]

Several geographical texts argue, therefore, that ecological conditions in Asia have directly led to inferior or underdeveloped social structures. Other books reverse this relationship, proposing that societal mismanagement is, in fact, the cause of environmental decay. Charles Middleton's *New and Complete System of Geography* (1777–8) argues that the Turks 'possessed themselves of the center regions of Asia, laying waste to a most delightful country, and converting its fruitfullest spots into barren wilderness'.[64] An anti-Ottoman theme pervades several texts: one alleges that the empire has turned the most 'fruitful Spot in all *Asia*' into a 'wild incultivated Desert'; another that it has 'destroyed all [the region's] ancient splendour'.[65] Some books are less critical of the rest of the continent: 'the other parts of the Asiatic territories continue in much the same situation as formerly'.[66] But others argue that almost all Asian societies squander natural resources and exhibit moral failings. The continent is 'bountiful and liberal to Mankind', but 'it furnishes not only every thing necessary for Life and Health, but all that Avarice, Vanity and Sensuality put a value upon'. Misusing or neglecting the bounties of nature, Asians are now 'swallow'd up in Luxury and Idleness', idolatry having 'drench'd them in all sorts of Vice'.[67]

---

[62] *Historical and Commercial System of Geography* (1800), 329. See also Guthrie, *Geographical Grammar* (1770), 440.

[63] [Conrad] Malte-Brun, *Universal Geography* [1st edn] (10 vols., Edinburgh and London, 1822–33), II, 17–24. For Hippocrates see *Ancient Medicine*, trans. Jones, 105–9, 115–17. Aristotle and, later, Montesquieu also offer similar theories, but ascribe Asian languor to excessive heat: Aristotle, *The Politics*, ed. Stephen Everson, trans. Jonathan Barnes (Cambridge, 1988), 165; Montesquieu, *The Spirit of the Laws* (1748), trans. Anne M. Cohler, Basia Carolyn Miller and Harold Samuel Stone (Cambridge, 1989), 234–7.

[64] Charles Theodore Middleton, *A New and Complete System of Geography* [1st edn] (2 vols., 1777–8), I, 5.

[65] *Complete System of Geography* (1747), II, 67; Fenning and Collyer, *New System of Geography* (1764–5), I, 6.

[66] Middleton, *New and Complete System of Geography* (1777–8), I, 5.

[67] *New General Atlas* (1721), 141–2.

Sometimes these arguments are presented concurrently. The anonymous *Complete System of Geography* (1747), for example, argues both that the rich Asian climate has generated inferior societies, and also that those societies have degraded the natural environment. In some respects, these assertions can be made to serve a consistent purpose. Asia's natural resources enabled a glorious past which in turn has facilitated the European present; and the continent is still rich enough to enable commercial opportunities. Latterly, however, the resources still extant are neglected or poorly managed, a fact which justifies European imperial incursion. But at root, a circular logic is at work because environmental conditions and social structures are seen as the ultimate cause of each other.[68] Geographical texts' presentation of Asia is thus somewhat unstable: it is both a resource-rich paradise which generates advanced cultures; and a sterile wasteland thanks to societal incompetence. This tension partly echoes wider early modern debates about the relationship between the natural environment and human activity.[69] Does the environment direct social activity, or do humans make their own history, partly by shaping the environment around them? As I have discussed elsewhere, these same debates also affect understandings of Europe in the period. Ideal environmental conditions – fertile soil, abundant rivers and so on – are sometimes seen as the cause of Europe's supposedly superior social development. But at the same time, Europe's *inferior* climate is said to have prompted greater social dynamism, principally because the challenge of overcoming privation has helped to accelerate progress. By offering different interpretations – often within a few pages of each other – geographical texts tap into wider contemporary controversies about environmental influence. [70] In their articles on 'Asia', we can see how these broad debates take on specific form, with consequences for how the continent and its people are understood by the literate British public.

Given widespread assumptions about Asia's environmental and societal decline, many geography books are interested in the causes of that supposed degeneration. One suggested reason is 'idolatry'.[71] Fenning and Collyer's *New System of Geography* (1764-5) blames 'Mahometans' in particular for the decay of the 'most fertile spots of Asia', but goes on to complain that almost the whole continent is 'involved in the grossest idolatry', from 'worshippers of Brama [sic]' to 'followers of Confucius'.[72] Denunciations of Islam are commonplace: it is described bluntly, for instance, as a 'stupid kind of religion'. But other faiths are also censured: 'in China, Japan, Siam, &c. they are, for the most part, heathens and idolators; have strange notions of the Deity, or rather of their deities, and use the most extravagant rites in the worship of

---

[68] Jan Golinski, *British Weather and the Climate of Enlightenment* (Chicago, 2007), 171–2.

[69] For an overview see Clarence Glacken, *Traces on the Rhodian Shore: Nature and Culture in Western Thought from Ancient Times to the End of the Eighteenth Century* (Berkeley, 1967).

[70] Stock, *Europe and the British Geographical Imagination*, 79–102, esp. 99–100. See also Nathaniel Wolloch, *History and Nature in the Enlightenment: Praise of the Mastery of Nature in Eighteenth-Century Historical Literature* (Farnham, 2011), 73–135.

[71] For early modern European attitudes to Islam, see David R. Blanks and Michael Frassetto (eds.), *Western Views of Islam in Medieval and Early Modern Europe: Perception of Other* (New York, 1999).

[72] Fenning and Collyer, *New System of Geography* (1764-5), I, 6.

them'. It is even argued that these 'idols, and superstitious ceremonies' are maintained by a priest class to subdue a credulous population.[73] These comments are especially interesting because they echo the anti-Catholic rhetoric also present in many geographical texts. The 'artifice and fraud' and 'absurd mummeries and superstitions' of Roman Catholicism are often ridiculed;[74] and it is even claimed that the Catholic clergy 'supress all scientific knowledge among the laity; and in order to keep them in ignorance and subjection, they brand all literary researches with the name of heresy'.[75] Many British geographical texts thus display the anti-Catholicism prevalent in wider British society of the period; Catholicism is so flawed that it replicates the errors of heathen idolators.[76] But it is perhaps more salient to reverse the comparison. Since geography books frequently exhibit a pro-Protestant worldview – suggesting, for instance, that 'Europe owes a great part of [its] superior civilization' to the Reformation – it is unsurprising that they should understand Asian religions in terms of more familiar Catholic faults.[77] In this way, religious practice in Asia can be rendered readily comprehensible and, at the same time, dismissed for its errors and deleterious effects.

Not all geographical books are quite so universal in their aggressions. John Payne's *Universal Geography* (1791) includes standard remarks about how 'Mahometans' have despoiled the natural environment; but it goes on to offer cautious praise for the 'more sagacious followers of *Confucius*' as well as the Zoroastrians who acknowledge 'but one Supreme Deity'.[78] Other texts go further still. Zoroastrians 'are sworn Enemies to all kind of Idolatry, Imagery, Temples, &c. which they look upon as derogatory to the supreme Being, who neither can nor ought to be represented by Images, nor confined in Temples'. '*Brahmans*, or *Brachmins*' are also

> very humane and benign, lead a contemplative Life, feed only upon Vegetables, and are so far from killing any living Creatures for their Use, or even noxious ones in their own Defence, that they build even Hospitals for the Maintenance of such, especially domestic ones, as are decay'd thro' Age, Accident or any other Infirmities.

If the praise for Zoroastrianism echoes typical Protestant hesitancy about icons and rich decoration, then the remarks about vegetarianism are more unexpected. In the very next paragraph, however, Christian pre-eminence reasserts itself. The book acknowledges that '*Asia* was the Theatre of the first

---

[73] Baldwyn, *New, Royal, Authentic, Complete and Universal System of Geography* ([1794?]), 1. See also Millar, *New, Complete, Authentic, and Universal System of Geography* ([1785?]), 6–7.

[74] Thomas Salmon and J. Tytler, *The New Universal Geographical Grammar* [4th edn] (Edinburgh, 1782), 87–8; William Guthrie, *A New Geographical, Historical and Commercial Grammar* [13th edn] (1785), 58.

[75] Millar, *New, Complete, Authentic, and Universal System of Geography* ([1785?]), 714.

[76] See Colin Haydon, *Anti-Catholicism in Eighteenth-Century England, c.1714–80: A Political and Social Study* (Manchester, 1993).

[77] *Glasgow Geography* (1819), III, 205. See Stock, *Europe and the British Geographical Imagination*, 70–5.

[78] Payne, *Universal Geography* (1791), I, 5.

Promulgation of Christianity', arguing that the faith spread rapidly 'as far as *India*' and 'was almost every where received and professed'. Unfortunately, societal and personal failings in Asian cultures caused it to decline. Chief blame belongs to 'the Unworthiness of those Converts' and subsequently 'the Churches of *Asia Minor* were abandoned to Persecution; and ... utterly destroy'd by the Inundation of the northern Barbarians, *Saracens, Tartars* and *Turks*'.[79] Faint praise for Asian religious cultures thus quickly reverts to reflections on the continent's societal shortcomings as well as implicit reaffirmation of Europe's role as the principal heir to spiritual truths.

Geographical texts also blame Asia's supposed shortcomings on its governmental structures, particularly the apparent prevalence of despotic empires.[80] As I noted above, geography books tend to understand European imperialism in terms of expansion, acquisition and the proper use of resources. Indeed, commercial activity was frequently understood – from the late seventeenth century onward – as a sign of social advancement and modern civilisation; and geography books often present European empires as an outgrowth of commercial exchange and enterprise.[81] Europeans, for example, 'have made themselves masters of the greatest part of the rest of the World, and sent thither numerous colonies ... Their commerce and navigation ... serve, as it were, to unite together the principal parts of the Earth.'[82] Asian empires, however, are understood differently, often by adapting ideas derived ultimately from Aristotle about the continent's propensity for absolute rule and slavery.[83] Asian polities are usually characterised as absolute monarchies ('when the power of the sovereign is not limited by law') or as outright despotisms ('when the government is very absolute'; the monarch ruling 'by his own arbitrary will').[84] According to Guthrie's *Geographical Grammar* (1770), 'many of the Asiatic nations ... could not conceive how it was possible for any people to live under any other form of government than that of a despotic monarchy'. This pattern means not simply that one can generalise about the continent, but also that Asian states and peoples are, fundamentally, very similar: 'in Asia, a strong attachment to ancient customs, and the weight of tyrannical power, bears

---

[79] *Complete System of Geography* (1747), ii, 67.

[80] The literature on so-called oriental despotism is vast. For overviews, see R. Koebner, 'Despot and Despotism: Vicissitudes of a Political Term', *Journal of the Warburg and Courtauld Institutes*, 14 (1951), 275–302; Joan-Pau Rubiés, 'Oriental Despotism and European Orientalism', *Journal of Early Modern History*, 9 (2005), 109–80.

[81] Istvan Hont, 'The Early Enlightenment Debate on Commerce and Luxury', in *The Cambridge History of Eighteenth-Century Political Thought*, ed. Mark Goldie and Robert Wokler (Cambridge, 2006), 253–76; Stock, *Europe and the British Geographical Imagination*, 229–32.

[82] Büsching, *New System of Geography* (1762), i, 58.

[83] For Aristotle's ideas about despotism and their early modern adaptations see Melvin Richter, 'Despotism', in *The Blackwell Encyclopaedia of Political Thought*, revd edn, ed. David Miller (Oxford, 1991), 119–22.

[84] *A Summary of Geography and History [...] For the Use of the Highest Class in the High School of Edinburgh* (Edinburgh, 1784), 7; R. Wynne ([ed.] and trans.), *Introduction to the Study of Geography* (1778), 2.

down the active genius of man, and prevents that variety in manners and character, which distinguishes the European nations'.[85]

Numerous geographical texts reproduce similar remarks about Asian despotism: 'despotism entirely prevails' in Asia; 'Asiatic governments are almost universally despotic'; and *'monarchical despotism* ... has all along been the established government over the whole of Asia'.[86] This insistence on the universality of despotism fuels wider cultural observations. Millar's *New, Complete, Authentic, and Universal System of Geography* ([1785?]), for example, asserts that Asia has fewer languages than other parts of the world 'chiefly owing to the very extensive empires comprised in it' – specifically, Persia, 'Great Mogul', China and Japan – 'each of which strives to introduce an uniformity of language among the subjects of it'.[87] Occasionally, one can find more measured, even generous remarks: 'the immense country of China', for example, is 'famous for the wisdom of its laws and political constitution' and 'for the singularity of its language, literature, and philosophy'.[88] But for most geography books, Asia is characterised by despotic government. Indeed, for Payne's *Universal Geography* (1791) even the 'dominions established here by the *Europeans'* have succumbed to this pattern: European territories 'have all an absolute and supreme authority; and the *European* governors have, in a great measure, the power of arbitrary princes'.[89]

There are various theories about why despotism is supposedly so prevalent in Asia. One common argument places the blame on environmental conditions. Europe is

> intersected with great numbers of mountainous ridges, which form natural boundaries to its kingdoms, and check the ambition of its princes. In Asia, these natural boundaries are placed at much greater distances from each other; hence the Asiatic empires are vastly larger than those of Europe, and of consequence their rulers being superior in wealth and power to the European monarchs, are proportionably more insolent, haughty, oppressive and cruel.[90]

Some texts expand this thesis. For Malte-Brun's *Universal Geography* (1822–33) 'it is not enough to say that the great plains with which Asia abounds, give the conquerors easier access'. There are other factors involved too: 'the want of

---

[85] Guthrie, *Geographical Grammar* (1770), 441, vii.

[86] Gordon, *New Geographical Grammar* (1789), 312; Pinkerton, *Modern Geography* (1802), ii, 13; Bell, *System of Geography* (1832), i, cxxx.

[87] Millar, *New, Complete, Authentic, and Universal System of Geography* ([1785?]), 6. Turkey and Muscovy are also mentioned as Asian empires, though 'the most considerable shares' of their territories are in Europe.

[88] Guthrie, *Geographical Grammar* (1770), vii. For similar remarks on the constitutionalism of China see Voltaire, *An Essay on Universal History*, 2nd edn, trans. Nugent (4 vols., 1759), iv, 297.

[89] Payne, *Universal Geography* (1791), i, 5.

[90] Salmon and Tytler, *New Universal Geographical Grammar* (1782), 90. See also Nicholas Hamel, *World in Miniature* (1800), 14; [James Millar], *Encyclopaedia Edinensis* (6 vols., Edinburgh, 1827), iii, 433. See Stock, *Europe and the British Geographical Imagination*, 86.

wood for building' means that 'habitations offer nothing firm and solid' and empires can freely rise and fall, because 'the want of strong places, open the road to sudden and rapid invasions'. Furthermore, these circumstances have affected the 'moral and political' character of Asians. 'The uniform influence of a climate, which imperiously determines the sorts of cultivation and food for each region, and the irresistible influence of religious superstition, despotic laws, and servile moods', have together changed the behaviour of Asian peoples. The 'animated and free emotions which in Europe inspire the breast' are absent from 'the soul of the Asiatic': their states 'do not feel the ardour and energy of true patriotism', and sovereigns presented 'only a vain show of resistance to the audacity of the conquerors'. 'Every thing', in short, 'combines to facilitate the total and frequent subjugation of these vast empires of the east.'[91]

Other geographical texts emphasise supposed behavioural differences between Asians and Europeans. After explaining that it is hard to discern a physical boundary between the continents, Pinkerton's *Modern Geography* (1802) asserts that the distinction 'if not strictly natural, is ethical, as the manners of the Asiatic subjects of Russia, and even Turkey, differ considerably from those of the European inhabitants of those empires'.[92] This statement implies that Asians and Europeans are different thanks to certain fixed characteristics, which remain constant even when they coexist under the same regime. Bigland's *Geographical and Historical View of the World* (1810) echoes this position: 'Turks, although settled in Europe, are Asiatic people; and their customs and manners are rather Asiatic than European. Prejudice, ignorance, and want of curiosity, gravity of deportment, and contempt of foreigners, are conspicuous traits in their national character.' European Armenians, by contrast, remain 'polite and sensible' under Ottoman rule: 'in amiableness of manners, and in purity of morals, they excel all other subjects of the Turkish empire'.[93] From this perspective, Asian despotism develops from the supposed qualities of Asian peoples; it is the system of government best suited to an ignorant and contemptuous populace. Another group of geography books, however, argues precisely the opposite: that despotism is not naturally suited to Asian peoples; it is imposed on them by tyrannical rulers and governmental convention. Millar's *New, Complete, Authentic, and Universal System of Geography* ([1785?]) says that

we will not pretend to determine, whether the reflection which is commonly cast on all the Asiatic nations, that they are naturally admirers of monarchy, be altogether just; since their princes have always kept them in such abject slavery and subjection, that they never had the least opportunity of displaying their love of liberty, which we suppose to be as congenial to them, as with the rest of mankind.[94]

---

[91] Malte-Brun, *Universal Geography* (1822–33), II, 21, 24.

[92] Pinkerton, *Modern Geography* (1802), I, 6.

[93] Bigland, *Geographical and Historical View of the World* (1810), IV, 114–15, 109.

[94] Millar, *New, Complete, Authentic, and Universal System of Geography* ([1785?]), 6. See also *Complete System of Geography* (1747), II, 67; Baldwyn, *New, Royal, Authentic, Complete and Universal System of Geography* ([1794?]), 1.

In seeking to explain the supposed prevalence of despotism in Asia, geograph-ical texts therefore offer a variety of theories, ranging from societal and envir-onmental influences to the 'natural and innate' qualities of Asian peoples.[95] This breadth reflects wider ideas of the period about nature and society, and especially the often opaque relationship between acquired behaviours and sup-posedly natural characteristics in early modern thought. Far from being irre-concilable opposites, the 'poles of an essentialised Nature and a capricious Environment' were often assumed to be ambiguously – and sometimes mys-teriously – interconnected. Purportedly fixed characteristics could be affected by external factors such as climate; and learned behaviours could come to seem innate, passed down through the generations. Consequently, ideas about manners and society were blended with '"absolutist notions" of inherit-ance and non-acquired "essence"'.[96] Discussion of 'Asia' in geographical texts reflects this fundamental ambiguity – which is why the books generalise about the innate qualities of individuals and populations, but also postulate the influence of external factors such as climate. Bigland's *Geographical and Historical View of the World* (1810), for example, argues that Asian 'customs and manners' are fixed regardless of governmental and social circumstance; and then suggests – on the very next page – that 'defects which appear in the national character, ought rather to be attributed to the baleful influence of a government ill-planned and worse administered'.[97] While ostensibly contradictory – especially to present-day readers – such moments reflect deep-seated debates in the period about human nature, social development and climatic influence, all of which inform how Asia is understood in popular geographical texts.

An emphasis on despotic empires is not, however, the only characterisation of Asian peoples and societies present in geography books. There is also sub-stantial interest in the so-called 'vagabond nations' or 'vagrant nations, who have no settled abode' within the continent.[98] If any people in Asia 'can be said to enjoy some share of liberty', says Adams's *New Royal System of Universal Geography* ([1794/6?]), 'it is the wandering tribes, as the Tartars and Arabs'. Arabs

alone possess liberty, on account of the sterility of their soil; independent themselves of revolution and change, they see, with unconcern, empires falling and rising around them. They remain unconquered by arms, by luxury, by corruption ... When men are obliged to wander for subsistence, despotism knows not where to find its slaves.

---

[95] *Complete System of Geography* (1747), II, 67.

[96] Kathleen Wilson, *The Island Race: Englishness, Empire and Gender in the Eighteenth Century* (2003), 8, cited in Paul Stock '"Almost a Separate Race": Racial Thought and the Idea of Europe in British Geographies and Histories, 1771–1830', *Modern Intellectual History*, 8 (2011), 3–29, at 5.

[97] Bigland, *Geographical and Historical View of the World* (1810), IV, 114–15.

[98] *Complete System of Geography* (1747), II, 68; Millar, *New, Complete, Authentic, and Universal System of Geography* ([1785?]), 6.

Although also wanderers, Tartars are less free: while 'a violent aristocracy always prevails', on occasion 'the fortune of one established a transient despotism over the whole'. Indeed, the whole region is defined by fear and violence: 'men are more afraid of men, in the solitudes of Tartary, than of beasts of prey'.[99] These are common assertions; other texts repeat them almost verbatim.[100]

Some geography books offer specific theories about the relative despotism and mobility of Asian peoples. Kelly's New and Complete System of Universal Geography (1814–17) argues that 'the northern tribes, who occupy the extensive regions of Tartary, are robust and active, hate idleness, and are continually roving about'. The 'inhabitants of the southern parts of Asia', by contrast, 'are so extremely indolent, that they never stir but with reluctance'. The book goes on to theorise a rivalry between these groups: northern Asians 'deem courage the greatest virtue, and athletic exercises the most essential mark of genius', whereas southern Asians are 'ingenious' and have 'brought several arts to great perfection'. Consequently, 'this disparity of disposition occasions them to despise each other, on account of that contrast which marks their characters' and because 'each imagines that his peculiar mode of life leads by the most direct road to earthly felicity'.[101] The idea that all Asian peoples are either independent wanderers or oppressed idlers, and that each group is associated with a specific topographical region, has a long legacy. The Thesaurus Geographicus (1695) offers the insight that 'the People of Asia have always been great Lovers of Pleasure and Ease, except some that dwell in the Mountains, and the Tartars. They are not usually so vigorous and active as the People of Europe or Africa.'[102] And the anonymous New General Atlas (1721) says that most Asians, 'except those who live in Tartary, and other Northern Parts, have always been accounted effeminate, and swallow'd up in Luxury and Idleness'.[103] One geographical text adopts a rudimentary formula: one can assess the relative 'Effeminacy' and 'Strength and Courage' of Asian people 'as they are seated nearer or further from the North. For it is plain, that the southern Climates produce not such robust Natures as the Northern ones.' This book also treats Europeans as normative: 'those Asiatics, who live near the same latitude with us, cannot be much inferior to us'; whereas 'those who live in the more southern regions of Asia' possess 'Ingenuity in various kinds of Workmanship, which our politest Mechanicks have in vain tried to imitate'.[104]

The general principle that Asians can be divided in two by location and style of government – and that these points of distinction are intimately related – is widespread by the early nineteenth century. Malte-Brun's Universal Geography (1822–33) considers the matter 'proved by physical geography, namely, that

---

[99] Adams, New Royal System of Universal Geography ([1794/6?]), 167.

[100] Historical and Commercial System of Geography (1800), 329–30; Smith, System of Modern Geography (1810–11), II, 755

[101] Kelly, New and Complete System of Universal Geography (1814–17), I, 7.

[102] Thesaurus Geographicus (1695), 412.

[103] New General Atlas (1721), 142.

[104] Complete System of Geography (1747), II, 67.

Asia has no temperate zone, no intermediate region between very cold and very hot climates. The slaves inhabit the hot, and the conquerors the elevated and cold regions.' Each group has a 'totally different physical and moral nature'.[105] The *Universal Geography* premises its observations on quotations from Montesquieu's *The Spirit of the Laws* (1748). Montesquieu argues that Asia is polarised between 'very cold' and 'exceedingly hot' parts of Asia, and that it lacks a temperate zone. 'From hence', he continues, 'it comes, that in Asia the strong nations are opposed to the weak; the warlike, brave, and active people touch immediately on those who are indolent, effeminate, and timorous: the one must therefore conquer, and the other be conquered.' This explains 'the slavery of Asia' and also why 'liberty in Asia never increases'.[106] Evidently, the *Universal Geography*'s arguments are dependent on Montesquieu's phrasing, but he is in no way the initiator of general theories about cold northern conquerors and warm southern idlers in Asia. Instead, these ideas are part of a much longer trend – evident in generations of geography books – which connects climate, governance and manners in order to define the distinctive features of the continent.

Overall, therefore, British geography books characterise Asia as a place with both too much and too little government, a continent of arbitrary despotisms and wandering 'vagabonds'. Most European states, by contrast, are said to have achieved an ideal form of government, usually described either as 'limited monarchies' (those states which limit a sovereign's power by law) or a 'mixed form' (which blends forms of government identified by classical authorities – monarchy, aristocracy and government 'of the people' – and fuses the advantages of each).[107] The implications of these assertions are complex. In some respects, geographical works stress the distinctiveness, even the strangeness, of Asia, particularly in its governmental arrangements. One text notes that while some Asian states have supposedly fixed boundaries and dimensions, in other parts of the continent – namely 'Russian, Chinese, Mongulean and Independent Tartary' – 'the bounds ... are unlimited, each power pushing on his conquests as far as he can'. It presents Asia as a chaotic and inchoate place; a place where, thanks to 'absolute monarchy', the power and territory of states are unlimited and unstable.[108] This contrasts with the characterisation of Europe as 'a system of political equilibrium' in which states coexist under a 'system of international law'.[109] Europe supposedly forms 'one complete whole – a great confederacy of states': any country seeking 'to

---

[105] Malte-Brun, *Universal Geography* (1822–33), II, 22. See also Bell, *System of Geography* (1832), IV, 28.

[106] Montesquieu, *The Spirit of the Laws, Translated from the French [...] with Corrections and Additions Communicated by the Author* (2 vols., Dublin, 1751), I, 328–9.

[107] Malte-Brun, *Universal Geography* (1822–33), VI, 81; Bankes, Blake and Cook, *New Royal, Authentic and Complete System of Geography* ([1787/88/90?]), 578. For the classical idea that government takes three forms – rule by one person, a few individuals or a larger group – see Herodotus, *Herodotus*, trans. A. D. Godley, Loeb Classical Library (4 vols., Cambridge, MA, 1920–5), I, 105–11; Aristotle, *Politics*, ed. Everson, trans. Barnes, 61–2. For more on monarchy and ideas of Europe see Stock, *Europe and the British Geographical Imagination*, 133–8.

[108] Adams, *New Royal System of Universal Geography* ([1794/6?]), 166–7.

[109] David Brewster (ed.), *Edinburgh Encyclopaedia* (18 vols., Edinburgh, 1830), IX, 239.

tyrannize' its neighbours exposes itself to 'chastisement', a point apparently demonstrated by various European conflicts which created 'a closer union ... sealed with the blood of all'.[110] A blasé interpretation of European history this may be, but the principle that Europe constitutes an ordered political system is commonplace in geographical texts.[111] Asia, by contrast, is at once unbalanced, lawless and subject to overweening despotic power, unconstrained by the norms of limited government and territorial restraint.

At the same time, however, geography books use precise frames of reference to make Asia comprehensible to a domestic audience. George Augustus Baldwyn's *New, Royal, Authentic, Complete and Universal System of Geography* ([1794?]) says that 'the principal monarchies or sovereignties of Asia, at present known to us, amount to forty two': six empires, thirty-three kingdoms, and three sovereignties 'established here by the Europeans'. The book almost immediately qualifies its apparent precision: it hastily mentions other imperial enclaves and 'independent ... nations'. But the effect is to present Asia as a known space which can be labelled with confidence. Moreover, the states themselves are familiar by type: all Asian polities are monarchies or empires, thus fitting neatly into categories of government derived from classical antiquity. Baldwyn's *System* anticipates potential objections – 'that Tartary is not under one government; that India, beyond the Ganges, is independent of the Great Mogul' – but it defers further discussion 'to void clogging our readers' memory with too many distinctions'. It then simplifies further, offering 'the most clear idea of the continent' in a series of tables. One shows only fifteen states on the Asian continental land mass and includes 'distance and bearing from London' as key information alongside size, cities and religion, an emphasis which makes European places and priorities the criteria through which to understand Asia.[112]

British geographical texts thus familiarise Asia by presenting it in European terms, and, at the same time, assert its distinctive characteristics. It is both strange and exotic, and fully knowable and exploitable. Indeed, the apparent conceptual difference between these perspectives is eroded: Asia's predictable 'otherness' becomes a comfortable cliché through which to understand it. Furthermore, from the mid-seventeenth century to the early nineteenth century, geography books present Asia in a remarkably consistent manner. This is not to say that they all reach identical conclusions, but rather that the same debates and (sometimes unresolved) tensions recur across the whole period covered by this article. These trends include: Asia as the 'cradle' of religious truth and social order, at once the origin of European civilisation and

---

[110] Thomas Myers, *A New and Comprehensive System of Geography* [1st edn] (2 vols., 1822), I, 14.

[111] Many texts reproduce William Robertson's theory that Europe formed 'one great political system' and a 'balance of power' at the dawn of the modern period. See Robertson, *History of the Reign of the Emperor Charles V*, I, x–xi; Guthrie, *Geographical Grammar* (1770), xlv–xlvi; Thomas Salmon and J. Tytler, *The New Universal Geographical Grammar* [2nd edn] (Edinburgh, 1778), 65; Bankes, Blake and Cook, *New Royal, Authentic and Complete System of Geography* ([1787/88/90?], 578. For the wider context see H. D. Schmidt, 'The Establishment of "Europe" as a Political Expression', *The Historical Journal*, 9 (1966), 413–41.

[112] Baldwyn, *New, Royal, Authentic, Complete and Universal System of Geography* ([1794?]), 2–3.

superseded by it; Asia as an abundant environment, but also under-exploited and degraded; Asia as a continent without meaningful government and subject to despotic excess. This might seem to be an unexpected conclusion: there were, after all, very significant developments in British commercial and imperial engagements with Asia and the wider world across this period.[113] But my contention is that because the themes discussed here are repeated so often, across a long period of time, and in texts which were read very widely, we can say with reasonable confidence that they represent the cultural frameworks though which Asia was understood in this period.

Geography books, then, allow us to appreciate the depth of certain ideas about Asia in British intellectual life: these are the commonplace notions which recurred in general reference material, were taught in schools and were encountered by everyday readers from monarchs to shopkeepers. And although some of these ideas – about the influence of climate, or the prevalence of despotism – are very familiar to scholarship, their consistent presence in popular geographical texts allows us to reassess how ideas may have circulated in early modern British intellectual culture. One possibility is that commonplace texts imitate and disseminate the arguments of prominent intellectuals. This is not always an easy contention to prove, in part because geography books so rarely cite their sources, but occasionally – as we have seen in the cases of Voltaire and Robertson – one can glimpse such influences. Robert Mayhew, for example, has proposed that Guthrie's *Geographical Grammar* (1770) incorporates arguments from key figures in the Scottish Enlightenment, especially David Hume, Adam Ferguson and Robertson.[114] The 1771 edition of the *Grammar* asserts the primacy of Greece and Europe in the phrase 'what Greece therefore is with regard to Europe, Europe itself is with regard to the rest of the globe'.[115] Mayhew traces this phrase to Hume's essay 'The Rise and Progress of the Arts and Sciences' which contends that '*Europe* is at present a Copy at large, of what *Greece* was formerly a Pattern in Miniature.'[116] Such instances potentially show how the ideas of prominent Enlightenment thinkers were distributed in wider British literate culture, often in ways which disguise their eminent exponents.

But there is an additional, perhaps more intriguing possibility which only comes into focus after an exhaustive survey of a great many sources. Prominent thinkers may in fact be mere participants – and not necessarily leaders – in sets of presumptions which permeated far more thoroughly throughout literate culture than might otherwise be assumed. Montesquieu's *The Spirit of the Laws* (1748) is certainly an important text; for some it

---

[113] See P. J. Marshall, *The Making and Unmaking of Empires: Britain, India and America c. 1750–1783* (Oxford, 2005); Jack P. Greene, *Evaluating Empire and Confronting Colonialism in Eighteenth-Century Britain* (Cambridge, 2013); David Veevers, *The Origins of the British Empire in Asia, 1600–1750* (Cambridge, 2020).

[114] Robert Mayhew, *Enlightenment Geography: The Political Languages of British Geography, 1650–1850* (Basingstoke, 2000), 175–80, cited in Stock, *Europe and the British Geographical Imagination*, 34.

[115] William Guthrie, *New Geographical, Historical and Commercial Grammar* [2nd edn] (2 vols., 1771), I, 85.

[116] [David Hume], *Essays, Moral and Political* [1st edn] (2 vols., Edinburgh, 1741–2), II, 71.

constitutes 'the most influential formulation of the view that climate has a determinant role in human society'.[117] But it is harder to claim that it drives the terms of debate about climate and Asian despotism in the eighteenth century when we can read scores of geographical texts articulating related ideas throughout the preceding and following centuries. Nor is it necessarily enough to identify the antecedents and successors of the great thinkers, tracing chains of influence and inspiration.[118] Instead, geographical works show us that celebrated figures are contributors to much wider networks of ideas, in which certain notions are repeated and reformulated across hundreds of commonplace texts, encountered, absorbed and debated by thousands of participant authors and readers. If this seems an obvious remark about public discourse in abstract terms, detailed analysis of popular materials such as geographical texts can make such assertions more concrete and demonstrable. It allows the terms of discussion about significant historical problems – what did early modern British people think about Asia? – to be set by broadly consumed texts in that period itself, rather than by individuals selected, sometimes retrospectively, as representatives of an epoch. Significant questions, of course, still remain, not least the potential connections between the ideas discussed here and wider imperial ideology and practice. To what extent did these commonplace perspectives on Asia inform ideas about empire, or Britain's commercial and colonial practice more widely? Clearly, such enquiries require confirmation using additional sources – not least, documents recording political decisions and justifications – and as such lie beyond the scope of this article. But my principal point is that geographical texts can open early modern British intellectual life to us more fully; they can help us to understand the principles on which British understandings of the wider world were founded.

Acknowledgements. I would like to thank the editors and anonymous readers for their comments on an earlier version of this article.

Competing interests. None.

---

[117] Nelson Moe, *The View from Vesuvius: Italian Culture and the Southern Question* (Berkeley, 2006), 23.

[118] See Robert Shackleton, 'The Evolution of Montesquieu's Theory of Climate', *Revue Internationale de Philosophie*, 9 (1955), 317–29; R. J. W. Mills, 'William Falconer's *Remarks on the Influence of Climate* (1781) and the Study of Religion in Enlightenment England', *Intellectual History Review*, 28 (2018), 293–315.

Cite this article: Stock P (2023). The Idea of Asia in British Geographical Thought, 1652–1832. *Transactions of the Royal Historical Society* 1, 121–144. https://doi.org/10.1017/S0080440123000026

Transactions of the RHS (2023), **1**, 145–158
doi:10.1017/S0080440123000038

ARTICLE

Work and Identity in Early Modern England

Mark Hailwood[1] and Brodie Waddell[2]

[1]Department of History, University of Bristol, Bristol, UK and [2]Department of History, Classics and Archaeology, Birkbeck, University of London, UK
Corresponding author: Email: m.hailwood@bristol.ac.uk

(Received 6 October 2022; revised 4 April 2023; accepted 12 April 2023; first published online 10 May 2023)

Abstract

How did work shape people's identity before industrial capitalism? It is a question that early modernists have never really got to grips with. Thanks to decades of research by social and cultural historians, we now have a much better understanding of how people in the past saw themselves and labelled those around them. But until recently scholars of early modern England have had surprisingly little to say about how a person's working life – their occupation, trade, vocation or livelihood – influenced their social identity. This essay is therefore an attempt to synthesise recent research on the subject into a more explicit historiographical intervention. Early modernists need to broaden their research to consider 'working identities' as a whole, rather than merely the narrower concept of 'occupational identities'. By exploring how work influenced a person's self-image and social role, we can reshape our understanding of broader social relations in this period and challenge some of the 'grand narratives' of early modern social and economic change.

Keywords: Labour; identity; class; gender; occupation

Identity has long been a key category of analysis for social and cultural historians of early modern England. But the exploration of occupational identity has not been especially central to this field. This relative neglect can probably be blamed on two prevalent assumptions. On the one hand, some scholars have dismissed 'occupational' identity as an anachronism in a society where many men and women had multiple jobs at the same time and repeatedly changed them over the course of their lives. On the other hand, some have regarded it as niche experience, confined to the small number of workers in formal craft guilds, where it supposedly slowed the emergence of broader forms of identity such as 'class'. There is some truth to both these views, but they also obscure much more than they reveal and neither justifies ignoring this important issue. Economic historians have eagerly counted occupational titles, but social and cultural historians have lagged behind in paying 'work' much heed.

Recently, however, early modernists have begun to explore the relationship between work and identity more carefully. As often as not they have found the occupational title a hindrance as much as a help, and one of the key findings of this new research is that occupations are only part of the picture of working identities. But as yet this scholarship remains fragmented and no clear overview of the topic has been produced.[1] This essay therefore represents an attempt to synthesise recent research on the subject – in England at least – into a more explicit historiographical intervention.[2] Although we bring in some examples from primary sources, the central purpose of this piece is to highlight the ways that existing literature, when brought together, can be seen as reconceptualising the relationship between work and identity, and pointing the way to a new agenda in this field. Recent work reveals, we argue, that early modernists need to broaden their research to consider 'working identities' as a whole, rather than merely the narrower concept of 'occupational identities'. And by exploring how work influenced a person's self-image and social role, scholarship on this subject has the potential to reshape our understanding of broader social relations in this period and challenge some of the 'grand narratives' of early modern social and economic change.

The essay consists of three sections: the first draws on recent research to introduce the idea of 'working identities' and the diverse ways people's work informed their sense of themselves. The second considers how this understanding of the relationship between work and identity might disrupt narratives of change in the early modern period. The third considers how working identities varied across gender, space, forms of 'free' and 'unfree' labour and different types of source material. We conclude by outlining an agenda for where we think further research into work and identity is most needed.

How did work inform identity in early modern England? The most explicit way was the according of occupational titles to men, a descriptor that sat alongside name and parish of residence as the most commonly deployed fragments of biographical information in a whole range of surviving legal and bureaucratic records from the period. These occupational descriptors were clearly central in framing the way contemporaries sorted and categorised individuals into larger groupings on the basis of their work, and their prevalence in the archive has made them a primary focus for quantitative approaches to the history of work.[3] Although contemporaries reached for them frequently, and historians

---

[1] The best survey of attitudes to work in the period is Keith Thomas, *Ends of Life: Roads to Fulfilment in Early Modern England* (Oxford, 2009), ch. 3, though it focuses on elite views.

[2] For a survey with a much wider chronological and geographical scope, see Catharina Lis and Hugo Soly, *Worthy Efforts: Attitudes to Work and Workers in Pre-industrial Europe* (Leiden, 2012).

[3] See the Cambridge Group for the History of Population and Social Structure's ongoing project on 'The Occupational Structure of Britain 1379–1911', https://www.campop.geog.cam.ac.uk/research/occupations.

can recover them relatively easily, recent research has increasingly questioned how much they can actually tell us about the relationship between individuals and their work. They are of limited value to historians of women's work, as female litigants and deponents in court records were generally accorded a marital status rather than an occupational label. Their value as guides to men's working lives has also come under scrutiny, with Tawny Paul arguing that their use in formal administrative records obscures the fact that few men could expect stable occupational identities in early modern society. Multiple and by-employment were much more common experiences of male working life, rendering single occupational titles as 'fictions of the archive' that are not an especially helpful starting point for unpacking the relationship between 'identity, masculinity and occupational plurality' that would have framed many men's sense of self. The early eighteenth-century diarist Edmund Harrold was a 'barber' by title, but cutting hair was just one job in a portfolio of employments that included wig making, 'cupping' (a medical service for lactating women), book dealing, money lending and dog muzzling.[4]

The rise of the 'verb-oriented' approach to the history of work has produced similar conclusions. This was initially developed to overcome the lack of occupational descriptors for women that precluded studying them through the 'noun-oriented' approach to workers in the past. Instead, historians search for archival references to people *doing* work activities.[5] They have shown that women were regularly doing many of the tasks associated with occupations that are usually only accorded to men in the records, including everything from butchery to ploughing. In the process of transforming our understanding of women's work across early modern Europe, this body of scholarship has also called for us to rethink men's work in a number of important ways: not least the relationship between occupational titles and the work tasks men actually undertook. Alex Shepard's study of church court records found a considerable discrepancy in many cases between occupational descriptors given and the specific work tasks men engaged in. For some individuals this was due to engagement in by-employments; for others it was the result of life-cycle changes, with men in old age still using an occupational title that did not reflect more recent shifts in the work they were able to undertake.[6] The Gender and Work project at Uppsala University also found that occupational titles routinely concealed a diversity of work activities in early

---

[4] K. Tawny Paul, 'Accounting for Men's Work: Multiple Employments and Occupational Identities in Early Modern England', *History Workshop Journal*, 85 (Spring 2018), 43, 29, 26. For a similar argument in relation to eighteenth-century Italy, see Beatrice Zucca Micheletto, 'Husbands, Masculinity, Male Work and Household Economy in Eighteenth-Century Italy: The Case of Turin', *Gender and History*, 27 (Nov. 2015), 752–72.

[5] Barbara Hanawalt, *The Ties that Bound: Peasant Families in Medieval England* (Oxford, 1986), 269–74; Sheilagh Ogilvie, *A Bitter Living: Women, Markets and Social Capital in Early Modern Germany* (Oxford, 2003); Maria Ågren (ed.), *Making a Living, Making a Difference: Gender and Work in Early Modern European Society* (Oxford, 2017); Jane Whittle and Mark Hailwood, 'The Gender Division of Labour in Early Modern England', *Economic History Review*, 73 (Feb. 2020), 3–32.

[6] Alexandra Shepard, *Accounting for Oneself: Worth, Status and the Social Order in Early Modern England* (Oxford, 2015), ch. 7.

modern Sweden: tailors, for instance, are recorded in their database as under-taking activities as diverse as building stables, selling salt, collecting rents, keeping inns and lending money, as well as mending clothes.[7] Results from the University of Exeter based project on Women's Work in Rural England, 1500–1700, show 'tailoring' activities as accounting for only 43 per cent of recorded work activities undertaken by tailors, with other categories such as commerce (14 per cent) and agriculture (12 per cent) also featuring promin-ently in the everyday working lives of these men.[8]

Despite this growing recognition that single occupational titles mask the complexities of men's working lives, they cannot be altogether dismissed by historians interested in working identity. Their widespread use suggests that contemporaries did find them a useful, if crude, tool for connecting work and selfhood, and that this went beyond mere administrative convenience. After all, single occupational titles featured heavily in a ballad literature that celebrated the occupational identity of bonny blacksmiths and the 'gentle craft' of shoemakers, identities that clearly appealed to some consumers of cheap print.[9] Similarly, while most women were primarily identified by their marital status in both official records and literary texts, titles such as 'shopkeeper', 'midwife', 'seamstress', 'milliner' and many others were occasion-ally deployed.[10] The argument here is that if historians direct their energies too narrowly onto the low-hanging fruit of occupational titles in their search for working identities, they will have little to say about the significant numbers of men and women for whom a single occupational title did little to capture the relationship between their work and their identity.

Instead, we need to be sensitive to other forms of what we might usefully call working identities, of which occupational identity was only one variant. Indeed, recent research has highlighted the existence of a number of working identities operating in early modern society, many of which were more effect-ive at incorporating the flexibility and instability that were characteristic of experiences of work in the period. One such for men was the identity of 'tradesman', which, as Hailwood has shown, was inclusive of a range of arti-sanal occupations, and even some unskilled ones such as porters. It featured prominently in a broadside ballad literature that emphasised experiences and values that cut across individual crafts to define a broad collective of work-ers as 'tradesmen'.[11] For an individual engaged in multiple or by-employment;

---

[7] Ågren, Making a Living, 35.

[8] 'Women's Work in Rural England, 1500–1700', earlymodernwomenswork.wordpress.com.

[9] Mark Hailwood, 'Broadside Ballads and Occupational Identity in Early Modern England', Huntington Library Quarterly, 79 (Jun. 2016), 188–93. For more on depictions of occupational groups in print see Edward P. Taylor, 'The Representations of Millers, Tailors, and Weavers in Popular Print, c. 1500 to c. 1700' (Ph.D. thesis, University of Exeter, 2017), https://ore.exeter.ac.uk/reposi-tory/handle/10871/29283.

[10] Amy Louise Erickson, 'Married Women's Occupations in Eighteenth-Century London', Continuity and Change, 23 (2008), 267–307; Shepard, Accounting for Oneself, 218–21; Laura Gowing, Ingenious Trade: Women and Work in Seventeenth-Century London (Cambridge, 2022), 35, 121, 223.

[11] Mark Hailwood, '"The Honest Tradesman's Honour": Occupational and Social Identity in Seventeenth-Century England', Transactions of the Royal Historical Society, 24 (Dec. 2014), 79–103.

or who moved between trades; or who transitioned over the life cycle from apprentice, to journeyman, to master, and then perhaps on to other forms of low-paid work, the 'tradesman' was an identity that could be sustained in the face of such vagaries much more readily than a narrow occupational title. Whilst 'tradesman' was an exclusively masculine identity, the same was not necessarily true of other working identities. To those whose working lives revolved around tasks that were insufficiently skilled to be considered artisanal, a working identity founded upon the notion of 'living by their labour' may have performed a similar function. Whilst the identity of 'labourer' was rarely claimed in the seventeenth century in the same way that 'tradesman' was, Alex Shepard has argued that labouring people – both male and female – were able to forge a sense of collective identity through an emphasis on their honesty, their industry and their relative freedom from dependence on others: something they saw as setting them apart from servants, despite the fact that labourers and servants were often engaged in very similar tasks.[12]

If both a labouring identity and a tradesman identity were relatively horizontal beasts – fostering solidarity between those of a broadly similar social status – other forms of working identity were more vertical in the bonds they encouraged. Most obviously and well known here are the craft guilds, which encouraged loyalty to a particular craft from the lowliest apprentice to the wealthiest master, often combining ostentatiously hierarchical rituals, such as guild feasts, with an emphasis on common purpose. Jasmine Kilburn-Toppin has shown, for example, that the 'design, furnishing, and ornamentation' of London's Livery Company halls 'celebrated and memorialised a distinctive craft culture of expertise and regulation, and honourable masculine artisanal identity'.[13] Brodie Waddell's recent work on the Essex clothier Joseph Bufton suggests that this form of working identity was not confined to formal urban guilds, but could have an equivalent in the small clothing towns of England in the notion of 'the trade'. Bufton's own position within the clothing trade is difficult to discern – very likely because he himself was subject to 'tumbling up and down in the world' – so it is unsurprising that he sought to promote an identity for male members of the clothing trade that was inclusive of combers, weavers and merchants alike, while excluding female spinners and unapprenticed 'intruders'.[14] 'The trade' represents another form of working identity that offered belonging to male workers whose precise position

---

[12] Shepard, *Accounting for Oneself*, ch. 5. On the importance of independence to labouring identities see also Keith Wrightson, *Earthly Necessities: Economic Lives in Early Modern Britain, 1470–1750* (New Haven, 2000). For more on the identities of servants as an occupational group, see Charmian Mansell, 'Beyond the Home: Space and Agency in the Experiences of Female Service in Early Modern England', *Gender and History*, 33 (2021), 24–49.

[13] Jasmine Kilburn-Toppin, *Crafting Identities: Artisan Culture in London, c. 1550-1640* (Manchester, 2021), 237. For company feasts, see her '"Discords Have Arisen and Brotherly Love Decreased": The Spatial and Material Contexts of the Guild Feast in Early Modern London', *Brewery History*, 150 (2013), 28–38.

[14] Brodie Waddell, '"Verses of My Owne Making": Literacy, Work, and Social Identity in Early Modern England', *Journal of Social History*, 54 (Fall 2020), 161–84.

within it was very likely to fluctuate over their working life. It also reminds us that both horizontal ('class') and vertical ('craft') solidarities were at work in early modern society.[15]

A notable feature of early modern working identities is that they often sought to overcome the complexities of working lives by emphasising sets of values or ethics shared by groups of workers, rather than highlighting shared experiences of doing specific occupations or tasks. The emphasis was less on *what* you did than on *how* you did it. Indeed, the 'tradesman' identity that featured in cheap print often did so with the prefix 'honest' attached, and grouped together a fairly disparate collection of workers by highlighting their shared ability to earn money with their hands, their commitment to good fellowship and their abhorrence of dishonest dealing.[16] Labouring people consistently put the stress on the fact that their work was 'honest', 'industrious' and 'painstaking', whilst downplaying the specifics of the varied and largely unskilled tasks they engaged in.[17] It was not the tasks themselves but rather the hard-working approach that defined them – and the idea of the 'industrious labourer' as a positive constituent of the commonwealth appeared to gain traction across the seventeenth century.[18] Garthine Walker and Jane Whittle have highlighted how the ability to effectively manage a household, and a distinct set of work skills were essential for women who sought to claim the title of 'good housewife'.[19] For some an emphasis on the 'godliness' of their approach to working life could be central to working identity. Joseph Bufton saw himself as a 'godly clothier' whose everyday work was closely guided by religious teachings, as did the eighteenth-century Leeds diarist Joseph Ryder – the 'watchful clothier' of Matthew Kadane's study.[20] For other eighteenth-century male diarists, as Paul has shown, it was the possession and application of knowledge and skill in working life that provided the basis of a stable working identity that 'transcended the precariousness of work' and its 'occupational fluidity'.[21] The importance of the distinction between skilled and unskilled workers, especially

---

[15] E. P. Thompson, 'Patrician Society, Plebeian Culture', *Journal of Social History*, 7 (Summer 1974), 396–7.

[16] Hailwood, '"The Honest Tradesman's Honour"'; Mark Hailwood, 'Sociability, Work and Labouring Identity in Seventeenth-Century England', *Cultural and Social History*, 8 (May 2011), 9–29.

[17] Shepard, *Accounting for Oneself*, ch. 5.

[18] Craig Muldrew, *Food, Energy and the Creation of Industriousness: Work and Material Culture in Agrarian England, 1550–1780* (Cambridge, 2011), ch. 7.

[19] Garthine Walker, 'Expanding the Boundaries of Female Honour in Early Modern England', *Transactions of the Royal Historical Society*, 6th Series, 6 (1996), 235–45; Jane Whittle, 'Women's Work and the Idea of Housewifery in the Memoirs of a Devon Yeoman, 1593' (Nov. 2020), https://history.exeter.ac.uk/research/economicandsocialhistory/blogdiscussiontimetable202021/womensworkandtheideaofhousewiferyinthememoirsofadevonyeoman1593.

[20] Waddell, 'Verses'; Matthew Kadane, *The Watchful Clothier: The Life of an Eighteenth-Century Protestant Capitalist* (New Haven, 2013).

[21] Paul, 'Accounting for Men's Work'. For more on knowledge, skill and work see James Fisher, 'The Master Should Know More: Book-Farming and the Conflict over Agricultural Knowledge', *Cultural and Social History*, 15 (2018), 315–31; Jasmin Kilburn-Tippin, 'Writing Knowledge, Forging Histories: Metallurgical Recipes, Artisan-Authors and Institutional Cultures in Early Modern London', *Cultural and Social History*, 18 (2021), 297–314. For an important new analysis of continental

to the sense of identity of the former, is well attested for later periods; it had fore-runners in the working identities of the early modern period, which likewise emphasised the approach to work rather than occupational specifics.[22] Early modern working identities – the honest tradesman, the industrious labourer, the good housewife, the godly clothier – hinged more often on the adjective than the noun.

Thinking in terms of working identities requires historians to recognise that these were often broader in scope than the occupational identities that we have traditionally sought when investigating the relationship between work and identity. Conventional analysis has seen working identities as a relatively insignificant form of social identity in this period because of the vagaries and variety of working lives. Recent research suggests instead that these factors shaped work-based identities in interesting ways, rather than simply undermining them. In part, this conclusion has been reached by approaching working identity in a more 'emic' way; investigating how contemporaries understood and described social identities and social groupings, rather than measuring the evidence against pre-existing templates such as occupational identity or class and finding them wanting.[23] That being said, we might then ask whether working identities were in fact more important, and more powerful, than some other forms of social identity that historians have tended to favour in their analyses of early modern society. The most obvious target here is the notion of 'sorts'.

Using the language of 'sorts' to describe early modern English social identities and social relations originates from a similar impulse to the one driving the argument above: that historians may be better served by adopting frameworks of analysis that would have been recognisable and meaningful to contemporaries.[24] 'Sorts' has therefore come to serve as a historicised alternative to the more general concept of class, and is now widely deployed by historians of the period. It has been particularly prominent in accounts that distinguish between the 'middling sorts' and the 'lower sort of people', and that highlight the process of 'social polarisation' occurring between these two groupings: a process which is seen as a – perhaps *the* – key development in the social history of early modern England.[25] Whilst thinking with 'sorts' has undoubtedly proven fruitful, there is a risk that it crowds out other ways of thinking about social identities and social relations that may have meant just as much, if not more, to contemporaries themselves.[26]

'author-practitioners', see Pamela H. Smith, *From Lived Experience to the Written Word: Reconstructing Practical Knowledge in the Early Modern World* (Chicago, 2022).

[22] John Rule, 'The Property of Skill in the Period of Manufacture', in *The Historical Meanings of Work*, ed. Patrick Joyce (Cambridge, 1987).

[23] Shepard, *Accounting for Oneself*, ch. 1.

[24] Keith Wrightson, 'Sorts of People in Tudor and Stuart England', in *The Middling Sort of People: Culture, Society and Politics in England*, ed. Jonathan Barry and Christopher Brooks (Basingstoke, 1994).

[25] This narrative is most closely associated with the work of Keith Wrightson, but for its wider influence see the essays in *Remaking English Society: Social Relations and Social Change in Early Modern England*, ed. Steve Hindle, Alexandra Shepard and John Walter (Woodbridge, 2013).

[26] Indeed, even the 'middling sort' did not necessarily see themselves clearly as such: Henry French, *The Middle Sort of People in Provincial England, 1600–1750* (Oxford, 2007).

What happens, then, if we put working identities at the centre of our thinking about social dynamics in this period? They have the potential, we would argue, to disrupt some of our existing models of social change. There is evidence, for instance, that working identities could cut across the model of polarising 'sorts'. One element of that model relates to a process of 'cultural polarisation' that was driven by rising rates of literacy among the 'middling sort', who came to increasingly inhabit a mental world shared with their reading and writing superiors – whilst simultaneously growing apart from the cultural mores of the lower-sort 'rabble that cannot read'.[27] But the rise of literacy and of cheap print tells a different story when viewed through the lens of working identity. For Joseph Bufton it was his own literacy skills that allowed him to participate in and promote – through reading, record keeping and the composition of poetry – a solidarity across the cloth working industry, bridging a gap between richer and poorer members of the trade.[28] For many more tradesmen the growth of the ballad market provided access to a corpus of material that promoted an identity based on values of honesty and manual work that cannot be described as straightforwardly middling – and was in many ways hostile to elements of the commercial middling sort as well as to the gentry.[29] In both of these cases, the rise of literacy and its associated products did not simply serve to reinforce a process of social polarisation, but fed into forms of social identity that often cut across a neat division between the middling and lower sorts.

A focus on work-based identities also serves to highlight key divisions within the 'lower sorts' in particular. The 'honest tradesmen' sought to distance themselves from groups they considered to be beneath them: the dependent and the idle in particular.[30] They very likely saw themselves as a cut above those who lived only by their labour, but they in turn asserted that their industry set them apart from idlers, and from the more dependent status of servants. Likewise, as we have seen, the distinction that contemporaries made between a 'good housewife' and an 'idle housewife' were as much about these women's diligence and household management as about their family's income or assets.[31] These identities could also cut across lines of gender at the same time as demarcating those between sections of the lower sorts, with Shepard finding that for labouring men and women 'their opportunities to forge solidarities in terms of honest industry were far greater than the formation of collective identities uniting labourers with servants'.[32] The distinction between the 'industrious' labouring man or woman and their poorer neighbours may also have been a key and growing division as the seventeenth century developed.[33] Paying greater attention to these working identities therefore reveals a series of solidarities and fault lines at play in early modern

---

[27] Keith Wrightson, *English Society, 1580–1680* (1982), ch. 7. The phrase is Richard Baxter's.
[28] Waddell, 'Verses'.
[29] Hailwood, '"The Honest Tradesman's Honour"'.
[30] Hailwood, 'Sociability, Work and Labouring Identity'.
[31] Walker, 'Expanding the Boundaries of Female Honour', 238–40.
[32] Shepard, *Accounting for Oneself*, 189.
[33] Muldrew, *Food, Energy and the Creation of Industriousness*, chs. 4 and 7.

social relations that do not map neatly onto the model of 'sorts' and social polarisation.

If thinking about working identities might cause us to question the emphasis placed on the rise of 'sorts', it also encourages us to reflect on other narratives of chronological change. Traditionally scholars have suggested that working identities in this period were shifting from a 'medieval' to a 'modern' form, with a narrow 'craft' consciousness giving way to a broader 'class' consciousness over the course of the early modern period. However, recent research has shown that this linear narrative cannot explain the many cross-currents of change and continuity in this period. For example, the decline of guilds as a source of men's working identity in the seventeenth century has probably been exaggerated, especially outside the mercantile elite of the London Livery Companies.[34] More importantly, as noted above, the rise of literacy among working people and the spread of cheap print likely strengthened rather than weakened many 'craft' and 'trade' identities, whilst at the same time encouraging broader alliances across occupational groupings. Among the wider population, Shepard has found people increasingly describing their own place in society by specifying how they earned a living, rather than how much they were worth, but rarely in a conventionally 'class conscious' way.[35] While we do not yet have a new narrative that can fully replace the 'craft' to 'class' teleology, newer scholarship is increasingly recognising and tracing the changing ways that people's work gave them a sense of identity. Further work in this vein has the potential to provide a deeper understanding of the genealogies of modern forms of class consciousness, and to encourage conversations about the nature of 'class' and working identity across the premodern/modern divide.

Although working identity was prevalent and powerful – much more prevalent and powerful than, for example, narrowly occupational identity – it was not universal or evenly distributed. A sixteenth-century husbandman, a seventeenth-century mantua maker and an eighteenth-century merchant might all have strong working identities, but they cannot be simply lumped together as 'workers'. Moreover, many of the conclusions that historians have drawn about these identities have been heavily influenced by the specific types of sources they have used. If we want to understand working identities, and develop new narratives of their development over time, we need to think more methodically about these variations.

The centrality of gender to both social identity and working life in early modern England is now well established by decades of scholarship, and recent research has shown that these two issues overlapped in highly gendered ways. As we have seen, focusing narrowly on formal occupational titles makes it appear that only men had meaningful working identities. Not only were these titles often restricted to men, it has become increasingly clear that they were often linked to specific ideals of patriarchal manhood and fraternal

---

[34] Brodie Waddell, *God, Duty and Community in English Economic Life, 1660–1720* (Woodbridge, 2012), 194–206.

[35] Shepard, *Accounting for Oneself*, ch. 7.

pride. When the wool combers of Coggeshall called upon each other to 'play the men' by supporting a common fund for workers in the trade in the 1680s, they were asserting an unambiguously masculine notion of occupational community.[36] However, working identity was also widespread among women. Sometimes this operated in similar ways to men, such as the many women in late seventeenth- and early eighteenth-century London who asserted formal occupational titles and laid claim to the Freedom of the City through the Livery Companies.[37] Most women worked in less formally organised trades, yet they too might be seen by those around them as defined by their livelihoods. Although the 'midwife', 'oyster wench', 'alewife' and 'marketwoman' may not have had a guild, they had a working identity that was just as potent as any wool comber's or shoemaker's.[38] In many other cases, women's working identities took very different forms from men's, but were no less important. This is most striking in the case of titles such as 'wife', 'housewife' or 'mistress' which were used constantly in this period. As Alex Shepard and Amy Erickson have shown, these were often as much occupational identities as they were marital statuses.[39] By treating them as such, we can integrate unpaid work into our understanding of working identities. Using gender as a category of analysis for approaching these questions ensures that formal male occupational designations are not assumed to be the norm, thus opening up many other expressions of working identity to analysis.

Geography was another important factor in shaping such expressions, yet few historians have made any attempt to decipher the relationship between 'place' and working identities. Craft loyalties in incorporated cities – especially in London – have rightly received attention. Thanks to long-standing institutional structures in the form of guilds, high levels of literacy and print availability, and an exceptional degree of occupational specialisation, many urban workers would naturally identify closely with their specific trade. But focusing on these environments risks making a particular form of work-based identity the standard against which all others are measured. The existence of fierce

---

[36] Waddell, 'Verses', 9.

[37] Erickson, 'Married Women's Occupations'; Laura Gowing, 'Girls on Forms: Apprenticing Young Women in Seventeenth-Century London', *Journal of British Studies*, 55 (2016), 447–73; Sarah Birt, 'Women, Guilds and the Tailoring Trades: The Occupational Training of Merchant Taylors' Company Apprentices in Early Modern London', *London Journal*, 46:2 (2021), 146–64; Gowing, *Ingenious Trade*.

[38] Eleanor Hubbard, *City Women: Money, Sex and the Social Order in Early Modern London* (2012), ch. 6; Tim Reinke-Williams, *Women, Work and Sociability in Early Modern London* (Basingstoke, 2014); David Pennington, *Going to Market: Women, Trade and Social Relations in Early Modern English Towns, c. 1550-1650* (Farnham, 2015); Charlie Taverner, 'Consider the Oyster Seller: Street Hawkers and Gendered Stereotypes in Early Modern London', *History Workshop Journal*, 88 (Autumn 2019), 1–23.

[39] Amy Louise Erickson, 'Mistresses and Marriage: or, a Short History of the Mrs', *History Workshop Journal*, 78 (Autumn 2014), 39–57; Shepard, *Accounting for Oneself*, especially ch. 6. For similar arguments in a continental European context, see Merry E. Wiesner, 'Spinning out Capital: Women's Work in Preindustrial Europe, 1350–1750', in *Becoming Visible: Women in European History*, ed. Renate Bridenthal, Susan Mosher Stuard and Merry E. Wiesner (Boston, MA/New York 1998), 216–17; Darlene Abreu-Ferreira, 'Work and Identity in Early Modern Portugal: What Did Gender Have to Do with It?', *Journal of Social History* (Summer 2022), 859–87.

craft loyalties can also be found among tradesmen in unchartered small towns and even rural areas, but here they took different forms due to the lack of formal institutional support. The cloth trade, for example, offered a powerful source of identity to many men in Essex, Gloucestershire and Somerset.[40] Likewise, Andy Wood and Simon Sandall have shown that free miners in the Peak District and the Forest of Dean had an exceptionally well-honed sense of fraternal unity.[41] Equally strong was the spirit of collective endeavour that emerged from maritime work, whether linked to a particular fishing village or to 'a floating factory' traversing the oceans.[42] However, it is less clear how locality and work intertwined in the identities of, for example, agricultural labourers. We know that they had a strong sense of place, but we still have much to learn about how this might have related to their sense of themselves as workers. For some, the links between their daily tasks, their long-term livelihoods, the local landscape and the particular 'customs' of their manor must have been very close indeed.[43] When we broaden our lens to include English men and women in places like Ulster, Massachusetts, Virginia or Jamaica, the importance of locality to self-identity becomes obvious. To be a 'servant' or 'yeoman' in one of these colonies potentially meant something very different from the same label in the metropole.

Approaching working life in England from an Atlantic perspective highlights an aspect of this topic that became much more significant in this period: the deepening cleavage between 'free' and 'unfree' labour. Servants hired on traditional annual contracts, as noted above, might be seen as 'dependent' yet their livelihoods still offered a potential source of pride and respect that was unavailable to the growing numbers of individuals whose work was explicitly coerced.[44] Poor 'masterless' young people were increasingly pushed into various forms of judicially imposed labour: compulsory service, pauper apprenticeships, houses of correction and workhouses.[45] Moreover, with the establishment of colonies in North America and the Caribbean, tens of thousands of English men, women and children were sent to labour overseas through various forms of bondage ranging from supposedly consensual

---

[40] Waddell, 'Verses'; David Rollison, *The Local Origins of Modern Society: Gloucestershire 1500-1800* (1992); Hailwood, 'Broadside Ballads', 196-7.

[41] Andy Wood, *The Politics of Social Conflict: The Peak Country, 1520-1770* (Cambridge, 1999); Simon Sandall, *Custom and Popular Memory in the Forest of Dean, c.1550-1832* (Atlanta, 2013).

[42] Peter Linebaugh and Marcus Rediker, *The Many-Headed Hydra: Sailors, Slaves, Commoners and the Hidden History of the Revolutionary Atlantic* (2000), 150; Cheryl A. Fury (ed.), *The Social History of English Seamen, 1485-1649* (Woodbridge, 2012); Cheryl A. Fury (ed.), *The Social History of English Seamen, 1650-1815* (Martlesham, 2017).

[43] Andy Wood, *The Memory of the People: Custom and Popular Senses of the Past in Early Modern England* (Cambridge, 2013).

[44] Mansell, 'Beyond the Home'.

[45] Tim Wales, '"Living at their own hands": Policing Poor Households and the Young in Early Modern Rural England', *Agricultural History Review*, 61 (2013), 19-39; Steve Hindle, *On the Parish: The Micro-Politics of Poor Relief in Rural England c.1500-1750* (Oxford, 2004), esp. ch. 3; Joanna Innes, 'Prisons for the Poor: English Bridewells 1555-1800', in *Labour, Law and Crime: An Historical Perspective*, ed. Francis Snyder and Douglas Hay (1987), 42-122.

long-term indentures to kidnapping or convict transportation.[46] Compulsion and coercion had always been a part of labour relations in England, but they became more salient as both domestic and colonial policies promoted forceful forms of labour discipline.

Of course a rising proportion of workers in the colonies were enslaved Africans and their descendants whose exploitation and oppression was far worse than anything experienced by white indentured servants or transported convicts. Their efforts to resist the commodification of their bodies and to assert control over their productive and reproductive labour remind us that a lack of records about people's self-identity should not be taken for passivity or inarticulacy.[47] Moreover, some of them ended up in England as 'servants' of ambiguous status, where many refused their assigned identity as permanently 'servile' workers through lawsuits or absconding.[48] Whilst historians have explored attitudes to forms of 'unfree' labour in colonial settings, what we do not yet know is how these trends shaped the identities of 'free' English workers in the metropole.[49] They could not help but be aware of the threat of coerced labour and the precarity of their own freedom, yet finding direct evidence of their attitudes towards this division is not easy. Literary scholars have shown one possible avenue by investigating the rise of racialised categories in drama, poetry and art, which often associated liberty with whiteness and servitude with blackness.[50] Furthermore, questions about the relationship between 'service' and 'consent' were already firmly embedded in English culture thanks to classical, biblical and medieval examples.[51] Even if not always overtly racialised, anxieties about servile bondage certainly circulated among English workers. In one late seventeenth-century ballad, for example,

---

[46] John Wareing, '"Violently taken away or cheatingly duckoyed": The Illicit Recruitment in London of Indentured Servants for the American Colonies, 1645–1718', *London Journal*, 26:2 (2001), 1–22; Anna Suranyi, '"Willing to go if they had their clothes": Early Modern Women and Indentured Servitude', in *Challenging Orthodoxies: The Social and Cultural Worlds of Early Modern Women*, ed. Sigrun Haude and Melinda S. Zook (Farnham, 2014); Misha Ewen, '"Poore Soules": Migration, Labour, and Visions for Commonwealth in Virginia', in *Virginia 1619: Slavery and Freedom in the Making of English America*, ed. Paul Musselwhite, Peter C. Mancall and James Horn (Chapel Hill, 2019).

[47] Jennifer L. Morgan, *Reckoning with Slavery: Gender, Kinship and Capitalism in the Early Black Atlantic* (Durham, NC, 2021), esp. ch. 6.

[48] Imtiaz Habib, *Black Lives in the English Archives, 1500–1677: Imprints of the Invisible* (Aldershot, 2008); Susan Dwyer Amussen, *Caribbean Exchanges: Slavery and the Transformation of English Society, 1640–1700* (Chapel Hill, 2007), ch. 6; Simon P. Newman, *Freedom Seekers: Escaping from Slavery in Restoration London* (2022).

[49] Simon P. Newman, *A New World of Labor: The Development of Plantation Slavery in the British Atlantic* (Philadelphia, 2013); Christopher L. Tomlins, *Freedom Bound: Law, Labor, and Civic Identity in Colonizing English America, 1580–1865* (Cambridge, 2010); Jennifer L. Morgan, *Laboring Women: Reproduction and Gender in New World Slavery* (Philadelphia, 2004).

[50] Kim F. Hall, *Things of Darkness: Economies of Race and Gender in Early Modern England* (1995); Ayanna Thompson (ed.), *The Cambridge Companion to Shakespeare and Race* (Cambridge, 2021).

[51] Urvashi Chakravarty, *Fictions of Consent: Slavery, Servitude, and Free Service in Early Modern England* (Philadelphia, 2022); Naomi Tadmor, *The Social Universe of the English Bible: Scripture, Society, and Culture in Early Modern England* (Cambridge, 2010), ch. 3; Michael Guasco, *Slaves and Englishmen: Human Bondage in the Early Modern Atlantic World* (Philadelphia, 2014), esp. ch. 1.

a 'Trappan'd Maiden' rhetorically laments that since arriving in 'Virginny' she has faced endless back-breaking labour and inhumane treatment: 'No rest that I can have, Whilst I am here a Slave'.[52] Legal freedom to choose one's employment and seek redress against abusive masters – the right of a 'freeborn Englishman' – thus may have become an increasingly important component in the identity of many workers, and further work on popular perceptions of this issue should be a high priority for scholars.[53]

We can only glimpse evidence of the role of work in social identity through the uneven and incomplete range of sources that have survived from the early modern period. Unfortunately, social and gender biases in literacy rates and related factors mean that relatively few working people have left us unmediated insight into how they saw themselves. Nonetheless, some such sources can be found in the archives, and innovative methodologies have made it possible to find traces of self-expression in other early modern records. The problem that has since arisen is the way each new study of this topic has tended to focus on a single type of source rather than analysing a wider range of contrasting genres. For example, the working identities that feature in diaries and other life-writing are naturally more individualist and nuanced than the occupational ideals promoted in commercial publications such as broadside ballads.[54] Likewise, self-descriptions in court depositions are conveniently numerous and socially inclusive, yet their inherent emphasis on 'worth' and credibility necessarily shapes the sorts of identities that are expressed in them.[55] We need to make more effort to draw comparisons across different genres to understand the nature of work-based identities. Expanding our source base to include other types of texts is a key first step. For instance, a different ideal of work and occupation might emerge in the self-descriptions used by petitioners in the thousands of surviving written requests submitted to local and national authorities, such as the 'verie good worke-man' who asked permission to build a cottage in Burton-by-Tarvin in Cheshire so that 'he might be readye to be helpfull to us his said neighbours in his worke as he hath bene hearetofore'.[56] Likewise, as Laura Gowing has shown, women's

---

[52] *The Trappan'd Maiden: Or, The Distressed Damsel. This Girl was cunningly trappan'd, Sent to Virginny from England* (1693–1695?), English Broadside Ballad Archive, ID 37023. For a detailed examination of the conceptual slippage between service and slavery, and the ways existing categories were used to forge new racialised ones, see Chakravarty, *Fictions of Consent*.

[53] For association between political and economic 'servitude' in this period, see Christopher Hill, 'Pottage for Freeborn Englishmen: Attitudes to Wage Labour in the 16th and 17th Centuries', in *Socialism, Capitalism and Economic Growth: Essays Presented to Maurice Dobb*, ed. Maurice Dobb and C. H. Feinstein (Cambridge, 1967); John Donoghue, *Fire under the Ashes: An Atlantic History of the English Revolution* (Chicago, 2013).

[54] For the former, see Paul, 'Accounting for Men's Work'. For the latter see Hailwood, 'Broadside Ballads'.

[55] Shepard, *Accounting for Oneself*, 10–27.

[56] 'Cheshire Quarter Sessions: 1618', in *Petitions to the Cheshire Quarter Sessions, 1573–1798*, ed. Sharon Howard, *British History Online*, www.british-history.ac.uk/petitions/cheshire/1618. For detailed examinations of paupers' self-presentation in petitions for relief, see Hindle, *On the Parish*, ch. 6; Jonathan Healey, *The First Century of Welfare: Poverty and Poor Relief in Lancashire, 1620–1730* (Woodbridge, 2014).

petitions for the privilege to practise a trade can provide insight into the distinctively gendered way they were forced to express their place in the City's trades.[57] We must pay particular attention to the differences between how people identified themselves as workers and how they were labelled by their neighbours, their social superiors and state officials. Now that the importance of these identities has been revealed, we need scholars to undertake direct comparisons between the widening range of sources to begin to piece together the multifaceted nature of working identities.

Working identity cannot – and should not – replace class, gender, race, religion or any of the other powerful concepts already central to historical analysis of early modern society. It does, however, have the potential to be more than merely an addition to the long list of potential categories by which scholars label their subjects.

Recent research on the power of work as a source of identity has – sometimes inadvertently – undermined common assumptions about social relations in this period. This article has been an attempt to bring together some of that scholarship to show more clearly how cumulatively it challenges a model of early modern society based on 'sorts of people' and unilinear 'social polarisation'. It has also highlighted the ways that new research on this topic will need to go further by adopting a wider frame of reference. Specifically, we need to better integrate our analyses of the various types of primary sources that we have available, explicitly comparing 'literary' and 'archival', 'self-created' and 'indirectly recorded', so as to better understand how the nature of the source shapes the expression of such identities. We need to know much more about variations in working identities across time, place, gender, forms of labour, and race. Again, direct comparisons between the evidence from early and late in the period, from city and country, from men and women, and from free and unfree workers, are vital because they will illuminate the limits of using the urban male artisan as the default standard of vocational pride. Examining how the rise of Atlantic colonialism and racialised slavery influenced the self-identity of English workers is particularly important for pushing this subfield beyond its parochial origins. New research along these lines – building on the recent scholarship highlighted above – could have major implications for our understanding of early modern society, and for long-term narratives about social change.

Finally, a reminder that this piece is intended as a spur to new research rather than an exhaustive review of a rapidly growing subfield. We have not tried to cover every issue and we expect that many further examples and counter-examples will have occurred to readers as they worked through this article. The task now is to marshal this evidence within a broader and stronger framework than has been used so far. A narrow focus on occupational titles or formal institutions vastly underestimates the way that work shaped social identity in the early modern period.

---

[57] Gowing, *Ingenious Trade*, ch. 6.

Cite this article: Hailwood M, Waddell B (2023). Work and Identity in Early Modern England. *Transactions of the Royal Historical Society* 1, 145–158. https://doi.org/10.1017/S0080440123000038

Transactions of the RHS (2023), **1**, 159–189
doi:10.1017/S0080440123000051

ARTICLE

Equality, Proportionality and Statistics: Political Representation from the English to the French and American Revolutions

Lars Behrisch

Department of History and Art History, Utrecht University, Utrecht, The Netherlands
Email: l.behrisch@uu.nl

(Received 23 October 2022; revised 23 May 2023; accepted 24 May 2023; first published online 26 June 2023)

Abstract

Debates on the proportionality of political representation surfaced repeatedly, and in similar forms, from the English to the American and French Revolutions. They contributed to shaping those revolutions' outcomes and, through them, to the emergence of modern democracy – especially so as they were linked up with voting rights: demands to make seats in assemblies more numerically proportionate to electorates – in other words, to weigh all votes equally – implied the equal weight of individual votes and thus also entailed calls for more equal standards regarding the right to vote. This did not yet signify voting rights for all: only specific categories of individuals – as a rule, male and propertied – were considered, even by the most 'enlightened' writers, to be politically entitled. Nevertheless, it was only one step from here to envisage voting rights for all individuals – or at least, for the time being, for all male individuals – as can also be seen in all three revolutions. If claims for more proportional and equal representation showed their full impact only on the American and French Revolutions, finally, this was due to the intervening emergence of statistics (or 'political arithmetic') as a tool of reflection and debate that gave numbers and calculations increasing persuasive power.

Keywords: History of democracy; voting rights; political equality; political arithmetic; revolutions

Introduction

Debates on the proportionality of political representation surfaced repeatedly, and in similar forms, in the 150 years from the English to the American and French Revolutions. They contributed to shaping those revolutions' outcomes and, through them, also to the emergence of modern democracy – the more so as they were closely linked to the issue of voting rights. Detailed retracing of those debates will show consistent patterns and reveal their specific contribution to those revolutions and to the (pre)history of modern democracy.[1]

As democracy is under pressure today, it is important to reconsider the historical conditions of its genesis. The idea that representative democracy is a necessary long-term outcome of history is not only challenged by populist parties; it has also been discredited, on a conceptual level, by postmodernist theory. This article shares this sceptical attitude towards the notion, prevalent among earlier generations, of an all-but natural, gradual gravitation towards democratic government during the seventeenth and eighteenth centuries. Recent studies on European states and regions have shown that neither Estate assemblies nor popular rebellions were usually poised for broader forms of political participation before the late eighteenth century. Until then, in fact, participation often became yet more restricted and oligarchical across Europe, including Britain.

This article will contribute to understanding the elements that *did* finally make modern representative democracy plausible and possible by focusing on one such element: the evolution of demands to make seats in assemblies more numerically proportionate to electorates, or, in other words, to weigh all votes cast more equally. As such demands implied the equal weight of individual voices and votes – self-evident to us but sharply contradicting traditional hierarchies and collective identities, so firmly entrenched at the time – they also entailed new demands for equal standards regarding the *right* to vote. Equal standards did not, though, mean voting rights for all: only specific categories of individuals – male and propertied or otherwise economically viable – were considered, even by the most 'enlightened' writers, to be entitled to equal political rights. Yet, it was just one more step from here to envisage voting rights for *all* individuals or at least, for the time being, for all male individuals. This can be seen in all three revolutions, too, although such rights were fully implemented only in the twentieth century.

Claims for more proportional and, as a corollary, more equal representation came to the fore in the English no less than in the American and French Revolutions but they had a major and lasting impact only on the latter two. An important clue to this divergence, it will be argued, lies in the timing of the emergence of statistics, or 'political arithmetic' as it was then called. The growing persuasive power of numbers and calculations, from the second half of the seventeenth century onwards, proved decisive to underpin the related notions of proportionality and standardised individual voting rights in the later eighteenth century. The same numerical rationality, as we will see, too, would ultimately make those notions gravitate towards universal voting rights.

The article will point to some pivotal moments and elements of the discussions around these issues. It will not, and cannot, offer a complete and

---

[1] There is as yet no overarching study of the debates on the proportionality of voting and representation during the early modern period. Studies dealing with specific contexts will be referred to in the course of the article.

coherent account of the subject over the 150 years that its (early) history covers. Such an account will require more in-depth research and a book-length presentation. Still, the present article seeks to show the acuity and continuity of debates on the proportionality of representation across those 150 years and their relevance for democracy's (pre)history.

Setting the frame: civil war and Commonwealth

In England, the creation of ever more parliamentary seats for boroughs, particularly over the sixteenth century, had led to a massive preponderance of borough over county seats and, thus, to a highly disproportionate representation of the electorate as a whole.[2] It had also led to a steady increase in 'rotten boroughs' with few voters, so that among the boroughs, too, representation was becoming ever more uneven. As a result of constituencies' extremely divergent size and composition, the soon-to-be-revolutionary 'Long' Parliament of 1640 was further away from evenly representing the country than any of its predecessors. Still, setting aside some temporary changes in the 1650s, only very few alterations were to be made over the next two centuries. As a consequence of uneven population growth, moreover, parliamentary representation would become ever more distorted. Most notoriously, but not exceptionally, before the reform of 1832 the industrialising cities of Birmingham and Manchester had no seats in Parliament at all.

This state of affairs had been a matter of criticism already in the sixteenth century – but this was more partisan than principled, reflecting corporate or personal indignation over the fact that one's own home had no seat in Parliament. Nor were complaints accompanied by remarks on the fact that, quite apart from their divergent sizes, voting rights, too, differed massively between boroughs. (In the counties, the electorate was at least nominally on the same footing across the country as all owners of freehold land worth at least forty shillings a year were entitled to vote.) In a number of disputed cases in the first decades of the seventeenth century, particularly in the 1620s, Parliament resolved in favour of a larger franchise. But this did not flow from overarching principles, either: the Commons tended to favour broader voting rights mainly so as to diminish court influence on particularly small elite electorates.[3] Generally speaking, the absence of any actual competition among candidates meant that voting rights were a symbolic much rather than a real asset. Mostly, local and regional elites agreed before an 'election' on the two candidates to be chosen, while contested – and, in this sense, proper –

---

[2] The number of ninety county seats was almost entirely stable (with two 'knights of the shire' from each county in England and one from each in Wales). The overall number of just over 500 seats in 1640 (and after) was merely nominal, though, as attendance rarely exceeded 300 (on two occasions in spring 1641, a peak of 379 members is recorded: William J. Bulman, *The Rise of Majority Rule in Early Modern Britain and Its Empire* (Cambridge, 2021), 73, 78. Generally, it was around or below 200 – which was roughly the number which the Commons Hall (St Stephen's Chapel) could seat with ease: David L. Smith, *The Stuart Parliaments 1603-1689* (1999), 24.

[3] Derek Hirst, *The Representative of the People? Voters and Voting in England under the Early Stuarts* (Cambridge, 1975), 44–89.

elections with more than two candidates were rare. As a result, neither the number of voters nor, as a corollary, the entitlement to vote was much of an issue. This began to change in 1640: with the broader political struggle, elections became more competitive on the level of candidates and, thus, also of voters.[4]

Popular participation in politics generally widened in the 1640s in the face of massive political and religious contestation, civil war and revolution. Beginning in 1640 with the election, after eleven years without Parliament, of the Short and, after its speedy dissolution, the Long Parliament, the public's minds and souls became objects of campaigning – and so did its financial and physical resources, as war broke out in mid-1642. Print poured out in hitherto unknown quantities, appealing to the people at large and spelling out their enhanced political role. This translated into active participation by urban populations who started to sign, and to bring forward, political petitions in their thousands.[5] Such mobilisation was most intense in London – but it would also permeate the New Model Army whose officers and soldiers saw themselves as a political force and religious vanguard in their own right, especially after the decisive defeat of royal forces at Naseby in 1645. It was in those two particular social orbits, too, and around that same time, that intellectual radicals, later labelled 'Levellers', emerged to propagate a consistently individualised and bottom-up vision of society – and, indeed, a degree of egalitarian popular sovereignty unprecedented in either historical practice or theory.[6]

With the mobilisation of a broader public and an incipient rhetoric of empowerment of 'the nation' and 'the people', the question of who had the right to vote took on more relevance, too. Yet, a generic concept of *the* franchise, beyond the multiplicity of local franchises, was still not immediately evident and was not spelled out even by those who appealed to 'the people' or 'the nation' as the ultimate source of political power. This was certainly due, to some extent, to the absence of general elections after 1640 (hence, the 'Long' Parliament). But there was also a conspicuous absence of calls for a broader 'franchise' by either side, be it only to court popular support – an absence relatively more conspicuous in the case of Parliament which, in its struggle for legitimacy with the king, claimed to be the true representative of the people. After the (first) end of civil war in 1646, though, a notion of 'the' national franchise emerged due to two interlinking discourses: an insistence on equal, proportionate representation among all constituencies, spelled out by the Levellers; and the New Model Army soldiers' demand for their own individual

---

[4] Mark A. Kishlansky, *Parliamentary Selection: Social and Political Choice in Early Modern England* (Cambridge, 1986); Hirst, *Representative of the People?*; Smith, *Stuart Parliaments*, 25–9.

[5] David Zaret, *Origins of Democratic Culture: Printing, Petitions, and the Public Sphere in Early-Modern England* (Princeton, 2000); John Walter, *Covenanting Citizens: The Protestation Oath and Popular Political Culture in the English Revolution* (Oxford, 2017); Gary S. De Krey, *Following the Levellers*, vol. 1: *Political and Religious Radicals in the English Civil War and Revolution, 1645–1649* (2017).

[6] Rachel Foxley, *The Levellers: Radical Political Thought in the English Revolution* (Manchester, 2013); De Krey, *Following the Levellers*; Lorenzo Sabbadini, 'Popular Sovereignty and Representation in the English Civil War', in *Popular Sovereignty in Historical Perspective*, ed. Richard Bourke and Quentin Skinner (Cambridge, 2016).

share in future politics. Both of these claims merged in the autumn of 1647, catalysed by half a year of conflict with a parliament that refused any kind of redress.

In October 1646, Leveller figurehead John Lilburne, imprisoned at the hands of Parliament, denounced the 'insufferable injury, and wrong, that is done unto thousands of the freemen of England' by the highly uneven representation of regions and localities: Cornwall had 'almost 50 Parliament-men; and Yorkshire twice as big, and three times as populous, and rich, not half so many' – not to mention 'my poor Country the Bishoprick of Durham' with no seats in the Commons at all.[7] Lilburne therefore thought it 'a great deale of more Justice and Equity ... to proportion out to every County, [i.e.] to chuse a proportionable number, sutable to the Rates, that each County by their Bookes of Rates are assessed, to pay towards the defraying of the Publique charge of the Kingdome'.[8] Counties should be weighted according to their tax yields for parliamentary seats, and the same distributive principle was to apply within them.[9] Such a general redistribution of seats could also end the other injustice: uneven voting rights. For whilst 'divers ... men of great estates in money and stock' had no voice, some boroughs featured 'scarse any but Ale-housekeepers, and ignorant sots, who want principles to chuse any man, but only those, that ... some ... great man ... recommends; or else who bribes them for their votes'.[10] Lilburne here advances standard arguments against giving the vote to the poor – as being ignorant, unprincipled and prey to bribery. Thus, his first call for fairer representation is, rather surprisingly, not at all a plea for equal voting rights but one for more proportionality and equality among those men who were economically viable and independent.[11]

Half a year later, the army took up the issue in the midst of its confrontation, political as well as religious, with Parliament's Presbyterian majority. In mid-June 1647, with the antagonism approaching its climax – and two weeks after Lilburne had repeated his views[12] – very similar statements appeared in the first overtly political 'Representation of the Army':

... that some Provision may be now made for such Distribution of Elections for future Parliaments, as may stand with some Rule of Equality or

---

[7] John Lilburne, 'London's Liberty in Chains discovered', in *Tracts on Liberty by the Levellers and Their Critics (1638-1660)*, 7 vols., ed. David M. Hart and Ross Kenyon (Indianapolis, 2014–18), vol. 3 (1646), 332.

[8] *Ibid.*, 333.

[9] Electoral districts within each county were to be made 'equally and proportionable by the common consent of the People thereof to divide it ... into *Divisions, Hundreds,* or *Wapentakes* ... sutable to the proportion that comes to their share' (*ibid.*; emphases in the original). Borough elections were implicitly abandoned altogether in this scheme.

[10] *Ibid.*, 332.

[11] On Lilburne's more inclusive statements and the question of the coherence of his views see below, n. 28.

[12] John Lilburne, 'Rash Oaths Unwarrantable'; see Philip Baker, 'The Franchise Debate Revisited: The Levellers and the Army', in *The Nature of the English Revolution Revisited*, ed. Stephen Taylor and Grant Tapsell (Woodbridge, 2013), 109.

Proportion, as near as may be, to render the Parliament a more equal
Representative of the whole, as for Instance, that all Counties or
Divisions and Parts of the Kingdom ... may have a Number of
Parliament-Men ... proportionably to the respective Rates they bear in
the Common Charges ... of the kingdom, ... or some other such like Rule.[13]

While the gist of the demand is clearly the same as Lilburne's, other potential
criteria than mere tax returns are envisaged now to provide proportionality
among constituencies. The same demand was included in the 'Heads of the
Proposals', a more fully fledged constitutional scheme published at the beginning of August, after the army had secured control over Parliament. Again,
it stressed that seats could be reapportioned on the basis of taxation – or
'according to some other rule of equality or proportion'.[14] The most obvious
alternative was the number of people (or voters) in the constituencies,
but this was not as yet spelled out: this only happened in the famous
Agreement of the People, a more radical constitutional scheme drawn up in
October 1647, to be discussed presently. The radicalising potential of such
an alternative, however, was already present, in the summer, in the soldiers'
demands for a continuing and equal share in national politics. These
demands were a reaction, at least in part, to parliamentary threats of dis-
bandment – and thus degradation to soldiers' former, mostly lowly and politically impotent status – and to the peremptory manner in which Parliament
was handling the soldiers' grievances. The latter, moreover, began to equate
their own case with the nation's: the 'Representation of the Army' urged the
defence of 'our owne and the peoples just rights, and liberties', with the aim
that 'we, and all the free-born people of this Nation' could live quietly.[15]
A few months later, in mid-October 1647, 'The Case of the Army Truly
Stated' would develop these juxtapositions further, bracketing 'the Army
[and] the poore oppressed people of the nation', the 'rights and freedomes
of our selves and the people' and, in short, 'our own & the peoples case'.[16]
Consistent with such bold and potentially radical rhetoric, the 'Case of the
Army' for the first time also explicitly asked for broad, and potentially
even full, (male) voting rights.[17]

---

[13] *Tracts on Liberty*, ed. Hart and Kenyon, vol. 4 (1647), 151f. The clause is only in a variant version of this 'Declaration, or, Representation'; see Baker, 'Franchise Debate', 109; John Cannon,
Parliamentary Reform 1640–1832 (Cambridge, 1973), 6.

[14] Samuel R. Gardiner (ed.), *The Constitutional Documents of the Puritan Revolution 1625–1660*, 3rd edn
(Oxford, 1906), 317. As a first step, seats of puny boroughs were to be given to major counties. In
due course, future Commons should continue 'to reduce the elections of members for that House to
more and more perfection of equality in the distribution' (*ibid.*, 318).

[15] *Tracts on Liberty*, ed. Hart and Kenyon, vol. 4 (1647), 146, 143.

[16] *Ibid.*, 241f.

[17] 'that all the freeborn at the age of 21. yeares and upwards, be the electors' (*ibid.*, 253). On the
origin of the document, see Philip Baker and John Morrill, 'The Case of the Armie truly re-stated',
in *The Putney Debates of 1647: The Army, the Levellers and the English State*, ed. Michael Mendle
(Cambridge, 2001); De Krey, *Following the Levellers*, 131–4. On the ambiguous subclause of the franchise stipulation, see below, n. 24.

Both strands of demands – for a more equal representation *and* for the soldiers' and, at least by extension, other men's voting rights – were to merge fully in the propositions made at the Putney debates in late October 1647. It was only here that *the* (national) 'franchise' became a topic proper, although even now the term was not employed.[18] The *Agreement of the People*, drawn up on the eve of the debate and serving as its starting point,[19] was silent on voting rights – but it did state for the first time explicitly, and prominently, that constituencies 'ought to be more indifferently proportioned according to the number of the inhabitants'.[20] Although all participants in the debate, including also the army leadership under Cromwell, essentially agreed on this, the clause led to the explosive opening question by General Henry Ireton: did it signify only 'that every man that is an inhabitant is to be equally considered' when creating proportionality among constituencies – something he might concur with – or was it *also* supposed to mean that every man was 'to have an equal voice in the election of the representers'?[21] In which case, he stated, 'I have something to say against it'.[22] The challenge was borne squarely by Maximilian Petty: 'We judge that all inhabitants that have not lost their birthright should have an equal voice in elections.'[23] The question of the franchise in the debate thus arose from the *Agreement*'s apportionment clause; and it was immediately divisive, with Ireton, Cromwell and other officers defending existing franchise regulations, and some officers, soldiers and civilians arguing for a sweeping franchise extension – possibly to include *all* adult males.

Ironically, the franchise debate at Putney is still almost as controversial now as it was then. Ever since its protocols surfaced in the late nineteenth century, it has elicited countless interpretations and counter-interpretations – but the specific content of the plea for franchise extensions has remained, and probably always will remain, something of an unassailable black box. The search for a coherent stance, especially on the side of the Levellers and/or the army 'radicals', is understandable in view of the later historical relevance of the franchise and also in view of the fascinating exchanges that the issue occasioned at Putney. The search might, however, be somewhat anachronistic: in

---

[18] The term seems to have been used only in the sense of local franchises throughout the 1640s (or else only in negative verbs, such as 'disfranchise'). Nor were there other generic terms, such as 'the vote'. At Putney, the usual terminology was '[a] voice[s] in [an] election[s]'.

[19] On the origins of the *Agreement* see below, esp. n. 27.

[20] The first stipulation of the *Agreement* reads, 'we declare ... that the people of England being at this day very unequally distributed by counties, cities and boroughs for the election of their deputies in parliament, ought to be more indifferently proportioned according to the number of the inhabitants: the circumstances whereof, for number, place, and manner, are to be set down before the end of this present parliament'. Andrew Sharp (ed.), *The English Levellers* (Cambridge, 1998), 93f.

[21] *Ibid.*, 102.

[22] *Ibid.* Later in the debate, Ireton (main author of the recent army 'Heads of the Proposals') put the officers' position succinctly: 'I think I agreed to this matter, that all should be equally distributed. But the question is whether it should be distributed to *all persons*, or whether the *same* persons that are the electors now should be the electors still, and it be equally distributed amongst *them*' (*ibid.*, 107; emphases in the original).

[23] *Ibid.*, 102. On Petty see below, n. 27.

contrast to the proportionality issue, the franchise question was so novel and so abruptly introduced, and it evolved so haphazardly during the debate – which is partly why it is so fascinating – that we cannot assume that individual speakers had arrived with a consistent view on it, let alone sharing a view between them. In any case, though, it seems by now generally acknowledged that the intricacies of the nuances in terminology and statement, conscious or fortuitous, are impossible to disentangle completely. The impression that clear pronouncements for a full male franchise *were* made during the debate is strong – but again, it might well be biased by the anachronistic assumptions of us modern readers, as first argued by Crawford B. Macpherson.[24] When it came to settling for a compromise after the debate, moreover, the soldiers were ready to exclude servants and receivers of alms, as long only as they themselves were given the vote regardless of their previous social status.[25]

Another, overlapping debate concerns the extent and timing of the influence of Leveller leaders and ideas on the army, the *Agreement* and the debates at Putney.[26] Those London political radicals most prominent in the context of the last two also seem to have created vital links, by the autumn of 1647, between the army and Leveller writings and ideas.[27] But while Leveller notions concerning individual rights, basic equality and popular sovereignty certainly exerted a strong influence, directly and indirectly, on New Model Army political radicalism, it is hard to establish an immediate contribution of their core figures – John Lilburne, William Walwyn and Richard Overton – to the *Agreement*, to the Putney debates and, indeed, to the discussion of the franchise.[28] In any case, crucial for our context is the point – not made in this

---

[24] Crawford B. Macpherson, *The Political Theory of Possessive Individualism: Hobbes to Locke* (Oxford, 1962), 107–36. He argued, among other things, that all general statements came with some addition or exception, such as Petty's 'all inhabitants that have not lost their birthright' or, in 'The Case of the Army', the subclause to 'all the freeborne' – namely, 'excepting those that have or shall deprive themselves of that their freedome, either for some yeares, or wholly by delinquency' (*Tracts on Liberty*, ed. Hart and Kenyon, vol. 4 (1647), 253) – that can be read as aiming at servants and apprentices, too. All concrete pronouncements on the franchise, during and beyond the debate, explicitly excluded at least servants and receivers of alms (see also below, n. 31).

[25] Baker, 'Franchise Debate', 112f.; Foxley, *Levellers*, 179.

[26] Foxley, *Levellers*, esp. 150–84, stresses a continuous and broad Leveller influence – and sees the Putney stance as endorsing a genuine Leveller insistence on full male voting rights (109f., 177f.). Baker, 'Franchise Debate', considers soldiers' demands to be more independent from Leveller influence – particularly their (at least at Putney) more radically egalitarian stance on the franchise (see also Philip Baker and Elliot Vernon, 'What Was the First *Agreement of the People*?', *The Historical Journal*, 53 (2010); Baker and Morrill, 'Case of the Armie').

[27] First and foremost, Maximilian Petty, John Wildman, Colonel (and MP) Thomas Rainborough and the soldier Edward Sexby. They seem to have been immediately involved, together with the army's 'New Agents', in the drafting of the *Agreement*: De Krey, *Following the Levellers*, esp. 130–6, 147–56 (arguing that the Levellers came into existence proper only in this context, 134–6, 155f.).

[28] None of them made a clear statement on the franchise in general. Lilburne's 'free-born Englishman' may stand for all men, as argued by Foxley, *Levellers*, 92–9; and Lilburne did assert his political role as a matter of principle: 'the poorest that lives, hath as true a right to give a vote as well as the richest and greatest' ('Charters of London', December 1646, in *Tracts on Liberty*, ed. Hart and Kenyon, vol. 3, 387; see also his 'Postscript to The freeman's freedom vindicated' of June 1646, in *English Levellers*, ed. Sharp, 31f.). But when it came to making concrete

way before – that against a background of evolving political radicalism, most consistently represented by the Levellers, it was only the convergence of a specific Leveller insistence on the proportionality of parliamentary representation, on the one hand, and of the soldiers' demand for their own voting rights, on the other, that first put 'the franchise' (and its enlargement) on the agenda. In this perspective, the franchise debate did not hinge on any specific Leveller notion – which doesn't seem to have existed – of who ought to be enfranchised. It did, however, hinge on their insistence on equal representation in Parliament irrespective of a person's social status or place of residence (if not of his economic viability). To this end, the uneven distribution of seats among counties and boroughs ought to give way to their strictly proportional distribution across the country. It has been said that the Levellers precociously conceived of a generalised 'liberty' pertaining to all individuals, in place of the various traditional collective liber*ties*.[29] In the same vein, it can be said that they framed an overarching national space of equal representation, fundamental for discussing *the* franchise – but not equivalent to its extension.

In fact, as we have already seen, while Lilburne wanted to end the inequality of representation, he consistently wanted to do so on the basis of tax yields – in 1646, again in 1647, and yet again in 1648, after population figures had already been mooted as the potentially better yardstick.[30] (It is also true, of course, that tax yields were much more easily available than population data.) Lilburne also wanted to synchronise voting rights across the nation: but rather than pleading for a full franchise, he had explicitly added a rationale for excluding the lowlier sort from the vote – a rationale mirrored by the contours of his more concrete franchise proposals.[31] It is obvious that a fiscally based proportionality of representation, on the one hand, and an individual economic (or fiscal) threshold for the right to vote, on the other, obeyed the same logic: those, and only those, who contribute materially to society and are not dependent on others should have an equal say in politics. Conversely, it also seems obvious that proportionality based on sheer numbers

---

proposals, Lilburne only referred to the rights of local (London) *freemen*, a more restricted category: Philip Baker, '*Londons Liberty in Chains Discovered*: The Levellers, the Civic Past, and Popular Protest in Civil War London', *Huntington Library Quarterly*, 76 (2013); idem, 'Franchise Debate', 108f., 115–21; Foxley, *Levellers*, 93f., 111f.; Hilary M. Larkin, *The Making of Englishmen: Debates on National Identity 1550–1650* (Leiden, 2013), 243, 245f. See also below, n. 31.

[29] Foxley, *Levellers*, 97–9.

[30] For Lilburne's 1648 proposals, see next footnote. Foxley, *Levellers*, 178, renders the relevant passage in 'Rash Oaths Unwarrantable' (May 1647, see above, n. 12) somewhat misleadingly: Lilburne here reiterated the plea made half a year before to base the apportionment of seats on tax contributions, not on population.

[31] The wording of that rationale, quoted above, points to the same sort of people that Lilburne's own version of the second *Agreement* (or else *Foundations of Freedom*, December 1648) would exclude – not only receivers of alms, servants and wage-earners, but also those not contributing to poor relief (*Tracts on Liberty*, ed. Hart and Kenyon, vol. 5 (1648), 318). Lilburne's version diverged from the officers' version of January 1649 (see below, n. 33) on a number of points, but not on this one (*Constitutional Documents*, ed. Gardiner, 363). Other Leveller declarations, including their renegade third *Agreement* of May 1649 (*English Levellers*, ed. Sharp, 170), would exclude at least alms-takers and servants. See also above, n. 28.

of people entailed a somewhat different logic – namely, to give the vote to all those very people, or at least to all adult men among them. For if each and every person was to count as '1' in apportioning parliamentary seats, it could seem just as logical that (at least) every man should also have the vote. Precisely this is the 'radical' reading of the Putney debates.

It was the first logic that was pursued into the Commonwealth period – at least in part, as the franchise extension envisaged by Lilburne, while endorsed by the army leaders, never materialised.[32] The plea for a more equally proportioned parliament, on the other hand, was not only given renewed rhetorical emphasis in 1649:[33] rather, after the 'Rump' Parliament had sat out any effective changes,[34] the 'Instrument of Government' of December 1653, establishing the Commonwealth of England, Scotland and Ireland together with the Protectorate, fixed 'proportions' among constituencies – according to their tax yields.[35] As a result, the elections of 1654 and 1656 were of a more proportionate nature than any others before the nineteenth century.

The apportionment reform died together with the Protector.[36] Yet, the dozen years in which it had been intensely discussed, and at least partly put into practice, had created templates to be evoked over and over again for many decades to come. As with other features of the republican experiment, they would also spur on more systematic reflection – reflection on how to

---

[32] On the franchise provisions in the second *Agreement* of 1648/9, see the previous footnote. Some minor and ambivalent adjustments were made in 1653, as the traditional forty-shilling threshold in county constituencies was turned into a £200 property threshold – which was higher, but less exclusive in terms of the *kind* of property owned. *Constitutional Documents*, ed. Gardiner, 411; Cannon, *Parliamentary Reform*, 17ff.; Blair Worden, *The Rump Parliament 1648-1653* (Cambridge, 1974), 158f. The changes were duly rescinded with the Restoration.

[33] The officers' *Agreement* (January 1649) urged to reapportion seats even more strongly than in its first, 1647 version. It also contained a list with appropriate numbers of MPs from each county and borough (*Constitutional Documents*, ed. Gardiner, 360-3), drawn up by Lilburne (see also his own version, in *Tracts on Liberty*, ed. Hart and Kenyon, vol. 5 (1648), 317f.; the changes made by the officers were relatively minor, see also Worden, *Rump Parliament*, 144). It was, in all likelihood, based on constituencies' tax yields, but this was not spelled out. Cannon, *Parliamentary Reform*, 10, identifies the 1636 Ship Money assessment as Lilburne's yardstick (see also Paul Slack, 'Government and Information in Seventeenth-Century England', *Past & Present*, 184 (2004), 49f.), stressing that his redistribution proposals 'were the most detailed and elaborate yet produced'.

[34] Worden, *Rump Parliament*, 146ff.; Cannon, *Parliamentary Reform*, 11ff. In 'Barebone's Parliament' of 1653 (with appointed, not elected, members), seats were already distributed according to tax burdens (*ibid.*, 13).

[35] Although there were now almost twice as many county as borough seats, boroughs still remained over-represented (at least partly because of partisan considerations which, conversely, left London conspicuously under-represented). Four hundred MPs from England and Wales were to be joined by thirty MPs each from Scotland and Ireland. *Constitutional Documents*, ed. Gardiner, 407-9 (quotation at 409); Cannon, *Parliamentary Reform*, 13ff.; Worden, *Rump Parliament*, 149ff., who stresses that the scheme had essentially been worked out by the Rump – and, by extension, followed up in Lilburne's and the 1649 officers' *Agreement* (see n. 33). See also David L. Smith, 'The *Agreements of the People* and the Constitutions of the Interregnum Governments', in *The Agreements of the People, the Levellers, and the Constitutional Crisis of the English Revolution*, ed. Philip Baker and Elliot Vernon (2012), esp. 240f., 245.

[36] Richard Cromwell's parliament (January 1659) was already elected according to ancient usage, the 'Humble Petition and Advice' of 1657 having de facto suspended the new rules.

make representation more proportional and equitable, and possibly also more egalitarian.

Arithmetical calculations and radical projections

Various proposals were made, between the mid-1640s and mid-1650s, to attribute seats to existing constituencies according to their population or their tax yields. In the ensuing decades, suggestions were made to make parliamentary representation yet more proportional by devising an entirely new electoral geography from the ground up, starting from the parishes.[37]

The most celebrated piece of seventeenth-century republican writing, James Harrington's *Commonwealth of Oceana* (1656), had its ideal republic organise 'the people, according [to] the places of their habitation, unto parishes, hundreds and tribes' for administrative and military purposes as well as for elections.[38] If 'tribes' are equated with counties, this hierarchy of units mirrored the situation in England. In Oceana, however, they were perfectly arithmetically proportioned – and not riddled by boroughs: 10,000 parishes made up 1,000 hundreds and 50 tribes. Propertied men from the age of thirty were to take part in annual elections at parish level.[39] Deputies elected here would then meet on the hundred level to elect a deputy for the tribe; finally, the tribe deputies chose seven deputies for a lower house, and two for a Senate.

Harrington's scheme was followed up and further developed by the polymath William Petty, co-inventor – together with his friend John Graunt – of statistics or what he termed 'political arithmetic'. Petty was intimate with some of the most pre-eminent protagonists of the incipient scientific revolution, in England as well as in the Netherlands and in Paris (where he assisted Hobbes), but he was also embroiled in the very midst of Commonwealth debates and realities of parliamentary elections.[40] Petty and Harrington rubbed shoulders in the latter's Rota club, one of the first coffee-house clubs in London, during the months before the Restoration.[41] The short-lived but celebrated club also had among its regulars Samuel Pepys, the political writer

---

[37] Some earlier apportionment proposals had envisaged the division of larger counties into electoral districts (see n. 9), but none of them envisaged 'a parish-based representational scheme' as claimed by Mark Knights, 'Locke and Post-revolutionary Politics: Electoral Reform and the Franchise', *Past & Present*, 213 (2011), 62 n. 89.

[38] James Harrington, *The Commonwealth of Oceana* and *A System of Politics*, ed. J. G. A. Pocock (Cambridge, 1992), 77.

[39] 'Elections' in Oceana being a mixture of actual choice and a lot-like ballot, similar to the system in Venice. On (the only relative) political equality in *Oceana*, see J. Colin Davis, 'Equality in an Unequal Commonwealth: James Harrington's Republicanism and the Meaning of Equality', in *Soldiers, Writers and Statesmen of the English Revolution*, ed. Ian Gentles, John Morrill and Blair Worden (Cambridge 1998).

[40] Ironically, for Richard Cromwell's parliament (January 1659), he was elected for West Looe (Cornwall), one of the most notorious 'rotten boroughs', with only a few voters: Ted McCormick, *William Petty and the Ambitions of Political Arithmetic* (Oxford, 2009), 112. Reduced by the reforms of 1653, it had been fully reinstated when they were undone (see n. 36).

[41] *Ibid.*, 128; Brian Cowan, *The Social Life of Coffee: The Emergence of the British Coffeehouse* (New Haven, 2005), 96ff.

Henry Neville and former Leveller John Wildman. Fellow member John Aubrey noted that Petty 'was a Rota man, and troubled Mr. James Harrington with his Arithmeticall proportions, reducing Politie to Numbers'.[42] More likely, it was Aubrey himself who was thus troubled – judging by his *Oceana*, Harrington was hardly less obsessed with numbers in politics.

For Petty, one of the 'impediments of Englands greatness' was

> the inequality of Shires, Dioceses, Parishes ... and other Precincts, as also the Representation of the People in Parliament; all which do hinder the Operations of Authority in the same manner, as a Wheel irregularly made, and excentrically hung; neither moves so easily, nor performs its Work so truely, as if the same were duely framed and poised.[43]

Petty's urge for proportional rationality was congenial with his approach to reform in many other political contexts, such as taxation and population policies. With the help of numerical data and arithmetical logic, England's – and indeed, a UK's – 'impediments' could all be solved at one stroke: 'May not the three Kingdoms be United into one, and equally represented in Parliament? ... Might not the Parishes, and other Precincts be better equalized. ... Might not the Taxes be equally applotted?'[44] To such an end, Petty suggested remoulding the 9,600 parishes of England, being of very different sizes, into 12,000 same-sized electoral 'precincts' or 'districts'. On this basis stood a pyramidal system similar to Harrington's – but with a radically egalitarian male franchise.[45] In another piece of writing, Petty went yet further.[46] He lowered the age threshold to eighteen and advanced a radically decimal logic – a logic or 'system' that simply 'is the best; because with such computation do we deal with

---

[42] *Aubrey's Brief Lives*, ed. Oliver L. Dick (Ann Arbor, 1962), 240.

[43] William Petty, *Political Arithmetick* (1690) (presumably composed in the early 1670s), 93.

[44] *Ibid.*, 95. The term 'precinct' was also used by Harrington (for a 'hundred'): Harrington, *Commonwealth of Oceana*, 83.

[45] 'that in each district all the males of above twenty-one years old may meet upon a certain day to choose a certain person who may represent them ... and that forty [each] of the said 12,000 may meet at 300 convenient places ... to elect 300 members for the Grand Council', after Edmund Fitzmaurice, *Life of Sir William Petty 1623-1687* (1895), 279, referring to a 1685 manuscript entitled 'An Opinion of what is Possible to be Done'. The immediate object of this proposal was one-half of a 'grand National Council' of some 600 members (the other half was to mirror the House of Lords and the county members of the Commons). But the subsequent insistence on electoral reform suggests that Petty envisaged radical adjustments for the existing parliament, too: he called for 'a new apportionment and election for the House of Commons', considering not only that '70,000 Persons, called London, send but eight Members, while 7 other persons send two, and some counties of equal Bigness and Wealth send ten times as many as others', but also that 'of all the Men in England of 21 years old, although they have all Right and Capacity to be made Members of either House of Parliament, yet scarce one-fifth part of them have power to elect Members for the House of Commons' (after *ibid.*, 279f.).

[46] Frank Amati and Tony Aspromourgos, 'Petty contra Hobbes: A Previously Untranslated Manuscript', *Journal of the History of Ideas*, 46 (1985). The translators give no date; McCormick, *William Petty*, 129 n. 41, suggests the last months before the Restoration, when the Rota club was meeting (October 1659 to February 1660).

numbers in arithmetic ... and because no one else clearly found a more suitable number system'.[47] Thus, 10,000 basic units or 'centumvirales', i.e. 100 men, formed 1,000 'chiliarchies', 100 'comitatus' and finally 10 provinces. An assumed total of one million adult men chimed with actual estimates for England – as well as with the figure in *Oceana*.[48] The latter's arithmetical rationality was driven to a perfectly decimalised end – and the analogy of, on the one hand, proportionality based on population and, on the other, a full franchise was fully spelled out: an analogy already present, if as yet obliquely, at Putney.

It was only after Petty's death and the publication of his eponymous *Political Arithmetick* in 1690 that his ideas became widely known and taken up, including more specific calculations on the proportionality of elections. Population and especially taxation data were contrasted with representation, such as by John Houghton who, in 1693, compared the number of MPs per county (including boroughs) with tax burden, acreage and number of houses – to conclude, not surprisingly, that they all matched quite badly.[49] Five years later, a similar table appeared, again comparing the number of MPs per county (with their boroughs) with both the land tax yields of 1693 and the subsidies of 1697 – with the result that the disproportion was even bigger if measured by the second than by the first: '6 Northern and 5 Western Counties' paid less than half of Middlesex and Essex, but occupied 216 seats in the place of a bare 16.[50] The under-representation of London and its environs preoccupied other authors of the time, too.[51]

If Houghton and others advanced hard data only on taxation,[52] it might have had less to do with an inclination towards taxation-based proportionality and more with the fact that such data were easier to obtain than regional population data.[53] This suggestion is further corroborated by the way in which Gregory King, the most important 'political arithmetician' after William Petty, adapted Harrington's pyramidal apportionment scheme to the administrative and fiscal realities of England.[54] Breaking down a rough total of £10 million in annual direct taxes, King attributed first-tier deputies to

---

[47] Amati and Aspromourgos, 'Petty contra Hobbes', 131.

[48] *Ibid.*, 130.

[49] Joanna Innes, 'Power and Happiness: Empirical Social Enquiry in Britain, from "Political Arithmetic" to "Moral Statistics"', in *idem*, *Inferior Politics: Social Problems and Social Policies in Eighteenth-Century Britain* (Oxford, 2009), 122f. Houghton, pharmacist and member of the Royal Society, published a weekly broadsheet with data on agriculture and trade. See also Knights, 'Locke and Post-revolutionary Politics', 80; Slack, 'Government and Information', 51, 61f.

[50] 'A Scheme of the Proportions', in Knights, 'Locke and Post-revolutionary Politics', 83; see also *ibid.*, 80f. The author, John Smart, worked at the London town clerk's office.

[51] *Ibid.*, 81.

[52] The number of houses listed by Houghton was probably also derived from tax data; see Innes, 'Power and Happiness', 122f.

[53] This is also stressed by Innes, 'Power and Happiness', 174; but more accurate population figures did become available from the early 1690s; see Slack, 'Government and Information', 62.

[54] In a manuscript composed in the second half of the 1690s (the 'Burns Journal'), printed in *The Earliest Classics: John Graunt and Gregory King*, ed. Peter Laslett (Farnborough, 1973), here 250 (of 291).

the parishes at the ratio of 1:£200.[55] These parish deputies were then to meet at the hundred level to elect a tenth of their number as the next tier of deputies – who then met at county level where, again, they would choose a tenth of them, so as to arrive at a total of 500 members of Parliament. The model did not require a complete remake of the administrative landscape, as Harrington's and especially Petty's schemes did, but it still apportioned each parliamentary seat to (roughly) an equal amount of taxes paid.[56]

As no new data became available, those of the late seventeenth century, especially those of King and of his colleague Charles Davenant (through whose publications many of King's figures and calculations first became accessible), were taken up time and again throughout the eighteenth century – together with much the same kind of political arguments against the distorted representation in Parliament.[57] After a national census bill had been thwarted by the House of Lords in 1753, only the census of 1801 began to supply reliable data for apportionment based on population[58] – as first attempted by the 1832 Reform Act, and even then only to a very rudimentary extent.

Proportionality and the franchise in the Enlightenment

Neither the radicalism of Harrington and Petty, nor the support by arithmetical precision and concrete data aimed at by him and his followers, characterised the ensuing political discourse in Britain or abroad. Characteristic, rather, was the more distanced and conservative stance of John Locke – who nevertheless helped to pass some of the seventeenth-century notions on proportionality on to eighteenth-century political thought. His *Second Treatise of Government*, written around 1680, noted the desirability of re-establishing the distorted balance between representation and constituency size (suggesting that an original balance was offset by later demographic and economic changes).[59] Locke further argued that, as Parliament could neither reform itself nor be reformed by the people who had ceded their power to it, that distorted

---

[55] Following Harrington, deputies on all the three levels were to be 'chosen by Ballot' (*ibid.*), but there was no further pronouncement on the franchise.

[56] This was possible because parishes, hundreds and counties, while serving as organisational units, were not given fixed numbers of deputies but numbers according to their relative tax yield. By the same token, it seems to be the first scheme that – possibly inadvertently – allowed for yearly reassessments and thus for changing fiscal, and indirectly demographic and economic, conditions.

[57] Innes, 'Power and Happiness', 174, mentioning Malachi Postlethwayt, James Burgh and John Wilkes. Only in 1783, on behalf of Wyvill's reform movement, were new data presented, followed in turn by yet more detailed research on the size of boroughs by the 'Society of Constitutional Information' in the 1790s (*ibid.*, 174f.).

[58] David V. Glass, *Numbering the People: The Eighteenth-Century Population Controversy and the Development of Census and Vital Statistics in Britain* (Farnborough, 1973).

[59] 'in tract of time this *Representation* becomes very *unequal* and disproportionate to the reasons it was at first establish'd upon': John Locke, 'The Second Treatise', in *Two Treatises of Government*, ed. Peter Laslett (Cambridge, 1960), § 157 (emphasis in the original).

balance had to be fixed by the executive, i.e. the king.[60] And in accordance with the general trend of the century – if not with Harrington and Petty – Locke saw the balance or 'true proportion' warranted by 'the assistance, which it [a constituency] affords to the publick', that is, its tax yields.[61]

The two clauses in the *Second Treatise* concerned with this theme have frequently been read as an explicit stance in favour of a property-based franchise. Yet, Locke's lack of clarity on the issue has caused much headache and discussion – not unlike Putney and the Levellers.[62] But against the background of the preceding half-century's debates on proportionality, the relatively greater weight he lends to *this* issue – and the absence of any explicit mention of 'the franchise' – appears much less puzzling: against that background, it can be argued that what was relevant for Locke, too, and for his 'fair and *equal Representative*',[63] was equality both among constituencies and among the voters in different constituencies: a *standardised* franchise, in other words, much more than any clearly specified (let alone broadened) electorate.

This can be further confirmed by placing Locke's stance in the context of the Exclusion Crisis and the early Whig electoral reform proposals that it engendered.[64] A bill brought forward by the first Earl of Shaftesbury, whose associate Locke had been since the mid-1660s, stipulated a radically standardised borough franchise:[65] every householder from the age of twenty-one who had 'payed and born his Scot and Lot towards the maintenance and defraying the Poor, and other publick Charges and Payments' was to have the vote.[66] This would have broadened the franchise in most boroughs while narrowing it down in some others (as further emphasised by an insistence on excluding all others)[67] – but, crucially, it would have equalised it among them.

---

[60] *Ibid.*, §§ 157, 158. To prove this, and its consistency with his constitutional theory, was clearly Locke's biggest concern here (just as the §§ are part of ch. XIII, 'Of the Subordination of the Powers').

[61] *Ibid.*, § 158. There is a conspicuous, and suspicious, cumulation here of the attribute 'true' in one sentence ('true proportion', based on 'true reason', would recreate the 'old and true' 'Legislative').

[62] §§ 140 and 158 are often considered as pleas for a restricted franchise. John Rawls, *Lectures on the History of Political Philosophy*, ed. Samuel Freeman (Cambridge, MA, 2007), 138–55, makes the case that such a stance for a property threshold is not inconsistent with Locke's theory of equality. Jeremy Waldron, *God, Locke, and Equality: Christian Foundations in Locke's Political Thought* (Cambridge, 2002), 114–19, detects more potential in Locke's political egalitarianism, but stresses that the legislature's specific make-up was not essential for him.

[63] Locke, 'Second Treatise', § 158 (emphasis in the original).

[64] See also Knights, 'Locke and Post-revolutionary Politics'.

[65] 'Bill for Regulating Elections of Members to serve in Parliament' (second reading, 5 April 1679), in *The Necessity of Parliaments, with Seasonable Directions for the More Regular Election of Parliament-Men* (1689), 25–31; see also Knights, 'Locke and Post-revolutionary Politics', 63f.

[66] 'Bill for Regulating Elections', 26. London, York, Norwich, Exeter and Bristol were, however, exempted from the regulation, with no further stipulations.

[67] The county threshold was to be heightened to a £200 property threshold – as had already briefly obtained under Cromwell (see above, n. 32, also for the implications) in whose Council of State Shaftesbury had sat.

Curiously, in a memorandum presumably also authored by Shaftesbury, two contrasting alternatives were put forward.[68] The first advocated a sharp restriction of voting rights: 'The power of Election [ought] to be fixed in the Optimacy only,' as most men were too easily 'misguided ... by their ignorance' and 'under the temptation of being Corrupted and Seduced by the inveiglements of a little Mony, or a Pot of Ale'.[69] The second alternative, however, suggested that the only way 'to bring an old irregular Structure into a convenient Uniformity' was 'by razing it to the Ground, and erecting a new Pile by some better contrived design'.[70] Such a design, apart from featuring a Harrington-style electoral pyramid, would rest on the premise that 'every individual Person in the Nation, has a Natural Right to Vote' and envisage the franchise for all male householders.[71] This would achieve 'a perfect Representative of the whole Body of the People, and also of every numerical person in the Kingdom'.[72]

To the extent that we can make sense of these contrasting schemes, it is again by acknowledging that the Whigs' goal was to rationalise representation by creating equality among voters – however these were to be defined. This meant, on the one hand, proportionality among constituencies, measured by the taxes they paid. On the other hand, it meant an equal – that is, a standardised – franchise, which they strove to obtain by legislation. In the 1690s, in fact, another electoral bill – drawn up, among others, by Locke – again envisaged a standardised borough franchise to be awarded to every man paying local taxes (scot and lot).[73] Rather than being radically egalitarian, again, the aim was to 'bring an old irregular Structure into a convenient Uniformity', to quote Shaftesbury. This uniformity was to be predicated on the payment of taxes – for more proportional constituencies as well as for the entitlement of individual voters. This was a standard that was not only relatively easy to measure but also one that local and central elites might agree upon.[74] If the move failed again, it was not because it was too egalitarian – but because the rationalising, standardising logic of proportionality and individual (or voter) equality contradicted the traditional logic of hierarchical and corporate rights.

The first logic was, broadly speaking, that of the European Enlightenment – and the equalising, while not egalitarian, stance of Locke and the Whigs was precisely that of all but a few Enlightenment thinkers.[75] They wanted

---

[68] Later published as Some Observations Concerning the Regulating of Elections for Parliament (1689). The original date (1679?) and Shaftesbury's authorship are not entirely certain; see Knights, 'Locke and Post-revolutionary Politics', 61f. (but Knights confusingly treats the 1679 bill and the pamphlet as identical here – and passes over the fact that the latter contained two radically contrasting schemes).

[69] [Shaftesbury], Observations, 10f.

[70] Ibid., 14.

[71] Ibid., 14–18 (quotation at 15). Apart from the fact that male householders were not 'every individual Person', there were also restrictions on eligibility, especially on the second (county) level.

[72] Ibid., 18.

[73] Knights, 'Locke and Post-revolutionary Politics', 66ff., esp. 68, 70. The county franchise was left untouched – but the franchise here was already at least formally equal (and the boroughs sent the vast majority of MPs).

[74] As emphasised also ibid., 75ff.

[75] The most obvious exception is of course Rousseau, but he rejected the idea of representation altogether. The nuances of eighteenth-century arguments on equality are discussed by John

representation to be more equal – but not shared by all. They wanted to see it untied from traditional categories of birthright and group membership – but they wanted it to be tied to economic independence, moral and intellectual capacity, personal achievement and individual contribution to the public weal (all of which were seen as closely linked). Enlightened thinkers, in other words, envisaged a new kind of social and political stratification: not inherited and collective but utilitarian and individual. It contrasted sharply with the traditional early modern logic of birth, and corporate, status and rights, while corresponding to the functional, materialist rationality of the Enlightenment. (By the same token – by obeying an essentially materialistic logic – such stratification was measurable and quantifiable, through property registers, tax lists or otherwise.) This vision of stratification undercut traditional birth and corporate hierarchies by putting the right to vote within each and every (male) individual's reach – based on his economic success. Here, then, was Locke's 'true proportion' and 'true reason';[76] here was his – and later the Americans' – 'no taxation without representation';[77] here were French revolutionary Sieyès's 'true shareholders' of society.[78]

This, too, was the gist of the entry on 'representation' in Diderot's *Encyclopédie*, authored by the German expatriate philosopher baron d'Holbach whose Paris salon was frequented by the crème of French and British philosophers.[79] For Holbach and the *Encyclopédie*, it was clear that 'the people' were to be represented proportionately – but proportionately according not just to their numbers but also to their usefulness.[80] Only the educated and wealthy, in fact – those who had a true understanding of, and true stake in, society and politics – ought to represent the people: 'It is in proportion of his possessions that the voice of the citizen should have weight in national assemblies.'[81] Indeed only they were to *be* represented, as 'it is property that makes the citizen … [He] acquires the right to be represented as a proprietor, in function of his possessions.'[82]

Carson, *The Measure of Merit: Talents, Intelligence, and Inequality in the French and American Republics, 1750-1940* (Princeton, 2007), 11–37.

[76] Locke, 'Second Treatise', § 158.

[77] *Ibid.*, § 140; see also § 142.

[78] 'les vrais actionnaires de la grande entreprise sociale', Emmanuel J. Sieyès, *Préliminaire de la constitution françoise. Reconnoissance et exposition raisonnée des droits de l'homme et du citoyen* (Paris, 1789), 37.

[79] Paul-Henri Thiry [Paul H. Dietrich], Baron d'Holbach, 'Représentans', in *Encyclopédie, ou Dictionnaire raisonné des sciences, des arts et des métiers*, ed. Denis Diderot, vol. 14 (Paris, 1765). His salon, an important caucus of *Encyclopédie* authors, existed over three decades from the middle of the century onwards. Holbach himself contributed hundreds of articles, mostly on matters of science.

[80] 'Le peuple composé … de la partie la plus nombreuse, la plus laborieuse, la plus utile de la société', *ibid.*, 144.

[81] 'c'est en proportion de ses possessions, que la voix du citoyen doit avoir du poids dans les assemblées nationales', *ibid.*, 145. See also *ibid.*, 144: 'il convient qu'ils [les sujets] aient des représentans, c'est-à-dire des citoyens plus éclairés que les autres, plus intéressés à la chose, que leurs possessions attachent à la patrie, que leur position mette à portée de sentir les besoins de l'état'.

[82] 'en un mot c'est la propriété qui fait le citoyen; … c'est toujours comme propriétaire, c'est en raison de ses possessions … qu'il acquiert le droit de se faire représenter', *ibid.*, 145.

This logic was translated, from the 1770s onwards, into attempts by French ministers to set up Provincial Assemblies to oversee taxation and streamline local administration. The original plan put forward, in particular, by physiocratic writers, saw these as consisting of regional landowners, noble and non-noble alike, representing taxpayers at large and looking beyond particularist spheres of interest. When Finance Minister Necker initiated two such *Assemblées provinciales* in the late 1770s, however, they were organised along the lines of the traditional three Estates and fully dominated by noble elites.[83] In early 1787, Finance Minister Calonne tried to take up the original idea of gathering landowners, regardless of rank, but this foundered on the resistance of the Assembly of Notables.[84] His successor Loménie de Brienne, finally, put almost twenty Assemblies – organised along the conventional lines – in place by the end of 1787.[85] Yet, just like Necker's prototypes, they featured a 'doubled Third' – they contained, that is, the same number of representatives from the Third as from the first two (clerical and noble) Estates together, thus prefiguring the form which the Estates General of 1789 would take. More than that, their members voted individually – 'by head' – rather than collectively by Estates,[86] thus anticipating the logic of the revolutionary Third Estate during the first two months of the Revolution. In this restricted way at least, the pre-revolutionary Provincial Assemblies translated a notion of individual, but functionally qualified, proportionality and equality into practice. Together with the lower-level, elected Municipal Assemblies that were set up during autumn 1787 they helped, on the eve of the Revolution, to spread an individual, property- or taxation-based logic of proportionality and representation among a large public.[87]

From Estates to Assembly: proportionality and equality in the French Revolution

The call for a revocation of the Estates General or some other form of 'national representation'[88] to solve the financial and political impasse of the monarchy

---

[83] Turgot (finance minister 1774–6) had the physiocrat Dupont de Nemours draw up a first plan. Necker (1776–81) had two prototype assemblies established in 1778/9, with members partly appointed and partly co-opted. Stephen Miller, *Feudalism, Venality, and Revolution: Provincial Assemblies in Late-Old Regime France* (Manchester, 2020); Peter M. Jones, *Reform and Revolution in France: The Politics of Transition, 1774–1791* (Cambridge, 1995), 38f.

[84] At the end of 1786, Calonne had also envisaged reinstalling the Provincial Estates of old (*États provinciaux*) to 'garner the support of landowning taxpayers who, through their regularly elected representatives, would be ... advising the government in a consultative capacity' (quoted after *ibid.*, 38).

[85] *Ibid.*, 40, 142. Again, first-time members were appointed, not elected.

[86] Loménie de Brienne here, too, followed Necker's model, while Calonne (and Turgot) had proposed that representation should not be organised by orders at all.

[87] Calonne had envisaged a 'physiocratic' landowner franchise for the *Municipalités*, too, but Loménie de Brienne would replace this with a taxpaying franchise (*ibid.*, 41, 144).

[88] Words of the abbé Morellet in late 1787, after *ibid.*, 140. The Assembly of Notables, convened in spring, had already been dubbed a 'National Assembly' (*ibid.*, 116), a term also used by Holbach in 1765.

was growing ever louder throughout 1787 – and at the end of the year, the king promised the convocation of an Estates General. After 175 years of slumber, however, they could not, in most people's eyes, simply be revived in their ancient form, as the government envisaged it: to accord the church and the nobility *each* the same weight as the entire rest of society – represented in the 'Third Estate' (*Tiers État*) – appeared just as anachronistic as insulting. At the same time, the new Provincial Assemblies pointed towards a fairer form of representation.[89] In the Alpine province of Dauphiné, in July 1788 – a few weeks after the 'Day of the Tiles', when citizens of the province's capital, Grenoble, had hurled roof tiles on the soldiers deployed in the streets – members of the three Estates assembled to reconvene their long-deceased Provincial Estates: but not, as in the past, with an equal number of representatives from each Estate but, following the Provincial Assemblies, with a 'doubled Third' and the vote 'by head'.[90] They proclaimed this to be the proper set-up for the upcoming Estates General, too. However, the central authorities insisted that these be modelled on their last convocation in 1614 – triggering a pamphlet war throughout autumn 1788 that pitted traditionalists against self-styled 'patriots' clamouring for a larger share of seats for the Third Estate.[91]

In this debate, arguments for more proportional forms of representation could be readily based on statistical, and in particular demographic, reasoning which had started to attract much general attention over the past decades.[92] In France, it was popularised in particular by the hefty debate over an alleged long-term depopulation of the kingdom – prompting Rousseau to ask, provocatively, for population counts to evaluate governments; and the government, in turn, to carry out yearly demographic surveys.[93] Such statistical reasoning and practice not only underscored the relevance of proportionality but also a notion of basic individual equality – implicit in the simple proposition to count each and every person as an identical '1' regardless of social rank (as well as, potentially, of sex and age). A decade before the Revolution, demographer Jean-Baptiste Moheau had stated that his discipline, by revealing the general laws of life, showed men 'naked' in their 'natural equality', without the trappings of society. There was no difference between kings and the

---

[89] It was widely held that they should be the model for the Estates General; see *ibid.*, 43, 119, 139ff.

[90] A doubled Third Estate and the vote by head already existed in the Estates of Languedoc, too.

[91] Among the 'patriots' were many nobles, and their central caucus (later dubbed 'Committee of 30') consisted of important members of the Paris *parlement* at odds with the latter's pronouncement (in September 1788) for the 'forms of 1614'. Timothy Tackett, *Becoming a Revolutionary: The Deputies of the French National Assembly and the Emergence of a Revolutionary Culture (1789-1790)* (Princeton, 1996), 89f.

[92] See Lars Behrisch, *Die Berechnung der Glückseligkeit. Statistik und Politik in Deutschland und Frankreich im späten Ancien Régime* (Ostfildern, 2016).

[93] On the *Enquête Terray* (starting in the early 1770s), Rousseau's call and the depopulation debate in general: Jean-Claude Perrot, *Une histoire intellectuelle de l'économie politique, XVIIe-XVIIIe siècles* (Paris, 1992), esp. 161ff.; Carol Blum, *Strength in Numbers: Population, Reproduction, and Power in Eighteenth-Century France* (Baltimore, 2002); Frederick G. Whelan, 'Population and Ideology in the Enlightenment', *History of Political Thought*, 12 (1991).

least of their subjects: they all shared the same needs and pleasures; they all shared 'the same beginning, the same end, one cradle, and one grave'.[94]

In autumn 1788, arguments starting from the numerical proportionality of equal citizens were forcefully brought forward by the eminent lawyer Guy-Jean-Baptiste Target. In his view, delegates ought to be sent 'from all parts of the kingdom according to wise rules and just proportions'.[95] Such proportions were absent in the past, as Target proved with a survey of membership figures since the fourteenth century: contrary to what traditionalists maintained, the historical record was a 'masterpiece of irregularity and chance' and could not serve as a rule.[96] Target did not advise a radical break. Nevertheless, as 'there are a million individuals in the two first orders, but ... twenty million in the Third Estate', the latter constituted 'almost the entire nation' and should therefore clearly outweigh clergy and nobility in the Estates General.[97] Much the same point was made by Protestant pastor (and future eminent revolutionary) Jean-Paul Rabaut Saint-Étienne: 'What is the Third Estate? It is the nation minus the clergy and the nobility,' made up of some 'twenty-four million Frenchmen'.[98] Thus, the muddled pedigree of tradition was now trumped by quantitative arguments – by the sheer 'dictates of reason and justice'.[99]

As already indicated by these examples, though, the concrete numbers employed varied, due to a lack of census data no less than to the bewildering array of territories recently added or (semi-)incorporated into the kingdom.[100] Emmanuel-Joseph Sieyès, taking up the argument in January 1789 in his *What Is the Third Estate?*, admitted that he knew no better what the 'true proportion' among the orders was – 'but, like everybody else, I will permit myself to make my calculations'.[101] The result was a maximum of 200,000 members of the first

---

[94] 'L'homme [est] ainsi vu à nu et dépouillé de toutes les prérogatives et distinctions qu'ont introduit [sic] les conventions sociales, ramené au sentiment de l'égalité naturelle; pour tout individu, mêmes besoins, mêmes plaisirs; les seules jouissances réelles pour les souverains, sont celles qu'ils partagent avec les derniers de leurs sujets; même commencement, même fin, un berceau, et un tombeau.' Jean-Baptiste Moheau, *Recherches et considérations sur la population de la France* [1778], ed. Eric Vilquin (Paris, 1994), 2.

[95] After Mitchell B. Garrett, *The Estates General of 1789: The Problems of Composition and Organization* (New York, 1935), 90. Garrett dates 'Les états généraux convoqués par Louis XVI', most likely authored by Target, to the end of October (*ibid.*, 88, 235); it went through several editions.

[96] After *ibid.*, 89. Target referred to regional proportions as well as to the ratio between Estates, showing that the proportion of the Third had fluctuated wildly over the centuries.

[97] After *ibid.*, 90. Target proposed a ratio of 1:1:3 (250 deputies each for the first two, 750 for the Third Estate).

[98] After *ibid.*, 92f. The 'Considérations sur les intérêts du tiers état adressées au peuple des provinces' were written around the same time and also printed repeatedly (*ibid.*, 233; see also *ibid.*, 93).

[99] *Ibid.*, 88, 92 (Garrett referring here to both Target and Rabaut Saint-Étienne).

[100] France's population in 1789 was around 28 million. Contemporary estimates (often not including recent territorial acquisitions) ranged between 20 and 25 million (Perrot, *Histoire intellectuelle*, 174).

[101] 'J'ignore, comme tout le monde, quel en est le véritable rapport; mais comme tout le monde, je me per-mettrai de faire mon calcul.' Emmanuel J. Sieyès, *Qu'est-ce que le tiers-état?*, 3rd edn [1789] (Paris, 1988), 71.

two orders, contrasting with no less than 'twenty-five to twenty-six million souls' belonging to the rest, i.e. the Third Estate.[102] Considering this numerical evidence, it would be plain 'absurdity' to insist on the first two Estates' conventional two-thirds majority: it would be just the same as to 'maintain that 2 plus 2 equals 5'.[103]

Although Sieyès used an argument previously deployed by others,[104] he gave it renewed rhetorical vigour and made it immensely popular on the eve of the elections to the Estates General. In the meantime, at the end of 1788, the king had given in to Finance Minister Necker to 'double the Third'; but as he shrank away from conceding the vote by head, too, the first two Estates would de facto retain their two-to-one majority.[105] As a result, this half-hearted concession only fuelled the debate that gripped the public, much rather than appeasing it. When the crucial issue of the vote by head was taken up after the Estates General had opened on 5 May, the stubborn and arrogant refusal of the first two Estates to even consider and discuss it gave the Third Estate a common cause – and made it 'become revolutionary'.[106] On 17 June, the Third Estate finally proclaimed itself the 'National Assembly', soon to be joined by most clergy as well as many nobles – on the rationale of its sheer numerical proportionality: 'This Assembly is ... made up of the deputies ... of at least ninety-six per cent of the nation.'[107]

But the picture is not yet complete. Omnipresent from the start was also the functional, utilitarian notion of proportionality – the notion that representation should also, if not chiefly, be proportional to individual and collective usefulness, measured by property and/or taxation. In a widely read 'Letter to the King' from the autumn of 1788, the precocious and much admired Estates of Dauphiné had argued that the Third Estate could not be denied the same number of deputies as the first two Estates together – considering not only that it

---

[102] *Ibid.*, 71–5 (quotation at 75). Later in the piece, he used the much lower figure of 20 million (see next footnote).

[103] 'Si donc on prétend qu'il appartient à la constitution française que deux cent mille individus fassent sur un nombre de vingt millions de citoyens les deux tiers de la volonté commune, que répondre, si ce n'est qu'on soutient que deux et deux font cinq? ... On ne peut ... arrêter que dix volontés n'en vaudront qu'une, contre dix autres qui en vaudront trente. Ce sont là des contradictions dans les termes, de véritables absurdités,' *ibid.*, 142.

[104] Apart from Target and Rabaut Saint-Étienne, quoted above, the argument had been made already in the context of the Assembly of Notables in spring 1787, when municipal officers from Montauban complained that the Third Estate was de facto not represented in the Assembly – in spite of the fact that 'il forme les quarante-neuf cinquantièmes parties de la Nation Françoise' (quoted after Bernd Klesmann, *Die Notabelnversammlung 1787 in Versailles* (Ostfildern 2019), 145).

[105] Necker's proposal for, and partial realisation of, Provincial Assemblies ten years earlier had already featured *both* a doubled Third and the vote by head (see n. 83), as did the Provincial Assemblies created in 1787.

[106] To borrow the apt title of Tackett, *Becoming a Revolutionary*.

[107] '[C]ette Assemblée est déjà composée des représentants envoyés directement par les quatre-vingt-seize centièmes, au moins, de la nation,' *Archives parlementaires de 1787 à 1860*, 1ère série, vol. 8 (Paris, 1875), 127. On this reasoning, see also Lynn Hunt, 'The 'National Assembly', in *The French Revolution and the Creation of Modern Political Culture*, vol 1: *The Political Culture of the Old Regime*, ed. Keith M. Baker (New York, 1978).

'comprises the majority of your subjects; [but also that] it pays most of the taxes; it possesses most of the property'.[108] Similarly, many local petitions stressed the Third Estate's taxpaying performance to emphasise its rights.[109] The geographical proportionality of future representation, too, was discussed along these lines. Target already recommended direct tax returns as the suitable criterion and advanced calculations – reminiscent of Gregory King – that broke up a national total of taxes into the numbers of deputies that each electoral district would send.[110] As a consequence of this general stance, the first national elections, in 1791, on the basis of the revolutionary constitution barely amended the mix of population and taxation criteria which had served to specify the weight of electoral districts back in 1789.[111]

And the same logic, once again, applied to voting rights. In December 1788, an anonymous author had already made the point that the 'model' Estates of Dauphiné were in fact predicated on a highly restrictive franchise that flew in the face of its high-minded assertions:

You have laid great emphasis on the numerical strength of the Third Estate and the mass of its wealth; you have insisted that, to render it justice, it must have a representation in the Estates General commensurate with its importance. Yet, by the article of your constitution which defines the qualifications for suffrage and eligibility, you ... exclude precisely that numerous class of citizens whose rights have served as a pretext for your demands. ... Thus your constitution, if taken as the model for that of the Estates General of France, will disqualify forty-nine fiftieths [98 per cent] of the ... nation.[112]

This criticism was as perceptive as it was rare. The notion that political entitlement depended primarily on utility, as measurable by property or taxes, simply prevailed on all levels. Sieyès, too, advanced the twofold argument of taxes and population to commend the Third Estate.[113] Then, in July 1789, he hammered

---

[108] 'Lettre écrite au roi par les trois ordres de la province de Dauphiné' (published in early November 1788), quoted after Garrett, Estates General, 131. An anonymous author observed that giving the Third Estate 'a number of deputies commensurate with its wealth and numerical strength' would have it send nineteen out of twenty deputies, something he thought unwarranted (ibid., 132f., quotation at 133).

[109] See the examples in Michael Kwass, Privilege and the Politics of Taxation in Eighteenth-Century France: Liberté, Egalité, Fiscalité (Cambridge, 2000), 301–3.

[110] The basic ratio of one deputy each from the first two Estates, and three from the Third, from each district (bailliage) was always to be identical. Garrett, Estates General, 90. On Gregory King, see above. Both systems were pyramidal, but Target apportioned deputies at the highest level and King first-tier electors.

[111] 'Que ce nombre [des députés] sera formé, autant qu'il sera possible, en raison composée de la population et des contributions de chaque bailliage', Archives parlementaires de 1787 à 1860, 1ère série, vol. 1, 2nd edn (Paris, 1879), 498 ('Résultat du conseil d'État du roi', 27 Dec. 1788). The same mixed logic was applied to the newly created départements in the elections to the 1791 legislature; see Melvin Edelstein, The French Revolution and the Birth of Electoral Democracy (Farnham, 2014), 210.

[112] 'Première lettre d'un citoyen aux trois ordres de Dauphiné' (Dec. 1788), quoted after ibid., 133f.

[113] Sieyès, Qu'est-ce que le tiers-état?, 71.

out the distinction, reflecting the general discourse, between 'active' and 'passive' citizens: only the first, paying a certain amount of taxes, were 'the true shareholders of the big social enterprise' – only they ought to have the vote.[114] The exclusion of a substantial minority (around a third) of adult men from the vote became enshrined in the 1791 revolutionary constitution. So did various tax-related thresholds for eligibility within a two-tiered electoral pyramid – also initiated, among others, by Sieyès (and possibly inspired by Harrington).[115] Both active and passive electoral rights in France would remain restricted in the constitutions of more than half a century to come. Only the Jacobin constitution of 1793 stipulated a universal male franchise, as well as fully spelling out demographic proportionality for electoral districts – but it remained a mere paper tiger.[116] The logic of weighing electoral districts *and* granting voting rights according to economic performance was yet to prevail.

Apportioning seats in the United States' Congress

With the United States' census of 1790 – following up on the Constitution, drawn up three years earlier – our story turns full circle. Not only was this the first national census successfully undertaken in the wider European world: it was set up to ensure the demographic proportionality of federal elections.

Americans used demographic data already as an argument for the viability of colonial resistance – not entirely unlike the advocates of the Third Estate in France on the eve of the Revolution. Already at mid-century, Benjamin Franklin had claimed that, thanks to ideal conditions, the American population was the fastest-growing in the world – doubling about every twenty years.[117] Franklin did not provide much evidence; but ten years later, Connecticut clergyman Ezra Stiles dug up New England parish records to substantiate such claims, adding a fair dose of divine providence.[118]

---

[114] Sieyès, *Préliminaire de la constitution*, 37 ('les vrais actionnaires de la grande entreprise sociale').

[115] Sieyès originally envisaged a three-tiered pyramid: *Qu'est-ce que le tiers-état?*, 138f.; S. B. Liljegren (ed.), *A French Draft Constitution of 1792 Modelled on James Harrington's Oceana* (Lund, 1932), 51, 55f.; Edelstein, *Electoral Democracy*, 44. On Harrington's possible influence, already suspected by contemporaries: Liljegren (ed.), *Draft Constitution*, 44–79; Rachel Hammersley, *The English Republican Tradition and Eighteenth-Century France: Between the Ancients and the Moderns* (Manchester, 2010), 164f.

[116] The 1793 constitution also abolished the two-tier system. The elections to the Convention, in August 1792, largely followed the earlier constitutional stipulations, except for a broader franchise (similar to that of 1789, but with a reduced age threshold of twenty-one) and the elimination of tax criteria for eligibility: Malcolm Crook, *Elections in the French Revolution: An Apprenticeship in Democracy, 1789–1799* (Cambridge, 1996), 80f.

[117] 'Observations Concerning the Increase of Mankind' [1751, published 1755], after Whelan, 'Population and Ideology', 53. A mere 80,000 English immigrants had already increased to a million and 'in another Century ... the greatest Number of Englishmen will be on this side [of] the Water' (after *ibid.*, 54).

[118] 'A Discourse of the Christian Union' [1761], after *ibid.*, 53f. The Israelites had multiplied, under similar exile conditions, from 70 descendants of Jacob to 3 million at Exodus time: a 14-year doubling rate, still somewhat superior to that of New Englanders.

The Stamp Act of 1765 called forth further calculations by Stiles who concluded from London's expectations of fiscal profits that 'the subjects in North America are reckoned by the Lords at about two million and a Quarter of souls'.[119] Among those 'souls', slaves counted, too, according to Stiles.[120] The figure – a third of current estimates for England's population – could be adduced in favour of colonial confidence and resistance, but also, on the other side of the Atlantic, to highlight Britain's paramount interest in keeping its grip on the colonies.[121]

A few years later, British moral philosopher Richard Price, a friend of Franklin's – who helped to turn his interests towards demographics, and his sympathies towards the colonies – feared that Americans, 'formerly an increasing number of friends', were 'now likely to be converted ... into an increasing number of enemies'.[122] The word 'number' was key, as the statement was made in a paper on demographics. Soon afterwards, in an influential analysis of finance and population data from all over Europe, Price reflected more systematically on the rapid growth of the colonial population.[123] His figures and calculations inspired Thomas Paine who, in his 1776 pamphlet *Common Sense* that gave a decisive final boost to American morale, declared both the swelling size and the mixed origin of colonials to be incontrovertible tokens for the viability of independence.[124]

The relevance of population data for political representation, on the other hand, surfaced in 1774 when the first Continental Congress met in Philadelphia. For days, it debated how many delegates should represent each of the thirteen colonies: ought they to be apportioned according to a colony's population – or to its population and wealth combined? Demographic figures were passed around and discussed; but in the end it was decided that, for the moment, all colonies would have the same weight. Still, the discussion spread outside Congress, prompting commentaries from various quarters. Ezra Stiles, for one, considered most numbers overestimated: the figure he now advanced,

---

[119] After James H. Cassedy, *Demography in Early America: Beginnings of the Statistical Mind, 1600–1800* (Cambridge, MA, 1969), 181.

[120] *Ibid.* The term 'slave(s)' will be employed in this article instead of 'enslaved person(s)' which has been criticised as a euphemism. See, e.g., Graeme Wood, 'Just Say "Slavery": Involuntary Relocation and Enslaved Person are Misguided Euphemisms', *The Atlantic*, 11 July 2022. The discussion is ongoing; but for the time being, the author endorses the point that the inhumane nature of the institution should continue to be fully expressed.

[121] Whelan, 'Population and Ideology', 54; Cassedy, *Demography in Early America*, 181, 189ff.

[122] Richard Price, 'Observations on the Expectations of Lives; the Increase of Mankind ...', quoted after *ibid.*, 184f. ('friends' and 'enemies' appeared in capital letters). The passage was censured when the Royal Society published Price's piece, delivered in 1769, in the *Philosophical Transactions*.

[123] 'Observations on Reversionary Payments' [1771]; see *ibid.*, 185. In 1774, Edward Wigglesworth calculated that by the year 2000, 'should their future population be as rapid as their past, the Americans would amount to [the following in capital letters] one thousand two-hundred and eighty millions' (after *ibid.*, 192) – or not much under the size of today's India and China.

[124] Thomas Paine, 'Common Sense' [1776], in *idem, Rights of Man, Common Sense and Other Political Writings*, ed. Mark Philp (Oxford, 2008), 36 ('our present numbers are sufficient to repel the force of all the world'), 22f. ('Europe, and not England, is the parent country of America', as 'not one third of the inhabitants ... are of English descent').

if slightly above the one he had referred to a decade earlier, was some 20 per cent below that of the Continental Congress, tallied from the colonies' specifications.[125] This discrepancy was most likely owed to their leaders' wish to increase their relative shares of representation.[126]

Already half a year later, when the Second Continental Congress met in spring 1775, another question of proportionality emerged: how much should each colony contribute to the defensive effort against Britain? The decision to apportion it according to population foreboded the later apportionment regulation of the Constitution; but for the time being, it remained dependent on the data provided by the colonies, unreliable and biased as they were – this time of course in the opposite direction, all trying to keep their contribution as small as possible.[127]

Shortly afterwards, however, the Articles of Confederation – discussed in Congress as soon as Independence had been declared but ratified by all colonies only by 1781 – stipulated that the common treasury, put up for defence and welfare, 'shall be supplied by the several states, in proportion to the value of all land within each state, granted to or surveyed for any Person'.[128] Thus, (landed) wealth was now chosen as the measuring stick for apportioning federal taxes. Apart from remaining unimplemented for practical reasons, this had not been everyone's preferred solution. In fact, in direct continuation of the provision of 1775, an alternative draft for the Articles read: '... shall be supplied by the several colonies in proportion to the number of inhabitants of every age, sex, and quality, except Indians not paying taxes'.[129] It would be *this* formula that would be taken over, in 1787, into the Constitution – which did not interfere with voting rights, arranged autonomously by each state[130] – but with three very substantial additions. First, seats in the House of Representatives were to be proportional to the number of inhabitants per

---

[125] Stiles came up with a total of 2.4 million (including 330,000 Blacks), against Congress's figure of just over 3 million. The data from Massachusetts, Connecticut, Rhode Island and New Jersey corresponded with his own, while the discrepancy was most pronounced for New York (250,000 and 156,000, respectively) and Virginia, the most populous state (640,000 and 400,000, respectively). Thomas Jefferson's statistically scrupulous 'Notes on Virginia' from the mid-1780s has figures closer to those of Congress – due mainly to his much higher number of slaves (270,000, on a near-par with non-slaves) than allowed for by Stiles (who estimated 100,000). Cassedy, *Demography in Early America*, 189f., 228.

[126] Within the colonies/states, too, and in their 1776/7 revolutionary constitutions, representation in lower houses began to gear towards population-based regional apportionment, with different kinds of compromise struck between hitherto under- (or un-)represented back countries and much more populated coastal areas and towns. See the overview in Willi P. Adams, *The First American Constitutions: Republican Ideology and the Making of the State Constitutions in the Revolutionary Era* (New York, 2001), 234ff.

[127] Only two colonies carried out a census to come up with precise figures (*ibid.*, 193).

[128] Articles of Confederation, Art. VIII.

[129] Original draft of Articles of Confederation, Art. XI, quoted after Cassedy, *Demography in Early America*, 193. (A resolution for a census did not come to pass, either.)

[130] As it was too difficult to settle for any general denominator, the Constitution only stipulated that voting rights for the House of Representatives in a given state should be those used for elections to its lower house.

state, too; second, a national census must be taken once every ten years to determine this number; third, ignominiously, slaves were not to be weighted fully but by a ratio – later referred to as the 'federal ratio' – of three-fifths.[131]

The weight accorded to slaves had been debated already in 1783 in reaction to an amendment proposal for the Articles of Confederation, aiming at the apportionment of taxes, that in turn revived the alternative draft just quoted.[132] Although the ensuing debate remained theoretical for the time being,[133] it was in this context that the ugly three-fifths compromise was hammered out. Virginia, spearheading the slave-holder states, wanted to count slaves only half so as to lower the prospective tax burden, while some New England states insisted on three-quarters; James Madison suggested the compromise of three-fifths. It was resorted to, four years later, at the Philadelphia Convention – and now linked with another compromise, namely, to use population *also* as the yardstick for apportioning seats in the House of Representatives. In this way, other potential indices – such as land values, unsuccessfully stipulated by the Articles of Confederation – were replaced with a single and essentially clear-cut unit. At the same time, as states were rewarded with seats *and* burdened with taxes in exactly the same measure, the double apportionment tool promised to avoid quarrels. Here was, in short, 'one of the classic checks and balances of the Constitution'.[134] As an integral part of it, the disgraceful three-fifths compromise worked for the Southern states, adding to their representation to the exact same degree as it did to their share of taxation.[135]

The cost of the double compromise, of course, was the absurd and macabre qualification of slaves as unevenly mixed entities of humans and property. The absurdly arbitrary figure highlighted the logical incongruity of the entire construction – as spelled out already by Madison who referred uneasily to the 'compromising expedient ... which regards them [the slaves] as inhabitants, but as debased by servitude below the equal level of free inhabitants ... [namely] as divested of two-fifths of the man'. In fact, Madison went further, asserting that 'if the laws were to restore the rights which have been taken away, the negroes could no longer be refused an equal share of representation

---

[131] Constitution, Art. 1, Section 2 § 3: 'Representatives and direct Taxes shall be apportioned among the several States ... according to their respective Numbers, which shall be determined by adding to the whole Number of free Persons, ... excluding Indians not taxed, three fifths of all other Persons.' Neither the term 'slaves' nor race or colour were mentioned here or anywhere else in the Constitution, but they were of course clearly implied.

[132] Its wording was conducive to such a debate as it also envisaged that 'in each Colony, a true account of [the inhabitants], distinguishing the white inhabitants, shall be triennially taken and transmitted to the Assembly [i.e., the Confederation Congress] of the United States' (after Cassedy, *Demography in Early America*, 193).

[133] New Hampshire and New York opposed the final draft, while changes to the Articles required unanimity.

[134] Margo J. Anderson, *The American Census: A Social History* (New Haven, 1988), 10.

[135] At the outset, to be sure, Southern states had demanded to count slaves fully (as persons) when it came to representation, and not at all (being property) for taxation, with the Northern states arguing the very opposite. For a detailed account see Michel J. Klarman, *The Framers' Coup: The Making of the United States Constitution* (Oxford, 2016), 265ff.

with the other inhabitants'.[136] That it would take another eighty years before slaves were formally freed, and at least nominally enfranchised, was partly the perverse effect of that same macabre compromise: it gave Southern states at least a third more seats in Congress than would have been the appropriate share of their free, white population.

Similar arguments, it may be noted, were exchanged in the French Caribbean colony of Saint-Domingue. In 1791, the mostly African-born slave majority, working on the sugar plantations, rose up in rebellion that ushered in the independent state of Haiti. Two years earlier, the white planters had claimed representation in the National Assembly – not just for their own number of some 30,000, which would barely give them one seat, but also for the almost twentyfold number of their slaves. The demand was duly spurned by Mirabeau: 'Do the colonies claim to class their negroes ... in the category of men or in that of beasts of burden? ... If [they] want the negroes ... to be men, they ought to free [them]; all ought to have the right to vote and to be elected.' He concluded sardonically that when fixing the numbers of deputies back in France, 'we have not taken into consideration the number of our horses or our mules'.[137]

Beginning in 1790, the decennial US census would enshrine racial distinctions – not only by way of the three-fifths compromise but also through the continuous imprint that its categories and tabulations left on the imagination of the new nation.[138] At the same time, though, it nurtured and enhanced a general statistical mindset – already prominent among revolutionary elites – by taking the notion of quantifying and calculating all things social and political to all corners of the federation. While Madison's urge to include not only demographic but also economic data was rejected for the time being,[139] the data of the first census, completed after eighteen months,[140] were used in myriad ways to present, analyse and debate the state of the nation.

---

[136] Alexander Hamilton, John Jay and James Madison, *The Federalist*, ed. George W. Carey and James McClellan (Indianapolis, 2001), no. 54 (12 Feb. 1788), 283, previous quotation at 284. See also *ibid.*, 283: slaves have a 'mixt character of persons and of property ... bestowed on them by the laws under which they live ... [and] it is only under the pretext, that the laws have transformed the negroes into subjects of property, that a place is disputed them in the computation of numbers'.

[137] Translated after René Koekkoek, *The Citizenship Experiment: Contesting the Limits of Civic Equality and Participation in the Age of Revolutions* (Ridderkerk, 2016), 75 n. 169.

[138] The census's sociocultural impact in the nineteenth century and beyond has been much discussed: see Anderson, *American Census*; Paul Schor, *Compter et classer. Histoire des recensements américains* (Paris, 2009).

[139] Anderson, *American Census*, 14. The census of 1800 saw some refinement (the age was now indicated for both sexes), but economic data requests – among others, by Jefferson – were again rejected (*ibid.*, 18).

[140] Not entirely satisfactorily, in Washington's eyes (*ibid.*, 14). Margo Anderson remarks that 'it is perhaps just as well that Madison's more ambitious census plans were not implemented ... the federal government could ill afford to fail in its first effort to count the population' (*ibid.*, 14). Still, compared to the regular failures, or else massive delays, of European endeavours of this kind, this was a major feat.

Notwithstanding many obstacles, delays and altercations,[141] the overall efficiency of census-based apportionment strengthened a general 'trust in numbers'[142] – in turn underpinning the viability and legitimacy of the new political system and its number-based compromises, core among them the famous 'Connecticut compromise' that balanced equal representation of the states, regardless of size, in the Senate and representation in numerical proportion to population in the House.[143] Madison's claim must have involved a fair degree of wishful thinking on his part – but would ultimately prove self-fulfilling: 'It is agreed on all sides, that numbers are the best scale of wealth and taxation, as they are the only proper scale of representation.'[144]

Conclusion

In a fine study, French historian Olivier Christin has traced the ways in which practices of decision-making by majorities in central political assemblies – together with a notion of the formal equality of individual votes – emerged in various contexts since the High Middle Ages.[145] He suggested, too, that gradually and cumulatively, such modes of voting *within* political assemblies would have fed into conceptions and practices of voting rights *outside* them. While Christin's nuanced panorama is fascinating and inspiring, however, he does not provide any specific suggestions as to how, when and why such a putative last step may have taken place.

It is true, to be sure, that there *is* a fundamental analogy between majority voting within assemblies and voting equality at large. Both rest on a quantitative, arithmetical logic. Both refer to some basic unit (such as the individual person), all manifestations of which are treated as equivalent so that they can be summed up into totals. A majority in an assembly can emerge only if all members are treated as equivalent: only then can their votes be counted as equal '1's and aggregated, thus yielding a majority and a minority. Like voting in assemblies, electoral proportionality, too, has to refer to a basic unit, to a general indicator that cuts across any distinctions that might otherwise exist among those who vote – that is, a quantitative indicator. Unlike in the case of majority voting in an assembly, it is true, the basic unit here need not be the individual person (or voter): it can also be predicated on some other kind of generalisable, quantifiable feature such as property, income or taxation – as

---

[141] Bringing about, among other things, the first presidential veto: see Anderson, *American Census*, 15ff.

[142] To use the title of the history of nineteenth-century US statistics by Theodore Porter, *Trust in Numbers: The Pursuit of Objectivity in Science and Public Life* (Princeton, 1995).

[143] With a strong bias towards the second in the mixed electoral college (Constitution, Art. 2, Section 1, § 2). In the states' ratification debates in 1787/8, numerical proportionality had been presented as a clear advantage over the Articles of Confederation (at least for the bigger states) – under whose stipulations the inhabitants of individual states 'are not represented in proportion to their numbers and importance' (quoted after Edmund S. Morgan, *Inventing the People: The Rise of Popular Sovereignty in England and America* (New York, 1988), 281).

[144] Hamilton, Jay and Madison, *The Federalist*, no. 54 (Madison, 12 Feb. 1788), 283.

[145] Olivier Christin, *Vox Populi: Une histoire du vote avant le suffrage universel* (Paris, 2014).

was mostly advocated by those talking about proportionality in the seventeenth and eighteenth centuries. But here, too – to create electoral proportionality – the most stable and plausible unit across time and space, the least ambiguous indicator, the smallest common denominator is ultimately the individual person.

In spite of this fundamental analogy, the findings of this article (if admittedly still of a cursory nature) do not suggest that there was a direct transition from concepts and practices of voting within assemblies to practices outside them. Majority voting in England's parliament did not engender any readiness on its behalf to allow for more equal representation among constituencies, nor a more equal, let alone egalitarian franchise: and this, in spite of the striking fact that the breakthrough of majority voting in Parliament, as recently documented by William J. Bulman,[146] occurred at the same moment in time – the early 1640s – and due to the same divisive political and constitutional issues as caused the rise in importance of majority voting for parliamentary members in electoral constituencies. In England as elsewhere, equality among individual voters at large does not seem to have sprung from a simple transfer onto a wider electorate of individualised, quantified majority decision-making at the centre. For a similar logic to gain ground within polities at large, it seems, a different kind of catalyst was more relevant: namely, the demand to make representation more proportionate, among constituencies no less than among those who were entitled to vote.

The very concept of representation, in fact – whenever it becomes a matter of contestation, reflection and debate – seems to gravitate towards some mode of proportionality. But just as the notion of simple numerical majorities among assembly members, conceived of as equals, required a leap of confidence in pre-modern societies – profoundly characterised as they were by concepts of corporate rather than individual rights and identities, and by many status hierarchies among them, reflecting supposedly innate differential 'qualities'[147] – so the idea of aggregating individuals or, for that matter, their sheer economic or taxpaying capacities clashed with the same all-pervasive belief in inherent, 'qualitative' differences, as embodied in traditional corporate identities and status distinctions. At the same time, a strong adherence to consensual decisions as the only way to reach good or even 'true' decisions[148] clashed with contested, adversarial decision-making by majority vote, within no less than outside assemblies.

---

[146] Bulman, *Rise of Majority Rule* (on parallels in time and causes, see in particular pp. 17, 32f.). Bulman also – and also only vaguely – suggests that majority voting in Parliament preceded, or else conditioned, majority rule (including elections) more generally (pp. 1f., 17f.). Unfortunately, Bulman did not take Christin's book on board.

[147] For the concept of growing procedural autonomy of the political sphere over and against the social, allowing the decoupling of decision-making procedures from participants' corporate and social status, see (with reference to Niklas Luhmann's systems theory) Barbara Stollberg-Rilinger, 'Einleitung', in *Vormoderne Politische Verfahren*, ed. *idem* (Berlin, 2001); *idem*, *Cultures of Decision-Making* (2016).

[148] See the works by Barbara Stollberg-Rilinger, Olivier Christin and William Bulman, as cited in nn. 145–7.

As a result, debates around proportionality emerged properly only in moments of fundamental political upheaval that challenged dominant discourses, conventions and hierarchies. This is what happened in the English revolution of the 1640s, when a major fissure at the top – reflected, too, in the surge of majority voting in Parliament – spread through the entire polity. As we saw, the demand for more proportionality among constituencies now emerged alongside a demand for giving all votes an equal weight (though not for giving the vote to all). The Levellers were the first, at mid-decade, to plead for parliamentary representation to be more proportionate to the relative weight of constituencies. They also demanded a more equal, that is, standardised franchise throughout the country. They did not, though, at least not explicitly, demand an *egalitarian* franchise, i.e. voting rights for all. This last step – taking the underlying quantitative logic to its end point – was tentatively made at the 1647 Putney debates, as the Levellers' demand for proportionality among constituencies and (entitled) voters merged with the claim of the parliamentary 'New Model' army's soldiers, seconded by some officers, for *their* political rights – bringing forth what sounds, at least, very much like a call for voting rights for all (men). It is revealing that this call, while so crucial and evident to us, arose only haphazardly as a spin-off of the debate on electoral proportionality. Accordingly, too, it was not followed up nearly as seriously, for the time being, by any of the protagonists involved.

But while the claim for broader voting rights made at Putney was not yet clearly formulated – and could not be, considering its utter novelty – it was brought forward more explicitly over the next decades. The least ambiguous pronouncement of all was made by William Petty. Not coincidentally, *he* was also the first to spell out the potential of statistics, or 'political arithmetic', as he christened it. Not coincidentally, either, his plea for a fully egalitarian (male) franchise was embedded in – and logically entirely conditioned by – the most stringent arithmetical proposal to date for establishing full electoral proportionality. But as on most other accounts, Petty's arguments in this field remained as yet largely ignored. For electoral proportionality to become a real issue, the underlying numerical logic of statistics or 'political arithmetic' needed to be more broadly endorsed. This happened in the last third of the eighteenth century, when a trust and belief in quantitative reasoning came strongly to the fore across Europe.[149]

As a consequence, it was only in the political ruptures of the American and French Revolutions that the arithmetical logic of proportionality and equality took on its full political vigour. It was against the background of a now widely shared belief in quantification and statistics that demographics could now be adduced as a core political argument: by Americans, to stress the viability and legitimacy of their resistance and independence; by the French, to argue for a larger political share of the 'Third Estate' – and finally to declare, in June 1789, that it represented the nation as a whole all by itself. In both cases, arguments of numerical proportion went hand in hand, too, with establishing a wider franchise (in the United States within the individual states, as

---

[149] See Behrisch, *Berechnung der Glückseligkeit*.

the Constitution did not meddle in this area). At the same time, following the strong emphasis on utilitarian merit and economic performance that had been dominant throughout the Enlightenment – and that lent itself just as easily and plausibly to quantification – the idea of material, or fiscal, rather than mere demographic proportionality still remained strong on both sides of the Atlantic. As a result, only the economically successful, or at least fully economically independent, men were generally seen as entitled to a full, active stake in politics.

And yet, there was no denying the contradiction and, ultimately, the logical incompatibility between political claims and stakes based on demographic proportionality – fully elaborated in apportioning seats in Congress by means of the national US census – and the political exclusion of major parts of the population. Already in the autumn of 1788, a critic of the Estates of Dauphiné pointed to their inconsistent, if not hypocritical, stance as they claimed more representation for the 'Third Estate', congruous with its numerical importance, while at the same time firmly restricting their own constituents' franchise. Earlier that same year, James Madison had admitted that the three-fifths compromise was a bad 'expedient' – and insinuated that slaves, counted as they were as 'inhabitants' in apportioning Congress seats, could only with a massive leap of (bad) faith be denied the franchise, let alone human rights. Nevertheless, for the time being, a full (male) franchise remained exceptional, such as in Vermont, joining the United States in 1791, or in the unimplemented Jacobin constitution of 1793. Yet, over the next century, the ultimate consequence of giving the vote to all men *was* drawn both in the United States and in France – if only in leaps and bounds and, for ex-slaves and their descendants, as yet largely on paper.

Women, too, remained excluded throughout the nineteenth century or even, such as in France, well beyond – arguably the most striking gap between the rhetoric of 'all inhabitants', employed both at Putney and in Philadelphia, or of Shaftesbury's 'every individual numerical Person' to be weighed in order to apportion representation, and actual political representation. But excluding women was simply so self-evident for most (if not all) early modern contemporaries, apparently grounded not only in society but indeed in 'nature', that it barely seemed to merit comment. As this sustained exclusion of women as well as of other major groups of people shows, the ultimate upshot of the arithmetical logic – namely, to include *all* individuals – has always been, and might always remain, strongly modified by many other political, social and cultural factors. Yet, as this article tried to argue, that logic *did* play an important role for the gradual broadening of democratic participation, kicking in during phases of political upheaval and, as the persuasive power of numbers steadily grew, becoming ever more difficult to reject.

Cite this article: Behrisch L (2023). Equality, Proportionality and Statistics: Political Representation from the English to the French and American Revolutions. *Transactions of the Royal Historical Society* **1**, 159–189. https://doi.org/10.1017/S0080440123000051

Transactions of the RHS (2023), **1**, 191–217
doi:10.1017/S0080440123000063

ARTICLE

The Incoherence of Empire. Or, the Pitfalls of Ignoring Sovereignty in the History of the British Empire

Jon Wilson[1] and Andrew Dilley[2]

[1]Department of History, King's College London, London, UK and [2]Department of History, University of Aberdeen, Aberdeen, UK
Corresponding author: Email: jon.wilson@kcl.ac.uk

(Received 25 August 2022; revised 26 May 2023; accepted 30 May 2023; first published online 10 July 2023)

Abstract

This article argues for an essentially political definition of empire with sovereignty at its core, which recognises that British assertions of sovereignty were multiple, mutually contradictory and thus, taken together, incoherent. Tracing the history of conflict between different archetypes of sovereign authority, we argue that imperial crises occurred when empire's different ideas were forced to speak to one another, during world war, for example. The emphasis here on sovereignty and incoherence contrasts with conceptions of the history of the British empire which assert to the contrary that empire was a coherent entity. Such coherence can, we argue, only be maintained by treating empire as a metaphor for broader conceptions of power and thus collapsing the history of empire into other totalising meta-concepts such as global capitalism or Western cultural dominance. Recognition of the incoherence of imperial sovereignty offers new, more nuanced, readings of central concerns in the literature such as imperial violence and the economics of empire.

Keywords: British; empire; sovereignty; law; constitutions; imperialism; colonialism; incoherence; decolonisation

As the British empire was an historic growth, corresponding to *no* principle, the application of any principle whatever to it would at once torpedo it.[1]

The name now loosely given to the whole aggregate of territory, the inhabitants of which, under various forms of government ultimately look to the British crown as the supreme head.[2]

---

[1] Israel Zangwill, *Principle of Nationalities* (1917), 34.
[2] *Encylopædia Britannica*, 1911 edition, s.v. 'British Empire'.

Empire is an essentially political concept, with sovereignty at its core. For the English and then British, empire was nothing more or less than the assertion of sovereign authority over territories throughout the world. To study empire is, unavoidably, to study this global assertion of sovereignty. Through the 400-year history of empire, sovereignty was exercised in multiple, often contradictory, forms. Idioms of sovereignty varied; there was no single British way of claiming territory. The 'British empire' was a jumble of different lands and societies, all ruled through different forms of government with differing claims to political power, ultimately unified by their common existence under the sovereignty of the Crown, as the 1911 edition of the *Encylopædia Britannica* recognised. Claims to sovereignty were articulated through an extraordinary range of idioms and practices, from violent conquest through treaties and concessions to the right of settler communities to govern themselves. The plurality of imperial sovereignty meant 'the empire' could never be a single power or space. It was not even a single 'project'.[3]

Incoherence was the essence of empire. Plural sovereignty is not just a helpful perspective for understanding empire. It was what Britain's empire actually was. Multiple and contradictory forms of sovereignty defined the very essence of Britain's empire, as the different idioms evolved in contrast and opposition to one another. While at times asserting primacy, none could ever subordinate others. Amidst this multiplicity of contradictory idioms, in practice, Britain's empire relied on the demarcation of different rules and different political philosophies for different spaces. Permanent separation was impossible. Tension between different forms of political authority occurred within the same territories, often from the start. Those tensions usually dissipated as one or another idiom dominated in any one place at one point in time. But large-scale crises, particularly the global wars which occurred in the eighteenth and twentieth centuries, forced competing idioms of imperial authority dominant in different regions into conflict.

Incoherence and plural sovereignty defined the empire as a political field and historical entity. Rather than debating rival theories about the driving force behind imperial expansion, endurance, demise and decline, we argue that the history of the British empire should focus on tracing the ever contested outworkings of the empire's inherent incoherence. This argument contrasts with most dominant approaches to writing the history of the British empire at a general level, since at least the late nineteenth century. As we show below, successive waves of literature have been premised on the assumption that empire was a coherent phenomenon. Until the middle of the twentieth century, histories of empire told an essentially political story about the assertion of sovereignty over territory throughout the world. While empire's practical multiplicity was of course not ignored, coherence was imparted through various assertions justifying empire through the supposedly benign motives and character of the British themselves, or the 'progress' purportedly fostered by imperial rule. Those ideological stories largely collapsed under

---

[3] J. Darwin, *The Empire Project: The Rise and Fall of the British World-System, 1830–1970* (Cambridge, 2009).

pressure from the failure of empire itself, and the dispersal of imperial sovereignty into a myriad of post-imperial forms. Subsequently, and rather than recognising the underlying incoherence exposed at the empire's end, scholars have tended to seek to preserve the unified field of imperial history by turning the concept of empire into a metaphor, and making it into a synonym for something else: modernity, globalisation, capitalism or white European racial or cultural dominance. The result is that, since the 1950s, where scholars have attempted a unified account of empire, this has tended to be achieved by pushing the assertion of direct political authority, necessarily plural and incoherent, into the background.[4] Thus, this article begins by tracing the impulse to coherence and the eventual neglect of sovereignty through successive strands of the history of Britain's empire, while acknowledging accounts that, we suggest, offer a more fruitful approach. A second section elaborates on sovereignty as a concept and offers a typology of the different and contradictory idioms of imperial sovereignty invoked during empire's 400-year history. The final section indicates how the approach outlined here might transform the history of empire.

Empire, and the effort to tell a coherent and unified story about it, played a central part in the professionalisation of the interrelated fields of history, law and politics in late nineteenth-century Britain's universities.[5] Writers of textbooks and lectures as well as political tracts strained against the geographical, ethnic and constitutional diversity of Britain's possessions, trying to explain how empire was governed by some kind of unified force. Their accounts in response were essentially political, defining empire as the territory over which the Crown held sway, often celebrating the 'special capacity for political organization' supposedly possessed by British peoples, as the Canadian educationist and supporter of imperial federation George Parkin put it.[6] Even so, the different tactics scholars used to assert coherence led to a series of contradictory arguments about the character of imperial authority.

From at least the late eighteenth-century crises of empire, the Crown-in-Parliament lay at the centre of accounts of the way empire was coordinated. Well into the nineteenth century, Parliament was seen as a body which drew together a multiplicity of communities and interests, in the British Isles and beyond. These perceptions were challenged by the rise of democracy in Britain where the will of the domestic population was increasingly seen as the ultimate arbiter of political power, by the growth of self-governing

---

[4] Since the 1960s, existential crises have punctuated drives to coherence in imperial history. See for instance G. Martin, 'Was There a British Empire?', *Historical Journal*, 15 (1972), 562–9; D. K. Fieldhouse, 'Can Humpty-Dumpty Be Put Back Together Again? Imperial History in the 1980s', *Journal of Imperial and Commonwealth History*, 12 (1984), 9–23; Douglas M. Peers, 'Is Humpty Dumpty Back Together Again?: The Revival of Imperial History and the "Oxford History of the British Empire"', *Journal of World History*, 13 (2002), 451–67.

[5] F. W. Maitland dated the 'serious endeavour to make historical study one of the main studies of the universities' to the 1870s: Maitland, 'The Teaching of History', in *Collected Papers*, ed. H. A. L. Fisher (1901), iii, 405–6.

[6] George Parkin, *Imperial Federation: The Problem of National Unity* (1892), 2.

assemblies in the colonies of white settlement, and by the growing rapidity of communication.[7] In the 1880s, the question of Irish Home Rule further charged the question. In this context, Cambridge legal scholar Albert Venn Dicey reasserted the importance of a single legislative body over all British territories. Dicey's doctrine of parliamentary sovereignty was a response to fears about fragmentation. It recognised the unequal power relations which existed between different territories, and then suggested that only a single, central legislative body could bind the disparate communities of empire together. That left, of course, even many white, supposedly 'civilised' imperial subjects (at least partially) disenfranchised.[8]

Dicey was arguing against an alternative vision, which saw the empire primarily as a network of self-governing 'British' communities that voluntarily coordinated their activities on a global scale. This underpinned the writings of a significant group writing in the early phases of professional history writing, including the Regius Professor of History at Cambridge between 1869 and 1895, J. R. Seeley; the Regius Professor of History at Oxford between 1892 and 1894, J. A. Froude; and the first Beit Professor at Oxford between 1905 and 1920, Hugh Egerton. In place of an empire bound together by the force of Parliament, Seeley thought imperial sovereignty emanated from the expansion of a vigorous, naturally energetic English culture and civilisation, through the diffusion of supposedly English racial bodies throughout the world. Seeley saw expansion as an essentially political process, noting that in contrast to the movement of Germans to America for example, England's migration 'carries across the seas not merely the English race, but the authority of the English government'. The resulting Greater Britain was an 'organism' whose 'organs ... are institutions, magistrates, ministers, assemblies'.[9] Rather than asserting coherence by privileging Westminster as Dicey had done, Seeley attempted to tell a unitary story about empire by marginalising parts he didn't think were racially British. 'The colonies and India are in opposite extremes,' he suggested. 'Whatever political maxims are most applicable to one, are most inapplicable to the other.' Seeley's solution to the intellectual conundrum was to diminish India's place within empire, arguing that its connection to Britain was a short-term phenomenon driven by Asian dynamics.[10] The West Indies, Cape Colony and Natal were seen as essentially settler-dominated, their non-white majorities ignored. The remainder of Britain's then still relatively small dependent empire was simply not mentioned.

Even so the maintenance of coherence amongst these scattered colonies of settlement became a source of anxiety. It was this which drove successive generations of imperial federalists – drawing directly on Seeley – to draw up rationalising

---

[7] See also D. S. A. Bell, 'Dissolving Distance: Technology, Space, and Empire in British Political Thought, 1770–1900', Journal of Modern History, 77 (2005), 523–62.

[8] On democracy see A. V. Dicey, 'Some Aspects of Democracy in England', North American Review, 137, 323 (1883), 317–26; A. V. Dicey, Lectures Introductory to the Study of the Law of the Constitution (1885), 91–105. For a later, more ponderous, reassertion of the principle of parliamentary sovereignty, see A. V. Dicey, Introduction to the Study of the Law of the Constitution (1915), xxv–xxxvii.

[9] J. R. Seeley, 'Georgian and Victorian Expansion', Fortnightly Review, 48 (1887), 48, 126.

[10] J. R. Seeley, Expansion of England ([1883] 1890 print), 176.

schemes to implement a unifying structure which would rationalise, equalise and combine the sovereign claims of Westminster and the quasi-sovereign claims made by what, in 1907, became known as dominions. Such schemes, implicit in Seeley's writings, found expression in the Imperial Federation League, and its successors such as Lionel Curtis's Round Table movement.[11] They consistently ran afoul of the aspirations to autonomy of the dominions, and unwillingness of the Westminster parliament to surrender power.

In his 1903 history of 'Greater Britain', Egerton asserted that 'steam and electricity' were already 'resisting separatist tendencies, promoting unity of interest'. Contrary to imperial federalists, Egerton argued that unity in practice could only occur through a set of messy concessions and compromises; practical moves towards a unified political structure would seem too domineering and push territories apart.[12] So a third answer to the empire's incoherence was simply to recognise the forces propelling autonomy for its constituent parts. Edward Freeman, J. A. Froude's predecessor as Regius Professor of History at Oxford, argued that the unity of race and political culture could only be preserved if a unitary point of sovereignty was abandoned, and British communities became separate sovereign states.[13] In fact this is exactly what happened. Self-governing territories were reconfigured into the interwar British Commonwealth of Nations, an entity more successfully anticipated by autonomist critics of imperial federation such as Richard Jebb or H. Duncan Hall.[14]

Salvaging unity by treating diversity as a virtue could extend beyond the white settler empire. In his wartime lectures on empire, the former colonial civil servant and historian Charles P. Lucas criticised German efforts at enforcing political uniformity through 'force, over-powering, and ... rigid system', arguing by contrast that 'toleration of diversity' and 'encouragement of diverse customs and characteristics' were distinctly English characteristics. With the importance of the Middle East during World War I in mind, this allowed Lucas to shift the core of empire from the (supposedly) racially homogeneous white-settler colonies to protectorates in which 'native' rulers governed under British 'supervision'.[15]

Throughout the interwar period, the continued centrality of sovereignty in conceptualising empire meant coherence was sidelined. The practical task of governing an incoherent and multiple imperial polity meant that the most prominent texts on the history and current politics of empire, even those intended to celebrate it, were catalogues of different forms of government in different places. The past and present of an incoherent empire could only be described through empirical discussion. Serious writing was dominated

---

[11] G. Martin. 'The Idea of "Imperial Federation"', in *Reaappraisals in British Imperial History*, ed. R. Hyam and G. Martin (Cambridge, 1975), 121–37; J. E. Kendle, *The Round Table Movement and Imperial Union* (Toronto, 1975); L. Curtis, *The Problem of the Commonwealth* (1916); D. Lavin, *From Empire to International Commonwealth: A Biography of Lionel Curtis*, (Oxford, 1995).

[12] H. Egerton, *The Origins and Growth of Greater Britain* (1903), 182, 190.

[13] E. A. Freeman, *Greater Greece and Greater Britain* (1886).

[14] Curtis, *The Problem of the Commonwealth*; R. Jebb, *Studies in Colonial Nationalism* (1905); H. D. Hall, *The British Commonwealth of Nations* (1920).

[15] Charles P. Lucas, *The British Empire: Six Lectures* (1916), 195–8.

by experts on particular places, or constitutionally focused scholars like Arthur Berriedale Keith, Ivor Jennings, Keith Hancock and Reginald Coupland. Thus Hancock's *Survey of Commonwealth Affairs* presented an entity originating from multiple expanding trading, plantation and settlement frontiers, divided between self-governing dominions, India and the rest; its problems of 'nationality' and 'economics' could only be analysed historically without obvious unity.[16] Jennings's 1938 essay 'The Constitution of the British Commonwealth' described 'the growth of diverse forms of political practice in different places, the failure of late nineteenth and early twentieth century initiatives for greater coordination, and the emptiness of all that was left of the sole uniform practice within empire, common allegiance to the Crown'.[17] In his 1935 *Governments of the British Empire*, Keith argued that their different political histories meant that both the functions of the Crown in each territory, and the political principles used to justify its authority were different.[18] The plural view of empire in interwar historiography reached its most expansive expression in the multi-volume *Cambridge History of the British Empire* which privileged empirical elaboration, and was divided between territory-specific volumes which prevented an overarching account.[19]

The momentum of interwar scholarship carried into the post-Second World War decades. In 1959, the young American historian of empire Philip D. Curtin surveyed 'The British Empire and Commonwealth in Recent Historiography' for the *American Historical Review*. Curtin observed the simultaneous importance of imperial history's worldwide sweep, and of the collapse of empire as a unitary field. The history of the empire as a whole had been replaced by two new, 'quite different frames of reference', Curtin suggested. On the one hand, broader studies of 'the impact of the west' globally, and on the other, national or regional histories of different parts of the globe that had once been ruled by Britain. For periods later than the late eighteenth century studied in Vincent Harlow's then recent work, Curtin thought there simply were 'no works of broad synthesis'.[20]

Curtin missed the themes and arguments originating in radical and Marxist writings which drove the rebirth of imperial history. From J. A. Hobson in 1901 onwards, a succession of radical and Marxist writers and scholars characterised the history of Britain's possessions overseas as a process, not a set of institutions, labelled 'imperialism' not empire.[21] For Hobson imperialism was

---

[16] W. K. Hancock, *Survey of British Commonwealth Affairs*, vol. 1: *Problems of Nationality, 1918-1936* (1937); W. K. Hancock, *Survey of British Commonwealth Affairs*, vol. 2: *Problems of Economic Policy, 1918-1939* (1942).

[17] H. Kumarasingham (ed.), *Constitution Maker: Selected Writings of Sir Ivor Jennings* (Cambridge, 2015), 2-15; I. Jennings, 'The Constitution of the British Commonwealth', *Political Quarterly*, 9 (1938), 465-79; W. D. McIntyre, *The Britannic Vision: Historians and the Making of the British Commonwealth of Nations, 1907-48* (Basingstoke, 2009), 181-7.

[18] A. B. Keith, *The Governments of the British Empire* (1935).

[19] J. H. Rose et al., *Cambridge History of the British Empire* (8 vols., Cambridge, 1929-59).

[20] Philip D. Curtin, 'The British Empire and Commonwealth in Recent Historiography', *American Historical Review* 66 (1959), 74, 76.

[21] Keith Hancock's much quoted remark that imperialism was 'no word for scholars' reflected the strength of the critique. See Hancock, *Survey*, ii, 1-3. In that volume, W. H. B. Court contributed an appendix on the 'Communist Doctrines of Empire', *ibid.*, 293-305.

not a synonym for empire but a broader aggressive and expansive disposition by the world's great capitalist powers. Still trying to find a coherent principle able to explain why Britain possessed the territory it did, Hobson still saw imperialism as a process of political assertion in which officials and capitalists cooperated to create a 'despotic' form of authority which undermined the democracy of Britain and supposedly self-governing colonies.[22] But the pre-1917 generation of Marxists that included Rudolf Hilferding, Nikolai Bukharin, Rosa Luxemburg and of course V. I. Lenin moved beyond Hobson's political focus to define imperialism as a phase in the development of a social and economic system, capitalism, characterised by the hegemony of finance capital and which culminated in the First World War.[23] Debates in the Comintern during the interwar period explicitly broke the connection between imperialism and political power. The possibility of the Western powers dismembering their empires and granting independence to colonies was entertained, and defined as a strategy to retain capitalist hegemony; the word 'decolonisation' was first coined in this context. The renunciation of sovereignty was seen as a tactic of imperialism.[24] The jumbling of claims about empire, imperialism and global capitalism continued in debates about development and underdevelopment in the Latin American *dependencia* tradition, in debates about neocolonialism, world systems theory and modernisation.[25]

In his 1959 essay, Curtin also missed the text many later saw later as the beginning of the rebirth of the history of empire for non-Marxist scholars in the UK, John Gallagher and Ronald Robinson's 1953 essay 'The Imperialism of Free Trade'. Intriguingly, Gallagher and Robinson explicitly started with the same premise as Seeley, suggesting that the 'history of nineteenth century Britain was the history of an expanding society'. But they castigated the post-Seeley historiography which 'regarded the empire of kinship and constitutional dependence as an organism with its own [coherent] laws of growth'. Instead of developing the emphasis on the diversities and contradictions which the scholarship of the 1930s and 1940s detected within the political constitution of empire, Robinson and Gallagher drew on the post-Hobson discussion of imperialism to replace the British interwar focus on sovereignty with vaguer notions of power. Imperialism not empire was the key category; and

---

[22] J. A. Hobson, *Imperialism: A Study* (1902); P. J. Cain, *Hobson and Imperialism: Radicalism, New Liberalism, and Finance 1887–1938* (Oxford, 2002).

[23] V. I. Lenin, *Imperialism: The Highest Stage of Capitalism* (Beijing, 1917; reprint, 1975); A. Brewer, *Marxist Theories of Imperialism: A Critical Survey* (1990).

[24] R. B. Remnek, *M.N. Roy and the Comintern, 1920–1924* (1977); for the career of the concept of imperialism, see D. K. Fieldhouse, '"Imperialism": An Historiographical Revision', *Economic History Review*, 14 (1961), 187–209.

[25] F. H. Cardoso, E. Faletto, and M. Urquidi, *Dependency and Development in Latin America* (Berkeley, 1979); A. G. Frank, *Capitalism and Underdevelopment in Latin America: Historical Studies of Chile and Brazil* (New York, 1969), 187–209; W. Rodney, *How Europe Underdeveloped Africa* (Washington, DC, 1981); I. M. Wallerstein, *The Modern World-System* (3 vols., 1974–89); S. Amin and B. Pearce, *Accumulation on a World Scale: A Critique of the Theory of Underdevelopment* (New York, 1974). For discussion, see Brewer, *Marxist Theories*; D. K. Fieldhouse, *The West and the Third World: Trade, Colonialism, Dependence, and Development* (Oxford, 1999).

imperialism was defined as the 'sufficient political function of ... integrating new regions into the expanding economy'. Although not originators of the term, their use of 'informal empire' as a category of domination essentially equivalent to formal empire was central to their reconceptualisation of the field: '[a] concept of informal empire which fails to bring out the underlying unity between it and formal empire is sterile'.[26] Their account of Britain's role in the partition of Africa, while seeking to explain the assertion of formal empire (or territorial sovereignty), presented this as an attempt to preserve a mid-Victorian informal empire.[27]

Informal empire never won universal acceptance.[28] Nonetheless, the concept remained central to subsequent synthetic accounts within the Robinson and Gallagher tradition: Peter Cain and Tony Hopkins's British Imperialism, 1688-2000, and John Darwin's trilogy on British and global empires. Although revising chronology and emphasising the metropolitan economy and the City of London, Cain and Hopkins place great emphasis on the concept of informal empire.[29] Taking Gallagher and Robinson to a logical conclusion, sovereignty's relevance to Cain and Hopkins's history of empire was purely negative: '[t]he distinguishing feature of imperialism is not that it takes a specific economic, cultural or political form but that it involves an incursion, or an attempted incursion, into the sovereignty of another state'.[30] Darwin reworked the tradition differently. In early work he questioned the assumption that informal empire and formal empire are interchangeable, but on the grounds that in many regions (China and Latin America) informal empire was all that the British state could achieve. Equally, Darwin's early work with constitutional historian Frederick Madden heightened attention to political institutions in Unfinished Empire.[31] Still, his essential concern has remained with imperialism not empire. As he put it in 1997, '[i]mperialism may be defined as the sustained effort to assimilate a country or region to the political, economic or cultural system of another power' and he reasserted '[t]he futility of trying to make sense of Victorian expansion in terms of territorial

---

[26] J. Gallagher and R. Robinson, 'The Imperialism of Free Trade', Economic History Review, 6 (1953), 1-2, 5, 6-7.

[27] R. Robinson, J. Gallagher and A. Denny, Africa and the Victorians: The Official Mind of Imperialism (1961). On the concept of informal empire, see B. Attard, 'Informal Empire: The Origin and Significance of a Key Term', Modern Intellectual History, (2022).

[28] For an overview of the debate on Robinson and Gallagher, see W.R. Louis (ed.), Imperialism: The Robinson and Gallagher Controversy (New York, 1976). For contrasting views on informal empire, see D. C. M. Platt, 'Further Objections to an "Imperialism of Free Trade", 1830-60', Economic History Review, 26 (1973), 77-91; W. M. Mathew, 'The Imperialism of Free Trade: Peru, 1820-70', Economic History Review, 21 (1968), 562-79; D. McLean, 'Finance and "Informal Empire" before the First World War', Economic History Review, 29 (1976), 291-305; P. Winn, 'British Informal Empire in Uruguay in the Nineteenth Century', Past & Present, 73 (1976), 100-26.

[29] P. J. Cain and A. G. Hopkins, British Imperialism, 1688-2000 (Harlow, 2001). See also R. E. Dumett, Gentlemanly Capitalism and British Imperialism: The New Debate on Empire (1999).

[30] Cain and Hopkins, British Imperialism, 1688-2000, 54.

[31] A.F. Madden and J. Darwin (eds.), Select Documents on the Constitutional History of the British Empire and Commonwealth, vol. 6: The Dominions and India since 1900 (1993); J. Darwin, Unfinished Empire: The Global Expansion of Britain (2012).

or formal empire alone'.[32] Darwin's *The Empire Project* charts the rise and fall of multi-pillared British efforts to construct a 'world system' which extended far beyond Britain's formal territorial possessions.[33] His *After Tamerlane* charted the construction, contestation and collapse of (mostly) European global power for which empire was generally a synonym.[34]

If economic expansion offered one substrate which historians identify as driving the epiphenomena of Britain's sovereign assertions overseas, culture was another. Given the attention to non-political power disparities in place from the 1960s onwards, it is if anything surprising that the cultural turn took time to gain traction. Edward Said and historians writing in the wake of his 1978 *Orientalism* associated empire with a broad process of cultural domination propagated by non-state actors, in Said's case particularly universities and research institutions, loosely attached to the actions of an imperial regime.[35] The 'new imperial history' emphasised the place of cultural categories, particularly race and gender, in metropolitan life, focusing on non-governmental institutions: private networks, public scholarly associations, universities, research centres, churches, clubs and missionary societies.[36] More recently, studies have increasingly turned to the construction of whiteness as the necessary corollary of such racial otherness.[37] These different strands of argument tend overall to corral empire (and imperialism and colonialism – both generally used synonymously) into a unified, coherent field that focused on ideas of racial otherness, with little or only token reference to the diverse and specific political forms with which imperial authority was asserted. As Catherine Hall put it,

the variety of forms of rule *was* [original emphasis] underpinned by a [our emphasis] logic of rule – colonial governmentality, what Partha Chatterjee calls 'the rule of colonial difference'. This was the rule that distinguished the colonizers from the colonised, that was predicated on the power of the metropole over its subject peoples.[38]

The main varieties of British imperial history written since the mid-twentieth-century collapse of empire deploy empire as an under-conceptualised

---

[32] J. Darwin, 'Imperialism and the Victorians: The Dynamics of Territorial Expansion', *English Historical Review*, 112 (1997), 614; and his earlier work on decolonisation which, for Darwin, was never just a matter of constitutional change, J. Darwin, *Britain and Decolonisation: The Retreat from Empire in the Post-war World* (Basingstoke, 1988), 5–17.

[33] J. Darwin, *The Empire Project: The Rise and Fall of the British World-System, 1830–1970* (Cambridge, 2009).

[34] J. Darwin, *After Tamerlane: The Global History of Empire since 1405* (2007), 4–45.

[35] E. W. Said, *Orientalism* (1978); E. W. Said, *Culture and Imperialism* (1993).

[36] K. Wilson, *A New Imperial History: Culture, Identity, and Modernity in Britain and the Empire, 1660–1840* (Cambridge, 2004); C. Hall, *Civilising Subjects: Metropole and Colony in the English Imagination, 1830–1867* (Oxford, 2002); C. Hall and S. O. Rose, *At Home with the Empire: Metropolitan Culture and the Imperial World* (Cambridge, 2006).

[37] B. Schwarz, *Memories of Empire*, vol 1: *The White Man's World* (Oxford, 2011); Onni Gust, *Unhomely Empire: Whiteness and Belonging* (2020).

[38] C. Hall, 'Introduction', in *Cultures of Empire: A Reader. Colonisers in Britain and the Empire in Nineteenth and Twentieth Centuries*, ed. C. Hall (Manchester and New York, 2000), 19, quoting P. Chatterjee, *The Nation and Its Fragments: Colonial and Postcolonial Histories* (Princeton, 1993), 10.

metaphor within arguments about diffuse and often loosely defined forms of global (economic and/or cultural) power. The problem is that there is no stable basis for defining what kind of phenomenon counts as empire. As Gallagher and Robinson declared to the delight of every undergraduate nihilist, '[t]he imperial historian is very much at the mercy of his [sic] particular concept of empire [which] decides what facts are of "imperial" significance'.[39] Of course they offered little justification for their particular concept, other than their own unassailable intellectual confidence. By disengaging with the idea of sovereignty, and replacing it with vague notions of power, the conceptual architecture of histories of empire has become disconnected from its subject.

In contrast to the way the field has been broadly conceptualised, the presence of sovereignty in the archive means it is never absent from the detailed historiography of Britain's empire. Historians of the end of empire still study a subject unavoidably punctuated by the constitutional and legal dimensions of the transfer of sovereignty; few textbooks are complete without a world map showing the (conventional) dates territories became independent.[40] Historians of the law and constitutions particularly emphasise the multiple and contested character of the empire's structures. Harshan Kumarasingham has reasserted the importance of constitutional history, and shown how messy practices of sovereignty were crucial to the choreography of the end of empire in South Asia and in its political legacies in a series of 'Eastminsters'.[41] With an approach very similar to that adopted in this article, Mark Hickford offers a detailed account of the multiple constitutional idioms in play in practice in one particularly contested polity, New Zealand.[42] Tightening the diffuse literature on the 'British world', Stuart Ward's recent epic study charts the end of global Britishness conceived as a 'civic identity', and in so doing frequently acknowledges the associated political languages (and, by extension, institutions).[43] Lauren Benton's work has highlighted the role of plural forms of law, showing that 'multisided legal contests were simultaneously central to the construction of colonial rule and key to the formation of larger patterns of global structuring'.[44] Alan Lester, Kate Boehme and Peter Mitchell's project mapping imperial government 'everywhere all at once', has shown the the

---

[39] Gallagher and Robinson, 'The Imperialism of Free Trade', 1.

[40] For succinct justification, see J. D. Hargreaves, Decolonization in Africa (1996), 2–3.

[41] H. Kumarasingham, 'The "Tropical Dominions": The Appeal of Dominion Status in the Decolonisation of India, Pakistan and Ceylon', Transactions of the Royal Historical Society, 6th ser., 23 (2013); H. Kumarasingham, 'Eastminster: Decolonisation and State-Making in British Asia', in Constitution-Making in Asia: Decolonisation and State-Building in the Aftermath of the British Empire, ed. H. Kumarasingham (2016), 1–36.

[42] M. Hickford, 'Designing Constitutions in Britain's Mid-Nineteenth Century Empire: Indigenous Territorial Government in New Zealand and Retrieving Constitutional Histories', Journal of Imperial and Commonwealth History, 46 (2018), 676–706.

[43] S. Ward, Untied Kingdom: A Global History of the End of Britain (Cambridge, 2023). Space prevents consideration of wider literature on the 'British world', except to note that practitioners often attempt to distinguish that 'world' from empire, without success. For overview and critique, see Rachel Bright and Andrew Dilley, 'After the British World', Historical Journal, 60 (2017), 547–68.

[44] Lauren Benton, Law and Colonial Cultures: Legal Regimes in World History, 1400–1900 (Cambridge, 2002), 3. See also L. A. Benton, A Search for Sovereignty: Law and Geography in European Empires,

entangled nature of a plural empire whose occasional empire-wide projects worked themselves out in different places in different ways.[45] Most expansively, Jane Burbank and Frederick Cooper ground their study of *Empires in World History* in the observation that 'empire presumes that different peoples within the polity will be governed differently' and that all empires were built on a 'politics of difference'.[46]

This recent literature reminds us that empires have, as Jens Bartelson puts it, 'long constituted the default mode of political organization on a planetary scale'.[47] The danger in overly general accounts such as Burbank and Cooper's is that we lose sight of the thinking about different forms of empire in different historical moments. Britain's empire shared its incoherent structure with other contemporary empires; our argument is not a claim for any form of exceptionalism. There are points of comparison between the multiplicity of Britain's imperial idioms and the myriad of political forms and discourses within the French, Dutch, Spanish, Portuguese, Japanese or American empires (to name a few). Many empires since the seventeenth century have been distinguished from their predecessors by the possession of different territories effected through mutually incompatible political idioms and practices. This distinguished Britain's modern empire (alongside other contemporary European empires) from earlier composite monarchies. All empires are plural; not all are incoherent. In states such as the early modern Habsburg empire or pre-1707 British Isles, monarchs were capable of accumulating territory without destabilising their relationship with earlier possessions. They could do so because possessions were held personally, without a strong sense of the aggregate polity beyond the person of the monarch.[48] The British empire's incoherence emerged with the proliferation of political idioms which could justify the exercise of political authority, potentially separate from the institution of the monarch. Idioms in other words to articulate sovereignty, to which we now turn.

As codified from at least the writings of Jean Bodin in the late sixteenth century, the concept of sovereignty expressed a belief in the existence of a final, absolute, perpetual and undivided authority within political society. That belief has been expressed in different ways. To give two famous descriptions: the nineteenth-century British jurist John Austin suggested that the sovereign was 'a determinate human superior' that themselves had no superior but

---

1400-1900 (Cambridge, 2009); Lauren Benton and Lisa Ford, *Rage for Order: The British Empire and the Origins of International Law* (2016).

[45] Alan Lester, Kate Boehme and Peter Mitchell, *Ruling the World: Freedom, Civilization and Liberalism in the Nineteenth-Century British Empire* (Cambridge, 2021).

[46] Jane Burbank and Frederick Cooper, *Empires in World History: Power and the Politics of Difference* (Princeton, 2010), 8, 10.

[47] Jens Barteson, 'The Empire to Sovereignty – and Back?', *Ethics and International Affairs*, 28 (2014), 252.

[48] J. H. Elliott, 'A Europe of Composite Monarchies', *Past & Present*, 137 (1992), 48–71. Elliott's approach is informed by H. G. Koenigsberger, 'Dominium Regale or Dominium Politicum et Regale', in his *Politicians and Virtuosi: Essays in Early Modern History* (1975).

'receive[d] habital obedience from the bulk of a given society'; the twentieth-century German Carl Schmidt defined the sovereign as 'he who decides on the exception'.[49] The point from these descriptions is that a particular person, group of people or institutions possess final authority; the concept of sovereignty implies that there is a choice about who or what that authority is. As the mid-twentieth-century historian of international relations F. H. Hinsley put it, the question of sovereignty addresses the 'problem of deciding the basis of government and obligation within a political community'.[50]

Many scholars argue that sovereignty is a modern concept, marking a break with a medieval world in which political authority was distributed between multiple, overlapping secular and religious authorities.[51] Its life is bound up with the history of modern, European, post-Reformation empires. It presupposes a world of multiple, separate political entities, each governed by a sovereign body not accountable to any external earthly body. By the second half of the twentieth century, sovereignty had become the key concept within a post-imperial world order in which ultimate political authority was distributed between nation states. But as late as the late 1940s, sovereignty remained a crucial term to the exercise of imperial power. To begin with, leaders from the Western empires thought imperial sovereignty was upheld by the United Nations Charter for example. In a debate on the future of the Dutch empire in Southeast Asia in February 1946, Britain's foreign secretary, Ernest Bevin, recognised the political aspirations of Indonesians but suggested that 'the sovereignty of the Netherlands [over the Dutch East Indies] was not questioned'.[52]

The concept of sovereignty has long frustrated historians and political philosophers, leading many to reject it as an analytical category.[53] Frustration emerges from the concept's ambiguity in two ways, both of which illuminate British imperial politics. First, sovereignty is both a normative and empirical concept. It indicates who or what should possess authority within any particular society: the people, king, parliament or whatever. But it also needs to have some kind of actual basis in power and institutions. A seemingly legitimate claim to authority alone is not sovereign power; king in exile is not a sovereign until able to control the institutions of administration. A generation of early twentieth-century political thinkers, led by French jurist Léon Duguit and English political theorist Harold Laski, argued that this ambiguity meant sovereignty should be replaced by a more realistic, empirical account of political

---

[49] John Austin, *The Province of Jurisprudence Determined* (Cambridge, [1832], 2009); Carl Schmitt, *Political Theology: Four Chapters on the Concept of Sovereignty* (Chicago, [1932] 2005), 1.

[50] F. H. Hinsley, *Sovereignty*, 2nd edn (Cambridge, 1986), 26

[51] For example, Charles McIlwain, *The Growth of Political Thought in the West* (1932), 392; Robert Jackson, *Sovereignty: The Evolution of an Idea* (2009), 1–24; Quentin Skinner offers a connected account of the origins of a modern concept of the state in *Foundations of Modern Political Thought*, vol. 2: *Reformation* (1978), particularly 350–5.

[52] Security Council Official Records, 1st year, 13th meeting, 9 February 1946, https://digitallibrary.un.org/record/636634 (accessed 26 May 2023).

[53] Benjamin Franklin in 1770 was not the last to feel 'quite sick of this our *Sovereignty*', quoted in David Armitage, *Foundations of Modern International Thought* (Cambridge, 2013), 216.

authority.[54] Sovereignty's focus on a single unitary point of legitimate authority was a 'metaphysical' or 'mystic' abstraction, which contrasted with the dispersal of real power amongst multiple institutions within a society. But politics is partly constituted by people's arguments about norms; about who can legitimately do what to whom. Grounded in both political ideas and political practice, the concept of sovereignty addresses the crucial interplay between these normative arguments and political reality.

The dual character of sovereignty as both normative and real allowed multiple idioms of sovereignty to proliferate within the empire. The validity of a particular idiom was never determined by purely empirical criteria, but blended fact, political aspiration and the ideas of necessity drawn from a particular political situation. For example, the idea that Britain's sovereignty in India came from conquest reflected a particular account of South Asian history, a desire to assert superiority and power, and a belief in the necessity of centralised violence as the only force able to maintain order in the subcontinent. The ambiguous mix of fact and norm meant that another very different concept of sovereignty, in this case that Britain governed with the consent of the governed for example, could be plausibly articulated at the same time.

There is, though, a second ambiguity. Sovereignty makes claims to both internal and external validation which can be very different from one another. European powers recognised sovereignty over each other's empires, as if each piece of imperial territory was a similar kind of entity. But the claims to legitimacy made within each particular territory might be very different, entailing the location of authoritative political power in one or another domestic institution. Bevin's comment in 1946 about the Netherlands' sovereignty over its Asian empire meant only that an external organisation such as the United Nations had no right to interfere in the Dutch government of its colonies; it eschewed any judgement about how Indonesia was ruled; what appeared from the outside as a coherent international order made up of equivalent sovereign states seemed from within each state to be constituted by multiple, incoherent idioms of sovereignty. Hannah Arendt pushed this to the extreme by arguing that the American revolution exploited the division between internal and external by 'reconcil[ing] the advantages of monarchy in foreign affairs with those of republicanism in domestic policy'. The early US state, she argued, abolished internal sovereignty altogether in favour of the diffusion of power through multiple institutions; but asserted a sense of itself as a strong, unified sovereign power that stood alongside the world's imperial powers externally.[55] In Britain's and other empires, externally recognised imperial sovereignty often coexisted with the very limited assertion of power over territory, sometimes involving little more than ambiguous agreements with local political hierarchies. At the fringes of imperial territory, frontiers were often purely notional agreements with other powers; the priority for empire's governors was to manage conflict with other states in the international arena, not

---

[54] Léon Duguit, 'Law and the Modern State', *Harvard Law Review* 31, (1917), 6; Harold Laski, *Studies in the Problem of Sovereignty* (New Haven, 1917), 4–5.

[55] Hannah Arendt, *On Revolution* ([1963] 1990), 153.

assert territorial power on a granular scale.[56] The form of empire in practice at any one moment was shaped by the complex and highly variable way claims to sovereignty were made and practised at different spatial scales. The possibility of different ways of discussing internal and external sovereignty multiplied the plural idioms available for empire's protagonists to discuss their authority.

As Michael Freeden points out, these claims to ultimate authority are usually made in time.[57] Arguments about who possesses final authority rely on stories about how that authority was first created. The disparate territories of the British empire shared their common submission before the Crown, but they articulated very different stories about *how* the authority of the Crown was created. Empire, in other words, was constituted not only by multiple claims to authority, but by equally multiple and contradictory histories of legitimate power; that's why the default form of imperial history has been the history of particular territories, not empire as a whole. Those histories provided a resource for protagonists from across empire to justify their actions and to challenge others'. But when brought too close to one another in the practical task of governance, they created tension and crisis.

The territories which composed the British empire went under a bewildering variety of names: dominions, colonies, protectorates, condominiums, mandates, dependencies, treaty ports, subordinate empires, territories and the like.[58] The language used to describe the relationship between Britain and its imperial territories matters because it expressed the plural forms in which British sovereignty was expressed. That language of sovereignty emerged from, but also shaped, institutions and practices of governance.

In order to begin to reconstruct the politics of incoherent sovereignty, the remainder of this section offers a typology of the language used in the British empire's different claims to sovereignty, each of which was made through different accounts of how authority was acquired. This is not to reproduce the reductionist meta-geographies or meta-chronologies often used to impart false coherence to the history of empire: settler/self-governing vs dependent/despotic; first, second, third, even fourth (!) British empires. Rather it is to describe the different competing forms claims of sovereignty could take. Within any location different idioms always coexisted, shifted and clashed, even though one or another form often achieved temporary dominance.

The starting point for our typology needs to be the early modern English Crown's claim to imperial authority over the independent, unitary realm of England itself. Most famously articulated in Henry VIII's Act in Restraint of Appeals (24 Henr. VIII c.12), the claim to empire had been made from the late fourteenth century onwards, when English alongside other European kings began to wear the closed imperial crown associated with the Holy

---

[56] For the ambiguities of imperial frontiers in north-east India, see Bérénice Guyot-Rechard, *Shadow States: India, China and the Himalayas, 1910–1962* (Cambridge, 2016), 31–58.

[57] Michael Freeden, *The Political Theory of Political Thinking: The Anatomy of a Practice* (2013), 119–22.

[58] M. I. Finley, 'Colonies: An Attempt at a Typology', *Transactions of the Royal Historical Society*, 5th ser., 26 (1976), 167–88.

Roman Emperor. Used to assert equivalent status to other European monarchies, England's imperial statutes gave its monarch ultimate authority. In the process they defined a territorially defined political community, 'a body compact of all sorts and degrees of people' which had a duty to obey the Crown. Even here, empire as sovereignty over one territory easily bled into claims to rule other territories. As David Armitage notes, within the British Isles such claims were first made by the Scottish monarch over the then Norwegian-ruled Western Isles. By the time Tudor England adopted them, they referred to the government of Wales and parts of Ireland, and claims to Scotland and sometimes territories beyond. The claim of unitary absolute monarchical authority relied on no single founding moment, but appealed to a history of continuous kingship, citing 'divers sundry old authentic histories and chronicles' to prove the continuity of English kingship well before the Norman conquest. Elements of this idiom endured for centuries.[59]

A second idiom, which became particularly popular during Britain's civil wars, challenged the unitary self-evidence of authority from the mere fact of monarchical continuity. This grounded sovereignty on the will of the people within a particular territory, making the Crown's authority conditional on the monarch's conformity to popular wishes. Here the people existed as an organised, geographically defined entity that gave the Crown its authority, but constituted the first and final arbiter of political decision-making. Like the Henrician monarch, this republican, self-governing people claimed a continuous existence before memory or written record, with the Norman conquest sometimes seen as an illegitimate usurpation.[60]

The invocation of an imperial monarch or imperial people were initially claims to English (or later British) sovereignty over the people in England (and later the United Kingdom). Both forms of sovereignty could, though, be transferred outside Europe, through conquest, settlement and often unequal acts of voluntary cession. These claims justified the attempt to assert domination, often through violence, of people and territories throughout the world. But they did so in different and mutually incompatible ways, which created very different relationships with local and migrant populations, and between overseas territories and the imperial metropolis.

Conquest, our third archetype, is often neglected as an explicit source of sovereign political authority; some scholars arguing indeed that it needed to be 'masked' by other principles of legitimacy.[61] But the explicitly violent subjugation of local states and peoples was an important principle used to publicly justify the establishment of sovereignty until at least the early twentieth century.[62]

---

[59] David Armitage, *The Ideological Origins of the British Empire* (Cambridge, 2004), 34; David Armitage, 'The Elizabethan Idea of Empire', *Transactions of the Royal Historical* Society, 6th ser., 14 (2004), 269–77.

[60] Lorenzo Sabbadini, 'Popular Sovereignty and Representation in the English Civil War', in *Popular Sovereignty in Historical Perspective*, ed. Richard Bourke and Quentin Skinner (Cambridge, 2016), 164–86.

[61] Gauri Viswanathan, *Masks of Conquest: Literary Studies and British Rule in India* (1990).

[62] For example, Mark Wilks, *Historical Sketches of the South of India* (1820), I, 438–42; William, H. Prescott, *History of the Conquest of Mexico* (1843), II, 43.

Sovereignty established through conquest relied on a story about an original conflict and a moment of defeat and submission in which authority was transferred to a new state. This was not necessarily a moment of complete upheaval. Repeating a centuries-long trope, Keith wrote in the 1930s that where the Crown came by 'cessation or conquest' into possession of the territories of a 'civilised power and in enjoyment of a code of law … it did not hold that the law was changed by mere fact of conquest or cessation'. Crucially, the Crown's assertion of sovereignty did create a new state; conquest didn't merely add an existing state to the monarch's possessions. But 'the common law remained that prevailing before the British acquisition'. Ambiguity imbued Keith's words, with the definition of a 'civilised power' and the identity of pre-existing law always open to debate, leading in practice to the multiplication of legal systems, as well as uncertainty about their boundaries in many parts of empire.[63]

The historical languages of sovereignty consequent on conquest were not simple. Conquest dominated imperial politicians' explanations of England's authority in eighteenth-century Ireland, although not unchallenged and with varying details and outworkings. Jonathan Swift wrote about 'the savage Irish, who our Ancestors conquered several hundred years ago', while from the 1730s Protestant soldiers who fought with King William proclaimed 'we … conquered [at] the Boyne'. But conquest troubled Whigs and liberal Protestants who struggled to legitimise Britain's connection to Ireland without it, but feared past force justified present and future violence. In response some conjured a benign form of conquest, 'into freedom and happiness' as the Irish attorney general put it in the 1820s.[64] Others, such as Thomas Macaulay, believed they were forced to accept its reality but also to condemn those who perpetuated the 'fatal heritage of malignant passions' into a post-conquest world.[65]

Conquest's complexity underlay discussions of India's relationship with Britain. The concept was first used to understand India's polity before the growth of British power, with the idea of Mughal conquest helping legitimate the notion of British conquest. It became, by the 1830s, the centrepiece of a Tory view of empire, articulated most clearly by members of the Duke of Wellington's circle, such as Charles Metcalfe. 'We are here by conquest, not by the affection of our subjects,' Metcalfe wrote in 1833.[66] Others, including again Macaulay, spoke again about the need for conquest to be tempered by conciliation and slow incorporation of Indians into British institutions. As with Ireland, Macaulay's role was to assimilate Tory arguments about hierarchy and violence into Whig narratives about constitutional progress.[67] By

---

[63] Keith, Governments of the British Empire, 12; see Jon E. Wilson, The Domination of Strangers (2008), for the British effort to govern with existing custom in Bengal.

[64] Sharon Korman, The Right of Conquest (Oxford, 2003), 46. Jacqueline Hill, 'The Language and Symbolism of Conquest in Ireland, c.1790–1850', Transactions of the Royal Historical Society, 6th ser., 18 (2008), 165–86.

[65] Thomas Macaulay, History of England from the Accession of James II, II (1848), xxx.

[66] 'Minute by Sir C.T. Metcalfe', 18 October 1830, Further Papers Respecting the East India Company's Charter, Parliamentary Papers, HC (1833) XXV, 18

[67] Kieran Hazzard, 'From Conquest to Consent: British Political Thought and India, 1818–1833' (Ph.D. thesis, King's College London, 2016).

the middle of the nineteenth century, conquest was part of the staple vocabulary used to discuss British rule, which most commentators thought needed to be acknowledged to make any line of reasoning convincing. Arguments against were, though, possible, Seeley's marginalisation of India's place in empire occurring through his denial of conquest.[68] Only from the 1920s did alternative themes replace conquest as the dominant idiom for Britons discussing the basis of British rule in India, as imperial administrators were forced to introduce principles to justify their framing of reforms which introduced Indians as partners in government. By 1929, a retired British officer could write to M. K Gandhi acknowledging some still believed Britain was 'in possession of India ... by right of conquest', but he thought most saw themselves 'as trustees of the whole population'.[69] Even then, the shift produced waves of published, eloquent anger amongst serving and former British officers committed to the idea that conquest was the basis of Britain's supposedly unilateral power in India.[70]

If conquest was the extraterritorial equivalent of monarchical absolutism, our fourth archetype, settlement, once called colonisation, was the extraterritorial equivalent of popular sovereignty. The early twentieth-century Cambridge University Press *History of the Australasian Colonies* described British sovereignty as not acquired 'by accident of dynastic title' but through the emigration of 'communities of kindred blood'. This form of sovereignty involved 'a movement of population and an extension of political power', as another early twentieth-century textbook put it.[71] Settlers constituted themselves as distant citizens of the imperial homeland, then defined their citizenship through their racial difference from 'local' populations and their common labour in the creation of a settler society. Settlement justified the extension of apparently British institutions such as representative assemblies. It was also used by settlers to oppose the encroachment of more authoritarian imperial institutions on what they saw as their rights.[72]

While conquest relied on the existence of a prior political structure which could be forced to submit, settlement depended on the settlers' denial of the existence of legally constituted political authority beforehand. That denial relied either on the fiction of *terra nullius*, empty land, the claim that land 'not possessed of any Christian Prince' had no legitimate regime, or that the supposed savagery and violence of indigenous regimes made coexistence impossible. In practice, settlement relied on the annihilation or displacement of existing polities and peoples. That meant that the sequence by which contemporaries described the emergence of sovereignty through settlement in

---

[68] Seeley, *Expansion of England*; 'Dissent by John Shepherd', 6 January 1849, *Correspondence Respecting the Disposal of Sattara State*, Parliamentary Papers, HC (1849) XXXIX, 137; James FitzJames Stephen, *Liberty, Equality, Fraternity* (1873).

[69] M. K. Gandhi, 'In Possession', in *Collected Works of Mahatma Gandhi* (New Delhi, 2005), XLV, 181

[70] For the Tory rearguard action, see A. L. Carthill, *The Lost Dominion* (1924).

[71] Edward Jenks, *A History of the Australasian Colonies* (Cambridge, 1912); Albert Kenner, *Colonization* (1908), 1.

[72] L. Veracini, '"Settler Colonialism": Career of a Concept', *Journal of Imperial and Commonwealth History*, 41 (2013), 313–33.

their histories of empire was often complex. Sovereignty in New South Wales began with military power, but was transferred to a migrant population as free, non-convict settlers moved in greater numbers and the aboriginal population was either annihilated or marginalised. In British North America, an initial phase of conquest was narrated first through a sequence of conflicts between European powers in which native Americans were involved, then as conflict when native American states refused to live peacefully with their European neighbours.[73]

European settlement in New Zealand occurred alongside the extension of British power over Maori by treaty, to begin with, but eventually involved violence. Here though, the importance of settlement as the source of authority made it impossible for Britons to avow conquest as the mode by which the Crown's authority was extended. Even in the most violent encounters with Maori warriors during the New Zealand Wars, British actions were defined as the opposite of conquest. In October 1863, British imperial officers tried to impose sovereignty over Maori in the Waikato area, who had retained their independence. But the imperial invasion of the region was not described as an act of conquest. Speaking to the representatives of settlers in October 1863, Governor Sir George Grey argued that fighting had been provoked by particularly belligerent groups of Maori seizing land which had long been 'peacefully occupied by our settlers', embarking on 'schemes of conquest and plunder' instead. While in India conquest could be explicitly celebrated, and was a common framework for talking about British rule, in New Zealand the importance of the idiom of settlement required conquest by the British to be denied, and a conquering mindset attributed to Maori. Clearly both positions could not be avowed consciously at the same time.[74]

A fifth category, plantations, involved the assertion of sovereignty in order to protect the 'settlement of capital', as Hugh Egerton put it.[75] Here, institutions were created in order to profit from the production of commodities, cultivated through the labour of enslaved or indentured non-citizens. As with settlement, the territory over which sovereignty was asserted was seen as empty land, able to be transformed through the agency of imperial authority. But that transformation did not occur through the 'settlement of men'. Instead institutions were created which allowed money to be invested controlling unfree labour, and then ensuring that labour force worked the land for its owners to profit. A tiny European population sometimes imagined themselves to be the members of a self-governing demos. But the most important relationship was the assertion of power over land and forced labour. Sovereignty was asserted through the legal definition of the subordinated population in slave

---

[73] Jan Kociumbas, *The Oxford History of Australia*, vol. II: *Possessions* (Sydney, 1992); Mark Francis, *Governors and Settlers: Images of Authority in the British Colonies, 1820-1860* (Cambridge, 1992); for the Canadian narrative see Jeffers Frith, *History of Canada* (Toronto, 1884); Charles Lucas, *A History of Canada, 1763-1812* (1909), 1-32.

[74] James Belich, *The New Zealand Wars and the Victorian Interpetation of Race Conflict* (Auckland, 1986); Sir George Grey to Legislative Council and House of Representatives, Enclosure in no. 42, 'Further Papers Relative to the Affairs of New Zealand', *House of Lords Papers* XII (i), 1864.

[75] Egerton, *Greater Britain*, 5.

codes and penal laws. While this form was dominant in the Caribbean, variants on such differential claims to sovereignty made by European settlers on non-Europeans could be found in various forms across the empire, for instance in the settler societies of British Africa and arguably eighteenth-century Ireland.[76] The imperial state's focus on extracting profit from natural and human resources at the expense of migrant or indigenous people and local economic development was paralleled in the approach in Newfoundland, where settlement was discouraged in order to retain a British monopoly on extracting fish.[77]

The three categories of conquest, settlement and plantation could all overlap with, but also run counter to, a sixth archetype which, in various incarnations, often underlay the story about empire which the British often told themselves: that imperial sovereignty was justified in the supposed advances and benefits delivered to those governed.[78] We have already encountered it in Whig attempts to soften high Tory claims to sovereignty by conquest whether in Ireland or India. Under the guise of the 'civilising mission' or concepts of 'trusteeship', this strand of underlying paternalism persisted in British discourses on empire. Trusteeship underpinned Edmund Burke's arguments on India in the 1780s, along with antislavery and nineteenth-century humanitarianism. It was a central element of Lord Lugard's 'Dual Mandate' and underpinned clashes between Southern Rhodesian and Kenyan settlers and the Colonial Office. As we saw a moment ago, in the minds of many it replaced 'the right of conquest' as the justification for British rule in India in the interwar period. The racialised justifications for colonial rule combined claims about its supposedly beneficent effects and its necessity given the supposed incapacity of subjects to govern themselves. In modified form such arguments justified the withholding of full autonomy from either imperial governors or impatient settlers. This form also transferred directly into the League of Nations mandate system.[79]

Seventh, sovereignty was acquired through the formally voluntary cession of authority through treaties with existing regimes. Often this supposedly

---

[76] For slave codes in Jamaica, see Mary Turner, *Slaves and Missionaries: The Disintegration of Jamaica Slave Society, 1787-1834* (1982); for Ireland as a plantation society ruled through a penal code, Ian McBride, *Eighteenth Century Ireland: The Isle of Slaves* (Dublin, 2009), ch. 5. For southern African examples, see Charles Van Onselen, *Chibaro: African Mine Labour in Southern Rhodesia 1900-1933* (1975); Rachel Bright, *Chinese Labour in South Africa, 1902-10: Race, Violence, and Global Spectacle* (Basingstoke, 2013).

[77] For this comparison, see C. P. Lucas, Review of 'A History of Newfoundland', *English Historical Review*, 11, 43 (1896), 602.

[78] For professional historians justifying empire, see P. Satia, *Time's Monster: History, Conscience and Britain's Empire* (Cambridge, 2020).

[79] R. Hyam, 'Bureaucracy and "Trusteeship" in the Colonial Empire', in *Oxford History of the British Empire*, vol. 4: *The Twentieth Century*, ed. J. M. Brown and W. R. Louis (Oxford, 1999), 255–80; A. N. Porter, 'Trusteeship, Anti-Slavery and Humanitarianism', in *Oxford History of the British Empire*, vol 3: *The Nineteenth Century*, ed. A. N. Porter (Oxford, 1999), 198–211; F. J. D. B. Lugard, *The Dual Mandate in British Tropical Africa* (1922); P. J. Cain, 'Character, "Ordered Liberty", and the Mission to Civilise: British Moral Justification of Empire, 1870-1914', *Journal of Imperial and Commonwealth History*, 40 (2012), 557–78.

consensual act of cession occurred after a moment of violence. Frequently the terms of exchange were unequal. But the claim that rights had been ceded rather than seized, and were based on treaty not conquest, shaped the history of later institutions, enabling subordinated populations to articulate their own claims with a language of historical legitimacy. This is the mode which structured sovereignty initially in New Zealand, before settlement emerged as the dominant idiom. According to the British interpretation of the text, in the 1840 Treaty of Waitangi Maori exchanged supreme sovereignty for protection of their right to property. The treaty framed the conversation between the British state and Maori in New Zealand throughout the nineteenth century, with Maori asking, and being reassured, about it being still in force during the New Zealand Wars, for example. Treaties structured the continual dialogue which occurred between India's 'native states' and the British regime, as rulers continually challenged what they saw as imperial administrators' breach of promises, a challenge they usually lost but sometimes won.[80] The capitulations, unequal treaties and other partial concessions of sovereignty which characterised Britain's imperial presence in the Ottoman Empire and China (key spheres of so-called 'informal empire') might be understood as a confined blend of conquest- and treaty-based sovereign authority where, again, the nature of British claims was deeply contested.[81] In practice, cession involved a complex blend of old and new, and the reconstruction and co-option of existing or (re)invented sovereignties into imperial structures.[82]

Eighth and finally, sovereignty over a territory could be founded on the authority of global institutions. The most obvious examples were the League of Nations and United Nations mandates of the 1920s and 1940s; but joint and complicatedly interwoven forms of authority were common beforehand, from international supervision of the sixteenth-century fisheries at Newfoundland to the treaty ports in nineteenth-century China. Transnational claims to sovereignty often involved a more abstract and universalistic language and created institutions which followed suit.[83] Thus the municipal council which administered the international settlement in Shanghai incorporated many forms familiar from elsewhere in the British empire, but functioned as a vehicle for what Isabella Jackson calls 'trans-national colonialism' administered by a multinational cast of actors within the matrix established by foundational treaties and concessions by China.[84] The collapse of imperial claims to legitimate sovereignty together with the growing emphasis on self-determination in the

---

[80] For an account of British power in India which privileges treaties, see Callie Wilkinson, *Empire of Influence: The East India Company and the Making of Indirect Rule* (Cambridge, 2023).

[81] Jurgen Osterhammel, 'Semi-colonialism and Informal Empire in Twentieth-Century China: Towards a Framework of Analysis', in *Imperialism and After: Continuities and Discontinuities*, ed. W. J. Mommsen and J. Osterhammel (1986), 290–314.

[82] For the resultant muddle in Africa, see W. M. Hailey, *An African Survey: A Study of Problems Arising in Africa South of the Sahara* (Oxford, 1938).

[83] Michael D. Callahan, *The League of Nations and Africa, 1914–1931* (Eastbourne, 2008); S. Pedersen, *The Guardians: The League of Nations and the Crisis of Empire* (Oxford, 2016).

[84] I. Jackson, *Shaping Modern Shanghai: Colonialism in China's Global City* (Cambridge, 2018); R. Bickers and I. Jackson (eds.), *Treaty Ports in Modern China* (2016).

twentieth century left little other than international trusteeship to justify imperial rule.[85]

This list of archetypes is not exhaustive or mutually exclusive, something we have sought to illustrate especially in our discussions of conquest and settlement. There were no stable boundaries between each one; each could be subdivided. Nor did each define the identity of any single area of imperial territory. Often, more than one claim was made for the same place at the same moment, sometimes in coalescence, and sometimes in argument, with others. A common pattern was for multiple idioms to be asserted when a territory first came under British sovereign authority, with one of these predominating through contest between different groups of governors, settlers and indigenous peoples. Crucially the claims to sovereign authority shaped the political institutions which asserted power in practice, as well as the other way round. The incoherence and multiplicity of imperial sovereignty is not just an idle curiosity for historians of political thought but ought to be central to the broader historical study of empire.

The empire's sweep encouraged its protagonists and subjects, supporters and opponents, to try to offer universal accounts of its rise, systematic character and, more recently, its fall. Such narratives ultimately always failed; telling stories relied on giving empire a single identity, which involved the suppression of other incompatible narratives. Reincorporating the incoherence of imperial sovereignty requires something more than merely recognising empire's complexity and diversity: it involves an account of how the fundamental instability and ever present clash between mutually incompatible idioms of sovereignty in turn shaped the politics and governance of the empire. Recognising this, we sketch in this final section, may help answer some of the big questions in the history of Britain's empire.

First, war. Violence within empire frequently occurred as governors and subjects who previously existed separately with incompatible but unacknowledged visions of empire were forced to confront their differences. War, often on a global scale against Britain's rivals and enemies, created the greatest sense of coordinated action with a defined purpose. The short-term exigencies and exertions needed to create such coherent action only accelerated the disruptive tendencies of multiple idioms of sovereign authority. Such periods coincided with major assertions of, and retreats from, imperial authority, and were followed by the empire's most serious crises.

The Seven Years War, for example, created an unsustainable tension between different visions of imperial sovereignty. In 1763, the conquest and cession of territory across North America through the exercise of British arms enabled British politicians to use a more militaristic idiom to justify a

---

[85] J. L. Pearson, 'Defending Empire at the United Nations: The Politics of International Colonial Oversight in the Era of Decolonisation', *Journal of Imperial and Commonwealth History*, 45 (2017), 525–49; M. Mazower, *No Enchanted Palace: The End of Empire and the Ideological Origins of the United Nations* (Oxford, 2009); R. Burke, *Decolonization and the Evolution of International Human Rights* (Philadelphia, 2010).

more systematic and absolutist form of power. Lord Egremont's June 'Report on Acquisitions in America' criticised the chaotic extension of settlement throughout the Americas, and set out a systematic plan which would govern through 'a considerable military force'. Political leaders in London imagined this North American empire of conquest would be regulated from Parliament. But settlers in the Americas thought sovereignty had been transferred in the physical migration of individual subjects, who then created their own new British institutions through contracts and charters which created new forms of 'civil body politic', as the Mayflower Compact put it. The American crisis began as the clash between an idea of empire as a composite monarchy made up of self-governing territories affiliated to the Crown without being subject to Whitehall, and an alternative notion of a political hierarchy controlled from the Crown-in-Parliament in London. The period of what Edmund Burke called 'salutary neglect' before the Seven Years War allowed incompatible ideas to develop without conflict. The unity required in war exposed the essential incoherence of empire, creating an almost terminal crisis.[86]

A similar dynamic occurred within other global conflicts. The First World War brought the empire together as a global belligerent in a way which had never occurred before. The representation in the imperial war cabinet of leaders from territories on five continents seemed to presage a broader form of imperial union. Yet in practice, efforts to marshal the diverse sovereignties of the empire in the First World War disrupted the possibilities of governance in the long term.[87] They led white-ruled dominions to assert greater autonomy based on their claim of having established democratic polities through settlement. Indian anti-imperialism was energised by the denial of Britain's Asian empire's equivalence to white settler self-governance in the name of the enduring importance of conquest as the basis of Britain's claim to exercise power. Such contradictions pushed empire to total collapse after World War II. New systems of coordination, often created in collaboration with the USA, wove imperial territories into a kind of mutual dependence which was unsustainable once peace forced politicians to reflect on the principles of legitimacy which sustained their rule.

Secondly, our emphasis on mutually incompatible idioms of sovereign authority helps explain the incidence and scale of violence more generally within empire. The violence associated with empire did not occur evenly. An attention to the concepts of sovereignty in operation at particular junctures provides suggestive ways to understand these variations in the scale of both endemic and episodic violence. First, the degree to which concepts of

---

[86] Lord Egremont, 'Report on the Acquisitions in America', 8 June 1763, https://www.solon.org/Constitutions/Canada/English/PreConfederation/lt_17630608.html (accessed 26 Jan. 2021). For a discussion of the American crisis as the clash between contradictory visions of empire, see J. G. A. Pocock, 'Empire, State and Confederation: The War of American Independence as a Crisis in Multiple Monarchy', in *A Union for Empire: Political Thought and the Union of 1707*, ed. John Robertson (Cambridge, 1995), 318–48.

[87] A. J. Stockwell, 'The War and the British Empire', in *Britain and the First World War*, ed. J. Turner (1988).

sovereignty conceived of populations as objects in the pursuit of some other objective, rather than subjects or citizens, affected the possibility for violence to be legitimated. Slave plantations treating the bulk of the population as property opened the way for extreme levels of coercion constrained only by metropolitan regulation.[88] In settler societies, endemic violence was concentrated on the frontiers of colonialism where indigenous peoples were marginalised and displaced; the importance of the apparently peaceful idiom of settlement in legitimating authority meant the scale of violence was frequently hidden, in many cases until long after the end of empire. Ironically, imperial power was at its most total, indeed sometimes genocidal, where violence was not explicitly recognised in the idiom used to justify sovereignty. Imperial violence against indigenous people in Australia and in India were both structured by idioms of racial difference; but their different practices and effects can only be understood by charting the multiple contradictory ways violence was justified.[89]

The multiple contradictory conceptions of sovereignty across empire accentuated the chance of clashes and provided alternative vocabularies through which challenges to the status quo might be mobilised. Many of the most violent episodes in imperial history occurred as groups of people who had imagined they inhabited the same polity realised their antagonists had a radically different conception of sovereignty. Participants in the 1857 rising in northern India rallied around idioms of Mughal sovereignty in response to British assertions of rights of conquest along with associated attempts to intervene at an all-India level. Here, actions which British officers saw as the necessary consequence of sovereignty acquired by conquest were regarded as illegitimate when viewed through the prism of the East India Company's bounded treaties with Mughal sovereignty.[90] Put schematically, 1857 saw a clash between our third (conquest) and fifth (treaty) archetypes of sovereign authority. The violence of the end of empire emerged from competing conceptions of national sovereignty which emerged out of or in response to different imperial idioms. The violence associated with the emergency in Kenya or continual violence in Southern Rhodesia emerged in contexts where imperial, settler and various African notions of sovereignty came into conflict with one another.[91] Rebellion and counter-rebellion occurred as protagonists' visions of authority clashed within an empire which proliferated incompatible ways of justifying and resisting sovereign power.

Third, attention to the incoherence of empire helps unpick the economic consequences of empire. Clashing conceptions of sovereignty produced no institutional coherence. Empire as a whole was not a project of development, nor the systematic producer of underdevelopment, although both of these

---

[88] Mary Turner, *Slaves and Missionaries: The Disintegration of Jamaican Slave Society, 1787-1834* (Kingston, Jamaica, 1998).

[89] Henry Reynolds, *The Other Side of the Frontier: Aboriginal Resistance to the European Invasion of Australia* (Ringwood, 1982).

[90] F. W. Buckler, 'The Political Theory of the Indian Mutiny', *Transactions of the Royal Historical Society*, 4th ser., 5 (1922), 71–100.

[91] D. Anderson, *Histories of the Hanged: Britain's Dirty War in Kenya and the End of Empire* (2006).

occurred at certain places and times. In some cases, notions of sovereignty were directly produced by particular efforts at economic exploitation. In the slave economy of the Caribbean, a system of comprehensive labour exploitation evolved in tandem with an associated plantation conception of sovereignty and institutions of political governance. Cecil Rhodes's British South Africa Company evolved a similarly comprehensive and geographically extensive system of Chibaro labour in its attempt to squeeze profits from gold mines in its territories.[92] Not all concepts of sovereignty were so tightly tied to such exploitative economic outcomes. Railways, for example, in India were primarily constructed for military and political ends, to secure conquest, with British capitalists constantly clamouring for more and different routes than those which were actually built.[93] But different concerns drove policy in different places. In tropical Africa and Australia, governments prioritised exports above defence: the north–south transcontinental line in Australia which Lord Kitchener argued was integral to the territory's defence was only completed in 2003.

Judged by growing output, the most economically successful portions of the empire, the settler dominions, were those portions where economic policy was increasingly determined domestically through representative institutions responding in a fluid way to global economic norms. This growth was grounded in the seizure of land from the indigenous population who were then largely excluded from growth because of their partial or total political and economic exclusion.[94] Elsewhere, the desire of imperial officers to maintain more absolutist idioms of imperial sovereignty usually (if not inevitably) constrained the involvement of local populations in institutions which would have facilitated development, or limited involvement to a small number of highly governed spaces such as port cities.[95] In much of Britain's African empire, colonial administrations constantly fretted that the social consequences of economic change would undermine their political control through neo-traditional elites.[96] In short, those writing the political economy of empire need to think closely about the economic impacts of the political institutions produced by incoherent sovereignty.

Finally, our approach helps explain the complex and uneven process by which empire ended and was replaced by a set of theoretically equal sovereign nation states.[97] The late 1940s saw the emergence of the first truly coherent global idea of world order. As the idioms of legitimacy which had justified

---

[92] Charles Van Onselen, *Chibaro: African Mine Labour in Southern Rhodesia, 1900–1933* (Gwelo, 1974).

[93] Jon Wilson, *India Conquered: Britain's Raj and the Chaos of Empire* (2016), 278–90.

[94] J. Belich, *Replenishing the Earth: The Settler Revolution and the Rise of the Anglo-World, 1783–1939* (Oxford, 2009); P. Wolfe, 'Settler Colonialism and the Elimination of the Native', *Journal of Genocide Research*, 8 (2006), 387–409.

[95] M. Mamdani, *Citizen and Subject: Contemporary Africa and the Legacy of Late Colonialism* (Princeton and Chichester, 1996); Tirthankar Roy, *A Business History of India: Enterprise and the Emergence of Capitalism from 1700* (Cambridge, 2018).

[96] B. Berman and J. Lonsdale, *Unhappy Valley: Conflict in Kenya & Africa* (1992), 77–95.

[97] For incoherence in early stages of the ending of empire, see Amanda Behm, 'Settler Historicism and Anticolonial Rebuttal in the British World, 1880–1920', *Journal of World History*, 26 (2015), 785–813.

the practice of empire collapsed, political leaders everywhere spoke a common language about popular sovereignty and national self-determination which assumed that every state was founded on the same principles of authority.[98] Even where imperial powers retained control after 1950, they exercised it in the name of nation-building, claiming to be preparing 'undeveloped' colonies for self-government. The last vestiges of empire paid homage to this new post-imperial world, imputing coherence to empire's diverse forms by claiming they were bound together through a shared liberal, developmental project after every other idiom had collapsed. Liberal imperialism thus triumphed as a way of explaining empire at the moment of its collapse.[99] Thereafter, the routes which different imperial territories took to becoming sovereign, self-governing nation states were very different. Incoherent sovereignty did not end at one, sharp juncture. For instance, for former settler colonies, decolonisation represented the evolution of imperial idioms which justified sovereignty through settlement and self-government into post-imperial nationhood, making it difficult to identify a single moment of 'independence' for societies like Australia, Canada and New Zealand.[100] Elsewhere, where British rule was justified with reference to military force or explicit racial hierarchies, a sharper rupture often needed to occur. In India, Africa and the Caribbean, the empire's sovereign idioms needed to be emphatically repudiated for the new state to fit into a global order of nation states based on popular sovereignty.

The empire's multiple forms of imperial sovereignty, and then the different routes which former imperial territories took to repudiate it, were a crucial legacy of empire. This multiplicity has shaped and limited in sharp degree the possibilities of the post-imperial Commonwealth, as Philip Murphy has charted.[101] They played out within new nation states, as multiple, contradictory idioms of authority left over from empire shaped the transition from empire to sovereign nationhood. Political leaders in territories where conquest was the dominant idiom had to deal with the status of subordinate polities which asserted that imperial suzerainty occurred through treaty. Different tactics were adopted, from the post-imperial Indian nation state's deployment of overwhelming violence against the state of Hyderabad's desire to remain autonomous, to the legal recognition of autonomous chieftaincies in West Africa.[102] In countries which succeeded to the authority of settler colonies, settler narratives have been challenged with stories of violence and dispossession

---

[98] See Jon Wilson, *Out of Chaos: A Global History of the Rise and Crisis of the Nation State* (forthcoming).

[99] Sarah Stockwell, 'Imperial Liberalism and Institution Building at the End of Empire in Africa', *Journal of Imperial and Commonwealth History*, 46, (2018), 1009–33; M. K. Chan, 'The Legacy of the British Administration of Hong Kong: A View from Hong Kong', *China Quarterly*, 151 (2009), 567–82.

[100] J. Davidson, 'The De-dominionisation of Australia', *Meanjin*, 32, (1979), 139–53; P. A. Buckner (ed.), *Canada and the End of Empire* (Vancouver, 2005).

[101] P. Murphy, *The Empire's New Clothes: The Myth of the Commonwealth* (2018).

[102] For Hyderabad, see Taylor Sherman, *State Violence and Punishment in India* (2009), 151–69; for the way leaders in South Asia drew on and recast imperial idioms, see H. Kumarasingham, *A Political Legacy of the British Empire: Power and the Parliamentary System in Post-colonial India and Sri Lanka*

coming from indigenous and aboriginal populations.[103] Inclusion in the nation in recent decades has involved a reckoning with these multiple histories which has had reverberations in national politics. In Britain, controversies about the imperial past mesh different political values with alternative historical narratives about the basis of the British empire's claim to authority over territory overseas. Empire's incoherence has, it seems, struck back even in the former metropole.

Imperial propagandists and scholars alike have tried to persuade themselves that the British empire was a coherent, albeit complex and diverse, entity. Such efforts misconstrue the nature of empire. The history of the British empire was always one in which mutually disruptive sovereignties and a maelstrom of political projects clashed, coalesced and contradicted one another. 'The empire' was an unstable field of difference and contestation, not a unit of common action. Its discrete practices of politics curtailed the possibility that the empire, in its century- and globe-spanning entirety, had clear coherent and unilineal effects.

The argument here is not that the British empire did not exist. Clearly it did, in the consciousness of its protagonists and critics, but also in the practical, material institutional means of asserting power over people and territory across the world. Its existence was central in shaping the history of the territories it encompassed and over which it exerted sovereignty. The point instead is that the history of empire as a whole should be approached as an exercise in charting the contests between mutually contradicting idioms of sovereignty and their practical outworkings in various locations, and the presence of the incoherence of empire as a potentially disruptive force in their histories.[104] With its focus on unevenness and plurality, such an analysis precludes the association of 'the British empire' with an abstract meta-concept such as capitalism, globalisation, modernity or Western civilisation. Crucially, it also precludes assertions of empire-wide continuity with the present, which fail to acknowledge the degree to which the period of decolonisation saw a collapse of the political and institutional forms that were empire, and the forms of legitimacy they relied on. Empire really did end. Other, post-imperial forms of global power emerged in its place. Reducing the history of empire to clashing monochrome parables for the present does a disservice to the past. But it also fails to offer a useful way of understanding the forces which shape the present. Far better that historians acknowledge the fundamental incoherence of empire, trace the multiple different ways our present is shaped by its effects and, as importantly, develop more sophisticated ways of understanding the transnational forms of power that shaped the post-imperial world which followed its collapse.

Acknowledgements. This article has been a long time in the making. We would like to thank participants at a workshop on an earlier draft at the University of Aberdeen in 2016, David

---

(2012); for West Africa, J. M. Allman, *The Quills of the Porcupine: Asante Nationalism in an Emergent Ghana* (Madison, 1993).

[103] L. Veracini, 'Decolonizing Settler Colonialism: Kill the Settler in Him and Save the Man', *American Indian Culture and Research Journal*, 41 (2017), 1–18.

[104] Armitage, *Ideological Origins*.

Edgerton, Michael Brown, Mike Kenny, Harshan Kumarasingham and anonymous reviewers for *TRHS* for comments and discussion. Andrew Dilley's contribution was supported in early phase by an Arts and Humanities Research Council Early Career Fellowship (AH/M00662X/1).

Cite this article: Wilson J, Dilley A (2023). The Incoherence of Empire. Or, the Pitfalls of Ignoring Sovereignty in the History of the British Empire. *Transactions of the Royal Historical Society* **1**, 191–217. https://doi.org/10.1017/S0080440123000063

Transactions of the RHS (2023), 1, 219–239
doi:10.1017/S0080440123000087

Gendered Violence, Victim Credibility and Adjudicating Justice in Augustine's Letters

Victoria Leonard

Centre for Arts, Memory and Communities, Coventry University, Coventry, UK
Email: victoria.leonard@sas.ac.uk

(Received 25 February 2023; revised 19 June 2023; accepted 20 June 2023; first published online 20 July 2023)

Abstract

In their focus on queer sexuality, letters 77 and 78 in Augustine's letter collection are unusual. Same-sex acts and sexual violence are mostly tightly controlled and deliberately erased in antiquity. This article looks again at the case of sexual abuse preserved in letters 77 and 78 between the monk Spes and the presbyter Bonifatius, applying modern critical understandings of gendered violence, victimisation and harm to reach beyond previous critical approaches that have seen the exceptionalism of the case as a reason not to engage with it. This research takes a new critical approach, re-situating the incident within the wider context of gendered violence in Augustine's letters. It engages with the case of sexual abuse solely between men intrinsically, and as a uniquely available point of comparison with sexual violence perpetrated by men against women. It examines how sexual violence is gendered, in Augustine's response, in the adjudication of the case and in the behaviours and expectations of both victim and perpetrator. Whilst working outwards from absence and silence is a central historiographical approach to gender and violence in the past, this article reaches new understandings by turning towards evidence that is usually siloed and working it back into a framework of sexual violence in Augustine's letters.

Keywords: Gendered violence; ancient history; early Christianity; letters

Around 402 CE, Augustine wrote *epistulae* 77 and 78, responding to the sounded alarm of Satan's disturbance of the Christian community at Hippo. Allegations of sexual harassment had surfaced, that a monk, Spes, had made 'unchaste and impure advances' to the priest Bonifatius.[1] Bonifatius had refused to consent or to suffer Spes's transgressive sexual behaviour in silence. But Spes made counter-allegations against Bonifatius, that he was the perpetrator of abuse not the victim, and the dispute had rumbled unhappily on.[2] *Epistulae* 77 and 78 bring the dispute into sharp focus, illuminating Augustine's awkward position as he tries to assert his episcopal authority whilst resolving tensions and maintaining the cohesion of his congregation. In their focus on queer sexuality, these letters are unusual. Same-sex acts and sexual violence are mostly tightly controlled and deliberately erased in antiquity. Until a problem becomes impossible to ignore, narratives, critiques and conversations addressing sexual violence and harassment are largely absent. The repression of sexual violence by ancient writers like Augustine means that this article is necessarily concerned with missing critiques, missing conversations, about what and who is missing, as well as what is more plainly evident. This article applies critical understandings of gendered violence, victimisation and harm to reach beyond previous approaches. It engages with the case of sexual abuse solely between men intrinsically, and as a uniquely available point of comparison with sexual violence perpetrated by men against women. The central objective of this research is to examine how sexual violence is gendered, in Augustine's response, in the adjudication of the case, and in the behaviours and expectations of both victim and perpetrator. Whilst working outwards from absence and silence is a central historiographical approach to sexual abuse, gender and violence in the past, this article reaches new understandings by turning towards evidence that is usually siloed and working it back into a framework of sexual violence in Augustine's letters.[3]

---

[1] 'motum inpudicum et immundum', ep. 78.2, in *Corpus Scriptorum Ecclesiasticorum Latinorum* [*CSEL*], *S. Avgustini epistulae, epistulae 31-123*, vol. 34.2, ed. Al. Goldbacher (Vindobonae, 1898), 333; all references to the main collection of Augustine's letters are to this edition. *Saint Augustine Letters*, vol. 1 (1-82), trans. Wilfred Parsons (Washington, DC, 1951), 376; all translations of the main collection of Augustine's letters are based on this translation, with my modifications. See 'Bonifatius 5', *Prosopographie de l'Afrique chrétienne (303-533)*, ed. André Mandouze (Paris, 1982), 148, and 'Spes', *ibid.*, 1091.

[2] In ep. 78.3, Augustine commented that the case had tortured him for a long time ('Cum enim me causa ista diu cruciasset'), CSEL 34.2, 334.

[3] Silence as a historiographical approach is a long-held aspect of feminist gender and women's history. For example, see Amy Richlin, *Arguments with Silence: Writing the History of Roman Women* (Ann Arbor, 2014). Rosemary Radford Ruether's foregrounding of male experiences as normative is resonant beyond the theological context of her discussion:

> It is precisely women's experience that has been shut out of hermeneutics and theological reflection in the past. This has been done by forbidding women to study and then to teach and preach the theological tradition. Women have not been able to bring their own experience into the public formulation of the tradition. Not only have women been excluded from shaping and interpreting the tradition from their own experience, but the tradition has been shaped and interpreted against them. The tradition has been shaped to justify their exclusion. The traces of the presence have been suppressed and lost from the public memory of the community. The androcentric bias of the male interpreters of the tradition, who regard maleness as normative humanity, not only erase women's presence in the past history

As opposed to other textual forms, Augustine's letters in particular can provide unique insight into sexual abuse. The reciprocity of textual exchanges with actors in communicative networks means that Augustine's letters often foreground his pragmatic response to queries and demands, whilst also preserving at least crystallised moments in the progression of cases. Most recent research has trended towards a methodology that centralises silence and absence. Ulriika Vihervalli reveals the biases in Augustine's responses to sexual violence towards sanctified women, and foregrounds the absence of complaints by non-sanctified persons.[4] Jennifer Barry highlights the persistence of victim-blaming, doubting of female voices, and undermining of accounts of sexual violence in Augustine's writings, approaches that extend far beyond an ancient context.[5] Midori Hartman demonstrates the inconsistencies in Augustine's approach to sexual violence depending on his rhetorical objective: his willingness to frame Christian women raped during the sack of Rome as martyrs in *epistula* 111 does not extend to his discussions in *De civitate Dei*.[6] The messiness and multidimensionality of sexual violence against women by men and same-sex sexual violence outside the sphere of the Church is largely unrepresented in Augustine's letters. If we can identify Augustine's generalised approach to sexual violence, it is responsive rather than preventative, and preoccupied with the aftermath of violence, particularly in the punishment of the perpetrator. Whilst the overwhelming majority of victims of sexual violence are women and girls, their experiences and needs are often overlooked, and their outcomes are not centralised: in most cases, what happens to the victim remains an unanswered question.[7]

Sexual abuse and violence have always been a fundamental aspect of ancient societies, but critical approaches to these overlooked topics are a relatively recent development. Whilst considerable attention has been given

---

of the community but silence even the questions about their absence. One is not even able to remark upon or notice women's absence, since women's silence and absence is the norm.

Rosemary Radford Ruether, 'Feminist Interpretation: A Method of Correlation', in *Feminist Interpretation of the Bible*, ed. Letty M. Russell (Oxford, 1985), 112–13. In her path-breaking article, Blossom Stefaniw steps on from Ruether's normative inequality, moving the discourse towards social justice and Critical Race Theory: Blossom Stefaniw, 'Feminist Historiography and Uses of the Past', *Studies in Late Antiquity*, 4 (2020), 260–83.

[4] Ulriika Vihervalli, 'Wartime Rape in Late Antiquity: Consecrated Virgins and Victim Bias in the Fifth-Century West', *Early Medieval Europe*, 30 (2022), 3–19.

[5] Jennifer Barry, 'So Easy to Forget: Augustine's Treatment of the Sexually Violated in the City of God', *Journal of the American Academy of Religion*, 88 (2020), 235–53, at 250.

[6] Midori Hartman, 'Sexual Violence, Martyrdom, and Enslavement in Augustine's Letter 111', in *Sex, Violence, and Early Christian Texts*, ed. Christy Cobb and Eric Vanden Eykel (Lanham, MD, 2022), 85–106, at 95.

[7] As Catharine MacKinnon argues, in most histories of sexuality 'the silence of the silenced is filled by the speech of those who have it and the fact of the silence is forgotten'. Catharine MacKinnon, 'Does Sexuality Have a History?', in *Discourses of Sexuality: From Aristotle to AIDS*, ed. Domna C. Stanton (Ann Arbor, 1992), 121. Linda K. Kerber acknowledges that interrogating silence allows us to 'indulge in unguarded hypotheticals, a stance that historians necessarily distrust': Linda K. Kerber, Review of Joan Wallach Scott, *Gender and the Politics of History*, *International Labor and Working-Class History*, 39 (1991), 94.

to rape in antiquity, research into other forms of sexual and gendered violence such as sexual abuse in warfare or domestic violence is atomised across an unconnected field that lacks a structural centre.[8] More specifically, Augustine's representations and responses concerning sexual violence have received increasing consideration in the last two decades, correlating with a greater scholarly focus on women and gender in his writings. But gendered and sexual violence more broadly in his letter collection have received less critical notice.[9] Scholarship has not entirely neglected the dispute between Spes and Bonifatius, but the exceptionalism of the case has been seen as a reason not to engage with it. Most notably, Danuta Shanzer's articles have treated it specifically and within a wider context of sexual scandals, but without any particular consideration of gender.[10] The perceived delicacy of events and Augustine's deliberate ambiguity about the sexual abuse deters scholarly attention, and the compulsion to turn away from the case in fifth-century Hippo informs modern critical responses.[11]

---

[8] On rape in antiquity, see Susan Deacy and Karen F. Pierce (eds.), *Rape in Antiquity* (1997); Susan Deacy, José Malheiro Magalhães and Jean Zacharski Menzies, *Revisiting Rape in Antiquity: Sexualised Violence in Greek and Roman Worlds* (2023); Rosanna Omitowoju, *Rape and the Politics of Consent in Classical Athens* (Cambridge, 2002); and Nancy Sorkin Rabinowitz, 'Greek Tragedy: A Rape Culture?', *EuGeStA*, 1 (2011), 1–21. For sexual violence in warfare, see Kathy L. Gaca, 'Continuities in Rape and Tyranny in Martial Societies from Antiquity Onward', in *Women in Antiquity: Real Women across the Ancient World*, ed. Stephanie Lynn Budin and Jean MacIntosh Turfa (2016), 1041–56; and Caryn A. Reeder, 'Wartime Rape, the Romans, and the First Jewish Revolt', *Journal for the Study of Judaism in the Persian, Hellenistic, and Roman Period*, 48 (2017), 363–85. For domestic violence, see Julia Hillner, 'Family Violence: Punishment and Abuse in the Late Roman Household', in *Approaches to the Byzantine Family*, ed. Leslie Brubaker and Shaun Tougher (Aldershot, 2013), 21–46; Leslie Dossey, 'Wife Beating and Manliness in Late Antiquity', *Past & Present*, 199 (2008), 3–40; and Margherita Carucci, 'Domestic Violence in Roman Imperial Society: Giving Abused Women a Voice', in *Violence in the Ancient and Medieval Worlds*, ed. Maria Cristina Pimentel and Nuno Simões Rodrigues (Leuven, 2018), 57–73.

[9] For recent discussion of Augustine and sexual violence, see Melanie Webb, '"Before the Eyes of Their Own God": Susanna, Rape Law, and Testimony in City of God 1.19', in *Reading Scripture as a Political Act: Essays on Theopolitical Interpretation of the Bible*, ed. Matthew A. Tapie and Daniel Wade McClain (Minneapolis, 2015), 57–82; Melanie Webb, '"On Lucretia Who Slew Herself": Rape and Consolation in Augustine's De ciuitate dei', *Augustinian Studies*, 44 (2013), 37–58; Margaret R. Miles, 'From Rape to Resurrection: Sin, Sexual Difference, and Politics', in *Augustine's City of God: A Critical Guide*, ed. James Wetzel (Cambridge, 2012), 75–92; Tianyue Wu, 'Shame in the Context of Sin: Augustine on the Feeling of Shame in "De Civitate Dei"', *Recherches de Théologie et Philosophie Médiévales*, 74 (2007), 1–31.

[10] Danuta R. Shanzer, 'Augustine's Epp. 77–78 (A Scandal in Hippo): Microhistory and Ordeal-by-Oath', *Reading Medieval Studies*, 40 (2014), 11–33, and Danuta Shanzer, 'Some Treatments of Sexual Scandal in (Primarily) Later Latin Epistolography', in *In Pursuit of Wissenschaft: Festschrift für William M. Calder III zum 75 Geburtstag* (Spudasmata, vol. 119), ed. Stephan Heilen *et al.* (Hildesheim, 2008), 393–414. See also Dennis E. Trout, *Paulinus of Nola: Life, Letters, and Poems* (Berkeley, 1999), 235–7.

[11] Daniel Edward Doyle's treatment is typical, avoiding the sexual violence at the centre of the case and approaching it instead through canon law: Daniel Edward Doyle, *The Bishop as Disciplinarian in the Letters of St. Augustine* (New York, 2002), 311–13. Jennifer Ebbeler's excellent work on Augustine's letter collection includes no mention of the case: Jennifer Ebbeler, *Disciplining*

Augustine's first resolve not to manage the dispute actively and to leave Spes and Bonifatius to God failed.[12] Members of Hippo's congregation refused to attend services whilst Bonifatius's name remained on the lists of presbyters, and Spes's attempts to lever to his advantage and attain promotion to the priesthood, either by Augustine directly or by letters of recommendation from Augustine to another bishop, were denied, intensifying Spes's complaints.[13] Spes argued that if he could not be ordained to the priesthood, then Bonifatius should be stripped of his clerical status. At this point, Bonifatius's desire to avoid further disturbance in the Church and his willingness to acquiesce in Spes's objections forced Augustine to act. He instructed Spes and Bonifatius to bind themselves, seemingly by an oath, to visit St Felix's shrine at Cimitile, Italy. Augustine intended that increased proximity to the divine in this holy place would disturb the perpetrator's guilty conscience, provoking him into miraculous confession. Augustine's role as bishop burdened him not only with the spiritual well-being of his community, but with arbitrating civil and ecclesiastical disputes in his own court, the *audientia episcopalis*.[14] Augustine's familiarity with Roman law is evident in his letters; he kept copies of laws and distributed them alongside letters where he needed to invoke legislative protocol.[15] His involvement in various types of legal arbitration runs like a thread throughout his letters. This was an addition to his workload that he did not always welcome – he complains to Alypius in *epistula* 9* how the civil punishment of crimes is neglected, wearing out the Church leadership as a result.[16] Augustine's letters show that his judicial activities were mainly (but not always) reserved for ecclesiastical rather than civil matters, and he arbitrated various disputes over landownership, inheritance and sexual violence within the Church.[17]

Christians: Correction and Community in Augustine's Letters (Oxford, 2012). See also Othmar Perler, *Les voyages de saint Augustin* (Paris, 1969), 244–5.

[12] Ep. 78.3, *CSEL* 34.2, 334: 'cogitaueram primo sic ambos deo relinquere'.

[13] Ep. 78.4. Doyle understands that the removal of Bonifatius's name from the list of presbyters equates to excommunication: Doyle, *Bishop as Disciplinarian*, 312. Augustine's ep. 60 to Aurelius (*c.* 401), written soon before epp. 77 and 78, reveals Augustine's resistance to monks who lever towards ordination.

[14] On the *audientia episcopalis*, see Noel E. Lenski, 'Evidence for the *Audientia episcopalis* in the New Letters of Augustine', in *Law, Society, and Authority in Late Antiquity*, ed. Ralph W. Mathisen (Oxford, 2001), 83–97; Henry Chadwick, *The Role of the Christian Bishop in Ancient Society: Protocol of the Thirty-Fifth Colloquy, 25 February 1979*, Center for Hermeneutical Studies in Hellenistic and Modern Culture, ed. Edward C. Hobbs and Wilhelm H. Wuellner (Berkeley, 1980); Maria Rosa Cimma, *L'episcopalis audientia nelle costituzioni imperiali da Costantino a Giustiniano* (Turin, 1989); Caroline Humfress, 'Bishops and Law Courts in Late Antiquity: How (Not) to Make Sense of the Legal Evidence', *Journal of Early Christian Studies*, 19 (2011), 375–400; John C. Lamoreaux, 'Episcopal Courts in Late Antiquity', *Journal of Early Christian Studies*, 3 (1995), 143–67; Kauko K. Raikas, 'St. Augustine on Juridical Duties: Some Aspects of the Episcopal Office in Late Antiquity', in *Collectanea Augustiniana: Augustine, Second Founder of the Faith*, ed. Joseph Schnaubelt and Frederick Van Fleteren (New York, 1990), 467–83.

[15] In ep. 114, Augustine wrote to the imperial official Florentius, appealing to the law in a case involving Faventius, and sending a copy of the law with the letter. With ep. 10* to Alypius, Augustine sent a copy of a law to prevent free people being kidnapped into slavery.

[16] Ep. 9*.2.

[17] See respectively ep. 8*, ep. 83 and ep. 9*.

Augustine's surviving letters that address the dispute between Spes and Bonifatius (*epistulae* 77 and 78) are representative of pressure points in the controversy where Augustine was forced to escalate his response, and his epistolary network heated up with increased communication. Although it is unattested, *epistula* 77 seems to be a reply to a ghost-letter, a letter from Felix and Hilarinus that does not survive.[18] Augustine is responding to specific points, such as the request for Bonifatius's name to be removed from the clergy register. *Epistula* 77 mentions a decree (*placitum*) about Spes and Bonifatius that could be read to Hilarinus and Felix, if they wish it.[19] This decree could record Spes and Bonifatius's commitment to travelling together to St Felix's shrine, demonstrating Augustine's active management of the case in the face of complaints from his congregation. Augustine's reference seems to suggest that the decree was sent with *epistula* 77, although, like the ghost-letter from Hilarinus and Felix, this is not confirmed by the extant letter.

In *epistula* 77, Augustine makes reference to Spes's request for letters from Augustine to another bishop, advising his promotion. Augustine rather obliquely explains his reasoning in sending Spes and Bonifatius to the shine of Felix at Nola, because if any divine revelation should identify the perpetrator, a trustworthy account could more easily be written to Augustine from there.[20] Dennis Trout has plausibly understood this as a tacit reference to Augustine's reliance on Paulinus of Nola to provide such documentation.[21] Trout also speculates about a ghost-letter that Augustine would have written to Paulinus in Nola, delivered by Spes and Bonifatius on their strained pilgrimage.[22] It seems probable that Augustine supplied a letter of recommendation to Bonifatius, counted here as another ghost-letter. At Bonifatius's request, the letter did not authenticate his clerical rank, enabling Bonifatius and Spes to be treated equally in an unknown place.[23] But unless Augustine's letter positively recommended Spes, which seems unlikely, Bonifatius's reception in Italy would already have been made partial by Augustine's letter.

Most critical approaches overlook the existence of an implied, unattested matrix of communications surrounding *epistulae* 77 and 78. Two observations can be made: first, in a case marked by obscurity, if we take into account these implied, ghostly texts, we already know more than we think we know. Secondly, the sexual violence on which the case centres is firmly marginalised, at least within the epistolary response. Augustine directs his rhetoric away from the shadowy acts that have caused the disturbance, concentrating instead on damage limitation. His

---

[18] For more on the important role of ghostly correspondence and resource exchange that is attested but not directly evident in Augustine's letter collection, see the database of late antique and medieval letter collections created by the European Research Council-funded 'Connected Clerics' Project (forthcoming, https://connectedclerics.com/index.html).

[19] Ep. 77.2, *CSEL* 34.2, 330.

[20] Ep. 78.3.

[21] 'It may well have been the presence of Paulinus at Nola, as much as the reputation of Felix, that led Augustine to single out this particular *locus sanctus* in 402.' Trout, *Paulinus of Nola*, 237.

[22] *Ibid.*

[23] We can read this concession to the perpetrator that further harms the victim as a form of safeguarding behaviour typically evident in the aftermath of violence.

management strategies are designed not to resolve the conflict, but to contain it, and to address its consequences, principally in his attempts to direct the collective response of Hippo's Christian community to Bonifatius and Spes.

Augustine's first line of defence is to redirect appeals and complaints from his resentful congregation, reframing their outrage and distress through Scripture (Matt. 24:12–13). Scandals such as these test and prove the faithful, and have been divinely foretold, Augustine writes.[24] This way lies salvation.[25] After reassurance that this is all part of God's mysterious plan, Augustine shifts towards defensively appealing to his position. He creates distance between his responsibility as bishop and how the case should be decided, asking how he as a man can judge clearly 'the secret acts of men'.[26] In emphasising the difference between sacred and profane justice, and the privacy of male sexual behaviour, Augustine represents himself as defeated in the case, justifying the deferral of judgement quite literally to God: 'While the case which has arisen between him and Spes is still subject to divine decision according to their degree ... who am I to dare to forestall the verdict of God?'[27] He appeals to legal precedents established in civil contexts whereby a case that is referred to a higher power cannot be altered to avoid prejudicing the higher judge. Thus, Augustine does not dare even to remove Bonifatius's name from the register of priests to avoid injuring the power of God with whom the case now rests.[28]

In this context of escalating tensions, increasing pressure to resolve the case, and Augustine's recusal, what type of justice can Spes and Bonifatius hope to receive? Although Augustine argues that the truth of the matter can only be revealed by divine judgement, he nevertheless advocates persuasively on behalf of Bonifatius, the accuser of Spes, as truth-teller. In *epistula* 77, Augustine writes that he has not found evidence of Bonifatius's wrongdoing, and he emphatically does not believe any such thing of him.[29] For Augustine, Spes is undoubtedly lost, whereas Bonifatius's reputation is only damaged. In *epistula* 78, Augustine explicitly defends Bonifatius's innocence, based on his refusal to consent to Spes's sexual harassment or to keep silent about it.[30] Augustine has unambiguously arrived at his verdict, finding that Bonifatius's conscience is clear. But Augustine's awareness that implementing his decision will not resolve the matter reveals how the conflict has widened beyond the individual to the group.[31] Mutual consensus has broken down, factionalism has intervened and deadlock has immobilised the dispute.

---

[24] Ep. 77.1, *CSEL* 34.2, 329.

[25] 78.1, *CSEL* 34.2, 331–3.

[26] Ep. 77.2, *CSEL* 34.2, 330: 'quis ego sum, ut audeam dei praeuenire sententiam in delendo uel supprimendo eius nomine, de quo nec suspicari temere mali aliquid episcopus debui nec dilucide iudicare homo de occultis hominum potui'. Parsons, *Letters*, vol. 1, 374.

[27] Augustine seems to employ a similar tactic of mobilising God in the adjudication of cases in ep. 65.1.

[28] Ep. 78.4.

[29] Ep. 77.2.

[30] Ep. 78.2.

[31] Shanzer understands that the conflict caused 'severe division and distress'. Shanzer, 'Microhistory', 17.

In his search for a resolution, Augustine represents himself as forced to supersede his own ecclesiastical arbitration with a divine justice that is intrinsically ambiguous. Parallels have been drawn between Augustine's resolution and the miracle of the ordeal in later medieval contexts, where innocence or guilt was determined through God's intervention (or lack of it) to protect the accused person.[32] Peter Brown describes the ordeal as 'a controlled miracle', and observes that it functioned as God revealing truth rather than any specific fact: 'He was judging the status of a person or of a group, whether they and their claims were "pure" and "just". He was not deciding whether a piece of land really belonged to a certain claimant.'[33] Brown sees that the individual issues were less at stake than the status in the community of the groups that had been brought into conflict, and Augustine's search for the miracle of God's revelation was intended to generate consensus through a resolution that could not be disputed.[34] Augustine's design to displace the dispute physically was intended to mitigate the unbearable antagonism that divided the community along partisan lines. St Felix's shrine offered a spectacular salve to the marginalisation of Spes and Bonifatius from the community by sin and the association of sin. Augustine envisions performative justice at the holy sanctuary that functions to ostracise Spes and Bonifatius, which will then enable their reintegration into the community at Hippo. Ultimately, it protects Augustine from being disenfranchised from his own congregation.

We can see, then, that Augustine's judicial solution was already slanted, and was not victim-centred.[35] Forcing a victim to undertake a long journey to a foreign place with their alleged perpetrator would compound their suffering and trauma, and would risk exposing them to further harm. A process that treats victim and alleged perpetrator as equivalents elides the power imbalance that is at the root of the perpetration of harm. Augustine's solution was convenient for the community at Hippo, alienated along fault lines of blame and uncomfortable with the association of sin and disreputability.[36] But it was not convenient for the victim. Theorist Sara Ahmed has highlighted how sexual harassment works by increasing the costs of fighting against something, making it easier to accept something than to struggle against it,

---

[32] Sister Wilfrid Parsons, *Letters*, vol. 1 *(1-82)* (Washington, DC, 2008), 374 n. 6; Peter Brown, *Augustine of Hippo: A Biography* (1967), 196.

[33] Peter Brown, 'Society and the Supernatural: A Medieval Change', *Daedalus*, 104 (1975), 135 and 137.

[34] 'The need for consensus and the pressure brought by consensus in relatively small groups are the leitmotivs of much early medieval religion. We see this in the cult of the relics. For to vest what was intrinsically ambiguous with final authority was part of a whole style of decision-making in the early centuries of the Middle Ages.' *Ibid.*, 140.

[35] Brown similarly perceives this slanting, describing Augustine's proposed resolution as 'a strangely subjective objectivity', as 'skin deep' and 'not impersonal. It was the projection of the needs of a group, and was thus sucked into the subjective values of the group.' *Ibid.*, 142.

[36] Augustine recognises that many in the community are troubled and grieved by the scandal. Ep. 78.2.

even if that acceptance is itself how the victim is diminished.[37] Bonifatius's desire to de-escalate his complaint in acquiescing in Spes's demand that he should be stripped of his clerical status is a concession that attempts to appease the perpetrator and safeguard against further harm. It indicates the high cost of holding Spes to account; the harassment as well as the process to resolve it was harmful. Ahmed reminds us that the term harass derives from the French *harasser*, to tire out, to vex.[38] To speak about harassment provokes further harassment, until the victim is worn down and stops pushing forward the allegation.

The sexual violence perpetrated against Bonifatius, and his attempt to bring Spes to account should be seen not as an anomalous or isolated incident, but as part of a process of victimisation and harm. Spes's response to Bonifatius's attempts to hold him accountable echoes a standardised pattern of perpetrator defence, commonly known as DARVO, an acronym that stands for Deny, Attack, and Reverse Victim and Offender.[39] This offensive reaction from perpetrators of wrongdoing, particularly sexual offences, includes denying the abuse, attacking the victim's credibility and reversing the roles of victim and offender, all of which Spes does effectively. Spes's manipulative denial gaslights his community into believing his victim status, and his attempts to reduce Bonifatius's clerical status seek to degrade his credibility. The disappearance of Bonifatius and Spes, both from Hippo and from our historical view, because of what Bonifatius tried to bring into view, was a necessary intervention from Augustine. His solution gives the appearance that the problem has been dealt with, enabling the community at Hippo to move forward. But the problem has not been dealt with, it has only been shifted onto another sphere, prolonging the dispute through stalling tactics that place a judicial resolution far beyond human control.

Epistulae 77 and 78 demonstrate that, for Augustine, justice is an afterthought. The letters crystalise not around specific allegations or criminal acts as we might expect, but around clerical status, ecclesiastical authority and individual and institutional reputation. The formal positioning of Spes and Bonifatius within the Church, namely Bonifatius's continuing position as a presbyter and Spes's attempts to force his own promotion to presbyterial level, is the principal issue of contention in both letters. Augustine's letters do not well represent the manoeuvrings that occurred before he put *stylus* to *chartus*, and there is a considerable logical gap between allegations of sexual harassment coming to light and Spes's opportunism in using the case to advance his status: it is an unusual position from which to negotiate. Really what *epistulae* 77 and 78 offer us is the opportunity to read a micro-incident

---

[37] Sara Ahmed, *Living a Feminist Life* (Durham, NC, 2017), 141. My own analysis of sexual harassment owes much to the valuable insights of Ahmed.

[38] *Ibid.*, 140.

[39] This theory was first developed by Jennifer J. Freyd, 'Violations of Power, Adaptive Blindness, and Betrayal Trauma Theory', *Feminism & Psychology*, 7 (1997), 22–32. For a more recent application, see Sarah J. Harsey and Jennifer J. Freyd, 'Defamation and DARVO', *Journal of Trauma & Dissociation*, 23 (2022), 481–9.

of victimisation and harm between individuals translated into professional opportunism that implicates a much wider communal group.

Augustine's arguably ineffective policy of containment includes attempts to conceal the controversy. He twice defends his actions for not bringing the case to the attention of the wider community, explaining that he did not want to trouble his congregation with 'sharp and useless sorrow'.[40] The case provoked a litigious and conservative response that reveals how pressing the threat of allegations of sexual harassment was to institutional and individual reputations. The Catholic Christian community at Hippo had been made vulnerable to attack by the dispute. As Augustine observes, those whose evil tongues are sweetened by these sorrows, especially Donatists, seize upon the example of a fallen monk to demonstrate the moral failure of all those sanctified within the Catholic Church. Augustine brackets male–male sexual harassment with adulterous women, making his point with an ill-fitting analogy that not all wives are cast off and not all mothers accused when one married woman commits adultery.[41] Augustine's epistolographic response shows that the case is first and foremost perceived as a threat: to his reputation as bishop, to Bonifatius's integrity as a presbyter, to the standing of Hippo's Christian community and to the wider Catholic Church. Epistula 78 especially, as a longer letter following on from epistula 77 and addressed to a much wider audience, is part of a top-down policy of damage control that seeks to retain institutional legitimacy by curtailing complaints from Hippo's Christian community, limiting the opportunity for the case to be mobilised by the opposition, and silencing the complainants Spes and Bonifatius through their physical removal.

Adjudicating abuse across Augustine's letters

Sexual violence in Augustine's letters features through male-specific narratives, where the values and experiences of men are foregrounded, and female victims are incidental at best. But where does this bias originate? Is it situated against victims and those who bring forward these discomfiting and difficult cases? Or does the bias run along gendered lines? Are male victims alongside male perpetrators treated differently from female victims and their male perpetrators? Do their expectations and outcomes differ, and is the justice accessible to victims consistent? The restricted scope of the evidence for sexual violence, especially where the perpetrator and victim are both male, means that it is not possible to reach absolute answers. But there are instructive comparisons to be made with other examples of sexual abuse against women and girls that Augustine adjudicated in the letter collection.

Pauline Allen has highlighted the disparity between classical letter-writing, where female addressees were almost exclusively close family members, and the fourth–sixth centuries CE, where letters were written to Christian

---

[40] Augustine defends himself against his decision not to inform the wider community: at ep. 78.4, CSEL 34.2, 378 ('ne uos atrociter et inaniter contristando turbarem'), and ep. 78.7.
[41] Ep. 78.6.

women more widely, without the need for close familial ties.[42] And this epistolographic shift in communication with women is certainly seen in Augustine, where no letters to female relatives including his mother, Monica, sister or 'concubine' survive, whereas letters to Christian women seeking advice or transporting relics on Augustine's behalf are evident in his collection.[43] Jennifer Ebbeler has noted how much of Augustine's correspondence with women is confined to the 'amorphous mass' at the end of the collection, and it is similarly notable how much more prominent sexual violence and slavery are in the Divjak collection.[44]

Unlike most other cases which involve female victims, the dispute between Spes and Bonifatius lingers on the determination of truth rather than the appropriate punishment for the perpetrator. Augustine writes *epistulae* 77 and 78 in the midst of the controversy, but his epistolographic interventions are typically staged late. *Epistula* 9* in the Divjak series shows Augustine responding not to the kidnap and rape of a consecrated virgin in a church, not to the punishment of her perpetrator by local clergy, not to the perpetrator's complaints at his punishment, not even to Pope Celestine's demand to have the clergy punished for beating the perpetrator, but to his colleague Alypius, who is now adjudicating the case.[45] As in *epistula* 77, Augustine throws up his hands at the case, asking what a bishop or the clergy is to do about these crimes committed by men. Whilst it is not clear if Augustine is referring to sexual crimes or crimes in general, he does not replicate his argument from *epistula* 77 that the inscrutability of the 'private acts of men' means that the

---

[42] Pauline Allen, 'Bishops and Ladies: How, If at All, to Write to a Woman in Late Antiquity', *Men and Women in the Early Christian Centuries*, ed. Wendy Mayer and Ian J. Elmer (Strathfield, 2014), 181.

[43] For critical discussion of Augustine's correspondence with women, see Maureen Tilley, 'No Friendly Letters: Augustine's Correspondence with Women', in *The Cultural Turn in Late Ancient Studies: Gender, Asceticism, and Historiography*, ed. Dale B. Martin and Patricia Cox Miller (Durham, NC, 2005), 40–62; Catherine Conybeare, 'Spaces between Letters: Augustine's Correspondence with Women', in *Voices in Dialogue: Reading Women in the Middle Ages*, ed. Linda Olson and Kathryn Kerby-Fulton (Notre Dame, 2005), 55–72; Joanne McWilliam, 'Augustine's Letters to Women', in *Feminist Interpretations of Augustine*, ed. Judith Chelius Stark (Pennsylvania, 2007), 189–202. For letters to and from women in late antiquity, see the important article by Julia Hillner, 'Empresses, Queens, and Letters: Finding a "Female Voice' in Late Antiquity?"', *Gender & History*, 31 (2019), 353–82.

[44] Ebbeler, *Disciplining Christians*, 19 n. 57. The Divjak letter series collates previously unknown Augustinian letters discovered by Johannes Divjak and published in 1981 in a series 1*–29*. Augustine, *Epistolae ex duobus codicibus nuper in lucem prolatae. Sancti Aureli Augustini Opera, Corpus Scriptorum Ecclesiasticorum Latinorum* (*CSEL*) 88, ed. Johannes Divjak (Vienna, 1981); all references to the Divjak collection of Augustine's letters are to this edition. *Saint Augustine. Letters. Vol. VI* (*1 *–29**), vol. 81, trans. Robert B. Eno (Washington, DC, 1989); all translations of the Divjak collection of Augustine's letters are based on this translation, with my modifications. For further discussion of the Divjak collection, see Claude Lepelley, 'La Crise de l'Afrique romaine au début du Ve siècle, d'après les lettres nouvellement découvertes de Saint Augustin', *Comptes rendus des séances de l'Académie des Inscriptions et Belles-Lettres*, no. 3 (1981), 445–63; *Les Lettres de saint Augustin découvertes par Johannes Divjak: communications présentées au colloque des 20 et 21 septembre 1982* (Paris, 1983); Henry Chadwick, 'New Letters of St. Augustine', *Journal of Theological Studies*, 34 (1983), 425–52.

[45] Ep. 9*.1.

case cannot be decided; the case has already been decided and there is no question of guilt. Instead *epistula* 9* is preoccupied with how to deal effectively and appropriately with perpetrators, weighing the options of corporeal punishment and excommunication.

As in *epistula* 9*, female victims of sexual violence are often overlooked or purposefully ignored in the letter collection, obscuring the fraught exercise of claiming victimhood that places women at the centre of the narrative.[46] The victim of the case in *epistula* 9*, the nun who was taken from her father's house to a church and raped, is given the briefest mention and remains anonymous.[47] Similarly, the nun at the centre of the case in *epistulae* 14* and 15* who was violently raped by Cresconius is hardly mentioned in Augustine's scramble to ensure that Cresconius is not punished excessively: 'I received a complaint against one of your men but I did not dare mention his name or his sacrilegious disgrace in this letter in case perhaps you become enraged to excess and punish him more violently than is fitting.'[48] Where the evidence against perpetrators does not rely on female victim testimony, as in *epistulae* 14* and 15*, Augustine can represent these cases as simple and reductive morality tales, and the focus can rest on punishing the perpetrator.

Female victims move towards the centre only where their testimony is questioned, as in *epistula* 18* where Augustine positions allegations against the deacon or priest Gitta made by an unnamed woman as potentially false. Augustine is writing to the Christian community at Membliba to explain why their request for Gitta to be their priest cannot be fulfilled; even if only some of what the woman alleged was true, it would be enough to discount Gitta from assuming the role. If she had lied and only what he confessed to was true, he still cannot be a cleric, since all Christians, and clerics especially, have to be innocent of illicit sexual intercourse.[49] It seems that the unnamed woman made allegations against Gitta not of consensual sexual relations but of

---

[46] For further discussion of victimhood, see Kate Manne, *Down Girl: The Logic of Misogyny* (2019), 220–48, specifically here 225.

[47] Ep. 9*.1, *Saint Augustine*, trans. Eno, 71: 'So the only source of concern in this affair which still bothers me is that I find it difficult to conceive how they who found him with that woman, a professed nun, whom he had taken from her father's house for the purpose of rape, refrained from doing him bodily harm.' *CSEL* 88, ed. Divjak: 'Unde solus mihi remansit de hac re scrupulus, quia difficile mihi videntur qui eum reppererunt cum illa femina, quam professam sanctimonialem ad ludibrium stupri de patria duxerat, ab eius corporali iniuria temperasse.' Shanzer ('Sexual Scandal', 397) argues that the case in ep. 9* did not involve rape, and that the letter is 'seriously misinterpreted' by Leslie Dossey. Leslie Dossey, 'Judicial Violence and the Ecclesiastical Courts', in *Law, Society, and Authority in Late Antiquity*, ed. Ralph W. Mathisen (Oxford, 2001), 111.

[48] Ep. 14*.2, *CSEL* 88, ed. Divjak: 'Habebam quod quererer de homine tuo, cuius nec nomen nec sacrilegum flagitium ausus sum his litteris intimare, ne forte gravius succenseres et atrocius vindicares quam decet.'

[49] Ep. 18*.1, *Saint Augustine*, trans. Eno, 124: 'For even if only some of the things which the woman said about him were true, that's the end of the matter; if she perjured herself and only what he himself confessed was true, he cannot be a cleric, since all Christians and, above all, all clerics, must be innocent of all illicit sexual intercourse, even all illicit kissing and embracing, and all impurity.' *CSEL* 88, ed. Divjak: 'Si enim aliqua [vera] sunt quae de illo mulier dixit, factum est; si autem illa etiam peierat et hoc solum de isto verum est quod ipse confessus est, nec is esse

sexual abuse, and that Augustine is actively partitioning out the allegations he is prepared to respond to.[50] As in the case of Spes and Bonifatius, sexual violence is only relevant where it intersects with clerical status, not at the point of perpetration, and not in response to the victim's complaints.

Victim credibility, clerical status and community division are issues that are again evident in *epistula* 13*, written by Augustine to the priest Restitutus about a cleric whom a nun has accused of rape.[51] The perpetrator strategy of DARVO is again evident here, and the letter foregrounds the counter-accusation from the cleric, that the nun who made allegations against him was in fact the perpetrator of sexual harassment. There are not two competing narratives here: the female's testimony is left entirely unrepresented, and we have to read the accusation of rape into the letter and ghost-letter that preceded it. Augustine has arrived at his judgement that the cleric is innocent after repeatedly interrogating him, but no mention is made of an interview with the female. Instead Augustine concludes that the nun should not be believed – this lost woman is looking for 'someone to get her hooks into', in Eno's memorable translation, as a way of shifting the blame for her dishonour.[52] Augustine's misogynistic stereotyping relies on a collective conception of women as victim as lascivious and vengeful, and the woman's own sexual immorality is represented as another man's crime. By shifting blame onto the victim, Augustine advocates that the cleric should not be condemned and that he should keep his position unless more evidence is uncovered to prove that he is lying – the woman's words alone are insufficient.

Besides victim-blaming, another effective rhetorical strategy Augustine mobilises is to spectacularly and deliberately miss the point, identifying the problem in *epistula* 13* as priests who travel alone, leaving themselves vulnerable to accusations of impropriety.[53] Augustine's response, to advocate against clergy moving around autonomously as a tool of prevention, echoes more recent institutional responses to sexual violence: knowledge avoidance, where the root causes of violence are sidestepped, and inadequate or irrelevant actions, represented as viable solutions, come before more difficult strategies of prevention.[54]

---

clericus potest, quoniam omnes Christiani, quanto magis clerici non solum ab illicito concubitu puri esse debent, verum etiam ab illicito osculo et ab illicito amplexu et ab omni immunditia.'

[50] Shanzer describes Augustine's response to the case as 'sympathetic and humane'. Shanzer, 'Sexual Scandal', 407.

[51] There must have been a time lag between the crime and accusation as the cleric was a deacon when it took place.

[52] Ep. 13*.3, *Saint Augustine*, trans. Eno, 111: 'This is the man's story. I conclude that he ought not to be condemned unless by chance it can be proved that he is lying. Don't let this woman's words be listened to and accepted against him because doubtless this lost woman is looking for someone to get her hooks into.' *CSEL* 88, ed. Divjak: 'Hactenus mihi confessus est homo, unde non eum iudico esse damnandum, nisi forte de mendacio convincatur et non verba illius feminae audiantur et accipiantur adversus eum, quia sine dubio perdita quaerit cui haereat.'

[53] Echoed in another of Augustine's letters, ep. 65. For further discussion, see below.

[54] For discussion of inadequate institutional responses to sexual violence in more modern contexts, see Allegra M. McLeod, 'Regulating Sexual Harm: Strangers, Intimates, and Social Institutional Reform', *California Law Review*, 102 (2014), 1553–1621.

In cases of sexual violence where victim testimony constitutes the central evidence against a male perpetrator, Augustine reveals his propensity to disbelieve female victims, compounding harm on an individual level with institutional betrayal. This is starkly distinct from his approach to the complainant when both perpetrator and victim are male; the female victim in *epistula* 13* is disbelieved because of the allegations she raised, whereas Bonifatius is believed principally *because* of the allegations he brings to light against Spes. This gendered disparity means that, for women, stating their victimisation publicly is an insecure method of gaining the sympathetic attention of invested third parties.[55] The perceived unreliability of female complainants in Augustine's letters is part of a wider nexus of bias where female victims are discredited, dismissed and subject to counter-accusations that deny their victim status.[56] The reflexive disbelief of women, otherwise known as testimonial injustice, occurs when a speaker receives an unfair deficit of credibility from a hearer as a consequence of the hearer's prejudice.[57] In *epistulae* 13* and 18*, Augustine endorses the counter-accusations made by male clergy against female victims, but where both victim and perpetrator are male, as in the case of Spes and Bonifatius, the original accuser is believed. The propensity to disbelieve the female victim, even to suspect them of perjury, is strong enough to dismiss their testimony even where the male cleric has admitted wrongdoing, as in *epistula* 18*. Augustine's letters reveal that allegations made by women from a subordinate ecclesiastical position are given substantially less credibility and are much less impactful than those made by male clerics.

The gendered disparity of victim credibility has wider consequences beyond the victim and perpetrator. In *epistula* 13*, Augustine advocates that the priest accused of sexual abuse should keep his position, ordering that the community should not let their love for the priest grow cold.[58] Augustine mobilises his own correspondence in defence of the priest, instructing the recipient to read his letter (*epistula* 13*) to the community and explain the incident so that they do not reject the priest; he is, after all, a good man who was confronted with temptation, which could happen to anyone. Augustine's approach, however, to a hostile congregation in *epistulae* 77 and 78 is very different. The community in Hippo is much less malleable and staunchly opposes Bonifatius's continuing presbyterial role. Accusations of sexual violence brought by a woman are easier for the alleged perpetrator to discount, and for individuals and groups responsible for adjudicating justice to ignore.

If we can identify a gendered disparity in victim credibility in Augustine's letters, how then is truth determined within the judicial process? In *epistula* 9* to Alypius, Augustine writes that when a case comes to judgement, those who deliver justice must first make enquiries and establish the facts of the

---

[55] Manne, *Down Girl*, 236.

[56] *Ibid.*, 222.

[57] Miranda Fricker, *Epistemic Injustice: Power and the Ethics of Knowing* (Oxford, 2007), 17.

[58] Ep. 13*.3.

case.[59] In *epistula* 13*, Augustine reveals how his investigative process relies on interrogation: he repeatedly probed the mind of the man accused of sexual abuse, attempting to intimidate him into confession through fear of divine judgement.[60] The deliberation of guilt is absent where the perpetrator of sexual violence was caught in the act and his crimes were publicly witnessed, such as in *epistula* 13*. It is difficult to know how guilt was assigned in the violent rape of a nun in *epistulae* 14* and 15*, but without mention of the possibility of the perpetrator's innocence or the reliance on victim testimony, it is likely that his crime was more widely witnessed. Augustine's determination of truth is constrained in *epistula* 18* by the moral standards required for ordination: Gitta's confession of illicit sexual relations is enough to discount him for the priesthood, and that is as far as Augustine needs to push to establish truth.

Augustine's letters often approach sexual violence through the lens of clerical disreputability, and whilst *epistula* 65 from Augustine to Sanctippus is concerned with embezzlement and immorality rather than sexual violence, it does illuminate Augustine's judicial processes when managing the case of a wayward cleric. The priest Abundantius has been suspended from his office for diverting money intended for the church, and for dining at the house of a woman 'of evil fame' (*malae famae mulierem*) on Christmas Eve rather than fasting.[61] Prompted by rumours of his reputation for moral deviance, Augustine explains that his first recourse is to gather evidence of Abundantius's wrongdoing, discovering his fraudulent use of church funds, which the priest admitted to. A colleague witnessed Abundantius's illicit activities on Christmas Eve and Abundantius could not deny his presence at the house of ill-repute, although how much he admitted to is unclear.[62]

In writing to Sanctippus as primate of Numidia, informing him of the case and explaining his actions, Augustine is following formal procedure and aiming for maximal transparency, perhaps in anticipation of a complaint from Abundantius which Augustine pre-emptively frames as a 'false report' (*fallacia*).[63] Augustine writes that he heard the case and gave a full account of his decision to suspend Abundantius from the priesthood, who has a year to plead his case, if he feels there is a case to answer. Augustine advocates for the punishment of clerics according to canon law established at the Council of Carthage (401), but complains that he is forced to adjudicate cases where evidence of wrongdoing is insecure or unknown. Augustine then refers to an earlier canonical law that instructs the case of a priest to be submitted to six bishops, and advocates that if his decision to suspend Abundatius from his priestly office is considered erroneous, any bishop is welcome to restore Abundatius to his clerical status by giving him a church within his own diocese.

---

[59] Ep. 9*.3.

[60] Ep. 13*.1.

[61] Ep. 65.1, *Saint Augustine*, trans. Parsons, 312. *CSEL* 34.2, ed. Goldbacher, 233.

[62] Ep. 65.1, *CSEL* 34.2, ed. Goldbacher, 233: 'negare non potuit, nam quae negauit, deo dimisi iudicans, quae occultare permissus non est'. *Saint Augustine*, trans. Parsons, 313: 'he could not deny being there, for what he denied I left to the judgement of God, and he was not permitted to conceal it'.

[63] Ep. 65.1. *Saint Augustine*, trans. Parsons, 313. *CSEL* 34.2, ed. Goldbacher, 233.

In *epistula* 65, Augustine's judicial processes are on display in the careful framing of his actions to his ecclesiastical senior. A report or rumour of clerical wrongdoing prompts evidence-gathering, followed by an interview with the alleged perpetrator with the aim of eliciting a confession, and eyewitness testimony is gathered. The case is then heard formally following the prescriptions of canon law, and an outcome is decreed, with an appeal permissible within one year.

In broad terms, we can see Augustine's judicial process working similarly in the case between Spes and Bonifatius, although the delay between evidence-gathering and the formal hearing means that the determination of guilt has not yet been concluded. Abundantius's admission of wrongdoing and eyewitness testimony are sufficient for Augustine to suspend his clerical status, and there appears to be no question over his guilt. Despite Augustine's clear conviction that Abundantius deserves punishment, he has Augustine's sympathy. Augustine writes to an anonymous priest who advocates for Abundantius to be allowed to return to his home church and live without clerical duties. Although Augustine advises against it, his treatment of Abundantius, who he suggests could be given a parish in another diocese, falls far short of uncompromising condemnation and represents a continued investment of resources in a disreputable former cleric. Augustine's disbelief of the female victim in *epistula* 13* and his defence of the rapist Cresconius in *epistulae* 14* and 15* indicate his predisposition to centre perpetrators, particularly of sexual violence, across the letter collection.

Just how significantly Augustine's treatment of victim and perpetrator is gendered and how this effects a particularly uneven distribution of justice is starkly illuminated if we turn to *epistula* 262 written to Ecdicia, a victim of domestic abuse who fled with her dependent child. Ecdicia wrote to Augustine for advice, and *epistula* 262 was Augustine's reply. Ecidicia and her husband had previously taken a vow of continence, although Augustine perceived that Ecdicia had defrauded her husband of the debt she owed him with her body by vowing continence without her husband's permission.[64] After they had lived chastely together for a long time, Ecdicia's husband broke his vow and committed adultery, for which Augustine vehemently blames Ecdicia, her lack of submissiveness and her immoderate almsgiving.[65] The bearer of *epistula* 262 told Augustine that when Ecdicia's husband learned that she had given away almost everything she possessed to two unknown monks, he cursed them and Ecdicia, alleging that they were not servants of God but of men who creep into other people's houses, leading Ecdicia captive and plundering her.[66] The strong overtones of sexual violence in the language of capturing and plundering complicate and tarnish Ecdicia's donation, degrading the ethical basis of her actions. Augustine strongly criticises Ecdicia for adopting widow's clothes, again without her husband's permission, and argues

---

[64] Ep. 262.2.

[65] Doyle is able to detect 'a touch of chauvinism' in Augustine's loading of blame on Ecdicia. Doyle, *Bishop as Disciplinarian*, 334.

[66] Ep. 262.5.

that Ecdicia's husband should have made her wear the clothing of a wife rather than a widow.[67] Augustine's rhetorical approach strongly resists the understanding of Ecdicia's behaviour as fulfilling core Christian values of chastity, poverty and almsgiving: her self-denial was only disobedient and reckless, and directly resulted in her husband's spiritual ruin.

Roman law interfered only in a minimal sense with violence within the home, as Julia Hillner has observed.[68] Domestic abuse and violence were not outlawed; at least within elite contexts, it was not the elimination of violence but the regulation of excessive violence that was emphasised.[69] Roman law distinguished between adultery, elopement and rape, but these categories were not defined by female consent. As Melanie Webb has highlighted, rape was not clearly or consistently distinguished from other forms of illegitimate sexual activity.[70] The issue of female marital consent was addressed in Roman law: a woman had to agree to a marriage in order for it to be valid.[71] Although such legislation has been described as 'superfluous and irrelevant', given that women were expected to obey the paterfamilias with regard to marriage, the consent of women appears to have been increasingly considered from the imperial period onwards.[72] Augustine's conservative response to Ecdicia does not give precedence to her agency or desire; he understands that marital continuity is the only solution to the situation. If Ecdicia truly wants to belong to Christ, she must not scorn her husband but reclaim him, clothing herself in lowliness of mind and offering a sacrifice of tears as if they were blood from a pierced heart.[73] Ecdicia must pour out devout and continuous prayers for him, and write an apology that begs forgiveness for disposing of her property without permission. Augustine rather disingenuously advocates that Ecdicia should not repent of giving to the poor, but that she excluded her husband from the good deed. Ecdicia should promise her husband that she will be

---

[67] Ep. 262.9. On Ecdicia's change of dress, see Kate Wilkinson, *Women and Modesty in Late Antiquity* (Cambridge, 2015), 46.

[68] Julia Hillner, 'Family Violence: Punishment and Abuse in the Late Roman Household', in *Approaches to the Byzantine Family*, ed. Leslie Brubaker and Shaun Tougher (Aldershot, 2013), 21. For more on domestic violence in antiquity, see Patricia Clark, 'Women, Slaves and the Hierarchies of Domestic Violence: The Family of St Augustine', in *Women and Slaves in Greco-Roman Culture*, ed. Sandra Joshel and Sheila Murnaghan (1998), 109–29; Carucci, 'Domestic Violence in Roman Imperial Society'; Dossey, 'Wife Beating and Manliness'.

[69] Hillner, 'Family Violence', 23.

[70] Melanie Webb, '"Before the Eyes of Their Own God": Susanna, Rape Law, and Testimony in City of God 1.19', ed. M. A. Tapie and D. W. McClain, *Reading Scripture as a Political Act: Essays on Theopolitical Interpretation of the Bible* (Minneapolis, 2015), 58.

[71] *Cod. Theod.* 3.10.1, 3.6.1 and 3.11.1. On women in Roman law, see Judith Evans-Grubbs, *Law and Family in Late Antiquity: The Emperor Constantine's Marriage Legislation* (Oxford, 1995); Antti Arjava, *Women and Law in Late Antiquity* (New York, 1996); Angeliki E. Laiou (ed.), *Consent and Coercion to Sex and Marriage in Ancient and Medieval Societies* (Washington, DC, 1993); and Susan Treggiari, *Roman Marriage: Iusti Coniuges from the Time of Cicero to the Time of Ulpian* (Oxford, 1991).

[72] Arjava, *Women and Law*, 35; and for the growing attention paid to consent in Roman law, see Mathew Kuefler, 'The Marriage Revolution in Late Antiquity: The Theodosian Code and Later Roman Marriage Law', *Journal of Family History*, 32 (2007), especially 347–52.

[73] Ep. 262.11.

subject to him in all things if he repents and resumes their continence together. Augustine's approach is intended to shame Ecdicia into compliance with a solution that would entirely remove her fragile agency and autonomy, and force her and her child back into an abusive situation.

Augustine's complex rhetorical position seeks to deny Ecdidia's victim-centred narrative, at first attacking her actions, and then reaffirming the theological basis for her good deeds with recourse to Scripture but condemning the way in which she fulfilled these good deeds. Augustine focuses his scrutiny only on her actions and not her husband's, holding her to impossible standards, and revealing his assumption that victims are answerable but perpetrators are not. Through an excessive display of himpathy, Augustine loads Ecdicia with responsibility to ameliorate the situation, which is contingent on her repentance and not her husband's, even though his behaviour is the more sinful.[74] Hillner has outlined how the rise of Christianity added a new dimension to the authority of the paterfamilias, making him responsible for the spiritual health of the household and the preparation of each member for the Final Judgement.[75] But Augustine pushes the responsibility for her husband's eternal salvation onto Ecdicia: through his adultery he has plunged headlong into deep destruction, which is something she has done to him. Augustine centres the perpetrator to such an extent that he effectively reverses the roles of victim and perpetrator: the woman who has fled harm with her dependent child is the perpetrator, and the husband with agency, resources and legal, spiritual and moral authority is the victim. Augustine's letter gaslights Ecdicia, obscuring the harms that have been perpetrated against her, which are in turn difficult for us to discern, but could include sexual harassment, verbal abuse, coercion and control, sexual violence or assault, and the threat of further harm. We know that in committing adultery and breaking his vow of continence in anger and indignation, Ecdicia's husband used his emotional response to control her. It was a hostile and aggressive act that was intended to degrade her, and Augustine's letter that layered blame on Ecdicia was further degrading.

Fleeing an abusive situation is difficult and frequently the result of a careful and sustained period of risk assessment. Often a last resort for victims of domestic violence is to reach out for help, as Ecdicia did in writing to Augustine. The period immediately before and after escape is the most dangerous for victims, including children, when they are most likely to be seriously harmed or murdered. Augustine's response is to emphasise that, as a married woman, Ecdicia had no right to dispose of her own property, to control access to her body, to resist the authority of her husband or to remove his son to an unknown place. He reminds Ecdicia chillingly that legal authority over her child rests with her husband, and that he cannot be denied custody of the child when he learns where Ecdicia has taken him:

---

[74] The term 'himpathy' derives from Manne, *Down Girl*.
[75] Hillner, 'Family Violence', 23.

As for your son, since you received him in lawful and honourable marriage, who does not know that he is more subject to his father's authority than to yours? Therefore, his father cannot be denied custody of him whenever he learns where he is and legally demands him.[76]

Augustine's coercion of Ecdicia is absolute; he makes her accountable not only for her husband's spiritual welfare but also represents that Ecdicia must reconcile with her husband for the spiritual sake of her son: 'Consequently, your union of hearts is necessary for him, so that as according to your will, he may be brought up and educated in the wisdom of God.'[77] Augustine sees that Ecdicia's choices to give away her possessions and flee her husband compromise her child's spiritual and economic future. Dependants like children are often mobilised against victims of domestic violence as weapons of abuse, and Augustine exploits this structure of oppression to force her and her child back into an abusive environment.

What capacity would Ecdicia have to resist Augustine's overbearing advice? Assessing the reach of Augustine's authority in a local and generalised sense in North Africa in the fifth century is fraught with difficulties, but it is unlikely that Ecdicia would have been able to brush off his instructions easily, especially when she and her child were isolated and vulnerable. Ecdicia lacks support from every single known adult actor within her immediate network. The bearer of her letter to Augustine discloses information about her donation that she had not included in the letter. The bearer could also disclose her family's location, further compromising her precarious position.[78] With the

---

[76] Ep. 262.11, *Saint Augustine*, trans. Parsons, 269. *CSEL* 57, ed. Goldbacher, 631: 'filium autem uestrum, quoniam de legitimis eum et honestis nuptiis suscepisti, magis in patris quam in tua esse potestate quis nesciat? et ideo ei negari non potest, ubicumque illum esse cognouerit et iure poposcerit'.

[77] *Ibid.*, 631: 'ac per hoc, ut secundum tuam uoluntatem in dei possit nutriri et erudiri sapientia, necessaria illi est etiam uestra concordia'.

[78] The bearer of Ecdicia's letter to Augustine, which does not survive, must have been an actor within Ecdicia's network and not Augustine's. The information about who delivered Augustine's reply to Ecdicia, ep. 262, has not survived. It does not always appear to be the case that a letter was delivered and a reply returned by the same bearer, although that would be logical here. More generally, the identity of the bearers of Augustine's letters has not been preserved. Bearers of letters were sometimes petitioners requesting Augustine to write specific letters on their behalf, which they would then deliver, and sometimes take other letters that were awaiting delivery from Augustine. For example, Augustine wrote ep. 178 to Hilarius at the request of Palladius, who had asked Augustine to recommend him to Hilarius. Palladius delivered the letter to Hilarius, as well as an oral message of news of Augustine. For more on letter bearers in late antiquity, see Pauline Allen, 'Prolegomena to a Study of the Letter-Bearer in Christian Antiquity', *Studia Patristica*, 62 (2013), 481–91; Sigrid Mratschek, 'Die ungeschriebenen Briefe des Augustinus von Hippo', in *'In Search of Truth': Augustine, Manichaeism and Other Gnosticism. Studies for Johannes van Oort at Sixty*, ed. Jacob Albert van den Berg, Annemaré Kotzé, Tobias Nicklas and Madeleine Scopello (Leiden, 2011), 109–22; Élisabeth Paoli-Lafaye, 'Messagers et messages. La diffusion des nouvelles de l'Afrique d'Augustin vers les régions d'au-delà des mers', in *L'information et la mer dans le monde antique*, ed. Jean Andreau and Catherine Virlouvet (Rome, 2002), 233–59; Pauline Allen, 'Christian Correspondences: The Secrets of Letter-Writers and Letter-Bearers', in *The Art of Veiled Speech: Self-Censorship from Aristophanes to Hobbes*, ed. Han Baltussen and Peter

weight of the institutional Church behind him, Augustine's reaction to Ecdicia's disclosure sidesteps responsibility for her well-being and safety, denying her justice and failing to hold her husband to account.[79]

Although it was legal for Roman men like Ecdicia's husband to have sexual relationships outside marriage, in *sermo* 392 Augustine preached that wives who know of their husbands' infidelity or broken vows of chastity should inform him directly.[80] Through Augustine, Christ orders shamelessly unchaste husbands to perform the humility of penance to absolve them of their sins. They should refrain from communion, and they are summoned before God's judgement. Augustine instructs wronged wives not to tolerate calmly their husbands' infidelities. Instead he demands they be jealous of their husbands, not for the sake of their bodies, but for the sake of their souls.[81] How can we reconcile what Augustine preaches here with his response to Ecdicia in *epistula* 262? In his sermon, Augustine is uncompromising in his condemnation of adulterous husbands, painstakingly setting out each circumstance in which infidelity is not allowed. Men who break the bonds of marriage are centred, but in *epistula* 262, Augustine reserves his criticism for Ecdicia only, blaming her for her husband's infidelity. In his sermon, Augustine argues that men compromise their eternal souls through infidelity, and that wives must not be indifferent but fight obstinately with them over their chastity. By comparison, Ecdicia's response of fleeing her husband appears self-interested and transgressive. Augustine's encouragement to women to inform him of their husbands' infidelities reveals the double standard in *epistula* 262, for when Ecdicia follows his request, Augustine blames her for it and makes her responsible for fixing the situation.

J. Davis (Philadelphia, 2015), 209–32; Pauline Allen and Bronwen Neil, *Greek and Latin Letters in Late Antiquity: The Christianisation of a Literary Form* (Cambridge, 2020), 96–115.

[79] 'Expectations for justice that go unmet … create another enormous category of aftermath nonevents … The dire circumstances of those for whom justice is passionately desired but is instead deferred or delayed because nothing happened to the perpetrators, makes it seem that the surviving victims are still powerless in the face of their persecutors. For them, Nothing has changed.' Susan A. Crane identifies nothing, a void in history that, whilst it has been present all along, has been overlooked and ignored. Her History of Nothing aims to map that void. Susan A. Crane, *Nothing Happened: A History* (Stanford, 2020), 18.

[80] *Serm.* 392.4: 'I myself, I repeat, am giving you orders: don't allow your husbands to go on fornicating. Bring your complaints against them to the Church. I don't say to the civil judges, to the governor, to the deputy, to the commissioner, to the emperor; but to Christ.' *Sermons*, trans. Edmund Hill, pt III, vol. 10 (New York, 1995), 423. 'ego, inquam, iubeo. Nolite uiros uestros permittere fornicari. Interpellate contra illos ecclesiam. Non dico, iudices publicos, non proconsulem, non uicarium, non comitem, non imperatorem; sed christum.' *Patrologia Latina* 39, col. 1711. Augustine notes in *sermo* 82 that women do come to him to tell him about their husbands' affairs: 'There are people who commit adultery in their own homes; they sin privately. Sometimes they are reported to me by their wives out of extreme jealously, sometimes out of a real concern for their husbands' salvation.' *Sermons*, trans. Hill, pt III, vol. 3, 375. *Serm.* 82.11. 'Sunt homines adulteri in domibus suis, in secreto peccant; aliquando nobis produntur ab uxoribus suis plerumque zelantibus, aliquando maritorum salutem quaerentibus: nos non prodimus palam, sed in secreto arguimus.' *Patrologia Latina* 38, col. 511.

[81] *Serm.* 392.4.

Conclusion

No further evidence concerning Ecdicia and her child survives, and it is impossible to know if she was forced to follow Augustine's advice and return to her husband, or if she managed to maintain her autonomy. In writing to Augustine and making him aware of the harms perpetrated against her as she must have done, Ecdicia advocated for herself, claiming entitlement to redress and sympathy, perhaps as the earliest attested victim of domestic abuse to flee with a child. *Epistula 262* stands out within the letter collection because the female assertion of agency and entitlement to acknowledgement of harm is unusual, and Augustine pushes back against it. Instead, women are explicitly and implicitly expected to provide a caring and sympathetic audience for men's victim narratives. In other words, one of the goods women are characteristically held to owe dominant men is their moral focus and emotional energy, something which abusive men often feel excessively entitled to.[82] Augustine's blaming of female victims for the sexual violence and domestic abuse perpetrated against them is an end-point conclusion within a thought-system of patriarchal entitlement and hostile misogyny where women are not entitled to acknowledgement and redress. Even raising an accusation of harm against a man is a dangerous transgression of the boundaries of gendered societal expectations.[83] This system is so complete in Augustine's fifth-century North Africa that only through comparison of his reaction to a male victim of sexual harassment can we see how polarised his conception of female and male victimhood is. Although this article seeks to highlight the framework of misogyny that was embedded in Augustine's epistemology, it does not argue that his response to Ecdicia was exceptional, or exceptionally heinous. Instead, Augustine's letters illuminate normative levels of violence in domestic and familial environments that are simultaneously interpersonal and structural, and that reflect the rigid hierarchisation of Roman society dominated by patriarchal thought systems and constructions of power.

---

[82] Manne, *Down Girl*, 231.
[83] *Ibid.*, 230–1.

Cite this article: Leonard V (2023). Gendered Violence, Victim Credibility and Adjudicating Justice in Augustine's Letters. *Transactions of the Royal Historical Society* 1, 219–239. https://doi.org/10.1017/S0080440123000087

Transactions of the RHS (2023), **1**, 241–265
doi:10.1017/S0080440123000099

ARTICLE

Archival Intimacies: Empathy and Historical Practice in 2023

Sarah Fox

School of History and Cultures, University of Birmingham, Edgbaston, Birmingham, UK
Email: s.fox.3@bham.ac.uk

(Received 27 February 2023; revised 28 June 2023; accepted 29 June 2023; first published
online 7 August 2023)

Abstract

This article explores the use of empathy in historical research. Using evidence collected from
a number of academic historians working in UK higher education institutions in 2022, this
article uses empathy as a window into historians' attitudes towards the professional self,
the appearance of objectivity and their relationship to the historical subject. It explores
the role of empathy in learning history, teaching history, in historical research including
the selection of sources, and in the communication of historical research to different audiences. It discusses empathetic historical approaches, suggesting that these can be categorised
into three distinct taxonomies: historical empathy, where the researcher engages with the
historical subject using professional detachment to manage their affective response; historicised empathy, where the researcher employs deep knowledge of historical context to
understand and appreciate the worldview of their historical subject; and empathy as historical approach, so person-centred (rather than system-centred) accounts of history. Finally,
this article tests its hypotheses by exploring histories in which empathy is absent.

Keywords: Empathy; eighteenth century; archive; historical methodology; letters

> The poetry of history lies in the quasi-miraculous fact that once, on this earth,
> once, on this familiar spot of ground, walked other men and women as actual
> as we are today, thinking their own thoughts, swayed by their own passions,
> but now all gone, one generation vanishing into another, gone as utterly as
> we ourselves shall shortly be gone, like ghosts at cockcrow.[1]

That 'this familiar spot of ground' can be occupied by people who seem at once
recognisable, yet also utterly different, drives much of the study of history,

---

[1] G. M. Trevelyan, 'Autobiography of an Historian', in *An Autobiography and Other Essays* (1949), 13.

from people searching online for the lives of their predecessors, to academic historians. In seeking to gain a deeper understanding of the past, historians of all stripes have to reconcile themselves to this fundamental dichotomy, setting aside their own self and their worldview in order to attempt to understand those of another. This 'ability to understand and appreciate another person's feelings', the 'quality or power of projecting one's personality into or mentally identifying oneself with an object of contemplation, and so fully understanding or appreciating it', is defined by the *Oxford English Dictionary* as 'empathy'. This article explores the role of empathy in academic historical research, asking the extent to which it shapes the topic of research, the way in which research is conducted, and the way that history is communicated to students, to academic audiences and to the public. It asks 'how does the historian in 2023 understand empathy?', presenting historians as an emotional community of sorts, and exploring historians' attitudes towards the professional self, the appearance of objectivity and their relationship to the historical subject.

Methodology

To explore these questions, I have gathered the reflections and experiences of eleven academic historians working in UK institutions in 2022.[2] These historians represent three key career stages: early career, mid-career and senior faculty. Most (though not all) specialise in histories of the eighteenth century, and all have worked with letters at some point in their careers. The letter archive is particularly fertile ground for thinking about empathy and the historical researcher. Letters are, after all, designed to create connections between a writer and reader across distance, and that distance can be temporal as well as geographical. As such, letters lend themselves to both an affective sense of connection and an empathetic methodological approach.

Each participant responded to a questionnaire containing nine questions (see Appendix). The use of questionnaires is uncommon in historical research, but has a number of advantages in collecting data on historical practice. Questionnaires allow respondents time to think about the questions being asked, prompting more reflective answers than might be obtained through conversation or interview.[3] The questionnaire contained entirely open questions, designed to gather narrative, qualitative information that I could then analyse. The questions were grouped thematically, covering the respondent's initial views on what empathy in historical research might be, their thoughts on learning and teaching empathy, and the role of empathy in their research. These themes are reflected in the structure of this article. Contributors were asked if they wished to remain anonymous in this article, but I took the decision to anonymise the entire data sample. Respondents are therefore referred to numerically when referenced, using the abbreviation R# in order to cite individual responses and opinions.

---

[2] Approved by the Research Ethics Team, University of Birmingham, ERN_2-22_0460.

[3] Gill Marshall, 'The Purpose, Design and Administration of a Questionnaire for Data Collection', *Radiography*, 11 (2005), 131–6.

A brief history of empathy

Empathy, writes philosopher Susan Lanzoni, is a technology of the self.[4] Early versions of empathy involved expanding the self to occupy an object. A translation of the German word *Einfühlung*, the term 'empathy' was used to describe the 'quality or power of projecting one's personality into or mentally identifying oneself with an object of contemplation, and so fully understanding or appreciating it'.[5] As such, aesthetic empathy was about expanding the self into, for example, the swell of a landscape, or the angles of a piece of furniture. In 1909, English psychologist Edward Titchener extended the basic concepts of aesthetic empathy to encompass the mind. He claimed that he not only observed gravity and modesty and pride in his patients 'but I feel or act them in the mind's muscles'.[6] Empathy therefore became the capacity to enter into the emotions of another person and to experience them in a way that reflected, if imperfectly, the emotions being observed. In 1958, psychologist Nathan Blackman suggested that empathy was the ability not to extend the self, but to put the self aside in order to more fully occupy the position of another.[7] Empathy then became the dominant psychological term used to denote the ability to understand the experience of others. This acquired particular importance in the post-war world of the atom bomb, and the cold war, where the threat of the self-immolation of the human race loomed, and understanding one's enemy took on a particular prominence.[8] Recent work on the neurological nature of empathy has identified a biological marker in the brains of primates that responds to the appearance of emotion in another. The 'mirror neuron' locates empathy in the body, yet it does not negate the contextual and relational elements of empathy. Brain mechanisms make us experience (as if replicating) the emotions of another but they remain grounded in our own experience.[9]

Acts of emotional projection, or of recognition, demand at the very least a shared social and cultural background with the object of enquiry. 'Reactions to the emotions of others', suggests historian of emotion Rob Boddice, 'are always part of a process of recognition.'[10] Modern empathy, he suggests, is 'projection, reception, and internal production' of emotion.[11] These three meanings and their associational experiences overlap, coexist and confuse each other, adding to a sense of slipperiness over what it means to empathise with another. Without a shared background, understanding, and therefore empathy, is difficult. Even relatively stable cultural norms such as maternity or parenthood

---

[4] Susan Lanzoni, *Empathy: A History* (New Haven, 2018), 280.

[5] OED   2a,   https://www.oed-com.ezproxyd.bham.ac.uk/view/Entry/61284?redirectedFrom= empathy#eid.

[6] 'Lectures on the Experimental Psychology of the Thought-Process by Edward Bradford Titchener', *Science*, 31:789 (1910), 224–6.

[7] Nathan Blackman, 'The Development of Empathy in Male Schizophrenics', *Psychiatric Quarterly*, 2 (1958), 546–53, at 547.

[8] Lanzoni, *Empathy*, 132.

[9] Rob Boddice, *The History of Emotions* (Manchester, 2018), 56.

[10] *Ibid.*, 184.

[11] *Ibid.*, 56.

are hugely affected by individual circumstance, as Emma Griffin has shown in her exploration of hunger and parenting in industrial England.[12] Moreover, in presuming to know how another human feels, those that claim empathy are also, albeit subconsciously, claiming the dominance of their own hierarchies of emotion and regimes of feeling in a way that can minimise, or reduce, the actual feelings of the person being empathised with.[13] It is necessary to know how to interpret an emotional dynamic in order to enter into it, and that knowledge is ingrained, learnt, practised and prescribed.[14] That interpretive context is essential to achieving an experiential understanding of another person.[15]

Empathy in history

Historians generally have an uneasy relationship with empathy. For many, empathy is inextricably linked to a sense of attachment to the past that is at once open to criticism, yet entirely necessary. E. H. Carr highlighted the need for 'some kind of contact' with the mind of the historical subject when writing, to avoid what he calls 'dry as dust factual histories'.[16] David Lowenthal discusses empathy as a type of deep connection to the past – a 'more than' approach – though he doesn't specify precisely what he understands empathy to be.[17] Ludmilla Jordanova talks about 'identification' evoking profound connections to the past, which she links to the emotional response of many historians to the material that they study to the point where the researcher may feel 'inside' their sources.[18] For others, however, this sense of connection or recognition should be approached with caution, lest it close the gap between 'now' and 'then'. John Tosh warned about the dangers of an empathetic approach to history making the past look too familiar. Using empathy to close the distance between researcher and historical subject, he suggests, distracts from the historian's job of accessing the fundamentally different mentalities of the people that we study and whose worldview we seek to understand.[19]

Michael Roper's article 'The Unconscious Work of History' situated empathy in experience, rather than in the mind. He defined empathy as 'the ability to imaginatively connect with the subjectivities of people in the past', drawing on Barbara Taylor's notion of 'species similarity'.[20] Yet this idea, of common

---

[12] Emma Griffin, 'Diets, Hunger, and Living Standards during the British Industrial Revolution', *Past & Present*, 239 (2011), 71–111, at 92–4.

[13] Jonathan Saha, 'Murder at London Zoo: Late Colonial Sympathy in Interwar Britain', *American Historical Review*, 121 (2016), 1468–91, at 1472.

[14] Boddice, *Emotions*, 184.

[15] Lanzoni, *Empathy*, 8.

[16] Edward Hallett Carr, *What is History?* (1987), 15.

[17] David Lowenthal, *The Past Is a Foreign Country: Revisited* (Cambridge, 2015), 64.

[18] Ludmilla Jordanova, *History in Practice* (2019), 45.

[19] John Tosh, *Why History Matters* (Basingstoke, 2008), 27.

[20] Michael Roper, 'The Unconscious Work of History', *Cultural and Social History*, 11 (2014), 169–93, at 174.

experiences across time, defined by species, is problematic. We do not experience our bodies in the same way as our historical subjects. For example, as Boddice described in his discussion of 'sight', the physical eye is part of a biological body and a sensory system that is historical and mutable.[21] Species similarity and shared experience has long been a subject of debate. As nineteenth-century physician Peter Mere Latham noted in his 1862 book on medical practice, the 'things of life and feeling ... are different from all things in the world besides'. His enquiry into the nature of pain, explored in depth by Joanna Bourke in *The Story of Pain*, shows how even something as universally 'felt' as pain is experienced in layers constructed individually – psychologically, bodily and socially.[22] Taylor argues in her work that 'our interpretations of past subjectivities draw on our imaginative identifications, conscious and unconscious, with the people we study'.[23] Yet subjectivity, particularly imagined subjectivity, is a source of some concern for historians, a hangover from post-structuralist debates about narrative and truth, traceable through the 'social turn' of the 1970s and 1980s, the cultural turn of the 1990s and the affective turn of current scholarship.

'The history of objectivity', wrote historians of science Lorraine Daston and Peter Galison, 'is the story of how and why various types of subjectivity become seen as dangerously subjective.'[24] In attempting to pry apart the relationship between knowledge and the self, they argue, objectivity became viewed as 'impartiality, disinterested ontology, epistemology, and character'.[25] Yet they were careful to point out the close contours of the relationship between objectivity and subjectivity. Objectivity and subjectivity, they argue, are expressions of a particular historical predicament, one that seeks to erase the historian as 'knower' with their associated skills and judgements.[26] At first glance, empathy, a method of knowing grounded in feeling and in imagination, appears to exist in direct opposition to objectivity. Rosa Belvedresi noted how 'it is generally believed that the affective bond that requires empathetic understanding puts objectivity at risk', before arguing that the opposite is in fact true. When historians don't pay attention to the affects in their work, she suggests, they risk confusing their own values with irrefutable data.[27] Stephen Gaukroger goes even further in his *Short Introduction* to objectivity. On the first page, he writes that 'objectivity requires the ability to shift perspective'.[28] An objective approach to any subject requires us to stand back from our perceptions, beliefs and opinions, to reflect on them and to subject them to scrutiny and judgement, he argues.

---

[21] Boddice, *Emotions*, 132.

[22] Joanne Bourke, *The Story of Pain: From Prayer to Painkillers* (Oxford, 2014); see introduction, 1–25.

[23] Barbara Taylor, 'Historical Subjectivity', in *Psyche and History*, ed. S. Alexander and B. Taylor (Basingstoke, 2012), 195–9.

[24] Lorraine Daston and Peter Galison, *Objectivity* (New York, 2010), 37.

[25] *Ibid.*, 378.

[26] *Ibid.*.

[27] Rosa E. Belvedresi, 'Empathy and Historical Understanding', in *Empathy: Emotional, Ethical and Epistemological Narratives*, ed. Richardo Guttierez Aguilar (2019), 169.

[28] Stephen Gaukroger, *Objectivity: A Very Short Introduction* (Oxford, 2012).

Empathy, I suggest, requires the same careful delineation between self and other, an awareness of affect and of evidence. Empathy, then, straddles the narrow line between subjectivity and objectivity in a way that awakens the intellectual fear described by Daston and Galison as a driving factor in the power of objectivity as an academic ideal. Historians' attitudes to empathy reflect our concerns about errors, or challenges to our objectivity and accuracy, anxiously anticipated along with the precautions that we take to mitigate them.[29]

If empathy is an act of projection, grounded in affect, in experience and in culture, is it actually possible to feel empathy for historical figures? How do historians read emotion and experience in history? What are we doing when we empathise? In his overview text *The History of Emotions*, Boddice talks about packing away his own empathetic response to his subject because he could not be sure that his response, for all its empathy, was hitting the right notes.[30] He continues, 'to be out of time and place is to risk a failure of empathy activation or a complete misreading of another's mind'. Boddice does not advocate an absence of empathy; instead, he suggests, 'just as we have to learn empathy for ourselves in the present, so we have to learn it differently for the past'.[31] Empathy requires effort, and care, and must be held apart from affect. That is not to dismiss affective forms of historical engagement. That flash of feeling in the archives is often what draws historians to the discipline. It has the capacity to change us, to take our research in new and interesting directions, to tap into parts of our own lives, touching us deeply and providing us with the means to touch others. If empathy is fully understanding and appreciating another's feelings, however, it requires historians to put our own affect and emotion aside. As Belvedresi concluded, 'empathy does not suppose the uncritical identification between historian and historical agent, but it does manifest the affective load that is displayed in the process of understanding'.[32] To cite Susan Lanzoni, 'Empathy marks a relation between the self and the other that draws a border but also builds a bridge ... we need the self to empathise, but we also have to leave it behind.'[33]

What historians mean when they describe empathetic approaches to their subject varies hugely. As we shall see throughout this article, empathy is particularly personal to the researcher and to the nature of the histories they research and write. Whilst working through the responses to my survey questions, I have sought to define three empathetic approaches to historical source material. These taxonomies are particularly visible when respondents discuss empathetic approaches to teaching, learning and researching history, though they fade away when writing history is discussed. They are by no means exhaustive, nor are they clearly defined. They blur and merge at their edges, and overlap in their practices, but they provide a framework to think about the methodological uses of empathy in historical research and, I hope, launch future discussion about the nature of empathy in our discipline.

---

[29] Daston and Galison, *Objectivity*, 372.
[30] Boddice, *Emotions*, 126.
[31] *Ibid.*, 126–7.
[32] Belvedresi, 'Empathy', 169.
[33] Lanzoni, *Empathy*, 17, 278.

Empathetic perspective

At their simplest, empathetic methodologies for studying history focus on people, rather than systems or places. Psychoanalyst and historian Thomas Kohut has suggested that historians think about empathy as a way of knowing grounded in evidence, logic and reason, as well as in harder-to-identify tools such as imagination, insight, sensitivity to people, emotional intelligence and emotional resonance. In thinking 'systematically and rigorously' about the nature of historian's empathy, Kohut premises the empathetic observational position as a way of writing empathetic history. This, he suggests, requires the researcher to write history from the perspective of the subject, rather than with the hindsight that generally characterises the discipline.[34] This approach is adopted by Katie Barclay in her 2018 article 'Falling in Love with the Dead'.[35] Barclay uses empathy as an historical tool in her attempts to fall in love with the distinctly unlovable (from a modern perspective) Gilbert Innes of Stowe. She tests both the limits and the analytical possibilities of empathy by empathising with a figure she has no sympathy for.

Historicised empathy

Historicised empathy requires the researcher to employ a deep knowledge of historical context in order to understand and appreciate the worldview of their historical subject. This type of knowledge is learned and cultivated over entire careers and forms the basis of all historical enquiry. Its application to empathetic approaches to history is therefore to be expected. Empathy is contingent upon knowing what is being encountered, therefore historicised empathy is contingent not just upon knowing or recognising what is being encountered but upon being also able to contextualise that knowledge through engagement with historical evidence.[36] It requires an immersion in the social, political, cultural and economic frameworks of the period under consideration, generally built over many years of study and research.

Historical empathy

Historical empathy more closely reflects philosophical and psychological definitions of empathy. The researcher engages with the historical subject using professional detachment to manage their affective response. Successful historical empathy requires the researcher to cultivate the cognitive capacity to take the perspective of another (through imagination) alongside the regulatory mechanisms that tone down the self-perspective and allow for the evaluation of the other-perspective.[37] Fritz Breithaupt describes this type of empathetic practice as 'co-experiencing the situation of another',

---

[34] Thomas Kohut, *Empathy and the Historical Understanding of the Human Past* (2020), 4.
[35] Katie Barclay, 'Falling in Love with the Dead', *Rethinking History*, 22 (2018), 459–73.
[36] Tracey Loughran, Kate Mahoney and Daisy Payling, 'Women's Voices, Emotion and Empathy: Engaging Different Publics with "Everyday" Health Histories', *Medical Humanities*, 48 (2022), 397.
[37] Boddice, *Emotions*, 126.

arguing that the term 'co-experiencing' retains a necessary sense of difference between the self and the subject.[38]

How do historians 'feel' about empathy?

To feel empathy with an historical subject is described by many respondents as seeing or recognising another's feelings and experiences. R8 describes empathy as 'a recognition of, or an emotional response to, the experiences of the historical actors we study'. For R6, empathy is the sense of 'holding a feeling in common with someone, or recreating someone's emotional state within oneself', whilst for R7 it is 'a controlled act of feeling'. R9 describes empathy as 'more than merely a feeling' but 'a sense of intertwining your own world view with others ... a sense of hearing the voices and experiences of those whose shoes you have not walked in'. Acknowledged but unspoken in these descriptions of empathy is the unilateral nature of this relationship. In this context, R8's use of the term 'recognition' is significant in locating the emotions that might be experienced in the archive firmly within the researcher. Emotion and affect can (and do) form part of the historicisation of empathy, but they are neither essential nor even desirable. Source material and historical approach are generally seen as important in defining empathetic approaches to history. R10 extrapolates, 'Perhaps I might do this [theorise explicitly about empathy] more if I worked on histories of emotion, or on histories that appeal to or relate on some level to the researcher?' Academic training is the medium through which these emotional responses to source materials might be controlled. Corfield and Hitchcock have recently described empathy as 'cool intellectual / emotional understanding without condoning or sympathising'.[39] As such, they suggest a level of detachment on the part of the researcher that forms part of an historian's professional toolkit.

If empathy is a way of knowing or understanding the emotional state of an historical actor, is it fundamentally a fiction? A way of claiming to know the unknowable? The line between empathy and imagination appears, at times, vanishingly thin and draws us back towards post-structuralist debates of the mid-twentieth century in which the nature of history and historical fact was cause for some concern amongst historians. R1 suggested that empathy is an attempt 'to understand the point of view of, including the attitudes, emotions and motivations of, the historical characters you are studying', yet this raises questions about the difficulty of 'knowing' more generally. Empathising with the historical subject requires imagination. Sarah Maza has argued, in her primer *Thinking about History*, that 'narrative and imagination are probably more central to history as a discipline than any other field of enquiry'.[40] Good history, she suggests, requires both a forensic attention to detail and meticulous research, coupled with a compelling narrative. It does not follow, however, that an imaginative narrative relies on an empathetic

---

[38] Fritz Breithaupt, *The Dark Sides of Empathy* (New York, 2019), 11.
[39] Penelope J. Corfield and Tim Hitchcock, *Becoming a Historian* (2022), 104.
[40] Sarah Maza, *Thinking about History* (Chicago, 2017), 233.

approach to history. In balancing the sometimes competing demands of narrative and historical evidence, historians become acutely aware of the limits of 'knowledge' and the need to be cautious in our assumptions, and critical of what we know in a way that is perhaps less marked in other disciplines. As such, empathy sharpens historical practice through both the way it is used in historical writing and as an historical tool.

The researching and writing of history encourages historians to reflect upon what survives, how insufficient the historical record can be in representing lives that have been lived, and ultimately how little we know. Archives reflect the dominant structures and hierarchies of the societies in which they are created. They are, therefore, never equal with the voices of the powerful represented at the expense of those of the oppressed. For some peoples, places or events, the archive – which is generally identified as the seat of historical knowledge – is deeply limited. In trying to access these histories, writers such as Saidiya Hartman have started to embrace imagination as a form of historical practice. Hartman seeks to 'elaborate, augment, transpose and break open archival documents so that they might yield a richer picture of the social upheaval that transformed black social life in the twentieth century'.[41] To understand the world as it was experienced by young black women at the turn of the century, to learn from what they knew, Hartman has 'pressed at the limits of the case file and the document, speculated about what might have been, imagined the things whispered in dark bedrooms, and amplified moments of withholding, escape, and possibility'. Hartman's imaginings and amplifications are grounded in the holdings of both institutional and personal archives, historicised and person-focused. Trial transcripts, portraits, newspaper clippings, oral histories, personal ephemera and institutional case files all contribute to her compilation of *Wayward Lives*.[42] 'My speculative and imaginative approach', she notes, 'is based on archival research and rigorous attention to sources.'[43] By grounding her imaginative narrative in the archive, Hartman creates the rich historical context on which historicised empathy is based. Hartman's willingness to discuss the imaginative elements of her work is perhaps grounded in her disciplinary background in literature and performance studies.

Empathy studies is a long-established and lively area of literary theory and research that explores empathy as an aspect of readers' responses to literature, authors' creative imagining and the textual cues that might deliberately invite or incite an affective response in the reader.[44] There are a number of parallels that can be drawn between literature and historical writing, not least the management of depictions of people on the page, the author as mediator of the voices of others and as director of the response of readers. Yet historians

---

[41] Saidiya V. Hartman, 'Notes on Method', in *Wayward Lives, Beautiful Experiments: Intimate Histories of Social Upheaval* (2019), 9–10.

[42] Hartman, 'Voices from the Chorus', in *Wayward Lives*, 165.

[43] *Ibid.*, 167.

[44] For an overview, see Suzanne Keen, 'Empathy Studies', in *A Companion to Literary Theory*, ed. David H. Richter (Oxford, 2018), 126–38.

appear less certain of the role of empathy in their histories, and its relationship with imagination and with objectivity. Historian Marisa Fuentes employs empathy to fill the archival silence of enslaved women in eighteenth-century Barbados. 'History', she writes, 'is produced from what the archive offers. It is the historian's job to substantiate all the pieces with more archival evidence, context, and historiography, and put them together into a coherent narrative form. The challenge this book has confronted is to write a history about what an archive does not offer.'[45] Fuentes questions traditional historical methods that 'search for archival veracity, statistical substantiation, and empiricism'. The search for more sources, she suggests, and reliance on the archive simply reproduces the silences experienced by the dispossessed in the eighteenth-century world by demanding the impossible. Historians must, she argues, relinquish the archive as the site of authority and reconcile themselves 'to allow for uncertainty, unresolvable narratives, and contradictions'.[46] Fuentes addresses these problems through empathy. She acknowledges the affective nature of her topic and its relation to the self: 'confronting sources that show only terror and violence are a danger to the researcher who sees her own ancestors in these accounts'.[47] The 'process of historicization', she continues, 'demands strategies to manage the emotional response one has to such brutality'.[48] This acknowledgement of her own affective response to her sources, and the setting aside of that emotion to focus on recovering the lives of her historical subjects, both demands and demonstrates historical empathy. Fuentes's focus on the context in which archival silences are produced and reproduced, and her person-centred interpretation of the systems and structures of colonial power are empathetic approaches to archival absences. She fills these silences by reading against the grain of the documents, grounding them in the deep contextual knowledge demanded by historicised empathy. As such, both Fuentes and Hartman show that imagination and empathy can be used to acknowledge history as a production as well as an accounting of the past, and therefore as a method to challenge both historical and current power structures. In order to claim authority, historical imagination is grounded in a deep knowledge of context based upon experience and robust research. As R2 suggested, imagination 'does not mean making things up, but offering hypotheses based on wider knowledge which will be considered convincing and likely to specialists'.

Miri Rubin has described empathetic approaches to history as being a 'move away from trying to understand "how it was" to trying to understand "how it was for him, or her, or them".[49] Whilst such an approach lends itself to first-person narratives such as letters, diaries or oral testimonies, Hartman and Fuentes show that it can still be applied to the documents that support

---

[45] Marisa J. Fuentes, *Dispossessed Lives: Enslaved Women, Violence, and the Archive* (Philadelphia, 2016), 146.

[46] *Ibid*, 12.

[47] *Ibid*, 146.

[48] *Ibid*, 147.

[49] Miri Rubin, 'What Is Cultural History Now?', in *What is History Now?*, ed. David Cannadine (Basingstoke, 2002), 80–94.

and perpetuate systems and structures of power, and indeed, to social systems and structures of power themselves. Account books, court documents, ship's records, have all been used to produce empathic accounts of the past that both centre the individual, and situate them in the structures that shape and define their lives. R1 describes this as 'reading between the lines, or against the grain of a text', to uncover the experiences of those recorded only indirectly in the sources. R2 describes this as 'putting aside our own emotions and allowing space for the perspective of another'. As such, empathetic approaches demand a level of nuance in interpretation that also makes for very messy history. It is possible to empathise with historical subjects on a number of different registers. As Sarah Maza is at pains to point out, 'History is always someone's story, layered over and likely at odds with someone else's: to recognise this does not make our chronicles of the past less reliable, but more varied, deeper and more truthful.'[50]

Learning empathy

All of the contributors to this article agreed that empathy forms part of their historian's toolkit, to varying degrees. The Quality Assurance Agency for Higher Education's 2022 Subject Benchmark Statement for History expects all graduating students in the UK to:

> understand how people have existed, acted and thought in the always-different context of the past. History involves encountering the past's otherness and learning to understand unfamiliar structures, cultures, and belief systems. These forms of understanding illuminate the influence of the past on the present; they also foster empathy, and respect for difference.[51]

The implication here is that simply studying history increases the student's capacity for empathy. It is, then, unsurprising that explicit discussion of empathy is largely absent from historical skills and methodological survey courses in the UK, though this may be changing as more institutions offer undergraduate and postgraduate courses on the history of emotions. For Sarah Maza, this is because 'historical research is impossible to teach. It is learned on the fly, just by doing it.'[52] Moreover, empathy is thought to be part of the human experience and therefore innate to the researcher. R6 described empathy as a skill 'in the sense that walking or whispering are skills: pretty basic to normal human functioning, even if not everyone is capable of doing it, and it can be done better or worse'. R5 called empathy 'a quality of a healthy human mind'. As such, it is reasonable to assume that students at both undergraduate and postgraduate levels are able to adopt an empathetic approach to history without the need for dedicated training. Yet the key feature of the

---

[50] Maza, *Thinking about History*, 234.

[51] Quality Assurance Agency for Higher Education, *Subject Benchmark Statement: History*, 5th edn (Gloucester, Mar. 2022), clause 1.7P. 4.

[52] Maza, *Thinking about History*, 3.

historical approach to empathy is control, and an understanding of the limits of feeling and recognition. This control, and the nuanced application of empathetic approaches to history, does need to be learned, and therefore also taught.

For most of the contributors to this article, their approach to empathy was honed and developed over the course of their university studies. Dominant historiographical and institutional trends must therefore be hugely influential in the development and application of historical approaches to empathy. The arrival of social approaches to history in the mid-twentieth century really heralded the arrival of critical person-centred histories that moved beyond biography. For R5, the arrival of 'history from below' in university curricula meant that 'one was presented with highly technical social science history, and narrative history'. 'The latter', they note, 'has survived, while the former, not so much.' R1, trained at a similar time, suggested that empathy was 'embedded in my general training as a social historian ... but it was not a word that was often used'. During the social and cultural 'turns' of the 1990s, R10 identified a long-established tendency for historical training to insist 'on a separation between past and present, and a reaching for some form of critical objectivity'. Perhaps this push for a form of objectivity more aligned with the social sciences arose from the 'social turn's' focus on individuals, or groups of previously under-studied people, as a way of defending such an approach against the remnants of post-structuralist approaches to history, and older, sociological forms of historical enquiry.

Age and life stage emerged as being hugely formative in empathetic approaches to historical work, further emphasising the developmental and progressive nature of empathy as a professional historical tool. R3 felt that their empathetic approach to family history 'happened by attrition, by reading more and more primary sources combined with my own life experience as I aged'. Life experience implies a level of maturity, of knowledge, and the decentring of the self that often comes with ageing. If empathetic history requires the centring of another's perspective at the temporary expense of your own, maturity if not chronological age may well be influential on a researcher's ability to do it well. R6 described learning empathetic historical approaches as a form of apprenticeship, suggesting that, as 'any attempt to express yourself to others entails some attempt to imagine what other people will feel and how they'll think', then 'learning some sort of empathy is part of learning to write, which I did a lot of, especially as a postgraduate student and postdoc'. R7 also raised career stage as crucial to the capacity to both feel and practise empathy, though they framed it not as academic 'youth' or apprenticeship, but as a response to employment security:

I suspect I developed empathy a bit later – when I was a bit older, a bit more secure in myself, and (crucially) free from the all-encompassing panic of not having a job. I suspect I found it quite hard to fully commit to the past when I wasn't sure about my own future, and the cultivation of empathy does require some breathing space.

Of course, career stage and life stage often but do not always coincide.

R7 was the only researcher to explore gender in their response to my survey. On reflection, this is perhaps surprising. Empathy has historically been seen as a stereotypically female trait. Recent studies have suggested, however, that the roots of this perceived difference are sociocultural, with women being more inclined to acknowledge empathetic qualities than men, rather than systematically exhibiting empathetic behaviours more frequently.[53] It might be expected, then, that female respondents would be more likely to identify themselves with empathetic research methods, though this is not the case. Instead, R7 linked a lack of empathy in their earlier work with their efforts to develop a 'hard-nosed professional persona' in a male-dominated subfield of research. In raising the spectre of a work persona, R7 encourages us to think about the way in which subfield, research environment and institutional culture may impact upon individual approaches to research.[54] The affective turn of the noughties has perhaps removed empathetic approaches to history from an association with overtly gendered approaches to academia.

Teaching empathy

Empathetic approaches to teaching history, it would appear, are largely implicit. Just as the contributors to this article did not learn 'empathy' as they might learn other methodological approaches to the study of history, most do not teach it either. Empathetic approaches to history are therefore acquired through practice or apprenticeship, rather than through guided application and teaching. Historicised empathy is grounded in a deep contextual know-ledge of a period or a subject, and it therefore makes perfect sense that empathy must be developed in tandem with that deep contextual knowledge. Developed skills must, however, be built from good foundations and several respondents achieve this by encouraging their students to explore their feelings of historical empathy through their recognition of the historical subject as 'other', and by thinking about their subject as both similar and different to themselves. R3, for example, asks undergraduate students 'to think about the fact that people in the past were not perfect, and that they often made irrational or impulsive decisions as we might today'; 'I don't actively create teaching materials or exercises that are designed to teach empathy but I do talk about them when we read primary sources.' R1 asked students 'to think about the person they are studying from their own point of view', and

[53] Charlotte S. Loffler and Tobias Greitemeyer, 'Are Women the More Empathetic Gender? The Effects of Gender Role Expectations', *Current Psychology*, 42 (2021), 220–31; Michael J. Clark, Anthony D. G. Marks and Amy Lykins, 'Bridging the Gap: The Effect of Gender Normativity on Differences in Empathy and Emotional Intelligence', *Journal of Gender Studies*, 25 (2016), 522–39; Leonardo Christov-Moore *et al.*, 'Empathy: Gender Effects in Brain and Behavior', *Neuroscience & Biobehavioural Reviews*, 46 (2014), 604–27.

[54] Vera Troeger has shown that only 20 per cent of the professoriate, and only 30 per cent of academics in the highest pay scale, identify as female. Vera E. Troeger, 'Productivity Takes Leave? Maternity Benefits and Career Opportunities of Women in Academia', Social Market Foundation (2018), 2 https://www.smf.co.uk/publications/productivity-takes-leave-maternity-benefits-career-opportunities-women-academia, accessed 24 Feb. 2023.

advocated discussion as the best format for thinking about empathetic approaches to history. R4 'sometimes asks students to imagine themselves into a particular historical subject-position'. The study of primary sources is central to these teaching exercises, as they provide students with an historical subject into whose world they can imagine themselves. R2, for example, will 'choose sources which have a particularly vivid personal event or gripping narrative that encourage students to focus closely on the person involved'. R3 also associates teaching empathy with sources, suggesting that their research focus on the history of the family demands that students think about interpersonal relationships. The prominence of sources in empathetic teaching practices mirrors respondents' discussions about the role of empathy in the selection of research topic and source material. Teaching empathetic historical approaches is therefore founded upon modelling good behaviour, upon discussion and upon the researcher's own empathetic approaches to history. Several contributors noted the importance of allowing time in seminars to explore 'the personal and the affective when discussing people's lives in the past' (R2).

Only R9 described themselves as having a defined pedagogic approach to teaching empathy to undergraduate students grounded in materiality. They 'buy objects on eBay and from junk shops or suppliers and then at the start of every seminar session get them to look and understand the object and the people who owned it or made it or held it for a time'. This approach encourages students to adopt an historical empathetic approach by placing themselves into the shoes of others. This imaginative approach to history can then be historicised by a discussion of context and evidence. R9's pedagogical approach causes them to reflect upon the dangers of the empathetic approach, something that has not been touched upon by other contributors. Empathy is often presented as implicitly morally positive. To be empathetic implies understanding, an essential humanness and an ability to connect with those that we encounter.[55] Yet this is not always the case. Empathy and its companion concepts, sympathy and compassion, have pointed to social disintegration, exclusion, stratification and chauvinism as much as they have pointed to cohesion, reciprocity and community-building.[56] Fritz Breithaupt highlights the ways that empathy can be manipulated, intentionally and unintentionally, to negative effect, particularly through spotlighting an individual at the expense of others, and deepening polarised divides. R9 sounded similar notes of caution in their survey responses, listing the dangers of the empathetic approach as 'the retreat of truth, the rise of identity politics and the mistaken sense that a single case or experience (with which we empathise) can tell us something either systematic or systemic'.

Empathy in the archive

If, as I have argued, the distinguishing feature of historicised empathy is its grounding in deep knowledge and historical context, it must have its roots

---

[55] Breithaupt, *The Dark Side*, 7.
[56] Boddice, *Emotions*, 128.

in the archive. After all, the archive is, as Carolyn Steedman has suggested, the central locus of the historian's authority. 'Without the archive', she writes, 'there is no historian.'[57] Ludmilla Jordanova similarly highlights the place of the archive in 'making' historians. The archive, she suggests, is where 'we become historians, develop identifications with our sources and inhabit other worlds'.[58] It is the seat of what R5 calls 'evidential authority, [which combines] with the authority created through narrative and empathy'. Archives shape historians and the histories that we write, and, as such, are sites of particular intimacy between researcher and subject.[59] The archive is therefore a charged space for historical researchers. It is where we touch the documents that our historical subjects have touched, it might be where we encounter physical reminders of the lives we study; a smudge in ink, a paw print, a cockroach.[60] Sometimes we find bodily evidence of our subjects: a lock of hair, a caul, a tear stain.[61] Such findings can have an affective impact, as when Sara Hiorns was moved to tears by an image of her subject.[62] This affective impact might stimulate a resonance between researcher and historical subject but this is distinct from historical empathy. Indeed, it is the control and distance inherent in historical empathy that allows historians to acknowledge and manage their affective impulses in response to the archive. If empathetic approaches to history take account of the messiness of our subjects' lives, then the detachment demanded by a historical empathetic approach goes some way towards neatening (or at least acknowledging) the messiness, or perhaps the humanness, of the historian.

Empathy and the letter archive

'Letters and lives are bound together,' wrote historian Claudine van Hensbergen, specifically of eighteenth-century familiar letters. Private correspondences, she suggests, offer a means for historians to 'recreate the character and opinion of the individuals who penned them'.[63] As R8 commented, 'there is, by the very nature of the letter's creation, separation, loneliness, longing

---

[57] Carolyn Steedman, *Dust* (Manchester, 2001), 145. See also Emily Robinson, 'Touching the Void: Affective History and the Impossible', *Rethinking History*, 14 (2010), 503–20.

[58] Jordanova, *History*, 209.

[59] *Ibid*, 209.

[60] For example, Caroline Davis, 'Eighteenth-Century Cockroach Found in Slave-Trading Ship Ledger', *The Guardian*, 15 Jun. 2022; Rachel Nuwer, 'Centuries Ago, a Cat Walked across This Medieval Manuscript', *Smithsonian Magazine*, 12 Mar. 2013, https://www.smithsonianmag.com/smart-news/centuries-ago-a-cat-walked-across-this-medieval-manuscript-1766202, accessed 22 Feb. 2023.

[61] Vicky Iglikowski-Broad, 'A Lock of Love', The National Archives Blog (2015), https://blog.nationalarchives.gov.uk/lock-love, accessed 22 Feb. 2023; Hertfordshire Archives and Local Studies, DE/Lw/F114, 'Locks of hair; Sir Charles' caul'.

[62] Roper, 'Unconscious Work', 170; Sara Hiorns, 'Crying in the Archive: The Story of Diana Bromley', History of Emotions blog, posted 21 Dec. 2015, https://emotionsblog.history.qmul.ac.uk/2015/12/crying-in-the-archive-the-story-of-diana-bromley.

[63] Claudine van Hensbergen, 'Towards an Epistolary Discourse: Receiving the Eighteenth-Century Letter', *Literature Compass*, 7 (2010), 508–18, at 511.

and that in itself appears, in the deceptive way of personal correspondence, to carry meaning down the centuries'. William Decker recognises that published volumes of letters are valued for their ability to create the illusion of historical subjects telling their own stories, rather than for their capacity to reconstruct the past.[64] This, he suggests, forms part of a fundamental fiction that letters offer intimacy and immediacy. We are, he argues, 'voyeurs of lives preserved in the letter genre's continuous present tense' and, as voyeurs, must contemplate the impact of our involvement in the epistolary form.[65] The historian's interpretation is only one of a number of interventions that shape the modern reading of past letters.

Archival practices are influential in mediating historians' interactions with their historical subjects. Archives of letters are generally shaped by archival sorting practices, attached to certain peoples, families or places. Letter collections may also be categorised, by the religious accomplishments of the writer, or their correspondents, by their gender, by the nature of their business. These imposed categorisations and attachments, essential to good archival practice, can obscure the nature and purpose of letter-writing, and alter the researcher's engagement (empathetic or otherwise) with the archive. Moreover, archival practice can give a false sense of the temporality of letters and letter-writing. When we can move immediately on to the next letter, when we already know the outcome of the correspondence (often from the online archive notes that we have studied before we visit), we do not think enough on the space between letters, the emotions of waiting, or of a missing letter. Letters, sociologist Liz Stanley argues, are disparate and fragmented.[66] They do not provide us with a whole picture of a life because they are only present where there is a separation, yet the temptation, particularly when presented with a collection of letters spanning several years, is to view them as whole despite the glaring absence of half the correspondence.

The nature of the letter archive offers researchers important opportunities to explore their own position in relation to their subject. In adopting an empathetic approach to history, particularly when using letters, historians become deeply familiar with their historical subject. In order to put aside our own feelings to take account of the perspectives of another, we need to be familiar with the experiences that shaped and formed those perspectives. Contextual knowledge forms the basis of much sociocultural historical research and is essential in creating the imaginative and narrative style that characterises good history. It is the foundation for an historicised empathetic approach to the history of past lives. The letter archive, however, facilitates a layering of historicised empathy and therefore a depth that can be difficult to achieve using other sources. The researcher will likely be familiar with the social, cultural, economic and political context of the world occupied by the writers of the letters that they are studying, but by immersing themselves

---

[64] William M. Decker, *Epistolary Practices: Letter-Writing in America before Telecommunications* (Durham, NC, 1998), 8.

[65] *Ibid*, 5.

[66] Liz Stanley, 'The Epistolarium: On Theorizing Letters and Correspondences', *Auto/Biography*, 12 (2004), 201–35, at 204.

in letter collections they may also become familiar with the writer's authorial voice, with their specific social, financial or political situation, the challenges that those situations present, with the nuances of their interpersonal relationships, and even with their physical and emotional state through the shape and strength of their handwriting. As such, the letter archive offers opportunities to explore empathetic historical approaches with particular richness and depth.

Shared experience with an historical subject does not necessarily lead to a more empathetic, or indeed a more accurate, historical account of their lives. Indeed, shared experience can actively obstruct empathetic approaches to history by blurring the separation between the researcher's feelings and those of their historical subject. As R6 acknowledged in their survey responses, 'their world is connected to ours, but it was also very different'. Yet, upon questioning, several respondents to the survey acknowledged a relationship between the people that they studied and their own experiences. For R6, the similarity lay in class position and the cultural capital that goes alongside class identity. R8 acknowledged that they only experienced strong affective responses when confronted with events that are 'almost inconceivably sad, or events/relationships that I feel strongly echo events/relationships in my own life'. R9 drew strong parallels between their upbringing, education and family background and the lives of their historical subjects, suggesting that they 'must have had their research design framed by empathy'. These statements would suggest that researchers are drawn to stories that resonate with their own experiences of life, though this appears to be neither deliberate nor is it a methodological tool for analysis or critique using, for example, auto-ethnographical techniques. As professional historians, well paid and highly educated, this subtle or underlying familiarity with the lives of their historical subjects is often obscured, for example where the subjects of the study are poor. In these situations, the researcher's lived familiarity with their subjects remains undiscussed. This is not, in itself, problematic. As we have seen, historical empathy is founded in the setting aside of one's own perspective to make space for that of another. This approach can be applied regardless of perceived similarity to or difference with the historical subject, allowing the historian to maintain the necessary emotional distance for good historical writing, though it should, perhaps, be more explicitly theorised about. The professional persona of 'the historian' means that whilst most historians think carefully and deliberately about their own position in relation to their subject, it is reasonably rare for this to be written about outside the context of historical primers.[67]

Source selection

The relationship between empathetic approaches to history and the selection of sources is a complex and intertwined one. Picking at the threads of this

---

[67] Jessica Hamnett, Ellie Harrison and Laura King, 'Art, Collaboration and Multi-sensory Approaches to Public Microhistory: Journey with Absent Friends', *History Workshop Journal*, 89 (2020), 246–69, at 255.

relationship leads to a 'chicken and egg' type scenario. Does the nature of the eighteenth-century letter lead historians to take an empathetic approach to the histories they write? Or does the empathetic approach draw us towards letters and life-writings as a way of accessing the first-person narratives that so much social and cultural history depends upon? Both iterations are visible in the survey responses. R1 suggested that empathy shapes the questions that one asks and attempts to answer. It is the historical question for R1 that informs the nature of the historical sources that an historian chooses to consult. Similarly, R2 noted 'I am drawn by the personal narrative, though I don't doubt that many historians are. I select the sources that are required to answer my research questions.' R4 and R9 felt that empathy did not have an impact on their selection of sources. They aligned with R6, who speculated that an empathetic approach was only necessary once the nature of suitable sources for answering the research question had been identified. They explained 'There's very often a personal aspect to the documents I work with – they are almost always written by named, known individuals. That makes it possible and necessary to read them with the kinds of practices I've discussed here already, which you might call empathetic.'

Other respondents felt drawn to certain types of sources, and this affective pull shaped the nature of their research questions. R3 argued that they were 'always trying to understand people's experiences, which I suppose is empathy of some kind ... I have always been most drawn to qualitative sources like correspondence and life-writing, which appear to give a more immediate connection to the writer.' R7 expressed a similar draw towards a type of source that demanded an empathetic approach. 'There was certainly an emotional/ personal element' to choosing to work with their current sources, remembering not only engaging with them as a child and a teenager, but being fascinated by the elements that now form the foundation for their research. They added, 'I strongly felt that [the sources] had been dismissed/not recognised as important sources of knowledge ... I definitely felt that these were sources that deserved to be handled more closely, read more sensitively, and that doing so also meant demonstrating respect for their readers.' R8 suggested that 'familiar letters by their very personal, intimate nature lend themselves more to empathetic responses than say the financial records of a factory, or minutes from a Church vestry meeting'. R5, however, believed that it is possible to 'squeeze empathy from any source, however apparently arid'.

R1 raised the difficulty of accessing the experiences of those who could not write letters, or produce direct written narratives of their lives. Empathy, for them, was important in 'trying to document the experiences of those at the bottom of the social scale who are often recorded only indirectly in the sources. This, then, involves reading between the lines, or against the grain, of the text.' In implying that empathy allows historians to access difficult histories, this comment again raises the spectre of imaginative approaches to history. Empathy, this suggests, can be used as a tool to fill in the silences and spaces of history. R11 also identified imaginative approaches to history, grounded in empathy and in historical context, as becoming important to their current project, noting that 'the speculative histories that recently emerged have been useful in allowing me to consider the need to get at the experiences of others (to underline their dignity and place in the world) and the difficulty of doing so, because ego documents do not exist for them'.

Writing empathically

Empathy was most likely to be explicitly conceived as an historical tool by respondents when discussed in relation to writing. For many, empathy was perceived as being an essential component of good communication. R1 suggested that empathy is 'about asking, and answering, the right questions, and is important in all forms of historical writing'. Ludmilla Jordanova called writing the 'most important interpretative act', as 'by crafting description and argument we integrate our ideas into an account'.[68] Despite not specifying *how* empathy shaped their historical writing, R5 agreed, suggesting that 'empathy is a technology that makes historical writing more powerful and effective'. R2 agrees that empathy can be an effective tool or technology, using it to 'help me focus on the people whose lives I am working on, and that can certainly be useful to drive forward the actual writing process (and, depending on the piece of writing, the narrative)'. For R2, empathy takes on a structural role by focusing the researcher's attention on the historical subject, reminding them that their empathetic approach to history is grounded in person-centred history.

Several respondents discussed the use of empathy as a way to stimulate an affective response in the reader, extending the connection between historian and historical subject to include their readers. R8 was specific about the intended affective impact of empathetic writing tools. They wrote, 'I think I tend to hinge writing around certain anecdotes I perceive that readers would find particularly shocking, or tear-jerking – I imagine I do this for dramatic effect.' R7 similarly suggested, 'I also probably do try to provoke empathy or other emotions in readers through stylistic tricks (don't we all?). I certainly admire people who are able to do this with a light touch ...' While such an approach sounds reasonably simple, it demands that the historian engage empathetically not just with their historical subject, but with their reader as well. As we saw earlier, R6 situates the development of empathetic approaches to history in writing practices, in that it requires a consideration of the reader's mindset as well as of the mindset of the historical subject. In thinking about empathy as a written practice, R6 extends their consideration of empathy in written work to explore the difficulties of encouraging a reader to engage empathetically with an historical figure:

On one hand, I want readers and audiences to be able to imagine themselves in [their historical subject's] shoes. On the other, I don't want them to 'empathise' so much with them that they don't see, or (perhaps even worse!) begin to rationalise and make excuses for their part in the defence and reproduction of class power. They were basically

---

[68] Jordanova, *History*, 208.

a bad person, a slave-owner, and an unashamed advocate of their family's interests above all other concerns.

Helen Sword, in her book on *Stylish Academic Writing*, suggested that historians were arch-manipulators of language in their written work despite a tendency to claim objective authorial stances. She suggested that 'of all the researchers in the ten disciplines that I surveyed, the historians were the most clearly subjective – manipulative even – in their use of language'.[69] This, she suggests, is despite historians being the least likely to openly acknowledge their authorial position through the use of personal pronouns. Hidden in this observation is, yet again, the narrow line that historians tread between creative and compelling narrative, and historical fact. Yet for David Lowenthal, 'emotional involvement enables the historian to communicate, without it his account is disjointed, insipid, unread'.[70] 'History bereft of shape and conviction', he suggests, 'would not be understood or attended to. Partiality and empathy warp knowledge, but distortion is essential to its conveyance – even to its very existence.'[71] R7 reinforced the importance of empathy to historical writing, drawing parallels between provoking empathy and the crafting of historical argument: 'In general, though, I think that provoking empathy in readers is much the same as presenting a historical argument effectively; it's about judicious selection and organisation of evidence as much as the explicitly drawn out interpretation.'

Accusations of manipulating historical sources through language can be countered by historians' ethical practices. Several researchers suggested that empathetic approaches to history helped them to maintain ethical research practices by reflecting on the way they treat the people around whom their research is focused. R4 conflated empathy with respect, arguing, 'I would say that maybe respect is a concept that shapes my writing process, in that whoever or whatever I am writing about, I would always want to treat that subject with the dignity I would have wanted to accord it if the people were still alive.' R7 also drew a comparison between writing about the living and writing about the dead. They responded, 'I try to write about people (living and dead) in ways that they would recognise as talking about their own lives, and not to over-determine my interpretation.' R3 wrote,

Empathy reminds me that the individuals I write about were not just historical subjects but that they were real. I feel a responsibility to tell their story with dignity and compassion ... and this makes me more concerned

---

[69] Helen Sword, *Stylish Academic Writing* (Cambridge, MA, 2012), 39. Sword surveyed over seventy academics from multiple disciplines on the characteristics of stylish academic writing; she analysed over 100 pieces of writing by authors considered exemplary in their field; she created a dataset of 1,000 academic articles, compiled from 100 articles each from international journals in the fields of medicine, evolutionary biology, computer science, higher education, psychology, anthropology, law, philosophy, history, and literary studies by selecting the twenty most recent articles from each of five different journals in each subject area.

[70] Lowenthal, *The Past*, 343.

[71] *Ibid*, 342.

to be not only accurate, which I hope I am anyway, but also to draw attention to subtleties in their experience.

For these respondents, empathy is not only a writing tool, it is also a method for ensuring ethical rigour in their research. The ethics of the eighteenth-century letter archive are decidedly slippery. Letter-writers are long dead, their letters freely available in archival collections. We are unable to ask the letter-writer's permission to read their work, we cannot easily trace their descendants to request these permissions, nor is there generally a requirement for us to do so.[72] If we could ask, would our eighteenth-century letter-writers agree to our using their correspondence in our work? Empathetic approaches to history, centred upon the letter-writer and their social world, go some way to allay historians' concerns about the ethics of using personal documents. R4 summarised this discomfort, and the role of empathy in countering it:

> It feels wrong to treat people – even ones who have been dead for a long time – merely as sources of information upon which we can build our careers. If we want the things that happened to people, or the things they said about their lives, to be available to us, it should be because we feel some sort of duty of care to show the significance of those people's lives to helping us understand something about what it means to be human.

Absent empathy

Throughout this article, I have depicted empathy as an important part of historical practice. I have suggested that empathy is a fundamental part of being human, is one element of historical training and has an important role in shaping or conveying history to our audiences. I have argued that empathy can be used as a structural tool shaping research topic, primary source selection and communication, and I have also suggested that empathy can be a method of approaching historical study. As such, I have made an argument for empathetic approaches to history being fairly central to the discipline. Is this fair, or does it reflect my own grounding in the 'affective turn', and my immersion in the letter archive? This final section of the article tests my arguments by asking: is it possible to write history without empathy?

For some respondents, empathetic approaches to history reflect the humanity of both the historian and the historical subject. As theologian John D. Wilsey wrote in a reflective article on his academic relationship to American diplomat John Foster Dulles, 'the dead do not surrender their humanity at their last breath'.[73] For Wilsey, the historical subject is a complex human, as is the historical researcher. As another, similarly complicated human, Wilsey argues,

---

[72] Françoise N. Hamlin, 'Historians and Ethics: Finding Anne Moody', *American Historical Review*, 125 (2020), 487–97, at 492.
[73] John D. Wilsey, 'A Lock of Hair, a Ruined Cabin, and a Party with Hitler: The Ethics of Communing with Dead People We Come to Love', *Fides et historia*, 52 (2020), 116–25, at 125.

empathy is *owed* by the researcher to the subject. As such, it is not possible to write history without empathy. R7 expressed very similar views when reflecting on the possibility of writing history without empathy:

> At a very basic level, I don't think it is possible to research and write history to a high level without some empathy, in the same way that it is not possible to participate in a satisfying human relationship without some degree of empathy. History *is* a human relationship. As the study of the human past, History is always in some way about people and what they did, felt, and thought. To attempt to reconstruct any aspect of the human past, we need to try to relate to what happened in human terms, and that surely must involve empathy in some way. That doesn't mean that researchers necessarily need to reflect much on empathy, to consciously explore it or try to provoke it, to display it, or even to acknowledge its value. But empathy has to be present in their endeavours to some degree to make the results of that research worthwhile. Otherwise, what do we have? A list of dates? An account of what happened devoid of meaning? How can we call that history in any meaningful sense?

R2 and R11 both raised the historian's duty to pay proper attention to the lives and experiences of their historical subjects. As such, they draw lines from empathetic history to ethical historical practice. R2 argued that

> Historical work without empathy would flatten the depth, range and wonder of past human experience; it would be unconvincing because it imposes a present-centred perspective onto the lives of those in the past; it would be inattentive to the lives of people in the past as they experienced them, an act that (if not of actual harm or violence) is at odds with the values that underpin our humanities discipline.

Of course, sometimes histories have the potential to be harmful and traumatic. R11 wrote:

> I think it [empathy] really matters in histories of enslavement, for example. As historians we need to understand that histories are often forms of trauma and violence, they unleash and animate a past which is deeply hurtful and atrocious. We must understand this to work with care and caution, we must know this power in our communication.

R10 also urged caution that 'contested, uncomfortable and challenging histories call perhaps for greater empathy in understanding how the past can shape the present and its ongoing legacies'. Historical trauma, and the narratives through which it has been told, has been shown to be 'a potential source of both distress and resilience' particularly for racial and ethnic minority populations and groups that experience significant health disparities.[74] Empathetic approaches to history, then, allow historians to ensure that the past and those that populate it are being treated carefully, fulfilling a duty of care not only to our historical subjects, but to those who read our histories.

Other respondents, however, suggested that the presence or absence of empathy is driven by the nature of the history being written, and the historian's engagement with it. R6 pointed out that:

> not all history is about capturing people's experience. No historian can do everything at once. There's also a lot of danger in 'empathetic' approaches that risk reifying the perspectives of particular actors (especially those with good sources) ... I'd go so far as to say that sometimes it's better to leave empathy out of the picture altogether.

R8 also raised the possibility that empathetic approaches to history run the risk of distorting the historian's necessary objectivity:

> I don't think I treat historical actors that I don't empathise with that differently – indeed, it is possible that I am more likely to misrepresent those I empathise with, because I perhaps read too much into certain situations. So personally, I don't think it matters if empathy is absent, because if it is present, it is likely misplaced.

This comment suggests that, for R8, empathy that is rooted in emotion has the potential to mislead. Their reflection reiterates the importance of explicit reflection about the relationship between the historian and their subject, and the need to ground empathetic approaches to history with a deep contextual knowledge. That contextual knowledge, for R10, is what allows historians to decide whether an empathetic methodology is appropriate for the histories they are trying to write:

> Good historical work shifts perspective, knows the limits of what the evidence can carry, is driven by effective questions and deeply aware of entangled contexts etc. Empathy may figure, but there are also circumstances in which empathy is inappropriate or can even become self-indulgent.

To some extent, it would appear that the puzzle of absent empathy returns us to our initial enquiry: how does the historian in 2023 understand empathy? When asked the question 'what is empathy?' most respondents gave answers that were slightly fuzzy at the edges. Empathy was described by many respondents using two or three different terms, particularly that it was a skill (in that it could be learned) and that it was a quality (in that most humans possess the capacity to empathise). Exploring absent empathy gives these answers much sharper edges. In the answers to this question,

---

[74] Nathaniel Vincent Mohatt *et al.*, 'Historical Trauma as Public Narrative: A Conceptual Review of How History Impacts Present-Day Health', *Social Science and Medicine*, 106 (2014), 128–36.

empathy was described in methodological terms, as a tool to be deployed in the correct circumstances and as a quality, or a marker of humanness.

Conclusion

So, how *does* the historian in 2023 understand empathy? It would appear that, as a profession, we're not entirely sure. Empathy is described as intimacy with the lives and minds of those we write about, but also distance. It can be, at once, a learnable, and transferable skill, an innate human quality, and a methodological approach to our academic discipline. Respondents described it as a tool that can be manipulated and bent to our purpose, and as a duty that we as historians owe to the past. Empathy is, it transpires, very personal. Historians' views of empathy are shaped by the histories that we study, by the prevalent school of thought at our institution, or in the discipline when we were trained, and by our own lives. Our gender, our age, our upbringing, our stage in the life cycle all have the potential to influence what we understand empathetic approaches to history to be. As Jordanova has suggested, 'historians' skills are developed and refined over a lifetime, becoming an integral part of the person'.[75]

Some historians conceptualise history as an historical tool, the professional detachment that we employ when we wish to understand the lives and actions of our historical subjects. It offers us a way of accessing histories that might be unpleasant, or difficult, or that fall outside traditional archival collections. As Richard Evans asked in *In Defence of History*, how can one 'understand' Hitler without a detached mode of cognition, a faculty of self-criticism and an ability to understand another's point of view?[76] Here the dichotomies of historical approaches to empathy become particularly marked. Empathy is described by respondents as a tool that allows them to stand alongside their historical subjects to try and understand their worldview. Yet, as Thomas Haskell has written, empathy is also distance, and 'the ability not to put oneself at the centre of a view of the world' where 'one's own self is just one object among many'.[77]

Empathy can be a type of historical knowledge, or a perspective of the past. To cite Tracy Loughran, 'a properly historicised empathy depends on the contextualisation that precedes and follows from engagement with historical evidence – in other words, from the fusion of "facts", interpretation, and imagination'. 'It is', she continues, 'an essential aspect of how historians engage with sources – how we respond to traces of the past.'[78] Finally, empathy can also be a methodological position, or an historical approach. Historians generally see empathetic histories as histories with people at their heart rather than systems or structures. Through their focus on people, empathetic histories can contradict system- or structure-based histories, but it would be

---

[75] Jordanova, *History*, 197.

[76] Richard Evans, *In Defence of History* (2018), 155.

[77] Thomas L. Haskell, 'Objectivity Is Not Neutrality: Rhetoric and Practice in Peter Nock's *That Noble Dream*', *History and Theory*, 29 (1990), 129–57, at 132.

[78] Loughran, Mahoney and Payling, 'Women's Voices', 397.

naive to suggest that empathetic histories sit outside social structures. The tendency of respondents to associate empathy with subjective, personal, human-centred histories reflects an interesting separation in the way historians have been trained to think about the relationship between emotion, the individual, and social structure that warrants further consideration and discussion.

As a profession, historians lack a general consensus on the role of empathy in historical research and in the practices of our discipline. Understandings of empathy in historical research are shaped by multifarious factors from the moment a historian's training begins as an undergraduate, and they shift and change throughout the professional life cycle. As such, understandings of empathy can be seen as reflective of the professional figure of the historian, the changing nature of the discipline, and our ongoing engagements with our historical subjects.

Appendix

1. What is empathy in your opinion, within the context of historical work/ your work as an historian?
2. Is empathy a skill? Or is it something different? A quality? Or a virtue?
3. Did you develop or learn empathy as part of your historian's training? How and when?
4. Do you teach empathy to your students? If so, how?
5. How does empathy shape your research?
6. How does empathy have an impact on the types of sources that you work with?
7. What role do you think empathy plays in your writing processes?
8. How is empathy important in communicating your research a) to academics? b) to other audiences?
9. What happens to historical work when empathy is absent? Does it matter?

Acknowledgements. My sincere thanks to the peer reviewers of this article and the journal editors, to Karen Harvey, Emily Vine, and audiences at the Department of History, University of Birmingham, and the North American Conference on British Studies (Chicago, 2022). Particular thanks to the respondents to my survey, who generously gave significant amounts of their time and energy to provide the empirical data for this article.

Financial support. This research has been completed as part of the project Material Identities, Social Bodies: embodiment in British letters *c*.1680–1820, Leverhulme Trust Research Grant RPG-2020-163.

Ethical standards. This research has been approved by the University of Birmingham's Research Ethics Team, reference ERN_2-22_0462.

Cite this article: Fox S (2023). Archival Intimacies: Empathy and Historical Practice in 2023. *Transactions of the Royal Historical Society* **1**, 241–265. https://doi.org/10.1017/S0080440123000099

Transactions of the RHS (2023), 1, 267–290
doi:10.1017/S0080440123000105

ARTICLE

Statues, Spatial Syntax and Surrealism: 'History' and Heritagescapes in Public Space

Pippa Catterall

School of Humanities, University of Westminster, London, UK
Email: p.catterall@westminster.ac.uk

(Received 14 January 2023; revised 28 June 2023; accepted 4 July 2023; first published
online 7 August 2023)

Abstract

The purpose of statues in public spaces has recently become a matter of controversy. Using
a 1937 quotation from the artist Paul Nash and the surrealist leader André Breton, this
paper explores the circumstances in which a statue is read as appropriately – 'in its right
mind' in their terms – situated in public space. In doing so, it draws primarily on examples
from Britain, Europe and North America during the rapid expansion in the number of statues in public space from the eighteenth century onwards. The rightmindedness of a statue
is shown as primarily determined not by the subject of the statue itself, or by its reception
among the public, but by ways in which public authorities and local elites authorise the use
of public space. Yet these authorities' understanding of the fit between a statue and public
space can vary over time. Shifts in the political context often prompt changes to where
statues are seen as appropriately located. However, picking up on Nash/Breton's phrase,
to place a statue in 'a state of surrealism' involves more than mere relocation. This is
shown to require additional disruption to a statue's artistic language and/or spatial syntax.

Keywords: Statues; memorialisation; surrealism; public space; heritage; vandalism; Paul
Nash

A statue in a street or some place where it would normally be found is just
a statue, as it were, in its right mind, but a statue in a ditch or in the
middle of a ploughed field is then an object in a state of surrealism.[1]

Exploring this state of surrealism was a major theme in the art of the British
landscape painter Paul Nash during the 1930s. It was then that he penned this
translation of the words of the French artist André Breton, one of the founding

---

[1] P. Nash, 'Swanage or Seaside Surrealism', in *Writings on Art*, ed. A. Causley (Oxford, 2000), 126.

fathers of surrealism. Jarring juxtapositions intended to subvert normative readings of space and vistas and thereby reveal a deeper reality became a characteristic of much of Nash's work during that challenging decade. They also continued after Nash, who had been a major war artist during the Great War, was again employed in that capacity by the Air Ministry during the Second World War. One of his most celebrated works from that period is *Totes Meer* (1940–1). Its punning title refers with bitter irony to a desolate landscape of warplanes which – having been destroyed – are clearly no longer in their right mind. It thereby sought to 'convey the feel of the war far more vividly than a photographic record could do'.[2]

Christopher Hussey, the architectural editor of *Country Life*, noted that Nash's contributions to the ensuing War Artists Exhibition 'are, in their queer way, the only pictures there that represent satisfactorily the fantastic night-mare element in this war'.[3] Jill Craigie's 1944 film *Out of Chaos* shows Nash sketching at the Cowley aircraft dump that inspired his painting. Her voiceover records how 'he felt that the terrific action taking place should be interpreted in a new way', capturing the reality of the Battle of Britain through a sombre rendering of 'This strange almost surreal world of fantastic shapes and twisted metal'.[4] Nash thereby sought to use allegorical and metaphorical artistic language to convey to the public the supervening realities of a battle that otherwise challenged attempts to provide adequate pictorial depiction. He took the savage beauty of the warplanes and showed them eerily relocated amidst the surrealism he readily found in nature.[5]

It is a moot point whether warplanes or statues are ever in their right mind. The notion of a statue's rightmindedness conjures up an image of it proudly shaping the nature of space by its occupation of it and representing and reifying a particular construction of reality as part of the normal and quotidian. Indeed, Nash/Breton imply that a statue is only rendered abnormal when it is not in spaces where it would be expected to be. Its meaning is thereby subverted not by the statue itself but its location. In certain spaces – such as city squares, parks or outside important buildings – statues are normative. Their presence is expected and unconsciously understood as conveying the significance of the site or even that of the town, city or country they thus adorn. The casual visitor assumes that they will see statues in such spaces. Accordingly, Daniel Defoe in 1724, when describing the sights of the City of London, listed various (generally royal) statues that already featured prominently in its streetscapes.[6] Not that these statues were well maintained: thirty years later an early London guidebook complained that 'All the Statues and Fountains are so much impaired by Time, that they want to be taken down.'[7]

---

[2] Sir Kenneth Clark speaking on J. Craigie (dir.), *Out of Chaos* (Two Cities Films, 1944), at 3.36–3.39. See https://player.bfi.org.uk/free/film/watch-out-of-chaos-1944-online (accessed 28 June 2023).

[3] C. Hussey to Miss Ramsden, 21 Aug. 1941, Tate Archive (henceforward TGA): Nash 7050, 453.

[4] Craigie (dir.) *Out of Chaos*. The Nash sequence is at 7.30–9.13.

[5] S. Bishop, 'The Spirit of Place: Paul Nash, a Painter in Wartime Oxford', *Oxford Art Journal*, 1 (1978), 42.

[6] D. Defoe, *A Tour through the Whole Island of Great Britain* (4 vols., 1983 [1724]), ii, 106–9.

[7] *London in Miniature* (1755), 205.

Defoe did not find this panoply of royal statues incongruous in public space, though he did consider some inferior in execution. In Robert Musil's celebrated satire, they are so much part of the scene that 'one doesn't notice them. There is nothing in the world so invisible as monuments.'[8] Similarly *The Times* in 1861 described the newly erected statue of General Sir Henry Havelock in London's Trafalgar Square as 'one of those uninteresting statues with which London is crowded, and of which we have nothing to say except that we never look at them twice, never think of them, never care to remember them'.[9] As Jay Winter observed of his Cambridge students' failure to spot the town's war memorial, these monuments simply become for much of the time 'white noise' in stone or bronze.[10] Even something as imposing as the Monument by London Bridge fades into the background for the office workers who daily pass it.[11] Obviously, a statue cannot have a mind, let alone be in its right one: instead, a statue's right to occupy space is conceded by the extent to which they are read and accepted as accustomed elements of the built environment. This does not mean, however much their originators might have hoped that they would invoke memory in public space, that they are necessarily visible, unless they are also controversial.

Although statues are thus everyday if frequently unnoticed features of public space, where they might be expected to be found changes over time and in different cultural settings. For instance, most of the oldest surviving statuary in Britain dates from Roman times and now can only be found in museums, collected in historic houses and gardens or long buried.[12] However, originally these vividly painted figures of emperors, gods and local dignitaries would have appeared in public spaces such as forums, military bases or baths. Following the departure of the legions in the fifth century, most statuary created for public spaces moved to different, interior settings. The vast bulk of it was either on or in public buildings known as churches. Facades of cathedrals were decorated with saints, angels and biblical figures as aids to faith. Inside parish churches there was stone statuary as memento mori to the wealthy benefactors who paid for the effigies placed in sacred space upon their tombs.[13] This type of memorialisation persisted even after the Reformation: most eighteenth-century monuments continued to be funerary.[14] Indeed, the creation of statuary

---

[8] R. Musil, *Posthumous Papers of a Living Author* (New York, 1987 [1936]), 61.

[9] *The Times* 7 Mar. 1861, cited in D. Cherry, 'Statues in the Square: Hauntings at the Heart of Empire', *Art History*, 29 (2006), 687.

[10] J. Winter, 'Sites of Memory and the Shadow of War', in *Cultural Memory Studies: An International and Interdisciplinary Handbook*, ed. A. Erll and A. Nünning (Berlin, 2008), 72–3.

[11] P. Catterall, 'Changing Attitudes to the Past: *Lieux de Mémoire* and Contested Histories', *Political Quarterly*, 88 (2017), 631–2.

[12] M. Polm, 'Museum Representations of Roman Britain and Roman London: A Post-colonial Perspective', *Britannia*, 209 (2016), 209–13; F. Poulsen, *Greek and Roman Portraits in English Country Houses* (Oxford, 1923); D. Kindy, 'Trio of "Astounding" Roman Statues Found beneath Mediaeval Church in England', *Smithsonian Magazine*, 3 Nov. 2021.

[13] See N. Saul, *English Church Monuments in the Middle Ages: History and Representation* (Oxford, 2009).

[14] Joan Coutu, *Persuasion and Propaganda: Monuments and the Eighteenth-Century British Empire* (2006), 14.

specifically for sacred spaces continued into the nineteenth century, instanced by the monument to the statesman William Huskisson paid for by public subscription and erected in Chichester Cathedral in 1832.

By then, however, a different type of statuary had begun to emerge. Patrons alluded to their education, aesthetic taste and awareness of classical heritage through the statues they commissioned. Aping what they saw as the tropes of classical civilisation as rediscovered during the Renaissance, they thereby acknowledged a particular reading of how the artistic language of statues should be articulated. Widely influential works such as Johann Joachim Winckelmann's *Geschichte der Kunst des Alterthums* (1764) elevated the white marble statuary of Roman antiquity as the epitome of beauty.[15] In a period during which Europeans were increasingly encountering and denigrating other peoples, a classical whiteness came to be celebrated as the authentic artistic language of statuary, even though this occluded the rich colour palette actually used in antiquity on statues to represent the varied peoples of the Roman world. Although traces of the original paint were noticed, they were routinely ignored.[16] Colour continued to be used on monuments in ecclesiastic settings in Counter-Reformation Europe. Otherwise, an aestheticised whiteness was emphasised and came to have enduring influence, not least during the statuomania that swept Europe during the nineteenth century.[17] Indeed, these artistic tropes were also exported by Europeans around the colonised world during this period. In this process, statues of colonisers served the same purposes of expressing hierarchies of power that had been served by the Roman archetypes these monuments were supposedly modelled on, only with an added racial dimension.[18]

The influence of the Renaissance changed the location as well as the artistic language of European statuary. Classical statues imported from Italy were by the seventeenth century established as centrepieces of formal French gardens,[19] a fashion subsequently adopted across the Channel. James II's much relocated statue, for instance, depicted him in Roman garb and was originally created to adorn the grounds of Whitehall palace in 1686.[20] It was predated by the first Renaissance-inspired equestrian statue in England, an image of his royal master Charles I commissioned for his private garden by Lord High Treasurer Richard Weston in 1633. After the restoration of the monarchy

---

[15] A. Potts, 'Foreword', in J. Winckelmann, *History of the Art of Antiquity* (Los Angeles, 2006), 27–30.

[16] M. Kotrosits, *The Lives of Objects: Material Culture, Experience, and the Real in the History of Early Christianity* (Chicago, 2020), 146–57; M. Bradley, 'The Importance of Colour on Ancient Marble Sculpture', *Art History*, 32 (2009), 427–57.

[17] This eventually provoked complaints, such as G. Pessard, *Statuomanie parisienne: Étude critique sur l'abus des statues* (Paris, 1911).

[18] See Z. Çelik, 'Colonial Statues and their Afterlives', *Journal of North African Studies*, 25 (2020), 711–26.

[19] C. Mukerji, 'The Political Mobilization of Nature in Seventeenth-Century French Formal Gardens', *Theory and Society*, 23 (1994), 660–70.

[20] Historic England, 'Statue of James II in front of the National Gallery West Wing', grade I monument, list entry 1217629, see https://historicengland.org.uk/listing/the-list/list-entry/1217629?section=official-list-entry (accessed 14 Jan. 2023).

this statue was moved into the public realm and its current prominent position on the edge of Whitehall in 1674–5.[21] By then it had been joined by another, purportedly of his son, Charles II. The then lord mayor, Sir Thomas Vyner, imported from Italy a statue originally of the Polish king John Sobieski. With a remodelled head it was erected in 1672 at Stocks Market, London. Defoe tells us that when one of the king's mistresses, the Duchess of Portsmouth, gave birth, the statue was adorned the following morning with a pillion to which was pinned the message 'Gone for a midwife'.[22] Further indignities followed as the statue was successively moved to an inn yard, then the Vyner estates in Lincolnshire and thence to other country locations.[23]

An even worse fate befell that of his nephew, William III, in Dublin. This was installed in 1701 on the eleventh anniversary of the Battle of the Boyne at which William had secured his kingdom, on the politically symbolic site of College Green, just by the Irish parliament. Its depiction of the king in Roman garb, at least among the classically educated elites of the era, established the rightmindedness of his statue both in terms of its setting and its appearance. This rightmindedness was, however, clearly contested from the outset. After various indignities, including being smeared with mud and having his truncheon broken off in 1710, William III's statue was finally removed following a bomb attack in 1928.[24]

By then, however, there were plenty of other examples of statues of William III, if not as widespread as those of his former enemy, Louis XIV, were around France.[25] Dublin's statue was unusual in being erected while the king was still alive, its equestrian referencing of ancient depictions of martial valour proving ironic when in 1702 William III died after falling from his horse. This did not stop the classically informed equestrian style remaining a common means of depicting him, invariably in Roman garb, in the growing number of statues commissioned in the 1730s and 1740s at a time of renewed Jacobite activity. Some, like the one in Bristol, were, as in Dublin, ordered by the city authorities. Others were paid for by private individuals. The one in the small Hampshire town of Petersfield certainly does not go unnoticed in a locale with few such monuments: it was restored by public subscription in 1912 and more recently described in the local press as having 'come to symbolise the town'. This was a new form of memento mori, whereby Sir William Joliffe in death associated himself with the cause of (Protestant) liberty by memorialising the king whose Glorious Revolution in 1688 had supposedly brought such liberty and certainly founded the regime under which these statues

---

[21] Historic England, 'Statue of Charles I', grade I monument, list entry 1357291, see https://historicengland.org.uk/listing/the-list/list-entry/1357291?section=official-list-entry (accessed 14 Jan. 2023).

[22] Defoe, *A Tour*, II, 106.

[23] '(lost) Charles II trampling Cromwell', London Remembers, https://www.londonremembers.com/memorials/charles-ii-trampling-cromwell (accessed 21 June 2023).

[24] Y. Whelan, 'The Construction and Destruction of a Colonial Landscape: Monuments to British Monarchs in Dublin before and after Independence', *Journal of Historical Geography*, 28 (2002), 514–17, 522–23.

[25] Coutu, *Persuasion and Propaganda*, 8.

appeared.[26] The politicised nature of this memorialisation is made clear by the words on the plinth on William III's statue in Hull. These homages to 'Our Great Deliverer' were not to record history but to impose a particular reading, favourable to the then regime, upon it. Liberty was thus symbolically associated with Protestantism, William III and his successors.[27]

In the later eighteenth century, William III's statues were joined by others in open public space. One such was an equestrian depiction of the Duke of Cumberland in Cavendish Square, funded by General William Strode in 1769. This statue of the 'Butcher of Culloden' was soon mocked both for its sanguinary associations and on aesthetic grounds. It was quietly removed in 1868 and the statue itself melted down.[28] Worse fates befell contemporary statuary in British North America. George III's statue erected in New York to celebrate the repeal of the Stamp Act in 1766 was torn down a decade later and used to make bullets to fight the British during the Revolutionary War.[29] It may be that 'Monuments, because they can be so public (in terms of commission, location and iconography) and because they are imbued with the notions of permanence, timelessness and posterity, are a perfect fit for empire,'[30] but they clearly only remain rightminded adornments of public space as long as that empire is uncontested.

Sculpture was nonetheless to be widely deployed to assert that empire during its Victorian zenith.[31] This was part of a contemporary statuomania, facilitated by new techniques of manufacture and replication,[32] that served differing purposes across Europe and North America. For instance, the trauma of loss or of defeat provided a context for the thousands of Civil War monuments that appeared in American cities and villages, both North and South, by the 1890s.[33] Increasingly, as the Harvard philosopher William James warned in 1897, these came to reflect not the meaning of that war, but a search for reconciliation across the White population, an occlusion of Black suffering and – in the South – a cathartic celebration of the supposedly noble Christian warriors who had fought in the Lost Cause of the Confederacy.[34] Meanwhile,

---

[26] Historic England, 'Statue of William III', grade I monument, list entry 1093567, see https://historicengland.org.uk/listing/the-list/list-entry/1093567?section=official-list-entry (accessed 21 June 2023); *Petersfield Post*, 14 Sept. 2021.

[27] Historic England, 'Statue of King William III and Flanking Lamps', grade I monument, list entry 1197697, see https://historicengland.org.uk/listing/the-list/list-entry/1197697?section=official-list-entry (accessed 21 June 2023).

[28] Survey of London, 'Cavendish Square 5: The Duke of Cumberland's Statue', 19 Aug. 2016, see https://blogs.ucl.ac.uk/survey-of-london/2016/08/19/cavendish-square-5-the-duke-of-cumberlands-statue (accessed 25 June 2023).

[29] Coutu, *Persuasion and Propaganda*, 3.

[30] Ibid., 8.

[31] See M. Droth, J. Edwards and M. Hatt (eds.), *Sculpture Victorious: Art in an Age of Invention 1837–1901* (New Haven, 2014).

[32] A. Dunstan, 'Reading Victorian Sculpture', *Interdisciplinary Studies in the Long Nineteenth Century*, 22 (2016), 7–8.

[33] D. Blight, *Race and Reunion: The Civil War in American Memory* (2001), 339.

[34] Ibid., 204, 267–71, 341–4. The Robert Gould Shaw memorial in Boston, the unveiling of which was the occasion for James's remarks, was almost unique in providing monumental recognition of the Black contribution to the Union war effort.

following German reunification some 500 statues of the architect of that process, Otto von Bismarck, dotted the country. These were part of the nation-building process that across Europe provided the principal impetus for the statuomania of the time. As Michalski remarks, Bismarck's statues are 'not in reality dedicated to him; they are monuments which the nation erected for herself, and which refer to Bismarck solely as a pretext'.[35] They did not so much memorialise the man himself as mark the territories he had incorporated into the *Kaiserreich*. The trauma of the defeat Bismarck inflicted on France in the process appears to explain the conspicuous absence of military figures from the form statuomania took there. This involved a rejection of the politicised and conservative overtones of such representations. Third Republic statues instead celebrated the genius of France's thinkers, statesmen and manufacturers. It is these statues, often quirkily showing their subjects in settings associated with them (for instance, Marat was depicted in the bathtub in which he was murdered), that Breton had in mind when writing in the 1920s of the rightmindedness of statues.[36]

A century later Tim Edensor suggested that the rightmindedness of many relics of Britain's Victorian statuomania is increasingly questionable. Consider the statuary of public squares across Britain, dominated as they continue to be by nineteenth-century figures. Manchester's Albert Square, for instance, features five Victorian worthies amidst one of the city's principal public spaces. Although some of these figures were nationally prominent, others had a purely local and ephemeral fame. Indeed, Edensor claims the survival into the present of that of James Fraser (Bishop of Manchester 1870–85) is surreal, a jarring reminder of a vanished and more religious era.[37]

During the Victorian statuomania, politicians, royal personages and military figures were joined in public spaces across Britain by reforming campaigners such as Fraser. Whether they continue to command public recognition depends on the cause they were identified with and the narrative purposes the statue served. Thus, monuments to William Wilberforce (erected 1883)[38] and Joseph Sturge (erected 1862)[39] in their respective native cities of Hull and Birmingham could easily be incorporated into a national narrative of defence of liberty amended to incorporate the abolition of slavery that, in the process, conveniently occluded Britain's leading part in the horrors of the transatlantic slave trade. They thereby supported a self-congratulatory approach to monumental national mythmaking. The iconography of Sturge's monument, with the supporting allegorical figure of Charity giving succour to an African infant, readily conveys the racialised narrative that freedom

---

[35] S. Michalski, *Public Monuments: Art in Political Bondage 1870-1997* (1998), 66–74.

[36] *Ibid.*, 25–47.

[37] T. Edensor, 'The Haunting Presence of Commemorative Statues', *ephemera*, 19 (2019), 55–9.

[38] Historic England, 'Statue of William Wilberforce in garden of Wilberforce House', grade II* monument, list entry 1197754, see https://historicengland.org.uk/listing/the-list/list-entry/ 1197754?section=official-list-entry (accessed 21 June 2023).

[39] Historic England, 'Statue of Joseph Sturge in front of Tube Investment House', grade II monument, list entry 1076324, see https://historicengland.org.uk/listing/the-list/list-entry/1076324? section=official-list-entry (accessed 21 June 2023).

was gifted by paternalist white figures to the childlike enslaved. A mythic figure is thus used to fix a mythic and whitewashed history.[40] This affirms in public space a reassuring and misleading narration of national virtue.

Those who struggled in causes which did not speak so easily to national myths, or were more contested, were less likely to be memorialised by the Victorians. This was the case even with those causes, like parliamentary reform, which could be related to the post-1688 national narrative of British liberty. Victorian statues of exemplary male statesmen monumentalised Parliament and its role in national life through their commemoration enacted in London's Parliament Square.[41] Yet it was not until Millicent Fawcett in 2018 joined what became during the twentieth century a more heterogeneous celebration of imperial and American great men that any women, or external campaigners for parliamentary reform, entered this throng.[42]

Political figures associated broadly with the Left are not conspicuously commemorated in British public space. It was not until 1964 that Tom Paine was memorialised, when the Thomas Paine Foundation of New York donated a statue of him to his native town of Thetford.[43] The statue of the Chartist leader Feargus O'Connor, erected after some controversy in Nottingham in 1859, is a rare example of Victorian memorialisation of campaigners for parliamentary reform. O'Connor's statue was authorised by the local council, who were also persuaded to renovate it in 1880.[44] However, the monument to an earlier campaigner for parliamentary reform, Henry 'Orator' Hunt, erected by Chartists from public subscriptions in 1842, was pulled down because of deteriorating stonework in 1888.[45] In contrast, that to Earl Grey, whose patrician Whig government passed the 1832 Reform Act, still stands impressively on its column in the centre of Newcastle upon Tyne. Campaigners are much less likely than office holders to have statues, but that does not necessarily reflect their relative historical significance. The happenstance of one monument's survival and the other's demise does not testify to history, but to the narrative inequality enacted by those who control power.[46] The prime determinant of the rightmindedness of a statue is thus not the statue itself, nor the attitudes of the public who view it, but the mindset of those authority figures who, since

---

[40] This is even more the case with the statue to the Earl of Derby erected in 1874; see M. Dresser, 'Set in Stone? Statues and Slavery in London', History Workshop Journal, 64 (2007), 185.

[41] G. Hicks, 'Parliament Square: The Making of a Political Space', Landscapes, 16 (2015), 164–70.

[42] M. Terras and E. Crawford, 'Introduction', in Millicent Garrett Fawcett: Selected Writings, ed. M. Terras and E. Crawford (2022), 1.

[43] A. McIntosh, 'The Great British Art Tour: Thomas Paine and his Upside-Down Rights of Man', The Guardian 26 Jan. 2021.

[44] P. Elliott, 'Nottingham Arboretum's Oldest Figure: The Troublesome Statue of Feargus O'Connor', NG Spaces, 20 Apr. 2010, see http://www.ng-spaces.org.uk/nottingham-arboretums-oldest-figure-the-troublesome-statue-of-feargus-oconnor (accessed 14 Jan. 2023); Historic England, 'Statue of Feargus O'Connor on South Side of Arboretum', grade II monument, list entry 1255246, see https://historicengland.org.uk/listing/the-list/list-entry/1255246?section=official-list-entry (accessed 27 June 2023).

[45] Transactions of the Lancashire and Cheshire Antiquarian Society, 7 (7 Dec. 1889), 325–6.

[46] M. Livholts, 'Immaterial Monuments, Narrative Inequality and Glocal Social Work: Towards Critical Participatory Arts-Based Practices', British Journal of Social Work, 52 (2021), 777.

Henri Grégoire during the French Revolution, have sought to establish the grounds on which they ought to be preserved.[47]

Statues and memorials do not just appear. Nor are they inert *tabulae rasae* waiting for the public to invest them with meaning and value through interaction with them. They must be conceived, paid for, maintained and, nowadays, win planning permission. Accordingly, the rightmindedness of a statue is generally a matter of official sanction. Statues thus express what the elites of a society choose to remember or occlude in public space. Thus, Victorian male elites celebrated their male heroes and role models. Women, if represented at all, were often anonymised eye candy in supporting roles: for example, draped in semi-naked mourning as the figure 'Grief' over the monument to Sir Arthur Sullivan in Embankment Gardens.[48] They were used as stereotyped representations of imperial geography or allegorical images of the sciences – such as around the Albert Memorial in Hyde Park – or of virtues, as at the base of the Victoria Memorial outside Buckingham Palace.[49] The queen the latter commemorates is one of the few named women from the era to be memorialised, the rightmindedness of her statues emphasised by their ubiquitous evocation of the age to which she gave its name. It was not until the twenty-first century that she began to be joined by her female contemporaries, an example being Monumental Welsh Women's current campaign to erect five statues of actual as opposed to allegorical women.[50]

Victoria's statues were undoubtedly seen as rightminded during the era of statuomania. This rightmindedness can, however, change. When Queen Victoria was empress of India her statue's pride of place on Delhi's Chandni Chowk in the heart of what had been the Mughal capital was only to be expected. After independence, its presence became a jarring reminder of former political realities.[51] The statue's former location reflected the power dynamics of the time. The relocation of the monuments of the British Raj to a retirement home for imperial statues in Delhi's Coronation Park marks the creation of a new normative site.[52] Their relegation to an imperial garden of remembrance enables the observer to still see them speaking not of present power structures but of a receding though still palpable past.

---

[47] See J. Sax, 'Heritage Preservation as a Public Duty: The Abbé Grégoire and the Origins of an Idea', *Michigan Law Review*, 88 (1990), 1142–69.

[48] Historic England, 'Sir Arthur Sullivan Memorial', grade II monument, list entry 1238072, see https://historicengland.org.uk/listing/the-list/list-entry/1238072?section=official-list-entry (accessed 21 June 2023).

[49] Historic England, 'Prince Consort National Memorial (Albert Memorial)', grade I monument, list entry 1217741, see https://historicengland.org.uk/listing/the-list/list-entry/1217741?section=official-list-entry (accessed 21 June 2023); Historic England, 'Queen Victoria Memorial', grade I monument, list entry 1273864, see https://historicengland.org.uk/listing/the-list/list-entry/1273864?section=official-list-entry (accessed 21 June 2023).

[50] 'Swashbuckling Poet Cranogwen is Third Woman in Wales to Get Statue', BBC News, 10 June 2023, see https://www.bbc.co.uk/news/uk-wales-65867326 (accessed 28 June 2023).

[51] The statue is now in a cobwebbed corner of Delhi College of Art. S. Pisharoty, 'The Crowned in the Corner', *The Hindu*, 15 June 2014.

[52] B. Groseclose, 'Indian Ironies or British Commemorative Sculpture and (Re)Shaped Memory', in *Memory & Oblivion*, eds. W. Reinink and J. Stumpel (Alphen aan den Rijn, 1999), 588.

Theomorphic statuary of various kinds adorned temples across India from long before the arrival of Europeans,[53] but the British rulers in the late nineteenth century added the symbolic use of statues of eminent men, usually authority figures, simultaneously so widespread in Europe. This practice of commemoration continued after Indian independence in 1947, although the subjects changed, especially with the confluence of Hindu revivalism and nationalism from the 1990s.[54] Indeed, in some areas local individuals and groups began unofficially to erect statues of figures they admired in prominent public locations. An example is the statue of the Dalit leader B. R. Ambedkar that M. Veeraraghavan put up on a village road. Consequent litigation in 2021 led to an order requiring the Tamil Nadu government to remove all such statues of political leaders and personalities in those places 'affecting or infringing the rights of the common people', such as roads, and relocate them to a 'Leaders Park'.[55]

Clearly, a statue can only fully be deemed to be in its right mind when its appropriateness in a particular space is acknowledged by the public authorities. Notwithstanding Nash/Breton's comments, this can be in a ditch, a field or a junkyard.[56] After all, James II's statue lay on its back amid weeds in the garden of Gwydyr House for a year. However, its re-erection in its (so far) penultimate location outside the New Admiralty building in 1903 renewed official recognition of its right to be in public space.[57]

Processes of political transition have historically been the main drivers of change to the rightmindedness of a statue. Consider the vicissitudes experienced by the statue of the German imperialist Hermann von Wissmann. This was erected in 1911 in the centre of Dar es Salaam, then capital of German East Africa. It was taken down when the British captured the territory during the Great War. As the result of the replacement of one imperial order by another, Wissmann's statue was no longer in its right mind in Africa. It was donated to Wissmann's alma mater, the University of Hamburg. Official sanction thus restored rightmindedness to the statue in its new location. Yet not for long. By the time of the student upheavals in Germany in 1968, Wissmann had come to be seen as a racist villain who played his part in his country's descent into genocidal violence. His statue was first attacked and then removed. It is only occasionally, and historically often through such violent actions, that protesters break into the narrative and alter a statue's rightmindedness. Wissmann's statue now lies broken and symbolically daubed with red paint. As such it was displayed in the exhibition on *Deutscher Kolonialismus* in the German Historical Museum in Berlin in 2016. Its rightmindedness has been re-established and metamorphosed in its maimed state now into a symbol of anticolonialism that is only in its right mind in a museum.[58]

---

[53] R. Davis, *Lives of Indian Images* (Princeton, 1997), 7–13.

[54] See K. Jain, *Gods in the Time of Democracy* (Durham, NC, 2021).

[55] 'Madras HC Orders Removal of Political Leaders' Statues from Public Places', *Deccan Herald*, 7 Oct. 2021.

[56] See A. Fauve, 'A Tale of Two Statues in Astana: The Fuzzy Process of Nationalistic City Making', *Nationalities Papers*, 43 (2015), 383.

[57] E. Gleichen, *London's Open-Air Statuary* (1928), 47–8.

[58] Catterall, 'Changing Attitudes to the Past', 635–6.

Statues are thus far from being neutral interventions in public space. Their rightmindedness generally reflects the exercise of public authority, even when retired to a museum. Their erection and retention enact what Laurajane Smith has called an authorised heritage discourse whereby these authorities establish what should be in the public realm, why it is important, what ought to be preserved and how.[59] Her analysis focuses upon archaeological sites, but it can also be applied to the public space which most statues inhabit. This authorised public space discourse is shaped by public bodies from churches to planning authorities, determining the nature of public space and the features it contains.[60]

Many of these features are legacies, sometimes highly problematic ones, from the Victorian era. As a result, there is in public space always a dialogic relationship between the residues from the past that statues – among other edifices – mark and the contested ways in which a society chooses to remember, memorialise or indeed forget that past.[61] These processes are not neutral, but part of the authorised heritage discourse. Built heritage, such as statues, involves a purposeful process of deeming certain features of the public realm as relevant to public memory.[62] The public's role in this process, except when protesting about what is included in public memory and how it is memorialised, is essentially a passive one. Instead, professional gatekeepers acting on behalf of public authorities determine what constitutes heritage and gets to be preserved. These gatekeepers designate and delineate the articulation of public memory in the public realm by creating what Garden has called 'heritagescapes'.[63] Through constructing these heritagescapes and protecting the elements within them, they play a major role in determining the rightmindedness of a statue. Take Oxford's Rhodes Building, listed in 1972. The right-wing novelist Evelyn Waugh might have felt it ought to be blown up because of its ugliness, yet the grounds on which this designation occurred reflected a statutory framework that continues to privilege supposed architectural merit. Nonetheless, the much-reviled statue of Cecil Rhodes which adorns its facade was included in the citation, because it 'serves as a major monument to Rhodes, a controversial figure, but of immense historical importance and whose legacies had a major impact on the University'.[64]

---

[59] See L. Smith, *Uses of Heritage* (2006).

[60] P. Catterall and A. Azzouz, *Queering Public Space: Exploring the Relationship between Queer Communities and Public Spaces* (2021), 13–14.

[61] S. Levinson, *Written in Stone: Public Monuments in Changing Societies*, 2nd edn (Durham, NC, 2018), 191–3.

[62] For instance, British regulations in 2021 require secretary of state approval for the removal of any statues; see K. McClymont, 'The Fall of Statues? Contested Heritage, Public Space and Urban Planning: An Introduction', *Planning Theory and Practice*, 22 (2021), 768.

[63] See M.-C. Garden, 'The Heritagescape: Looking at Landscapes of the Past', *International Journal of Heritage Studies*, 12 (2006), 394–411.

[64] Historic England, 'The Rhodes Building (North Range), Oriel College', grade II* monument, list entry 1046662, see https://historicengland.org.uk/listing/the-list/list-entry/1046662 (accessed 14 Jan. 2023).

The Rhodes Building is a monument to the man who paid for it. Similar donations have long been means of establishing a personal legacy to posterity. In medieval times benefactors paid for abbeys and chantries for the good of their souls and, less successfully, their earthly renown.[65] Rhodes was making a more effective and secular payment for the sake of his posthumous reputation. The residue from the past represented by his statue results from his determination to memorialise himself. Rhodes may have been of historical importance, yet so were many people who are not thus memorialised. Furthermore, being of historical importance does not necessarily connote meriting commemoration. After all, there are plenty of figures whose historical importance sees them memorialised only in the distinctive location of chambers of horrors. Historical importance is not what has, until recently, rendered rightminded the occupation of Oxford's public space by Rhodes's statue. That rightmindedness was instead purchased by Rhodes himself and then officially recognised by a listing which inscribed it into the heritagescape of Oxford.

Listing changes the status of such statues. Like Goodhart's Law – that the process of observing a phenomenon changes the nature of what is observed – the decision to list also seems to change public understanding of what has been listed. Listing articulates which residues in the public realm are worth preserving and thereby inserts them into an inherited legacy of the national past. This process is reinforced by narratives such as that provided by Historic England designating 'commemorative monuments' somehow as 'our history made manifest'.[66] Such statements officially encourage a tendency to treat statues as signifiers, embodying the person or the past they reference, and assert the presumed historical value of statues as unproblematic, their rightmindedness obvious and innate.

Yet that rightmindedness is also historically contingent. With regime change, whether imperial or political, rightmindedness can rapidly disappear. Henri Grégoire coined the term vandalism to critique attacks on cultural artefacts as betrayals of revolutionary principles, in his report to the French National Convention in 1794.[67] Such iconoclasm, often officially sanctioned, can be traced back to antiquity.[68] It can also be an outlet for social protest. As Marschall notes of contemporary South Africa, there,

for many, a commemorative monument is not recognized as a dignified public symbol with a specific political "message," but rather as a generic

---

[65] See M. Richards, 'Chapels and Chantries in Late Mediaeval and Early Modern Besançon: The Record Book of Jean Ferreux, Chaplain', *Journal of Mediaeval History*, 20 (1994), 121–32.

[66] Historic England, press release about 'Commemorative Structures', 4 Dec. 2017, https://historicengland.org.uk/images-books/publications/dlsg-commemorative-structures (accessed 14 Jan. 2023).

[67] A. Merrills, 'The Origins of "Vandalism"', *International Journal of the Classical Tradition*, 16 (2009), 155–6.

[68] S. Frank and M. Ristic, 'Urban Fallism: Monuments, Iconoclasm and Activism', *City*, 24 (2020), 554–5; S. Connor, 'Killing or "De-activating" Egyptian Statues: Who Mutilated Them, When and Why?', in *Statues in Context: Production, Meaning and (Re)uses*, ed. A. Masson-Berghoff (Leuven, 2019), 281–302.

and largely meaningless piece of urban infrastructure, erected and maintained by the state at high cost, while the needs of the poor are blatantly ignored.[69]

However, when the targets are seen as symbolising not a political regime but an aspect of the national story, conflicts over the rightmindedness of statues can become embattled in identity politics. This is particularly the case when the authorised discourse is so internalised that challenges to it elicit an angry backlash. Identification with the nation can lead to perceived threats to its emblems being seen as personally threatening as well.[70] In Britain and America in 2020, challenges presented to the rightmindedness of certain statues by Black Lives Matter accordingly prompted a determination to protect what these statues are deemed to embody, particularly on the political Right. For instance, prominent far-right politician Nick Griffin was among the fifty men who turned up in Shrewsbury to 'defend' the statue of one of the founders of British India, Robert Clive,[71] after 10,000 had signed a petition for its removal. In claiming that 'It's nothing to do with racism, we're proud of our town and its history and want to stand up for it,' they rhetorically enlisted history and civic identity as the purportedly acceptable grounds on which to continue to recognise the rightmindedness of Clive's statue within the town.[72]

Elsewhere some went even further. Consider the bleach thrown in Bristol on the statue of Jamaican actor and playwright Alfred Fagon, a few days after the statue of slave trader Edward Colston was forcibly torn down in the same city. In resorting to the crude racist trope of seeking to bleach Fagon's blackness, the perpetrator(s) also symbolically rejected the rightmindedness of his memorialisation and the way in which the only statue of a Black person in the city unselfconsciously conveyed in public space a broader narrative of Britain's imperial past and Bristol's place in it.[73]

Statues do not represent history or memory, but they do impact upon public understandings of how history and memory are represented. That they are erected, maintained and in some cases listed also provides a statement from public authorities that their subjects are deemed worthy of remembrance.[74] Such a claim might be bolstered by inscriptions lauding their merits and

---

[69] S. Marschall, 'Targeting Statues: Monument "Vandalism" as an Expression of Sociopolitical Protest in South Africa', *African Studies Review*, 60 (2019), 216.

[70] See J. Hearn, 'National Identity: Banal, Personal and Embedded', *Nations and Nationalism*, 13 (2007), 657–74.

[71] Historic England, 'Statue of Lord Clive', grade II monument, list entry 1254926, see https://historicengland.org.uk/listing/the-list/list-entry/1254926?section=official-list-entry (accessed 21 June 2023).

[72] C. Bentley, '"Statue Defenders" Gather around Robert Clive in Shrewsbury', *Shropshire Star*, 13 June 2020.

[73] T. Cork, '"Bleach Attack" on Bristol Actor's Statue Shocks Community', *Bristol Post*, 11 June 2020.

[74] Historic England first listed monuments to Black people in 2016 (Catterall, 'Changing Attitudes to the Past', 637). In 2022 Fagon's statue was added to that list. Historic England, 'Statue of Alfred Fagon', grade II monument, list entry 1482464, see https://historicengland.org.uk/listing/the-list/list-entry/1482464?section=official-list-entry (accessed 23 June 2023).

invoking public acclaim,[75] gestures (such as Thomas Guy's hand outstretched to a sick pauper) or allegorical characters.[76] Merely being represented in a statue can indicate that such remembrance is worthy among a public for whom that statue is otherwise most of the time simply Winter's 'white noise' in stone.

The statue, in the process, becomes in the imagination the person they represent and the past they are felt to evoke. Statues become avatars, invested with psychic value. Historically, of course, statues have always served this function: hence the warnings against the resulting idolatry of men or gods contained in the Book of Wisdom and the iconoclasm of medieval Christianity and Islam.[77] Statues may be simply representations, but they are intended to embody otherwise hard-to-grasp abstractions. Surrealists like Breton recognised this quality in the Third Republic statues of interwar Paris, feeling that they imbued the places they inhabited with magical qualities.[78] They did so by conveying abstractions charged with social as well as religious meaning, such as national identity. National identity is not something you can point to or easily define, but – according to Historic England – it can be made manifest in a monument.

An example is the way in which statues of Sir Winston Churchill, particularly the one in London's Parliament Square, are identified with the Second World War. The meaning invested in that statue has steadily morphed. From being an embodiment of national survival in 1940–1, it has become more implausibly a symbol of the supposed national victory achieved (with scant acknowledgement of the contribution of Americans, Russians, the empire and Commonwealth, Poles and many others) in 1945. This misappropriation of history has become powerfully lodged in the national myth. National virtue has become entwined with the personal merit having a statue is deemed to represent. Attacks on the statue – including graffiti drawing attention to Churchill's racism and role in the Bengal famine of 1943 that appeared following the Black Lives Matter protests of 2020 – are thus read as impugning the nation itself. Both in these attacks and in the defensive cordon that first volunteers and then the police established around the statue, what was being contested was not history but narratives of the nation.[79] In the process much is occluded, with 1945 transformed from the deliverance from dire peril Churchill then invoked, into a narrative of triumphal white Britishness. For instance, it was found in 2018 that only 22 per cent of the British public were aware of the thousands of Muslims who fought and died for Britain in two world wars, an ignorance reinforced by their absence from the memorialisation of that conflict in public space and exploited by Islamophobic far-right

---

[75] Cherry, 'Statues in the Square', 686.

[76] Dresser, 'Set in Stone?', 171–3.

[77] See J. Noyes, *The Politics of Iconoclasm: Religion, Violence and the Culture of Image-Breaking in Christianity and Islam* (2013).

[78] Michalski, *Public Monuments*, 47.

[79] J. Peat, 'Protect Churchill at All Costs', The London Economic, 14 Mar. 2021: see https://www.thelondoneconomic.com/news/protect-churchill-at-all-costs-police-surround-statue-as-protesters-march-on-parliament-square-257639 (accessed 14 Jan. 2023).

groups.[80] Gravesend's statue to Squadron Leader Mahinder Singh Pujji, funded by the local Sikh community and erected in 2014 four years after his death, is a rare and belated example of memorialisation of the overlooked contribution to the war effort of Britain's ethnic and religious minorities. It has since been joined by several other memorials of Sikh contributions to Britain's armed forces. By writing this representation of their community into the heritage-scape, Sikhs also encoded their place in and contribution to contemporary British society.[81]

As this example shows, the erection of statues of historical figures primarily expresses the associations the groups who caused them to be made seek to draw from history for themselves, often long after their subject's demise. Take two examples from Bristol. The first is the statue of Edmund Burke erected in 1894, nearly a hundred years after his death. This was funded by W. H. Wills, the local tobacco magnate who was elected Liberal MP for Bristol East the following year, and unveiled by his party leader, the then prime minister, Lord Rosebery.[82] The prime motive of the city elites who supported this was to emphasise the importance of their city by adorning it with statues of significant figures associated with Bristol, even though for Burke himself his brief experience as MP for the city in 1774–80 was a far from happy one.

The second example concerns two radically different twentieth-century representations of the fifteenth-century Venetian explorer John Cabot. At least the later one of these, erected in 1985, is close to the site of the docks from whence Cabot sailed across the Atlantic, rather than right outside the City Hall. Yet the prime reason for his representation there is still to claim lustre for the city by association with Cabot's exploits: as the accompanying plaque puts it, 'In May 1497 John Cabot sailed from this harbour in the Matthew and discovered North America'. This asserts for Bristol a historical claim to fame, but only from a distorting European perspective. The falseness of this claim is testified by the signs of human activity Cabot brought back with him.[83]

This statue may have been, for Bristol city council, rightmindedly commemorative. Yet this act of commemoration still distorted the past. Clearly, even when not hagiographic, commemoration is not history.[84] Notwithstanding Historic England's views, the most historically aware of commemorative monuments, such as those to the Holocaust, are more concerned with responding to and learning from history, rather than telling or manifesting it.[85] As pieces of

---

[80] R. Sheikh, 'Forgotten Muslim Soldiers of World War One "Silence" Far Right', BBC News, 9 Nov. 2018: see https://www.bbc.co.uk/news/uk-46124467 (accessed 14 Jan. 2023).

[81] A. Banse, 'Sikh Soldiers' Valour and Laurels in the UK', *Sikh Review*, 69/11 (2021), 57–65.

[82] See the description of the unveiling in Roslyn scrapbook, Bristol Archives: 17563/1/369, https://archives.bristol.gov.uk/records/17563/1/369 (accessed 26 June 2023).

[83] I am grateful to Evan Jones, co-director of the Cabot Project at the University of Bristol (https://www.bristol.ac.uk/history/research/cabot, accessed 21 June 2023), for this information.

[84] K. Savage, 'The Politics of Memory: Black Emancipation and the Civil War Monument', in *Commemoration and the Politics of National Identity*, ed. J. Gillis (1994), 135–6.

[85] See J. Young, 'The Texture of Memory: Holocaust Memorials and Meaning', *Holocaust and Genocide Studies*, 4 (1989), 63–76.

art, they seek to produce an emotional rather than intellectual response. Most statues should be seen as texts which often tell one-sided stories, hence the addition in 2021 adjacent to the column topped by a statue of Henry Dundas in Edinburgh of interpretative material to draw attention to his deliberate role in delaying the abolition of the slave trade.[86] Statues do not in themselves represent history, or present historical narratives. Indeed, the teaching of history is rarely among their initial purposes. Insofar as they reflect history, it is the history of memorialisation, not of what is memorialised.

Accordingly, it is curious that so much effort has been invested recently in trying to base the rightmindedness of statues on their supposed ability to represent history. After all, many of the most controversial statues were clearly erected with the explicit and politicised intention of misrepresenting history. Consider the Confederate statuary and monuments targeted for protests in recent decades. These articulated in public space the political project of bolstering a Lost Cause ideology and the racialised power relations of the Jim Crow era of the late nineteenth century, long after the Civil War they purportedly memorialised.[87] This project was carried out by appropriating classical motifs and allegorical figures, a process which established their aesthetic rightmindedness within a Western artistic canon by applying a bogus veneer of heroic virtue and refinement. It also drew upon imperial iconography dating back to Rome but mediated through contemporary imperial practice in Europe.[88] In some cases, this reflected a dramatic shift in intentions: for instance, lobbying by various interest groups led to the simple obelisk memorial originally planned as the Confederate Soldiers Memorial at the state capitol in Arkansas being replaced by a more elaborate monument, complete with an angel improbably holding a victory wreath towering over it.[89] Such strategic positioning alongside seats of political power established a visual culture which brooked no dissenting images. Indeed, the statues of Confederate generals that until recently lined Richmond's Monument Avenue intentionally articulated this politicised visual culture.[90]

The decision to erect a statue is certainly a statement by a particular society – or more commonly the authorities therein – of what they consider important to reflect in public space which then, over time, becomes a legacy for

---

[86] 'Edinburgh's Dundas Statue to Be Dedicated to Slavery Victims', BBC News, 11 June 2020, https://www.bbc.co.uk/news/uk-scotland-edinburgh-east-fife-52997858 (accessed 26 June 2023). A Shropshire county council press release on 19 Nov. 2021 indicated plans for something similar alongside Clive's statue in Shrewsbury (https://newsroom.shropshire.gov.uk/2021/11/robert-clive-statue-in-the-square-shrewsbury-an-update, accessed 21 June 2023). However, such interventions can themselves prove controversial, as pointed out in Levinson, *Written in Stone*, 22–3, 41–2.

[87] Levinson, *Written in Stone*, 174.

[88] Blight, *Race and Reunion*, 267–70.

[89] F. Latimer, 'Arkansas Listings in the National Register of Historical Places: The Confederate Soldiers' Monument and the Monument to Confederate Women in Little Rock', *Arkansas Historical Quarterly*, 60 (2001), 305–8. These monuments were listed in 1996.

[90] See K. Edwards and E. Howard, 'Monument Avenue: The Architecture of Consensus in the New South, 1890–1930', *Perspectives in Vernacular Architecture*, 6 (1997), 92–110. Ironically, the only monument left standing on Monument Avenue now is that of the African American tennis star Arthur Ashe.

succeeding generations. Whether the resulting statues come in any meaningful sense to represent history is another matter. Consider a British equivalent of Wissmann, the statue of Edward Colston in Bristol. The Victorians who erected it in 1895, a year after the statue to Burke was unveiled and 174 years after Colston's death, were supposedly commemorating the latter's philanthropy to the city. Yet there were more important Bristol philanthropists who have no monument, such as Richard Reynolds, perhaps because of his outsider status as a Quaker. Colston was very much an insider, and it was the elites in the web of local charitable societies, Liberal associations and other civic bodies who were the prime movers and funders behind his statue, notwithstanding the misleading claim on its plinth that it was 'Erected by citizens of Bristol'.[91] There was an oblique reference to the source of Colston's philanthropy at the unveiling, but it was not until Carole Drake's 1993 installation *Commemoration Day* that the collective amnesia that his wealth came from slave trading was challenged, as she presented the shadow cast by Colston's statue sucking in 'the histories of thousands of black children, men and women ... to present an uncomplicated, unsullied image of Colston as a benign patriarch'.[92]

When that statue was torn down on 7 June 2020 by protesters for whom its presence in public space was not rightminded but an affront, there was nevertheless much complaint that the past was somehow thereby distorted. Yet, as the historian Joanna Burch-Brown had earlier pointed out, what was at stake was not an unrecoverable past, but the way in which the existing memorialisation of Colston imposed one particular and deeply misleading reading of it.[93] In that sense, John Cassidy's rendering of Colston was a patina, a meta-narrative for public consumption that obscured the monstrous reality of Colston's actions. The statue itself became an absurd distortion of its theme of philanthropy that subverted the meaning of the past far more thoroughly than the violent act of removal to which it was eventually subjected. Recumbent and now stored in a museum,[94] like that of Wissmann, it has arguably recovered a kind of right-mindedness, though one imbued with a very different meaning.

Like Colston's simulacrum, statues often hide in plain sight uncomfortable historical truths. James II's statue might still be accepted as rightminded, but its subject was governor of the Royal African Society through which Colston operated.[95] This grim reality remains disguised by the classical veneer of the statue. Artistically it is thus very different from the efforts of surrealism

---

[91] R. Ball, 'Myths within Myths ... Edward Colston and that Statue', Bristol Radical History Group, 14 Oct. 2018, https://www.brh.org.uk/site/articles/myths-within-myths (accessed 26 June 2023); S. Jordan, 'The Myth of Edward Colston: Bristol Docks, the Merchant Elite and the Legitimisation of Authority 1860–1880', in *A City Built upon Water: Maritime Bristol 1750–1880*, ed. S. Poole (Bristol, 2013), 175–96.

[92] Cited in Bluecoat Library, Liverpool, 'Trophies of Empire', https://www.thebluecoat.org.uk/library/event/trophies-of-empire (accessed 26 June 2023).

[93] J. Burch-Brown, 'Defenders of Colston Are The Ones Airbrushing the Past', *Bristol Post*, 30 Apr. 2017.

[94] McClymont, 'The Fall of Statues?', 770.

[95] W. Pettigrew, *Freedom's Debt: The Royal Africa Company and the Politics of the Atlantic Slave Trade, 1672–1752* (Chapel Hill, 2013), 25.

to 'resolve the heretofore contradictory conditions of dream and of reality into an absolute reality, a super-reality'.[96] Rather than being surreal in an artistic sense, statues like those of Colston or James II might instead be seen as sub-real. They are sub-real because, through flattering its subject to deceive its audience, they hide rather than reveal reality. Many historic statues combine ideational and material facets to the same effect. They often express a meta-narrative both explicitly in the inscription and allegorically in the supporting features. Yet the foregrounding of this unproblematic meta-narrative simply reinforces their one-dimensionality. Meanwhile, the emphases on virtues found on the plinths of Colston and others reduce their subjects to mere, and misleading, exemplars. The humanity – the hopes and dreams Breton aimed to encapsulate – is drained from these superficial representations. Indeed, Taussig suggests that the smug strategic forgetting reflected in these monuments positively cries out to be lampooned or desecrated.[97]

This sub-reality is also expressed in the perennial referencing of classical imagery in conventional statuary. One example of subverting this imagery and its idealised allegorical and objectified representation of the female form is the nude pose struck by the artist Dora Carrington alongside one such statue in Garsington Manor in 1917.[98] This deliberate juxtaposition was not self-consciously surreal, yet Carrington achieved the same objective Nash invoked by imagining a statue in a ploughed field by contrasting the female statue with her own naked body.

A similar, also temporary, intervention was effected by the disabled artist Jason Willsher-Mills placing his 2021 self-portrait *I Am Argonaut* – a rendering of a body very much outside the classical canon Winckelmann featured – in dialogue with Peter Trimming's conventional 2009 rendering of Folkestone's most famous son, the seventeenth-century physician William Harvey.[99] Both by changing the artistic language and by invading the spatial syntax Carrington and Willsher-Mills, in their different ways, subverted the normative readings of ornamentation, commemoration and celebration that rightminded statues generally seek to convey.

This raises the question of how far such interventions can be interpreted as taking a rightminded statue and rendering it surreal. Nash's own work does not give many clues on this. Rather than producing permanent pieces of public statuary, he instead delighted in finding natural ready-mades in the English countryside, such as *Marsh Personage*,[100] exhibited at the 1936 International Surrealist Exhibition.[101] Two years later he invoked the super-reality of

[96] G. Hugnet and M. Scolari, 'In the Light of Surrealism', *Bulletin of the Museum of Modern Art*, 4/2–3 (1936), 20.

[97] M. Taussig, *Defacement, Public Secrecy and the Labor of the Negative* (Stanford, 1999), 20–1.

[98] The photograph adorns the cover of A. Chisholm (ed.), *Carrington's Letters* (2017).

[99] Creative Folkestone, 'Jason Willsher-Mills', see https://www.creativefolkestone.org.uk/artists/jason-wilsher-mills (accessed 21 June 2023).

[100] *Marsh Personage* (1934), TGA Nash 7050, 757, see https://www.tate.org.uk/art/archive/items/tga-7050ph-757/nash-black-and-white-negative-marsh-personage (accessed 27 June 2023).

[101] I. Cassels, '"Surrealism Found Me": British Surrealism and Encounter', *Cambridge Quarterly*, 50 (2021), 12–14; P. Nash, 'The Nest of the Wild Stones', in *The Painter's Object*, ed. M. Evans (1937), 38–9.

these discoveries in pointing out that they 'belong to the world that lies visibly about us. They are unseen merely because they are not perceived.'[102] The virtuous narratives loudly proclaimed by rightminded statues can be seen as intended to ensure that these underlying realities remain unseen. Nash hints as much in his early surreal work *Token* (1929–30),[103] both through the title and the way in which a classical figure of a mother and child is bisected by an artist's easel, expressing the artificiality of much public statuary. Accordingly, rendering a statue into a state of surrealism does not necessarily require its physical relocation to a ditch. Instead, a statue can be seen as surreal when the disruption of its spatial syntax and/or readings of its artistic language make that which is occluded in conventional renderings perceptible.

One such occluded theme in the Victorian statuary with which London still throngs is the human impact of empire. *Fons Americanus* by the African American artist Kara Walker, installed in the Tate Modern in 2019, was a rare, brief and belated reference to this. Its punning title both reflected its presentation as a giant fountain and the role of Britain as the source of black chattel slavery in North America. This monument provided a depiction of those enslaved people who perished in their thousands on Colston's ships. Its references to Western classicism indicated that it largely worked by disrupting the expected artistic language. This parody of the Victoria Memorial outside Buckingham Palace thus served as a temporary bat-squeak of protest against the chorus of imperial statues permanently proclaiming in London's public spaces a one-sided and white celebration of empire.[104]

Another example of ironic parody is Meekyoung Shin's 2012 version of Cumberland's statue, only this time made of soap, symbolically washing away the bloody deeds of its subject as it gradually eroded in wind and rain. The primary effect of these interventions is to subvert the meaning of the parodied original. They reveal what was originally hidden, in Shin's case figuratively as the armature of the statue became visible as it weathered. In this revived state Cumberland's statue was placed in a state of surrealism that worked more thoroughly because it also returned this parody to Cumberland's original plinth.[105]

Some artists have sought to disrupt artistic language and spatial syntax even when carrying out a commission. As an authorised statue, Charles Robb's 2004 rendering of Charles La Trobe, the first governor of Victoria,[106] could be seen as rightminded. Yet it is also surreal in the various ways it subverts and plays with artistic conventions. Even entitling it *Landmark* evokes a

---

[102] P. Nash, 'Unseen Landscapes', *Country Life*, 73 (1938), 526–7.

[103] *Token* (1929–30), National Galleries of Scotland: GMA 2984, see https://www.nationalgalleries.org/art-and-artists/725 (accessed 27 June 2023).

[104] P. Catterall, 'On Statues and History: The Dialogue between Past and Present in Public Space', LSE British Politics and Policy, 18 June 2020, https://blogs.lse.ac.uk/politicsandpolicy/statues-past-and-present (accessed 14 Jan. 2023).

[105] Survey of London, 'Cavendish Square 5'.

[106] Monument Australia, 'Charles Joseph La Trobe', https://www.monumentaustralia.org.au/themes/people/government---colonial/display/98916-charles-joseph-la-trobe (accessed 14 Jan. 2023).

super-reality by referring both to its status as a work of art rather than act of commemoration and to multiple puns about its purpose as a marker of the university that commissioned the statue and bears La Trobe's name, the landing of Australian settlers and the ensuing territorial claims of coloniality. It also literally inverts the classical imagery commonly used to express in stone or bronze encomiums to eminent figures. The statue plays upon the viewer's expectations of this artistic registry by placing upside down, with the plinth at the top, an image which otherwise seems conventional in appearance.[107] This representation calls into question the appropriateness of the coloniality of this art, whilst simultaneously drawing attention to La Trobe's promotion of European culture during what was otherwise widely seen as an ineffective governorship. It also required the artist to eschew the heavy materials commonly used for such statues in favour of fibreglass and polystyrene, in the process also challenging the bombastic claims made by so many of the monuments parodied by Landmark. Additionally, it addresses the record of its subject himself, the coloniality of its form and location, and the tensions between the authority such monuments demand and the lack of attention they habitually receive because their rightmindedness makes them unremarkable and unnoticed.

Robb's Landmark uses spatial syntax and different materials rather than methods of representation to subvert the artistic language of the conventional Western statue form. Arguably, this is a characteristic approach taken by the most successful attempts to place statues in a state of surrealism. Several of these interventions reflect efforts to come up with an artistic language to express a response to the demise of communism in Eastern Europe. One such is Jerzy Kalina's Przejście (Monument to the Anonymous Passer-by). First installed temporarily in Warsaw in 1977, it was re-erected in Wrocław in 2005 on the anniversary of the imposition of martial law in Poland in 1981. Kalina describes his work as 'ritual actions'. By the time Przejście appeared, he had made a name for himself as a Catholic artist opposed to the communist regime.[108] To express this ritual act of opposition, Kalina's work disrupts both the spatial syntax and the artistic language. The first is expressed in two ways. Unusually for such a monument, action is encoded in the work both by its title (the Polish word for passage) and the installation of its fourteen statues either side of a crossing. Furthermore, on one side these figures are disappearing into the ground, whilst on the other side they are re-emerging. There is no inscription or interpretation, leaving the viewers themselves to read the symbolic meaning of the work through the religious and cultural connotations of journeys, oppression and deliverance that it references. This extended spatial syntax is also one of the ways in which the work subverts customary understandings of such monuments and the artistic language in which they

---

[107] Robb thus realised a version of what Claes Oldenburg had earlier proposed when suggesting in 1965 the concept of a gigantic inverted and submerged statue of President Kennedy: Michalski, Public Monuments, 173.

[108] M. Sitkowska, 'Jerzy Kalina', Culture.pl, June 2002, https://culture.pl/en/artist/jerzy-kalina (accessed 14 Jan. 2023).

are expressed. The other is achieved by the conspicuous anonymity of Kalina's figures, emphasised by the shabby ordinariness of their appearance. That very ordinariness itself subverts viewers' expectations of what a rightminded statue should be, in the process drawing attention to the theme of the monument. In this case it is not the deeds of a famous man, but the shabby deeds of an authoritarian regime.

As with *Landmark*, the entitling of Kalina's monument emphasises that this is consciously a work of art. This inverts the historical occlusion of the artist in the creation of statuary as they are often not even mentioned in the inscriptions. It also stresses the artificiality of statues. They are simulacra, not their subjects themselves. Both Robb and Kalina's work also use their human subjects to critically engage with wider themes. *Landmark*'s inversion suggests the impact of unseen external forces, in this case the imperial power of Britain on the other side of the world, just as the semi-buried state of Kalina's figures references the submersion of the human spirit under Poland's communist regime.

This wider context is also central to David Cerny's *Man Hanging Out* (1996). Installed suspended by its hand from a pole above the streets of the Czech town of Olomouc in 1997, it achieves this effect primarily by disrupting the spatial syntax. It is very deliberately not where such a statue would be expected to be found. Nor is it a celebration of its subject, Sigmund Freud, though it arguably references Freud's contribution to the origins of surrealism through his pioneering work on psychology and dreams and Cerny certainly regarded Freud as 'the intellectual face of the 20th century'.[109] Instead, the statue's suspension alludes to the need to suspend belief in the material realities commonly conveyed by statuary and see the hidden meta-narratives. Unlike a rightminded statue to Freud – such as Oscar Nemon's 1971 depiction of him seated near to his final home in Hampstead – the precarious situation of Cerny's figure conveys the thinker's attempts to grasp the working of the mind, the fragility of psychology and the potential isolation of the intellectual at the end of the twentieth century. It also alludes to Freud's own sceptical attitudes towards the consolatory illusions of monuments and their tendency to encourage nostalgia and 'neglect of what is real and immediate'.[110]

Cerny made his name not by creating monuments but by disrupting them. In 1991 he was arrested for what was deemed an act of vandalism, painting pink a Soviet tank in Prague that served as a memorial to liberation by the Red Army during the Second World War.[111] This was also a deliberate subversion of the artistic language and interpretation of a monument, rendering it surreal. This process of modifying a monument that has hitherto been accepted as rightminded is thus a third means – in addition to the examples

---

[109] Open Concept Gallery, 'Man Hanging Out by David Cerny', http://www.openconceptgallery.org/portfolio/man-hanging-out-by-david-cerny (accessed 14 Jan. 2023).

[110] Cited in Cherry, 'Statues in the Square', 684.

[111] 'Artist David Cerny: "I Painted Tank Pink to Get a Girl"', Radio Free Europe, 11 Apr. 2010, see https://www.rferl.org/a/Provocateur_Artist_David_Cerny_I_Painted_Tank_Pink_To_Get_A_Girl/2008892.html (accessed 26 June 2023).

given above of new works that seek to achieve this either intrinsically or via ironic parody – to place a statue in a state of surrealism. *Pace* Nash/Breton, the spatial syntax of a site does not have to be materially altered to effect this. Modification serves as a clandestine means for protesters to change how a statue is presented and perceived. A notable example is the statue of Gladstone in London's East End. Local myth maintains that this monument erected to the then prime minister in 1882 at the expense of Theodore H. Bryant, proprietor of the nearby match factory, was smeared with blood by his female workers during the landmark matchgirl strike of 1888. Ever since, Gladstone's hands have continually been painted red – a symbolic attribution of guilt – as a small act of resistance. This is a monument on a monument whereby a statue established and authorised by the rich and powerful has its meaning subtly altered by an unauthorised and popularly expressed addition.[112]

Another example of the application of paint as means to disrupt a statue's meaning is the red ball and chain attached to Colston's statue in an ironic reference to slavery in 2018.[113] Through a simple modification the statue's one-dimensional veneer of historical occlusion was fundamentally altered, albeit only briefly before this addition was removed by officialdom. Cerny's efforts demonstrate that monuments to the Red Army in the former Eastern bloc have been prominent targets for this kind of intervention. For example, that erected in the King's Gardens in Sofia in 1954 has since 2011 been repeatedly painted. These interventions have taken various forms, though the most striking was when its mixture of Soviet soldiers and Bulgarian peasants were reimagined as Captain America, Santa Claus and assorted other icons of Americana. This provided both an ironic reference to the superhero pretensions of so many rightminded statues – not least those expressing the socialist realism of the Soviet era – as well as a commentary on the growing influence in post-cold war Eastern Europe of American culture. It reinterpreted the monument in the contemporary. Such interventions are far closer to the purposes of history – to explicate the past in the present – than most rightminded statues. To underline this point, underneath a graffito proclaimed 'In Pace with the Times'.[114]

The statues that throng in public spaces are not generally there to explicate the past to the present. Indeed, many of them deliberately occlude that past, instead celebrating what those elites who erected them wished to laud and thereby marking, not the histories of their subjects, but the history of memorialisation. Accordingly, the rightmindedness of a public statue is principally determined by authorised public space discourse which determines what gets represented and preserved in the heritagescape of public space.[115]

---

[112] 'Vandalism and the Red Hands of William Gladstone', *East End Review*, 16 Nov. 2014, https://www.eastendreview.co.uk/2014/11/16/vandalising-gladstone (accessed 23 June 2023).

[113] Michael Young, 'Ball and Chain Attached to Edward Colston's Statue in Bristol City Centre', *Bristol Post*, 6 May 2018.

[114] K. Patowary, 'The Painted Monument to the Soviet Army in Bulgaria', *Amusing Planet*, 4 Feb. 2015, https://www.amusingplanet.com/2015/02/the-painted-monument-to-soviet-army-in.html (accessed 14 Jan. 2023).

[115] Levinson, *Written in Stone*, 54.

Although such public monuments are necessarily freighted with political meanings, inscribing them into public space all too often constitutes an erasure rather than a representation of the past that hides in plain sight problematic histories behind superficial and celebratory aesthetics.[116]

This reflects a tendency to read them as representations of a past that is gone, a reading which fails to recognise the ways in which the legacy of imperial figures like Rhodes or Frederick Roberts shapes the continuing racial stereotyping and inequalities experienced in contemporary Britain. Such a reading, confining imperialism to the past, also occludes the ways in which global power relations, expressed explicitly through Roberts's Victorian deployment of military might, 'have been replaced by new informal empires of economic and political influence' which are much more shadowy, difficult to personalise in a statue and impenetrable in form.[117]

Few indeed are the monuments which have sought to make visible in public space these new imperialistic economic realities. Even the symbolic juxtaposition of Kristen Visbal's *Fearless Girl* (2017) with the celebration of global capitalism captured by Arturo Di Modica's *Charging Bull* (1989) outside the New York stock exchange simply and controversially sought to include women in the visual representation of these power structures.[118] Nonetheless, Di Modica clearly felt challenged by the ways in which this intervention disrupted his monument's spatial syntax, yet his efforts to get *Fearless Girl* moved remain ongoing.

As Nash/Breton suggest, location is thus clearly an important factor in the rightmindedness of a statue. However, the appropriateness of a statue occupying a prime site clearly can change over time. This may be because a space has changed: a statue of medical pioneer Edward Jenner was placed in Trafalgar Square in 1858 but moved four years later as the space became increasingly an imperial celebration of military figures rather than the forum of arts and sciences its creator, John Nash, had originally intended.[119] More frequently, these alterations occur because of shifts in political order or military defeat.[120] This process may also be driven by growing public awareness of the sub-real nature of much public statuary, prompted by protesters pointing out that the virtues they one-dimensionally claim for their subjects are at best problematic and at worst bogus.[121] In such circumstances, the authorities may decide that a statue is no longer rightminded in public space but only in a

---

[116] See R. Drayton, 'Rhodes Must Not Fall? Statues, Postcolonial "Heritage" and Temporality', *Third Text*, 33 (2019), 651–66.

[117] P. Enslin, 'Monuments after Empire? The Educational Value of Imperial Statues', *Journal of Philosophy of Education*, 54 (2020), 1343.

[118] G. Bellafante, 'The False Feminism of "Fearless Girl"', *New York Times*, 16 Mar. 2017.

[119] Cherry, 'Statues in the Square', 680.

[120] Levinson, *Written in Stone*, 6–12.

[121] This reaction against the banality of many statues is not necessarily new. *The Times* (7 March 1861) noted of statues like that of Havelock: 'if they excite any positive feelings in our minds, it is a wish that some happy chance may relieve us of the greater part of our street statuary', cited in Cherry, 'Statues in the Square', 687. For William Thackeray's similar comments in 1842 see Whelan, 'Construction and Destruction', 514.

museum. Such statues become repurposed rather than surreal. Notwithstanding Nash/Breton, a statue is not placed in a state of surrealism simply by moving it. A piece of Roman statuary found in a ploughed field is not surreal but, like Shelley's deserted *Ozymandias*,[122] an outdated reflection of long-past power relations. What makes statues surreal are deliberate interventions intended to subvert their artistic language and/or spatial syntax. Thereby the simple narratives of power, public service or virtue usually portrayed by rightminded statues are replaced by more complex readings. In the process those often-unnoticed denizens of our streets, rightminded statues – not to mention the narratives that they hide – can become visible and controversial, thereby actually speaking to the discourse of public space.

Acknowledgements. I am grateful to: the editors and anonymous referees of this journal for their very helpful comments; Evan Jones, who leads on the Cabot Project at the University of Bristol, for information about the material here drawn from that city; Sam Edwards of Manchester Metropolitan University for an invitation to present at a conference there in 2018 the initial ideas on which this paper is based; John Carman of the University of Birmingham for insights into authorised heritage discourse; and the late Malcolm Chase, whose work on Chartist memorialisation first alerted me to the complexities of the politics of representation in public space.

Competing interests. None.

---

[122] Connor, 'Killing or "De-activating" Egyptian Statues', 295.

Cite this article: Catterall P (2023). Statues, Spatial Syntax and Surrealism: 'History' and Heritagescapes in Public Space. *Transactions of the Royal Historical Society* **1**, 267–290. https://doi.org/10.1017/S0080440123000105

Transactions of the RHS (2023), **1**, 291–313
doi:10.1017/S0080440123000166

ARTICLE

Creeping up on the Roman Provincial

Ben Wiedemann

Fitzwilliam College, University of Cambridge, Cambridge, UK
Email: bw423@cam.ac.uk

(Received 4 November 2022; revised 11 July 2023; accepted 18 July 2023; first published online 17 August 2023)

Abstract

Around the year 1200, the court of the Roman pope produced a list of all the bishops – and hence of all the cities – in the Christian world. For the next three centuries this text was copied and updated by kings, priests, lawyers and academics across Europe. The numerous surviving manuscripts of this text – the so-called 'Roman provincial' – have received some attention from scholars, but the sheer number of manuscripts has meant that any attempt to catalogue and study them en masse is all but destined to fail. This article suggests a different approach: that the most interesting feature of the provincial manuscripts is their differences; the ways in which copyists changed the ecclesiastical and political geography of Europe to meet their own preferences and expectations. Political geographers and modern historians have long been aware of 'contested cartographies' and battles over borders on maps; by studying the Roman provincial we can apply such lenses to the medieval world too. Thirteenth-century kings were quite as aware as we are that maps and lists constitute, rather than just describe, political realities.

Keywords: Medieval history; medieval papacy

Lists are interesting. Although some colleagues who grapple with the excitement of legal cases, battles, internecine village disputes or high politics might yet dispute this statement, many would now accept it.[1] Lists structure our world: they both describe and constitute reality (at least in the minds of the readers). For Jack Goody, they were characteristic of a literate rather than oral culture: how could a list exist in a purely oral society? Lists

---

[1] See, inter alia, POLIMA: Le pouvoir des listes au Moyen Âge; http://polima.huma-num.fr/ (accessed 22 Aug. 2022); Jack Goody, *The Domestication of the Savage Mind* (Cambridge, 1995 [1977]), especially 74–111; Umberto Eco, *The Infinity of Lists: From Homer to Joyce*, trans. Alastair McEwen (2009).

encourage categorisation and division, hence reflecting the concerns of the list-maker, irrespective of how peculiar such divisions might seem to readers from other cultures.[2]

Many societies have lists; the Middle Ages were no different. Around 1200, the papal court – the courtiers, administrators and clerics who formed the jurisdictional apex of medieval Christendom – put together a text. This was the so-called Roman provincial, the *Provinciale Romanum*, a list of all the bishops in the Christian world. As a list of all the bishops, the Roman provincial was also a list of all the cities in Christendom. Of course, this was not the first such list: earlier lists of all the bishops and all the cities in the world had been written and copied since antiquity.[3] But around 1200 a new list was made. This list, the Roman provincial, would continue to be copied, altered and updated until 1500.[4]

The Roman provincial listed all the bishops in the world. The bishops were divided up both geopolitically and by province. So, for example, most manuscripts of the provincial read:[5]

In Anglia	In England
Archiepiscopus Cantuarien' h(os) h(abet) s(uffraganeos)	The archbishop of Canterbury has these suffragans:
Londonien'	London

---

[2] Goody, *Domestication of the Savage Mind*, 74–111; See, famously, the short (fictional) story by Jorge Luis Borges, 'The Analytical Language of John Wilkins', in *Other Inquisitions, 1937-1952*, trans. Ruth Simms (Austin, 1964), 101–5, and, of course, Michel Foucault, *The Order of Things: An Archaeology of the Human Sciences*, trans. Alan Sheridan (2002 [1970]), xvi–xxvi.

[3] Fabrice Delivré, 'Du nouveau sur la "Liste de Florence": la chronique du Pseudo-Godel (v. 1175) et la préhistoire du *Provinciale Romanum* du xiiie siècle', *Bibliothèque de l'École des chartes*, 167 (2009), 353–74.

[4] For scholarship on the provincial, see Delivré, 'La chrétienté en liste. Genèse et fortunes du provincial de l'Église romaine (xiie–xve siècle)', in *Écritures grises. Les instruments de travail des administrations (xiie-xviie siècle)*, ed. Arnaud Fossier, Johann Petitjean and Clémence Revest (Paris, 2019), 497–529; Florian Mazel, *L'évêque et le territoire. L'invention médiévale de l'espace (v[e]-xiiie siècle)* (Paris, 2016), 359–63; Dominique Iogna-Pratt, 'The Meaning and Usages of Medieval Territory', *Annales HSS (English Edition)*, 72 (2017), 91–100; Benedict Wiedemann, 'The Joy of Lists: The *Provinciale Romanum*, Tribute and *ad limina* Visitation to Rome', *Revue d'histoire ecclésiastique*, 116 (2021), 61–97; Heinrich Börsting, *Das Provinciale Romanum mit besonderer Berücksichtigung seiner handschriftlichen Überlieferung* (Lengerich, 1937); Götz-Rüdiger Tewes, 'Das spätmittelalterliche Papsttum und die Problematik der Raumerfassung', in *Raum und Raumvorstellungen im Mittelalter*, ed. Jan Aertsen and Andreas Speer (Berlin, 1997), 603–12, at 608; Hans-Joachim Schmidt, 'Raumkonzepte und geographische Ordnung kirchlicher Institutionen im 13. Jahrhundert', in *Raumerfassung und Raumbewußtsein im späteren Mittelalter*, ed. Peter Moraw (Stuttgart, 2002), 87–125, at 102–5; idem, *Kirche, Staat, Nation: Raumgliederung der Kirche im mittelalterlichen Europa* (Weimar, 1999), 234–48; Peter Linehan, 'Utrum reges Portugalie coronabantur annon', A politica portuguesa e as suas relacoes exteriores, 2° Congresso historicao de Guimares (3 vols., Guimares, 1997), II, 387–401, reprinted in idem, *The Processes of Politics and the Rule of Law: Studies on the Iberian Kingdoms and Papal Rome in the Middle Ages* (Aldershot, 2002).

[5] This example is taken from Vatican City, Bibliotheca Apostolica Vaticana, Ross 476, f. 52v.

Roffen'	Rochester
Cicestren'	Chichester
Wintonien'	Winchester
Exonien'	Exeter
Wellen' et uniti	Wells and, united,
Bathonien'	Bath
Lincolnien'	Lincoln
Saresbinien'	Salisbury
Wigornien'	Worcester
Hereforden'	Hereford
Conventren'	Coventry
Lichfelden'	Lichfield
Norwicen'	Norwich
Elien'	Ely
Meneven' ...	St David's
Landaven'	Llandaff
Bangoren'	Bangor
De Sancto Asaph'	St Asaph
Archepiscopus Eboracen' h(os) h(abet) *s(uffraganeos)*	The archbishop of York has these suffragans:
Dunelmen'	Durham
Carleocen'	Carlisle
Candidecrise [*sic*]	Galloway

There is a geopolitical heading (*In Anglia* – 'In England') and then divisions by provinces – Canterbury and York. The cities of England and Wales are enumerated in order. The internal logic of the provincial is thus fairly simple: the list is divided by polity and by ecclesiastical province; by both secular and ecclesiastical unit; by both king and archbishop. This logical division, as well as being observable from the manuscripts, is also confirmed by one of our earliest literary references to the provincial. Gerald of Wales, in one of his frequent attempts to get the diocese of St David's recognised as an archdiocese (and as the metropolitan of the other Welsh dioceses, none of which were – according to Gerald – subject to Canterbury), appealed to Pope Innocent III. When Gerald was in Rome, around 1199, Innocent called on his copy of the Roman provincial to check the status of St David's.

Innocent

ordered his register to be brought, where the Cathedral Churches, both
metropolitans and their suffragans, from all the world of the faithful
and every kingdom are enumerated in order. And when he turned to
the kingdom of the English, it was written there in this manner and
read: 'The metropolitan of Canterbury has these suffragan churches:
Rochester, London', and so on in order. But with the suffragan churches
of England all enumerated, [and] with a rubric 'concerning Wales' [De
Wallia] interposed, it continued in this manner: 'In Wales, the Church of
St David's, Llandaff, Bangor and St Asaph'. When this was heard, the
pope suggested, as if taunting and mocking, 'See! The Church of St
David's is numbered with the others'.

Gerald replied: 'But that [Church] and the others of Wales are not numbered in the same manner as the others, that is to say, in the accusative,
as the suffragans of England. If they had been, then they could indeed
have been considered subject'.

To which the pope said 'You saw that well. But there is something else
which similarly works for you and your church, that is to say, the inserted
rubric, which is never added to the register, except where there should be
a transition either from kingdom to kingdom or from metropolitan to
metropolitan'. 'That's true!', said Gerald, 'And Wales is a part of the
Kingdom of England, not a kingdom itself'.[6]

We can see fairly clearly that this register was a provincial. The bishops under
a metropolitan archbishop are subject to that archbishop, and a rubric denotes
either a change in political unit, or a change from archiepiscopal province to
archiepiscopal province.

Although, in the example above, the provincial manuscript merely includes
an abbreviation mark at the end of each diocese (e.g. Londonien'), those manuscripts that do not abbreviate overwhelmingly seem to give place names rather
than groups of people. So, for example, Bamberg, Staatsbibliothek [BS], Msc.
Can. 91 gives Londoniensem – 'London', a city, rather than 'the Londoners'.
The provincial – from the manuscripts I have looked at – envisages bishops
as bishops of dioceses rather than as bishops of groups of people. In this article, I have only expanded the place names where the original manuscript has
done so.

The provincial was divided geopolitically. The overall layout of the provincial is very consistent across the manuscripts. Most (although not all) manuscripts of the provincial begin with a list of all the churches in the city of
Rome which had cardinals, beginning of course with the cardinal-bishops,
and then list the archbishops and bishops of the provinces of Italy, Sicily
and Istria, then the rest of Croatia and the Dalmatian coast; Hungary;
Poland; Germany, Austria and Livonia; Burgundy and Lotharingia; modern-day

---

[6] 'Giraldi Cambrensis De iure et statu Menevensis ecclesiae dialogus', in Giraldi Cambrensis opera,
ed. J. S. Brewer, James F. Dimock and George F. Warner (8 vols., 1861–91), III, 165–6.

France; Spain and Portugal; England; Scandinavia; Scotland and Ireland; Sardinia; and then the dioceses *ultra mare* – beyond the sea, in Jerusalem and the Holy Land.[7]

When one considers that any list betrays the worldview of its compiler, it is easy to see how this layout gave rise to the view that the provincial created,

> in the form of lists and tables, an administrative order establishing con-tinuity with the center via concentric circles, like a "new empire, in which papal authority radiated outward, *urbi et orbi*, over all the provinces and bishoprics of Christendom.[8]

The recent scholarship on the provincial – from, inter alia, Fabrice Delivré and Florian Mazel – has tended to take this view: that the layout of the provincial makes it a conceptual tool of papal monarchy, whereby Rome is at the centre of the world and Christendom – under the authority of the pope – radiates out to the periphery. Delivré, the scholar who has focused most on the provincial itself and its manuscripts in recent years, has significantly advanced our understanding of the genesis and use of the text.[9] Delivré's work on the genesis of and precursors to the provincial, and his overview of the fortunes of the provincial are excellent, in terms of identifying manuscripts and proving that the provincial was first compiled around the year 1200. Florian Mazel, on the other hand, was less interested in the provincial per se, and more focused on whether and how it contributed to his arguments as to how the medieval Church pioneered the creation of 'space' (identifying social identities or political authority with particular territory). For Mazel, the provincial represented the theocratic papacy's new territorial understanding of Christendom; the imperial papacy saw itself at the head of the Church and the World: 'not only ... a mental image of the *orbis christianorum* ruled by Rome, but also ... a true instrument of government at the service of the pope and the Curia, as evidenced by its [the provincial's] copying into a series of administrative tools with diplomatic or fiscal purposes'.[10] The provincial is, for Mazel, a conceptual and practical tool of papal monarchy, part of the mus-cular, activist, post-Gregorian papacy's desire to govern the world from Rome.

There is value to that view – the view that the purpose of the provincial was to make Christendom 'legible' to the pope; a sort of James Scott *avant le lettre*.[11] Certainly, I am willing to believe that such could have been the intention of the original compiler of the provincial at the papal court, in the years before 1200.

---

[7] On this 'itinerary', see Valérie Theis, 'Se représenter l'espace sans carte: Pratiques d'écriture de la Chambre apostolique au xive siècle', in *Entre idéel et matériel: Espace, territoire et légitimation du pou-voir (v. 1200–v. 1640)*, ed. Patrick Boucheron, Marco Folin and Jean-Philippe Genet (Paris, 2018), 329–64.

[8] Iogna-Pratt, 'Medieval Territory', 97, quoting Delivré. See also, for example, Jean-Philippe Genet, 'Introduction', in *Entre idéel et matériel*, ed. Boucheron *et al.*, 11–27.

[9] Delivré, 'Du nouveau sur la "Liste de Florence"', 353–74; *idem*, 'La chrétienté en liste', 497–529.

[10] Mazel, *L'évêque et le territoire*, 360–3.

[11] James Scott, *Seeing Like a State: How Certain Schemes to Improve the Human Condition Have Failed* (New Haven, 1998).

Let us say, however, that the intent of the provincial was indeed to lay out all the bishops and cities of Christendom and to emphasise Roman centrality and papal supremacy, to make the world legible to the City. Even if that is the case, papal control of that image vanished as soon as the first copy of the provincial left the Curia. Copyists outside the Roman court – and most manuscripts of the provincial must have been copied outside the immediate papal sphere – could change and alter the picture presented by the provincial to fit their own views of what the world should look like.

Manuscripts of the provincial are found everywhere: royal courts, episcopal and archiepiscopal administrations, lawyers' handbooks, works of theology, in monasteries, and in chronicles. Most of these copyists were not papal scribes. As soon as the first visitor to the papal court copied the first provincial, and carried it outside Rome, and had it copied again, the papal court lost control of the spread of the provincial. And, as well as losing control of the spread of the provincial, the Curia lost control of what the provincial said. When a scribe in England or France made a copy of the Roman provincial, they had the ability to alter the political and ecclesiastical geography of Europe to bring it into line with what they thought it ought to be.

The provincial is arguably interesting as a tool of papal power, but *the many different manuscripts of the provincial* are also interesting because they tell us about 'contested cartographies': battles over borders, and differing ideas about what precisely is inside a particular political or ecclesiastical unit. A provincial copied in one place can have a very different idea of what Europe looks like compared to a contemporary provincial copied somewhere else.

This methodology – of 'Cartographic Struggle' rather than 'seeing like a state' (to put it crudely) – is fairly easy to understand: lists, like maps are not objective statements of the world but political claims, ways of acting upon and changing the world, at least partially constitutive of political realities.[12] An article in the *Washington Post* in 2020 drew attention – apparently with surprise – to Google Maps' policy of, for example, altering the borders of Kashmir depending on whether one accesses Google Maps from within India or not.[13] The scholarship on cartographic struggle over the last thirty or so years has offered fascinating insights into how modern societies use maps as weapons; we would be foolish to assume that pre-modern societies did not do the same with both lists and maps.[14] Mapping and 'counter-mapping' – the 'appropriation of the cartographic discourse of a dominant power to oppose and challenge its views on territories' – are present within

---

[12] Fundamental is the work of John B. Hartley: see 'Deconstructing the Map', *Cartographica*, 26 (1989), 1–20; and 'Maps, Knowledge, and Power', reprinted in Hartley, *The New Nature of Maps: Essays in the History of Cartography*, ed. Paul Laxton (2001), 51–81.

[13] Greg Bensinger, 'Google Redraws the Borders on Maps Depending on Who's Looking', *Washington Post*, 14 Feb. 2020: https://www.washingtonpost.com/technology/2020/02/14/google-maps-political-borders/ (accessed 22 Aug. 2022).

[14] Reuben S. Rose-Redwood, 'Governmentality, Geography, and the Geo-coded World', *Progress in Human Geography*, 30 (2006), 469–86, at 479; Nick Blomley and Jeff Summers, 'Mapping Urban Space: Governmentality and Cartographic Struggles in Inner City Vancouver', in *Governable Places: Readings on Governmentality and Crime Control*, ed. Russell Smandych (Aldershot, 1999), 261–86.

the provincial manuscripts.[15] This dynamic – conflicts over what the world is supposed to look like, played out through different manuscripts of the Roman provincial – is to me a much more profitable way of approaching the provincial than purely as a tool of papal authority.

This approach also frees us from aiming to construct stemmatic diagrams, or to reconstruct the 'original' ur-Text of the provincial.[16] While it is useful still to identify provincial manuscripts which seem to share a common exemplar, a full stemmatic diagram is probably impossible; I intend to move forward by studying different manuscripts and attempting to explain their differing worldviews.

It should be admitted that the two viewpoints – cartographical struggle and seeing like a state – are not necessarily opposed. If one accepts that different copyists could change the picture of the world presented in the provincial to bring it into line with the world as they thought it ought to be, then logically the copyists at the papal Curia could do exactly that, and use the text to curate an image of the centrality of papal monarchy.[17] Some provincials, *Roman* provincials in the geographical rather than nominative sense, must indeed present the papacy as the centre of world and 'papal authority radiat[ing] outward, *urbi et orbi*, over all the provinces and bishoprics of Christendom'.

What, however, does taking a more localist view – believing that local copyists could simply change what the provincial said – do to our view of the supposedly monolithic 'papal monarchy'? Really all it does is bring it into line with how most scholars of the papacy see the period formerly known as the 'papal monarchy'. The pope was not, and never could be, an absolute ruler. Papal letters and documents were issued at the initiative of petitioners. As soon as a papal missive left Rome, its realisation was left up to those in the provinces. Papal instructions could be ignored, or enforced in selective ways, as local agents wished.[18] The pope could do nothing to prevent it. As with the papal monarchy in general, so with the provincial: local agency matters most.

The sources

I do not know how many manuscripts of the provincial are still extant: certainly more than a hundred, probably hundreds. The earliest manuscripts survive from the early thirteenth century – soon after the list was first compiled – and the latest from the late fifteenth century. Without a full catalogue of all the surviving manuscripts – a vast task, manageable only by a well-funded team working for years – I can only speak about those I have seen,

---

[15] Daniel Foliard and Nader Nasiri-Moghaddam, 'Contested Cartographies: Empire and Sovereignty on a Map of Sistān, Iran (1883)', *Imago Mundi*, 72 (2020), 14–31.

[16] The title of this paper is self-consciously taken from Martin Brett's classic article 'Creeping up on the *Panormia*'; many of the points he made about the manuscripts of the *Panormia* (an important canon law compilation of the late eleventh or early twelfth century) are equally true for the provincial, if not more so. Martin Brett, 'Creeping up on the *Panormia*', in *Grundlagen des Rechts. Festschrift für Peter Landau zum 65. Geburtstag*, ed. Richard Helmholz *et al.* (Paderborn, 2000), 205–70.

[17] I owe this point to one of the anonymous reviewers.

[18] Benedict Wiedemann, *Papal Overlordship and European Princes, 1000–1270* (Oxford, 2022), 1–20, 167.

around fifty or so manuscripts. Fifty seems to me to be a significantly large sample from which to draw some conclusions about the provincial, as I have done in this article.

Large numbers of provincials survive in the Bibliothèque nationale de France [BnF], the British Library [BL] and the Bibliotheca Apostolica Vaticana [BAV]. Smaller numbers exist in various other archives, such as the Staatsbibliothek in Munich. Then there are numerous archives with one copy of the provincial: St John's College, Cambridge, for example. The provincial was certainly copied as far northwest as Scotland, and probably as far east as Poland.[19] The nature of medieval manuscript survival means that, unsurprisingly, more fifteenth-century provincials seem to survive than fourteenth-century provincials, and likewise for fourteenth- and thirteenth-century provincials, although this is only my impression.

In general, provincials appear in manuscripts bound up with other texts. Provincials are not infrequently found in manuscripts of Martin of Troppau's Chronicle of the Popes and Emperors, presumably because both aspired to some sort of universal scope.[20] Worcester, Cathedral Library, F 38 contains a provincial as well as texts on pastoral care (e.g. the *Speculum iuniorum*) and Buonaguida of Arezzo's *Summa* on dispensations and privileges. Hereford, Cathedral Library, P.VII.3 copies a provincial into a manuscript which also contains glosses and commentary on Gratian. The register of Andrea Sapiti, a fourteenth-century proctor at the papal Curia, contains a provincial.[21] Formularies of the various departments of the papal Curia often contained a provincial, especially the chancery, the chamber and the penitentiary.[22] Occasionally, however, one finds a provincial in a stand-alone *libellus*, such as Cambridge, St John's College, G.9.

As well as appearing as a text in itself, medieval writers used and mentioned the provincial in other works, as we have already seen with Gerald of Wales. Gervase of Tilbury mined it for geographical information for his *Otia Imperialia* (s.xiii[in]).[23] Alexander Minorita found it a helpful resource when he wrote his commentary on the Apocalypse (c. 1235–40s).[24] Jean de Saint-Victor used his house's provincial manuscripts when compiling the

---

[19] See Cambridge, Corpus Christi College [CCCC], 171A (c. 1440s) and Wrocław, Wrocław University Library [WUL], R 262 (s.xv[1]).

[20] Wolfgang-Valentin Ikas, *Fortsetzungen zur Papst- und Kaiserchronik Martins von Troppau aus England*, 2nd edn (Hannover, 2004), 87–8 n. 17.

[21] *Il registro di Andrea Sapiti, procuratore alla curia avignonese*, ed. Barbara Bombi (Rome, 2007), no. 32, pp. 151–87.

[22] Chancery: Michael Tangl, *Die päpstlichen Kanzleiordnungen von 1200-1500* (Innsbruck, 1894), 3–32; *Der Liber Cancellariae Apostolicae vom Jahre 1380*, ed. Georg Erler (Leipzig, 1888), 16–43; Penitentiary: e.g. BAV, Ott. Lat. 333; Chamber: Emil Göller, 'Der *Liber Taxarum* der päpstlichen Kammer', *Quellen und Forschungen aus italienischen Archiven und Bibliotheken*, 8 (1905), 113–73, 305–343, at 152–6.

[23] Gervase of Tilbury, *Otia Imperialia: Recreation for an Emperor*, ed. S. E. Banks and J. W. Binns (Oxford, 2002), xlvi, 216–25, 272–85, 298–305, 312–15, 346–7.

[24] Alexander Minorita, *Expositio in Apocalypsim*, ed. Alois Wachtel (Weimar, 1955), 53, 156, 445.

Memoriale historiarum (s.xiv[1]).[25] In 1417, at the council of Constance, the English and French delegations argued over the voting rights of the English, whether England was a true 'nation'. Both sides drew on the provincial to buttress their case.[26] At the very end of the Middle Ages, Mercator used it for his *Atlas*.[27] These uses of the provincial – in many different texts, for many different purposes – all potentially demonstrate both the ubiquity and authoritativeness of the provincial. These writers all had access to a text (or multiple texts) of the provincial, and they all thought it was sufficiently 'right' to be mined for information to support their arguments.

Interestingly, Latin was not the only language of the provincial: Munich, Bayerische Staatsbibliothek Cgm 1112 (dating from *c.* 1475) is in German; and BL, Egerton 1500 (*c.* 1321–4) contains a Provençal or Occitan version of the provincial. Based on an analysis of the other texts in the Egerton codex, Catherine Léglu and Alexander Ibarz have plausibly suggested that Egerton 1500 was produced for 'an Occitan-speaking court with anti-English, pro-French interests, that was linked by marriage to the family of Robert of Naples'.[28] This provincial then was copied for a lay audience, not for churchmen. On Léglu's point of having anti-English interests, it is worth noting that the Occitan translation of the list of kings who have the privilege of being crowned and anointed (a list very often found in the provincial) misses out the king of England completely; normally the English king is one of the four kings who can be crowned and anointed, along with Sicily, France and Jerusalem.[29] Perhaps this was an intentional change to downgrade English royalty.

---

[25] BnF, Latin 15010, f. 43r; Isabelle Guyot-Bachy, *Le* Memoriale historiarum *de Jean de Saint-Victor. Un historien et sa communauté au début du XIVe siècle* (Turnhout, 2000), 365–7.

[26] *Magnum Oecumenicum Constantiense Concilium de universali ecclesiae reformatione, unione et fide*, ed. Hermann von der Hardt (6 vols., Frankfurt/Leipzig, 1696–1700), v, 57–103; *The Council of Constance: The Unification of the Church*, trans. Louise Loomis, ed. John H. Mundy and Kennerly Woody (New York, 1961), 315–24, 329, 335–49; *Unity, Heresy and Reform, 1378-1460: The Conciliar Response to the Great Schism*, ed. and trans. Christopher Crowder (1977), 109–26. The scholarship on this is considerable: see Andrea Ruddick, 'The English "Nation" and the Plantagenet "Empire" at the Council of Constance', in *The Plantagenet Empire, 1259-1453*, ed. Peter Crooks, David Green and W. Mark Ormrod (Donington, 2016), 109–27; Jean-Philippe Genet, 'English Nationalism: Thomas Polton at the Council of Constance', *Nottingham Medieval Studies*, 28 (1984), 60–78; Robert Swanson, '*Gens secundum cognationem et collectionem ab alia distincta?* Thomas Polton, Two Englands, and the Challenge of Medieval Nationhood', in *Das Konstanzer Konzil als europäisches Ereignis: Begegnungen, Medien und Rituale*, ed. Gabriela Signori and Birgit Studt (Ostfildern, 2014), 57–87; Louise Loomis, 'Nationality at the Council of Constance: An Anglo-French Dispute', *American Historical Review*, 44 (1939), 508–27.

[27] Gerardi Mercatoris, *Atlas etc*, ed. Jodocus Hondius (Amsterdam, 1607), 287, 399; Marina Rajaković, Ivka Kljajić and Miljenko Lapaine, 'Map Projection Reconstruction of a Map by Mercator', in *Cartography from Pole to Pole: Selected Contributions to the XXVIth International Conference of the ICA, Dresden 2013*, ed. Manfred Buchroithner, Nikolas Prechtel and Dirk Burghardt (Berlin, 2014), 31–44, at 35.

[28] Catherine Léglu, 'A Genealogy of the Kings of England in Papal Avignon: British Library, Egerton MS. 1500', *eBritish Library Journal* 2013, article 18, at p. 20; Alexander Ibarz, 'The Provenance of the *Abreujamens de las estorias* (London, British Library, Egerton MS. 1500) and the Identification of Scribal Hands (c. 1323)', *eBritish Library Journal* 2013, article 12.

[29] BL, Egerton 1500, f. 67v.

The diversity of contexts for surviving provincial manuscripts makes it hard to generalise about who copied them and for whom. Secular rulers definitely kept copies, most obviously the thirteenth-century Capetian kings of France, as I will show later in this article, and the court affiliated to Robert of Naples which produced Egerton 1500. The different organs of the papal Curia kept many copies, that is clear, and those copyists must have been papal scribes and notaries (or, in some cases, freelancers working at the Curia). Many – perhaps most, at least most surviving – copies probably come from ecclesiastical institutions: abbeys, monasteries and episcopal chanceries, copied with chronicles, formularies or other texts. Whether that is because medieval ecclesiastical archives in general tend to have a better survival rate than secular archives is uncertain.

Does the creation of the provincial around the year 1200 attest to a new desire to list the world at that time? Certainly, it does seem that listing was a particular interest: the proliferation of estate surveys from the twelfth and thirteenth centuries attests to that. Tom Bisson's argument in *The Crisis of the Twelfth Century* that there was a growth in accountancy and accountability from the later twelfth century has a corollary that running accounts must have been kept to enable 'true' accounting.[30] Bisson's argument, however, does not really apply to the provincial. The provincial is not a new tool, but an improvement on existing lists; the provincial text composed around the year 1200 is not the first attempt to list all the bishops in Christendom. Fabrice Delivré has explored the immediate precursor to the Roman provincial, the 'Florence List'. The Florence List, in turn, made use of the *Notitia Galliarum* (composed around 400) as well as other texts.[31] Thus the provincial is not a new paradigm but essentially an improved version of similar lists which had already been being compiled for centuries. Rather than being part of sudden desire to list the world, the provincial exists as the latest in a long series of attempts to codify the bishops and cities of Christendom. Florian Mazel would, I think, point out that the creation of a new list at this time – even if not fundamentally different in conception from existing lists of bishops and cities – is itself worthy of comment, attesting to a desire or need at this time for the papacy to 'create' space; the provincial is, for Mazel, part of the territorialisation and imperialisation of the medieval Church and papacy which occurred following the Investiture Contest.[32]

Battles in the manuscripts

If, as I argued above, cartographical struggle rather than 'seeing like a state' is the more profitable approach, then the next question is: can we actually see and explain any cartographic struggles in our provincial manuscripts? Without wanting to multiply examples to the point of tedium, I will spend

---

[30] Thomas N. Bisson, *The Crisis of the Twelfth Century: Power, Lordship, and the Origins of European Government* (Princeton, 2009); Benedict Wiedemann, 'The Character of Papal Finance at the Turn of the Twelfth Century', *English Historical Review*, 133 (2018), 503–32.

[31] Delivré, 'Du nouveau sur la "Liste de Florence"', 353–74.

[32] Mazel, *L'évêque et le territoire*, 360–3.

most of the rest of this article going through some case studies where I think one can see precisely such struggles and differences.[33] First we will look at how France is portrayed in thirteenth-century provincials; then we will turn to Scotland across the entire later Middle Ages; then the development of how Iberia and Brittany were described; and finally the view of Christendom offered by an Eastern provincial, from Wrocław. These sections, though on the face of it unconnected, illustrate the different ways in which the world in the provincial could change: the rubrics and layout could be intentionally changed, with the aim of advancing political claims. The provincial could be accidentally changed, to bring a real but surprising aberration into line with perceived normalcy. Over time, the descriptions of parts of the world might become more developed and detailed. And finally (albeit perhaps obviously), provincials written in one part of the world might display considerable interest and knowledge about their locality, but utter ignorance about a place far away about which the copyist knew nothing. That trend probably even afflicted the papal Curia itself – we err in assuming that the pope really knew chapter and verse about his most distant dioceses.

Francia in the thirteenth century: royal politics

Several of our earliest provincials survive in the milieu of the Capetian royal court. In the registers of Philip II Augustus (r.1190–1223) there is a provincial, probably copied around 1220. The editors of Philip's registers believed that the provincial in BnF Latin 6191 (also copied in 1220) was copied from a similar exemplar to the version in Philip's registers.[34] The provincial in BnF Latin 6191 bears a number of similarities to a provincial copied into BL Additional MS. 34254. The most obvious similarity is that, halfway through the provincial proper (the list of all the dioceses in Christendom), BnF Latin 6191 includes a list of which English dioceses are contiguous with each other. BL Additional 34254 also includes this list after the provincial. So, for example: *Notandum est quod Cantuariensis diocesis conterminatur Roffen', Cicestren', Lindonien'* (sic) – 'Note that the diocese of Canterbury borders Rochester, Chichester and London'. The order of dioceses is the same in both BnF Latin 6191 and BL Additional 34254: Canterbury; Rochester; London; Chichester; Winchester; Bath; Exeter; Salisbury; Worcester; Hereford; Chester; York; Durham; Carlisle; Norwich; Ely – BnF Latin 6191 misses out Worcester and Durham, however. This list is pretty uncommon – the only other provincial manuscript I have seen which includes it is BnF Latin 4910, a fourteenth-century manuscript which I suspect is copied from the same exemplar as BnF Latin 6191.[35] Consequently, I suspect that BnF Latin 6191, BL Additional 34254 and the

---

[33] The nature of this article is such that I do not intend to provide exhaustive references for every case study, since doing so would constitute a comprehensive bibliography to thirteenth-, fourteenth- and fifteenth-century European ecclesiastical and secular politics.

[34] *Les registres de Philippe Auguste*, ed. John W. Baldwin *et al.* (Paris, 1992), 355–6.

[35] Wiedemann, 'Joy of Lists', 84–5. It is also found in Bartholomew Cotton's *Historia Anglicana*: *Bartholomaei de Cotton, Monachi Norwicensis, Historia Anglicana (AD 449–1298), necnon eiusdem Liber de Archiepiscopis et Episcopis Angliae*, ed. Henry Luard (1859), 417–18.

provincial in Philip's registers all share a fairly close common exemplar (as probably does the later BnF Latin 4910).

They are also close to each other in time. BnF Latin 6191 and the provincial in Philip's register date from 1220. The provincial in BL Additional 34254 was probably copied in c. 1221–2. The same hand that copied the provincial has also made a list of all the previous bishops of every English see by name. Although later hands have updated the list, the original hand appears to name the bishops down to 1221–2 (Eustace de Fauconberg, r.1221–8, is listed as the current bishop of London, and Ranulf of Warham, r.1217–22, as current bishop of Chichester), hence a date of around 1221–2 seems likely.[36] The interest, in this manuscript, in English ecclesiastical affairs (listing the past bishops of English dioceses) suggests that this manuscript was copied in England by an English scribe, although I would not care to be any more specific than that.[37]

So, we have here three provincials, probably sharing a fairly close common exemplar, copied fairly close in time, but two originating from the Capetian court and one from England. The closeness of timing and transmission makes the difference between them – or between their conceptions of European geopolitics – all the more jarring.

In BnF Latin 6191, copied for the Capetian chancery, there is a heading *In Francia* – 'In France' – and then are listed continuously the archiepiscopal cities of Lyons, Sens, Reims, Rouen, Tours, Bourges and Bordeaux, and all the cities of the suffragan bishops of those archdioceses. Auch and Narbonne are listed separately – under the heading 'In Gascony' – but otherwise Francia in this manuscript looks fairly similar to *l'hexagon*, modern-day France. The provincial in Philip Augustus's registers takes an even more expansive view of Francia.[38] Under the heading *In Francia* comes every archdiocese from Lyons to Narbonne (and hence all of their suffragan cities and bishops). BL Additional 34254 does not quite share this interpretation. To the copyist of BL Additional 34254 – probably based in England – only Lyons, Sens and Reims (and their suffragan cities) were *In Francia*. Rouen and Tours (and their suffragans) were 'In Normandy'; Bordeaux, Bourges and Auch were 'In Aquitaine', and Narbonne was *In Gothia* – the lands in the south also known as Septimania or Languedoc.

BL ADDITIONAL 34254	BNF LATIN 6191	PHILIP AUGUSTUS'S REGISTER
In France (*In Francia*)	In France (*In Francia*)	In France (*In Francia*)
Lyons	Lyons	Lyons

---

[36] Wiedemann, 'Joy of Lists', 90–1.

[37] Although note that it was acquired by the BL from a German antiquarian in 1892: Nicholas Vincent, *Peter des Roches: An Alien in English Politics, 1205-1238* (Cambridge, 1996), 98 n. 50.

[38] On Francia vs. *Rex Francorum*, see John Baldwin, *The Government of Philip Augustus: Foundations of French Royal Power in the Middle Ages* (Berkeley, 1986), 360–1. There seems little doubt that Francia designated the broader French kingdom to Philip and his courtiers.

Sens	Sens	Sens
Reims	Reims	Reims
In Normandy (*In Normannia*)		
Rouen	Rouen	Rouen
Tours	Tours	Tours
In Aquitaine (*In Aquitania*)		
Bourges	Bourges	Bourges
Bordeaux	Bordeaux	Bordeaux
In Gascony (*In Wasconia*)		
Auch	Auch	Auch
In Languedoc (*In Gothia*)		
Narbonne	Narbonne	Narbonne

There may be any number of reasons why such variation in rubrics occurred. A fairly obvious one springs to mind, however. Prior to 1202–5, the king of England had also been duke of Normandy, duke of Aquitaine and count of Touraine and Poitou. Philip Augustus of France, however, seized Normandy, Touraine, and Anjou and Poitou north of the Loire, and both Philip and his successor Louis VIII (r.1223–6) had designs on Aquitaine. The king of England would be reduced to a rump duchy of Gascony.[39]

Around 1220, therefore, the Capetian court preferred to obliterate the existence of Normandy as a separate political unit, and Aquitaine was likewise either to be erased or reduced down merely to 'Gascony'. Those territories which had been under the authority of the English kings and their sons – broadly corresponding to the ecclesiastical provinces of Rouen (Normandy), Tours (Touraine and Brittany) and Bordeaux (Aquitaine/Gascony), most obviously – were now merely part of Francia. The copyist of our English provincial, however, preferred an older view, where Normandy and greater Aquitaine were still distinct from Francia; perhaps one day to be reclaimed.

And it is not simply a case of the Capetian provincials reflecting reality and the English provincial looking back to a lost past. The Capetian provincials put the Poitevan bishoprics – Poitiers, Saintes, Angoulême, Périgueux (all suffragans of Bordeaux) – unequivocally in Francia, whereas in BL Additional 34254 they were 'In Aquitaine' – the king of England's duchy. A few years after these provincials were written, in 1224, Louis VIII made war on Poitou, capturing La Rochelle and receiving the allegiance of most of the county.[40] Louis realised the claim made in the Capetian provincials in 1220: that

---

[39] David Carpenter, *The Minority of Henry III* (1990), 374–5; idem, *Magna Carta* (2015), 199–203; Baldwin, *The Government of Philip Augustus*, 191–6.

[40] Carpenter, *Minority*, 343–75; Maurice Powicke, *King Henry III and the Lord Edward: The Community of the Realm in the Thirteenth Century* (2 vols., Oxford, 1947), I, 171–6.

Poitou was part of Francia, not Aquitaine; part of his domain, not the king of England's.

The political conflicts of the early thirteenth century were played out through diplomacy and on the battlefield, but also through the Roman provincial. Did Normandy and Aquitaine still 'exist' or was Francia the prime political unit of Western Europe? Of what precisely 'France' – Francia – consisted varied, depending on which provincial one looked at.

At this stage, we might ask whether the headings in the provincial manuscripts actually mattered to the kings of France and England. Fortunately, Florian Mazel has found evidence that they did, at least later in the thirteenth century.[41] In 1297, the King of France, Philip IV (r.1285–1314), was seeking to incorporate the city of Lyons within his sphere of influence. To do this, he had to find justifications and proofs that the city had always been under the authority of the French king. One of his scribes hit upon the evidence of the Roman provincial. Around August 1297 the French administration sent a list of proofs that Lyons was part of the kingdom of France to Pope Boniface VIII. One item stated:

> It is found in the register of the Roman Court – a transcript of which is said to be among the registers of the French court – that the archdiocese of Lyons is in the kingdom of France, and is enumerated among the archdioceses of the kingdom of France.[42]

Since the Roman provincial said that the archbishop of Lyons was in France, then the whole city of Lyons must be too. Philip IV appealed to the authority of the Roman provincial when seeking to expand the royal reach. The rubrics of the provincial mattered, and could be interpreted as reflecting geopolitical and regnal divisions, as well as ecclesiastical ones.

The Scottish Church in the provincial: Church politics

BL Additional 34254, BnF Latin 6191 and the provincial in Philip Augustus's registers are remarkable for another reason: their presentation of the Scottish Church, which all of them get 'wrong', at least as far as historians of medieval Scotland would probably judge. Those familiar with the Scottish Church will know that, between c. 1192 and 1472, most of the Scottish dioceses were anomalous within the universal Church: St Andrews, Glasgow, Caithness, Dunkeld, Dunblane, Brechin, Aberdeen, Moray, Ross and possibly Argyll and Whithorn

---

[41] Mazel, L'évêque et le territoire, 371.

[42] Acta imperii Angliae et Franciae, 1267–1313, ed. Fritz Kern (Tubingen, 1911), no. 274, pp. 201–6; see also ibid., no. 270, pp. 198–9. While this claim was accurate for the provincials kept by the Capetian court (e.g. Les registres de Philippe Auguste, ed. Baldwin et al., 367; BnF Latin 6191; BnF Latin 4910), it was not universally true: BL, Cotton, Galba, E IV (s.xiv^{in}) put Lyons 'In Burgundy' rather than In Francia (f. 153v); and Innocent III also implicitly assumed Lyons was outside the French realm when he told Philip II that 'even if he [Peter of Capua, the papal legate] had departed beyond the bounds of the kingdom of the French (fines regni Francorum), he had not left the boundaries of his legation, because not only in the kingdom of the French, but even in the provinces of Vienne, Lyons and Besançon, he had received the solicitude of legation enjoined on him by us', X. 1. 30. 7., Corpus Iuris Canonici, ed. Emil Friedberg (2 vols., Leipzig, 1879), II, 185.

too (de facto) were exempt dioceses. They did not owe obedience to any superior other than the pope. This unusual ecclesiastical exemption was granted to them by the pope at the end of the twelfth century in a privilege, *Cum universi*. By this they were freed from the archbishop of York, who claimed jurisdiction over the Scottish dioceses.[43] In 1472 St Andrews was raised to the rank of archdiocese, followed closely by Glasgow, and the structure of the Scottish Church fell into line with that elsewhere in Christendom: bishop – metropolitan archbishop – pope.[44]

Some early provincials get this right. BS, Msc. Can. 91, for example, lists the eleven Scottish dioceses, and next to each one writes *qui est domini pape* – 'this belongs to the lord pope', that is to say, these dioceses were exempt. The Capetian provincials take a different tack, however. Both claim that Argyll is exempt, but none of the other Scottish dioceses. Instead, St Andrews is raised to the rank of an archdiocese and the other Scottish bishops are listed as suffragans of St Andrews. This might be the moment to reiterate that these provincials were copied in *c.* 1220, some 252 years before St Andrews was actually made an archbishopric. It is possible that this was a knowing and intentional change by a copyist who was supportive of St Andrews' claims to be an archdiocese, but it is equally likely that our copyist (unaware of the complexities of the Scottish situation) was simply tidying up, bringing Scotland into line with what they knew the ecclesiastical hierarchy *ought* to look like.

BL Additional 34254 is more subtle. If we turn back to the geographical order of the provincial (which I gave in the introduction), we see that almost every provincial manuscript lists England, then Scandinavia (Denmark – Norway – Sweden), then Scotland. BL Additional 34254 has – uniquely – moved Scotland to immediately after England. Thus BL Additional 34254 reads:

Archiepiscopus Eboracensis hos habet	The archbishop of York has these
Dunelmensem	Durham
Carleocensem	Carlisle
In Scotia	In Scotland
Episcopatus Sancti Andree	The diocese of St Andrews
Glascuensis	Glasgow
Candide Case	Galloway
Dulcheldensis	Dunkeld
Dunblanensis	Dunblane
Brechinensis	Brechin

[43] Dauvit Broun, *Scottish Independence and the Idea of Britain: From the Picts to Alexander III* (Edinburgh, 2007), 124–46; Andrew D. M. Barrell, 'Scotland and the Papacy in the Reign of Alexander II', in *The Reign of Alexander II, 1214–49*, ed. Richard Oram (Leiden, 2005), 157–77, at 172–4.

[44] Leslie MacFarlane, 'The Primacy of the Scottish Church, 1472–1521', *Innes Review*, 20 (1969), 111–29, at 111.

Aberdonensis	Aberdeen
Murensis	Moray
Rosmarchinensis	Ross
Catanensis	Caithness
Aregaithel qui est domini pape	Argyll, which belongs to the lord pope

As with the Capetian provincials, BL Additional 34254 claims that only Argyll is exempt. Unlike the Capetian provincials, however, BL Additional 34254 does not make St Andrews an archdiocese. The logical conclusion to draw, if one follows the internal organisation of the provincial, is that Argyll is exempt but all the other Scottish dioceses are subject to the most recent preceding archbishop, since the heading for that archdiocese would read: 'The archbishop of X has these suffragans' and the Scottish bishops would follow underneath. Normally, that would mean the Scottish bishops were subject to the archbishop of Uppsala in Sweden, since in most provincial manuscripts Scotland immediately follows Sweden. But, because the copyist of BL Additional 34254 has moved the Scottish bishops to come immediately after England, this has the effect of making all the Scottish bishops (bar Argyll) suffragan to York. The list, as given above, seems unequivocal: 'the archbishop of York has these', then Durham and Carlisle; then the heading 'In Scotland' to show we are moving into a different political unit, a different kingdom; then the ten Scottish bishops, all implicitly dependent on York. The copyist of BL Additional 34254 has undone the terms of *Cum universi* and made the Scottish Church once more subject to York. They have not, however, claimed that Scotland is subject to England: the heading *In Scotia* makes it clear that it is a separate political unit, but not a separate ecclesiastical unit.

Admittedly, in the light of Gerald of Wales's testimony above, we should note that the English suffragan dioceses of York are given in the accusative and the Scottish dioceses in the nominative – might this have given a clever advocate of Scottish ecclesiastical independence a line of argument for their position? Potentially yes: grammatically the Scottish dioceses do not agree with the *hos ... [suffrageneos]* subject to York. They might not be covered. Perhaps the copyist neglected to change the Scottish dioceses from the nominative to the accusative when they moved the Scottish bishops (which was rather careless). Nonetheless, I do think that here, in BL Additional 34254, there has been an attempt to rewrite the ecclesiastical history of Scotland and make York (doubtless rightfully, in our copyist's eyes) into the metropolitan archbishop of Scotland.

By the fifteenth century at the latest, Scottish copyists of the provincial were happy to play the English at this game. Cambridge, Corpus Christi College [CCCC], 171A is the first volume of the manuscript of Walter Bower's *Scotichronicon*, written in Inchcolm in the 1440s.[45] As well as the *Scotichronicon* – the chronicle of the Scots – CCCC 171A contains a provincial. Originally, this

---

[45] Walter Bower, *Scotichronicon*, gen. ed. D. E. R. Watt (9 vols., Edinburgh and Aberdeen, 1987–98), VIII: *Books XV and XVI*, ix–x.

provincial, like most provincials, listed the Scottish dioceses as exempt. However, a later hand has noted the 1472 elevation of St Andrews to an archdiocese and included the dioceses of the Orkneys and the Isles as 'In Scotland' and under St Andrews. Even more interesting, however, is a comment in the original hand regarding the English dioceses.

Archiepiscopus Eboracen' hos habet suffraganeos:	The archbishop of York has these suffragans:
Dunelmen'	Durham
Carleonen' vel Cardoneten'	Carlisle
qui debet esse suffraganeus episcopo Glasguen'	who ought to be subject to the bishop of Glasgow

The copyist here decided to assert that either the territory of the bishop of Carlisle, or the bishop of Carlisle himself, ought to be subject to Glasgow. This was a claim in keeping with the rest of the *Scotichronicon*. Book XI of the *Scotichronicon*, in its account of the pleading of Scottish proctors before Pope Boniface VIII in 1301 that Scotland was not subject to England, noted that:

when King David of Scotland [David I, r.1124–53] died at Carlisle in peaceful possession of the counties of Cumbria, Northumbria and Westmorland ... King Henry of England [Henry II, r.1154–89] violently invaded and occupied the said counties ... and on his own authority, as it seems, erected a cathedral church at Carlisle, a place which previously had been of the diocese of Glasgow ...[46]

The claims of Glasgow over Carlisle had a history older than the *Scotichronicon*. The chronicle of Lanercost in its entry for 1258, recounted the attempts of John de Cheam, Bishop of Glasgow, to expand Glasgow's authority over Carlisle in the 1260s. The parts of the Lanercost Chronicle up to 1297 are believed to be based on a now lost Franciscan chronicle (subsequently added to by a canon of Lanercost).[47]

John de Cheam succeeded Bishop William of Bondington in the Church of Glasgow, having been collated by the pope and consecrated in the curia; [he was] born in southern England, but greatly hostile to England, for in his last days, with increasing cupidity, he was claiming an ancient right in Westmorland, in prejudice to the church of Carlisle, saying that up to the Rere Cross in Stainmore pertained to his diocese ...[48]

---

[46] Bower, *Scotichronicon*, vi: *Books XI and XII*, ed. Norman F. Shead *et al.*, 154–5.
[47] A. G. Little, 'The Authorship of the Lanercost Chronicle', *English Historical Review*, 31 (1916), 269–79, at 272–4.
[48] *Chronicon de Lanercost MCCI–MCCCXLVI*, ed. Joseph Stevenson (Edinburgh, 1839), 65.

The Rere Cross, or Rey Cross, is a stone cross between Barnard Castle and Penrith, close to the borders between Cumbria, North Yorkshire and County Durham. If Glasgow's episcopal authority stretched to the Rey Cross, then a huge swathe of northwest England would fall under the ecclesiastical jurisdiction of the bishop of Glasgow. Probably not coincidentally, this area, Cumbria and Westmorland, was an occasional claim of the kings of Scotland. David I had ruled Cumbria, and even exercised authority over a 'a greater Scoto-Northumbrian realm extending to the Ribble and the Tyne', although Henry II then regained control of northern England in the second half of the twelfth century.[49] Alexander II (r.1214–49) seems to have sought rule of the same counties when he joined the baronial revolt against King John in 1215–17. The twenty-five barons of the Magna Carta security clause recognised Alexander's claims to the northern counties, and Alexander was apparently invested with Northumberland. Practically, Alexander exercised considerable power in the north, especially in Cumbria, until driven out by King John.[50] Scottish royal hegemony over northern England was far from unimaginable.

The legacy of these claims to northwest England is written into the *Scotichronicon*'s provincial. The claim of the provincial is not too extreme – Carlisle *'ought'* to be subject to the bishop of Glasgow' – but it reflects a long-standing belief that the diocese of Carlisle rightly belonged to Glasgow, and perhaps also reflected the Scottish kings' claims to Northumberland, Cumbria and Westmorland. Again, it was apparently thought that the provincial was the place to record those claims; the authoritative text for the political and ecclesiastical geographies and jurisdictions of Europe. What was woven through the text of the provincial was woven through the lands of Christendom.

Spain (and Brittany) over the centuries

When we turn our attention to the rubrics used for the Iberian peninsula, we see not so much conflict between competing interpretations, but more development over time. The early provincials, from the first half or so of the thirteenth century, tended not to separate out the Iberian kingdoms. Until the fifteenth century, there were a number of Christian kingdoms on the peninsula: Portugal; Castile-León (divided 1157; reunited 1230); Aragon-Catalonia and Navarre. Of course, there were also the Islamic states in the south, but these were not included in the Roman provincial. During the first half of the thirteenth century, there were also four ecclesiastical provinces in Iberia: the archbishop of Braga in Portugal; Tarragona in Aragon-Catalonia; and Toledo and Compostela in Castile-León. Seville was reconquered in 1248, and in the early fourteenth century Zaragoza was also raised to the level of metropolitan archbishop by John XXII.[51] The early thirteenth-century provincials do

---

[49] Keith Stringer, 'Kingship, Conflict and State-Making in the Reign of Alexander II: The War of 1215–17 and Its Context', in *The Reign of Alexander II, 1214–49*, ed. Richard Oram (Leiden, 2005), 99–156, at 101.

[50] Carpenter, *Magna Carta*, 404–5; Stringer, 'War of 1215–17', 117–46.

[51] Peter Linehan, *Spain, 1157–1300: A Partible Inheritance* (Malden, MA, 2008), 69; *idem, History and the Historians of Medieval Spain* (Oxford, 1993), 507. On John's reforms, see also Fabrice Delivré, 'Les

not really bother to note which dioceses and archdioceses were in which kingdom; the regnal divisions of Iberia did not seem to concern our copyists.

BL Additional 34254 gave all the Iberian dioceses under the headings 'In Catalonia' (for the province of Tarragona) and 'In Spain (*Hispania*)' for the provinces of Braga, Compostela and Toledo. BnF Latin 6191 simply listed Tarragona, Toledo, Braga and Compostela as *In Hispania*; and BnF Latin 5011 also put all four ecclesiastical provinces under *Hispania*. Ditto for BnF Latin 8874. Paris, Bibliothèque Sainte-Geneviève, 792 – which probably dates to the first half of the thirteenth century – noted that Tarragona was *In Hyspania*, but Toledo, Braga and Compostela were in *Tolleranus*, presumably meaning *Tolletanus* – Toledo.[52] This peculiar division might have been intended to emphasise the claims of Toledo to be primate of Spain, and hence holding jurisdiction even over the archbishops of Braga and Compostela.[53] *Hispania* was hardly an unknown term in the thirteenth century: the Visigoths had called their kingdom *Hispania*.[54] By the eleventh century Gregory VII could address Alfonso VI of Castile-León as 'King of the Spains' (*rex Hispaniarum*), presumably reflecting both the break-up of the peninsula into multiple kingdoms – multiple 'Spains' – and the fact that Alfonso dominated all of them.[55] Innocent III's chancery in 1210 sent a privilege to Rodrigo Jiménez de Rada, Archbishop of Toledo and 'primate of the Spains' (*Hyspaniarium primas*), confirming his primacy 'through the kingdoms of the Spains' (*per Hyspaniarium regna*).[56] Whether of course this 'Spain', or these 'Spains', included the Islamic states in the south is open to question. Nonetheless, *Hispania*, or *Hispaniae*, seems to have been a term covering the Christian Iberian realms in general. Initially therefore, in the thirteenth-century provincials, it appears that there was very little attempt to map the specific Iberian regnal divisions onto the Spanish and Portuguese Church, and into the provincial.

A century later that had changed. The provincial in Venice, Bibliotheca Nazionale Marciana, Lat. Z. 399 (=1610) – part of Paolino Veneto's *Compendium gestarum rerum regnorumque originem*, illustrated in Avignon and probably dating from between 1321 and 1326 – offers a rather more

---

dioceses méridionaux d'après le *Provinciale Romanum* (xiie–xve siècle)', in *Lieux sacrés et espace ecclésial (ixe–xve siècle)*, ed. Julien Théry (Toulouse, 2011), 395–420.

[52] Wiedemann, 'Joy of Lists', 66 n. 6, suggests a date in the later 1210s, but I am inclined to think the manuscript is slightly later than this.

[53] On the primacy dispute, see Fabrice Delivré, 'The Foundations of Primatial Claims in the Western Church (Eleventh–Thirteenth Centuries)', *Journal of Ecclesiastical History*, 59 (2008), 383–406, at 390–3; Linehan, *History and the Historians*, 269–87, 352–84; Robert Benson, 'Provincia = Regnum', in *Prédication et propagande au Moyen Age: Islam, Byzance, Occident*, ed. George Makdisi, Dominique Sourdel and Janine Sourdel-Thomine (Paris, 1983), 41–69, at 44–9.

[54] Janna Bianchini, 'Re-defining Medieval Spain', *English Historical Review*, 126 (2011), 1167–79, at 1168.

[55] *Das Register Gregors VII.*, ed. Erich Caspar (2 vols., Berlin, 1920–3), MGH Epp. sel. II, II, no. 7.6, pp. 465–7.

[56] *Die Register Innocenz' III. 13. Jahrgang (1210/1211). Texte und Indices*, ed. Andrea Sommerlechner et al. (Vienna, 2015), no. 5, pp. 10–15.

complicated picture of Iberia.[57] First of all, there are multiple rubrics: the arch-dioceses of Tarragona, Zaragoza and, oddly, Toledo are *In regno Aragonie et Cathalonie* – 'In the kingdom of Aragon and Catalonia'. Compostela is *In regno Castelle et Legionis* – 'In the kingdom of Castile and León' – and Braga and Seville are *In regno Portugallie* – 'in the kingdom of Portugal'. Even below those general rubrics, there is more specificity. Several of Zaragoza's suffragan dioceses are noted as being *isti erant Tarragon'* – 'these belonged to Tarragona'; that is, they were subject to the archbishop of Tarragona until the elevation of Zaragoza to archdiocesan status. Among those bishops subject to Braga, five – Coimbra, Viseu, Ourense, Lamego and Tui – all have noted next to them *In regno Legionis* – 'in the kingdom of León'. Although the accuracy of all this detail is questionable (was Coimbra really in León? was Seville really in Portugal?), there has clearly been an attempt here to indicate the regnal divisions of fourteenth-century Iberia.

BAV, Ott. Lat. 333, dating to around 1346, makes a slightly better fist of the Iberian peninsula.[58] Tarragona and Zaragoza are 'In Aragon and Catalonia'; Toledo is 'In Spain' (*In Yspania*); Compostela is 'In the kingdom of Castile and León' and Braga and Seville are 'In the kingdom of Portugal'. Within the provinces, the dioceses of Huesca, Tarazona, Calahorra, Segovia and Segorbe-Albarracín were seemingly noted as 'In the kingdom of Navarre'; Evora is 'In the kingdom of Portugal', as are Lisbon and Guarda; while Lamego, Tui, Lugo, Astorga and Mondoñedo are all 'in the kingdom of León'. There are still quibbles (surely Huesca and Tarazona were actually in Aragon-Catalonia?) but there is a pretty clear recognition of the peculiar reality of peninsula politics; ecclesiastical provinces did not match up fully with regnal polities; the suffragan bishops of an archbishop in one kingdom were not necessarily all in the same kingdom.

A similar process is visible when provincials came to the archdiocese of Tours and the duchy of Brittany. Although Tours was – obviously – in Touraine, most of the suffragan bishops of Tours were in Brittany. Fourteenth-century provincials often noted this, but it is clearest in the later fifteenth-century provincial in BAV, Ott Lat 65: Le Mans and Angers are listed as subject to Tours; Saint-Brieuc, Saint-Malo, Dol and Rennes followed, but were noted as *In Brittania Galllicana* – 'in Gallic Brittany'. The remaining dioceses – Nantes, Quimper, Vannes, Léon and Tréguier – were 'in Britannic Brittany' (*in Britania Britonice* or *in Brittania Brittonizante*). The distinction here is a linguistic rather than a political one: Britannic Brittany corresponds to Lower Brittany, where Breton was spoken, while Gallic Brittany is the French-speaking Upper Brittany. Whether Nantes could be said to be in Breton-speaking Brittany is open to question, but otherwise Quimper, Vannes, Léon and Tréguier correspond to the (apparently slightly arbitrary)

---

[57] Catherine Léglu, '"Just as Fragments are Part of a Vessel": A Translation into Medieval Occitan of the Life of Alexander the Great', *Florilegium: Journal of the Canadian Society of Medievalists/Société canadienne des médiévistes*, 31 (2014), 55–76, at 57; *Paolino Veneto: storico, narratore e geografo*, ed. Roberta Morosini and Marcello Ciccuto (Rome, 2020).

[58] Cf. Olomouc, Statni Archiv, C/O 422.

four modern dialects of Breton (Kernev, Vannetais, Léon and Treger).[59] Indeed, the modern decision to use dioceses to divide Brittany linguistically seems to have a medieval precedent in the provincial. Fourteenth-century and later provincials sought to map secular political (in Iberia) and linguistic (in Brittany) divisions onto ecclesiastical provinces.

The view from the east

The provincial manuscript from the furthest east (at least, the furthest east known to me) is Wrocław, Wrocław University Library [WUL], R 262. It dates from the first half of the fifteenth century and comes from the Bibliotheca Rehdigeriana, the library collected by the Wrocław native and bibliophile Thomas Rehdiger in the sixteenth century.[60] The picture which WUL R 262 presents is the reverse of that often found in Western provincial manuscripts: WUL R 262 has a pretty good idea of what the ecclesiastical province of Gniezno should look like, but a slightly more questionable view of what, for example, the ecclesiastical province of Canterbury looks like.

WUL R 262 is very nearly the only provincial I have seen which even has the correct number of dioceses under the archbishop of Gniezno, six: Cracow; Poznań; Wrocław; Płock; Włocławek; Lebus. As a comparison, BL Additional 34254, the English provincial from *c.* 1221–2, lists nine bishops under Gniezno, as does the mid-fourteenth-century provincial in the registers of Pope Clement VI (Vatican City, Archivum Apostolicum Vaticanum [AAV], Reg. Avin. 57, ff. 446r–450v). The extra dioceses are invariably accidental duplicates. BL Additional 34254 has, for example: Włocławek; Wrocław; Lebus; Włocławek (again, as Kuyavia); Płock; Cracow; Poznań; Płock (again, as Mazovia); and either Kamień Pomorski or Włocławek yet again (as Pomerania). Kamień Pomorski is not listed in WUL R 262, probably because (as the copyist of the Polish provincial presumably knew) it was an exempt diocese, not subject to the archbishop of Gniezno at all, and politically Kamień was not part of the kingdom of Poland but more-or-less the diocese of the duchy of Pomerania.[61]

---

[59] L. A. Timm, 'Modernization and Language Shift: The Case of Brittany', *Anthropological Linguistics*, 15 (1973), 281–98, especially 286–7; Ian Press, 'Breton', in *The Celtic Languages*, 2nd edn, ed. Martin J. Ball and Nicole Müller (Abingdon, 2009), 427–87, at 427–30.

[60] Adam Poznański, 'Medieval Manuscripts at the Wrocław University Library: An Overview of the Collections and their Digital Preservation', *Gazette du livre médiéval*, 64 (2018), 87–90, at 88.

[61] Przemysław Nowak, 'Das Papsttum und Ostmitteleuropa (Böhmen-Mähren, Polen, Ungarn) vom ausgehenden 10. bis zum Beginn des 13. Jahrhunderts', in *Rom und die Regionen. Studien zur Homogenisierung der lateinischen Kirche*, ed. Jochen Johrendt and Harald Müller (Berlin, 2012), 331–70, at 349; Jacek Maciejewski, 'A Divided Diocese at the End of the Christian World: The Case of the Bishopric of Włocławek', *España Medieval*, 45 (2022), 15–30; Broun, *Scottish Independence and the Idea of Britain*, 132–3; Winfried Irgang, 'Libertas ecclesiae und landesherrliche Gewalt – Vergleich zwischen dem Reich und Polen', in *Das Reich und Polen: Parallelen, Interaktionen und Formen der Akkulturation im Hohen und Späten Mittelalter*, ed. Alexander Patschovsky and Thomas Wünsch (Stuttgart, 2003), 93–118, at 97–9; Jerzy Wyrozumski, 'Poland in the Eleventh and Twelfth Centuries', in *New Cambridge Medieval History*, IV: *c.1024–c.1198*, pt 2, ed. David Luscombe and Jonathan Riley-Smith (Cambridge, 2004), 277–89, at 283–4.

The western provincials almost invariably were unaware of the status of Kamień Pomorski as an exempt diocese, with the exception of the provincial of Clement VI. Even Clement's provincial, however, duplicated some of the Polish dioceses: Płock is listed twice (once as Mazovia) and there is a bishop of Pomerania, even though both Włocławek and Kamień Pomorski are listed separately. WUL R 262 is one of the very few provincials I have seen which get Gniezno province right at all.

However, WUL R 262 makes an interesting error in its description of England. The cities of Coventry and Lichfield are listed consecutively but with a note next to them: *isti sunt coniuncti et exempti* – 'these are joined and exempt'. Coventry and Lichfield were indeed unified – it is not uncommon for provincials to note dioceses which have been unified – but they certainly were not exempt. I do not know of any source which suggests that the bishop of Coventry and Lichfield was exempt from the jurisdiction of the archbishop of Canterbury. What we have here is simply the inverse of the English provincials which had only a vague idea how many bishops there were in Poland; Polish provincials were unclear on whether all the English bishops were actually subject to Canterbury and York. Indeed, since almost every provincial I have seen gets the number of Polish bishops and cities wrong – including the provincial in the registers of Clement VI and the list of tribute-paying ecclesiastical institutions in the 1192 papal *Liber censuum* (which might have had the same base list as the *c.* 1200 provincial) – it seems almost certain that even the Curia *did not know how many dioceses there were supposed to be in Poland*.[62] That is quite a radical – though very plausible – inference.[63]

The conclusion here might seem obvious: provincials were more likely to get their local geography 'right' and more distant geography 'wrong'. But that is an important conclusion; it demonstrates that different manuscripts did vary depending on where they were written. If the provincial from Wrocław corrected the ecclesiastical geography of Poland, what else did the copyist change? If the English provincial totally misunderstood how many bishops there were in Poland, what else did he get wrong? Only further research will tell.

Conclusion

This essay might appear to be a collection of slightly disconnected observations; but these illustrations are intended to show the variation and richness of the provincial manuscripts; no two are the same; the reasons for changes are multiplex; and it is the changes which matter. The analysis I am advocating

---

[62] BAV, Vat. Lat. 8486, ff. 38r–38v; Paul Fabre, Louis Duchesne and Guillaume Mollat (eds.), *Le Liber censuum de l'Église Romaine* (3 vols., Paris, 1889–1952), I, 150–1. Wrocław; Lebus; Włocławek/Kuyavia (written over an erasure); Płock; Cracow; Poznań; Płock (again, as Mazovia); and Kamień Pomorski (as Pomerania), the bishop of which apparently owed an annual census of one gold piece.

[63] On the relationship between the papacy and the Polish Church, see Agata Zielinska and Igor Razum, 'The Papacy and the Region, Church Structure, and Clergy', in *Oxford Handbook of Medieval Central Europe*, ed. Nada Zečević and Daniel Ziemann (Oxford, 2022), 457–82.

here is, of course, complicated. It is very difficult to locate the time and place of production for most provincials accurately. This means that trying to work out who might have altered the text – and their motivation to do so – is often speculative. Nonetheless there are cases where we can be fairly confident of the who and the when, which allows us to put forward an argument for the why. And that is more or less how most historians always work.

The provincial was the authoritative text for the geopolitical and ecclesiastical organisation of Christendom between the thirteenth and fifteenth centuries; that was why copyists sought to amend it, to bring it into line with what they thought, or 'knew', the world ought to look like. This is one avenue of future research on the provincial, and I believe it to be potentially the most interesting.

However, pursuing this approach also necessitates a holistic approach to the provincial manuscripts: what can the other material in the manuscripts tell us about (1) the copyist and their milieu; (2) what their interests and aims might have been in keeping (and altering) a provincial? The obvious example is Bower and the *Scotichronicon*, discussed above. We can reasonably link his account in the chronicle proper about Glasgow's claims to Carlisle with the statement in his provincial asserting that Carlisle should be subject to Glasgow.

The number, richness and variation of manuscripts which include a provincial will provide plenty of avenues for comparison of differences between provincials, and evidence for why copyists made changes. The task is a huge one – it seems likely that the surviving number of provincial manuscripts is in triple figures. The potential rewards, however, are significant: an insight into the way that many people in the high Middle Ages saw their world – or how they wanted to see it.

Acknowledgements. My thanks to the anonymous reviewers of this journal, and to Patrick Zutshi and Rebecca Severy for their comments on this article. I am also grateful to audiences at the International Medieval Congress in Leeds; the Cambridge Medieval History Seminar; the Late Medieval Seminar at the Institute of Historical Research, London; the Graduate Centre for Medieval Studies at the University of Reading's Summer Symposium 2023; and the Fitzwilliam College History Society.

Cite this article: Wiedemann B (2023). Creeping up on the Roman Provincial. *Transactions of the Royal Historical Society* 1, 291–313. https://doi.org/10.1017/S0080440123000166

Transactions of the RHS (2023), **1**, 315–326
doi:10.1017/S008044012300004X

The Limits of the History of Western Sport in Colonial India

Subhadipa Dutta*

Department of History, West Bengal State University, Barasat, India
Email: subhadipa_dutta@yahoo.com

(Received 15 December 2022; revised 6 May 2023; accepted 8 May 2023; first published
online 31 May 2023)

Abstract

This historiographical review considers a corpus of literature which examines the spread of
modern Western sport within and beyond the locus of public schools, princely playgrounds
and club greens in colonial India. While locating the old historiographical problems and new
social historical interpretations, a great deal of attention has been paid to foregrounding significant research areas that are less catered to in existing scholarships. As well, this review
contends that the eagerness to examine colonial interventions in the sports field without tracing the conflict and negotiation between two different – pre-colonial and colonial – ideas of
leisure and body cultural movements expounds an incomplete history of Western sport in
modern India. While doing so, it urges a rectification of the methodology of current academic
studies in which vernacular literary sources are treated as a 'passive mediator' merely reflecting the popular enthusiasm for sport. It concludes that this 'reflectionist' approach is a
hindrance to research work on the diffusion of Western sports in colonial India, which recognises the emergence and development of a new sporting culture as the discursive formation
that surrounded the ideological meanings and images of the literary construction of sport.

Keywords: Western sports; Indian historiography; revisionist interpretation;
literary construction of sport; colonial India

Serious studies of the introduction of modern Western sports and their
associated ideologies into colonial India are comparatively recent in origin,
dating back mainly to the 1980s, though research in this field had begun
much earlier. Just like in other arenas of Indian historiography, since the introduction of post-colonial studies in the early 1980s the sport historian's craft
has witnessed substantial epistemological and methodological changes.
Post-coloniality has prompted a number of eminent social historians to

---

* The original version of this article was published with an error in the author's name. A notice
detailing this has been published and the error has been rectified in the online and print PDF.

move their focus specifically on to power relationships, cultural socialisation and informal resistance in the colonial play field. They have begun to investigate how modern sporting interventions were driven by a profound conviction of European racial, physical and moral superiority. While positioning themselves at the top of the hierarchy of the human race, laying claim to the appropriate physical strength and sporting spirit, the European colonisers often portrayed the colonial subjects as the effeminate, non-sporting 'Other', moral and racial inferiors who needed to be reformed, improved and civilised through novel sport. It has thus become crucial to understand the ways in which modern Western sport was introduced as an instrument of social control to bring order, discipline and virility to disorderly, undisciplined and feeble 'Orientals'. But, in the context of an anti-colonial nationalist stance, the colonised were not always fascinated to 'mimic' the manly gestures and leisure pursuits of their white masters. Then, it has also become essential to know the ways in which indigenous people adopted and adapted 'new' sporting techniques and practices. Recent scholarly enquiries have also found it appropriate to ponder sport as an arena in which the colonised inhabitants confronted and challenged the hyper-masculinity of imperial ideology, cultivated their own physical strength and prowess and gradually developed a self-image of confidence and pride as keys to achieve freedom and popular sovereignty. Their acts of subversion instead of simple imitation are therefore considered as the central loci of analysis in recent studies, specifically in revisionist historiography. Moreover, precise engagement with indigenous emotions and reactions often leads these social historical interpretations to look beyond an adult male-oriented narrative of colonial sport and, in a passing manner, consider the presence of women and children in sporting space as a relatively significant theme of history writing. In essence, sport is now viewed not merely as a site of imperialist hegemony and command, but also as a site of wider social, political and cultural contestations – those which were instrumental in shaping distinctive and varying identities in a non-Western hemisphere.

This historiographical review seeks to identify some of these most important views on sport's colonial past and trace out the changes that link them, with a specific focus on their limitations. In this review, an attempt is made to look beyond the overarching impact–response framework to mark the sharper reverse of pre-existing historical trends. The inference entails that without taking note of a rich pre-colonial matrix, in which diffused sporting ideals and idioms were drafted and grafted, no effort to understand the sporting scenario of colonial India can be comprehensive and complete. Last but not least, while appreciating the recent scholarly engagement with vernacular literary sources, this study questions the long-drawn 'reflectionist' method in which vernacular materials are used as a 'passive mediator', simply reflecting the indigenous consciousness of Western sport. Therefore, this review avers a genuine need to consider the diffusion of Western sport in colonial India as a discursive formation that encompassed the ideological meanings and images of the literary construction of recreational pastime.

Early historical (and sociological) studies of subcontinental sport during the colonial era often engaged with one of the most popular team games, cricket.

These early accounts usually tell the stories of gymkhanas, tournaments, associations and activities of the leading cricket personalities within a colonial sociocultural setting.[1] Perhaps the first meaningful attempt to analyse the importation and adaptation of an 'Anglo-Saxon' sport to a colonial society comes through the writings of Richard Cashman. He has provided detailed discussion of the social background of early patrons and players of cricket, the segregation of clubs on racial lines, crowd behaviour and resistance and the edifying and unifying forces of the game. According to him, the stark identification of cricket as a peculiarly alien game – which required manliness, stamina and doggedness for success on the pitch – somehow intensified a desire among the 'native' princes and others to come to terms with this 'gentlemanly' pastime and its ruling cultural characteristics. To these local people, cricket became an identifier of social status and a means of access to the politicocultural edifice of the Raj.[2] It is interesting to note that there was no direct cultural critique of this foreign sport during the heyday of nationalist movements. Thus, as it seems, through the conscious use of modern sport as a social safety valve, the colonial authority was often able to reduce tensions which could have been detrimental to the consolidation and perpetuation of empire. One scholar goes a step further to say that it was the elaboration of cultural power through sport – a crucial practice of the colonial 'informal authority system' – which ultimately enabled Britain to sustain its vast imperial preserve for so long in India.[3]

A different way of looking at sport as a social, didactic and ecclesiastical phenomenon in British India comes from the works of J. A. Mangan. He has analysed the relationship between athleticism and public school ideals in the broader context of physical culture and imperialism. According to him, the introduction of organised sports into various parts of the subcontinent was integrated with the colonial civilisation and conversion mission, or more specifically with the ethos and tradition of 'muscular Christianity'. From the mid-nineteenth century onwards, sport was considered by the colonisers as an instrument for training and disciplining 'unruly' male students. In consequence, the colonial authority began to deploy various modern sports among the colonised people in such a way that they could learn them (along with their associated virtues) and mould themselves into loyal supporters of the empire. The so-called 'games ethic' held pride of place in the pedagogical priorities of the public schools and mission colleges in India. The Anglo-Saxon educators and missionaries, who administered these institutions, involved themselves in integrating the games ethic with their educational programmes in order to inculcate moral order, *esprit de corps* and manly attributes

---

[1] Mihir Bose, *The Magic of Indian Cricket: Cricket and Society in India* (London and New York, 2006 [1986]); Edward Docker, *History of Indian Cricket* (Delhi, 1976); Alan Ross, *Ranji: Prince of Cricketers* (1983).

[2] Richard Cashman, *Patrons, Players and the Crowd: The Phenomenon of Indian Cricket* (New Delhi, 1980).

[3] Brian Stoddart, 'Sport, Cultural Imperialism, and Colonial Response in the British Empire', *Comparative Studies in Society and History*, 30 (1988), 649–73.

into 'native' pupils.[4] A good many studies of modern Indian sporting pursuits have reinforced this interpretation, with minor differences and shades of emphasis.[5] Looking outside the narrow confines of schools or similar institutions, Cashman has revealed that there are many contested areas where the ideology of sport could be inculcated effectively. According to him, 'games and the games ethic were significantly adapted when they were taken out of the closed environment of the school to wider society with its different values and demands'.[6]

During the last few decades, another popular game that has been attracting substantial attention from the practitioners of social history is soccer, or 'association football'. For example, a collection of essays has pointed out the crucial role played by imperialism, nationalism and communalism in the introduction, organisation and popularisation of this game in colonial South Asia.[7] Many of the contributions in that particular volume dealt with the history of football from above, or from the perspective that concentrates comprehensively on the role of proselytisers. The event that has grabbed most serious attention is the defeat of the East Yorkshire Regiment (a British military team) by the Mohan Bagan Athletic Club (a Calcutta-based Bengali team) in the decisive match of the Indian Football Association Shield of 1911. Tony Mason and Paul Dimeo are among the earliest to have noticed the nationalist, racialist and political significance of this indigenous triumph against the British on the sport field. They have depicted the celebration of this indigenous sporting prowess as a mode of acceptance of the English moral system introduced through the Anglo-Indian schools and colleges and submission to the cultural imperialism of the British.[8] This vision regarding the participation of indigenous communities in modern Western sport and their success on the ground offers a provocative, but Eurocentric view. In this interpretation, sporting dynamism belongs solely to the imperial metropole, leaving the colonial periphery to participate submissively in the process of diffusion, unable to make any original contribution of its own.[9] But, in the past two decades,

---

[4] See J. A. Mangan, *The Games Ethic and Imperialism: Aspects of the Diffusion of an Ideal* (2003 [1986]), 122–41; *idem, 'Manufactured' Masculinity: Making Imperial Manliness, Morality and Militarism* (2012); *idem*, 'Soccer as Moral Training: Missionary Intentions and Imperial Legacies', in *Soccer in South Asia: Empire, Nation, Diaspora*, ed. Paul Dimeo and James Mills (2013), 41–56.

[5] For instance, see Allen Guttmann, *Games and Empires: Modern Sports and Cultural Imperialism* (New York, 1994), 32–40; Richard Holt, *Sport and the British: A Modern History* (Oxford, 1992 [1989]), 203–79.

[6] Richard Cashman, 'Cricket and Colonialism: Colonial Hegemony and Indigenous Subversion?', in *Pleasure, Profit, Proselytism: British Culture and Sport at Home and Abroad, 1700–1914*, ed. J. A. Mangan (London and Totowa, NJ, 1988), 258–71, at 263–64.

[7] See chapters in *Soccer in South Asia*, ed. Dimeo and Mills.

[8] Paul Dimeo, 'Football and Politics in Bengal: Colonialism, Nationalism, Communalism', *ibid.*, 57–74; Tony Mason, 'Football on the Maidan: Cultural Imperialism in Calcutta', *The International Journal of the History of Sport*, 7 (1990), 85–96.

[9] Luise Elsaesser has recently shown that British imperialism not only created cultural space for the diffusion and absorption of Western sport (such as cricket, rugby and horse racing) in the colonial peripheries, but also made room for the transmission and appropriation of non-Western sport (such as polo) in the imperial metropole. The British uptake of the Indian game of polo (in India

despite differences between their respective thematic perspectives, Indian scholars have gone beyond this Eurocentric argument.

Modern sport appears in an entirely different hue in the writings of Indian scholars. In his essays on the social history of cricket in colonial Bombay, Ramachandra Guha has treated sport as a 'relational idiom', a sphere of activity that articulates, in concentrated form, the values, prejudices, divisions and unifying symbols of a society. In doing so, he elaborates how the fissures and tensions of a deeply divided society shaped the varying characters, patterns and forms of cricket.[10] In his book, Guha has extensively engaged with the politics of race, caste and religion that infiltrated the sporting space. He has charted the multifaceted roles of these constituent elements in the process of indigenisation of cricket.[11] The many dimensions of the indigenisation of an English summer game are also seriously considered by Arjun Appadurai. For him, indigenisation of cricket 'is often a product of collective and spectacular experiments with modernity, and not necessarily of the subsurface affinity of new cultural forms with existing patterns in the cultural repertoire'.[12]

Ashis Nandy has engaged with the cultural and psychological manifestations of cricket and foregrounded the discursive functions of the game which reveal 'more about the players, the consumers and the interpreters of the game than about the intrinsic nature of the game'.[13] He has reckoned that the underlying rhythms and mythic structure of the game aided indigenous people to come to terms with colonial modernity. During the process of modernisation, the game not only was appropriated by locals, but also allowed them to critique their alien rulers and find the ruling elites wanting.[14] Satadru Sen focuses on the career of Kumar Shri Ranjitsinhji (1872–1933), a ruling prince and a celebrity athlete, as an imperial subject, and reveals through his life and career certain unavoidable tensions within the British–Indian encounter during the late colonial era – tensions that made Ranjitsinhji a marginal man, a 'creature of indeterminate identity'.[15] The latest addition to this burgeoning literature on cricket has sought to understand the ways in which the idea of 'India' took shape through a momentous sporting journey of the first 'national' cricket team to the heart of empire. It strikingly contends that the nation on the cricket field was originally constituted by, and not against, the forces of empire long before India became independent.[16]

---

and Great Britain) during the colonial period demonstrates how the meaning of sport changed across cultures and within cultures across time. The global transfer of sporting culture was never a one-way traffic. Luise Elsaesser, '"Dashing about with the Greatest Gallantry": Polo in India and the British Metropole, 1862–1914', *Sport in History*, 40 (2020), 1–27.

[10] Ramachandra Guha, 'Cricket and Politics in Colonial India', *Past & Present*, 161 (1998), 155–90.

[11] Ramachandra Guha, *A Corner of a Foreign Field: The Indian History of a British Sport* (Gurgaon, 2014 [2002]).

[12] Arjun Appadurai, *Modernity at Large: Cultural Dimensions of Globalization* (2005 [1996]), 90.

[13] Ashis Nandy, *The Tao of Cricket: On Games of Destiny and Destiny of Games* (New Delhi, 2000 [1989]), 2.

[14] *Ibid.*, 7.

[15] Satadru Sen, *Migrant Races: Empire, Identity and K. S. Ranjitsinhji* (Manchester, 2004).

[16] Prashant Kidambi, *Cricket Country: An Indian Odyssey in the Age of Empire* (Oxford, 2019).

There is no doubt that these academic attentions devoted to cricket have broadened our understanding of a so-called 'colonial' game, its intricate relationship with wider social spectra and its contribution to the formation of unique national identities. But most of these studies considered the game, in its early years on the subcontinent, as mainly an elite preoccupation that only slowly entered the mass domain.[17] Appadurai, on the other hand, has pointed to the social paradox cricket represented in its early history in colonial India: 'It was honed as an instrument of elite formation, but like all complex and powerful forms of play, it both confirmed and created sporting sodalities that transcended class.'[18] Certainly, sport in colonial India invites multiple subalternities in many ways.[19] From the outset, there were several real-life versions of Bhuvan and Kachra of the blockbuster Hindi movie *Lagaan: Once upon a Time in India* (2001) – versions that articulate an active, non-elite engagement with modern sporting pursuits throughout the colonial period.[20]

The revisionist construction of a colonial sport history from below has gone far beyond the Eurocentric limit and recognised the importance of sport as an arena for articulation of an 'indigenous brand of nationalism'. Boria Majumdar has looked at sport and nationalism from the perspective of the recipients of sporting ideology.[21] He has shown that with the brutal suppression of the 1857 Uprising, 'political action against the might of the colonial state was doomed to failure. As the Raj grew more secured than ever, it was time to devise new ways to challenge colonial superiority.'[22] In the absence of an armed uprising, sport emerged as an arena where imperial supremacy was challenged and subverted. In a piece on football in colonial Bengal, Majumdar has coined the term 'Brown ethic' to signify 'a secularized, de-Christianized version of the muscular Christian ethos promoted by devoutly religious upper caste/class Hindus thousands of miles away from the British metropole for purposes of resistance against the very "muscular Christian" colonial masters'.[23] In doing so, he has discarded the monolithic understanding of the games ethic (and associated principles of muscular Christianity) found in Western scholarship, which is central to the perspective that concentrates exclusively on the proselytisers. Elsewhere, Majumdar, with his co-author, is more forthright: 'Ultimately, the impact of the public school games-playing ethos seemed of limited significance in promoting the game among the Indian masses. In fact, the process by which

---

[17] Projit B. Mukharji, 'The Early Cricketing Tours: Imperial Provenance and Radical Potential', in *Sport in South Asian Society: Past and Present*, ed. Boria Majumdar and J. A. Mangan (2005), 15–26, at 24.

[18] Appadurai, *Modernity at Large*, 92.

[19] See chapters in *Subaltern Sports: Politics and Sport in South Asia*, ed. James H. Mills (2005).

[20] Boria Majumdar, 'Politics of Leisure in Colonial India, "*Lagaan*": Invocation of a Lost History?', *Economic and Political Weekly*, 36 (2001), 3399–404.

[21] Boria Majumdar, *Twenty-two Yards to Freedom: A Social History of Indian Cricket* (New Delhi, 2004); idem, *Lost Histories of Indian Cricket: Battles off the Pitch* (2006).

[22] Boria Majumdar, 'Imperial Tool "for" Nationalist Resistance: The "Games Ethic" in Indian History', in *Sport in South Asian Society*, ed. Majumdar and Mangan, 48–65, at 50.

[23] Boria Majumdar, 'Tom Brown Goes Global: The "Brown" Ethic in Colonial and Post-colonial India', *The International Journal of the History of Sport*, 23 (2006), 805–20, at 805–6.

the game was appropriated and assimilated by various Indian groups at various places is a much more complex story.'[24] Majumdar's endeavour to discover the 'lost' history of cricket, against the broader sociocultural life of a sprawling nation, reveals that colonial subjects often played for reasons more multifarious than simply trying to emulate their white masters.[25]

As far as the social history of Bengal is concerned, Mrinalini Sinha has shown that the colonial discourse characterised Western-educated Bengali middle-class men as an artificial and unnatural class of person: in short, effeminate, non-sporting and non-martial Bengali *babus*.[26] Kausik Bandyopadhyay has indicated that the urban and suburban middle-class Bengalis, who mostly served the British as officials, clerks or professionals and could not show their anti-British resentment in public, always looked for opportunities to return the compliment. The football ground was considered a non-violent space to hit back at the alien masters. Bandyopadhyay has also demonstrated that the colonial games ethic itself, like the cultural-racist superiority of the West, was surpassed and nullified by its so-called inferiors at its own standard.[27] Thus, while discarding the assumption that in having recourse to modern Western sport the colonised actually followed a 'route of mimicry',[28] Bandyopadhyay has visualised a growing number of sporting Bengalis who played, watched and read about football as the makers of their own cultural politics rather than as passive clients of the cultural politics of ruling whites.

In this regard, Bandyopadhyay's latest contribution is noteworthy as it narrates a different indigenous response to modern Western sport. Drawing on the writings of Mahatma Gandhi (1869–1948), he has divulged an aversive individual reaction which questioned the 'civilising' values of Western sports and their relevant functioning in the overall development of the Indian population.[29] However, while analysing the interplay between Gandhi and cricket, Bandyapadhyay does not pay heed to the underlying decisive criteria that determined Gandhi's labelling of Western sport as an insignificant and barbaric practice. A closer look at Gandhi's statements on popular Western sport reveals that he evaluated the acceptability of a game on the basis of spirituality and its connection with the everyday practices of ordinary people. To him, modern Western sport was nothing but a separate competitive arena for displaying physical strength and vigour. He marked this virility without mental excellence and spiritual connection as brutal. On the other hand, alongside some indigenous sports, he advocated for the laborious daily chores of

---

[24] Boria Majumdar and Kausik Bandyopadhyay, *Goalless: The Story of a Unique Footballing Nation* (New Delhi, 2006), 18.

[25] See, particularly, Majumdar, *Twenty-two Yards to Freedom*; idem, *Lost Histories of Indian Cricket*.

[26] Mrinalini Sinha, *Colonial Masculinity: The 'Manly Englishman' and the 'Effeminate Bengali' in the Late Nineteenth Century* (Manchester, 1995).

[27] Kausik Bandyopadhyay, *Playing for Freedom: A Historic Sports Victory* (New Delhi, 2008); idem, *Scoring off the Field: Football Culture in Bengal, 1911–80* (2011), 1–107.

[28] For such Eurocentric comment, see Paul Dimeo, 'Colonial Bodies, Colonial Sport: "Martial" Punjabis, "Effeminate" Bengalis and the Development of Indian Football', *The International Journal of the History of Sports*, 19 (2002), 72–90, at 84.

[29] Kausik Bandyopadhyay, *Mahatma on the Pitch: Gandhi and Cricket in India* (New Delhi, 2017).

common people, such as agriculture and walking, as suitable alternatives to modern English games. He considered these exercises as the source of innocent pleasure as well as beneficial for the appropriate physical and mental development of the Indians.[30] This consideration signals a different, alternative perspective of sport, which was essentially conjoined with pre-existing cultural elements of traditional indigenous society. The connotation of spirituality, innocent pleasure and demotic connection can be found in the pre-colonial literary representations of play. Gandhi's ideological and political standpoints drove him to select several pre-colonial concepts as the decisive criteria for appropriate sport. In this process, Gandhi was not exceptional. During the high noon of nationalist programmes, many Western-educated Indian intelligentsias' aversive attitude to Western sport was based on the pre-colonial values and ideas of play. By concentrating mainly on the nationalist act of the adoption of Western sports, revisionist scholarship has developed an essential but partial narrative of sporting nationalism. This academic tendency created a lacuna that hides the multilayered and fluid nature of sport existing in Indian national consciousness.

It should be borne in mind that almost all the above attempts to look beyond the sport field have largely failed to consider the complex gendered matrix underlying the various projects of sporting nationalism – a matrix that often influenced and transformed through the involvement of women in sport. In other words, the nationalist construction and prescription of play activities for cultivating feminine virtues allotted for women remains unexplored in these narratives of 'manly' colonial sport. There is one major exception to this trend. Suparna Ghosh Bhattacharya has sought to examine the colonial condition within which sporting opportunities for Indian women were facilitated. She also draws attention to an inescapable contrariety of nationalist patrifocal opinion regarding the participation of women in sporting activities in colonial Bengal.[31]

In the above discourses, sport is also considered as a participatory and rivalrous area for adults. But should one consider an adult-oriented history of sport to be the history of colonial India's entire population comprising a huge number of boys and girls? It is the historians of colonial childhood who have noticed the imperialist and nationalist insistence on the pedagogic role of sport in ensuring the development of a child's body in a disciplined and predictable way. Satadru Sen has focused on the introduction of physical education in colonial boarding schools and established a connection between two contested sites in the empire: the school on the one hand and the body of

---

[30] *Ibid.*, 48–51.

[31] Suparna Ghosh Bhattacharya, 'Physical Education in the Curriculum: The Case Study of Bethune College', *The International Journal of the History of Sport*, 26 (2009), 1852–73; *idem*, 'Women and Sports in Colonial Bengal: A Process of Emotional and Cultural Integration?', in *Asia Annual 2008: Understanding Popular Culture*, ed. Kausik Bandyopadhyay (New Delhi, 2010), 257–71; *idem*, 'Sport, Gender and Socialization: The Experience of Jewish and Parsee Women in Colonial and Post-colonial Bengal', in *The Baghdadi Jews in India: Maintaining Communities, Negotiating Identities and Creating Super-diversity*, ed. Shalve Weil (London and New York, 2019), 125–41.

the students on the other.[32] Sudipa Topdar has placed weight on diverse pedagogical concerns and experiences in order to accentuate the implication of the use of physical education in colonial schools as a non-coercive cultural means of governance and reform.[33] Anindita Mukhopadhyay has observed how the playground of modern, urban educational institutions carried with it a new logic of pedagogy and training, which emphasised rule-bound action, strong self-identity with team and organised sense of competition. She has evidently identified a physicality of space 'reserved specifically for "games", akin to, yet not quite synonymous with, "play"' – one which became 'a marker of a colonial structuring and remoulding of space which had entered India via colonialism, and which became intrinsic to all the educational institutions that have put down roots in urban India'.[34] It was this new regime of field sports which began to orient the 'native' male body towards a modern space – a value-neutral space where young bodies lost their cultural symbols and became equal.

The history of subcontinental sport has mainly limited its complex study to the significance of organised, orderly and competitive activity that conforms to the modern Western criteria and values of 'real' sport. Considerable efforts are made to show how rationalised, achievement-oriented and rule-bound sport was implemented in India in order to elucidate the grand project of imperialism as well as anti-colonial nationalism. Although such studies highlight the social, political and cultural contexts of this implementation, they do not give adequate attention to the process through which modern Western sporting culture was introduced and utilised for colonising or nationalising the 'native' mind and body. This process deserves thorough scholarly engagement as there was no readily available empty space for the seamless and dominant application of the modern, specialised and structured concept of sport in an indigenous society which already had some distinct views of sport.[35] Addressing the traditional indigenous views and their complex encounters with the modern Western understanding of sport is necessary to comprehend the complexities of reception and rejection of modern Western competitive sport. It is undeniable that sport played an eclectic role in modern Indian society. But the question which also needs to be explored is how modern sport mingled with the significant issues of pre-modern society. While

---

[32] Satadru Sen, 'Schools, Athletes and Confrontation: The Student Body in Colonial India', in *Confronting the Body: The Politics of Physicality in Colonial and Post-colonial India*, ed. James Mill and Satadru Sen (2004), 58–79.

[33] Sudipa Topdar, 'The Corporeal Empire: Physical Education and Politicising Children's Bodies in Late Colonial Bengal', *Gender and History*, 29 (2016), 176–97.

[34] Anindita Mukhopadhyay, *Children's Games, Adults' Gambits: From Vidyasagar to Satyajit Ray* (Hyderabad, 2019), 361.

[35] In contrast to the historiography of modern Western sport in colonial India, few studies on the traditional indigenous manner of recreational activities and their changing colonial forms undeniably make the mentionable exceptions in this direction. For example, see Joseph S. Alter, *The Wrestler's Body: Identity and Ideology in North India* (Oxford, 1992); idem, 'Kabaddi, a National Sport of India: The Internationalism of Nationalism and the Foreignness of Indianness', in *Games, Sports and Cultures*, ed. Noel Dyck (Oxford, 2000), 83–115.

recent histories of the introduction of modern sporting culture remain silent when they come across such an issue, their unstated identification of indigenous tradition as an empty vessel – which did not allot any effective, important and noticeable place for sport – somehow implies a quick, seamless and unquestionable penetration of modern Western sport into Indian society.

Slowly but steadily, a few scholars of subcontinental sport have recognised this inherent paradox of colonial sport studies. Ronojoy Sen's monograph is exceptional among recent studies of the Indian approach to modern Western sport, as it traces the roots of serious indigenous engagement with sporting activity in the pre-British era. Using two great Indian epics (the *Mahabharata* and the *Ramayana*) and other literary sources, Sen has shown how various ancient and medieval sports like wrestling, archery, polo and hunting were intertwined with the contemporary hegemonic issues of caste-based hierarchy, royal diplomacy and the culture of nobility. He highlights the fact that the idea of sport as entertainment had gradually emerged in pre-colonial Indian society and stimulated the associated cultural advancement of performance and spectatorship. After the establishment of British rule in India, this sporting culture encountered the forces of colonialism, nationalism and race-, caste- and gender-based identity politics. Sen narrates this complex encounter and its resultant influence in shaping the modern Indian involvement in sport.[36] However, it would not be wrong to say that Sen's study renders an important but one-dimensional narrative of Indian sport. His endeavour to trace pre-colonial Indian sporting pursuits and their ideological underpinnings has been influenced by the dominant modern Western definition of sport. He has concentrated only on those activities of pre-colonial India which almost abide by the rules and structure of modern competitive sport. His narrow focus on finding instances of specific identical sporting practices impels him to overlook the multiple literary ways through which sports were defined in the traditional indigenous texts. Thus, he reveals a slightly superficial narrative of the sporting culture in India that ultimately indicates a unilinear method of diffusion for the modern Western model of sport in a non-Western landscape.

The traditional Indian notion of sport was never confined to any particular definition. There were a number of vernacular terms (that are very much in use today) which conveyed how people spent their spare time in India. For example, apart from denoting specific achievement-driven, competitive amusements or actions, the multipurpose and contradictory application of the words *krira* and *khela* (sport) in Bengali literature indicates an indigenous existence of a miscellaneous and diverse sporting culture.[37] In the colonial condition, modern Western notions and practices of sport encountered these varied indigenous understandings of sport rather than any one traditional approach to recreational pastime. Therefore, addressing the vernacular linguistic application of the word sport is crucial to comprehend the complex and

---

[36] Ronojoy Sen, *Nation at Play: A History of Sport in India* (New York, 2015).

[37] See, specifically, Manjita Mukharji, 'Metaphors of Sport in Baul Songs: Towards an Alternate Definition of Sports', *The International Journal of the History of Sport*, 26 (2009), 1874–88.

multivalent local responses to Western games and the resultant development of the modern Indian definition of sport. It is against this context that the use of vernacular literary sources is felt essential to write an expressive history of Western sport in colonial India, as such materials mediate a changing indigenous attitude to body cultural movements. This is where the importance of the revisionist scholarship lies. While emphasising the distinct objectives of local people in the diffusion of modern Western sport in colonial India, the revisionist scholars recognise the significance of vernacular literary sources. Their analyses have found vernacular source materials significant as they bring out the attitude and role of the colonised in the process of appropriation of modern Western sport.

However, it should also be pointed out that the revisionist historians are chiefly concerned about why the indigenous attitude towards modern Western sport appeared in the vernacular texts. But they have neither investigated how modern Indian consideration of Western games functioned in public life through literary mediums nor tried to locate how vernacular literature tended to shape the indigenous perception of sport. Thus, it can be said that the revisionist interpretation of vernacular literature largely follows what Jeffrey Hill has termed 'reflectionist theory', which implies that 'the textual source being studied only reflects an already existing reality'.[38] Over the past few decades, some eminent scholars working outside the subcontinent have put a big question mark over this reflectionist method of history writing.[39] Their pioneering works have moved from the interpretation of textual source as merely the passive mediator of the broader issues towards the notion of 'active text' or seeing the literary text as a 'cultural artefact that is itself capable of producing "reality" in the same way as other historical evidence'.[40] Their analyses of literary texts make us aware of the complex meanings of the messages inherent in the linguistic construction of creative writing, which essentially tends to determine knowledge and understandings of sporting activities. Such an analytical approach to literary sources holds minimal sway over studies of modern sport in colonial India. Since recent academic studies try to capture the significance of literary evidence only on the basis of tracing the mere reflection of the popular indigenous enthusiasm for serious sporting programmes, they hardly recognise the active agential role of the vernacular literary texts that not only illustrated the contemporary popular approach to sport but also in diverse and strategic ways shaped and influenced the cult of modern sport in India. The revisionist engagement with literary sources effectively explores the crucial question, why did vernacular writings

---

[38] Jeffrey Hill, *Sport and the Literary Imagination: Essays in History, Literature, and Sport* (Oxford and Bern, 2006), 21–2.

[39] See John Bale, *Anti-sport Sentiments in Literature: Batting for the Opposition* (London and New York, 2008); Anthony Batman, *Cricket, Literature and Culture: Symbolising the Nation, Destabilising Empire* (London and New York, 2016 [2009]); Hill, *Sport and the Literary Imagination*; Jeffrey Hill and Jean Williams, 'Introduction', *Sport in History*, 29 (2009), 127–31; Michael Oriard, *Dreaming of Heroes: American Sports Fiction, 1868–1980* (Chicago, 1982); idem, *Reading Football: How the Popular Press Created an American Spectacle* (Chapel Hill, 1993).

[40] Hill, *Sport and the Literary Imagination*, 27.

on sport emerge as a popular trend in a colonial context? But the existing works do not extend their exploration to scrutinise how the very urge for creating and expressing specific knowledge of sport was manoeuvred through such writings. Raising and exploring this question is crucial as, along with knowing the distinct causes of the popular adoption and adaption of Western sports in a local society, it is also important to grasp the unique indigenous ways through which the complex process of local development of the global model of sport worked. Therefore, it would not be an exaggeration to say that there is a definite need to break away from the prevalent academic habit and extend the scope of understanding of the sporting past of colonial India.

Acknowledgements. I would like to thank Kausik Bandyopadhyay, my supervisor, who proficiently taught me and encouraged my engagement with many of the issues addressed in this historiographical review. My thanks are also due to the editors and anonymous readers for their comments on an earlier version of this review.

Competing interests. None

Author biography. Subhadipa Dutta is a Ph.D. candidate at the Department of History, West Bengal State University, Barasat, India. Her interdisciplinary research lies at the crossroads of sport sociology, literary history and childhood studies, with a focus on pre-colonial and colonial Bengal. She has published in journals including *Folklore* and the *Journal of the History of Childhood and Youth*.

Cite this article: Dutta S (2023). The Limits of the History of Western Sport in Colonial India. *Transactions of the Royal Historical Society* 1, 315–326. https://doi.org/10.1017/S008044012300004X

Transactions of the RHS (2023), **1**, 327
doi:10.1017/S0080440123000075

ERRATUM

The Limits of the History of Western Sport in Colonial India – ERRATUM

Subhadipa Dutta

doi:10.1017/S008044012300004X, Published by Cambridge University Press, 31 May 2023.

The article has been updated to correct an error in the author's name since the original publication.

The publisher apologises for the error.

Dutta, S. (2023). The Limits of the History of Western Sport in Colonial India. *Transactions of the Royal Historical Society*, 1-12. doi:10.1017/S008044012300004X

Cite this article: Dutta S (2023). The Limits of the History of Western Sport in Colonial India – ERRATUM. *Transactions of the Royal Historical Society* **1**, 327–327. https://doi.org/10.1017/S0080440123000075

Transactions of the RHS (2023), **1**, 329–347
doi:10.1017/S0080440123000117

Decolonising Universities? Myth-Histories of the Nation and Challenges to Academic Freedom in Aotearoa New Zealand

Miranda Johnson

University of Otago, Dunedin, Otago, New Zealand
Email: miranda.johnson@otago.ac.nz

(Received 12 May 2023; revised 11 July 2023; accepted 13 July 2023; first published
online 25 August 2023)

Abstract

Can decolonising the university create possibilities for new stories to come into being, in the wake of the devastation wrought by colonisation? In Aotearoa New Zealand a particular instance of decolonising universities is under way. This is one that highlights how engagement with decolonising approaches may end up harming academic work. In New Zealand, public universities have involved themselves in negotiating a delicate compromise between activism and the demands of the state. This compromise brings into question the robustness of institutional autonomy and academic freedom. Conjoining the activist idea of decolonising with language that refers to a distinctive form of state governance foregrounding a political relationship between the Crown (executive government) and Māori, several universities have committed themselves to a 'Treaty partnership' with Māori. The idea is rooted in recent interpretations of the colonial Treaty of Waitangi/Te Tiriti o Waitangi, signed in 1840. The Treaty is and has been a contested text, event and idea. When universities invoke a particular idea of the Treaty as if it is a consensus view in order to advance social objectives, they risk thwarting the role and responsibility of academics, and particularly historians, to the common good as 'critic and conscience' of society.

Keywords: Academic freedom; decolonising; New Zealand; universities; indigenising

[T]he issue that concerns us is not who has the power to tell the story –
however important that might be; it is rather how power shapes what any
true story could possibly be.[1]

---

[1] Jonathan Lear, *Radical Hope: Ethics in the Face of Cultural Devastation* (2006).

Can decolonising the university create possibilities for new stories to come into being in the wake of the devastation wrought by colonisation? This is the hope of academics responding to wider social activism as well as internal debates about cultural imperialism. Those in former imperial metropoles and various postcolonial and settler colonial locations have called for universities to decolonise themselves by fostering new stories and storytellers. They make forceful arguments for the need to undo existing power structures which marginalise issues of race and representation. They aim to remake universities as places of substantive freedom for a much wider diversity of scholars and subjects than has conventionally been the case.[2]

In Aotearoa New Zealand a particular instance of decolonising universities is under way. This is one that, while promising the telling of new stories, also highlights contradictions in decolonising aspirations. In this south Pacific archipelago, annexed to the British Empire in the mid-nineteenth century, universities are conjoining the activist idea of decolonising with language that refers to a distinctive form of state governance that foregrounds a political relationship between the Crown (executive government) and Māori. Several universities have committed themselves to a 'Treaty partnership' with mana whenua,[3] that is Māori iwi (tribes) who hold local territorial authority. By so doing, universities seem to be ceding some of their autonomy to an iwi positioned outside of the institution, while at the same time universities mimic expressions of state power-sharing that are only a few decades old and that are the subject of considerable political dispute.

The idea of being a 'Treaty partner' is rooted in more recent interpretations of the colonial Treaty of Waitangi/Te Tiriti o Waitangi, signed in 1840. The Treaty was one basis for annexation of the islands to the British Empire. Despite its historic role in annexation, in recent decades its meaning has been rehabilitated: the Treaty has come to be regarded as the founding document of a bicultural nation. The current story told about the Treaty is that, in two somewhat different language texts, it allowed for British governance while guaranteeing Māori certain rights. This included, in the Māori language text, the ongoing right to exercise rangatiratanga, which is variously translated, sometimes as 'sovereignty' as well as 'chiefly authority'.[4] Today, the Treaty is invoked in law and public policy to signify reparation and biculturalism, referring to indigenous Māori culture and that of the mainly British settler descendants, or Pākehā. The Treaty also evokes Māori political and social goals including power-sharing, autonomy and equality, even when these might be in tension with each other.

While politically useful to an extent, this story of the Treaty assumes a consensus about the past. This is one that affirms a present-day view rather

---

[2] See for example Gurminder K. Bhambra, Dalia Gebrial and Kerem Nişancıoğlu (eds.), *Decolonising the University* (2018).

[3] Note that because the Māori language is an official language of New Zealand, Māori language terms are not italicised in English-language publications. I have followed that local convention in this essay.

[4] See for example Claudia Orange, *The Story of a Treaty: He Kōrero Tiriti* (Wellington, 2023).

than examining different meanings of the Treaty in different historical contexts. When such a consensus underwrites a political project and institutional change – the conjoining of the decolonising project with a state political process – it needs to be questioned and carefully analysed.

The consensus view of the Treaty is premised on a myth-history that underwrites current institutional claims to decolonising in the name of 'Treaty partnership'. While this myth-history draws on real events (such as the making of the Treaty itself), it retells such events in terms of a story of what *ought* to have occurred. Thus, it is written with a view to enacting its ideals in the present, rather than seeking to examine the messy complexities of past realities. By presenting a myth-history as agreed-upon fact, the *colonial* Treaty can thereby be reimagined as a framework for decolonisation in contemporary university settings.

Yet the Treaty is and has been a contested text, event and idea. Recent university policies invoke a particular, static, idea of the Treaty as if debate about it has been resolved. Ironically, the writing of a critical and rigorous constitutional history, one that may seek to question the role and significance of the Treaty and examine its many lives, is likely to be regarded as an act of bad faith in such a context. The academic historian faces moral dilemmas and unknown pitfalls in pursuing such a critical account. Moreover, the achievement of wider institutional goals via an unquestioned myth-history threatens to lead to conformity of opinion. While these university policies aim to advance social objectives, they risk thwarting the role and responsibility of academics, and particularly historians, as 'critic and conscience' of society.

The challenge that I describe is different from that faced in the United Kingdom and Florida, where right-wing governments have conflated 'academic freedom' with a broader 'free speech' agenda. Amia Srinivasan has recently pointed out that the former is 'the freedom to exercise academic expertise in order to discriminate between good and bad ideas, valid and invalid arguments, sound and hare-brained methods'. This is what she argues is under 'attack' from the new *Higher Education Act* in Britain according to which universities may be forced into compliance with the 'right's doublethink around free speech'.[5] What I analyse in this essay likewise throws up questions of how universities are or are not autonomous from the state and politics, although the context is very different. I associate the current challenges in Aotearoa New Zealand with a politics of progressive nationhood in a fraught postcolonial context. I am not describing – and do not believe this to be – an 'attack' on academic freedom. Instead, public universities are negotiating a delicate compromise between activism and the demands of the state in the wake of colonisation. But a good-faith effort to right historical wrongs may have the unintended consequence of circumscribing the 'freedom to exercise academic expertise'. This may happen by limiting the choice of research and teaching topics and by reshaping individual academics' ability to carry

---

[5] Amia Srinivasan, 'Cancelled: Amia Srinivasan Writes about Free Speech on Campus', *London Review of Books*, 45 (29 June 2023), https://www.lrb.co.uk/the-paper/v45/n13/amia-srinivasan/cancelled.

out such work in a way that they see fit according to their varied expertise, interests and skills.

Universities and 'Treaty partnership'

The predicament for historians and other scholars has become clearer as universities in Aotearoa New Zealand have announced new vision statements and strategic plans. These claim to be led by principles of the Treaty – usually referring to the Māori word 'tiriti' to indicate allegiance to a particular interpretation. For instance, according to its 'Vision 2040' interim statement, the University of Otago 'aspires to be a Tiriti-led university'. 'Te Tiriti' is the 'foundation document of our nation' and this institution will now be trying to 'liv[e] up to' the 'kind of relationship it originally envisaged'. This includes 'advancing Māori development aspirations' and 'integrating te ao Māori, tikanga Māori, te reo Māori and mātauraka Māori' into teaching, learning, research and support services.[6] Other universities have also emphasised the importance of the Treaty in institutional commitments. Massey University's 'Strategy 2022–2027' makes a similar set of claims about being a Tiriti-led institution:

> As a Tiriti-led University we are committed to demonstrating authentic leadership in contemporary Aotearoa New Zealand as we uphold Te Tiriti o Waitangi, the founding document of our nation, and its principles through our practice. We see this as a critical requirement to advance more inclusive and socially progressive outcomes for Aotearoa New Zealand. We will achieve this through provision of well-resourced Te Tiriti education, including research, teaching and collaborations that emphasise Te Tiriti-informed partnerships.[7]

Why this emphasis on being 'Tiriti-led'? The answer is to be found in part in relation to broader political developments in New Zealand. In the absence of a single document, or collection of documents, that we could refer to as the constitution of New Zealand, the Treaty of Waitangi/Te Tiriti o Waitangi has achieved such a status. This has occurred in a distinctive context, for a particular purpose: to establish legitimate terms of cohabitation between two peoples, who have at times opposed each other in the past (sometimes violently), and now seek to reconcile without giving up important differences that make them distinct. According to this story, while the Treaty marks the beginning of a new nation, it has also preserved cultural continuities. This idea is significant for how the Treaty is put to work in present-day policy-making and in forging a broader political consciousness: invoking the Treaty seems to invite the new without destroying the old. Remarkably, this idea of the Treaty has permeated much of public life in the country.

---

[6] University of Otago, 'Vision 2040' (approved as an interim final version by University Council, 29 Nov. 2022). 'Mātauraka' is the southern spelling for the term 'mātauranga' used elsewhere in the country.

[7] Massey University, 'Strategy 2022–2027', 6.

The interpretation of the Treaty as foundational to biculturalism, though now appearing as timeless orthodoxy, is only one of many that have been made by historians, lawyers, politicians, activists, rangatira (traditional leaders) and others over time. In other historical contexts, the Treaty was ignored or marginalised, or accorded a blithely symbolic meaning in making claims about the unity of the nation. Māori have interpreted the Treaty in many different ways since 1840: as a compact guaranteeing equal citizenship; or as a promise by which the state might be held to account, particularly in regard to land loss and rights to fishing and harvesting; but also as an event entailing considerable duplicity, one to be contested and even refuted. Even at an important meeting of chiefs and government ministers in 1860, just twenty years after the signing of the Treaty and on the verge of war, Māori understanding of the Treaty's terms and promises was not settled and their speeches did not even reference the Treaty extensively, as Lachy Paterson has carefully examined.[8]

A common activist slogan in the late 1970s and 1980s was 'the Treaty is a fraud'.[9] The slogan, associated with the activist group the Waitangi Action Committee, responded to the emphasis from the 1970s onwards that the 'two texts' (in fact there are a number of versions of Treaty documents), one in the English language and one in the Māori, appear to differ markedly, partly in meaning as well as in intent. Of particular concern for historians has been how sovereignty, government and possession were translated by missionaries at Waitangi and elsewhere, and how these ideas were understood at the time and subsequently.

Since the 1970s, following a seminal article published by the public historian Ruth Ross in the *New Zealand Journal of History* in 1972, the differences in meaning between the two language versions have preoccupied lawyers, judges, activists and historians.[10] In a recent book, Bain Attwood shows that Ross's argument in this unexpectedly influential article came to be misinterpreted.[11] Nonetheless, he traces how her 'minor' argument that the Māori text – or 'te Tiriti' – was the original text, since this was the one that many, though not all, rangatira in 1840 signed, laid the groundwork for a major reinterpretation of the Treaty. This is one that has underpinned the work of the Waitangi Tribunal, established in 1975 to inquire into Māori grievances regarding breach of the Treaty and recommend redress. It has also been highly influential in the courts and public policy.

While the different language texts have been the focus of considerable attention and debate, what has received much less attention in the public and political spheres is the quite radical change over time in political and

---

[8] Lachy Paterson, 'The Kohimārama Conference of 1860: A Contextual Reading', *Journal of New Zealand Studies*, 12 (2011), 29–46.

[9] For a discussion, see Ranginui Walker, *Ka Whawhai Tonu Matou: Struggle without End* (Auckland, 2004), ch. 11.

[10] R. M. Ross, 'Te Tiriti o Waitangi: Texts and Translations', *New Zealand Journal of History*, 6 (1972), 129–57.

[11] Bain Attwood, '*A Bloody Difficult Subject': Ruth Ross, te Tiriti o Waitangi and the Making of History* (Auckland, 2023).

constitutional meanings ascribed to the idea of the Treaty, as Attwood forcefully demonstrates. It is primarily the *matter* of this difference – that is, the historicity of Treaty interpretation and its plural (though not necessarily endless) meanings – to which I draw attention.[12] The Treaty has been, and should continue to be, the subject of reinterpretation and even contestation.

Yet such interpretive dissensus – which is ongoing – becomes difficult to discuss and debate openly when te Tiriti is presented as a set of incontestable, fixed, principles by which a university defines itself. Indeed, it is as if, by becoming 'Tiriti-led', universities in Aotearoa New Zealand are proposing that their interpretation of the Treaty is *the* framework by which academic work – teaching and research – is to be assessed and valued, however vague and ill-formed. Both of the university statements quoted earlier refer to te Tiriti – that is the Māori version and what Ross viewed as the original text. Both universities represent their particular responsibilities to te Tiriti in terms of advancing Māori language and knowledge, custom and law. Further, these universities argue that in order to make good on the obligation to uphold the original relationship envisaged in the Treaty, they will be partnering with mana whenua. In the case of the University of Otago, it will be 'proactively partnering with Kāi Tahu as mana whenua' and those iwi in other locations where the university has a presence.[13]

It is the claim to be 'proactively partnering' with mana whenua that the political scientist Dominic O'Sullivan has drawn attention to in critiquing Otago's vision statement. Universities, he writes, should not be adopting the role of Treaty partner as if they are delegated Crown representatives. Doing so turns academics into something more like public servants. It does not do enough to recognise their role as critic and conscience of society. Universities are independent institutions, emphasises O'Sullivan, places where ideas need to be tested and debated by academics who are not constrained by the codes of conduct imposed on public servants.[14]

I am not privy to the discussions among senior leaders of universities about why they have decided to engage in Tiriti-led partnerships. However, it is clear from publicly available documents that partnership *is* centrally important. Variations on the term 'partner' and 'partnership' are used at least twenty-four times in Otago's interim statement. The keyword is primarily used in reference to a partnership with mana whenua, but also to refer to other 'partnering' activities. For instance, the university aims to partner with 'communities in Te Waipounamu [the South Island] and Aotearoa New Zealand, the Pacific, and beyond to undertake research, teaching, and service that supports their needs'. Further underlining the idea that such actions are, in fact, core values, the statement explains that 'community and partnership' is something that the

---

[12] On this point, see also Michael Belgrave, *Historical Frictions: Māori Claims and Reinvented Histories* (Auckland, 2005), esp. ch. 2.

[13] University of Otago, 'Vision 2040', 20. See also Massey University, 'Priority 8 – Create, Honour and Sustain Meaningful Connections and Partnerships', in 'Massey Strategic Plan 2022–2027', 16.

[14] Dominic O'Sullivan, 'NZ Universities Are Not Normal Crown Institutions – They Shouldn't Be "Tiriti-Led"', *The Conversation*, 21 Mar. 2023. See also *idem, Sharing the Sovereign: Indigenous Peoples, Recognition, Treaties and the State* (Singapore, 2021).

university 'foster[s]'. This includes partnerships with industry and other local body authorities and so on. 'Partnership' is now something that the university seems to be extensively involved in with a variety of communities and entities, in order to meet those communities' needs as well as (at least implicitly) reap some benefits.[15]

But what does 'partnership' mean and what does it entail? The vagaries in these statements make it hard to work out what exactly is being envisaged. The scale at which partnerships is imagined matters. A bounded, specific project undertaken by an academic research team or class in partnership with a particular indigenous entity in order to, for instance, co-design a museum exhibition is a very different proposition to that of enacting an ongoing partnership between two major institutions. In that case, we might ask whether two very different partners do in fact share the same values and means of enacting them. One partner is an educational and knowledge-producing institution with a long European and colonial history, publicly funded to be of service to New Zealand society, and both legislatively required and conventionally understood to guarantee academic freedom. As the often-cited 'Statement of Principles on Academic Freedom and Tenure' by the American Association of University Professors (1940) asserts, 'Institutions of higher education are conducted for the common good and not to further the interest of either the individual teacher or the institution as a whole.' Further, '[t]he common good depends upon the free search for truth and its free exposition'.[16]

The other partner is a community defined by ancient lines of whakapapa (genealogical descent) seeking to uphold its mana, or authority, in the wake of dispossession and more recently following extensive monetary and cultural settlements with the Crown. Why would or should this institution be expected to be of service to wider society and uphold the common good? Do these different partners operate with equality and even capacity? Does one partner now have advisory or even veto power over the decisions of the other? Does this work both ways – and should it? A more recent plan from the University of Otago that outlines goals to 2030 only underlines that the partnership with iwi will require 'shifts in the way we teach, learn, research, engage and work as we bring together te ao Māori [the Māori world] and the traditional university world in a way that both honours the ideals of our Scottish heritage and upholds tino rangatiratanga'.[17] As I have already pointed out, rangatiratanga might be interpreted variously as the authority and dignity of the tribe through to an acknowledgement of the tribe's political sovereignty.

The significance of partnership as a core practice and value of the university thus raises a number of questions about the institution's autonomy and what we mean by this concept. Is the value of such partnership primarily to be found in enacting the obligations of the university to society – a claim

---

[15] University of Otago, 'Vision 2040'.

[16] American Association of University Professors, 'Statement of Principles on Academic Freedom and Tenure', AAUP, https://www.aaup.org/report/1940-statement-principles-academic-freedom-and-tenure.

[17] University of Otago, 'Pae Tata: Strategic Plan to 2030', 12.

that would imply some sturdiness and confidence on the part of the university but may place obligations on iwi that they may not wish to uphold? The proposition speaks to a wider set of debates in a variety of democratic societies where greater participation, particularly from under-represented groups, is being sought and nurtured in institutional and public settings in order to renew democracy. These debates are important and urgent but surely still leave many questions of justice in unequal societies unanswered.[18]

It is also possible that the frequent reference to partnership and partnering speaks to institutional vulnerability and even perhaps to an erosion of autonomy, on the part of the university at least. This seems particularly pertinent given the funding deficit and financial crisis in many universities in New Zealand, which are 'chronic[ally] underfunded'.[19] Several institutions are currently initiating widespread staff redundancies because they are in deficit.[20] Taking this context seriously is important for understanding the purpose of and critiquing the unintended consequences of the university's Treaty-led policy, for it is in an ongoing period of fiscal decline that partnership with a number of entities has come to seem valuable. Furthermore, this context forces questions about the material conditions necessary for realising academic freedom, as ongoing staffing and subject cuts mean that many departments are unable to offer the kinds of classes and courses and undertake the breadth of research that enacting such freedom would ideally entail.

That said, O'Sullivan is right to point out that the idea of a university engaging in a partnership as part of its aspiration to become 'Tiriti-led' is different in kind and poses particular challenges to notions of autonomy and freedom in the academic context. There is value in thinking seriously about and questioning this policy shift for a number of reasons, including whether it will achieve the kinds of social change that it aspires to do, and whether it meets larger goals universities might pursue, such as a renewal of democratic life and the valuing and protection of scholarly work in contributing to such a renewal.

Treaty partnership and the state

But where does this idea of Treaty partnership come from? Partnership between the Crown and Māori came to be regarded as a key 'principle' in interpreting the Treaty in the mid-1980s. It arose in part from a claim that the

---

[18] See for example Danielle Allen, *Justice by Means of Democracy* (Chicago, 2023).

[19] Brian S. Roper, 'Protect Otago – Save Our University!', ISO Aotearoa, 8 May 2023, https://iso.org.nz/2023/05/08/protect-otago-save-our-university/ See also Roper, 'Neoliberalism's War on New Zealand's Universities', *New Zealand Sociology*, 33 (2018), 9–39.

[20] On 27 June 2023, the New Zealand government announced top-up funding for universities but it is unlikely to be enough to stop redundancies – voluntary and possibly forced – from going ahead. See 'Big Job Losses at Victoria and Otago Universities to Go Ahead Despite More Government Funding', *Stuff*, 28 June 2023, https://www.stuff.co.nz/national/education/300915606/big-job-losses-at-victoria-and-otago-universities-to-go-ahead-despite-more-government-funding.

Treaty promised an ongoing relationship between Māori and the Crown, given public voice by key Māori leaders. This argument contrasted with the alternative contemporary claim mentioned earlier that the 'Treaty is a fraud'. But in significant ways, the idea of a Treaty relationship built on the efforts of generations of iwi leaders, while also reshaping interpretations of those earlier claims. Since the late nineteenth century, leaders had brought claims about dispossession to governments of the day. Some of those had been inquired into in the past, and some payments had even been made, but these were minimal and had not been accompanied by a broader shift in public understanding of colonial dispossession and its effects. In the late twentieth century, a new generation of Māori leaders aimed to achieve a broader transformation in the understanding of political authority, and even sovereignty, as shared, not unitary.[21]

The Treaty of Waitangi Tribunal, a specially designed permanent commission of inquiry tasked with investigating Māori claims of breach of the Treaty, became a central institution in this transformation. While the *Treaty of Waitangi Act* (1975) that established the tribunal is often referred to today as the moment when the Treaty began to be given real statutory meaning, the political philosopher Andrew Sharp viewed the tribunal as a way of 'avoiding rather than confronting the continued Māori demand that the Treaty should be "ratified" ... It was instituted too, as a means of negotiating, perhaps even evading, Māori claims that many statutes ... were in breach of the Treaty.'[22] What made the Tribunal into a much more significant institution was, as Sharp put it, the 'continuing and growing Māori demand for justice' and the role of some key leaders.[23] This pressure resulted in a significant amendment in 1985 which allowed for inquiries into breaches of the Treaty going back to 1840. The amendment opened the floodgates to hundreds of claims – more than the Cabinet of the day had contemplated.[24]

As well as investigating breaches of the Treaty, the Waitangi Tribunal was tasked with defining key principles of the Treaty. Presided over by justices of the Māori Land Court – led at the time by the chief judge Edward (Eddie) Taihakurei Durie – as well as eminent scholars, business leaders and others, the tribunal began to undertake this work in the early 1980s, defining several principles, key among which are partnership and protection. 'Partnership' refers to how the Crown should enact major policy as well as legislative and even constitutional change in the various branches of the state in consultation with Māori and in order to uphold its own honor. 'Protection' refers to how the Crown must protect Māori interests, and has primarily been invoked in reference to property. Both these principles have been used by the tribunal to evaluate the actions of the settler state in the past as well as in the present

---

[21] Richard Hill, *Maori and the State: Crown-Maori Relations in New Zealand/Aotearoa, 1950-2000* (Wellington, 2009).

[22] Andrew Sharp, *Justice and the Māori: Māori Claims in New Zealand Political Argument in the 1980s* (New York, 1990), 74.

[23] *Ibid.* See also Miranda Johnson, *The Land Is Our History: Indigeneity, Law and the Settler State* (New York, 2016).

[24] Alan Ward, *An Unsettled History: Treaty Claims in New Zealand Today* (Wellington, 1999).

in order to recommend forms of redress.[25] Although envisaged as being comple-
mentary, the two principles might also conflict with one another. Partnership
acknowledges Māori political autonomy, whereas protection acknowledges
inequality, even subordination, in the relationship of Māori to the Crown, particularly given the history of land dispossession. A third principle of 'participation' concerns 'empowering Māori communities to achieve their aspirations'.[26]

The principle of partnership was further entrenched in *New Zealand Maori
Council v Attorney-General* (1987), colloquially known as the 'lands case'. In
their decision, which upheld the appeal, the justices of the Court of Appeal
stated that the 'Treaty signified a partnership between races'. The case concerned key aspects of the *State-Owned Enterprises Act* (1986), particularly the
matter of whether land and other assets that might become the subject of
future Waitangi Tribunal inquiries would be transferred to the newly established state enterprises, whence they could be sold into private hands and
therefore would no longer be available to be returned to iwi as part of a
Treaty settlement process. In entrenching the principle of partnership, the
Court of Appeal referred to the Māori version and understanding of the
Treaty, and its 'spirit' of intent, as made in 'utmost good faith'.[27]

In making these interpretations, the court observed the influence of broader
social changes. Whereas just twenty years earlier, ministers of the Crown
argued to *remove* legislative recognition of distinctive Maori land title, by the
mid-1980s, the court argued, 'the emphasis is much more on the need to preserve Maoritanga, Maori land and communal life, a distinctive Maori identity'.[28] The court admitted a diversity of opinions among Māori and cited a
1980 Royal Commission into Māori lands that had emphasised the contextual
and contingent interpretations of key concepts. Nonetheless, underlined the
Court of Appeal in 1987, 'it is equally clear that the Government, as in effect
one of the Treaty partners, cannot fail to give weight to the "philosophies
and urgings" currently and, it seems, increasingly prevailing'.[29]

Still, at the time of the 'lands case', only a few acts of Parliament made
reference to the Treaty of Waitangi and its principles.[30] Notably, for our
purposes, the transformative *Education Act* of 1989, which established a new
vision of primary and secondary education and outlined the role, function
and responsibilities of tertiary education institutions, did not reference the

---

[25] Janine Hayward, '"Flowing from the Treaty's Words": The Principles of the Treaty of Waitangi',
in *The Waitangi Tribunal: Te Roopu Whakamana i te Tiriti o Waitangi*, ed. Janine Hayward and Nicola
R. Wheen (Wellington, 2009), 29–40.

[26] New Zealand Law Commission Te Aka Matua o te Ture, *Justice: The Experience of Māori Women*,
Report 53 (Wellington), 1999.

[27] *New Zealand Maori Council v Attorney-General and Others*, 1987, 6 New Zealand Administrative
Reports 353 at 35.

[28] *Ibid.*

[29] *Ibid.*, at 36.

[30] These included the aforementioned *Treaty of Waitangi Act*, the *State-Owned Enterprise Act 1986*
that was the subject of the Court of Appeal case, and the *Conservation Act 1987*, which was to be
'interpreted and administered as to give effect to the principles of the Treaty of Waitangi'.
Conservation Act 1987, s. 4.

Treaty in relation to tertiary education responsibilities.[31] In the next three decades, however, reference to the principles of the Treaty and to the principle of
partnership became ubiquitous in new and amended legislation, and across the
public service more generally. What had been defined as a relationship
between Māori and the Crown, or the executive government, became something to be recognised and upheld by various branches of the state, its bureau-
crats and increasingly other actors in civil society too.

Yet Treaty principles were not everywhere and universally supported. In a
paper prepared for a hui in 1991, lawyer and activist Moana Jackson offered a
contrary perspective. The Tino Rangatiratanga Hui was set to discuss a possible
claim to the Waitangi Tribunal on education. But, insisted Jackson, the terms of
the Treaty of Waitangi act 'have placed Treaty issues firmly within a context of
Pakeha law and Crown control. The effect of this process has been to redefine
the textual guarantees of the Treaty into a set of "principles" which actually
diminish the rights of Maori and facilitate increased control over Maori.'[32]

Other academics helped to extend the applicability of the version of the
Treaty that emphasises the Māori text and the importance of Treaty principles
in education. In an address to the Vice-Chancellor's Forum in Kuala Lumpur in
2009, the psychiatrist Mason Durie emphasised sustained progress in the incorporation of 'indigeneity (a distinctive indigenous perspective)' into education
alongside increasing participation in and some influence over mainstream university education by Māori. Durie, the brother of Eddie Durie, the former chair-
person of the Waitangi Tribunal, emphasised the importance of the Treaty in his
analysis of the 'context for change'. By the late 1980s, he argued, the 'Crown's
Treaty obligations were seen to apply to all sectors and to extend to agencies
funded by the Government such as public schools and universities'.[33]

However, the Treaty was not given statutory expression in regulating
education until 2020. In the *Education and Training Act* (2020), and the
accompanying Tertiary Education Commission (TEC) strategy, we can see how
the flowering of an idea that universities could and perhaps should be engaging
in their own partnerships with mana whenua has come about – although the
force impelling such innovations is in fact not clearly spelled out in the policy
documents. As O'Sullivan rightly points out, this act affirms academic freedom
and institutional autonomy. Section 267 further affirms 'the freedom of academic staff and students, within the law, to question and test received wisdom,
to put forward new ideas, and to state controversial or unpopular opinions'.
However, the act also includes a new section 9, 'Te Tiriti o Waitangi'. This section
states that the education system '*honours* Te Tiriti o Waitangi and *supports* Māori–

---

[31] The only related reference in that statute is where it lays out the responsibility of the minister
to provide a tertiary education strategy that addresses 'the development aspirations of Maori and
other population groups'. *Education Act 1989*, s. 159 AA 'Tertiary Education Strategy'.
[32] Moana Jackson, 'Maori Education Perspectives on a Claim to the Waitangi Tribunal: A Paper
Prepared for Tino Rangatiratanga Hui 1991 on Behalf of Nga Kaiwhakamarama I nga Ture/
Wellington Maori Legal Service Inc', Wellington, 1991 (n.p.).
[33] Mason Durie, 'Towards Social Cohesion: The Indigenisation of Higher Education in New
Zealand', paper for the 'How Far Are Universities Changing and Shaping Our World?' conference,
Vice-Chancellors' Forum in Kuala Lumpur, 2009, 12.

Crown Relationships'. It further asserts that the minister of education and the minister for Māori–Crown relations: Te Arawhiti

> *may*, for the purpose of providing equitable outcomes for all students, and after consulting with Māori, jointly issue and publish a statement that specifies what the Ministry, TEC, NZQA [New Zealand Qualifications Authority], the Education Review Office, and Education New Zealand must do to give effect to public service objectives (set out in any enactment) that relate to Te Tiriti o Waitangi.[34]

The verbs 'honour' and 'support' and the proposition that different ministries 'may' give effect to te Tiriti, are all somewhat vague, and they are not used to explicitly redefine the clauses guaranteeing academic freedom. Turning to the 'Statement of National Education and Learning Priorities (NELP) and Tertiary Education Strategy (TES)' of 2020, we find the language of honouring Te Tiriti o Waitangi is prominent. Tertiary education providers are required to 'ensure that strategies, behaviours, actions, services and resourcing *reflect* a commitment to Te Tiriti o Waitangi'.[35] While the act and policy document do not expressly state that universities must engage in Treaty partnerships, it is possible to see how honouring Te Tiriti and supporting Māori–Crown relationships might be interpreted in this way. This may explain why, at some universities, students are required to demonstrate allegiance. Admission to the Bachelor of Teaching at the University of Otago requires demonstration of a 'commitment to Te Tiriti o Waitangi'.[36] Yet in contrast to the vaguer language used in relation to universities, Te Pūkenga, the centralised organisation of what were formerly independent polytechnics, is statutorily required to engage in '*meaningful* partnerships with Māori employers and communities and to reflect Māori–Crown partnerships to *ensure* that its governance, management, and operations give effect to Te Tiriti o Waitangi'.[37] The language in this section is much stronger.

There was little comment in parliament, or in the media, on section 9 when the new 'Education and Training' bill was being debated in the House. Discussion focused primarily on the centralisation of the polytechnics. The minor attention paid to the introduction of a Treaty clause speaks perhaps to the ubiquity of such clauses in recent legislation and government policy-making. What was notably absent in 1987 was run-of-the-mill by 2020. But, recalling O'Sullivan's criticisms, we might still want to question the idea that a university should be upholding 'Māori–Crown relationships' and what this might mean in practice.

---

[34] *Education and Training Act 2020*, s. 9 (c). Emphases added.

[35] 'Statement of National Education and Learning Priorities (NELP) and Tertiary Education Strategy (TES)', 2020, https://www.education.govt.nz/our-work/overall-strategies-and-policies/the-statement-of-national-education-and-learning-priorities-nelp-and-the-tertiary-education-strategy-tes. Emphasis added.

[36] See for example Regulations for the Degree of Bachelor of Teaching (BTchg), 'Learning and Teaching Aka Ōtakou', University of Otago Te Whare Wānanga o Otāgo, https://www.otago.ac.nz/courses/qualifications/btchg.html#regulations.

[37] *Education and Training Act 2020*, s. 9 (g). Emphases added.

Further, we could debate whether such a notion contravenes institutional autonomy and the provisions guaranteeing academic freedom. We might recall again, as the 1987 Court of Appeal did even if in passing, that the Treaty has been a contested idea and that interpretations of it are shaped by present-day goals, values and aspirations. Is it the role of a university and those it employs to uphold the 'prevailing' or governing hegemony, or rather to question it?

Myth-histories of the nation

The political commitments outlined above have shaped and are in turn shaped by a powerful myth-history of the nation's past. In part, this finds past precedents for Treaty partnership in order to embed aspirations for present-day power-sharing as a feature of New Zealand identity, rather than as a novel or recently invented phenomenon. As Attwood puts it, the Treaty thus comes to serve as a 'foundational' or, in Nietzschean terms, a 'monumental' history. This is one that is useful for law and legal scholars, who now refer to the Treaty as a source of law.[38] We can see this foundational aspect permeating the University of Otago's 'Vision 2040' statement. When we read that the Treaty is '*the* foundation document of our nation' (i.e. not one of several possible texts); that the university is 'living up to the expectations of Te Tiriti' (which are assumed to be uncontestable); and that doing so permits of a 'kind of relationship [te Tiriti] originally envisaged' (when historians have debated extensively what *was* being envisaged in 1840 and to what purpose), we are being asked to believe in a story of timeless consensus – a story of legal foundationalism.

But the Treaty, its meaning and intentions, and what came next, are an ongoing matter of debate and dispute by historians. As well as Attwood, these include Tony Ballantyne, James Belich, Michael Belgrave, Lyndsay Head, Mark Hickford, Damen Ward and others. Their work on the nineteenth century puts the Treaty in its historical place and examines its disputed meanings and uses. For instance, as Ballantyne observes in his contribution to the *New Oxford History of New Zealand* (2009), while there is 'no doubt that the signing of the Treaty was a crucial watershed … to structure our understandings of nineteenth-century politics around the Treaty would present a thin and, in many ways, anachronistic reading of the young colony's political landscape'.[39]

However, at the same time that a sophisticated and critical historiography about the Treaty has developed, the mythic consciousness that finds in the Treaty a foundation for partnership – among other principles – has blossomed. Crafted in activist networks, represented in compelling visual media and even repeated in some academic scholarship, a myth-history presents political aspirations for Treaty partnership and imagines a bicultural citizenry as something that should have been nourished in the past. Some historians including

---

[38] Attwood, '*A Bloody Difficult Subject*', 113. See also Bain Attwood, *Empire and the Making of Native Title: Sovereignty, Property and Indigenous People* (Cambridge, 2020).

[39] Tony Ballantyne, 'The State, Politics and Power, 1769–1893', in *The New Oxford History of New Zealand*, ed. Giselle Byrnes (Melbourne and New York, 2009), 100.

Claudia Orange and recently the lawyer Ned Fletcher have contributed to this mythic history. Moana Jackson, earlier a critic of what the Treaty offered Māori politically, more recently argued that stories of the 'hopes that iwi and hapū placed' in the Treaty present an opportunity for the development of a 'different and unique decolonisation discourse' premised in an 'ethic of restoration'.[40] It is also represented on government websites, in Treaty workshops and training manuals, and schools. It is almost as if this past becomes more real the more strongly aspirations for the present are yearned for.

In other words, this myth-history is not simply a vernacular. It is embedded in policy and political institutions. Further, it is a creature of the institution that was created to investigate claims of breach – primarily the histories of dispossession – in the first place, that is, the Waitangi Tribunal. The historian W. H. Oliver identified aspects of what he called a particular kind of counterfactual history-writing at work in the tribunal, and about which he had become worried. He had conducted research for Māori claimants in the 1990s and been involved in other aspects of the tribunal's work. In a provocative essay published in 2001, he charged the tribunal with imposing a 'retrospective utopia' on historical events. It had created an implausible but highly attractive 'alternative past' in which

European settlement in (rather than of) New Zealand is depicted as dependent upon Maori consent and should and could have led to a regime characterised by partnership, power-sharing and economic well-being for Maori as well as Pakeha. In that scenario, colonists become tangata Tiriti, the people of the Treaty, and their presence in the country is conditional upon the invitation extended by the tangata whenua, the people of the land, an invitation made by Maori to further their own purposes. This is the 'future' that was promised in 1840 and, because the promise was subsequently broken, it is the 'past' New Zealand did not have. But it remains the 'future' to which the country may still aspire.[41]

Oliver's critique resonates with the charge of 'presentism'. This is one commonly made by historians, levelled at historical narratives that reflect an author's own concerns more than those of past peoples. In the case of the tribunal, Oliver contended that the history being written was determined more by the application of present-day judicial principles to the past than by trying to understand the past in its own terms or by its own norms. The actual reports the tribunal produces in making its recommendations on inquiries – hundreds if not thousands of pages long and that include dense empirical detail on dispossession and other grievances – are not themselves widely read by New Zealanders. Nonetheless the tribunal has played a significant

---

[40] Moana Jackson, 'Where to Next? Decolonisation and the Stories in the Land', in Bianca Ellington et al., *Imagining Decolonisation* (Wellington, 2020).

[41] W. H. Oliver, 'The Future behind Us: The Waitangi Tribunal's Retrospective Utopia', in *Histories, Power and Loss: Uses of the Past – A New Zealand Commentary*, ed. Andrew Sharp and Paul McHugh (Wellington, 2001), 10.

role in public life, as we have seen. Thus, the particular 'presentism' in tribunal historiography that Oliver diagnosed was potentially quite influential as well as being quite distinctive. In his account, the tribunal was not, for instance, exactly engaged in Whig history – telling a story of past contentions in order to ratify a present-day political consensus, as the English historian Herbert Butterfield put it.[42] This was history shaped for and by an *aspiration* to a better relationship between Māori and the Crown. It was not a fait accompli, although it is often represented as such.

In the midst of turbulent Treaty politics at the turn of the millennium, Oliver suggested that the tribunal was not so much ratifying the present, as producing an alternative past in order to imagine a past future that could have been and that still could be. By generating this 'retrospective utopia', tribunal historiography projected a political vision of partnership not only backward but also forward in time, he claimed. As a historian, Oliver had qualms about this project, though he appreciated its political and moral value in the present-day context. He was concerned that by creating a history framed in terms of what the Crown *ought* to have done (and not just what it did do), the 'alternative past' that the tribunal imagined – the past in which state actions would have been consonant with the principles of the Treaty of Waitangi – distorted the actual past. Principles defined in contemporary terms were applied to past events 'irrespective of the values and norms of the period in which they were performed'. Even more problematic, he suggested, was the 'millennialist' shape given to the historical account produced when purportedly timeless principles were applied to other times.[43] What happens, Oliver's argument might lead us to ask, when a millennialist account, one that fosters a laudable feeling of revival among a colonised people, is authored by *the state*? One thing that might happen is that the colonised – now recognised as a people who should and could have been accorded equal status and rights if the Treaty principles had been properly observed – become responsible for their own colonisation. Indeed, in one of its reports, Oliver observed, the tribunal muses on what 'consensual annexation' might have looked like.[44]

Oliver would have preferred a critical historical account of what the state did, not a fanciful one of what it ought to have done. The tribunal, he argued, presented an alternative past as something to which New Zealanders could still aspire; it was not lost or forgotten but could be retrieved and activated. His critique sparked critical responses in turn from other historians who themselves worked as researchers in tribunal processes.[45] Yet they did not engage specifically with what I think Oliver put his finger on: a broader political sensibility that engendered in so many people the desire to participate in finding a better history for a newly bicultural nation.

---

[42] Herbert Butterfield, *The Whig Interpretation of History* (1931).
[43] Oliver, 'The Future behind Us', 12.
[44] *Ibid.*
[45] For a discussion, see Miranda Johnson, 'Biculturalism and Historiography in the Era of Neoliberalism: A View from Aotearoa New Zealand', *Ethnohistory*, 70 (2023), 167–85.

We have seen such aspirational politics in the remaking of New Zealand's past implicit in the various public policy documents and strategies discussed earlier. Thus, the critique that Oliver levelled at the tribunal's work might be expanded to thinking about how a story of the Treaty was made and disseminated. This was one that privileged political optimism over self-critique, the mythification of foundational texts ahead of grappling with complex historical contexts, a preference for consensus over ongoing reckoning with dissensus, and increasingly in various institutions beyond those of the Crown an assumption of partnership.

The stakes are high. This narrowed-but-longed-for version of the Treaty, now adopted in university policy, stands in for a view of the past that minimises what actually happened, which cannot be contained in any one text or interpretation. Such a view of the past fails to explore how we might create new spaces for interpreting the varied and disputed meanings and legacies of colonial history today. Notably, when the University of Otago's 'Vision 2040' statement alludes to 'moving beyond' our 'colonial heritage' in the making of a Tiriti-led future, I am left wondering how it might be possible for us to continue to critically examine and analyse colonialism in a larger sense. No historian believes that history is something we 'move beyond' since we dedicate our working lives to trying to understand what has gone before. As we often tell our students, this is no antiquarian interest, but necessary if we are to better understand where we find ourselves in the present, although this is not a straightforward exercise.

I deem such inquiry to be vitally important. The process of settler colonisation and accompanying ideologies of colonialism radically transformed Māori community life and selfhood. Even the term of collective identity, 'Māori', is a colonial construction.[46] Like other indigenous peoples in similar contexts, Māori experienced dispossession, cultural and linguistic loss, as well as political and economic marginalisation. Colonial processes and ideologies entailed changes in the conceptions of self and community of the settler colonisers, too, as they laid claim to what they perceived as a 'new world', one of their making. The making of a new world entangled indigenous people and newcomers in a variety of relationships – intimate, social, economic, political – in ways that do not neatly fit the binary categories of 'Crown' and 'Māori'.

In philosopher Jonathan Lear's account, a breakdown in a way of life wrought by settler colonialism presents one of the most challenging predicaments that human societies can face. Haunted by the phrase attributed to the Crow leader Plenty Coups, Lear's contemplation on how to understand such a predicament offers us something more meaningful than 'moving beyond' colonialism. In the late nineteenth century, Plenty Coups's people were forced onto the reservation, and he is supposed to have said that 'after that nothing happened'. As Lear writes, the problem as the philosopher comes to understand it in ontological terms is not 'who has the power to tell the story – however important that might be; it is rather how power shapes what any true story

---

[46] See for example the extensive work of Lyndsay Head and Lachy Paterson on the crafting on Māori modernity in the nineteenth century, and James Belich, *Making Peoples: A History of the New Zealanders, from Polynesian Settlement to the End of the Nineteenth Century* (1996).

could possibly be'. In the face of cultural devastation, one framing idea of selfhood dies and with it even the possibility of a true story as previously intelligible. But this does not mean all hope is lost. The past can still inform the present. For what might happen is that a new Crow poet might be born who can 'take up the Crow past and ... project it into vibrant new ways for the Crow to live and to be'.[47]

When documents such as the University of Otago vision statement say, rather tritely, that the university will 'move beyond' a colonial heritage, what is missed is the radical destruction that colonialism has wrought. More significantly, such assertions *fail to appreciate the possibility of radical hope* that might arise in the wake of such destruction. The vision attendant on 'moving beyond' a past that is perceived to be holding New Zealanders back, or is embarrassing or shameful, avoids an ongoing confrontation with the ways these complex, messy and murky histories continue to ensnare communities, the ways they make everyone morally complicit, driving many to contest as well as try to understand what has come before. Such efforts, when undertaken by historians, may not lead directly to where a country finds itself today.

Power and the simplification of the past

In New Zealand, efforts to decolonise research practices are over twenty years old. Linda Tuhiwai Smith's touchstone book, *Decolonizing Methodologies: Research and Indigenous Peoples*, first published in 1999, set a new agenda for academic research conduct, brought into question what counted *as* academic knowledge and sought to revalue indigenous knowledge. Smith argued that in a settler colonial context like New Zealand, where academic research has been closely associated with the extraction of knowledge from Māori communities, research practice should be reshaped to ensure that any benefits flowed to and not away from them.

Since Smith published her book, support for Māori-led research has become a stated core objective of funding bodies and university processes. A wider objective of decolonising or, more specifically, 'indigenising' the university has enlisted many academics in a progressive cause.[48] This is one that intends to make New Zealand institutions more diverse in terms of staff and students. Universities also aim to foster the recuperation of indigenous knowledge, language and customary principles. Yet in practice, pursuing such objectives has raised profound questions about the conventions of evidentiary-based methods in many disciplines and about the freedom of academics to choose topics and how they research them. Decolonising requires considerable changes to research methods, processes of grant-making, and hiring practices as well as changes to curricula and pedagogy. In response to those advocating decolonisation of the university in other places, critics have voiced concerns about the reshaping of research protocols and disciplinary norms and expectations to meet, as some claim, the spirit of the times. They question whether

---

[47] Jonathan Lear, *Radical Hope: Ethics in the Face of Cultural Devastation* (Cambridge, MA, 2006), 31.
[48] Te Kawehau Hoskins and Alison Jones, 'Indigenous Inclusion and Indigenising the University', *New Zealand Journal of Educational Studies*, 57 (2022), 305–20.

'decolonising' in fact threatens established notions of academic freedom, as well as the quality of scholarship and teaching, by enforcing new orthodoxies that due to their progressive objectives become difficult to challenge.[49]

This problem is manifesting in institutional processes in New Zealand. In some instances, universities are requiring academic staff to present their research plans to a centralised committee for approval based on objectives associated with being Tiriti-led, before research can be funded, undertaken and published. As the Treaty becomes the framework for decolonising, it is not hard to imagine work critical of the story being told about it being externally obstructed. Recently, some scholars raised questions about the centring of mātauranga Māori in science curricula, which sparked acrimony and formal complaints within the Royal Society of New Zealand.[50] Public funding bodies and internal university research grants require academics to produce statements about how their work does or does not contribute to Māori knowledge and communities – irrespective of topic. As I have discussed elsewhere, these demands may dampen critique and even stymie the development of particular research topics as academics censor themselves.[51]

These requirements place scholars in difficult predicaments. Many of the goals associated with te Tiriti in its current interpretation are ones that I share, including the advancement and development of the capabilities of Māori students and staff, the growth and enhancement of Māori language and knowledge, and so on. Yet current university policy makes it hard for me to engage in the sort of critique that I think is valuable without appearing to be opposing these goals, since they are framed by the idea of a Tiriti-led university and the commitment to partnership. Even to question such goals is seen to be acting in bad faith – churlish at best, racist at worst.

However, not to question issues of such fundamental importance also seems like bad faith. To be required to uphold an orthodoxy, when there is no room made for contestability or an awareness of the many historical lives of the Treaty as an idea, feels oppressive to me and also dangerous. Many of the specific terms by which the decolonising of universities is being undertaken, such as becoming Tiriti-led, in fact reflect policies instigated by the New Zealand government and across the public bureaucracy. 'Decolonising' can look very similar to other increasingly hegemonic forms of governance.

We do not and cannot know whether this current notion is the 'best' version of the Treaty, one that really will help us to achieve all those social and educational goals. We must probe the limits of ideas, values and principles by analysing them from different experiential perspectives and by examining evidence that may even bring the value of those ideas into question. Furthermore, the vision of decolonising the university often simplifies a

---

[49] See for example D. Abbot et al., 'In Defense of Merit in Science', *Journal of Controversial Ideas*, 3 (2023), 1–26.

[50] See 'He Pānui Statement', *Royal Society*, 20 May 2022, https://www.royalsociety.org.nz/news/he-panui-statement. See also John Ross, 'Royal Society Drops Action against Controversial Letter Writers', *Times Higher Education*, 11 Mar. 2022, https://www.timeshighereducation.com/news/royal-society-drops-action-against-controversial-letter-writers.

[51] Johnson, 'Biculturalism and Historiography'.

complex social situation. We are invited to 'move beyond' the difficulties and not to dwell on the messy complexities of the past and their meanings for the present. Indeed, we are asked to cede our equally messy freedoms to do so, ones that are never established for all times but themselves always-in-negotiation with others. This kind of decolonising perhaps enables a certain kind of clean, unburdened freedom in a Nietzschean sense, in which we are not overwhelmed by a sense of a looming past and an unknown future. But I cannot help but feel that it gets us off the hook of making difficult decisions in the present.

I believe that acting in good faith as a scholar involves upholding commitments to truth and honesty, even if we often fall short. For historians, this demands an attempt to understand and interpret the past while remaining aware of the interpretive stakes of present-day political and social values. We write our histories in the language of our contemporaries, and what we write is inevitably shaped by the debates and larger forces of our times. But this does not mean that we should write our histories exclusively in the moral terms of our contemporaries or intentionally *for* the purposes of supporting a particular argument or demand that we find most compelling among them.

Beyond learning languages, how to navigate archives, reading widely and thinking reflectively about method and approach, the most important training a historian undertakes involves an ethical self-practice. That is, of learning how to conduct one's scholarly self in the acknowledgement of present demands without letting such demands overdetermine what is significant about research into the past. This in turn requires avoiding 'the respective positions of hegemonic appropriation and incommensurability', instead cultivating a 'sensitivity to difference and alterity', as philosopher Jerome Veith outlines.[52] Such a sensitivity is neither rigid nor craven. For historians it means exercising judgement wisely, not favouring a particular community we admire or to which we belong, nor distorting past realities in order to advance a cause in which, in our life as a coeval citizen, we may strongly believe. At the same time, practising this historical method is not about adopting a view from nowhere (or, omnisciently, a view of everywhere); it is reflective on its own situatedness in historical time. This kind of sensitivity and self-reflection seems particularly important in our contemporary world when individuals and groups often seek legitimation through the narrow selection of particular precedents, to the exclusion of other ways of thinking, feeling and valuing. I would like to work in, and for, a university that respects and upholds, that enhances and protects, the ethical practice of this kind of scholarly good faith.

Acknowledgements. I presented an early version of this essay to the Philosophy Programme, University of Otago, and appreciate the feedback I received. Thanks in particular to Catherine Abou-Nemeh, Greg Dawes, Michael Goodman, Dolores Janiewski and Tosh Stewart, and the anonymous reviewer for the journal for suggestions and advice.

---

[52] Jerome Veith, *Gadamer and the Transmission of History* (Bloomington, 2015), 145ff.

Cite this article: Johnson M (2023). Decolonising Universities? Myth-Histories of the Nation and Challenges to Academic Freedom in Aotearoa New Zealand. *Transactions of the Royal Historical Society* **1**, 329–347. https://doi.org/10.1017/S0080440123000117

Transactions of the RHS (2023), 1, 349–352
doi:10.1017/S0080440123000178

CAMBRIDGE
UNIVERSITY PRESS

THE COMMON ROOM

Stuart Ward's Untied Kingdom: A Global History of the End of Britain

Saima Nasar

History Department, University of Bristol, Bristol, UK
Email: saima.nasar@bristol.ac.uk

(Received 18 June 2023; revised 21 July 2023; accepted 21 July 2023; first published
online 25 August 2023)

Abstract

Unpicking Britishness on a global stage: a review of Stuart Ward's *Untied Kingdom*.

Keywords: Britain

British history can only be understood, as J.G.A. Pocock noted, as 'the inter-action of several peoples and several histories'.[1] Ever since its inception as a common political unit in 1707, Britain has been firmly embedded in a number of far-reaching political entities.[2] Tied to its empire, the development of the Commonwealth, and later the European Union, Britain cannot simply be described as an island nation lacking in global, albeit volatile, connections. Yet, how these political entities have shaped Britain and what it means to be British continues to be revisited by politicians, academics, journalists, and everyday Britons. From Norman Tebbit's 'cricket test' to 'progressive patriot-ism' and 'national renewal', one thing is clear: British national identity is notoriously difficult to define. Stuart Ward's *Untied Kingdom* thus importantly questions the changing historical meanings of Britishness. At a time when 'the slow death of Britain' is being declared by observers from across the political spectrum, Ward turns his sharp historical lens to 'the changing historical contingencies of being British and the deeper ruptures over time that have brought matters to a precarious impasse'.[3] In his panoramic study, Ward

---

[1] J. G. A Pocock, 'The Limits and Divisions of British History: In Search of the Unknown Subject', *American Historical Review*, 87 (1982), 313.

[2] https://archive.discoversociety.org/2016/07/05/viewpoint-brexit-class-and-british-national-identity (accessed June 2023).

[3] See Gavin Esler, *How Britain Ends: English Nationalism and the Rebirth of the Four Nations* (2021). Stuart Ward, *Untied Kingdom: A Global History of the End of Britain* (Cambridge, 2023), 2.

astutely examines the linkages between the end of empire and the 'slow depletion of shared British sentiment' since the Second World War.[4]

Ward's study is organised into three sections: part one covers the overseas projections of imperial identity, part two traces the various registers of Britishness including ideas of 'home', belonging and subjecthood, and part three turns to the repercussions of imperial expansion and retreat. The disintegration of the British world-system at the end of empire is critically explored in fifteen core chapters. The chronological, geographical and theoretical terrain covered is impressive, ambitious and vital.

The book's chapter on Kenyan Asians 'Coming Home to England' was of particular interest to me given my own research on East African Asians in diaspora. The chapter is a masterclass in critically unpicking Britishness on a global stage.[5] It achieves this by embracing a wide cast of historical actors. Ward recognises the long historical relationship between the South Asian diaspora in East Africa and the British imperial state. When Kenya gained independence in December 1963, Jomo Kenyatta's post-independence government sought to redesign its citizenship laws. It asked its South Asian minority population to prove their nationalist credentials by applying for citizenship, and a cut-off date of two years was given to submit these applications. Citizenship was not therefore conferred on everyone irrespective of territorial or generational claims. Dual citizenship was prohibited, which meant that applicants had to renounce all other nationality claims. Subsequently, only an estimated 48,000 South Asians registered as Kenyan and approximately 20,000 applied for Kenyan citizenship. For a number of reasons, including fears that they might one day be made stateless should the Kenyan government revoke their Kenyan citizenship, an estimated 100,000 South Asians opted to retain their British passports. They were able to do so because Kenya's South Asians were 'Citizens of the UK and Colonies' following the passage of the 1948 Nationality Act.

As Ward notes, questions of citizenship, belonging and loyalty remained at the forefront of public debate thereafter. South Asians were, at this time, popularly conceived as a permanent, bourgeois, immigrant minority in Kenya, who had enjoyed significant economic success in an imbalanced colonial society. When, in July 1967, the National Assembly passed the Kenya Immigration Bill, it cancelled the permanent resident certificates that entitled non-citizens to work in the country. Instead, a work permit policy was instated. Then in October 1967, a Trade Licensing Bill was proposed. This meant that trade in specific goods, such as sugar and other staple items, was restricted to citizens. Skilled and semi-skilled occupations commonly held by Kenya's South Asians similarly required trade licences. The passage of these reforms deeply impacted Kenya's South Asian British passport holders. Almost 500 South

---

[4] Ward, *Untied Kingdom*, 3.
[5] Interestingly, the East African Asian diaspora in Britain is remarkably dispersed. Their settlement in Britain spanned across the Four Nations.

Asians emigrated from Kenya to Britain each week. By March 1968, an 'exodus' took place, with 18 percent of the South Asian population choosing to emigrate from Kenya in the space of six months.[6]

The 'Kenyan-Asian Crisis' that ensued caused great alarm in Britain. Sensationalist claims that a group of 200,000 South Asians would 'swarm' Britain's borders failed to account for the fact that there were under 100,000 South Asian British passport holders in Kenya at the time. As Ward observes, politicians such as Enoch Powell and Duncan Sandys labelled the resettlement of Kenyan Asians in Britain as an unwelcome imperial hangover. In doing so, Ward lays bare the racialised rhetoric that shaped popular discourse on race, immigration and Britishness in the post-war years. What is encouraging to see in this retelling of the 'crisis' is the centring of Kenyan Asian voices and experiences. Ward begins the chapter with the unfortunate saga of twenty-two-year-old British passport holder Ranjan Vaid, who spent nine days travelling 17,069 miles between London, Nairobi, Johannesburg, Athens and Vienna because she was not in possession of an entry permit and did not therefore have the freedom of entry into Britain. Vaid was finally admitted into Britain by Home Secretary James Callaghan, who described this as an 'exceptional' concession.[7] Vaid's messy and exhausting journey is used to map the tremors of decolonisation felt not just in Britain, but also by global Britons.

Ward expertly explains how 'Greater Britain' was a composite structure that was forged by both internal and external factors. The end of empire in parts of Africa and Asia required a radical rethinking of what it meant to be British and who could claim Britishness. The view that the 'empire was striking back' in the form of communities of racialised subjects migrating to the colonial metropole served as a driver to remap and tighten the criterion of Britishness. Ward shows how Britain's borders were hastily renegotiated in 1968 in order to deliberately keep out Kenyan Asians. The legal concept of 'patriality' was introduced in the 1968 Commonwealth Immigrants Act, which served to exclude Britain's racialised global population, while keeping the door open for 'white Britons abroad'. Ward helpfully sketches the implications of this, especially in terms of what it signalled for Britain as a now former imperial power in East Africa. That a Labour government deliberately pushed legislation through in an attempt to curb Kenyan Asian migration – despite Labour so strenuously opposing the 1962 Commonwealth Immigrants Act – reflected the political climate of post-war Britain when racial minorities were often framed as a social and political problem despite being victimised by the state.[8] Britain loudly declared that she was unwilling to offer sanctuary to her own displaced

---

[6] See Sana Aiyar, *Indians in Kenya: The Politics of Diaspora* (Cambridge, MA, 2015).

[7] *New York Times*, 11 Feb. 1970.

[8] See, for example, responses to the 1958 Notting Hill riots when Black Britons who were targeted for attack were then singled out by the state as incompatible with the British way of life. See Kennetta Hammond Perry, '"Little Rock" in Britain: Jim Crow's Transatlantic Topographies', *Journal of British Studies*, 51 (2012), 155–77.

passport holders unless compelled to against her will.[9] The Act certainly tested the image of Britain as a country of asylum.

There is a limited but significant body of scholarship on Kenyan Asians. Sana Aiyar and Randall Hansen provide important historical analysis of migration, mobility and belonging.[10] What is remarkable about Ward's contribution is his ability to contextualise the episode in wider local and global currents – something he skilfully achieves across all fifteen chapters of this book. Ward explains the importance of local and national dynamics by taking into account the 1967 devaluation of sterling and the 1968 acceleration of Britain's military withdrawal from East of Suez. He explains how the image of a 'defeated nation pulling up the drawbridge' contributed to a renegotiation of national belonging and identity. It is perhaps also worth mentioning Britain's turn to Europe and its attempts to join the European Economic Community during this period, but altogether Ward offers an instructive template in doing global histories. As the current prime minister, Rishi Sunak, and the leader of the Scottish National Party, Humza Yousaf, both have Kenyan Asian heritage, it is clear to see that this history has critical afterlives. *Untied Kingdom* is required reading for students and scholars of Britain, empire and its messy entanglements.

---

[9] It is not uncommon for issues of statelessness to be discussed when retelling the story of Kenyan Asians. It is important to note, however, that Kenyan Asians were not altogether barred from entering Britain. A quota system was put in place that would permit 1,500 entry vouchers for heads of families. During a parliamentary debate, the Home Secretary confirmed: 'They are our citizens. What we are asking them to do is form a queue.' See J. G. Collier, 'The Commonwealth Immigrants Act 1968 – A British Opinion', *Verfassung und Recht in Übersee / Law and Politics in Africa, Asia and Latin America*, 2 (1969), 457–68.

[10] Aiyar, *Indians in Kenya*; Randall Hansen, 'The Kenyan Asians, British Politics, and the Commonwealth Immigrants Act, 1968', *The Historical Journal*, 42 (1999), 809–34.

Cite this article: Nasar S (2023). Stuart Ward's *Untied Kingdom: A Global History of the End of Britain*. *Transactions of the Royal Historical Society* 1, 349–352. https://doi.org/10.1017/S0080440123000178

Transactions of the RHS (2023), **1**, 353–356
doi:10.1017/S0080440123000130

Toward the Final Curtain: Glimpses of an End Foretold

Brendan O'Leary (iD)

University of Pennsylvania, Philadelphia, PA, USA
Email: boleary@upenn.edu

(Received 23 June 2023; revised 13 July 2023; accepted 14 July 2023; first published online 7 August 2023)

Abstract

Review of *Untied Kingdom: A Global History of the End of Britain*, by Stuart Ward (Cambridge: Cambridge University Press, 2022)

Keywords: United Kingdom; imperialism; colonialism; Ulster unionism; counter-insurgency

In *Untied Kingdom*, Stuart Ward, a professor of history at Copenhagen, and of Australian extraction, retells the story of the decolonisation of the British Empire against the to-be-determined question of whether the UK itself will unwind. His is a well-told narrative of related endings.

One is the end of the idea of *Greater Britain*, first propagated by Charles Dilke in the late nineteenth century, and romanticised more recently in erudite word-clouds by New Zealander J. G. A. Pocock, a doyen of the history of early modern political thought.

Another is the end of the *British* Commonwealth of Nations, originally an imperial confederation into which many sought to restructure the 'white dominions' – with significant sentimental success in British Canada and the British Antipodes. Acceptance was much less evident in South Africa, despite being championed by Jan Christian Smuts. Over time, neither the racially excluded non-whites, nor the Boers, the other white settler community, found 'Britishness' to their liking. The British identity was insufficiently democratic or liberal for the former, and too liberal and insufficiently racist for the latter. Unobserved by Ward, in 1921 Ireland was forced to accept Commonwealth membership as a means to oblige it to recognise 'the Crown', and in hopes of controlling its foreign and defence policy. Article 1 of the 1921 treaty provided that 'Ireland shall have the same constitutional status in the Community of Nations known as the British Empire as the Dominion of Canada, the Commonwealth of Australia, the Dominion of New Zealand, and the Union of South Africa.' Article 2 specified that 'the law, practice and constitutional usage' related to Canada would apply to the Irish Free State. The latter clause would be skilfully exploited by the new state to establish its sovereignty more quickly than Lloyd George and Conservatives had hoped.

The exit of the Irish Free State from the UK is not one of Ward's major case studies of British endings – admittedly these were so numerous in the twentieth century that he may be entirely excused, but it was the first, and it was accompanied by an unjust partition, and that became a precedent for British withdrawals from India and Palestine.

At independence, India, further away than Ireland and benefiting after 1945 from British weakness and Soviet and US promotion of self-determination, could not be coerced into any British definition. There were just not enough Britons. The fitful transition to 'the Commonwealth' took place at Nehru's insistence. 'Bitter-ender' resistance to the change of name came from those 'more British than the British themselves', the Australians and the New Zealanders. India also became a member as a republic, a right that had been denied to Ireland.

Another end to Greater Britain occurred through the punctuated withdrawal of the UK from the Commonwealth as a market for goods ('imperial preference') and as a zone of freedom of movement.

Bidding to join the European Economic Community in 1961, the UK abandoned its obligations to the Commonwealth, a task not completed until 1973. The 'imperial subject' was also downsized as British citizenship was incrementally defined and confined – through tacit rather than explicit racism. Citizenship was confined to those *from* Great Britain and Northern Ireland, and their immediate descendants, with special franchise and movement arrangements for the white Commonwealth and the Irish-born.

Ward elegantly relates other endings, notably the slow replacement of British symbols – flag, emblem, anthem – in the white commonwealth and the Caribbean, matched by faster-paced transitions where British settlers had been less numerous or powerful. 'Cosmologies of our own' accompanied the formation of many new nation states.

Ward does not register all retentions: British 'sovereign bases' in Cyprus now have their own Protocol in the UK's withdrawal from the European Union. Also missing is a sustained treatment of the insurgencies that speeded the termination of the British Empire: in Ireland, Iraq, India, Kenya, Cyprus, Malaya, Aden and elsewhere. He is fully aware of them, and of the atrocities generated. The Mau Mau insurgency is noted, and its brutal suppression; equally commendably he emphasises the often-forgotten destruction rained on Egyptians in the invasion of the Suez Canal by the UK, France and Israel.

Ward knows the facts and the historiography but does not draw on Caroline Elkins's parallel panorama, *Legacy of Violence: A History of the British Empire* (it is in his bibliography), or her earlier work with Susan Pedersen on *Settler*

Colonialism in the Twentieth Century. Charles Townshend's *Britain's Civil Wars: Counterinsurgency in the Twentieth Century* is also overlooked; generally impartial and accurate, it displays too much sympathy with the British counter-insurgents for my taste.

Crudely summarising, the British fought to keep their empire where they could, especially where they had strategic interests (albeit subject to constant redefinition). Elsewhere, they were relatively fast-paced downsizers when the costs of retention were judged too high. John Seeley's significantly titled *The Expansion of England* (1883) infamously suggested that 'We seem, as it were, to have conquered and peopled half the world in a fit of absence of mind.' In fact, there was as much mindfulness and ruthlessness in winding up much of the empire as there had been in its construction, and Ward fully recognises that.

The book's style is literary. Most chapters are started with telling vignettes, rescuing episodes from obscurity: for example, sailing Sikhs refused admission to Canada by British Columbian officials and courts in 1914, and a governor of Kenya permanently gifting a hunting lodge to Princess Elizabeth to encourage future royal visits. The Fleming brothers (one the inventor of James Bond) are deployed to open a discussion of receding frontiers after the withdrawal from Suez under American orders, while the brutal hanging of three founding members of the Zimbabwe African National Union (ZANU) by Ian Smith's Rhodesia, just before its unilateral declaration of independence, opens an account of the failure of British justice.

The author is also a British-style historian; that is to say, he reads other historians and evidently does not read social scientists much. No data are presented in tables; surveys are reported in sentences; the figures are photographs. Conceptual precision and clear theory-testing are avoided, and his methodology is sometimes as loose as the empire under scrutiny. All that is especially evident in his treatment of Northern Ireland. He 'sidesteps' the 'conceptual logjam' over whether Ireland ought to be considered a [past] colony. There is no such logjam, just a clear difference between those willing to define, operationalise, and test against evidence, and those who fear that lurking beneath any notion of colonialism is a notion of decolonisation that they find unwelcome.

Ward wants to argue that the decline of Greater Britain has impacted the core: the United Kingdom of Great Britain and Northern Ireland. That is plausible, but he cannot sidestep the colonial question. Ulster unionists feared that the withdrawal of British support from white settlers – in Kenya and Rhodesia – and sudden British withdrawals ('scuttles') from India and the Middle East set terrifying precedents.

True, but they had these fears because they knew their own standing derived from past settler colonialism, of which they were palpably proud (and from a biased partition, for which the Conservatives were largely responsible), and because they knew that most of the downsizing British of Great Britain had little sympathy for them. To many of the British of Great Britain, the Ulster British were, and sometimes remain, embarrassing reminders of what their ancestors had been like.

Many Irish nationalists and republicans also took comfort from the evident weakening of the British Empire, seeing the same precedents in similar light. Neither unionists nor nationalists were fools.

And the British army sent in 1969 to keep the peace between them soon behaved as it had done in Aden, Cyprus, Kenya and Malaya, guided by counter-insurgency strategy and tactics taught at Sandhurst – and that too helps explain the 'explosiveness' (Ward's word) of 'the Troubles'. Here it is evident that Ward is too reliant on some recent historians of Ireland who collectively share more hostility to Irish republicanism than to British imperialism – and the British army.

The rest of this decade is set to be an interregnum in which the twilight of the Union of Great Britain and Northern Ireland will be visible, but the new cannot yet be born. In these years Ward's book should be read both by those who wish to preserve the Union of Great Britain and Northern Ireland, and those who would like to see Irish reunification.

Untied Kingdom will remind readers that there have been several disastrous exits from past British commitments: Brexit is just one sample. Sovereign Ireland can certainly afford Northern Ireland, but its government must plan for the contingent possibility of an irresponsible British withdrawal, as well as prepare to make a success of reunification through the referendums provided for in the Good Friday Agreement.

Author biography   Brendan O'Leary is Lauder Professor of Political Science at the University of Pennsylvania. His most recent book is *Making Sense of a United Ireland* (2022). The paperback edition of *A Treatise on Northern Ireland* (three volumes) was published in 2020.

Cite this article: O'Leary B (2023). Toward the Final Curtain: Glimpses of an End Foretold. *Transactions of the Royal Historical Society* **1**, 353–356. https://doi.org/10.1017/S0080440123000130

Transactions of the RHS (2023), **1**, 357–361
doi:10.1017/S0080440123000142

Celtic Nationalisms and the Global Break-up of Britain

Ben Jackson

Faculty of History, Oxford University, Oxford, UK
Email: benjamin.jackson@univ.ox.ac.uk

(Received 12 June 2023; revised 15 July 2023; accepted 17 July 2023; first published
online 7 August 2023)

Abstract

This response to Stuart Ward's *Untied Kingdom* examines his treatment of Scottish and
Welsh nationalisms. This is a crucial part of the book because it is here that Ward completes his narrative arc, which depicts the loss of empire as a fundamentally destabilising force for the UK state and its basis in a shared British identity. So how should we
think about the pressure that decolonisation places on British identity within Britain?
While admiring much of Ward's treatment of this question, this response suggests that
he underestimates the importance of post-war social democracy as a possible alternative basis for British identity and the decay of that social democracy as a causal factor in
the rise of Scottish and Welsh nationalisms.

Keywords: British Empire; Scottish nationalism; Welsh nationalism; social democracy

Untied Kingdom is a truly panoramic work. Stuart Ward has given us a new
perspective on twentieth-century Britain by placing the regular fare of domestic
political and social history in conversation with the history of the British Empire
and in particular its settler colonies. He has written an account of global Britain
that follows the trajectory of Britishness from its zenith across the world in the
early twentieth century to its late twentieth-century retreat, as the British
imperial project broke up and British national identity began to seem thinner
and less compelling within the UK itself. The crucial innovation in Ward's
approach is that he connects late twentieth-century political turmoil within
Britain – perceptions of national economic decline; tensions over race and
immigration; the Northern Irish troubles; the rise of Scottish and Welsh
nationalisms – to the global break-up of the British Empire and the rise of distinct
national identities in states such as Australia, Canada and New Zealand, which

had formerly seen themselves as fundamentally British. The book is a magnificent achievement, the fruit of massive research across five continents, full of fascinating details and perceptive judgements that cumulatively build into a compelling overall case. Given such a vast canvas, it feels rather parochial to focus on the final chapters of the book and on the question of how Scottish and Welsh nationalisms fit into Ward's argument. Yet this part of Untied Kingdom is crucial because it is here that Ward completes his narrative arc, which depicts the loss of empire as a fundamentally destabilising force for the UK state and its basis in a shared British identity.

In this response to the book, I want to press on the question of precisely how Ward thinks that this instability within the UK relates to the wider process of decolonisation. As he frankly states, 'making sense of the interconnections between the course of events unfolding overseas and the decades-long push for the dissolution of the United Kingdom cannot be a straightforward matter of cause and effect'.[1] That gives a flavour of the subtle, multifaceted approach taken by the book, and the nuanced position that Ward outlines on the rise of Scottish and Welsh nationalisms in the UK after the 1960s. So how should we think about the pressure that decolonisation placed on British identity within Britain?

The overall thrust of Ward's argument is put most clearly in the conclusion of the book, which disarmingly starts, 'being British was always something of a stretch'.[2] Ward acknowledges here that the four nations inhabiting the British Isles do represent a different case from the other territories of the British world, since their 'geographic proximity' means that they will always have to collaborate in some way. But Ward argues that while something that looks like a 'British state' may therefore persist in some form in the future, it also means that the rationale for such a state will ultimately be 'a matter of political expediency' rather than 'anything more' and that 'centrifugal pressures' will continue to impress themselves on that political structure.[3] Implicit within Untied Kingdom is the assumption that British identity was inextricably bound up with the imperial project and that no plausible alternative basis for that identity could be found once decolonisation was underway. In my view, this leaves out of the picture one important alternative candidate for revitalising Britishness: the project of building a social democratic British state that bound together citizens across England, Scotland and Wales through an activist industrial policy, nationalisation of key industries, and of course the creation of the welfare state (the case of Northern Ireland I put to one side here since it raises a much more complicated set of issues). This new model of Britishness was certainly limited and compromised in various ways and, as Ward shows, was itself implicated in imperialism, but it did provide a new rationale for the state that was more domestic than international in orientation

---

[1] S. Ward, Untied Kingdom: A Global History of the End of Britain (Cambridge, 2023), 487.
[2] Ibid., 480.
[3] Ibid., 488.

and which foregrounded a more egalitarian and inclusive politics than had been evident before the 1940s.[4]

There is a telling comparison to be made between *Untied Kingdom* and David Edgerton's *Rise and Fall of the British Nation* (2018). Ward positions himself against Edgerton's book, but the two deserve to be read together for years to come on undergraduate and graduate syllabi as titanic contrasting accounts of twentieth-century British history. Edgerton regards the mid-twentieth century as the period in which a novel British project of national economic development rose to prominence, with the state newly committed to industrial and technological modernisation, protectionism and (eventually) social welfare (although Edgerton is less convinced than other historians that the welfare state was the key state innovation of this era). For Edgerton, the British nation was in fact invented after the 1930s, as the UK shed its global pretensions and became, briefly, an autarkic developmental state.[5] So Edgerton and Ward agree that the mid-twentieth century saw a fundamental reorientation in British state practices and cultural attitudes. But they disagree over whether anything coherent emerged out of that reorientation. For Ward, Britishness then suffered a slow puncture, as it started to deflate internally as well as externally. For Edgerton, in contrast, a new Britain was forged out of industrial and social modernisation that was in many respects successful. In Edgerton's view, it took the shock of Thatcherism and economic globalisation to smash apart this British nation. I don't agree with everything Edgerton says, but in this respect I am more sympathetic to his position than Ward's. I do think that an imperfect but recognisable form of social democracy emerged in Britain in this period, although I would be more inclined to connect this to the institutions of the welfare state and a new idea of shared social citizenship rather than Edgerton's focus on industrial modernisation (and hence to deploy the descriptor 'social democracy', a term that Edgerton himself is reluctant to use).[6]

What does all of this have to do with Scottish and Welsh nationalism? One powerful explanation for the rise of these nationalisms in the late twentieth century has been precisely that they were borne out of the 1970s and 1980s crisis of social democracy. As structural economic change and government strategy converged on a deindustrialised and more economically unequal Britain, the left in Scotland and Wales (whether formally aligned with nationalist parties or not) increasingly turned to Scottish and Welsh national identity to mobilise support against an apparently distant, uncaring UK state.[7] We don't hear a lot about this interpretation in Ward's book, partly because his chronological focus ends more or less in the 1970s, so the ructions of the

---

[4] The classic statement of this case with respect to Scotland is T. Devine, 'The Break-up of Britain? Scotland and the End of Empire', *Transactions of the Royal Historical Society*, 16 (2006), 163–80.

[5] D. Edgerton, *The Rise and Fall of the British Nation* (2018).

[6] D. Edgerton, 'What Came between New Liberalism and Neoliberalism? Rethinking Keynesianism, the Welfare State and Social Democracy', in *The Neoliberal Age? Britain since the 1970s*, ed. A. Davies, B. Jackson and F. Sutcliffe-Braithwaite (2021), 30–51.

[7] R. Finlay, 'Thatcherism, Unionism and Nationalism: A Comparative Study of Scotland and Wales', in *Making Thatcher's Britain*, ed. B. Jackson and R. Saunders (Cambridge, 2012), 165–80.

Thatcher era remain distant echoes. But this is also partly because his attention to the discourse of Plaid Cymru and the Scottish National Party (SNP) in the 1960s and 1970s leads him to emphasise instead a rhetoric of post-imperial crisis as the dominant ideological note of Scottish and Welsh nationalisms. As Ward shows, the point of this rhetoric was largely not to suggest that Scotland and Wales were de facto colonies of England, as deserving of emancipation as those other colonies enjoying their new-found independence, though of course this point was made in the more demotic variants of nationalism.[8] Although it offered an irresistible rhetorical charge, the question of whether Scotland and Wales were colonies faced serious objections, not least the inconvenient fact that the Scots and the Welsh had systematically benefited from, and participated in, British imperialism. The more sophisticated nationalist argument, Ward notes, was that Britain was an intrinsically imperial state that had been denuded of all meaning and purpose by the loss of empire. In a sense, then, the leaders of Plaid Cymru and the SNP agreed with Ward *avant la lettre*: for them there was no rationale for the British state beyond imperial plunder and paternalism. This was also the case that Tom Nairn elevated to a new intellectual level in his influential essays for *New Left Review*, eventually collected in his 1977 book, *The Break-up of Britain*.[9]

But this raises an important point about the politics of Scottish and Welsh nationalism before the 1980s. Nairn's critique of the imperial British state was ultimately aimed at pushing beyond what he saw as the watered-down 'labourism' that held back a more authentic socialism from breaking through at a British level. But unlike Nairn, and unlike the predominantly working-class supporters of the Labour Party who lived in industrial conurbations, nationalist voters and activists of the 1960s and 1970s were often ambivalent or hostile towards socialism and were drawn much more heavily from rural and small-town Scotland and Wales. As Malcolm Petrie has recently argued with respect to Scotland, they held political views that were in fact antagonistic to the centralised economic planning that had emerged from the war.[10] Tom Nairn had not yet become the guiding star of a left-wing nationalism in the period Ward writes about.

In other words, the politics of left and right are a necessary component of a full account of the trajectory of Scottish and Welsh nationalisms. Nationalists aligned themselves against the big UK state and against European integration in the 1960s and 1970s as a protest against centralising social democracy. In the

---

[8] A helpful survey of this theme with respect to the SNP, published too late for Ward to take account of, is S. Mullen and E. Gibbs, 'Scotland, Atlantic Slavery and the Scottish National Party: From Colonised to Coloniser in the Political Imagination', *Nations and Nationalism*, 29 (2023), 922–38. The debate in Wales is discussed in M. Johnes, *Wales: England's Colony?* (Cardigan, 2019).

[9] T. Nairn, *The Break-up of Britain* (1977); B. Jackson, *The Case for Scottish Independence: A History of Nationalist Political Thought in Modern Scotland* (Cambridge, 2020), 61–89.

[10] M. Petrie, *Politics and the People: Scotland 1945-79* (Edinburgh, 2022), 52–131. On Wales, see A. Edwards, *Labour's Crisis: Plaid Cymru, the Conservatives and the Challenge to Labour Dominance in North-West Wales, 1960-74* (Cardiff, 2011), 109–52; L. McAllister, *Plaid Cymru: The Emergence of a Political Party* (Bridgend, 2001), 37–72.

1980s and 1990s they presented themselves as against the big UK state and for European integration as a protest against Thatcherism. It is the latter formulation of Scottish nationalist ideology that has proved to be durable and ultimately helped the party to its greatest-ever victories after winning the Scottish Parliament from Labour in 2007.[11] Yet this also shows that the crisis of Britishness that Ward details is tied up with the seismic changes in British political economy after the 1970s. My impression is that Ward is less invested in the salience of the domestic left–right party divide within the UK because, in many of the case studies that he investigates, it is all too evident that Labour governments have been as complicit as Conservative governments in pursuing, say, a racialised immigration policy or a quasi-colonial foreign policy. Ward's account of Harold Wilson's governments will make difficult reading for those commentators and politicians who have become preoccupied with rehabilitating Labour's time in office in the 1960s and 1970s. Nonetheless, if we want to understand the rise and fall and rise of challenges to Britishness from Scottish and Welsh nationalisms after the 1960s, we do also need to follow David Edgerton in paying careful attention to the creation and then decay of the Britain of the National Health Service, the National Coal Board and the National Union of Mineworkers.

None of this is intended to detract from the importance and interest of Ward's book. Indeed, a more ecumenical way to read his argument would be that, by placing these domestic disputes in a wider global frame, he is entering a plea for greater balance between the domestic and the global in how we talk about the rise of Scottish and Welsh nationalisms and about the fortunes of British national identity in the late twentieth century. If that is his intent, then he is surely right to direct our attention to the wider global context in which the internal critique of Britain took shape. The parallels he explores between nation-building in Australia, Canada and New Zealand and the resurgence of nationalist sentiment within Scotland and Wales are illuminating. He also convincingly documents the saturation of that nationalist political discourse with references to postcolonial state-building. While the historiographies of Scotland and Wales are increasingly engaged by the relationship between those nations and empire, the reverberations of decolonisation have been largely left out of the study of late twentieth-century Scottish and Welsh nationalisms. Among the many other accomplishments of *Untied Kingdom*, Stuart Ward has performed an invaluable service in forcing historians of these movements to take their international context more seriously and to connect them to a much larger crisis of global Britishness after the Second World War.

---

[11] I have discussed this in greater detail in Jackson, *Case for Scottish Independence*, especially 90–127.

Cite this article: Jackson B (2023). Celtic Nationalisms and the Global Break-up of Britain. *Transactions of the Royal Historical Society* 1, 357–361. https://doi.org/10.1017/S0080440123000142

Transactions of the RHS (2023), **1**, 363–368
doi:10.1017/S008044012300018X

Unravelling Britishness

Wendy Webster

Department of History, University of Huddersfield, Huddersfield, UK
Email: w.h.webster@hud.ac.uk

(Received 31 May 2023; revised 21 July 2023; accepted 21 July 2023; first published
online 25 August 2023)

Abstract

This piece follows Stuart Ward's *Untied Kingdom* as it traverses a collapsing British Empire
and an increasingly disunited United Kingdom to tell the complex history of Britishness in
retreat across the world, mainly between 1945 and the early twenty-first century. It
reviews some of the shifting meanings of Britishness that Ward charts in different contexts, different territories and at different moments in this history and the dwindling resonance of Britishness almost everywhere. It reviews other main themes that thread
through the book: language, migration, race, belonging and unbelonging, nationalism, violence, and the impact of imperialism and colonialism on cultures, societies and mindsets.

Keywords: Britishness; imperialism; Englishness; archives; nationalism

The Coronation of Queen Elizabeth II in 1953 marked a high point in the narrative of
the British Commonwealth – after 1948 increasingly called simply 'the
Commonwealth'. There was considerable success in associating it with modernity,
youth and optimism, particularly through the figure of a glamorous young Queen
and through the timing of the news that Commonwealth men had reached the sum-
mit of Everest which appeared in the press on Coronation morning. Stories showed
the movement of people, loyal addresses and gifts from Empire and Commonwealth
to London and then a reverse movement in November 1953 when Elizabeth II began
a six-month tour of the Empire/Commonwealth and became the first reigning
monarch to set foot in Australia and New Zealand. Scenes of cheering crowds in
London in June 1953 were succeeded by scenes of cheering crowds in Bermuda,
Jamaica, Fiji, Tonga and New Zealand in November and December and then, in
1954, by cheering crowds in Australia and countries in South Asia, Africa and the
Mediterranean. The Commonwealth promised to maintain Britishness as a global
identity through transforming and modernising its imperial dimension.

By the time that Elizabeth II was succeeded by her son, Charles III, most of this was gone. At the Coronation in May 2023, the highly rehearsed ceremony in Westminster Abbey remained. Troops and dignitaries from across the Commonwealth were present and the flags of every Commonwealth nation. People from the United Kingdom who participated in the ceremony were of diverse ethnicities and religions. But since 1953, the Union Jack had been lowered in independence ceremonies in Asia, Africa and the Caribbean and the new flags of independent nations raised. Some had opted to become republics and more announced their intention to do so during Coronation week. Many nations in the Commonwealth had acquired new flags, new names, new national anthems and other national symbols to replace those associated with Britishness. New national histories had been written. In 2023, it was no longer possible to produce an image of rejoicing in a worldwide Commonwealth. Britishness had lost its charm across the world.

In his new book, *Untied Kingdom*, Stuart Ward sets out the history that produced these contrasting Coronations – the history of the end of the British Empire – tracing this history in all its complexity and contradictory impulses at different moments. His focus is on the retreat of Britishness as 'a credible marker of globally resonant values, beliefs, history, culture, ethnicity and civic identity', mainly in the period from 1945 to the early twenty-first century. At the heart of the book is the question of whether the end of the British Empire produced a climate in which Britishness lost its charm across the United Kingdom as well as across the Commonwealth. The book's subtitle, *A Global History of the End of Britain*, indicates the main argument. The end of Empire was integral to the process through which Britishness ceased to be a unifying identity for the peoples of Scotland, Wales and England (it had never been a unifying identity for the people of Northern Ireland). The disenchantment with Britishness indicated by the rise of Scottish and Welsh nationalism has to be set in this context – the dismantling of Britishness across the world – to be fully understood. Britishness is now history in the former Empire: even if pockets of British sentiment survive, they don't amount to very much and unfinished business is mainly confined to Gibraltar and the Falklands/Malvinas. The break-up of Britain is also unfinished business, but Ward argues that it is well advanced.

The term 'Commonwealth' was increasingly used for the British Empire during the Second World War, often 'British Commonwealth of Nations'. This shift was meant to emphasise a British world of progress, welfare and development as opposed to an imperialism of domination, militarism and conquest. In the aftermath of war, 'don't mention the Empire' became a watchword, but the language of Empire and Commonwealth became extraordinarily varied and confused. At least in part this was because negotiations of a new vocabulary in a Commonwealth that was quickly extended to include Ceylon, India and Pakistan were often secret, so that many people remained ignorant of the labels they were supposed to be using or avoiding. Confusion was compounded by the fact that in these negotiations, no agreement could be reached about the name of the organisation to which they all belonged. The disagreement turned on the term 'British'. India would have nothing to do with this term and did not want any part in an organisation that was described by it. The Indian government was prepared to join the Commonwealth only as a republic and only if 'British' was excluded from the name. Australia and New Zealand, who were not consulted, wanted to keep 'British'. The British government was prepared to lose 'British' if that ensured that India joined the Commonwealth. In the end, what people called the organisation to which they all belonged was left as a matter of individual preference and choice. 'British' became optional.

This negotiation about names is one of the 'little deaths' of 'Britain-in-the-world' that Ward charts in six central chapters of his book. Race is a central feature of many episodes in this history of 'little deaths' and *Untied Kingdom* provides an absorbing account of the varied fates of Britishness within different white racial communities. The negotiations over names suggested that notions of white racial prestige and superiority remained deeply embedded in these communities. In Australia and New Zealand, Britishness remained a key allegiance in the aftermath of war when both governments continued to operate immigration policies designed to keep out people of colour and to encourage (and fund) the entry of white Britons. In Rhodesia, the white racial community rebelled against the British government, declaring their independence from Britain and casting themselves as the true representatives of values that Britain had betrayed. In South Africa, the rise of anti-British Afrikaner nationalism to political ascendancy brought a government intent on the introduction of apartheid and a break with British connections. These policies cast the minority English-speaking population adrift, many of them reluctant to lose the benefits and privileges of the white population by making common cause with people of colour against apartheid.

The idea of the Commonwealth obscured the slavery, violence, atrocities and exploitation embedded in Britain's imperial history. The British narrative of a transition to Commonwealth presented this as an 'orderly withdrawal' from Empire – the final fulfilment of a British mission to prepare colonies for independence, and a gift graciously bestowed by the British. Ward highlights British violence in Kenya through a chapter on a 'little death' which begins with a cameo about Queen Elizabeth – one of the cameos at the beginning of each chapter that engage the reader with stories of individuals or groups caught up in the retreat of Britishness. Elizabeth was gifted a home in Kenya by the Kenyan colonial government but spent only two nights there, her visit cut short by the news of her father's death and her accession to the throne. By the time of her Coronation, there was ongoing colonial war in Kenya, and she never stayed in her home there again. Ward juxtaposes the story of the home she had vacated with the media narrative of colonial war, one in which the homes of white British settlers were under siege. As a place violated by insurgents, where British settlers were murdered, 'home' was stripped of its associations with domestic order and pleasures. Through its focus on black violence against white, this narrative distracted attention from British violence and brutal repression of the insurgency, but Ward brings to light considerable unease in the British media about British brutality. It is notable that the army, sent in to quell black insurgency in Kenya in the 1950s, was not sent to quell white rebels in Rhodesia, after their declaration of independence.

Australian migrants and visitors making the journey from Australia to Britain sometimes thought of arrival at a place thousands of miles away that they had never seen before as 'going home'. But in the post-1945 period, 'Commonwealth immigrants' were not associated with Australians or other white Commonwealth migrants but with black and Asian people arriving in Britain who were rarely viewed as internal migrants moving within a common British world from one part of the Empire/Commonwealth to another. 'Home' recurs as a key term in the histories of migration to Britain traced in *Untied Kingdom*. Caribbean migrants discovered an unhomely place when they were often expecting a motherland. Unbelonging is perhaps the most common theme in their accounts of experiences of Britain. Those who had thought of themselves as British in Caribbean colonies encountered a place where there was little acknowledgement of the long history that connected them to Britain and recast their identities in different ways including a shift to an identity as West Indian.

Belonging and unbelonging is a theme that runs through *Untied Kingdom*, developed particularly through discussion of Commonwealth Immigrants Acts from 1962 and through the stories of Caribbean and Kenyan Asian migration to Britain. In Australia and New Zealand, immigration policies designed to keep out people of colour were justified as preserving the 'British character' of their societies. The 1962 Commonwealth Immigrants Act in Britain was designed for the same purpose, one that was made explicit only in memoranda by government ministers. The 1968 Commonwealth Immigrants Act was more explicit through its patriality clause which permitted entry only to those with a parent or grandparent born in the United Kingdom – a requirement that many white people in the Commonwealth could meet but few people of colour. Ward brings the theme of unbelonging vividly to life in a cameo on Ranjanbala Vaid, a Kenyan Asian woman who arrived at Heathrow airport to join her brother in London but was refused entry under the terms of the 1968 Act. Over nine days, she shuttled between a range of airports on flights that took her to Germany, Switzerland, South Africa and Kenya – to some of these destinations several times. She was refused entry at all airports. It was only because of the media publicity attracted by her journey that she was finally granted entry to Britain.

Historians have neglected the part played by the end of the British Empire in the rise of nationalism in Scotland and Wales and in violent conflict in Northern Ireland. Ward fills in some of the gaps and silences. In Northern Ireland, he argues, nationalists were emboldened by the loss of British power and anticolonial struggles in other parts of the world which gave legitimacy to their cause. At the same time, Britain's retreat from long-standing commitments in the world unnerved Ulster unionists. Would they be next? Would Britain betray and abandon their kith and kin in Northern Ireland as they had abandoned them in Rhodesia? In Scotland and Wales, Ward sets the claims to independence made by Scottish and Welsh nationalists in the wider perspective of the dismantling of Britishness across the world. The mounting evidence that Britishness had lost its charm, that its economy had declined and its military withdrawn, that its power and prestige had diminished along with its role on the global stage – these developments, he argues, fostered nationalism in Scotland and Wales and the desire to uncouple from a British identity.

Ward notes a shift to the language of Englishness by those who opposed the arrival of Kenyan Asian migrants – an Englishness identified as increasingly embattled and threatened. In Leicester where many of the early arrivals settled, this language was prominent in letters written to the *Leicester Mercury*, a regional paper with a large circulation, where letter-writers gave vent to their feelings on the fate of the native-born Englishman (never woman) who would be 'a second-class citizen in an Afro-Asian community', with immigrants given priority over him in all things. One letter-writer asserted that 'our only hope lies in forming an English Nationalist party'.

The term 'English nationalism' makes no appearance in *Untied Kingdom*, and England and Englishness are largely missing from the account of Scottish and Welsh nationalism. What was the response to them from England and what was their response to English nationalism? The terms 'England' and 'Britain' are often used interchangeably by the English and in Anglocentric (sometimes London-centric) versions of British history. Ward comments that this elision did not extend to the British Empire which was never named 'English' – his book pays close attention to questions of language. The elision did not extend either to the 'Global Britain' slogan that the Conservative government came up with in the wake of Brexit in an attempt to refurbish the idea of Britain's global role. Ward offers a wonderfully comprehensive account of the many polls and referenda held across the Commonwealth and the United Kingdom to settle questions about Britishness – usually with outcomes that were far from decisive. But polls which showed that people in England were more likely to identify as British than people elsewhere in the United Kingdom are missing. So is the question of why, unlike the populations of Scotland and Wales, there was no referendum asking the population of England whether they wanted a devolved assembly or independence,. English dominance in the Union – geographically larger and with a much larger population, but with a wide range of internal regional differences and considerable London exceptionalism – is also missing. The very wide variety of hybrid and multiple identities evident in the histories of British imperialism and of migration within the British Empire/Commonwealth are neglected.

To write *Untied Kingdom*, Ward went on a tour of the former Empire that resembled Queen Elizabeth's tour of the Empire/Commonwealth after her Coronation. His purpose was very different: to visit archives and libraries. In many National Archives across the former Empire, writing by elite and powerful white men (often with fancy titles) has piled up, carefully preserved. By comparison, writing by people of colour is thin on the ground – most of it by men. Ward went outside National Archives to retrieve their writing from a wide range of documentary records and newspapers. Among these is the prison writing of the Reverend Ndabaningi Sithole who was one of the founders of the Zimbabwe African National Union – a breakaway movement from the Zimbabwe African People's Union. Writing by women of colour remains elusive, and it would be impossible to know anything about the story of

Ranjanbala Vaid's nightmare journey without the newspaper and other press sources that Ward carefully pieces together – in which *Time* called her a 'girl'. There needs to be acknowledgement of the wide range of work that has drawn on oral history to retrieve a range of voices, including those of women involved in the Zimbabwe African National Union and the Zimbabwe African People's Union.

In a shortish piece, it is impossible to do justice to the complexities of the global history traced in *Untied Kingdom*. Vivid in detail, bold in scope and exhaustively researched to cover a vast topic across vast territory, this is a must-read for all those interested in the multiple meanings of Britishness in different territories and different contexts at different moments, and in the histories of imperialism, decolonisation and their impact on cultures, societies and mindsets. It is a landmark study for the history of post-war Britain.

Cite this article: Webster W (2023). Unravelling Britishness. *Transactions of the Royal Historical Society* **1**, 363–368. https://doi.org/10.1017/S008044012300018X

Transactions of the RHS (2023), **1**, 369–372
doi:10.1017/S0080440123000191

Paradox Postponed

Erin F. Delaney

Pritzker School of Law, Northwestern University, Chicago, IL, USA
Email: erin.delaney@law.northwestern.edu

(Received 17 June 2023; revised 21 July 2023; accepted 24 July 2023; first published online 18 August 2023)

Abstract

A review of Stuart Ward's *Untied Kingdom*

Keyword: Constitutionalism

In a riveting and wide-ranging narrative, Stuart Ward tells a story of Britishness that transcends Britain. From Sagana Lodge in Kenya to the sugar factories of Queensland, from Government House in Rhodesia to the *Komagata Maru* anchored off the coast of Vancouver, Ward documents the 'little death[s]' of 'Britain-in-the-world' (p. 14) from the 1940s to the 1970s.[1] He then takes his readers back to London, Edinburgh, Cardiff and Belfast – deftly providing point and counterpoint in the dialogical process of identity formation or, perhaps more accurately, identity loss. In elaborating the grand aspirations and painful shortfalls of the very idea of 'being British', *Untied Kingdom* does more than trace the end of empire; it highlights the ways in which empire's end has complicated the 'politics of recognition' within the United Kingdom itself.

The ambition of the book lies in the very task of pinning down such a shape-shifting concept as Britishness. As Ward concludes at the book's end, 'at no time during its roughly three hundred years of popular currency did it provide watertight categories of inclusion or resonate uniformly from one constituency to the next' (p. 480). He describes a 'system of logic predicated on the export of English constitutional liberties for the presumptive benefit of all who resided under the British flag', but one so fundamentally flawed in its simultaneous adoption of 'racial, religious and ideological barriers to inclusion' (p. 482) that the flaws often overwhelmed the aspirations. The meaning of Britishness is thus left contextual and contestable.

---

[1] Ward's time frame mirrors that of the narrative of John Mortimer's *Paradise Postponed* (1985) to which the title of this response alludes.

This paradox of Britishness that Ward highlights is also that of British constitutionalism: How could liberal, democratic commitments operate within and alongside empire? And when, in the face of competing illiberalism, they failed abroad (as they most clearly did), did that failure work a corruption at home? The starkest example of these tensions is found in Ward's chapter on Rhodesia (ch. 9). He explains how Ian Smith's Unilateral Declaration of Independence in November 1965, issued in defiance of the British government's expectations of 'unimpeded progress towards majority rule' (p. 266), reflected certain colonial expectations of Britishness, rooted in long-standing preference for the 'White Dominions'. In this, Ward proposes, Smith claimed to represent the true mantle of Britishness, in solidarity with the British people, if not the British government. At least initially, racialism held some sway; in London, Harold Wilson 'ruled out the use of the British armed forces in the event of a white rebellion' (p. 267), allowing an internally inconsistent, contradictory and uncertain compromise position to take hold between the two governments.

Although politics may have allowed a moral dodge, eventually the question of the legal legitimacy of the usurping Smith regime was presented to the courts. And there, the more pointed question was joined: was *British* justice *white* justice? Was 'white Rhodesia ... an integral component of an organic chain of global British justice, or [was it] a rogue entity' (p. 283)? The Rhodesian judges, educated in Britain, ultimately legitimised the Smith regime by denying the authority of both the Privy Council and the Queen while using the language of responsible government to enforce the white supremacist claims.

This decision marked 'the end of the road for white Rhodesia's British credentials' (p. 285), resulting in a final break with the United Kingdom. The principles of British justice, flouted in Rhodesia, were understood as central to Britishness in Britain itself, eventually outweighing in importance the illiberal and racist elements of the imperial project. But the book is replete with other examples where claims of British (or historically English) liberties are sublimated to racial preferences – on entry to Canada and Australia, and in the evolution of limitations on immigration to the United Kingdom itself (themes that continue to resonate in the politics of migration today).

Ward engages with many of the toughest aspects of the paradox of Britishness, never shying away from the ways in which racialisation and racism impact the story. But he devotes less attention to the meaning of 'English constitutional liberties' and the span and contradictions of British constitutional practice. The conundrum of constitutionalism lurks in the shadows throughout the book, and it may well have deserved being brought into the light. As Harshan Kumarasingham has pointed out, '[s]uch hallowed principles of liberty and highlights of English constitutional history did not effortlessly flow to the empire'.[2] Nor were they left unaltered by the recipients. How should we evaluate or even understand decolonisation constitutions, with their bills of

---

[2] H. Kumarasingham, 'Written Differently: A Survey of Commonwealth Constitutional History in the Age of Decolonisation', *Journal of Imperial & Commonwealth History*, 46 (2018), 877.

rights and claims to democratic inclusiveness,[3] written by British civil servants who had never visited the countries in question?[4] And is there something distinctive about the transition to independence in former *British* colonies, such that we can meaningfully identify a 'Commonwealth constitutionalism'?[5]

The absence of explicit constitutional engagement is felt even more keenly when looking at the question from a domestic perspective: what does this paradox mean for constitutionalism in the United Kingdom today? How has empire shaped (or how does it shape) British constitutionalism as practised at home? The flexibility inherent in the unwritten constitution has always allowed the imperial constitution to operate at a remove from the domestic.[6] For example, Paul Scott has recently argued that the Privy Council, in both its political and judicial formations, is the reason that, even today, 'the UK is able to remain an Empire without being required to acknowledge that fact directly within its constitutional order'.[7] It is therefore possible (and, by some, possibly preferred) to focus solely on domestic machinations, keeping Westminster and London at centre stage.[8]

Ward's central contribution is his deep commitment to the global lens – a framing less often used in domestic discussion. In her own recent book, *The Gun, the Ship and the Pen*, Linda Colley suggested that the British Empire was one reason that Britain didn't develop its own single-document written constitution in the nineteenth century. Because it could draw on its colonies' resources to avoid raising taxes or conscripting troops at home, Britain did not face the pressures that forced formal constitutionalisation elsewhere.[9] Colley's intervention demonstrates well that these constitutional questions are not only for lawyers; historians have an essential role to play. The grand scope of Ward's project, and the existing element of constitutionalism within

---

[3] See Charles Parkinson, *Bills of Rights and Decolonization* (Oxford, 2007) (discussing British enthusiasm for including bills of rights in new constitutions, notwithstanding 'hostility' to the concept for the United Kingdom itself).

[4] Ivor Jennings, *Approach to Self-Government* (Cambridge, 1956), 1.

[5] Note, for example, the efforts of the 'Keith Forum on Commonwealth Constitutionalism', University of Edinburgh, https://www.law.ed.ac.uk/research/research-projects/keith-forum-commonwealth-constitutionalism (accessed 20 Jul. 2023).

[6] Twenty years ago, Stephen Howe wrote that 'the emerging historiography of Britain's "internal decolonization" remains at present empirically weak, conceptually cloudy, and often unhelpfully polarized'. Stephen Howe, 'Internal Decolonization? British Politics since Thatcher as Post-colonial Trauma', *Twentieth Century British History*, 14 (2003), 286.

And it is still contested. To my mind, Ward wisely sidesteps the questions of whether the nations that make up the United Kingdom should be considered 'colonies' of England – or even whether to think about the process of devolution as decolonisation in any sense – in order to retain the nuances of the 'far more complex reality'. *Ibid.*, 5.

[7] Paul Scott, 'The Privy Council and the Constitutional Legacies of Empire', *Northern Ireland Legal Quarterly*, 71 (2020), 261.

[8] Cf. generally H. Kumarasingham (ed.), *Constitution-Maker: Selected Writings of Sir Ivor Jennings* (Cambridge, 2014), 1–18.

[9] Linda Colley, *The Gun, the Ship, and the Pen* (New York, 2021), 73, 215. For further discussion of Colley's argument, see Erin F. Delaney, 'Of Constitutions and Constitutionalism', Balkinization (27 Oct. 2021), https://balkin.blogspot.com/2021/10/of-constitutions-and-constitutionalism.html.

his definition of Britishness, would have provided a powerful platform for analysis.

Though his focus is on identity, identity itself becomes quickly enmeshed in the constitutional ramifications of its demands: devolution, Scottish and Welsh independence, power sharing in Northern Ireland, English nationalism, Brexit. Ward convincingly argues that these more 'domestic' unravellings are not a function of an external 'end of Empire', foisting declinism on the metropole. Rather, they emanate from the same central instability of a concept, *Britishness*, whose capaciousness and grand potential ultimately served to undermine its ability to provide meaning. And he suggests, in his final sentences, that the future is bleak for the British state in its current form. Ward does not take the next step, to ask how this 'pervasive sense of an ending' (p. 288) relates to today's constitutional malaise, and whether, or in what ways, British constitutionalism may itself be undone by British imperialism. This is the paradox postponed – and the one with which the people(s) of the United Kingdom will have to wrestle.

Cite this article: Delaney EF (2023). Paradox Postponed. *Transactions of the Royal Historical Society* 1, 369–372. https://doi.org/10.1017/S0080440123000191

Transactions of the RHS (2023), **1**, 373–380
doi:10.1017/S0080440123000129

THE COMMON ROOM

Untidy Kingdom: A Reply by the Author

Stuart Ward (ID)

University of Copenhagen, Copenhagen, Denmark
Email: stuart@hum.ku.dk

(Received 26 June 2023; accepted 13 July 2023; first published online 7 August 2023)

Abstract

Author's response to the issues raised in the contributions to The Common Room round table on *Untied Kingdom: A Global History of the End of Britain* (2023)

Keywords: empire; decolonisation; Britishness; global history; United Kingdom

There is an episode in *Untied Kingdom* that goes right to the heart of the argument. It is January, and an unruly white mob have converged on the capital, their sights squarely set on the seat of executive power. What had started as dim conjecture has snowballed into an unshakable conviction. Something precious was not just being taken from them but removed by stealth by the cynical agencies of their own government. The paltry police presence assigned to keep them in check proves woefully inadequate as they set about illegally penetrating the inner sanctum of sovereignty itself.

This is not the United States Capitol in January 2021. It is January 1953, and the scene is the forecourt of Government House in Nairobi where, seventy years ago, hundreds of white Kenyan settlers in a state of high agitation took it upon themselves to break into the official residence of the British governor, Sir Evelyn Baring. It was not a 'stolen election' that fired their indignation, but a string of violent attacks on white homesteads by Mau Mau insurgents that compelled them to take matters into their own hands.

The burden of their grievance was unmistakable. When a cordon of African troops was hurriedly assembled to reinforce the barricaded doors, a wave of visceral anger spilled forth. 'There, there, they've given the house over to the f——n——s, the bloody bastards,' cried one particularly frantic woman, capturing in a single stream of invective the raw racial resentments on display.[1]

---

[1] Stuart Ward, *Untied Kingdom: A Global History of the End of Britain* (Cambridge, 2023), 152–4.

As Wendy Webster's pathbreaking work has shown, the settler home had long served as a potent symbol of the struggle for colonial order.[2] In the local idiom, 'giving over the house' was tantamount to the wholesale abdication of white authority, exposing the fragility and indeed absurdity of the settlers' claim to East Africa as an extension of Britain overseas. For these nervous stakeholders at the edge of empire, getting the house in order was not just about stiffening the resolve of an irresolute British government. It was a matter of shoring up the frontiers of Britishness itself.

In her lead essay in this fascinating 'Common Room', Webster affirms that race was a key driver of the drawn-out sequence of events that sealed the fate of Britishness as a global civic idea. The unedifying spectacle at Government House Nairobi in January 1953 was in no sense an isolated occurrence, but an early flashpoint in a wider existential challenge to the empire's intricate web of privilege and patrimony.

Webster further suggests that 'writing by elite and powerful white men' provides the dominant register in Untied Kingdom – perhaps a little too dominant – which she ascribes to the book's over-reliance on skewed archival collections that have allowed such material to 'pile up' at the expense of a more diversified historical record.

I would put it down to more calculated considerations arising from one of the book's key claims. If 'the exaltation of the "British race" was to be Britain's undoing', then serious engagement with its widely dispersed constituencies was always going to be a major part of the undertaking.[3] Making meaningful connections across disparate parts of the globe meant tuning in to a certain bandwidth – and not just that of 'powerful' men (as the fleeting example above suggests).

But the book aspires to do more than that. Many of the episodes documented in Untied Kingdom are concerned, not just with white British subjectivities per se, but with dynamic patterns of white reaction – constantly in dialogue with the unnerving implications of non-white challenges to racial authority. This could take the form of forthright assertions of the right to inclusion, such as Gurdit Singh's resounding claim to British subjecthood as he sailed into Vancouver harbour in May 1914 (ch. 2). It could also comprise the more mundane matter of Learie Constantine's right to stay in a London hotel in the 1940s (ch. 6).[4] But it also included moments of outright disenchantment with the promise of British rights and freedoms, such as the dramatic pivot to universal norms among Indigenous activists in the 1950s and 1960s (ch. 7), or the more direct resort to violent 'confrontation' among all manner of dissident groups (chs. 9, 13).

These are the fault lines that determined the source selection in Untied Kingdom, where each chapter is animated by the politics of 'misrecognition' between rival claimants to land, status, self-determination or simply belonging. What makes the Nairobi episode so emblematic is the triangulation of

---

[2] See especially her Englishness and Empire, 1939-65 (Oxford, 2005).

[3] Untied Kingdom, 4.

[4] Ibid., 48, 159-63.

black agency, white reaction and the overburdened expectations of Greater Britain. The irony is hard to miss: a settler community so incensed by Mau Mau farm invasions that they mount a makeshift home invasion of their own – discarding the very homely precepts of 'order' that underpinned their paradigmatic status.

What interested me most about these moments was the divisions and hesitations they invariably laid bare. For days afterwards, the letter pages of Nairobi's *East African Standard* churned with controversy over whether the Government House protest had gone too far. 'This is a British Colony', wrote one wary correspondent, 'and it is expected that the high ideals and principles of the British Way of Life should flow from the British people in this country.'[5] As with many other similar episodes, subtle cracks were revealed whenever lobbying for white interests became too fervent or forthright.

Saima Nasar's piece commends the 'centring of Kenyan Asian voices and experiences' in what was arguably the paradigmatic post-imperial encounter – the Wilson government's panicked move in March 1968 to close off Britain's entry gates to non-resident holders of British passports. The Kenyan Asians were far from the only British subjects to assume this precarious status. But as Nasar rightly points out, the unique circumstances in which they found themselves ultimately 'served as a driver to remap and tighten the criterion of Britishness'.

Had I been forced to cut just one chapter of *Untied Kingdom*, this one would have been the last to go – because it so vividly captures the deep entanglements between British identities abroad and their metropolitan variants, right down to the level of local politics (in this case, the fierce local objections to Kenyan Asian arrivals in Leicester). Just as white Kenyans became even whiter (and less British) under pressure, so too the legitimate claims of Kenyan Asians could weaken the hold of Britishness in favour of a reconfigured Englishness – framed by the local citizenry in narrower, nativist terms as a 'breed', 'people' or 'nation'. Invoking England as a small, overcrowded 'country' became a useful rhetorical ploy for keeping offshore Britons at bay. Loopholes could be devised for returning white settlers and itinerant Australasians, but only by emphasising a personal, 'patrial' connection to the downsized territorial unit of England.

Such semantic slippages are a mainstay of *Untied Kingdom* because they reveal the inherent tensions between the veneration of liberal values and the founding premise of racial inequality.[6] Packaging far-flung ethnic affinities in the language of hallowed constitutional principle was a crucial mechanism for draping Britishness in the garb of universalism – wide, capacious, inclusive – while screening out the disparities. With the influx of Commonwealth migrants, however, the wide-open spaces that had sustained centuries of outward expansion became a potential liability – and the sails were duly trimmed.

Erin Delaney's contribution highlights this 'conundrum of constitutionalism', perceptively stripping my argument back to its fundamentals. She

---

[5] *Ibid.*, 154.
[6] *Ibid.*, 481.

observes that the 'paradox of Britishness' was 'also that of British constitution-alism' – both grappling with glaring moral and legal inconsistencies in the effort to project universal ideals. She therefore wonders why the book stops short of engaging explicitly with 'the span and contradictions of British constitutional practice'. The direct constitutional implications, she says, are largely 'postponed', tending to 'lurk in the shadows' rather than illuminate the central premise.

It is an astute observation, and my response would be to make a fine distinction. The paradox of Britishness in all its myriad forms operated at an altogether more fluid level of conceptual rigour than its more formal constitutional counterpart. One of the reasons I opted for Charles Dilke's *Greater Britain* as a framing device was the striking imprecision that characterised his thinking – and that of many of his emulators. Though himself steeped in the myth of British constitutionalism, he chose not to enfold his theme in the language of a legislator or constitutional layer.

Legal specialists certainly could (and did) frame the issue in these terms, but for the vast assortment of laypeople who breathed life into the idea, it was about the 'high ideals and principles of the British Way of Life' (in the misty formulation of the *East African Standard* correspondent cited above). That is to say, it was the vaguely perceived *myth* of British constitutionalism – as distinct from the clearly adumbrated principles and practice thereof – that animated a popular sense of entitlement to an unbounded British world.

But the distinction is of course hazardous, and I accept Delaney's point that 'identity itself becomes quickly enmeshed in the constitutional ramifications of its demands'. This was especially apparent whenever the worlds of myth and legal measures collided. For the most part, the blurred lines of British subject-hood were perfectly primed to the needs of settler colonialism. Hazy moral categories could enjoy a wide net of legal and constitutional protection, while evading practical restraints whenever the strict application of principle threatened to impede the march of 'progress'. Difficulties arose, however, when it came to arbitrating legal disputes – not least between settlers and Indigenous peoples – where conceptual rigour and clear demarcation lines were procedurally crucial.

As Delaney points out, this is essentially what I was trying to show in the chapter on Rhodesia in the 1960s (ch. 9), but there is of course a larger story yet to be told – about a pervasive *disenchantment* with British constitu-tionalism itself in the long aftermath of decolonisation, resonating throughout Britain's dismantled empire and reverberating all the way to the contemporary crisis of the Union.

Which brings me to the other key claim of the book – that the receding frontiers of Britishness not only put paid to the myth of Greater Britain abroad, but also punctured the long-term viability of unionism in the United Kingdom. As Ben Jackson notes in his penetrating line of questioning, it was more a 'slow puncture' than a sudden implosion, the full implications of which remain to be seen. But enough air has escaped from the pressure cham-ber to permit the fundamental question: how did the passing of empire furnish the broader context and conditions for the 'break-up of Britain'?

Jackson recognises that *Untied Kingdom* eschews easy answers, steering clear of the correlation-equals-causation trap. But he is also left wondering precisely how political and constitutional 'instability within the UK relates to the wider process of decolonisation' – if not by way of direct causation. Specifically, he raises concerns that the global optics of *Untied Kingdom* run the risk of obscuring the internal political dynamics of devolution, especially since the Thatcher era – perhaps missing the crux of the matter entirely.

T. M. Devine was by no means the first to frame the question in either/or terms, but he is among the more forthright in his conviction that Mrs Thatcher had 'an infinitely greater claim to be the midwife of Scottish devolution than the factor of imperial decline'.[7] David Edgerton's towering *The Rise and Fall of the British Nation* is less explicit in this regard, but it also persistently discounts the effects of 'residual imperialism' in the post-war era, arguing throughout that the internal dynamics of a revived British nation 'trumped' empire at every turn. For Edgerton, too, it was the great sell-off of national assets under Thatcher that marked 'the end of British economic nationalism', ushering in 'something new, and not particularly British'.[8]

Jackson makes the valid point that my book pays scant attention to the finer details of devolutionary politics since the 1980s. Wendy Webster makes a similar observation about the simmering tensions of English nationalism in recent decades. These issues are obviously crucial for grasping the detail and complexity of the UK's current constitutional impasse, but they are not in my main line of sight because they do not – to my mind – present themselves as alternatives to the wider, decolonising processes and pressures brought to light in *Untied Kingdom*.

Rather than dismiss all that went before Mrs Thatcher (or most of what transpired beyond Britain's borders), my aim was to gauge the ebbing tide of Britishness over a much longer time frame, intersecting at three key junctures: empire, union and 'a plethora of distinct localities' around the world.[9] No two countries or contexts followed the same causal sequence, but all shared deeper structural similarities and a remarkable capacity to influence each other's outcomes. For my purposes, the distinctive inner workings of devolutionary politics in the UK – once the early fault lines and the political momentum had clearly revealed themselves – are but one manifestation of the inherent weakness of British sentiment worldwide since the onset of decolonisation.

Thus, the specifics of recent party politics in Scotland were never the principal 'investment' (as Jackson astutely puts it) – just as the contemporary legacies for Zimbabwe, say, or New Zealand never made it into the main frame. The goal was to take a much larger view of the dimensions and complexity of the social entity coming apart at the seams.

---

[7] T. M. Devine, 'The Break-up of Britain? Scotland and the End of Empire', *Transactions of the Royal Historical Society*, 16 (2006), 163–80, at 163, 166.

[8] David Edgerton, *The Rise and Fall of the British Nation: A Twentieth Century History* (2018), 18, 25, 255, 269, 316, 385–6, 458, 471.

[9] *Untied Kingdom*, 480.

Jackson ascribes to *Untied Kingdom* the view that 'no plausible alternative basis for [British] identity could be found once decolonisation was underway'. I would put it differently. Any number of plausible ideas jostled for attention, from social democratic modernisation (Jackson's preferred formula) to Thatcherite neoliberalism (as much a contender for British hearts and minds as the wrecking ball Edgerton and others make of it). Add to the mix the romance of the new Europe, the third way of 'cool Britannia', the restorative Britonism of Gordon Brown or even the fatuous talk of 'taking back control' in the Brexit era, and it becomes clear that there has been no lack of imagination or innovation.

The problem, as Australia's Donald Horne observed of Britain in the late 1960s, was that 'nothing seemed to stick'.[10] Ideas abounded, but viable, enduring and, above all, consensual alternatives that could bind the Union in the face of the exogenous forces acting upon it were thin on the ground already fifty years ago and remain so today as the old myths of shared wartime endeavour continue to fade. But crucially, national separatism, for all its obvious advances, has equally struggled to muster a convincing majority or a coherent way forward, and not just in Britain – the running has not been all one way.

None of this diminishes Jackson's key intervention – that 'the politics of left and right are a necessary component of a full account of the trajectory of Scottish and Welsh nationalism'. I can only agree, but the operative word is 'trajectory', evoking fluctuating contingencies and shifting political fortunes over time, rather than a self-sufficient, watertight accounting for the deeper fissures themselves. These, I would argue, emerged well before Thatcher's tenure during the long recessional of imperial Britishness. Which is perhaps another way of saying that Jackson's 'more ecumenical' reading of *Untied Kingdom* accords largely with my own.

Brendan O'Leary's critique tilts intriguingly in the opposite direction. Far from suggesting that *Untied Kingdom* makes more of global decolonisation than the evidence might warrant, he considers the approach needlessly timid – at least as far as Northern Ireland is concerned. Historians 'cannot sidestep the colonial question', he argues, especially when it comes to the role of Ulster unionists in fanning the flames of 'the Troubles' in the late 1960s. As evidence mounted in these years of the UK government's diminished commitment to holding forward positions abroad, unionists were forced to reckon with the knowledge that 'their standing derived from past settler colonialism, of which they were palpably proud'.

For a book that makes such compelling connections, O'Leary wonders why it seems in such a hurry to get past the question of whether Ireland constituted a 'colony'. The answer lies partly in the many narrative and structural choices that comprise such a multi-pronged study (which hares to chase, which to leave alone), combined with a certain apprehension about becoming caught in the partisan crossfire.

---

[10] *Ibid.*, 344.

That is to say, if it could be shown that the eclipse of British affinities and allegiances worldwide made an immediate, measurable impact in Northern Ireland regardless of whether it be deemed a 'colony', a more compelling or persuasive case might productively emerge – or so I imagined.[11] It was to avoid becoming lost in the thicket of entrenched positions that I sought to evade the 'conceptual logjam' (perhaps 'endemic disagreement' would have been a better characterisation) – in the hope that the book might indeed be 'read both by those who wish to preserve the Union of Great Britain and Northern Ireland, and those who would like to see Irish re-unification'.

Having made that conscious choice, however, I am inclined to agree that there are limits to how far a distinction can be maintained between the late-colonial *context* and the conditions of colonialism itself.[12] The book draws on an abundance of evidence of Ulster unionists readily identifying with the plight of embattled Britons offshore. Though this hardly constitutes conclusive proof of Northern Ireland's irreducible status as a 'colony', there is at least a conspicuous resemblance that unionists themselves have always found deeply unsettling.

O'Leary also raises more fundamental concerns about the conceptual imprecision inherent in the subject itself. Or as he himself puts it, the 'methodology is as loose as the empire under scrutiny'. But if 'clear-theory testing' is avoided in *Untied Kingdom*, it is more a matter of the unwieldy dimensions of the subject than a disinclination to consult social scientists. If ever a topic refused to conform to expectations, revealing the heterogeneity of the past and the stubbornness of historical actors, it is surely the infinite permutations and serial flaws of an expansive British compact conspicuously falling short of its own standards.[13]

My approach was to turn the terminological looseness around – presenting, not an impediment to analytical precision, but a large part of the solution as to why Britishness lost so much traction in the post-war world.[14] By attending to what Saul Dubow terms the 'fissile multiplicity of forms' that Britishness took – traversing class, country, ethnicity, indigeneity, gender, ideology and countless localities – it became clear how imperial Britishness defied stable analytical categories, and why its shape-shifting properties could not withstand the unprecedented scrutiny of empire's end.[15]

Such a resolution will not satisfy everyone, but it is adhered to rigorously throughout to make sense of a diverse patchwork of allegiances that might otherwise seem aberrant or superficial. In short, there is method in the pervasive ambiguity, allowing original perspectives to emerge that diverge from received wisdom. Whereas Linda Colley's classic account revealed the components of a coherent Britishness 'forged' within the island fortress of a

---

[11] *Ibid.*, 383.

[12] Which is essentially the ploy devised on p. 386 of *Untied Kingdom*.

[13] Sebastian Conrad, *What Is Global History?* (Princeton, 2016), 131.

[14] *Ibid.*, 41.

[15] Saul Dubow, 'How British Was the British World? The Case of South Africa', *Journal of Imperial and Commonwealth History*, 37 (2009), 1–27, at 14.

people compelled 'to look anxiously and inquiringly inwards', a far more diffuse, scattered and contingent Britain emerges from the pages of *Untied Kingdom*.[16]

Untidy Kingdom might have been a better title. The rich and varied selection of critical interventions in this *Transactions* Common Room underlines the multivalent nature of British selfhood and the extraordinary elasticity of its powers of signification. That five readers could be drawn in so many directions is revealing in itself – not least of the diversity of perspectives that need to be kept in play when considering the fading resonance of Britain-in-the-world and its implications for the contemporary United Kingdom.

All of which serves as a reminder that any attempt to contain the subject in a single volume will necessarily be partial and incomplete – and perhaps itself a little untidy – leaving abundant room for further exemplification, elaboration and, of course, lively debate. It only remains to thank the contributors sincerely for their penetrating and provocative insights, and for taking the time to present them in such a stimulating format.

---

[16] Linda Colley, *Britons: Forging the Nation* (1996), 4, 18.

Cite this article: Ward S (2023). Untidy Kingdom: A Reply by the Author. *Transactions of the Royal Historical Society* 1, 373–380. https://doi.org/10.1017/S0080440123000129